Mathematics of Finance

$$I = Prt \tag{6-1}$$

$$S = P(1 + rt) \tag{6-2}$$

$$i = \frac{j}{m} \quad \text{and} \quad n = m \times (\text{Number of years in the term}) \tag{8-1) \& (8-3}$$

$$FV = PV(1 + i)^n \quad \text{and} \quad PV = FV(1 + i)^{-n} \tag{8-2}$$

$$FV = PV(1 + i_1)(1 + i_2)(1 + i_3)\cdots(1 + i_n) \tag{8-4}$$

$$i = \sqrt[n]{\frac{FV}{PV}} - 1 = \left(\frac{FV}{PV}\right)^{1/n} - 1 \tag{9-1}$$

$$n = \frac{\ln(FV/PV)}{\ln(1 + i)} \tag{9-2}$$

$$f = (1 + i)^m - 1 \tag{9-3}$$

$$i_2 = (1 + i_1)^{m_1/m_2} - 1 \tag{9-4}$$

$$FV = PMT\left[\frac{(1 + i)^n - 1}{i}\right] \tag{10-1}$$

$$PV = PMT\left[\frac{1 - (1 + i)^{-n}}{i}\right] \tag{10-2}$$

$$c = \frac{\text{Number of compoundings per year}}{\text{Number of payments per year}} \tag{10-3}$$

$$i_2 = (1 + i)^c - 1 \tag{9-4c}$$

$$n = \frac{\ln\left(1 + \frac{i \times FV}{PMT}\right)}{\ln(1 + i)} \quad \text{and} \quad n = -\frac{\ln\left(1 - \frac{i \times PV}{PMT}\right)}{\ln(1 + i)} \tag{10-1n) and (10-2n}$$

$$FV(\text{due}) = PMT\left[\frac{(1 + i)^n - 1}{i}\right] \times (1 + i) \tag{13-1}$$

$$PV(\text{due}) = PMT\left[\frac{1 - (1 + i)^{-n}}{i}\right] \times (1 + i) \tag{13-2}$$

$$PV = \frac{PMT}{i} \tag{12-1}$$

$$FV = PMT\left[\frac{(1 + i)^n - (1 + g)^n}{i - g}\right] \tag{12-2}$$

$$PV = PMT\left[\frac{1 - (1 + g)^n(1 + i)^{-n}}{i - g}\right] \tag{12-3}$$

$$\text{Bond price} = b(FV)\left[\frac{1 - (1 + i)^{-n}}{i}\right] + FV(1 + i)^{-n} \tag{15-1}$$

1) Maslows
2) grapevine
3) manage grid.

BUSINESS MATHEMATICS IN CANADA

third edition

F. ERNEST JEROME

McGraw-Hill Ryerson

Toronto Montréal New York Burr Ridge Bangkok Bogotá Caracas Lisbon London Madrid Mexico City Milan New Delhi Seoul Singapore Sydney Taipei

McGraw-Hill
Ryerson Limited

A Subsidiary of The ***McGraw-Hill*** *Companies*

BUSINESS MATHEMATICS IN CANADA
Third Edition
F. Ernest Jerome

ISBN: 0-07-560940-1

1 2 3 4 5 6 7 8 9 10 VH 0 9 8 7 6 5 4 3 2 1 0

Printed and bound in the USA.

Publisher/Editorial Director: Evelyn Veitch
Senior Sponsoring Editor: Lynn Fisher
Associate Sponsoring Editor: Jason Stanley
Copy Editor: Laurel Sparrow
Production Coordinator: Madeleine Harrington
Senior Marketing Manager: Jeff MacLean
Marketing Manager: Bill Todd
Cover and Interior Design: Kyle Gell
Art Direction: Dianna Little
Cover Image: D. Stoecklein/Firstlight
Page Layout: Carlisle Communications, Ltd.
Printer: Von Hoffman Press, Inc.

Canadian Cataloguing in Publication Data

Main entry under title:
Jerome F. Ernest
Business Mathematics in Canada
3rd Canadian ed.
Includes index.

ISBN 0-07-560940-1

1. Business Mathematics-Canada. I. Title.
HF5691.J47 1999 650'.01'513 C99-932279-6

Credits:

Chapter 1 Canadian Press CP Frank Gunn; Chapter 2 Canadian Press CP Tom Hanson; Chapter 3 Associated Press AP Rudi Blaha; Chapter 4 Canadian Press CP Mike Ridewood; Chapter 5 Canadian Press CP Joe Bryksa; Chapter 6 Associated Press AP Charlotte Fiorito Ho; Chapter 7 Canadian Press CP Frank Gunn; Chapter 8 Canadian Press CP Alessandro Trovati; Chapter 9 Canadian Press CP Frank Gunn; Chapter 10 Canadian Press CP Jacques Boissinot; Chapter 11 Canadian Press CP Jacques Boissinot; Chapter 13 Canadian press CP Frank Gunn; Chapter 14 Canadian Press WFP Phil Hossack; Chapter 15 Canadian Press CP Jeff McIntosh; Chapter 16 Photograph courtesy of Cary Moretti © 1998.

To Seth, David, Kristen, Rachel, and Kevin

About the Author

F. Ernest Jerome taught courses in business mathematics, personal financial planning, corporate finance, mutual funds, and security analysis while professor of Finance and Quantitative Methods at Malaspina University–College in Nanaimo, British Columbia. After earning degrees in physics and oceanography, Professor Jerome obtained an MBA at the University of British Columbia, where he was awarded the Schulich Fellowship for Entrepreneurship. He holds a Chartered Financial Planner designation, and received the 1987 Outstanding Achievement Award from the Canadian Institute of Financial Planning.

Preface

Most business administration programs in Canadian colleges include an introductory course in business mathematics or mathematics of finance. *Business Mathematics in Canada* is intended for use in such courses. The text's primary objective is to support the learning of mathematics (other than statistics) needed to succeed in such fields as accounting, finance, management, marketing, and business information systems.

The overall approach is to identify and build upon unifying and integrative concepts. For example, the *Valuation Principle* is the basis for determining the market value of Treasury Bills, annuities, mortgages, bonds, and preferred shares. Several applications involve the concept of *economic equivalence* of alternative payment streams. Students are encouraged to work with a few fundamental formulas rather than to search through a large inventory of formulas for a customized version for each particular case.

It is intended that the text be adaptable to either a one- or a two-semester course in business mathematics. Chapter and section headings preceded by an asterisk (*) may be omitted with no loss of continuity or lack of preparation for later topics. The text is suitable for courses that emphasize either an algebraic approach or a preprogrammed financial calculator approach to compound interest problems. Instructions are given in the use of the basic financial functions for five popular models: SHARP EL-733A, SHARP EL-735, TEXAS INSTRUMENTS BA 35, TEXAS INSTRUMENTS BA II PLUS, and HEWLETT-PACKARD 10B. Both algebraic and financial calculator solutions are presented for most example problems in compound interest.

Changes in the Third Edition

This third edition is a major revision of *Business Mathematics in Canada.* Much of the exposition has been rewritten to make it more concise and easier to read. The new features and enhancements are:

Full Colour Design

The most obvious change is the use of colour for both functional and aesthetic purposes. Key elements of diagrams and graphs are more readily identified and remembered through the use of colour. Colour helps to indicate related items or features. Students also find a full-colour text more appealing to use.

A Few Topics Dropped or Moved to Appendixes

Chapters 17 and 18 of the second edition have been eliminated because the vast majority of colleges do not cover them in business math courses. (The Canada Student Loan topic has been retained and integrated with Chapter 7.) Reflecting their declining importance in everyday commerce, promissory notes, end-of-month dating, and receipt-of-goods dating have been moved to appendices. Equivalent payment streams are now covered only in a compound interest environment. Five appendices in the second edition have been deleted.

New Diagrams

One-third of the 51 figures in the List of Figures are new in the third edition. See, for example, Figures 8.1, 8.2, 10.3, and 10.5.

More Point-of-Interest Features

Fifteen of the 26 Point of Interest vignettes are new. Most of the other nine retained from the second edition have been substantially revised. Their purpose remains the same—to illustrate the application and misapplication of mathematics in business and personal finance. Generally speaking, the vignettes are shorter than in the second edition, and they are written to actively involve the student. More than half of the vignettes ask explicit questions that focus classroom discussion and the reader's thinking. See, for example, the Points of Interest in Sections 10.3 and 11.1. Many of these Points of Interest may be used as case studies.

Cases

Eight of the chapters end with a case study. A case study requires a more in-depth analysis and the integration of two or three topics from the current and possibly the preceding chapters. For example, the case study at the end of Chapter 3 involves rate of return on investment (Chapter 2), currency conversion (Chapter 3), and weighted average (Chapter 1).

Additional Problems

Several new problems have been added at the basic level of difficulty. Problems continue to be rated according to degree of difficulty. Problems preceded by a single bullet (◆) are more difficult than problems without a bullet. The double bullet (◆◆) problems are the most challenging.

Approximately 40 of the new problems are from course materials of the **Canadian Institute of Financial Planning** and the **Institute of Canadian Bankers**. These are the two organizations most active in the delivery of financial planning courses in Canada. The sample problems demonstrate that the topics covered in a business math course are important to these professional bodies. By solving these problems, students also gain confidence in their ability to succeed in industry-specific professional courses. An icon in the margin indicates problems derived from these sources.

Concept Questions

About half of the sections include Concept Questions. These questions exercise students' intuition, and test their understanding of concepts, principles, and relationships among variables.

Caught-in-the-Web Boxes

A new boxed element in the third edition provides a brief commentary about a Web site relevant to the topic under discussion. It may be a source of up-to-date data, a useful online calculator, an instructive chart or graphic, etc. For example, see the Caught-in-the-Web boxes in Sections 3.5 and 13.1.

www.Exercise.com

Nine chapters include an optional Web-based exercise. Typically, it is based on a Web site previously mentioned in a Caught-in-the-Web box. See, for example, the www.Exercise.com at the end of Chapter 13.

New Supplements

PowerPoint Presentation Slides and a Computer Test Bank are new supplements for the third edition.

Instructions for Specific Financial Calculator Models

New tables in the appendixes to Chapters 8 and 13 present instructions for using the basic financial functions of the **SHARP EL-733A, SHARP EL-735, TEXAS INSTRUMENTS BA 35, TEXAS INSTRUMENTS BA II PLUS,** and **HEWLETT-PACKARD 10B.**

Notation Change for Compound Interest

We have changed from the S_n, A_n, R notation (imported from actuarial science) to the *FV, PV, PMT* notation used by financial calculators, spreadsheet software, and many finance texts. A broader rationale for the change is given at the beginning of Section 8.5.

Treatment of Deferred Annuities

Deferred annuities are integrated with ordinary annuities and treated as a two-step application. (In the second edition they were treated as a special case with its own set of formulas.)

General Annuities Introduced Later

Some users of the second edition felt that students did not get enough practice with simple annuities in Chapter 10 before general annuities were introduced in Section 10.3. In the third edition, general annuities are introduced in Section 10.5 after students have had extensive practice with *both* the future value and the present value of ordinary simple annuities (including deferred annuity applications).

Segregation of Annuities Due

Some colleges do not have enough time to cover annuities due. The theory and applications of annuities due are confined to Chapter 13 in the third edition so these colleges can work around the topic more readily.

Simpler Treatment of Currency Conversion and Exchange Rates

The notation used for exchange rates in the second edition has been dropped. Currency conversion problems are now solved by explicitly setting up a proportion (rather than by using the exchange rate as a conversion factor).

Constant-Growth Annuities

The payments in many periodic-payment series increase over time because they are formally or informally linked to prevailing price levels. Indexed pensions are an example of a formal linkage; rent and property insurance premiums are examples of informal linkages. A constant-growth annuity is a much better approximation of these payments than a fixed-payment annuity. This new optional topic appears in Section 12.2.

Other Key Features

The third edition of *Business Mathematics in Canada* retains the features that have been popular in earlier editions.

Many Canadian Applications

Throughout the exposition, Example problems, Exercise problems, and Points of Interest, the book presents a wide range of applications of mathematics in Canadian business and finance. Every effort has been made to reflect current practices. Real financial instruments and real economic data are frequently used.

Wide Selection of Problems

Each section of a chapter is followed by a set of problems for applying and reinforcing the new material. The text contains over 2000 problems and concept questions. Considerable effort has been made to make the problems instructive, practical, realistic, and interesting.

Tips and Traps

Boxed elements inserted at appropriate points in the text draw the student's attention to simplifications, pitfalls, short-cuts, calculator procedures, and common errors.

"Point of Interest" Vignettes

Each chapter contains at least one intriguing illustration of the application or misapplication of mathematics in business or personal finance.

Graphs and Diagrams

This text presents more graphs and diagrams with the expository material than other texts.

Financial Calculator Compatibility

Any basic financial calculator model may be used with this text. Specific instructions for five popular models are provided in appendices.

Cash-Flow Sign Convention

All financial calculators (as well as the financial functions in most spreadsheet software) employ a cash-flow sign convention. Unique among currently available textbooks, we explain and faithfully use the cash-flow sign convention.

Practical Math Review

Review topics in Chapters 1, 2, 3, and 5 are integrated with practical applications. The review also incorporates the sort of "messy" coefficients and numbers that will be encountered in later chapters (and in real life). Instructions are provided on the number of figures required in intermediate steps to ensure the desired degree of accuracy in the final result.

End-of-Chapter Elements

Each chapter concludes with a set of review problems, a self-test exercise, a summary of notation, key formulas, and a list of key terms. In the third edition, some chapters also include a case study and/or an Internet exercise.

Inside-Cover Summaries

For easy reference, the key formulas are summarized on the inside front cover. Frequently used algebraic symbols are listed on the page facing the back cover. A tear-out formula card is included for use in tests or for posting at the student's workstation.

Supplements

Visit the Booksite and Online Learning Centre at www.mcgrawhill.ca/college/jerome for Web-based resources for both faculty and students. The Instructor site is password-protected, and contains **PowerPoint presentation files,** test questions, on-line solutions to problems in the text, and Web links to related sites. The Student site contains Internet applications questions, Web links to related sites, and self-testing quick-quiz material organized on a chapter-by-chapter basis.

A **Student's Solutions Manual** presents full solutions to the odd-numbered problems and Concept Questions.

The **Instructor's Solutions Manual** contains solutions to all Concept Questions, problems, Point-of-Interest questions, and case studies in the text.

The **PowerPoint Presentation** slides are available to instructors, on request, who adopt *Business Mathematics in Canada,* Third Edition. There is a file for each chapter, which contains slides related to each chapter, including key formulas and figures.

The **Computer Test Bank** contains word problems from the text and multiple-choice questions. Instructors receive special software for creating examinations from the test bank questions. The software also lets instructors edit test items and add new questions to the test bank.

SPATS

The **Spreadsheet Applications Template (SPATS) Diskette** found in the back of the text contains formatted templates for solving problems that are flagged by a diskette icon in the text's margin.

Pageout is the McGraw-Hill Ryerson Web site-development centre. This Web page-generation software is free to adopters and is designed to help faculty create on-line courses, complete with assignments, quizzing, links to relevant sites, lecture notes and more in a matter of minutes.

Acknowledgments

The third edition is the compound future value of contributions from many dedicated teachers. Thanks again to the following reviewers of the first and second editions.

John Anderson
Richard Gray
Velvet McGarrigle
Margaret Beresford
Rick Hird
Barbara Moore
Michael Conte
Bonnie Kerr
Colleen Quinn
Garry Dorash
Rick Knowles
Angelina Sbrocca
Millard Evans
Veronica Legg
Stanley Shaw
Ed Fox
John Mayer
Ed Zuke

Over the years, faculty at Seneca College and Mohawk College have been especially helpful in providing feedback and suggestions. Colleen Quinn (Seneca College), John Anderson (Red River College), and Gillian Leek (Mohawk College) deserve special mention for their contributions.

A new debt of gratitude is owed to the following educators for their thorough review of the manuscript for the third edition. Their suggestions have made this edition a better text.

Margaret Beresford	Kwantlen University College
Ross Bryant	Conestoga College
Charles Cox	St. Lawrence College
Kenneth Deck	Canadore College
Frank Gruen	British Columbia Institute of Technology
James Hebert	Red River College
Dorothy Kubsch	Northern Alberta Institute of Technology
Gillian Leek	Mohawk College
Henry Maclean	Humber College
Colleen Quinn	Seneca College
Jackie Shemko	Durham College
Janice Stang	Southern Alberta Institute of Technology
Carol Ann Waite	Sheridan College

The following individuals and organizations provided technical and professional information helpful in making *Business Mathematics in Canada* reflect current business practices.

David Burbach	Fidelity Investments Canada Limited
Peter Casquinha	The Institute of Canadian Bankers
David Chilton	Financial Awareness Corporation
Tim Hague	Templeton Management Ltd.

Sookie Ham	Templeton Management Ltd.
Greg Jerome	PriceWaterhouseCoopers
Rusty Joerin	Malaspina University–College
Knut Larsen	Canadian Institute of Financial Planning
Michael McGowan	McGowan and Associates
Pat O'Dwyer	Cunningham's Saturn Saab Isuzu
Robert Redmile	Canada Trust
Rick Thurmeier	Investors Group

I also wish to thank the staff at McGraw-Hill Ryerson. This includes: Evelyn Veitch, Editorial Director and Publisher; Lynn Fisher, Senior Sponsoring Editor; Jason Stanley, Associate Sponsoring Editor; Jenna Wallace, Associate Editor; Kelly Dickson, Editorial Services Manager; Jeff MacLean, Marketing Manager; Thom Hounsell, Director of Digital Applications; and others who I do not know personally, but who made important contributions. Laurel Sparrow of Top Copy Communications did a superb job of editing the manuscript.

I appreciate the technical support of Ted Waugh who, on more than one occasion, brought about reconciliation between my computer and me when the relationship got particularly nasty. Vitaly Lomov was particularly helpful in checking problem solutions and in preparing the Instructor's Solutions Manual.

Finally, I want to thank my family for their support during this long and arduous project. In particular, my wife has accepted a reduced social life, a distracted husband, and the tedium of proofreading hundreds of pages with remarkably good humour. I am most grateful for her understanding and assistance.

F. Ernest Jerome

List of Figures

SECTION ________

List of Figures *(continued)*

List of Tables

SECTION ________

Points of Interest

List of Cases

Brief Contents

Chapter

Contents

(Chapters or sections preceded by an asterisk * may be omitted without loss of continuity.)

7. Applications of Simple Interest 248

8. Compound Interest: Future Value and Present Value 288

9. Compound Interest: Further Topics and Applications 350

10. Ordinary Annuities: Future Value and Present Value 390

11. Ordinary Annuities: Payment Size, Term, and Interest Rate 440

12. Annuities: Special Situations 478

CHAPTER OUTLINE

*(Sections or chapters preceded by an asterisk * may be omitted without loss of continuity.)*

LEARNING OBJECTIVES

After completing this chapter, you will be able to:

- Perform arithmetic operations in their proper order
- Convert fractions to their percent and decimal equivalents
- Maintain the proper number of digits in calculations
- Solve for any one of percent rate, portion, or base, given the other two quantities
- Calculate the gross earnings of employees paid a salary, hourly wage, or commission
- Calculate the simple average or weighted average (as appropriate) of a set of values
- Perform basic calculations of the Goods and Services Tax, Harmonized Sales Tax, provincial sales tax, and real property tax

1

Review and Applications of Basic Mathematics

MOST ROUTINE CALCULATIONS IN BUSINESS are now performed electronically. Does this mean that mathematical skills are less important or less valued than in the past? Definitely not—the mathematics and statistics you study in your business program are more widely expected and more highly valued in business than ever before. Technology has empowered us to access more information more readily, and to perform more sophisticated analysis on the information. To take full advantage of technology, you must know what information is relevant, what analysis or calculations should be performed, how to interpret the results, and how to explain the outcome in terms your clients and colleagues can understand.

Both clients and employers expect higher education and performance standards than in the past from advisors and middle managers. Increasingly, employers also expect managers and management trainees to undertake a program of study leading to a credential recognized in their industry. These programs usually have a significant mathematics component.

As an illustration of the preceding points, consider the financial services industry. Each segment of the industry offers career-oriented education. The Institute of Canadian Bankers (ICB) offers more than 130 courses in 14 programs to financial services professionals. Each year, there are over 25,000 course registrations. To help prospective students determine if their mathematical skills are adequate for certain programs, the ICB's course calendar contains a mathematics self-test. This test is the subject of the Point of Interest box later in Section 1.2. The ICB offers resource materials and workshops to people who need to upgrade their math skills.

Naturally, a college course in business mathematics or statistics will cover a broader range of topics (often at a greater depth) than you might need for a particular industry. This broader education opens more career options to you and provides a stronger set of mathematical skills for your chosen career.

1.1 Order of Operations

In evaluating an expression such as

$$5 + 3^2 \times 2 - 4 \div 6$$

there is potential for confusion about the sequence of mathematical steps. Do we just perform the indicated operations in a strict left-to-right sequence, or is some other order intended? To eliminate any possible confusion, mathematicians have agreed on the use of brackets and a set of rules for the order of mathematical operations. The rules are:

1. Perform operations within brackets (in the order of Steps 2, 3, and 4 below).
2. Evaluate the powers.[1]
3. Perform multiplication and division in order from left to right.
4. Perform addition and subtraction.

To help remember the order of operations, you can use the acronym "BEDMAS" representing the sequence: **B**rackets, **E**xponents, **D**ivision, **M**ultiplication, **A**ddition, and **S**ubtraction.

Example 1.1A *Exercises Illustrating the Order of Mathematical Operations*

a. $30 - 6 \div 3 + 5 = 30 - 2 + 5$
$= 33$

Do division before subtraction and addition.

b. $(30 - 6) \div 3 + 5 = 24 \div 3 + 5$
$= 8 + 5$
$= 13$

Do operation within brackets first; then do division before addition.

c. $\dfrac{30 - 6}{3 + 5} = \dfrac{24}{8}$
$= 3$

Brackets are implied in the numerator and the denominator.

d. $72 \div (3 \times 2) - 6 = 72 \div 6 - 6$
$= 12 - 6$
$= 6$

Do operation within brackets first; then do division before subtraction.

e. $72 \div (3 \times 2^2) - 6 = 72 \div (3 \times 4) - 6$
$= 72 \div 12 - 6$
$= 6 - 6$
$= 0$

Do operations within brackets (the power before the multiplication); then do division before subtraction.

f. $72 \div (3 \times 2)^2 - 6 = 72 \div 6^2 - 6$
$= 72 \div 36 - 6$
$= 2 - 6$
$= -4$

Do operation within brackets first, then the power, then division, then subtraction.

---

[1] A power is a quantity such as 3^2 or 5^3 (which are shorthand methods for representing 3×3 and $5 \times 5 \times 5$, respectively). Section 2.2 presents a review of powers and exponents.

g. $4(2-5)-4(5-2) = 4(-3)-4(3)$
$= -12 - 12$
$= -24$

Do operations within brackets first, then multiplication, then subtraction.

Exercise 1.1

Answers to the odd-numbered problems are at the end of the book.

Evaluate each of the following.

1. $20 - 4 \times 2 - 8$

2. $18 \div 3 + 6 \times 2$

3. $(20 - 4) \times 2 - 8$

4. $18 \div (3 + 6) \times 2$

5. $20 - (4 \times 2 - 8)$

6. $(18 \div 3 + 6) \times 2$

7. $54 - 36 \div 4 + 2^2$

8. $(5 + 3)^2 - 3^2 \div 9 + 3$

9. $(54 - 36) \div (4 + 2)^2$

10. $5 + (3^2 - 3)^2 \div (9 + 3)$

11. $\dfrac{8^2 - 4^2}{(4 - 2)^3}$

12. $\dfrac{(8 - 4)^2}{4 - 2^3}$

13. $3(6 + 4)^2 - 5(17 - 20)^2$

14. $(4 \times 3 - 2)^2 \div (4 - 3 \times 2^2)$

15. $[(20 + 8 \times 5) - 7 \times (-3)] \div 9$

16. $5[19 + (5^2 - 16)^2]^2$

1.2 Fractions

Definitions

In the fraction $\frac{3}{4}$, the upper number (3) is called the **numerator** (or dividend) and the lower number (4) is the **denominator** (or divisor). In a **proper fraction,** the numerator is smaller than the denominator. An **improper fraction** has a numerator that is larger than the denominator. A **mixed number** contains a whole number plus a fraction. **Equivalent fractions** are fractions that are equal in value (even though their respective numerators and denominators differ). An equivalent fraction may be created by multiplying both the numerator and the denominator of a given fraction by the same number.

Example 1.2A *Examples of Types of Fractions*

a. $\frac{6}{13}$ is a proper fraction.

b. $\frac{17}{13}$ is an improper fraction.

c. $2\frac{4}{13}$ is a mixed number.

d. $\frac{5}{13}$, $\frac{10}{26}$, $\frac{15}{39}$, and $\frac{20}{52}$ are equivalent fractions. Note that the second, third, and fourth fractions may be obtained by multiplying both the numerator and the denominator of the first fraction by 2, 3, and 4, respectively.

Example 1.2B *Calculating an Equivalent Fraction*

Find the missing numbers that make the following three fractions equivalent.

$$\frac{7}{12} = \frac{56}{?} = \frac{?}{300}$$

Solution

To create a fraction equivalent to $\frac{7}{12}$, both the numerator and the denominator must be multiplied by the same number. To obtain 56 in the numerator of the second equivalent fraction, 7 must be multiplied by 8. Hence, the denominator in $\frac{7}{12}$ must also be multiplied by 8, making it $12 \times 8 = 96$. Therefore,

$$\frac{7}{12} = \frac{7 \times 8}{12 \times 8} = \frac{56}{96}$$

To obtain the denominator (300) in the third equivalent fraction, 12 must be multiplied by $\frac{300}{12} = 25$. The numerator must also be multiplied by 25. Hence, the equivalent fraction is

$$\frac{7 \times 25}{12 \times 25} = \frac{175}{300}$$

In summary,

$$\frac{7}{12} = \frac{56}{96} = \frac{175}{300}$$

Decimal and Percent Equivalents

The *decimal equivalent* value of a fraction is obtained by simply dividing the numerator by the denominator. Then shift the decimal point two places to the right and add the % symbol to express the fraction in *percent equivalent* form.

TIP *Adding or Subtracting Fractions*

To add or subtract any but the simplest of fractions, the easiest approach is to first convert each fraction to its decimal equivalent value. Then add or subtract the decimal equivalents as required. For example,

$$\frac{5}{12} + \frac{23}{365} = 0.41667 + 0.06301 = 0.4797 \text{ to four-figure accuracy}$$

Example 1.2C *Finding the Decimal and Percent Equivalents of Fractions and Mixed Numbers*

Convert each of the following fractions and mixed numbers to its decimal equivalent and percent equivalent values.

a. $\frac{2}{5} = 0.4 = 40\%$ **b.** $\frac{5}{2} = 2.5 = 250\%$

c. $2\frac{3}{4} = 2.75 = 275\%$ **d.** $\frac{5}{8} = 0.625 = 62.5\%$

e. $1\frac{3}{16} = 1.1875 = 118.75\%$ **f.** $\frac{3}{1500} = 0.002 = 0.2\%$

Rounding of Decimal and Percent Equivalents

The decimal equivalent of a fraction will often be an endless series of digits. Such a number is called a *nonterminating decimal.* Sometimes a nonterminating decimal contains a repeating digit or a repeating group of digits. This particular type of non-terminating decimal is referred to as a *repeating decimal.* A shorthand notation for repeating decimals is to place a horizontal bar over the first occurrence of the repeating digit or group of digits. For example,

$$\frac{2}{9} = 0.222222\ldots = 0.\overline{2} \quad \text{and} \quad 2\tfrac{4}{11} = 2.36363636\ldots = 2.\overline{36}$$

When a nonterminating decimal or its percent equivalent is used in a calculation, the question arises: How many figures or digits should be retained? We prefer not to write down or to enter in our calculator more digits than necessary. The following rules provide sufficient accuracy for the vast majority of our calculations.

RULES FOR ROUNDING NUMBERS:

1. Keep one more figure than the number of figures required in the final result. (When counting figures for the purpose of rounding, do not count leading zeros used only to properly position the decimal point.)
2. If the first digit dropped is 5 or greater, increase the last retained digit by 1.
3. If the first digit dropped is less than 5, leave the last retained digit unchanged.

Suppose, for example, the answer to a calculation is expected to be a few hundred dollars and you want the answer accurate to the cent. In other words, you require five-figure accuracy in your answer. To achieve this accuracy, the first rule says you should retain (at least) six figures in numbers[2] used in the calculations. The rule also applies to intermediate results that you carry forward to subsequent calculations. The consequence of rounding can be stated in another way—if, for example, you use a number rounded to four figures in your calculations, you can expect only three-figure accuracy in your final answer.

The instruction in Rule 1 about not counting "zeros used only to properly position the decimal point" is based on the following reasoning. A length of 6 mm is neither more nor less precise than a length of 0.006 m. (Recall that there are 1000 mm in 1 m.) The leading zeros in 0.006 m do not add precision to the measurement. They are inserted to locate the decimal point. Both measurements have one-figure accuracy. Contrast the preceding case with measurements of 1007 mm and 1.007 m. Here each zero comes from a decision about what the digit should be (rather than where the decimal point should be). These measurements both have four-figure accuracy.

[2] Some values may be known and written with perfect accuracy in less than five figures. For example, a year has exactly 12 months or an interest rate may be exactly 6%.

TRAP *NUMBER OF FIGURES VS. NUMBER OF DECIMAL PLACES*

Do not apply the first rounding rule in terms of the number of *decimal* places. It is the total number of figures (other than leading zeros) in a measurement or value that limits the accuracy of calculations which use the value.

TIP *OPTIMAL USE OF YOUR CALCULATOR*

Whenever possible, use the memory register(s) in your calculator to store intermediate results. This will save time and eliminate the possibility of keystroke errors upon data re-entry. It also virtually eliminates the introduction of rounding errors since most calculators retain two or three more figures internally than are shown in the display.

Example 1.2D *Fractions Having Repeating Decimal Equivalents*

Convert each of the following fractions to its decimal equivalent value expressed in the repeating decimal notation.

a. $\frac{2}{3} = 0.6666\ldots = 0.\overline{6}$

b. $\frac{14}{9} = 1.5555\ldots = 1.\overline{5}$

c. $6\frac{1}{12} = 6.08333\ldots = 6.08\overline{3}$

d. $3\frac{2}{11} = 3.181818\ldots = 3.\overline{18}$

e. $5\frac{2}{27} = 5.074074\ldots = 5.\overline{074}$

f. $\frac{5}{7} = 0.714285714285\ldots = 0.\overline{714285}$

Example 1.2E *Calculating and Rounding the Decimal Equivalents of Fractions*

Convert each of the following fractions and mixed numbers to its decimal equivalent value rounded to four-figure accuracy.

a. $\frac{2}{3} = 0.6667$

b. $6\frac{1}{12} = 6.083$

c. $\frac{173}{11} = 15.73$

d. $\frac{2}{1071} = 0.001867$

e. $\frac{17{,}816}{3} = 5939$

Example 1.2F *Applying the Rules for Rounding*

Maintaining the minimum number of figures at each step, evaluate

$$\$140\left(1 + 0.11 \times \frac{113}{365}\right) + \$74\left(1 + 0.09 \times \frac{276}{365}\right)$$

a. Accurate to the nearest dollar

b. Accurate to the nearest cent

Solution

The minimum number of figures required in the calculations is determined by the number of figures required in the answer. Therefore, we must first make a crude estimate of the answer. For this sort of estimate, it is sufficient to determine whether the answer is of the order of a few dollars, tens of dollars, or hundreds of dollars—an "error" of 20% or 30% is quite acceptable. In this example, we first note that the expressions inside both sets of brackets have values slightly larger than 1. After multiplication by the respective dollar amounts, the first term will be about \$150 and the second term about \$80. Therefore, the answer will be in the neighbourhood of \$200 to \$250.

a. For the answer to be accurate to the nearest dollar, it must have *three*-figure accuracy. The Rules for Rounding require that intermediate results have a minimum of *four* figures.

$$
\begin{aligned}
&\$140\left(1 + 0.11 \times \frac{113}{365}\right) + \$74\left(1 + 0.09 \times \frac{276}{365}\right) \\
&= \$140(1 + 0.11 \times 0.3096) + \$74(1 + 0.09 \times 0.7562) \\
&= \$140(1.034) + \$74(1.068) \\
&= \$144.8 + \$79.03 \\
&= \$223.83 \\
&= \$224 \qquad \text{to the nearest dollar}
\end{aligned}
$$

b. Two additional figures must be retained. Keep six digits in intermediate results in order to achieve five-figure accuracy in the answer.

$$
\begin{aligned}
&\$140\left(1 + 0.11 \times \frac{113}{365}\right) + \$74\left(1 + 0.09 \times \frac{276}{365}\right) \\
&= \$140(1 + 0.11 \times 0.309589) + \$74(1 + 0.09 \times 0.756164) \\
&= \$140(1.03405) + \$74(1.06805) \\
&= \$144.767 + \$79.0357 \\
&= \$223.80 \qquad \text{to the nearest cent}
\end{aligned}
$$

Note: By using a calculator's memory wisely, it is possible to obtain the answer in Example 1.2F without having to manually re-enter any intermediate results. However, if your solution is to be read and understood by someone else, you should present sufficient detail to reveal the steps in the solution.

Evaluating Complex Fractions

A **complex fraction** is a fraction containing one or more other fractions in its numerator or denominator. In simplifying complex fractions, particular attention should be paid to the correct order of mathematical operations as discussed in Section 1.1.

Example 1.2G Evaluating Complex Fractions

Evaluate the following complex fractions accurate to the cent.

a. $\dfrac{\$1265\left(1 + 0.115 \times \frac{87}{365}\right)}{1 + 0.125 \times \frac{43}{365}}$

$= \dfrac{\$1265(1 + 0.02741096)}{1 + 0.01472603}$

$= \dfrac{\$1265(1.027411)}{1.014726}$

$= \dfrac{\$1299.675}{1.014726}$

$= \$1280.81$

The quantity in brackets and the denominator are each slightly larger than 1. The answer is likely to be between \$1000 and \$2000.

For six-figure accuracy in the answer (to the cent), keep seven figures in intermediate results. Both 0.02741096 and 1.027411 have seven-figure accuracy.

b. $\dfrac{\$425\left(1 + \frac{0.10}{12}\right)^3}{\left(1 + \frac{0.09}{12}\right)^2}$

$= \dfrac{\$425(1.00833)^3}{1.00750^2}$

$= \dfrac{\$425 \times 1.02520}{1.01506}$

$= \$429.25$

The answer is likely to be in the \$400 to \$500 range. Therefore, we need five-figure accuracy. Maintain six figures in intermediate results.

POINT OF INTEREST

Mathematical Competencies Expected for Certain Courses Offered by the Institute of Canadian Bankers

The Institute of Canadian Bankers (ICB) offers several programs to financial services personnel. The programs and courses are described on the ICB Web site and in its annual catalogue. Both the Web site and the catalogue include a mathematics self-test whose "questions indicate the level of mathematical skills expected in order to pursue certain courses offered by the Institute of Canadian Bankers to professional bankers." The test has sections on arithmetic, algebra, graphs, time value of money, probability, and statistics. The test's preamble advises that "students should also be familiar with a financial calculator (Sharp EL733)."

Several questions from the arithmetic, algebra, and time value of money sections of the ICB self-test are presented in the appendix to this chapter. Any of these questions you are unable to answer now will seem straightforward by the time you complete Chapter 11. Self-test questions on probability and statistics (not presented in the appendix) are in the "less difficult" part of the range of problems you will encounter in a statistics course.

The ICB self-test illustrates that your college business mathematics and statistics courses will put you in a strong position to handle the mathematical aspects of a wide range of industry-based programs.

CAUGHT IN THE WEB

The Institute of Canadian Bankers Web site is at www.icb.org. From the home page you can access descriptions of the ICB's programs and courses.

You can also link to the full mathematics self-test through the home page or go directly to www.icb.org/self_test/default.htm. The test is presented in a multiple choice format. You can answer the questions online and have the test automatically scored.

Concept Questions

1. If you want four-figure accuracy in your answer, what minimum number of figures must be retained in the values used in the calculations?
2. For an answer of approximately $7000 to be accurate to the cent, what minimum number of figures must be maintained in the values used in the calculations?
3. If an answer of the order of five million dollars is to be accurate to the nearest dollar, how many figures must be maintained in the calculations?
4. If an interest rate (which could be greater than 10%) is to be calculated to the nearest 0.01%, what minimum number of digits must be retained in the numbers used to calculate the interest rate?
5. Give three examples of values which have only two or three digits but nevertheless are known with perfect accuracy.
6. If a time period of approximately five years is to be calculated to the nearest month, how many figures must be retained in the numbers used in the calculations?

Exercise 1.2

Answers to the odd-numbered problems are at the end of the book.

Convert each of the following fractions and mixed numbers to its decimal equivalent and percent equivalent values.

1. $\frac{7}{8}$ **2.** $\frac{65}{104}$ **3.** $\frac{47}{20}$ **4.** $-\frac{9}{16}$

5. $\frac{-35}{25}$ **6.** $1\frac{7}{25}$ **7.** $\frac{25}{1000}$ **8.** $\frac{1000}{25}$

9. $2\frac{2}{100}$ **10.** $-1\frac{11}{32}$ **11.** $\frac{37.5}{50}$ **12.** $\frac{22.5}{-12}$

Convert each of the following fractions and mixed numbers to its decimal equivalent and percent equivalent values expressed in the repeating decimal notation.

13. $\frac{5}{6}$ **14.** $-\frac{8}{3}$ **15.** $7\frac{7}{9}$ **16.** $1\frac{1}{11}$

17. $\frac{10}{9}$ **18.** $-\frac{4}{900}$ **19.** $-\frac{7}{270}$ **20.** $\frac{37}{27}$

Round each of the following to four-figure accuracy.

21. 11.3845 **22.** 9.6455 **23.** 0.5545454 **24.** 1000.49

25. 1.0023456 **26.** 0.030405 **27.** 40.09515 **28.** 0.0090909

Convert each of the following fractions and mixed numbers to its decimal equivalent and percent equivalent values rounded to five figures.

29. $\frac{1}{6}$ **30.** $\frac{7}{6}$ **31.** $\frac{1}{60}$ **32.** $2\frac{5}{9}$

33. $\frac{250}{365}$ **34.** $\frac{15}{365}$ **35.** $\frac{0.11}{12}$ **36.** $\frac{0.095}{12}$

Evaluate each of the following accurate to the cent.

37. $\$92\left(1 + 0.095 \times \frac{112}{365}\right)$

38. $\$100\left(1 + 0.11 \times \frac{5}{12}\right)$

39. $\$454.76\left(1 - 0.105 \times \frac{11}{12}\right)$

40. $\dfrac{\$790.84}{1 + 0.13 \times \frac{311}{365}}$

41. $\dfrac{\$3490}{1 + 0.125 \times \frac{91}{365}}$

42. $\dfrac{\$10{,}000}{1 - 0.10 \times \frac{182}{365}}$

43. $\$650\left(1 + \frac{0.105}{2}\right)^2$

44. $\$950.75\left(1 - \frac{0.095}{4}\right)^2$

45. $\dfrac{\$15{,}400}{\left(1 + \frac{0.13}{12}\right)^6}$

46. $\dfrac{\$550}{\left(1 + \frac{0.115}{2}\right)^4}$

47. $\dfrac{\$6600\left(1 + 0.085 \times \frac{153}{365}\right)}{1 + 0.125 \times \frac{82}{365}}$

48. $\dfrac{\$780\left(1 + \frac{0.0825}{2}\right)^5}{\left(1 + \frac{0.10}{12}\right)^8}$

49. $\$1000\left[\dfrac{\left(1 + \frac{0.09}{12}\right)^7 - 1}{\frac{0.09}{12}}\right]$

50. $\dfrac{\$350}{\frac{0.0975}{12}}\left[1 - \dfrac{1}{\left(1 + \frac{0.0975}{12}\right)^5}\right]$

51. $\dfrac{\$9500}{\dfrac{\left(1 + \frac{0.075}{4}\right)^5 - 1}{\frac{0.075}{4}}}$

52. $\$45\dfrac{\left[1 - \dfrac{1}{\left(1 + \frac{0.0837}{2}\right)^4}\right]}{\frac{0.0837}{2}} + \dfrac{\$1000}{\left(1 + \frac{0.0837}{2}\right)^4}$

1.3 The Basic Percentage Problem

Often we wish to compare a portion or part of a quantity to the whole amount. One measure of the relative size is the fraction

$$\frac{\textit{Portion}}{\textit{Base}}$$

where the term *Base* is used to represent the whole or entire amount. The fraction is called the *Rate*. That is,

THE BASIC PERCENTAGE FORMULA

$$\textit{Rate} = \frac{\textit{Portion}}{\textit{Base}} \quad \text{(1-1)}$$

This relation is also used more generally to compare a quantity (the *Portion*) to some other standard or benchmark (the *Base*). In these cases the *Portion* may be larger than the *Base*. Then the *Rate* will be greater than 1 and the percent equivalent *Rate* will be more than 100%.

Given any two of the three quantities: *Portion, Base,* and *Rate,* you can calculate the unknown quantity by rearranging formula (1-1). For example, multiplying both sides by *Base* gives

$$Portion = Rate \times Base$$

Dividing both sides of this rearranged equation by *Rate* gives

0.306849315

$$Base = \frac{Portion}{Rate}$$

TIP *AVOIDING "FORMULA CLUTTER"*

Do not create "formula clutter" by attempting to memorize rearranged versions of the same formula. Instead, learn the basic relation and rearrange it as required. Even learning the basic relation need not and should not be an exercise in memorization. The "basic relation" is merely a mathematical statement of an idea or a definition. With rare exceptions, there is a logical and intuitive basis for the idea or definition. To truly learn and understand mathematics, you should focus on the idea, the logic, and the intuition that lead to a formula. If you understand the idea and logic, you can readily express it in mathematical form.

Let's illustrate this approach with formula (1-1). The "need" is to determine the *relative* size of two quantities. "Relative" implies a comparison by *division.* Logically, one of the quantities must be chosen as the standard to which the other will be compared. Intuition suggests that we put this standard in the denominator. (This is the only way we will obtain a relative size of 2 if the "other quantity" is twice as large as the "standard.")

In the process of converting an idea to mathematical form, we usually introduce short names or symbols to represent the quantities involved. Ideally, a name or symbol should suggest the quantity it represents. In formula (1-1), *Base* suggests the standard (or basis) for the size comparison. *Portion* is a good name for suggesting a part of the *Base.* We continue to use *Portion* for other comparisons (instead of creating another formula having only one variable's name changed). Finally, *Rate* was chosen to represent the entire fraction or relative size[3].

TIP *DISTINGUISHING BETWEEN BASE AND PORTION*

The key to solving percentage problems is to distinguish between the *Base* and the *Portion.* The *Base* is always the standard or benchmark to which the *Portion* is being compared. In the wording of problems, the quantity following "of" is almost always the *Base.*

TRAP *DECIMAL EQUIVALENT OF RATES SMALLER THAN 1%*

When a *Rate* is less than 1%, students sometimes forget to move the decimal two places to the left in order to obtain the decimal equivalent *Rate.* For example, be clear on the distinction between 0.25% and 25%. The former is just $\frac{1}{4}$ *of* 1%—the latter is 25 *times* 1%. Their decimal equivalents are 0.0025 and 0.25, respectively. In terms of equivalent fractions, 0.25% equals $\frac{1}{400}$, while 25% equals $\frac{1}{4}$.

---

[3] Admittedly, *rate* does not particularly suggest "relative size." However, the term is commonly used in this formula because of the widespread use of *rate* in business to describe a portion as a percentage of the whole amount. Examples are commission *rate,* tax *rate, rate* of return, interest *rate,* etc.

Example 1.3A Using the Basic Percentage Formula

a. What is $40\frac{1}{4}\%$ of \$140.25?

b. How much is $0.08\overline{3}\%$ of \$5000?

c. What percentage is 7.38 kg of 4.39 kg?

d. 250% of what amount is \$10?

Solution

a. We are asked to calculate a part *(Portion)* of a given whole *(Base)*. Rearranging formula (1-1) to isolate *Portion,* we obtain

$$Portion = Rate \times Base = 40.25\% \text{ of } \$140.25 = 0.4025 \times \$140.25 = \$56.45$$

Therefore, \$56.45 is $40\frac{1}{4}\%$ of \$140.25.

b. Again the *Rate* and *Base* are given.

$$Portion = 0.08\overline{3}\% \text{ of } \$5000 = 0.0008\overline{3} \times \$5000 = \$4.17$$

Thus, \$4.17 is $0.08\overline{3}\%$ of \$5000.

c. We are given both the *Portion* and the *Base* for a comparison. Here 7.38 kg is being compared to the reference amount (*Base*) of 4.39 kg. The answer will be greater than 100% since the *Portion* is larger than the *Base.*

$$Rate = \frac{Portion}{Base} = \frac{7.38}{4.39} = 1.681 = 168.1\%$$

Thus, 7.38 kg is 168.1% of 4.39 kg.

d. Now the unknown is the amount to which \$10 is being compared. Therefore, the unknown is the *Base.* Rearranging formula (1-1) to isolate *Base* gives

$$Base = \frac{Portion}{Rate} = \frac{\$10.00}{2.50} = \$4.00$$

Therefore, 250% of \$4.00 is \$10.00.

Example 1.3B A Word Problem Requiring the Basic Percentage Formula

A battery manufacturer encloses a 50-cent rebate coupon in a package of four AAA batteries retailing for \$4.29. What percent rebate does the coupon represent?

Solution

In effect, the question is asking you to compare the rebate to the retail price. Therefore, the retail price is the *Base* in the comparison.

$$Rate = \frac{Portion}{Base} = \frac{\$0.50}{\$4.29} = 0.117 = 11.7\%$$

The manufacturer's percent rebate on the batteries is 11.7%.

TIP *UNITS OF PORTION AND BASE*

The preceding example demonstrates that the *Portion* and *Base* must have the *same* units when calculating *Rate*.

Concept Questions

1. What is the percent *Rate* if a quantity is four times the size of the *Base?*
2. What is the percent *Rate* if a quantity is $\frac{1}{1000}$ of the *Base?*
3. If the percent *Rate* is 1000%, what multiple is the *Portion* of the *Base?*
4. If the percent *Rate* is 0.01%, what fraction is the *Portion* of the *Base?*

Exercise 1.3

Answers to the odd-numbered problems are at the end of the book.

Calculate dollar amounts accurate to the cent and percent amounts to three-figure accuracy.

1. Calculate 1.75% of $350.
2. Calculate $6.\bar{6}\%$ of $666.66.
3. What percent is $1.50 of $11.50?
4. What percent is 88¢ of $44?
5. $45 is 60% of what amount?
6. $69 is 30% of what amount?
7. What is 233.3% of $75?
8. What is 0.075% of $1650?
9. $134 is what percent of $67?
10. $1.34 is what percent of $655?
11. 150% of $60 is what amount?
12. $0.58\bar{3}\%$ of $1500 is what amount?
13. $7\frac{1}{2}\%$ of what amount is $1.46?
14. $12\frac{3}{4}\%$ of what amount is $27.50?
15. What percent of $950 is $590?
16. What percent of $590 is $950?
17. 95% of what amount is $100?
18. $8\frac{1}{3}\%$ of what amount is $10?
19. 30 m is what percent of 3 km?
20. 500 g is what percent of 2.8 kg?
21. How much is $\frac{1}{2}\%$ of $10?
22. 0.75% of $100 is what amount?
23. $180 is 120% of what amount?
24. $559.35 is 113% of what amount?
25. $130\frac{1}{2}\%$ of $455 is what amount?

26. 0.0505% of $50,000 is what amount?

27. $281.25 is 225% of what amount?

28. 350% of what amount is $1000?

29. $10 is 0.5% of what amount?

30. $1.25 is $\frac{3}{4}$% of what amount?

31. A sales manager received a bonus of $7980 on the year's sales of $532,000. What was the bonus as a percent of sales and as a percent of her base salary of $45,000?

32. 113 of Freightway Trucks' employees belong to the Teamsters' Union; the remaining 31 employees are not union members. What percent of employees are in the union?

33. In a basketball game, the Langara College Falcons scored 54.$\overline{54}$% of 33 shots from the 2-point zone, 46.$\overline{6}$% of 15 attempts from the 3-point distance, and 79.3% of 29 foul shots (1 point each). How many points did the Falcons score?

34. Marilyn's net or take-home pay is 65% of her gross salary. If her take-home pay for May was $2000, what was her gross salary for the month?

35. Actual expenses of $169,400 for the most recent fiscal quarter were 110% of budgeted expenses. What were the budgeted expenses?

36. The $6\frac{1}{2}$% commission on the sale of a house was $13,975. What was the selling price of the property?

37. A property sold for 250% of what the vendors originally paid for it. What was that original price if the recent selling price was $210,000?

38. The fixed annual dividend on a company's preferred share is 8% of the share's original issue price (par value). If the annual dividend is $3.50, what is the par value of a share?

39. An individual's annual Registered Retirement Savings Plan (RRSP) contribution limit is the lesser of $13,500 or 18% of the previous year's earned income. At what level of earned income will $13,500 be the maximum contribution?

•40. Stan is a real estate salesperson. He receives 60% of the 6% commission that the real estate agency charges on sales. If his income for the past year was $75,000, what was his dollar volume of sales for the year?

•41. A stockbroker is paid 45% of the commission her firm charges her clients. If she personally received $134.55 on an $11,500 transaction, what is the firm's commission rate?

•42. A mortality rate indicates the fraction of individuals in a population who are expected to die in the next year. If the mortality rate among 35-year-old males is 0.34%, what is the expected number of deaths per year among a province's total of 50,000 such males? If 35-year-old males constitute 0.83% of the overall population in a city of 1.45 million, how many deaths of such males are expected in that city in a year?

*1.4 Payroll

An employee's remuneration may be based on an hourly wage, a salary, or a rate of commission. In some cases, earnings are based on a combination of a commission with a wage or a salary. This section will deal only with the calculation of *gross earnings*—the amount earned in a period before any deductions.[4]

Salaries

Where employment tends to be predictable and steady, an employee typically receives a salary quoted in terms of a biweekly, a monthly, or an annual amount. A monthly salary is usually paid on a monthly or semimonthly basis.[5] An annual salary may be paid at monthly, semimonthly, biweekly, or weekly intervals. For monthly and semimonthly pay periods, the gross earnings per pay are calculated by dividing the annual salary by 12 and 24, respectively.

A complication arises when an annual salary is paid at weekly or biweekly intervals. It occurs because a year does not contain exactly 52 weeks or 26 fortnights. A 365-day year contains 52 weeks *plus 1 day.* A leap year is 2 days longer than 52 weeks. Therefore, every fifth or sixth year will have 53 Fridays, the customary payday for weekly and biweekly payrolls.

The most commonly used approach is for the employer to divide the annual salary by the actual number of paydays falling in the calendar year. That is,

$$\text{Periodic gross pay} = \frac{\text{Annual salary}}{\text{Number of paydays in the year}}$$

With no change in annual salary, weekly gross earnings will then drop by about 2% in going from a 52-pay year to a 53-pay year. This can be difficult to explain to employees.[6]

---

[4] Employers are required by law to withhold income tax and the employee's share of Canada Pension Plan contributions and employment insurance premiums. By agreement with the employees or their union, an employer may also deduct and remit various insurance premiums, union dues, and pension plan contributions.

[5] Provincial employment standards usually provide that, if requested by the employees, monthly salaries be paid no less frequently than semimonthly. Some employers satisfy the requirement by providing a midmonth advance of approximately half the monthly take-home pay.

[6] A few employers use another approach. The periodic gross pay is obtained by dividing the annual salary by the *average* number of pay periods in a year. Since every fourth year is a leap year, the average length of a year is 365.25 days. This average length contains

$$\frac{365.25 \text{ days}}{14 \text{ days}} = 26.0893 \text{ biweekly pay periods}$$

or

$$\frac{365.25 \text{ days}}{7 \text{ days}} = 52.1786 \text{ weekly pay periods}$$

Assuming that an employee's base salary remains the same, this method results in no change to the periodic gross pay when a year contains an extra payroll date.

Example 1.4A Calculating Biweekly and Weekly Payments from Annual Salaries

An employee's annual salary is $45,000. Determine the gross earnings each payday in a year that has:

a. 26 biweekly paydays
b. 27 biweekly paydays
c. 52 weekly paydays
d. 53 weekly paydays

Solution

a. $\text{Biweekly gross pay} = \dfrac{\text{Annual salary}}{\text{Number of paydays in the year}} = \dfrac{\$45{,}000}{26} = \$1730.77$

b. Biweekly gross pay $= \$45{,}000 \div 27 = \$1666.67$

c. Weekly gross pay $= \$45{,}000 \div 52 = \$865.38$

d. Weekly gross pay $= \$45{,}000 \div 53 = \$849.06$

Hourly Wages

In jobs where the amount of work available is irregular or unpredictable, or where overtime is a common occurrence, employees are typically paid an hourly wage. Usually, a collective agreement between the employer and employees sets the number of hours per day (typically $7\frac{1}{2}$ or 8) and hours per week (typically $37\frac{1}{2}$ or 40) beyond which higher overtime rates apply. If no such agreement exists, federal or provincial employment standards apply.[7] The most common overtime rate, 1.5 times the regular hourly rate, is usually referred to as "time and a half."

Each province recognizes certain general holidays (often called "statutory" holidays, or "stat" holidays). New Year's Day, Good Friday, Canada Day, Labour Day, Thanksgiving Day, Christmas, and Boxing Day tend to be common to all provinces. Employees receive their normal pay for a statutory holiday *not* worked. If an employee is required to work on a stat holiday, she must be paid *at least* 1.5 times her regular wage rate. This is *in addition to* her regular wages for the day.

Gross earnings for a pay period are obtained by adding overtime and "stat" holiday pay to the regular pay. That is,

$$
\begin{aligned}
&\text{Regular hourly rate} \times \text{Regular hours}\\
&+ \text{Overtime hourly rate} \times \text{Overtime hours}\\
&\underline{+ \text{Stat holiday hourly rate} \times \text{Stat holiday hours worked}}\\
&= \text{Gross earnings}
\end{aligned}
$$

[7] For example, the Canada Labour Code applies to any "work, undertaking, or business that is within the legislative authority of Parliament."

When counting an employee's hours, remember the following points:

- Among "regular hours," always include the usual length of a working day for a statutory holiday falling in the pay period.
- If an employee works on a stat holiday, count the hours actually worked as "statutory holiday hours worked." Do not include them in "overtime hours" even if the employee exceeds the limit on regular hours for the pay period.

Sometimes wages in production and manufacturing jobs are structured to create an incentive for higher productivity. A *piecework rate* is based on the unit of production, such as $1 per garment sewn, or $2 per typed page, or $15 per ton of output.

$$\text{Piecework earnings} = \text{Number of units produced} \times \text{Piecework rate}$$

Example 1.4B Calculating the Gross Earnings of an Hourly Paid Employee

Steve is paid $18.30 an hour for his work on an assembly line. The regular work-week is 37.5 hours (five 7.5-hour shifts). In the most recent biweekly pay period (midnight Friday to midnight of the second following Friday), he worked full shifts from Monday to Friday of both weeks. The first Monday of the pay period was a statutory holiday. In addition, he worked 6 hours on the first Saturday. Overtime is paid at $1\frac{1}{2}$ times the regular rate and statutory holiday time at "double time." What will be Steve's gross pay for the period?

Solution

Steve should be credited with 7.5 *regular* hours for the statutory holiday whether he works it or not. These hours also count toward the 37.5 hours-per-week threshold at which overtime rates kick in. In addition to regular pay for the "stat" holiday, Steve will be paid twice his hourly rate ($2 \times \$18.30 = \$36.60$) for hours actually worked on a statutory holiday. (These hours *do not* count toward the 37.5 hours-per-week threshold for overtime eligibility.) Steve's hourly rate for overtime is $1.5 \times \$18.30 = \$27.45$.

The given information and calculations are summarized in the following table.

Week 1	Sat.	Mon.	Tue.	Wed.	Thur.	Fri.	Total	Hourly rate	Gross pay
Regular hours	6	7.5	7.5	7.5	7.5	1.5	37.5	$18.30	$686.25
Overtime hours						6	6	$27.45	$164.70
"Stat" holiday hours		7.5					7.5	$36.60	$274.50
Week 2	**Sat.**	**Mon.**	**Tue.**	**Wed.**	**Thur.**	**Fri.**	**Total**		
Regular hours		7.5	7.5	7.5	7.5	7.5	37.5	$18.30	$686.25
Overtime hours									
"Stat" holiday hours									
								Total:	$1811.70

Steve's gross pay for the two-week period will be $1811.70.

Example 1.4C *Calculating Gross Earnings Including a Piecework Wage*

An orchardist pays apple pickers \$5.50 per hour plus \$3.00 for each 100 kg of apples picked during an 8-hour shift. If a worker picks, on average, 180 kg of apples per hour for a 40-hour workweek, what will be the gross earnings for the week?

Solution

$$\begin{aligned}\text{Gross earnings} &= \left(\begin{matrix}\text{Hourly}\\\text{rate}\end{matrix} \times \begin{matrix}\text{Number}\\\text{of hours}\end{matrix}\right) + \left(\begin{matrix}\text{Piecework}\\\text{rate}\end{matrix} \times \begin{matrix}\text{Number}\\\text{of units}\end{matrix}\right)\\ &= (\$5.50 \times 40) + \$3.00\left(\tfrac{180}{100} \times 40\right)\\ &= \$220 + \$216\\ &= \$436\end{aligned}$$

The worker's gross earnings for the week will be \$436.

Commissions

For sales positions, it is standard practice to base at least a portion of the salesperson's remuneration on sales volume. If earnings are calculated strictly as a percent of sales, the salesperson is working on *straight commission.* A *graduated commission* structure pays progressively higher commission rates at higher levels of sales. A salesperson who receives a basic salary and a commission on sales is working on a *salary plus commission* basis. In some arrangements, the commission is paid only on sales exceeding a minimum level called the *quota.*

Example 1.4D *Calculating Gross Earnings Based on a Salary Plus Commission*

James manages a men's clothing store for a national chain. His monthly remuneration has three components: a \$1500 base salary, plus 2% of the amount by which the store's total sales volume for the month exceeds \$20,000, plus 8% of the amount by which his personal sales exceed \$2000. Calculate his gross compensation for a month in which his sales totaled \$4950 and other staff had sales amounting to \$54,630.

Solution

Base salary	\$1500.00
Commission on total store volume:	
0.02(\$54,630 + \$4950 − \$20,000)	791.60
Commission on personal sales:	
0.08(\$4950 − \$2000)	236.00
Total compensation	\$2527.60

James's gross earnings for the month are \$2527.60.

Example 1.4E *Calculating Gross Earnings Based on a Graduated Commission*

Tanya sells mutual funds for Pacific Financial Services Ltd. The "load" or commission charged on mutual fund sales averages 7%. Tanya works on a graduated commission structure in which she receives 40% of the gross commission on the first \$50,000 worth of mutual funds sold in a month, and 60% of the gross commission on additional sales. What will her earnings be for a month in which she sells \$90,000 worth of mutual funds?

Solution

Commission on first \$50,000:	
$0.40 \times 0.07 \times \$50{,}000$	\$1400
Commission on next \$40,000:	
$0.60 \times 0.07 \times \$40{,}000$	1680
Total earnings	\$3080

Tanya will earn \$3080 from the sale of \$90,000 worth of mutual funds in one month.

Exercise 1.4

Answers to the odd-numbered problems are at the end of the book.

1. Patricia's annual salary of \$29,400 is paid weekly. Her regular workweek is 35 hours. What hourly rate would she be paid for overtime at time and a half during a year containing:

   a. 52 paydays? **b.** 53 paydays?

2. Lucille receives an annual salary of \$37,500 based on a 37.5-hour workweek.

   a. What is Lucille's hourly rate of pay in a year with 26 paydays?

   b. What would be her gross earnings for a pay period in which she worked 9 hours of overtime at $1\frac{1}{2}$ times the regular rate of pay?

3. Morris is paid an annual salary of \$38,600 based on a 35-hour workweek.

   a. What is his equivalent hourly wage in a year having 27 biweekly paydays?

   b. What would be his total remuneration for a 2-week period in that year if he worked 10.5 hours of overtime at double time?

4. Ross's compensation is to be changed from an hourly rate of \$15.75 for a 40-hour week to a salary paid semimonthly. What should he be paid semimonthly in order for his annual earnings to remain the same? Assume there are exactly 52 weeks in a year.

5. Allison's regular hourly rate of pay is \$17.70. She is paid time and a half for all work on weekends and for any time over 7.5 hours on weekdays. Calculate her gross earnings for a week in which she works 4.5, 0, 7.5, 8.5, 6, 6, and 9 hours on Saturday to Friday, respectively.

6. Sam is paid \$24.50 per hour as a power plant engineer. He is paid $1\frac{1}{2}$ times the regular rate for all time exceeding 8 hours in a day or 40 hours in a week. Statutory holidays worked are paid at double time. What were his gross earnings for a week in which he clocked 8, 9.5, 8, 8, 10, 0, and 8 hours on Saturday to Friday, respectively, where Monday was a statutory holiday?

7. Mary sews for a clothing manufacturer. She is paid \$6.25 per hour plus a piece rate that depends on the type of garment in production. The current production run is men's shirts, for which she is paid \$2.25 for each unit exceeding her quota of 20 shirts in an 8-hour shift. What will be her total pay for a regular workweek in which her output on successive days was 24, 26, 27, 28, and 30 shirts?

8. Herb packs fish in 500-g cans on a processing line. He is paid \$8.25 per hour plus \$0.18 per kilogram for production in excess of 500 kg in a 7.5-hour shift. How much will he earn per day if he packs 250 cans per hour?

9. A shoe salesman is paid the greater of \$450 per week or 11% of sales.

a. What will be his earnings for a week in which sales are \$4236?

b. At what volume of sales per week will he start to earn more from the commission-based compensation?

10. Sharon is a manufacturer's representative selling office furniture directly to businesses. She receives a monthly salary of \$2000 plus a 2.2% commission on sales exceeding her quota of \$150,000 per month.

a. What are her earnings for a month in which she has \$227,000 in sales?

b. If her average monthly sales are \$235,000, what straight commission rate would generate the same average monthly earnings as her current basis of remuneration?

11. Julio is paid on a graduated commission scale of 5% on the first \$20,000 of sales in a month, 7.5% on the next \$20,000, and 10% on all additional sales.

a. What will he be paid for a month in which his sales are \$54,880?

b. What fixed commission rate would result in the same earnings for the month?

12. Karen works in a retail computer store. She receives a weekly base salary of \$300 plus a commission of 3% of sales exceeding her quota of \$20,000 per week. What were her sales for a week in which she earned \$630.38?

13. Jason's gross pay for August was \$3296.97 on sales totalling \$151,342. If his base salary is \$1500 per month, what is his rate of commission on sales exceeding his monthly quota of \$100,000?

14. Tom sells mutual funds on a graduated commission structure. He receives 3.3% on the first \$50,000 of sales in a month, 4.4% on the next \$50,000, and 5.5% on all further sales. What will be his gross earnings for a month in which he sells \$140,000 worth of mutual funds?

•15. Daniella's gross monthly earnings are based on commission rates of 4% of the first \$40,000 of sales, 5% of the next \$50,000, and 6% of all additional sales for the month. What was her sales total for a month in which she was paid \$5350?

•**16.** Trevor earns a base monthly salary of \$2000 plus a commission of 3% on sales exceeding his monthly quota of \$25,000. He receives a further 3% bonus on sales in excess of \$50,000. What must his sales be in order to gross \$4000 per month?

1.5 Simple and Weighted Averages

Simple Average The type of average initially encountered in basic mathematics is called the *simple average.* To calculate the simple average, simply (of course) add the values for all the items and then divide by the number of items. That is,

$$\text{Simple average} = \frac{\text{Sum of the values}}{\text{Total number of items}}$$

This average should be used in cases where each item has the *same* importance or each value occurs the *same* number of times.

Weighted Average We will now consider a situation requiring a different approach to averaging. Suppose you operate a seasonal business that employs 10 people during the peak period of July, August, and September. Only two employees are retained during the rest of the year. Is the average number of people employed during the year $\frac{10+2}{2} = 6$? No—a simple average of "10" and "2" is not appropriate because these two employment levels lasted for different lengths of time. The value "2" should influence the average more than the value "10." More precisely, each employment value should influence the average in proportion to its duration. Mathematicians have a rather odd way of expressing this sort of idea. In this case, they say: "Each employment level should be *weighted* by the time period for which it lasted." Consequently, we assign a *weighting factor* of three months to the value "10" and a weighting factor of nine months to the value "2." Then the *weighted average* number of employees during the year is calculated as follows:

$$\frac{(3 \times 10) + (9 \times 2)}{3 + 9} = 4.0$$

In the numerator, each of the two employment values (10 and 2) is multiplied by its weighting factor (three months and nine months, respectively). The two products are then added. Finally, the sum of the products is divided by the sum of the weighting factors.

In general, *a weighted average should be calculated when the values being averaged have differing relative importance, or when some values occur more often than others.*

$$\text{Weighted average} = \frac{\text{Sum of (Weighting factor} \times \text{Value)}}{\text{Sum of weighting factors}}$$

The preceding word equation[8] implies three steps for calculating a weighted average:

1. First multiply each of the "Values" by its "Weighting factor." The weighting factors represent the relative importance of each value, or the number of times each value occurs.
2. Add all of the products calculated in Step 1.
3. Finally, divide the Step 2 result by the sum of the "Weighting factors."

Weighted averages are frequently encountered in business. For example, the Toronto Stock Exchange's TSE 300 index is based on a weighted average price of the shares of 300 companies. Accountants may use the weighted average price paid for goods to determine the overall value of a firm's inventory. Several more examples will be presented in this section's Example problems and Exercise problems. When calculating weighted averages, you need to make careful decisions about what values should be averaged and what numbers should be used for the weighting factors. The following flow chart suggests an approach in which you answer key questions before the "number crunching" begins.

Figure 1.1 *Approach for Problems on Averages*

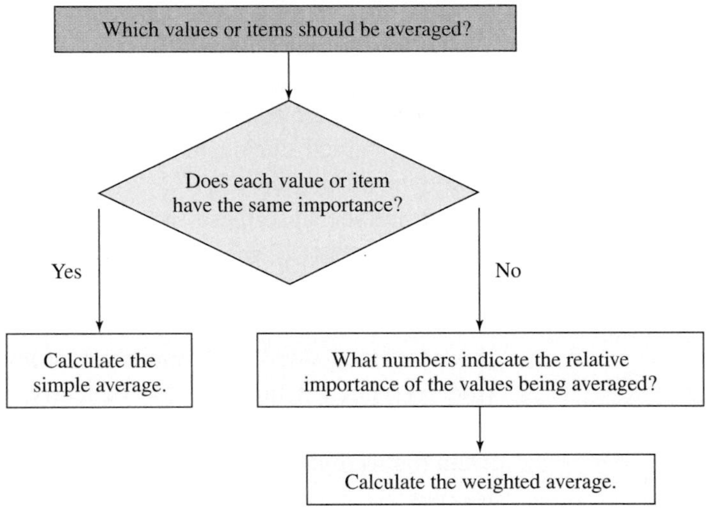

Example 1.5A *Calculation of Simple and Weighted Averages*

Northern Transport has 86 drivers each earning \$15.90 per hour, 14 clerical staff members each earning \$12.35 per hour, and 8 mechanics each earning \$24.67 per hour.

a. What is the simple average of the three hourly rates?

b. Calculate the weighted-average hourly rate earned by the three categories of employees.

---

[8] Note that if each of the "Values" has the same importance, then each weighting factor is "1." The "Weighted average" formula then reduces to the "Simple average" formula.

Solution

a. Simple average $= \dfrac{\$15.90 + \$12.35 + \$24.67}{3} = \$17.64$

b. Each hourly rate should be assigned a weighting factor reflecting the relative importance of that rate. The greater the number of employees receiving a particular wage rate, the more importance should be given to that rate. It is natural, then, to use the number of employees receiving an hourly rate as the weighting factor.

$$\text{Weighted average} = \frac{(86 \times \$15.90) + (14 \times \$12.35) + (8 \times \$24.67)}{86 + 14 + 8}$$

$$= \frac{\$1367.40 + \$172.90 + \$197.36}{108}$$

$$= \$16.09$$

The weighted average is less than the simple average because a high proportion of the employees earn the lowest hourly rate.

Example **1.5B** *Calculating a (Weighted) Grade Point Average*

Most colleges compute a grade point average (GPA) as the overall measure of a student's academic achievement. To compute the GPA, each letter grade is first converted to a grade point value. Each course's grade point value is then weighted by the number of credits the course carries.

The table on the left gives City College's scale for converting letter grades to grade point values. The table on the right presents Louise's courses and grades. Calculate her GPA.

Letter grade	Grade point value
A	4.0
A−	3.7
B+	3.3
B	3.0
B−	2.7
C+	2.3
C	2.0
C−	1.7
D	1.0

Course	Credits	Grade
English 100	3	B+
Math 100	4	B
Business 100	2	A
Economics 120	3	B−
Accounting 100	4	C+
Marketing 140	2	A−
Computing 110	3	C
Total	21	

Solution

The values to be averaged are the grade point scores Louise has achieved on her seven courses. However, these values are not given in a ready-to-use list. A new table should be constructed presenting the grade points earned on each course. (See the first three columns in the following table.)

A simple average of the grade point values is not appropriate because some courses carry more credits than others. A 4-credit course should count twice as much in the average as a 2-credit course. Therefore, each course's grade point score should be weighted by the number of credits that course carries (Column 4). The first step in the calculation of the weighted average is to multiply each value by its weighting factor (Column 5). In the second step, the products in Column 5 are added.

Course	Grade	Grade points earned (Values)	Credits (Weighting factors)	(Weighting factor) × (Value)
English 100	B+	3.3	3	9.9
Math 100	B	3.0	4	12.0
Business 100	A	4.0	2	8.0
Economics 120	B−	2.7	3	8.1
Accounting 100	C+	2.3	4	9.2
Marketing 140	A−	3.7	2	7.4
Computing 110	C	2.0	3	6.0
Total:			21	60.6

The third and last step is to divide the total in Column 5 by the total in Column 4. Hence,

$$\text{GPA} = \frac{60.6}{21} = 2.89$$

Louise's grade point average is 2.89.

Example 1.5C *Calculating the Weighted-Average Rate of Return for an Investment Portfolio*

One year ago, Mrs. Boyd divided her savings among four mutual funds as follows: 20% was invested in a bond fund, 15% in a money market fund, 40% in a Canadian equity fund, and 25% in a global equity fund. During the past year, the rates of return on the individual mutual funds were 10%, 4%, −2%, and 15%, respectively. What was the overall rate of return on her portfolio?

Solution

A simple average of the four rates of return is not the appropriate calculation because Mrs. Boyd invested different amounts of money in each mutual fund. The −2% return on the equity fund should have twice the influence of the 8% return on the bond fund because she invested twice as much money in the equity fund as in the bond fund. Therefore, we should choose weighting factors that reflect the relative amount of money invested in each mutual fund.

Mutual fund	Rate of return (Values)	Fraction of money invested (Weighting factor)	(Weighting factor) × (Value)
Bond fund	10%	0.20	2.0%
Money market fund	4%	0.15	0.6%
Canadian equity fund	−2%	0.40	−0.8%
Global equity fund	15%	0.25	3.75%
	Total:	1.00	5.55%

The overall or weighted-average rate of return on the portfolio was

$$\frac{5.55\%}{1.0} = 5.55\%.$$

Example 1.5D *Calculating the Weighted Average of a Varying Investment in a Business*

As of January 1, Alan had already invested \$63,000 in his business. On February 1 he invested another \$5000. Alan withdrew \$12,000 on June 1 and injected \$3000 on November 1. What was his average cumulative investment in the business during the year? (Assume that all months have the same length.)

Solution

A common error made in this type of problem is to attempt, in some way, to average the amounts that are contributed to or withdrawn from the business. We should instead average the cumulative balance of the invested funds. The amounts contributed and withdrawn from time to time are used only to revise the cumulative investment.

Period	Cumulative investment	Number of months
Jan. 1–Jan. 31	\$63,000	1
Feb. 1–May 31	\$63,000 + \$5000 = \$68,000	4
June 1–Oct. 31	\$68,000 − \$12,000 = \$56,000	5
Nov. 1–Dec. 31	\$56,000 + \$3000 = \$59,000	2

A weighted average should be calculated since the various amounts are invested for differing lengths of time. Each cumulative investment should be weighted by the number of months for which it lasted.

$$\text{Average investment} = \frac{(1 \times \$63{,}000) + (4 \times \$68{,}000) + (5 \times \$56{,}000) + (2 \times \$59{,}000)}{12}$$

$$= \$61{,}083$$

Alan's average investment in the business was \$61,083.

Concept Questions

1. In what circumstance should you calculate a weighted average instead of a simple average?
2. What condition must be met for the weighted average to equal the simple average?
3. How must you allocate your money among a number of investments so that your portfolio's overall rate of return will be same as the simple average of the rates of return on individual investments?
4. Suppose that, one year ago, you invested $20,000 in mutual fund A and $10,000 in mutual fund B. Which fund had the higher rate of return in the past year if the weighted average of the two rates of return exceeds the simple average? Present your reasoning.
5. X is less than Y. If the simple average of X and Y exceeds the weighted average, which of X and Y has the larger weighting factor? Present your reasoning.

Exercise 1.5

Answers to the odd-numbered problems are at the end of the book.

1. A survey of 254 randomly chosen residences in a city revealed that 4 had four television sets, 22 had three sets, 83 had two sets, 140 had one set, and 5 had no TV set at all. Based on the survey, what would you estimate to be the average number of TV sets per household?
2. An investor accumulated 1800 shares of Corel Corporation over a period of several months. She bought 1000 shares at $15.63, 500 shares at $19.00, and 300 shares at $21.75. What was her average cost per share? (*Note:* Investors who purchase shares in the same company or the same mutual fund at more than one price must eventually do this calculation. Tax rules require that the capital gain or loss on the sale of any of the shares be calculated using the weighted-average price paid for all of the shares rather than the particular price paid for the shares actually sold.)
3. A hockey goalie's "goals against average" (GAA) is the average number of goals scored against him per (complete) game. In his first 20 games in goal, O. U. Sieve had one shutout, two 1-goal games, three 2-goal games, four 3-goal games, seven 4-goal games, two 6-goal games, and one 10-goal disaster. Calculate his GAA.
4. Serge's graduated commission scale pays him 3% on his first $30,000 in sales, 4% on the next $20,000, and 6% on all additional sales in a month. What will be his average commission rate on sales for a month totalling:

   a. $60,000? **b.** $100,000?
5. The Royal Bank offers an "add-on option" on fixed-rate mortgages. The option allows the customer to borrow additional funds partway through the term of the mortgage. The interest rate charged on the combined mortgage debt becomes the weighted average of the old rate on the former balance and the current competitive rate on new mortgage financing. Suppose

Herschel and Julie had a mortgage balance of \$37,500 at $9\frac{1}{2}\%$, when they borrowed another \$20,000 at 8%. What interest rate will they be charged by the Royal Bank on the new consolidated balance?

6. Margot's grades and course credits in her first semester at college are listed below.

Grade:	C+	B−	B+	C−	B	C
Credits:	5	3	4	2	3	4

Using the Letter Grade to Grade Point Value conversion table in Example 1.5B, calculate her grade point average for the semester.

7. The distribution of scores obtained by 30 students on a quiz marked out of 10 is listed below.

Score:	10	9	8	7	6	5	4	3	2	1
Number of students:	2	6	9	7	3	2	0	1	0	0

What was the average score on the test?

8. Sam's transcript shows the following academic record for four semesters of part-time college studies. Calculate his cumulative GPA at the end of his fourth semester.

Semester	Credits	GPA
1	6	3.5
2	9	3.0
3	12	2.75
4	7.5	3.2

9. The "age" of an account receivable is the length of time that it has been outstanding. At the end of October, a firm has \$12,570 in receivables that are 30 days old, \$6850 in receivables that are 60 days old, and \$1325 in receivables that are 90 days old. What is the average age of its accounts receivable?

10. One year ago, Dan allocated the funds in his portfolio among five securities in the proportions listed in the table below. The rate of return on each security for the year is given in the third column of the table.

Security	Proportion invested	Rate of return for the year
Company A shares	15%	14%
Province B bonds	20	10
Company C shares	10	−13
Units in Fund D	35	12
Company E shares	20	27

Calculate the rate of return for the entire portfolio.

11. One of the methods permitted by Generally Accepted Accounting Principles for reporting the value of a firm's inventory is *weighted-average inventory pricing.* The Boswell Corporation began its fiscal year with an inventory of 156 units valued at $10.55 per unit. During the year it made the purchases listed in the following table.

Date	Units purchased	Unit cost
February 10	300	$10.86
June 3	1000	10.47
August 23	500	10.97

At the end of the year, 239 units remained in inventory. Determine:

a. The weighted-average cost of the units purchased during the year.

b. The weighted-average cost of the beginning inventory and all units purchased during the year.

c. The value of the ending inventory based on the weighted-average cost calculated in *b.*

12. Suppose a group of consumers spends 30% of its disposable income on food, 20% on clothing, and 50% on rent. If over the course of a year the price of food rose 10%, the price of clothing dropped 5%, and rent rose 15%, what was the average price increase experienced by these consumers?

13. The gross profit margin on the sale of an item is the percentage of the selling price remaining after paying the wholesale cost of the item. A restaurant owner had set prices so that the gross profit margin is 67% on appetizers, 45% on entrees, 70% on desserts, and 50% on beverages. If the distribution of revenue is 10% from appetizers, 50% from entrees, 25% from beverages, and 15% from desserts, what is the average gross profit margin?

•14. The balance on Nucorp's revolving loan began the month at $35,000. On the eighth of the month another $10,000 was borrowed. Nucorp was able to repay $20,000 on the twenty-fifth of the 31-day month. What was the average balance on the loan during the month? (Use each day's closing balance as the loan balance for the day.)

•15. A seasonal manufacturing operation began the calendar year with 14 employees. It added seven on April 1, eight on May 1, and 11 more on June 1. Six were laid off on September 1 and another 14 were let go on October 1. What was the average number of employees on the payroll during the calendar year? (Assume that each month has the same length.)

•16. Marcel must temporarily invest some extra funds in his retail business every fall to purchase inventory in preparation for the Christmas season. On September 1 he already had a total of $57,000 invested in his business. On October 1 he invested another $15,000, and on November 1 he injected

$27,000. He was able to withdraw $23,000 on February 1, $13,000 on March 1, and $6000 on May 1. What was the average investment in the business during the period from September 1 to August 31? (Assume that each month has the same length.)

•17. When a company calculates its earnings per common share for its financial statements, it uses the weighted-average number of common shares outstanding during the year. Suppose Enertec Corp. began its fiscal year (January 1 to December 31) with 5 million shares outstanding. On March 1, it sold a new public offering of 1 million shares. On June 1, employees and officers exercised stock options resulting in the issue of 500,000 common shares. On November 1, another 750,000 shares were issued when holders of convertible bonds chose to exercise the conversion privilege. What was the average of the number of common shares outstanding during the year? (Assume that each month has the same length.)

*1.6 Taxes

A **tax rate** is the percentage of a price or taxable amount that must be paid in tax. The dollar amount of the tax payable is

$$\textit{Tax payable} = \textit{Tax rate} \times \textit{Taxable amount}$$

This word equation is really just a variation of formula (1-1):

$$\textit{Portion} = \textit{Rate} \times \textit{Base}$$

Goods and Services Tax (GST)

The Goods and Services Tax (GST) is a federal sales tax charged on the vast majority of goods and services. The tax is paid by the purchaser of the good or service to the seller. Consequently, a business *collects* the GST on the goods and services it sells, and *pays* the GST on the goods and services it purchases. When the business files its GST return, it remits only the amount by which the tax collected from sales exceeds the tax paid on purchases. If, in a reporting period, the GST collected from sales happens to be less than the GST paid by the business on its purchases, Revenue Canada will refund the difference to the business.

The tax rate for the GST is 7%. The provinces of Nova Scotia, New Brunswick, and Newfoundland have agreed with the federal government to blend their provincial sales taxes with the GST in a single Harmonized Sales Tax (HST). The HST is administered by the federal government through Revenue Canada. The 15% rate for the HST applies to the same base of goods and services as the GST. The federal component of the 15% HST rate is 7% and the provincial component is 8%.

Example 1.6A *Calculation of the GST or the HST Payable by a Business*

Ace Appliance Repair files GST returns quarterly. During the first quarter of the year, Ace billed its customers $17,650 for labour, $4960 for parts, and then added on the GST. In the same period, Ace paid \$3250 to suppliers for parts, \$1800 for rent, \$673 for utilities, \$594 for truck repairs, plus the GST on these goods and services.

a. What GST must be remitted by Ace (or refunded by Revenue Canada) for the first quarter?

b. Repeat part *a* for the case where Ace also bought a new truck for \$24,000 on the last day of the quarter.

c. Repeat part *a* for the case where Ace pays HST instead of GST.

Solution

a. GST collected = 0.07(\$17,650 + \$4960) = \$1582.70
GST paid = 0.07(\$3250 + \$1800 + \$673 + \$594) = \$442.19
GST remittance payable = \$1582.70 − \$442.19 = \$1140.51

b. GST paid on the truck purchase = 0.07 × \$24,000 = \$1680
This GST credit exceeds the net GST calculated in part *a*. Hence, Ace will qualify for a refund.

GST refund receivable = \$1680.00 − Answer in part *a*
= \$1680.00 − \$1140.51
= \$539.49

c. HST collected = 0.15(\$17,650 + \$4960) = \$3391.50
HST paid = 0.15(\$3250 + \$1800 + \$673 + \$594) = \$947.55
HST remittance payable = \$3391.50 − \$947.55 = \$2443.95

Provincial Sales Tax (PST)

All provinces except Alberta and the three provinces participating in the HST charge a sales tax at the *retail* level. This tax typically applies to a somewhat narrower range of goods and to a considerably more restricted range of services than the GST. The various provincial sales tax (PST) rates are presented in Table 1.1. In Ontario and the western provinces, the tax rate is applied to the retail price. That is,

$$\text{PST} = \text{Sales tax rate} \times \text{Retail price}$$
(in Ontario and the western provinces)

In Quebec and Prince Edward Island, the PST is calculated on the combination of the retail price *plus* the GST. That is,

$$\text{PST} = \text{Sales tax rate} \times (\text{Retail price} + \text{GST})$$
(in Quebec and Prince Edward Island)

With the PST calculated this way, a consumer pays provincial sales tax on the GST—tax on a tax!

Table 1.1 *Provincial Sales Tax Rates (as of May 1, 1999)*

Province	Tax rate
Alberta	0%
British Columbia	7
Manitoba	7
Ontario	8
Prince Edward Island	10
Quebec	7.5
Saskatchewan	6

Example **1.6B** *Calculating the PST*

Calculate the PST on a \$100 item in

a. Ontario.
b. Quebec.

Solution

a. PST = 0.08 × \$100 = \$8.00
b. In Quebec the PST is based on the list price plus GST.

$$\text{GST} = 0.07 \times \$100 = \$7.00$$

$$\begin{aligned}\text{PST} &= 0.075 \times (\$100 + \text{GST}) \\ &= 0.075 \times \$107 \\ &= \$8.03\end{aligned}$$

Property Tax

Real estate property tax is not a sales tax, but rather an annual tax paid by the owners of real estate. Property taxes are paid to municipal and regional governments to cover costs of municipal services, public schools, policing, etc. Tax rates are set by municipal and regional governments, and by other agencies (such as school boards) authorized by the provincial government to levy property taxes. Municipal and regional governments also establish criteria for determining the taxable value (known as the *assessed value*) of real property.

Property tax rates in most provinces are quoted as a mill rate. A **mill rate** indicates the amount of tax per \$1000 of assessed value. For example, a mill rate of 13.732 means a tax of \$13.732 per \$1000 of assessed value. The percent equivalent of this mill rate is 1.3732%.

The annual tax on a property is calculated by multiplying the assessed value of the property by the decimal equivalent of the mill rate. The *decimal* equivalent of a mill rate is $\frac{\text{Mill rate}}{1000}$.

$$\text{Property tax} = \frac{\text{Mill rate}}{1000} \times \text{Assessed value of the property}$$

Example 1.6C Calculating the Property Tax on a Residential Property

A homeowner's tax notice lists the following mill rates for various local services and capital developments. If the assessed value of the property is $164,500, calculate each tax levy and the current year's total property taxes.

Tax rate	Mill rate
Schools	6.7496
General city	7.8137
Water	0.8023
Sewer and sanitation	0.7468

Solution

$$\begin{aligned}\text{School tax levy} &= \frac{\text{Schools mill rate}}{1000} \times \text{Assessed value}\\ &= \frac{6.7496}{1000} \times \$164{,}500\\ &= \$1110.31\end{aligned}$$

Similarly

$$\begin{aligned}\text{General city levy} &= \frac{7.8137}{1000} \times \$164{,}500 = \$1285.35\\ \text{Water levy} &= \frac{0.8023}{1000} \times \$164{,}500 = \$131.98\\ \text{Sewer levy} &= \frac{0.7468}{1000} \times \$164{,}500 = \$122.85\\ \text{Total property taxes} &= \$1110.31 + \$1285.35 + \$131.98 + \$122.85\\ &= \$2650.49\end{aligned}$$

Example 1.6D Calculating a Mill Rate

The town council of Concord has approved a new capital levy component of the property tax to pay for a new recreation complex. The levy must raise $400,000 in each of the next 10 years.

a. If the total assessed value of properties within Concord's jurisdiction is $738 million, what mill rate (to five-figure accuracy) must be set for the capital levy?

b. As a result of the capital levy, what additional tax will be paid each year by the owner of a property assessed at $200,000?

Solution

a. Since

$$\text{Tax rate} = \frac{\text{Tax payable}}{\text{Taxable amount}}$$

Then

$$\text{Capital levy tax rate} = \frac{\text{Required total tax}}{\text{Total assessed value}}$$

$$= \frac{\$400{,}000}{\$738{,}000{,}000}$$

$$= 0.00054201$$
$$= 0.54201 \text{ mill}$$

b. $$\text{Additional property tax} = \frac{\text{Capital levy mill rate}}{1000} \times \text{Assessed value}$$

$$= \frac{0.54201}{1000} \times \$200{,}000$$
$$= \$108.40$$

Exercise 1.6

Answers to the odd-numbered problems are at the end of the book.

1. Johnston Distributing, Inc. files quarterly GST returns. The purchases on which it paid the GST and the sales on which it collected the GST for the last four quarters were as follows:

Quarter	Purchases	Sales
1	$596,476	$ 751,841
2	967,679	627,374
3	823,268	1,231,916
4	829,804	994,622

Calculate the GST remittance or refund due for each quarter.

2. Sawchuk's Home and Garden Center files monthly GST returns. The purchases on which it paid the GST and the sales on which it collected the GST for the last four months were as follows:

Month	Purchases	Sales
March	$135,650	$ 57,890
April	213,425	205,170
May	176,730	313,245
June	153,715	268,590

Calculate the GST remittance or refund due for each month.

3. Calculate the price, including both GST and PST, that an individual will pay for a car sold for $21,900 in:

a. Alberta **b.** Ontario **c.** Quebec

4. How much more will a consumer pay for an item listed at $1000 (pretax) in Quebec than in British Columbia?

•**5.** In its most recent operating quarter, Robertson's Footwear had sales of $87,940. All sales are subject to GST, but $28,637 of the total represented PST-exempt sales. Calculate the PST that must be remitted if Robertson's is located in:

a. Saskatchewan **b.** Prince Edward Island

•**6.** Prepare a table showing the single tax rate for each province in Table 1.1 that is equivalent to the combined effect of the GST and PST on retail purchases. (Hint: Find the after-tax price of a $100 item in each province.)

7. What will be the taxes on a property assessed at $227,000 if the mill rate is 16.8629?

8. **a.** What is the percent equivalent of 0.1 mill?

b. If the mill rate increases by 0.1 mill, what will be the dollar increase in property taxes on a $200,000 home?

9. The assessment on a farm consists of $143,000 for the house and $467,000 for the land and buildings. A mill rate of 15.0294 applies to residences, and a rate of 4.6423 applies to agricultural land and buildings. What are the total property taxes payable on the farm?

10. The assessment on a property increased from $185,000 last year to $198,000 in the current year. Last year's mill rate was 15.6324.

a. What will be the change in the property tax from last year if the new mill rate is set at 15.2193?

b. What would the new mill rate have to be for the dollar amount of the property taxes to be unchanged?

•**11.** The school board in a municipality will require an extra $2,430,000 for its operating budget next year. The current mill rate for the school tax component of property taxes is 7.1253.

a. If the total of the assessed values of properties in the municipality remains at the current figure of $6.78 billion, at what value must next year's school mill rate be set?

b. If the total of all assessed values rises by 5% over this year's aggregate assessment, at what value must next year's school mill rate be set?

•**12.** The total assessed value of property in Brockton has risen by $97 million from last year's figure of $1.563 billion. The mill rate last year for city services was 9.4181. If the city's budget has increased by $750,000, what mill rate should it set for the current year?

Appendix: Questions from an Institute of Canadian Bankers Self-Test

The following questions indicate the level of mathematical skill expected in order to pursue certain courses offered to professional bankers by the Institute of Canadian Bankers[9]. (Refer to the Point of Interest box at the end of Section 1.2.)

ARITHMETIC

1. The sales discount on the original price of an alarm clock is 10%. If you have a \$5 credit note and the original price of the alarm clock is \$25, how much will you pay to purchase the clock?
2. What is the value of 10^3?
3. What is the value of $(1 + 0.5)^3$?
4. There are 15 customer service representatives and 6 managers in a financial institution. What is the ratio of customer service representatives to managers?
5. There are 15 customer service representatives and 6 managers in a financial institution. What percentage (to the nearest whole number) of the overall staff is made up of customer service representatives?
6. Yesterday the value of a stock was \$13.75. Today it is \$13.50. What is the percentage change in the price of the stock between yesterday and today (2 decimal places)?
7. What is the value of $0.36^{1/2}$?
8. Calculate the average of \$425, \$550, \$475, \$550, and \$400.
9. Evaluate: $6 \times \dfrac{1}{10^1} + 7 \times \dfrac{1}{10^2} + 8 \times \dfrac{1}{10^4}$.
10. A client has a first mortgage amounting to \$100,000 at an annual rate of 8% and a second mortgage of \$50,000 at a rate of 10% annually. Calculate the weighted-average mortgage rate that the client faces.

ALGEBRA

1. Solve $12 + 2x = 8$ for x.
2. A telemarketer gets a base salary of \$100 per week plus \$8 per unit sold. Write an equation representing her weekly earnings (y) based on the number of units sold (x).
3. The perimeter P of a rectangle is the sum of its four sides. The formula for the perimeter of the rectangle is $P = l + l + w + w$. The best way to write this formula is:

   a. $P = 2lw$ **c.** $P = 2l + 2w$

   b. $P = (l + w)^2$ **d.** $P = l^2 + w^2$

---

[9] Source: *Institute of Canadian Bankers.* Reprinted with permission.

4. The cost of two orders of a hamburger and French fries is \$5.50. If the price of an order of fries is \$1.25, which of the following equations can be used to find the price of a hamburger (represented by x)?

   a. $2(x + 1.25) = 5.50$
   b. $2x + 1.25 = 5.50$
   c. $(2 \times 1.25) + x = 5.50$
   d. None of these

5. Solve the following equation for x: $4x + 2400 = 2200(1 + 0.02x)$

Time Value of Money

1. You have \$20,000 worth of five-year investment certificates that have just reached maturity. If the annual rate of interest on these certificates was 8%, find the original amount invested.
2. An investment earns you an annual compound interest rate of 3.5%. Starting with a deposit of \$15,000, what will be the future value of your investment two years from now?
3. You agree to lend your daughter \$100 at an interest rate of 6.5% compounded annually for a period of one year. How much interest must she pay you at the end of the year?
4. Calculate (to three decimal places) the discounting factor $(1 + i)^{-n}$ when the interest rate i is 12% and the compounding period n is four years.
5. You decide to open an account in your daughter's name on January 1, 2001, with a deposit of \$1000. Starting February 1, you add \$50 at the beginning of every month. On December 31, 2001, how much money will you have if the account provides a return of 4% compounded monthly?
6. What is the value of $[(1+i)^n - 1] \div i$, when the annual interest rate is 18% compounded semiannually and the period is two years? (three decimal places)
7. You decide to begin contributing \$1200 to your retirement savings plan at the end of every year. At an interest rate of 5% compounded annually, how much will you accumulate in 20 years?
8. You want an investment that will earn you \$100 every month for a period of two years. If the annual interest rate is 6% compounded monthly, how much money should you invest for that purpose?
9. A customer invests \$4400 at a simple interest rate of 2.75% per annum. At withdrawal the original deposit is worth \$4800, indicating that revenue of \$400 was accumulated. Determine how long the money was invested.

Review Problems

Answers to the odd-numbered review problems are at the end of the book.

1. Evaluate each of the following:
   a. $(2^3 - 3)^2 - 20 \div (2 + 2^3)$ b. $4(2 \times 3^2 - 2^3)^2 \div (10 - 4 \times 5)$
   c. $\$213.85\left(1 - 0.095 \times \frac{5}{12}\right)$ d. $\frac{\$2315}{1 + 0.0825 \times \frac{77}{365}}$
   e. $\$325.75\left(1 + \frac{0.105}{4}\right)^2$ f. $\frac{\$710}{\left(1 + \frac{0.0925}{2}\right)^3}$
   g. $\$885.75\left(1 + 0.0775 \times \frac{231}{365}\right) - \frac{\$476.50}{1 + 0.0775 \times \frac{49}{365}}$
   h. $\$859\left(1 + \frac{0.0825}{12}\right)^3 + \frac{\$682}{\left(1 + \frac{0.0825}{12}\right)^2}$
2. What percent of \$6.39 is \$16.39?
3. 80% of what amount is \$100?
4. $\frac{3}{4}$% of what amount is \$1.00?
5. Six in. is what percent of 2 yds.?
6. The actual profit of \$23,400 for the most recent fiscal quarter was 90% of the forecast profit. What was the forecast profit?
7. Luther is paid an annual salary of \$56,600 based on a $37\frac{1}{2}$-hour workweek.
   a. What is his equivalent hourly wage in a year having 26 biweekly paydays?
   b. What would be his total remuneration for a two-week period of that year if he worked 4.5 hours of overtime at time and a half?
8. Sonja is paid \$32.50 per hour as a veterinarian. She is paid $1\frac{1}{2}$ times the regular rate for all time exceeding $7\frac{1}{2}$ hours in a day or $37\frac{1}{2}$ hours per week. Work on a statutory holiday is paid at double time. What were her gross earnings for a week in which she worked 6, 0, 3, $7\frac{1}{2}$, 9, $7\frac{1}{2}$, and 8 hours on Saturday to Friday, respectively, and the Monday was a statutory holiday?
9. Lauren's gross pay for July was \$3188.35 on net sales totaling \$88,630. If her base salary is \$1000 per month, what is her rate of commission on sales exceeding her monthly quota of \$40,000?
10. One year ago Helga allocated the funds in her portfolio among five securities in the amounts listed in the following table. The rate of return on each security for the year is given in the third column of the table.

Security	Amount invested	Rate of return for the year
Company U shares	\$ 5000	30%
Province V bonds	20,000	−3
Company W shares	8000	−15
Units in Fund X	25,000	13
Company Y shares	4500	45

Calculate the rate of return for the entire portfolio.

11. The fiscal year for Pine Valley Skiing Ltd., the owner of a downhill skiing facility, ends on June 30. The company began the recently completed fiscal year with its summer maintenance crew of seven. It took on six more employees on September 1, hired another 18 on November 1, and added 23 more on December 1. Eleven employees were laid off on March 1, 20 were let go on April 1, and another 16 left on May 1, leaving only the permanent maintenance personnel. What was the average number of employees per month working for Pine Valley during the fiscal year? (Assume that each month has the same length.)

Self-Test Exercise

Answers to the self-test problems are at the end of the book.

1. Evaluate each of the following:

a. $96 - (6 - 4^2) \times 7 - 2$

b. $81 \div (5^2 - 16) - 4(2^3 - 13)$

c. $\dfrac{\$827.69}{1 + 0.125 \times \frac{273}{365}} + \$531.49\left(1 + 0.125 \times \dfrac{41}{365}\right)$

d. $\$550.45\left(1 + 0.0875 \times \dfrac{195}{365}\right) - \dfrac{\$376.29}{1 + 0.0875 \times \frac{99}{365}}$

e. $\$1137\left(1 + \dfrac{0.0975}{12}\right)^2 + \dfrac{\$2643}{\left(1 + \frac{0.0975}{12}\right)^3}$

2. 167.5% of what amount is $100?

3. Through a mechanism (on Canadian Individual Tax Returns) known as the "Old Age Security clawback," an individual receiving Old Age Security (OAS) benefits must repay an increasing proportion of these benefits to the federal government as the individual's net income rises beyond a certain threshold. If the OAS clawback is 15% of net income exceeding $54,000, at what amount of net income must a taxpayer repay all $4500 of OAS benefits received in the year?

4. Jason earns an annual salary of $61,000 as an executive with a provincial utility. He is paid biweekly based on 26 pay periods in the year. During a strike, he worked 33 hours more than the regular 75 hours for a two-week pay period. What was his gross pay for that period if the company agreed to pay 1.5 times his equivalent hourly rate for overtime?

5. Marion receives a monthly base salary of $1000. On the first $10,000 of sales above her monthly quota of $20,000, she is paid a commission of 8%. On any additional sales, the commission rate is 10%. What were her gross earnings for the month of August, in which she had sales amounting to $38,670?

6. Ms. Yong invested $16,800 in a Canadian equity mutual fund, $25,600 in a U.S. equity mutual fund, and $31,000 in a global fund that holds a variety of foreign securities. If in the subsequent six months, the value of the units in the Canadian fund dropped by 4.3%, the U.S. fund declined by 1.1%, and the global fund rose by 8.2%, what was the overall rate of return on Ms. Yong's mutual fund portfolio for the six-month holding period?

◆ **7.** Anthony began the year with $96,400 already invested in his Snow 'n Ice retail store. He withdrew $14,200 on March 1 and another $21,800 on April 1. On August 1, he invested $23,700, and on November 1 he contributed another $19,300. What was his average cumulative investment during the year? (Assume that each month has the same length.)

www.Exercise.com

INSTITUTE OF CANADIAN BANKERS MATHEMATICS SELF-TEST

Take the Institute of Canadian Bankers mathematics self-test online at www.icb.org/self_test/default.htm. At the end of the test, click on the "Correction" button to have the test automatically scored (and also generate a list of questions that were incorrectly answered). Don't expect to get a high score. Your business math and statistics courses will fix that! At the end of this course, take the test again to gauge your progress.

Summary of Notation and Key Formulas

RULES FOR ROUNDING NUMBERS:

1. Keep one more figure than the number of figures required in the final result. (When counting figures for the purpose of rounding, do not count leading zeros used only to properly position the decimal point.)
2. If the first digit dropped is 5 or greater, increase the last retained digit by 1.
3. If the first digit dropped is less than 5, leave the last retained digit unchanged.

(1-1)

$$\textit{Rate} = \frac{\textit{Portion}}{\textit{Base}}$$

$$\textit{Simple average} = \frac{\textit{Sum of the values}}{\textit{Total number of items}}$$

$$\textit{Weighted Average} = \frac{\textit{Sum of (Weighting factor} \times \textit{Value)}}{\textit{Sum of weighting factors}}$$

List of Key Terms

Complex fraction *(p. 9)*
Denominator *(p. 5)*
Equivalent fractions *(p. 5)*
Improper fraction *(p. 5)*
Mill rate *(p. 33)*
Mixed number *(p. 5)*
Numerator *(p. 5)*
Proper fraction *(p. 5)*
Tax rate *(p. 31)*

CHAPTER OUTLINE

LEARNING OBJECTIVES

After completing this chapter, you will be able to:

- Simplify algebraic expressions
- Solve linear equations in one variable
- Solve "word problems" that lead to a linear equation in one unknown
- Solve problems involving a single percent change
- Calculate returns from investments in terms of both dollars and percentages
- Solve problems involving a series of compounding percent changes
- Determine the overall effect of compounding a series of percent changes or rates of return on investment

CHAPTER

2

Review and Applications of Algebra

ALGEBRA IS A BRANCH OF MATHEMATICS in which letters or symbols are used to represent various items (variables). Quantitative relationships (equations) can then be expressed in a concise manner. Algebra has rules and procedures for working with these equations. The rules enable us to calculate values of unknown variables and to derive new relationships among variables.

Algebra is vital to applications of mathematics to business. We (or our computers) make use of equations describing relationships among real-world variables. If your algebraic skills are rusty, you may need to spend more time doing exercises in the first four sections of the chapter than is allotted in your course schedule.

We begin by reviewing basic terminology, techniques for simplifying algebraic expressions, and the procedure for solving a linear equation in one unknown. Our refurbished skills will then be employed in word problems and in applications of percent change, rate of return on investment, and compounding percent changes.

2.1 Operations with Algebraic Expressions

Definitions

We will use a simple example to illustrate some basic language of algebra. Suppose you work in the payroll department of a large retail store. Every month you must calculate each employee's gross earnings. The sales staff are paid a base salary of \$1000 per month plus a commission of 4% of sales. The gross earnings of a salesperson in a month are calculated using:

$$\$1000 + 0.04 \times (\text{Sales for the month})$$

The only quantity that varies from one salesperson to another, and from one month to another, is the amount of each individual's sales. "Sales for the month" is therefore the mathematical *variable* in this calculation. In algebra we use a letter or symbol to represent a mathematical variable. With s representing "sales for the month," we can write the following algebraic expression for the gross monthly earnings:

$$\$1000 + 0.04s$$

An **algebraic expression** indicates the mathematical operations to be carried out on a combination of numbers and variables. To obtain any salesperson's gross earnings, we substitute that person's sales for the month as the value for s. The expression tells us to first multiply the sales by 0.04 and then add \$1000.

The components of an algebraic expression that are separated by addition or subtraction signs are called **terms.** This particular expression has two terms: \$1000 and $0.04s$. An expression containing only one term is called a **monomial.** A **binomial** expression has two terms, and a **trinomial** has three terms. The name **polynomial** is often used for any expression with more than one term.

Each term in an expression consists of one or more **factors** separated by multiplication or division signs. (Multiplication is implied by writing factors side by side with no multiplication symbol between them.) The numerical factor in a term is called the **numerical coefficient,** and the variable factors together are called the **literal coefficient.** The first term in our sample binomial contains only one factor, \$1000. The second term contains two factors: the numerical coefficient 0.04 and the literal coefficient s.

Example 2.1A *Identifying the Terms, Factors, and Coefficients in a Polynomial*[1]

$3x^2 + xy - 6y^2$ is a trinomial.

Term	Factors	Numerical coefficient	Literal coefficient
$3x^2$	$3, x, x$	3	x^2
xy	x, y	1	xy
$-6y^2$	$6, y, y$	-6	y^2

[1] Exponents and powers will be discussed in Section 2.2. For now, it is sufficient to recall that a^2 means $a \times a$, a^3 means $a \times a \times a$, and so on.

Addition and Subtraction

Sometimes an algebraic expression may be simplified by adding or subtracting certain terms before any values are substituted for the variables. Terms with the same *literal* coefficients are called **like terms.** Only like terms may be directly added or subtracted. Addition or subtraction of like terms is performed by adding or subtracting their numerical coefficients while keeping their common literal coefficient. For example, $2xy + 3xy = 5xy$. Adding or subtracting like terms is often referred to as *collecting* or *combining* like terms.

Example 2.1B *Simplifying Algebraic Expressions by Combining Like Terms*

a. $3a - 4b - 7a + 9b$
$= 3a - 7a - 4b + 9b$
$= (3 - 7)a + (-4 + 9)b$
$= -4a + 5b$

$3a$ and $-7a$ are like terms; $-4b$ and $9b$ are like terms. Combine the numerical coefficients of like terms.

b. $0.2x + 5x^2 + \frac{x}{4} - x + 3$
$= 5x^2 + (0.2 + 0.25 - 1)x + 3$
$= 5x^2 - 0.55x + 3$

Convert numerical coefficients to their decimal equivalents; then combine like terms.

c. $\frac{2x}{1.25} - \frac{4}{5} - 1\frac{3}{4}x$
$= 1.6x - 0.8 - 1.75x$
$= -0.15x - 0.8$

Convert numerical coefficients to their decimal equivalents; then combine like terms.

d. $\frac{3x}{1.0164} + 1.049x - x$ — Evaluate the numerical coefficients.
$= 2.95159x + 1.049x - x$
$= (2.95159 + 1.049 - 1)x$ — Combine like terms.
$= 3.0006x$

e. $x\left(1 + 0.12 \times \frac{241}{365}\right) + \frac{2x}{1 + 0.12 \times \frac{81}{365}}$ — Evaluate the numerical coefficients.
$= 1.07923x + \frac{2x}{1.02663}$
$= (1.07923 + 1.94812)x$ — Combine like terms.
$= 3.02735x$

Multiplication and Division

Multiplication The product of a monomial and a polynomial is obtained by multiplying *every term* of the polynomial by the monomial. To obtain the product of two polynomials, multiply *every term* of one polynomial by *every term* of the other polynomial. For example,

$$(a + b)(c + d + e) = ac + ad + ae + bc + bd + be$$

After all possible pairs of terms are multiplied, like terms should be combined.

Example 2.1C *Multiplication of Algebraic Expressions*

Expand each of the following expressions by carrying out the indicated multiplication.

a. $-x(2x^2 - 3x - 1)$
$= (-x)(2x^2) + (-x)(-3x) + (-x)(-1)$
$= -2x^3 + 3x^2 + x$

Multiply each term in the trinomial by $(-x)$. The product of two negative quantities is positive.

b. $3m(4m - 6n + 2)$
$= 3m(4m) + 3m(-6n) + 3m(2)$
$= 12m^2 - 18mn + 6m$

Multiply each term in the trinomial by $(3m)$. In each product, first multiply the numerical coefficients and then multiply the literal coefficients.

c. $(7a - 2b)(3b - 2a)$
$= 7a(3b - 2a) - 2b(3b - 2a)$
$= 21ab - 14a^2 - 6b^2 + 4ab$
$= 25ab - 14a^2 - 6b^2$

Multiply each term of the first binomial by the second binomial. Combine the like terms.

d. $(x - 2)(2x^2 - 3x - 4)$
$= x(2x^2 - 3x - 4) - 2(2x^2 - 3x - 4)$
$= 2x^3 - 3x^2 - 4x - 4x^2 + 6x + 8$
$= 2x^3 - 7x^2 + 2x + 8$

Multiply each term of the binomial by the trinomial. Combine the like terms.

Division When dividing a polynomial by a monomial, *each term* of the polynomial must be divided by the monomial.

Although there are a few cases in this book where a monomial or a polynomial is divided by a polynomial, you will not be required to perform the division algebraically. Instead, do the division *after* numerical values are substituted for the variables.

TRAP *Cancelling Common Factors in Division*

When cancelling a common factor, remember that *every term* in the numerator and *every term* in the denominator must be divided by that common factor. A common error made when dividing a polynomial by a monomial is to cancel one of the factors in the denominator with the same factor in just one of the terms in the numerator. The common factor must be cancelled in *every term* in the numerator.

TIP *Checking the "Legality" of Algebraic Manipulations*

If you are in doubt about the legitimacy of a manipulation on an algebraic expression, you sometimes can check it as follows. Substitute a numerical value for the variable in both the original expression and in the expression obtained from your dubious manipulation. If the resulting values are equal, it is highly probable that your manipulation was legal. For example, suppose you attempt the simplification

$$\frac{4x + 2}{2} \rightarrow 2x + 2$$

where you have divided the 2 in the denominator into only the numerical coefficient of x. (This common error was brought to your attention in the preceding Trap.) If you pick an arbitrary value to substitute for x, say $x = 3$, the value of the original expression is $\frac{(12+2)}{2} = 7$ but the value of the derived expression is $6 + 2 = 8$. Since the values differ, the simplification was either illegal or incorrectly carried out.

Example 2.1D *Division by a Monomial*

Simplify each of the following expressions.

a. $\dfrac{36x^2y}{60xy^2}$

$= \dfrac{3(12)(x)(x)y}{5(12)(x)(y)y}$ Identify factors in the numerator and denominator.

$= \dfrac{3x}{5y}$ Cancel factors that appear in both the numerator and the denominator.

b. $\dfrac{48a^2 - 32ab}{8a}$

$= \dfrac{48a^2}{8a} - \dfrac{32ab}{8a}$ Divide each term in the numerator by the denominator.

$= 6a - 4b$ Cancel factors that appear in both the numerator and the denominator.

c. $\dfrac{225(1+i)^4}{75(1+i)^2}$

$= \dfrac{3(75)(1+i)^2(1+i)^2}{75(1+i)^2}$ Identify and cancel factors that are common to both the numerator and the denominator.

$= 3(1+i)^2$

Substitution

Substitution means assigning a numerical value to each of the algebraic symbols in an expression. Then evaluate the expression by carrying out all the indicated operations. Referring back to our earlier example of the algebraic expression for the gross monthly earnings of the sales staff in the retail store, you can calculate any salesperson's earnings by substituting his or her actual sales figure for s in the expression

$$\$1000 + 0.04s$$

Example 2.1E *Evaluating Algebraic Expressions after Substituting Numerical Values for the Variables*

Evaluate each of the following expressions for the given values of the variables.

a. $8p - 9q$ for $p = 2.5$, $q = -6$

b. $3x^2 - 7x - 4$ for $x = -3$

c. $P(1 + rt)$ for $P = \$100$, $r = 0.09$, $t = \dfrac{7}{12}$

d. $(1 + i)^m - 1$ for $i = 0.05$, $m = 2$

e. $\dfrac{S}{(1 + i)^n}$ for $S = \$1240$, $i = 0.025$, $n = 4$

f. $R\left[\dfrac{(1 + i)^n - 1}{i}\right]$ for $R = \$2000$, $i = 0.0225$, $n = 3$

Solution

a. $8p - 9q = 8(2.5) - 9(-6)$ Replace p by 2.5 and q by -6.

$= 20 + 54$

$= 74$

b. $3x^2 - 7x - 4 = 3(-3)^2 - 7(-3) - 4$

$= 3(9) + 21 - 4$

$= 27 + 17$

$= 44$

c. $P(1 + rt) = \$100\left(1 + 0.09 \times \dfrac{7}{12}\right)$

$= \$100(1 + 0.0525)$

$= \$105.25$

d. $(1 + i)^m - 1 = (1 + 0.05)^2 - 1$

$= 1.05^2 - 1$

$= 1.1025 - 1$

$= 0.1025$

e. $\dfrac{S}{(1 + i)^n} = \dfrac{\$1240}{(1 + 0.025)^4}$

$= \dfrac{\$1240}{1.025^4}$

$= \dfrac{\$1240}{1.103813}$

$= \$1123.38$

f. $R\left[\dfrac{(1 + i)^n - 1}{i}\right] = \$2000\left[\dfrac{(1 + 0.0225)^3 - 1}{0.0225}\right]$

$= \$2000\left(\dfrac{1.0225^3 - 1}{0.0225}\right)$

$= \$2000\left(\dfrac{1.0690301 - 1}{0.0225}\right)$

$= \$2000(3.068006)$

$= \$6136.01$

Exercise 2.1

Answers to the odd-numbered problems are at the end of the book.

Simplify each of the following and collect the like terms.

1. $(-p) + (-3p) + (4p)$

2. $(5s - 2t) - (2s - 4t)$

3. $4x^2y + (-3x^2y) - (-5x^2y)$

4. $1 - (7e^2 - 5 + 3e - e^3)$

5. $(6x^2 - 3xy + 4y^2) - (8y^2 - 10xy - x^2)$

6. $(7m^3 - m - 6m^2 + 10) - (5m^3 - 9 + 3m - 2m^2)$

7. $2(7x - 3y) - 3(2x - 3y)$

8. $4(a^2 - 3a - 4) - 2(5a^2 - a - 6)$

9. $15x - [4 - 2(5x - 6)]$

10. $6a - [3a - 2(2b - a)]$

•11. $\dfrac{2x + 9}{4} - 1.2(x - 1)$

•12. $\dfrac{x}{2} - x^2 + \dfrac{4}{5} - 0.2x^2 - \dfrac{4}{5}x + \dfrac{1}{2}$

•13. $\dfrac{8x}{0.5} + \dfrac{5.5x}{11} + 0.5(4.6x - 17)$

•14. $\dfrac{2x}{1.045} - \dfrac{2.016x}{3} + \dfrac{x}{2}$

•15. $\dfrac{P}{1 + 0.095 \times \frac{5}{12}} + 2P\left(1 + 0.095 \times \dfrac{171}{365}\right)$

•16. $y\left(1 - 0.125 \times \dfrac{213}{365}\right) + \dfrac{2y}{1 + 0.125 \times \frac{88}{365}}$

•17. $k(1 + 0.04)^2 + \dfrac{2k}{(1 + 0.04)^2}$

•18. $\dfrac{h}{(1 + 0.055)^2} - 3h(1 + 0.055)^3$

Perform the multiplication or division indicated in each of the following expressions and collect the like terms.

19. $4a(3ab - 5a + 6b)$

20. $9k(4 - 8k + 7k^2)$

21. $-5xy(2x^2 - xy - 3y^2)$

22. $-(p^2 - 4pq - 5p)\left(\dfrac{2q}{p}\right)$

23. $(4r - 3t)(2t + 5r)$

24. $(3p^2 - 5p)(-4p + 2)$

25. $3(a - 2)(4a + 1) - 5(2a + 3)(a - 7)$

26. $5(2x - y)(y + 3x) - 6x(x - 5y)$

27. $\dfrac{18x^2}{3x}$

28. $\dfrac{6a^2b}{-2ab^2}$

29. $\dfrac{x^2y - xy^2}{xy}$

30. $\dfrac{-4x + 10x^2 - 6x^3}{-0.5x}$

31. $\dfrac{12x^3 - 24x^2 + 36x}{48x}$

32. $\dfrac{32a^2b - 8ab + 14ab^2}{2ab}$

33. $\dfrac{4a^2b^3 - 6a^3b^2}{2ab^2}$

34. $\dfrac{120(1 + i)^2 + 180(1 + i)^3}{360(1 + i)}$

Evaluate each of the following expressions for the given values of the variables. In Problems 39 to 43 and 45 to 50, calculate the result accurate to the cent.

35. $3d^2 - 4d + 15$ for $d = 2.5$

36. $15g - 9h + 3$ for $g = 14$, $h = 15$

37. $7x(4y - 8)$ for $x = 3.2$, $y = 1.5$

38. $I \div Pr$ for $P = \$500$, $I = \$13.75$, $r = 0.11$

39. $\dfrac{I}{rt}$ for $r = 0.095$, $I = \$23.21$, $t = \dfrac{283}{365}$

40. $\dfrac{N}{1 - d}$ for $N = \$89.10$, $d = 0.10$

•**41.** $L(1 - d_1)(1 - d_2)(1 - d_3)$ for $L = \$490$, $d_1 = 0.125$, $d_2 = 0.15$, $d_3 = 0.05$

42. $P(1 + rt)$ for $P = \$770$, $r = 0.013$, $t = \frac{223}{365}$

43. $\frac{S}{1 + rt}$ for $S = \$2500$, $r = 0.085$, $t = \frac{123}{365}$

44. $(1 + i)^m - 1$ for $i = 0.0225$, $m = 4$

45. $P(1 + i)^n$ for $P = \$1280$, $i = 0.025$, $n = 3$

46. $\frac{S}{(1 + i)^n}$ for $S = \$850$, $i = 0.0075$, $n = 6$

•**47.** $R\left[\frac{(1 + i)^n - 1}{i}\right]$ for $R = \$550$, $i = 0.085$, $n = 3$

•**48.** $R\left[\frac{(1 + i)^n - 1}{i}\right](1 + i)$ for $R = \$910$, $i = 0.1038129$, $n = 4$

•**49.** $\frac{R}{i}\left[1 - \frac{1}{(1 + i)^n}\right]$ for $R = \$630$, $i = 0.115$, $n = 2$

•**50.** $P(1 + rt_1) + \frac{S}{1 + rt_2}$ for $P = \$470$, $S = \$390$, $r = 0.075$, $t_1 = \frac{104}{365}$, $t_2 = \frac{73}{365}$

2.2 Rules and Properties of Exponents

The use of exponents allows us to write algebraic expressions containing repeated factors in a more concise form. If n is a positive integer, then a^n is defined by

$$a^n = a \times a \times a \times a \quad \text{to } n \text{ factors}$$

In this notation, a is called the **base,** n is called the **exponent,** and a^n is read as "a raised to the power n" or "a raised to the exponent n." The value obtained for a^n is referred to as "the nth power of a" or sometimes just as "the **power**." That is,

$$\text{Power} = \text{Base}^{\text{Exponent}}$$

We will use powers extensively in later chapters for compound interest calculations.

Example 2.2A *Evaluating Powers with Positive Integral Exponents*

a. $3^4 = 3 \times 3 \times 3 \times 3 = 81$
The base is 3, the exponent is 4, and the power is 81.
The fourth power of 3 is 81.

b. $0.1^4 = 0.1 \times 0.1 \times 0.1 \times 0.1 = 0.0001$

c. $\left(\frac{3}{4}\right)^3 = \left(\frac{3}{4}\right)\left(\frac{3}{4}\right)\left(\frac{3}{4}\right) = \frac{3 \times 3 \times 3}{4 \times 4 \times 4} = \frac{27}{64}$
$= (0.75)(0.75)(0.75) = 0.421875$

d. $(1.035)^3 = 1.035 \times 1.035 \times 1.035 = 1.108718$

e. $(-2)^3 = (-2)(-2)(-2) = -8$
An odd power of a negative base is negative.

f. $(-0.9)^4 = (-0.9)(-0.9)(-0.9)(-0.9) = 0.6561$
An even power of a negative base is positive.

TIP *Using a Calculator's Power Function*

Use the following sequence of keystrokes to evaluate 1.62^5 with the power function key (y^x).

$$1.62 \; \boxed{y^x} \; 5 \; \boxed{=}$$

If the symbol y^x sits above a calculator key (rather than on it), the power function is the secondary function of the key. The keystroke sequence is then

$$1.62 \; \boxed{2nd} \; \boxed{y^x} \; 5 \; \boxed{=}$$

Rules of Exponents A few mathematical operations involving powers occur so frequently that it is convenient to have a set of rules that provide shortcuts. The derivation of the following rules of exponents is straightforward and may be found in any introductory algebra text.

Rules of Exponents:

1. $a^m \times a^n = a^{m+n}$
2. $\dfrac{a^m}{a^n} = a^{m-n}$
3. $(a^m)^n = a^{m \times n}$
4. $(ab)^n = a^n b^n$
5. $\left(\dfrac{a}{b}\right)^n = \dfrac{a^n}{b^n}$

TRAP *Common Errors to Avoid*

Note the following inequalities in order to avoid some frequently made errors.

$(a + b)^n \neq a^n + b^n$ $\qquad a^n - a^m \neq a^{n-m}$

$(a - b)^n \neq a^n - b^n$ $\qquad a^n + a^m \neq a^{n+m}$

Example 2.2B *Using the Rules of Exponents to Simplify Algebraic Expressions*

Simplify the following expressions.

a. $3^2 \times 3^3 = 3^{2+3} = 3^5 = 243$ Rule 1

b. $y^5 \times y^4 = y^{5+4} = y^9$ Rule 1

c. $(1 + i)^6 \times (1 + i)^{11} = (1 + i)^{6+11} = (1 + i)^{17}$ Rule 1

d. $\dfrac{1.01^8}{1.01^5} = 1.01^{8-5} = 1.01^3 = 1.030301$ Rule 2

e. $\dfrac{(1+i)^{20}}{(1+i)^8} = (1+i)^{20-8} = (1+i)^{12}$ Rule 2

f. $\dfrac{x^5 \times x^{14}}{x^9} = x^{5+14-9} = x^{10}$ Rules 1 and 2

g. $(k^4)^5 = k^{4\times 5} = k^{20}$ Rule 3

h. $(3^2)^4 = 3^{2\times 4} = 3^8 = 6561$ Rule 3

i. $\dfrac{(p^4 \times p^2)^3}{\left(\dfrac{p^8}{p^5}\right)^2} = \dfrac{(p^6)^3}{(p^3)^2}$ ← Rule 1 (numerator), ← Rule 2 (denominator)

$= \dfrac{p^{18}}{p^6}$ ← Rule 3 (numerator), ← Rule 3 (denominator)

$= p^{12}$ Rule 2

j. $(5q)^3 = 5^3q^3 = 125q^3$ Rule 4

k. $\left(\dfrac{0.5}{x}\right)^2 = \dfrac{0.5^2}{x^2} = \dfrac{0.25}{x^2}$ Rule 5

l. $\left(\dfrac{3x^6y^3}{x^2z^3}\right)^2 = \left(\dfrac{3x^4y^3}{z^3}\right)^2$ Rule 2

$= \dfrac{3^2x^{4\times 2}y^{3\times 2}}{z^{3\times 2}}$ Rules 4 and 5

$= \dfrac{9x^8y^6}{z^6}$

m. $\left(\dfrac{b^5 - b^3}{b^2}\right)^2 = \left(\dfrac{b^5}{b^2} - \dfrac{b^3}{b^2}\right)^2$

$= (b^3 - b)^2$ Rule 2

No further simplification is possible using the rules of exponents.

Zero, Negative, and Fractional Exponents Zero, negative, and fractional exponents must have the following meanings in order to be consistent with the definition of a^n and the first three rules of exponents. (The justifications for these interpretations are presented in the appendix to this chapter.)

ZERO, NEGATIVE, AND FRACTIONAL EXPONENTS:

$$a^0 = 1 \qquad a^{-n} = \frac{1}{a^n} \qquad a^{1/n} = \sqrt[n]{a}$$

$$a^{m/n} = (\sqrt[n]{a})^m = \sqrt[n]{a^m}$$

TIP

USING THE POWER FUNCTION KEY WITH NEGATIVE AND FRACTIONAL EXPONENTS

For a negative exponent, press the "sign change" key, (+/–), *after* you enter the exponent. For example, to evaluate 1.62^{-5}:

1.62 (y^x) 5 (+/–) (=)

For a fractional exponent, first calculate the decimal equivalent of the fraction and save it in the calculator's memory. Later, when you would normally enter the exponent manually, recall its value from the memory.

Example 2.2C *Evaluating Powers for Zero, Negative, and Fractional Exponents*

Simplify or evaluate the following.

a. $7.132^0 = 1$

b. $(0.001)^0 = 1$

c. $(0.001)^{-1} = \dfrac{1}{0.001} = 1000$

d. $(1 + i)^{-n} = \dfrac{1}{(1 + i)^n}$

e. $\left(\dfrac{x}{y}\right)^{-2} = \dfrac{1}{\left(\dfrac{x}{y}\right)^2} = \dfrac{1}{\dfrac{x^2}{y^2}} = \dfrac{y^2}{x^2} = \left(\dfrac{y}{x}\right)^2$

f. $\left(-\dfrac{4}{5}\right)^{-2} = \left(-\dfrac{5}{4}\right)^2 = (-1.25)^2 = 1.5625$

g. $(1.0125)^{-5} = \left(\dfrac{1}{1.0125}\right)^5 = (0.987654)^5 = 0.93978$

h. $(1.0125)^{1/5} = \sqrt[5]{1.0125} = (1.0125)^{0.2} = 1.00249$

i. $\left(\dfrac{3}{2}\right)^{3/2} = 1.5^{3/2} = \sqrt{1.5^3} = \sqrt{3.375} = 1.8371$

$= 1.5^{1.5} = 1.8371$

j. $\$175(1 + 0.05)^{3.5} = \$175(1.18621) = \$207.59$

k. $\$321(1 + 0.025)^{-8} = \$321(0.8207465) = \$263.46$

l. $\dfrac{(1 + 0.0075)^{59.65} - 1}{0.0075} = \dfrac{1.5615918 - 1}{0.0075} = 74.87891$

m. $\dfrac{1 - (1.025)^{-30}}{0.025} = \dfrac{1 - 0.4767426}{0.025} = 20.93029$

Exercise 2.2

Answers to the odd-numbered problems are at the end of the book.

Simplify each of the following.

1. $a^2 \times a^3$

2. $(x^6)(x^{-4})$

3. $b^{10} \div b^6$

4. $h^7 \div h^{-4}$

5. $(1 + i)^4 \times (1 + i)^9$

6. $(1 + i) \times (1 + i)^n$

7. $(x^4)^7$

8. $(y^3)^3$

9. $(t^6)^{1/3}$

10. $(n^{0.5})^8$

11. $\dfrac{(x^5)(x^6)}{x^9}$

12. $\dfrac{(x^5)^6}{x^9}$

13. $[2(1 + i)]^2$

14. $\left(\dfrac{1 + i}{3i}\right)^3$

•15. $\dfrac{4r^5t^6}{(2r^2t)^3}$

•16. $\dfrac{(-r^3)(2r)^4}{(2r^{-2})^2}$

•17. $\left(\dfrac{3a^3b^2}{a - b}\right)^4$

•18. $\left(\dfrac{3}{2x^2}\right)^2\left(\dfrac{6x^3}{5^2}\right)\left(-\dfrac{x}{5}\right)^{-1}$

•19. $\dfrac{(-2y)^3(x^4)^{-2}}{(x^{-2})^2(4y)^2}$

•20. $\dfrac{[(x^{1/3})(x^{2/3})x]^{3/2}}{(8x^3)^{2/3}}$

Evaluate each of the following expressions to six-figure accuracy.

21. $8^{4/3}$

22. $-27^{2/3}$

23. $7^{3/2}$

24. $5^{-3/4}$

25. $(0.001)^{-2}$

26. $0.893^{-1/2}$

27. $(1.0085)^5(1.0085)^3$

28. $(1.005)^3(1.005)^{-6}$

29. $\sqrt[3]{1.03}$

30. $\sqrt[6]{1.05}$

•31. $(4^4)(3^{-3})\left(-\dfrac{3}{4}\right)^3$

•32. $\left[\left(-\dfrac{3}{4}\right)^2\right]^{-2}$

•33. $\left(\dfrac{2}{3}\right)^3\left(-\dfrac{3}{2}\right)^2\left(-\dfrac{3}{2}\right)^{-3}$

•34. $\left(-\dfrac{2}{3}\right)^3 \div \left(\dfrac{3}{2}\right)^{-2}$

35. $\dfrac{1.03^{16} - 1}{0.03}$

36. $\dfrac{(1.008\overline{3})^{30} - 1}{0.008\overline{3}}$

•37. $\dfrac{1 - 1.0225^{-20}}{0.0225}$

•38. $\dfrac{1 - (1.00\overline{6})^{-32}}{0.00\overline{6}}$

39. $(1 + 0.0275)^{1/3}$

40. $(1 + 0.055)^{1/6} - 1$

2.3 Solving a Linear Equation

Definitions An **equation** is a statement of the equality of two algebraic expressions. A large majority of the applications and problems encountered in this book will result in an equation containing a single variable or unknown. If this variable's exponent is 1, the equation is a **linear equation** in one unknown. If the variable appears with an exponent other than 1, the equation is **nonlinear.**

A particular numerical value for the variable that makes the two sides of the equation equal is a **root** or solution of the equation. A linear equation in one variable has only one root; a nonlinear equation may have more than one root. The process of determining the root or roots of the equation is called *solving the equation.*

Example 2.3A *Examples of Linear and Nonlinear Equations*

a. $3x - 7 = 5 - 9x$ is a linear equation.

b. $x^2 - x = 12$ is a nonlinear equation because x has an exponent different from 1 in one of the terms.

c. $\$150(1 + i)^4 = \$219.62$ is a nonlinear equation because of the presence of terms in i^4, i^3, and i^2 when $(1 + i)^4$ is expanded.

d. $2^x = 32$ is a nonlinear equation because x is in the exponent.

Solving a Linear Equation in One Unknown The procedure involves three steps:

1. Separate like terms, leaving terms containing the variable on one side of the equation and the remaining terms on the other side of the equation.
2. Combine the like terms on each side of the equation.
3. Obtain the root or solution by dividing both sides of the equation by the numerical coefficient of the variable.

TIP *Both Sides of an Equation Must Get the Same Treatment*

An important principle to keep in mind is that both sides of the equation must be treated in exactly the same way in order to preserve the equality. For example, if you subtract an amount from the right side of an equation, you must also subtract the same amount from the left side of the equation. You can take the square root of one side of an equation if you also take the square root of the other side.

After you calculate the root of an equation, you can verify its value by substituting it in the original equation. The root is correct (and is said to *satisfy* the equation) if the resulting values of both sides of the equation are equal.

Example 2.3B *Solving Linear Equations in One Unknown*

Solve the following equations and verify the solutions.

a. $8x - 11 = 5x + 4$ **b.** $0.5x - 0.75 + 7x = 3x + 1.5$

Solution

a.

$8x - 11 = 5x + 4$	
$8x - 11 - 5x = 5x + 4 - 5x$	Subtract $5x$ from both sides so that terms in x will be on the left side only.
$3x - 11 = 4$	Note that moving $5x$ from the right side to the left side with a change of sign also produces this result. It is more efficient to use this shortcut (called *transposition*).
$3x - 11 + 11 = 4 + 11$	Add 11 to both sides so that numerical terms will be on the right side only.

$3x = 15$ — Transposing the term "−11" with a change of sign from the left side to the right side produces this same result.

$\frac{3x}{3} = \frac{15}{3}$ — Divide both sides by the numerical coefficient of x.

$x = 5$

Verification:

Left-hand side (LHS) $= 8x - 11$	Right-hand side (RHS) $= 5x + 4$
$= 8(5) - 11$	$= 5(5) + 4$
$= 29$	$= 29$

Since LHS = RHS, $x = 5$ is the root or solution.

b. $0.5x - 0.75 + 7x = 3x + 1.5$

$0.5x + 7x - 3x = 1.5 + 0.75$ — Transpose $3x$ to the LHS and -0.75 to the RHS, and change their signs.

$4.5x = 2.25$

$x = \frac{2.25}{4.5}$ — Divide both sides by the numerical coefficient of x.

$= 0.5$

Verification:

LHS $= 0.5(0.5) - 0.75 + 7(0.5) = 0.25 - 0.75 + 3.5 = 3.0$
RHS $= 3(0.5) + 1.5 = 1.5 + 1.5 = 3.0$
Since LHS = RHS, $x = 0.5$ is the solution.

Example 2.3C *Solving a Linear Equation Having "Messy" Coefficients*

Solve the following equation for x (accurate to the cent). Verify the solution.

$$\frac{x}{1 + 0.11 \times \frac{75}{365}} + 2x\left(1 + 0.11 \times \frac{92}{365}\right) = \$1150.96$$

Solution

In this equation, the numerical coefficients are not simple numbers as in the previous examples. These coefficients should be reduced to a single number (which may not be an integer) by performing the indicated operations. Then carry on with the usual three-step procedure for solving a linear equation in one unknown.

$$\frac{x}{1.0226027} + 2x(1.0277260) = \$1150.96$$

$$0.9778969x + 2.0554521x = \$1150.96$$

$$3.0333489x = \$1150.96$$

$$x = \frac{\$1150.96}{3.0333489}$$

$$= \$379.44$$

Verification:

$$\begin{aligned}\text{LHS} &= \frac{\$379.44}{1 + 0.11 \times \frac{75}{365}} + 2(\$379.44)\left(1 + 0.11 \times \frac{92}{365}\right)\\ &= \frac{\$379.44}{1.0226027} + 2(\$379.44)(1.0277260)\\ &= \$371.05 + \$779.92\\ &= \$1150.97\\ &= \text{RHS}\end{aligned}$$

The \$0.01 difference between the LHS and the RHS arises from rounding the solution $x = \$379.4354$ to the nearest cent and then using the rounded value for the verification.

Exercise 2.3 *Answers to the odd-numbered problems are at the end of the book.*

Solve the following equations. The solutions to Problems 13 to 18 should be accurate to the cent.

1. $10a + 10 = 12 + 9a$

2. $29 - 4y = 2y - 7$

3. $0.5(x - 3) = 20$

4. $\frac{1}{3}(x - 2) = 4$

5. $y = 192 + 0.04y$

6. $x - 0.025x = 341.25$

7. $12x - 4(2x - 1) = 6(x + 1) - 3$

8. $3y - 4 = 3(y + 6) - 2(y + 3)$

9. $8 - 0.5(x + 3) = 0.25(x - 1)$

10. $5(2 - c) = 10(2c - 4) - 6(3c + 1)$

11. $3.1t + 145 = 10 + 7.6t$

12. $1.25y - 20.5 = 0.5y - 11.5$

•**13.** $\frac{x}{1.1^2} + 2x(1.1)^3 = \$1000$

•**14.** $\frac{3x}{1.025^6} + x(1.025)^8 = \$2641.35$

•**15.** $\frac{2x}{1.03^7} + x + x(1.03^{10}) = \$1000 + \frac{\$2000}{1.03^4}$

•**16.** $x(1.05)^3 + \$1000 + \frac{x}{1.05^7} = \frac{\$5000}{1.05^2}$

•**17.** $x\left(1 + 0.095 \times \frac{84}{365}\right) + \frac{2x}{1 + 0.095 \times \frac{108}{365}} = \$1160.20$

•**18.** $\frac{x}{1 + 0.115 \times \frac{78}{365}} + 3x\left(1 + 0.115 \times \frac{121}{365}\right) = \$1000\left(1 + 0.115 \times \frac{43}{365}\right)$

2.4 Solving Word Problems

In the preceding section, we reviewed the procedure for solving a linear equation. With practice, solving an equation becomes a mechanical procedure that follows a fairly routine series of steps. However, *practical* applications of mathematics rarely come as a given equation that needs only to be solved. Instead, a problem is presented to us in a more informal descriptive manner. We must deduce mathematical relationships from the given information and from our broader knowledge of general concepts and principles.

It is a large step to go from just solving a *given* equation to *creating* an equation from a word problem and then solving it. Constructing an algebraic equation from given information cannot be reduced to mechanical steps (such as those listed in Section 2.3 for solving a linear equation). We can, however, outline a general approach for solving word problems.

A General Approach for Solving Problems

Particularly if you are having difficulty with a word problem, use the following procedure to reduce the solution to more manageable steps.

Step 1: *Read the entire problem* to gain a sense of the topic involved and what is being asked. For example, you might find that the problem involves a loan repayment and you are asked to determine the size of the monthly payment.

Step 2: Now take pencil and paper in hand. On a second reading, *extract and label the given data. Identify the unknown quantity and choose a symbol for it. Draw and label a diagram if appropriate.* There are standard symbols for many quantities. These should be used to label numerical values as they are extracted. Otherwise, use one or two words to identify each value. Choose a symbol to represent the unknown quantity. Diagrams are particularly useful in problems involving multiple payments over a period of time. Incorporate as much data as possible in the diagram.

Step 3: *Identify the principle, concept, or idea that can be used to construct a word equation.* This may be a fundamental principle of broad application, or it may be a unique relationship stated or implied in the problem itself. The principle or idea provides a basis for writing a word equation tailored to the particular problem. An example of a word equation is

$$\text{Profit} = \text{Revenues} - \text{Expenses}$$

Step 4: *Convert the word equation to an algebraic equation and substitute the values extracted in Step 2.* Replace the words and phrases in the word equation with algebraic expressions or numerical values.

Step 5: *Solve the equation* and write a concluding statement that directly responds to the question asked.

SUMMARY OF THE STEPS FOR SOLVING WORD PROBLEMS

1. Read the entire problem.
2. Extract and label the data. Identify the unknown quantity and specify its symbol. Draw and label a diagram if appropriate.
3. Identify the principle, concept, or idea that can be used to construct a word equation. The word equation relates the given data to the unknown quantity.
4. Convert the word equation to an algebraic equation, and substitute the values extracted in Step 2.
5. Solve the equation.

TIP *Overcoming That Old "I-just-can't-seem-to-get-started" Feeling*

Have you ever stared and stared at a word problem without getting anywhere? (If you have, you belong to a rather large club.) Think about how you have approached word problems in the past. Did you begin by trying to find a formula in which to substitute the given numbers? If so, you were really trying to do Steps 1, 2, 3, and 4 all at once! It's not surprising that you got stumped on problems of even moderate difficulty. Even if you happen to hit on the right formula and calculate the right answer, the "formula-browsing" approach is not an effective way to "do" mathematics. It omits Step 3, where you bring mathematical ideas and concepts to bear on a problem. For problems of any complexity, you should use our five-step ladder instead of trying to leap tall problems in a single bound.

TIP *Good Work and Study Habits*

1. **Keep current with assigned readings and problems.** Mathematics is cumulative—the concepts in today's class are likely to be built upon in the next class. If you do not complete the assigned work needed to fully grasp new material, you impair your ability to understand further topics in the next class.
2. **There is no substitute for "doing" math.** Would you expect to learn how to hit a golf ball by watching Tiger Woods play golf on TV? Of course not. No matter how good the instruction, there always seems to be some unexpected glitches and surprises when we try something on our own. Mathematics is no different. It is one thing for you to *follow* the steps in someone else's solution—it is quite another matter to *create* the solution yourself. By doing problems, you discover gaps in your understanding. The most valuable and enduring form of learning comes when you run head-on into difficulties, and then clear up the misunderstandings or deficiencies that caused them. Always remember, you learn more from a problem with which you have some difficulty than from one you solve with ease.
3. **Be fearless!** Experiment with ideas for solving a problem as fearlessly as you mess around with new computer software. (After all, nothing can be inadvertently deleted, nothing can crash, you can't catch a virus, and there are no fatal errors!) Draw diagrams (in Step 2 of the problem-solving procedure) as fearlessly as in playing Pictionary. Be fearless about asking your instructor and classmates questions to promptly clear up any difficulties you encounter in assigned problems.

The following examples illustrate the five-step approach for solving word problems.

Example 2.4A

A retailer reduced his prices by 15% for a fall sale. What was the original price of an item on sale at $123.25?

Solution

Step 1: Read the problem. (This step is assumed hereafter.)

Step 2: Extract and label the data. Identify the unknown and define its symbol.

Discount rate = 15% Sale price = \$123.25

Let P represent the original price.

Step 3: Identify the idea that connects the data with the unknown. Write the word equation.

Sale price = Regular price − Price reduction
= Regular price − (Discount rate × Regular price)

Step 4: Convert the word equation to an algebraic equation.

$$\$123.25 = P - 0.15P$$

Step 5: Solve the equation.

$$\$123.25 = 0.85P$$

$$P = \frac{\$123.25}{0.85} = \$145.00$$

The original price of the item was \$145.00.

Example 2.4B

A manufacturing plant has in its inventory 1800 Type A gaskets and 2560 Type B gaskets, with a combined value of \$12,234. If a Type A gasket costs 50 cents less than three times the cost of a Type B gasket, what is the unit cost of each type of gasket?

Solution

Step 2: Number of Type A = 1800 Number of Type B = 2560

Total value = \$12,234

Cost of Type A = 3(Cost of Type B) − 50 cents

Let b represent the cost, in dollars, of a Type B gasket.

Step 3: Total cost = (Quantity of A × Cost of A) + (Quantity of B × Cost of B)

Step 4: $\$12{,}234 = 1800(3b - \$0.50) + 2560b$

Step 5: $\$12{,}234 = 5400b - \$900 + 2560b$

$$\$13{,}134 = 7960b$$

$$b = \frac{\$13{,}134}{7960} = \$1.65$$

The cost of a Type B gasket is \$1.65, and the cost of a Type A gasket is 3(\$1.65) − \$0.50 = \$4.45.

Example 2.4C

Tom, Dick, and Harry formed a business partnership. Whenever additional capital is required, their agreement requires Dick to contribute 50% more than Tom, and Harry to contribute three-fifths as much as Dick. If an injection of \$5000 is required, how much should each partner contribute?

Solution

All three partners' contributions are initially unknown. However, if any one partner's contribution is known, the other two can be calculated using the relative sizes provided. Therefore, the solution may be set up in terms of a single variable.

Step 2: Dick = 1.5(Tom), Harry = $\frac{3}{5}$(Dick)

Capital required = \$5000

With interrelated quantities such as these, the quantity chosen as the solution variable should be the one in terms of which the others can most easily be expressed. Since Harry's contribution is in terms of Dick's, and Dick's contribution is in terms of Tom's, Tom's contribution should be the variable. Let T = the amount of Tom's contribution.

Step 3: Sum of the three contributions = \$5000

Step 4: $T + 1.5T + \frac{3}{5}(\text{Dick's contribution}) = \$5000$

$$T + 1.5T + \frac{3}{5}(1.5T) = \$5000$$

Step 5:

$$T + 1.5T + 0.9T = \$5000$$
$$3.4T = \$5000$$
$$T = \frac{\$5000}{3.4} = \$1470.59$$

Tom should contribute \$1470.59, Dick should contribute 1.5(\$1470.59) = \$2205.88, and Harry should contribute $\frac{3}{5}$(\$2205.88) = \$1323.53.

POINT OF INTEREST

THE MOTHER OF ALL WORD PROBLEMS

In 1998 the federal government passed a minor reduction in the federal income surtax. An income surtax is an extra tax calculated as a percentage of the income tax you are already paying. (You read it right—income tax on income tax!) One description of the surtax reduction is quoted verbatim below.

> *"Effective July 1, 1998, the 3% surtax will be reduced by the amount by which \$250 exceeds 6% of the amount an individual's basic federal tax payable exceeds \$8333. As the change becomes effective July 1, 1998, the maximum surtax reduction for 1998 is only half of the actual surtax reduction calculated."*

Quick now! What was your 1998 federal surtax reduction if your 1998 basic federal tax payable was \$9000?

Exercise 2.4 *Answers to the odd-numbered problems are at the end of the book.*

1. A web site had $\frac{2}{7}$ more hits last month than in the same month of the preceding year. If there were 2655 hits last month, how many were there one year earlier?

2. The retail price of a pair of skis is \$295.20. This includes a markup of four-fifths of the wholesale cost. What is the wholesale cost?

3. The price tags in Annie's Flower Shop include the 7% Goods and Services Tax (GST). How much GST will she report for a plant sold at \$39.95?

4. A stockbroker's commission on a transaction is 2.5% of the first \$5000 of the transaction amount and 1.5% of the remainder. What was the amount of a transaction that generated a total commission of \$227?

5. A caterer has the following price structure for banquets. The first 20 meals are charged the basic price per meal. The next 20 meals are discounted by \$2 each and all additional meals are each reduced by \$3. If the total cost for 73 meals comes to \$810, what is the basic price per meal?

•6. A firm received a bill from its accountant for \$1655, representing a combined total of 41 "billable" hours for both the Certified General Accountant (CGA) and her accounting technician, for conducting the firm's audit. If the CGA charges her time at \$60 per hour and the technician's time at \$25 per hour, how many hours did each work on the audit?

•7. For developing a roll of 36-exposure film, Green's One-Hour Photos charges \$2 less than $1\frac{1}{2}$ times the \$9.50 charge for developing a 24-exposure roll. The total charge on a batch of 24 rolls came to \$288.50. How many rolls of each type were developed?

•8. A \$12,000 performance bonus is to be divided between two store managers. The manager of Store A is to receive \$1500 less than twice the bonus paid to the manager of Store B. How much should each manager be paid?

•9. Joan, Stella, and Sue have agreed to form a partnership. For the original capital investment of \$32,760, Sue agrees to contribute 20% more than Joan, and Joan agrees to contribute 20% more than Stella. How much will each contribute?

•10. The annual net income of the SGR partnership is to be distributed so that Sven receives 30% less than George, and Robert receives 25% more than George. If the past year's net income was \$88,880, what amount should be allocated to each?

•11. It takes 20 minutes of machine time to manufacture Product X and 30 minutes of machine time to manufacture Product Y. If the machine operated 47 hours last week to produce a combined total of 120 units of the two products, how many units of Y were manufactured?

•12. The tickets for a hockey game cost \$9.50 for the red section and \$12.75 for the blue section. If 4460 tickets were sold for a total of \$46,725, how many seats were sold in each section?

••13. Mr. Parker structured his will so that each of his four children will receive half as much from the proceeds of his estate as his wife, and each of 13 grandchildren will receive one-third as much as each child. After his death, \$759,000 remains after expenses and taxes for distribution among his heirs. How much will each child and grandchild receive?

••**14.** To coordinate production in a three-stage manufacturing process, Stage B must be assigned 60% more workers than Stage A. Stage C requires three quarters as many workers as Stage B. How should the foreman allocate 114 workers among the three stages?

••**15.** Fred has centralized the purchasing and record-keeping functions for his three pharmacies in a single office. The annual costs of the office are allocated to the three stores. The Hillside store is charged $1000 less than twice the charge to the Barnett store. The Westside store is charged $2000 more than the Hillside store. What is the charge to the Westside store if the cost of operating the central office for a year is $27,600?

•**16.** $100,000 is to be distributed under a firm's profit-sharing plan. Each of three managers is to receive 20% more than each of 26 production workers. How much will each manager and production worker receive?

••**17.** José works in a toy manufacturing plant. The wooden toy he fabricates requires three steps: cutting, assembly, and painting. Assembly takes two minutes longer than half the cutting time, and painting requires half a minute longer than half the assembly time. How long does each step require if José made 72 units in 42 hours of work?

2.5 Application: Percent Change

When a quantity changes over a period of time, the amount of the change is often expressed as a percentage of the initial value. That is,

$$\text{Percent change} = \frac{\text{Final value} - \text{Initial value}}{\text{Initial value}} \times 100\%$$

We can write a more compact formula if we define the following symbols:

V_i = Initial (or beginning or original or old) value
V_f = Final (or ending or new) value
c = Percent change (or its decimal equivalent)

Then

PERCENT CHANGE (2-1)

$$c = \frac{V_f - V_i}{V_i} \times 100\%$$

Note that when a quantity doubles, the percent change is 100%. If it triples, the percent change is 200%, and so on.

TIP *ORDER MATTERS*

The order of the final and initial values in the numerator is important—it determines the sign of the percent change. If a quantity decreases in size, its percent change is negative.

To illustrate a point on language, consider the example of a company whose sales declined from \$4 million in Year 1 to \$3 million in Year 2. The percent change in sales is

$$\frac{\text{Year 2 sales} - \text{Year 1 sales}}{\text{Year 1 sales}} \times 100\% = \frac{\$3 \text{ million} - \$4 \text{ million}}{\$4 \text{ million}} \times 100\%$$
$$= \frac{-1}{4} \times 100\%$$
$$= -25\%$$

We can say either "the sales changed by −25%" or "the sales decreased by 25%" from Year 1 to Year 2. The direction of the change may be indicated either by an algebraic sign or by a descriptive word such as "rose," "fell," "increased," or "decreased." However, it would be redundant and confusing to say that "the sales decreased by −25%."

Example 2.5A Calculating the Percent Change

The share price of Klondike Resources rose from \$2 on January 1, 1998 to \$4 on December 31, 1998. It fell back to \$2 by December 31, 1999. Calculate the percent change in share price during 1998, during 1999, and during the entire two-year period.

Solution

For 1998,

$$c = \frac{\text{Dec. 31, 1998 price} - \text{Jan. 1, 1998 price}}{\text{Jan. 1, 1998 price}} \times 100\% = \frac{\$4 - \$2}{\$2} \times 100\% = 100\%$$

Similarly, for 1999,

$$c = \frac{\$2 - \$4}{\$4} \times 100\% = -50\%$$

For the entire two years,

$$c = \frac{\$2 - \$2}{\$2} \times 100\% = 0\%$$

The share price increased by 100% in 1998 and then decreased by 50% in 1999. For the entire two-year period, there was no net price change.

TRAP *Percent Changes Are Not Additive*

As the preceding Example demonstrates, the net percent change for a series of intervals cannot be obtained simply by adding the percent changes for the individual intervals. The reason is that the base for the percent change calculation is different in each interval.

Example 2.5B Calculating the Percent Change in a Percentage

A chartered bank is raising the interest rate on its Visa card from 9% to 11%. What will be the percent increase in the interest charges on a given balance?

Solution

The interest charges will increase proportionately with the rise in the interest rate. The interest rate change must be calculated in relative terms [using formula (2-1)], not in absolute terms (11% − 9% = 2%). Therefore, the percent change in interest charges will be

$$c = \frac{V_f - V_i}{V_i} \times 100\% = \frac{11\% - 9\%}{9\%} \times 100\% = \frac{2}{9} \times 100\% = 22.\bar{2}\%$$

Calculating V_i or V_f When c is Known Sometimes the percent change and either the initial value or the final value are known. To calculate the remaining unknown, formula (2-1) should be rearranged to isolate the unknown variable. After multiplying both sides of (2-1) by V_i, we obtain

$$cV_i = V_f - V_i$$

where c is now in its decimal equivalent form. Transposing V_i to the left side gives

$$V_i + cV_i = V_f \qquad \text{and then} \qquad V_i(1+c) = V_f$$

Therefore, if c and V_i are known, V_f may be calculated using

$$V_f = V_i(1+c) \qquad \text{(2-1a)}$$

Dividing both sides by $(1+c)$ gives a version of formula (2-1) appropriate for calculating V_i when c and V_f are known.

$$V_i = \frac{V_f}{1+c} \qquad \text{(2-1b)}$$

Keep in mind that the three formulas designated (2-1), (2-1a), and (2-1b) are just three versions of the *same* mathematical relationship. Given any one of them, the other two may be derived merely by rearranging the given equation.

TIP *Signs Matter*

Whenever the percent change represents a decrease, a negative value must be substituted for c in formulas (2-1a) and (2-1b).

Example 2.5C Calculating V_i Given V_f and c

What amount when increased by 230% equals \$495?

Solution

We are given $c = 230\%$ and $V_f = \$495$. Note that the decimal equivalent of c is $c = 2.3$. Two solutions are presented. The first is based on a version of formula (2-1). The second is a more intuitive algebraic approach working from first principles.

Method 1: Substituting in formula (2-1*b*).

$$\text{Initial amount, } V_i = \frac{V_f}{1 + c} = \frac{\$495}{1 + 2.3} = \$150$$

Method 2: Creating and solving an algebraic equation.

Let x represent the initial amount. Express in mathematics the fact that the initial amount (x) increased by 230% (add $2.3x$) equals \$495. That is,

$$x + 2.3x = \$495$$
$$3.3x = \$495$$
$$x = \frac{\$495}{3.3} = \$150$$

Therefore, \$150 increased by 230% equals \$495.

Example 2.5D Calculating V_f Given V_i and c

How much is \$9550 decreased by 0.75%?

Solution

The initial amount is \$9550, and we need to calculate the final amount after a decrease of 0.75% ($c = -0.0075$). As in the previous example, two solutions are presented.

Method 1: Substituting in formula (2-1*a*).

$$\text{Final amount, } V_f = V_i(1 + c) = \$9550[1 + (-0.0075)] = \$9550(0.9925) = \$9478.38$$

Method 2: Formulating and solving an algebraic equation.

Let x represent the final amount. The initial amount (\$9550) decreased by 0.75% of the initial amount (subtract $0.0075 \times \$9550$) equals the final amount (x). That is,

$$\$9550 - 0.0075 \times \$9550 = x$$
$$x = \$9550 - \$71.625 = \$9478.38$$

\$9550 decreased by 0.75% is \$9478.38.

Example 2.5E Calculating V_i Given V_f and c

For the fiscal year just completed, a company had sales of \$157,500. This represents a 5% increase over the prior year. What were the sales in the prior year?[2]

Solution

We are given the "final" sales and need to calculate the "initial" sales.

Method 1: Substituting in formula (2-1*b*).

$$\text{Prior year's sales, } V_i = \frac{V_f}{1+c} = \frac{\$157{,}500}{1+0.05} = \$150{,}000$$

Method 2: Formulating and solving an algebraic equation.

Let x represent the prior year's sales. The most recent year's sales (\$157,500) represent the prior year's sales (x) plus a 5% increase ($0.05x$). That is,

$$\$157{,}500 = x + 0.05x = 1.05x$$

Then

$$x = \frac{\$157{,}500}{1.05} = \$150{,}000$$

The sales in the prior year totalled \$150,000.

Exercise 2.5

Answers to the odd-numbered problems are at the end of the book.

Calculate the missing value for Problems 1 through 12.

Calculate dollar amounts in Problems 1 to 37 accurate to the cent, and percent amounts throughout accurate to the nearest 0.01%.

Problem	Initial value	Final value	Percent change
1.	\$95	\$100	?
2.	\$100	\$95	?
3.	35 kg	135 kg	?
4.	135 kg	35 kg	?
5.	0.11	0.13	?
6.	0.095	0.085	?
7.	\$134.39	?	−12
8.	112 g	?	112
9.	26.3 cm	?	300
10.	0.043	?	−30
11.	?	\$75	200
12.	?	\$75	−50

[2] It is tempting but incorrect to reason that the prior year's sales must be 100% − 5% = 95% of \$157,500 (which is \$149,625). The 5% increase in sales means that

Most recent year's sales = 105% of (Prior year's sales)

rather than

Prior year's sales = 95% of (Most recent year's sales)

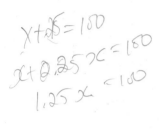

13. $100 is what percent more than $90?
14. $100 is what percent less than $110?
15. What amount when increased by 25% equals $100?
16. What sum of money when increased by 7% equals $52.43?
17. $75 is 75% more than what amount?
18. How much is $56 increased by 65%?
19. $754.30 is what percent less than $759.00?
20. 77,787 is what percent more than 77,400?
21. How much is $75 increased by 75%?
22. $100 is 10% less than what number?
23. What amount when reduced by 20% equals $100?
24. What amount when reduced by 25% equals $50?
25. What amount after a reduction of $16.\overline{6}\%$ equals $549?
26. How much is $900 decreased by 90%?
27. How much is $102 decreased by 2%?
28. How much is $102 decreased by 100%?
29. $750 is what percent more than $250?
30. $250 is what percent less than $750?
31. How much is $10,000 increased by $\frac{3}{4}\%$?
32. How much is $1045 decreased by 0.5%?
33. What amount when increased by 150% equals $575?
34. What amount after being increased by 210% equals $465?
35. How much is $150 increased by 150%?
36. How much is $10 increased by 900%?
37. The total cost of a coat, including GST and provincial sales tax totalling 15% of the ticket price, was $148.35. What was the ticket price of the coat?
38. The population of Lotustown increased by 24% over the last five years. If the current population is 109,500, what was the population five years ago?
39. Becker Tools sold 32,400 hammers at an average price of $7.55 in 1998 and 27,450 hammers at an average price of $7.75 in 1999. What was the percent change from 1998 to 1999 in:
    - **a.** The number of hammers sold?
    - **b.** The average selling price?
    - **c.** The revenue from the sale of hammers?
40. An investor purchased shares of Digger Resources at a price of $0.55 per share. One year later, the shares traded at $1.55, but they fell back to $0.75 by the end of the second year after the date of purchase. Calculate the percent change in the share price:
    - **a.** In the first year
    - **b.** In the second year
    - **c.** Over both years

41. The current quarter's sales of 599 units represent a 6% increase over the previous quarter. How many units were sold in the previous quarter?

42. In a 35%-off sale, the reduced price of a dress was $122.85. What was the regular price of the dress?

43. The price of the common shares of Campbell Mines fell by $1 in 1998 and by the same amount in 1999. If the share price was $4 at the end of 1998, what was the percent change in share price each year?

44. A wholesaler sells to retailers at a 27% discount from the suggested retail price. What is the suggested retail price of an item that costs the retailer $100?

45. The revenues of Petrocorp in the most recent quarter were $4.360 million, which represents an 18% increase over revenues for the same quarter in the previous year. What is the dollar amount of the year-to-year increase in revenues?

46. A commission salesperson's rate of commission increased from 7% to 8% of net sales. What will be the percent increase in commission income if the volume of sales is unchanged?

47. A chartered bank dropped the interest rate it charges on consumer loans from 10.5% to 9.75%. What is the percent reduction in the dollar amount of interest on these loans?

48. During the past 15 years the price of milk has increased by 280%. If the price is now $1.30 per litre, what is the dollar amount of the price increase per litre?

49. The price of the shares of Nadir Explorations Ltd. fell by 76% in the past year, to the current price of $0.45 per share. In dollars and cents, how much did the price of each share drop in the past year?

50. A piece of machinery has depreciated by 55% of its original purchase price during the past four years, to the current value of $24,300. What is the dollar amount of the total depreciation during the last four years?

•51. The owner listed a property for 140% more than she paid for it 12 years ago. After receiving no offers during the first three months of market exposure, she dropped the list price by 10%, to $172,800. What was the original price that the owner paid for the property?

•52. A car dealer normally lists new cars at 22% above cost. A demonstrator model was sold for $17,568 after a 10% reduction from the list price. What amount did the dealer pay for this car?

2.6 Application: Returns From Investments

There are two ways you can benefit financially from an investment. The first is by receiving **income**—money you receive without selling any part of the investment. Examples are interest from bonds, dividends from shares, and rent from real estate. Aside from the income, an investment may grow in value. The increase in value of the investment (not including income) is called the **capital gain.**

Figure 2.1 *The Components of Investment Returns*

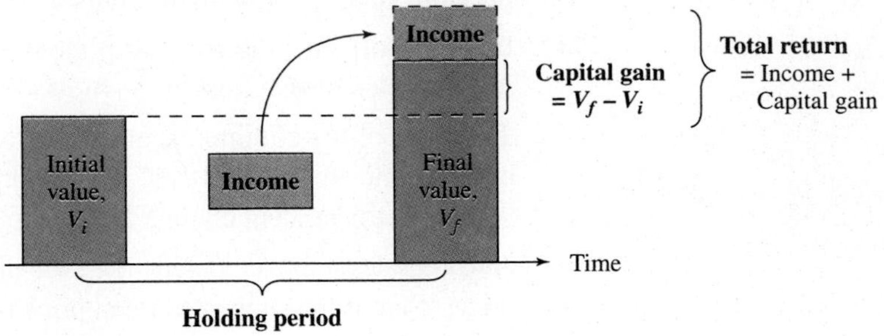

A typical investment scenario is represented in Figure 2.1. The initial value (or beginning value) of the investment is V_i. In finance, the term **holding period** is used for the time interval over which we are calculating the income and capital gain. Income may be received at one or more points during the holding period. The final value of the investment at the end of the holding period is V_f. The capital gain is the increase in value, $V_f - V_i$. (If the value of an investment declines during the holding period, the capital gain will be negative, indicating a **capital loss**.) The sum of the income and capital gain from the investment is called the **total return**. In summary,

$$\text{Capital gain} = \text{Final value } (V_f) - \text{Initial value } (V_i)$$
$$\text{Total return} = \text{Income} + \text{Capital gain}$$

The income, capital gain, and total return amounts defined above are all in terms of dollars. When discussing and comparing the performance of investments, investors prefer to express these amounts as a percentage of the initial value, V_i. Accordingly, we define:

$$\text{Income yield} = \frac{\text{Income}}{V_i} \times 100\%$$

INVESTMENT YIELDS AND RATE OF TOTAL RETURN (2-2)

$$\text{Capital gain yield} = \frac{\text{Capital gain}}{V_i} \times 100\% = \frac{V_f - V_i}{V_i} \times 100\%$$

$$\text{Rate of total return} = \text{Income yield} + \text{Capital gain yield}$$
$$= \frac{\text{Income} + \text{Capital gain}}{V_i} \times 100\%$$

TIP *WATCH FOR KEY WORDS*

The words "yield" and "rate" indicate amounts calculated as a percentage of the initial investment. Particular names may be used for specific types of income yield. For example, shareholders refer to a stock's "dividend yield," while bond investors speak of a bond's "current yield."

In everyday life, terms are sometimes used with less precision than in an academic environment. For example, "yield" may be dropped from "capital gain yield" when investors discuss capital gains.

Example 2.6A *Calculating Investment Returns When There Is a Capital Loss*

Richard purchased 1000 shares of Canadian Petroleum Ltd. on February 17 at $14.50 per share. On March 31 and June 30, dividends of $0.25 per share were paid. On the following September 1, the shares were trading on the stock market at $13.25. For the February 17 to September 1 holding period, what was Richard's:

a. Income yield (dividend yield)?

b. Capital gain yield?

c. Rate of total return?

d. Total return (in dollars)?

Solution

Since the shares are identical to one another, the income yield, percent capital gain, and rate of total return on a single share is the same as on 10 shares or on 1000 shares. We will do the calculations in (a), (b), and (c) in terms of a single share. The dollar amount of the total return (part d) depends on the actual number of shares owned.

a. Richard receives two $0.25 dividends from each share during the holding period.

$$\text{Income yield} = \frac{\text{Income}}{V_i} \times 100\% = \frac{2(\$0.25)}{\$14.50} \times 100\% = 3.448\%$$

b. $$\text{Capital gain yield} = \frac{\text{Capital gain}}{V_i} \times 100\% = \frac{\$13.25 - \$14.50}{\$14.50} \times 100\% = -8.621\%$$

That is, Richard has a capital loss[3] of 8.621% up to September 1.

c. $$\begin{aligned}\text{Rate of total return} &= \text{Income yield} + \text{Capital gain yield}\\ &= 3.448\% - 8.621\%\\ &= -5.173\%\end{aligned}$$

d. $$\begin{aligned}\text{Total return} &= \text{Rate of total return} \times \text{Initial investment, } V_i\\ &= -0.05173 \times 1000(\$14.50)\\ &= -\$750.09\end{aligned}$$

The negative total return means that, up to September 1, Richard has *lost* $750.09 on the investment. (The capital loss exceeds the dividend income by $750.09.)

---

[3] Since Richard still owns the shares, the capital loss is sometimes described in everyday language as a "paper" loss. The proper terminology in finance and accounting is "unrealized capital loss." When an investment is actually sold for less than the initial investment, it becomes a "realized capital loss." A capital gain may similarly be described as "unrealized" or "realized."

The total return can also be obtained by simply adding the total dividend income to the total capital gain. That is,

$$\begin{aligned}\text{Total return} &= 1000(\$0.50) + 1000(\$13.25 - \$14.50)\\ &= \$500.00 + 1000(-\$1.25)\\ &= -\$750.00\end{aligned}$$

The \$0.09 difference between the two answers results from rounding the rate of return on investment to four figures. Consequently, we can be assured of only three-figure accuracy in the total return. Therefore, the last reliable figure in \$750.09 is in the dollar position.

Example 2.6B *Calculating Investment Returns When There Are Expenses*

One year ago, Pierre purchased a rental house for \$129,000. During the past year, he collected \$825 per month in rent. In the same period, he paid \$1563 for property taxes and a total of \$1149 for maintenance and other expenses. The current appraised value of the property is \$135,000. What is Pierre's:

a. Income yield?

b. Capital gain yield?

c. Rate of total return?

d. Total return?

Solution

When there are expenses associated with an income-earning investment, the *net* income (after expenses) should be used in calculating the income yield.

a. Net income for the year = 12(\$825) − \$1563 − \$1149 = \$7188

$$\text{Income yield} = \frac{\$7188}{\$129{,}000} \times 100\% = 5.572\%$$

b. $$\text{Capital gain yield} = \frac{\$135{,}000 - \$129{,}000}{\$129{,}000} \times 100\% = 4.651\%$$

c. Rate of total return = 5.572% + 4.651% = 10.223%

d. Total return = Income + Capital gain = \$7188 + \$6000 = \$13,188

Example 2.6C *Calculating V_f Given V_i, Income, and Rate of Total Return*

An investor is prepared to buy common shares of Eagle Brewing Ltd. at the current share price of \$11.50 if he can expect at least a 15% rate of total return over the next year. Assuming that the company repeats last year's \$0.40 per share dividend, what will the minimum share price have to be one year from now for the investment objective to be achieved?

Solution

Given: $V_i = \$11.50$ Rate of total return = 15% Income = \$0.40

We want to determine what V_f must be one year from now for the rate of total return to be 15%. If the annual dividend is \$0.40 per share,

$$\text{Income yield} = \frac{\$0.40}{\$11.50} \times 100\% = 3.478\%$$

The rest of the 15% rate of total return must come from capital gain. That is,

$$\text{Capital gain yield} = 15\% - 3.478\% = 11.522\%$$

Hence,

$$\text{Capital gain} = 0.11522 \times V_i = 0.11522 \times \$11.50 = \$1.33 \text{ per share}$$

and

$$V_f = V_i + \text{Capital gain} = \$11.50 + \$1.33 = \$12.83$$

The share price must be at \$12.83 one year from now for the investor to achieve the minimum desired rate of total return (15%).

POINT OF INTEREST

FALSE PROFITS AND BULL MARKETING

The following tale speaks volumes about how little scrutiny is given to claims of investment performance. It also reveals how readily both producers and consumers of popular media suspend critical analysis in the face of a good story.

In 1994 Hyperion published *The Beardstown Ladies' Common-Sense Investment Guide.* The book describes the homespun stock-picking methods of an investment club of sixteen women living in Beardstown, Illinois (population 6000). We are told they range in age from 41 to 87. According to the book's introduction, "their hand-picked portfolio of fewer than 20 stocks has earned an average annual return of 23.4%" over the preceding 10 years (1984–1993). This return was almost twice the rate of return earned by the benchmark Standard & Poor's 500 (S&P 500) portfolio, and more than twice the average annual return achieved by professional mutual fund managers! Naturally the story found great appeal among the general public—a group of savvy septuagenarians emerging from the Illinois cornfields to trounce Wall Street's overpaid MBAs. (The book also contained neat recipes such as Ann's Kentucky Cream Cake and Helen's Springtime Pie.)

The Beardstown Ladies became celebrities almost overnight. The book was at the top of the *New York Times* bestseller list for three months and eventually sold over 800,000 copies in seven languages. The Beardstown Ladies were the subject of articles in scores of publications and appeared as guests on several television talk shows including *Donahue.* Four more books followed in rapid succession. (The most recent—*The Beardstown Ladies Pocketbook Guide to Picking Stocks*—appeared in 1998 and continued to "milk" the 23.4% annual return.) Along the way, the geriatric gurus produced their own home video titled *Cookin' up Profits on Wall Street.* After reviewing the video, the late great movie critic Gene Siskel wrote what proved to be a prescient one-liner: "Wait till you see what these ladies are up to!"

In early 1998, Shane Tristch, a managing editor at *Chicago Magazine,* set about writing yet another warm fuzzy story about the lovable ladies from Beardstown. However, he was troubled by the following disclaimer which appeared in the front material of the Beardstown Ladies' first book.

> *"Investment clubs commonly compute their annual "return" by calculating the increase in their total club balance over a period of time. Since this increase includes the dues that the members pay regularly, this "return" may be different from the return that might be calculated for a mutual fund or a bank. Since the regular contributions are an important part of the club philosophy, the Ladies' returns described in this book are based on this common calculation."*

The "dues" refer to regular contributions of new money that most investment clubs require from each member. In the case of the Beardstown Ladies, each member contributed $25 per month right from the start in 1984. Anyone with a basic knowledge of investing should have an "Excuse me?" moment upon reading the disclaimer. It is preposterous to treat new injections of investment capital as part of the total return from a portfolio! Frankly, it is highly doubtful that this method of calculating returns is "commonly" used by investment clubs.

Tristch wrote an article for the March 1998 issue of *Chicago Magazine* exposing the flaw and challenging the claim of a 23.4% average annual return. The Beardstown Ladies allowed the international accounting firm Price Waterhouse to audit their records. Instead of the 23.4% average annual return, Price Waterhouse determined that the average annual rate of return was a sickly 9.1%. This was far short of the publicized 23.4% return and well short of the 14.9% annual return on the unmanaged S&P 500 portfolio. The Ladies beat the S&P 500 in only two of the 10 years. The Beardstown Ladies and their publisher had built an empire based on a profoundly flawed calculation that went unchallenged for four years!

The saga soon took another bizarre turn. Price Waterhouse also discovered that the Beardstown Ladies did not, in fact, calculate their rate of return using the method indicated in the book's disclaimer. What did happen was this. In 1992 the Ladies bought a software package and entered their data going all the way back to the start-up of the club in 1984. In 1993, they used the software to calculate the average annual rate of return for the entire 10-year period. Or so they thought. In fact, they unwittingly (we are told) obtained the average annual rate of return for just two years, 1991 and 1992. As fate would have it, 1991 was their one and only outstanding year (with a return of 54.4%).

Several questions remain unanswered. Among them, why did the Beardstown Ladies' publisher accept their performance numbers at face value (along with the unlikely proposition that a group of inexperienced investors outperformed the market and professional investment managers by a 2-to-1 margin over a 10-year period)?

Concept Questions

1. What is meant by a "capital loss"?
2. What is meant by the "total return" from an investment?
3. Can the income yield from an investment be negative? Explain or give an example.
4. Is it possible for the capital gain yield to be worse than 100%? Explain or give an example.
5. Is it possible for a capital loss to be worse than −100%? Explain or give an example.
6. Give an example of an investment that cannot generate any income.

Exercise 2.6

Answers to the odd-numbered problems are at the end of the book.

Calculate the missing quantities in Problems 1 through 16. Calculate yields and rates of return to the nearest 0.01%. Calculate dollar amounts correct to the cent.

Problem	Initial value	Income	Final value	Income yield	Capital gain yield	Rate of total return
1.	$100	$10	$110	?	?	?
2.	100	10	90	?	?	?
3.	90	10	86	?	?	?
4.	135	0	151	?	?	?
5.	1367	141	1141	?	?	?
6.	879	280	1539	?	?	?
7.	2500	200	0	?	?	?
8.	1380	250	2875	?	?	?
•9.	2000	?	2200	5%	?	?
•10.	4300	?	3950	?	?	−5%
•11.	3730	250	?	?	?	5%
•12.	1800	50	?	?	150%	?
•13.	?	?	1800	?	−40%	−30%
•14.	?	100	?	5%	15%	?
•15.	1600	?	?	8%	?	0%
••16.	?	150	2700	?	?	80%

17. One year ago, Art Vandelay bought Canadian Pacific shares for $37 per share. Today they are worth $40 per share. During the year, Art received dividends of $0.60 per share. What was his income yield, capital gain yield, and rate of total return for the year?
18. Rose purchased units of the Trimark Fund one year ago at $24.10 per unit. Today they are valued at $25.50. On the intervening December 31, there was a distribution of $0.83 per unit. ("Distribution" is the term used by most mutual funds for income paid to unitholders.) Calculate Rose's income yield, capital gain yield, and rate of total return for the year.
19. The market value of Stephanie's bonds has declined from $1053.25 to $1021.75 per bond during the past year. In the meantime she has received

two semiannual interest payments of \$35. Calculate Stephanie's income yield, capital gain yield, and rate of total return for the year.

20. Vitaly's shares of Dominion Petroleum have dropped in value from \$36.75 to \$32.25 during the past year. The shares paid a \$0.50 per share dividend six months ago. Calculate Vitaly's income yield, capital gain yield, and rate of total return for the year.

21. Jack bought 10 Government of Canada bonds in a new series issued at \$1000 each. Each bond pays \$47.50 interest six months after issue and every six months thereafter. One year later Jack sold the bonds for \$1034 each. For the entire year, what was his:

a. Income yield?

b. Capital gain yield?

c. Total return (in dollars)?

d. Rate of total return?

22. Bernice purchased 15 bonds from her broker for \$1025 each. These bonds each pay semiannual interest of \$42.50. Over the next $1\frac{1}{2}$ years, the price of the bonds declined to \$980 because of rising interest rates. Over the entire 18-month period, what was her:

a. Capital gain yield?

b. Total return (in dollars)?

c. Rate of total return?

23. Jeff purchased some Mitel preferred shares on the Toronto Stock Exchange (TSE) for \$13.50. The shares pay a quarterly dividend of \$0.50. Nine months later the shares were trading at \$15.25. What was Jeff's rate of total return for the nine-month period?

24. Lily bought 200 shares in Maritime Trust Co. at \$29.37 just before it paid a dividend of \$0.60 per share. Rumours of loan losses sent the shares tumbling to \$24.50 only three months after she purchased them. For these three months, what was her:

a. Capital gain yield?

b. Rate of total return?

•25. Mr. Furlan purchased an older home for \$75,000 and spent another \$15,000 on repairs and renovations soon after the purchase date. Two months after the purchase, he rented the house for \$700 per month net of all expenses except property taxes, which came to \$1550 for the year.

a. If he "flips" the property one year after purchase for \$110,000, what will be his rate of total return for the year? Treat the initial repairs and renovations as part of the original investment.

b. What is his rate of total return if a 6% real estate commission on the sale of the house is deducted from the sale proceeds?

•26. Mrs. Wilson bought a duplex a year ago for \$160,000 using \$40,000 of her own money and \$120,000 borrowed from the bank on a mortgage loan. She collected monthly rents of \$575 and \$550 from the two units, net of all expenses except property taxes ($2173) and interest on the mortgage ($10,127). If the property has increased in value to $170,000, what is Mrs. Wilson's rate of total return, net of expenses, for the year on her personal investment of $40,000?

•27. One year ago, Morgan invested $5000 to purchase 400 units of a mutual fund. He has just noted in the *Financial Post* that the fund's rate of return on investment for the year was 22% and that the current price of a unit is $13.75. What amount did the fund distribute as income per unit during the year?

•28. Lori can buy Government of Canada bonds paying $50 interest every six months for $1090. What market price of the bonds one year from now would produce a rate of total return of 12%?

•29. As a consequence of rising interest rates, Union Gas bonds have produced a capital loss of 8% and a rate of total return of only 1% for the past year. If the bonds pay interest of $52.50 every six months, what is their current price?

••30. The *Globe and Mail* Report on Business noted that the shares of Compact Computers produced a 55% rate of total return in the past year. The shares paid a dividend of $0.72 per share during the year, and they currently trade at $37.50. What was the price of the shares one year ago?

••31. Ed can buy a duplex for $230,000. He would borrow 60% of the funds and pay interest charges totalling $12,400 on the mortgage during the next year. Repairs and maintenance would average $300 per month, and annual property taxes would be $2400. If property values increase 6% in the next year, what monthly rental income would the property have to generate for Ed to earn a 15% rate of total return on his personal investment?

2.7 Application: Compounding Percent Changes and Rates of Return

Suppose you read that a stock's price rose by 10% in 1998 and 20% in 1999. Does this mean the overall price increase for the two-year period was 10% + 20% = 30%? No—the understanding behind these numbers is that the *Base* for the 10% increase was the price at the beginning of 1998, whereas the *Base* for the 20% increase was the stock's price at the beginning of 1999. Since the two percent changes have different *Bases,* they cannot be added to accurately obtain the overall percent increase.

In this section, you will learn how to combine a series of percent changes. Let us continue with the preceding example to see what general inferences can be made. Suppose the stock's price was $15.50 at the beginning of 1998. The price at the end of 1998 was

$$V_f = V_i(1 + c) = \$15.50(1 + 0.1) = \$17.05$$

This is also 1999's beginning price to which the 20% increase applies. Hence, the price at the end of 1999 was

$$V_f = V_i(1 + c) = \$17.05(1 + 0.2) = \$20.46$$

The two-year percent increase in the stock's price was

$$c = \frac{V_f - V_i}{V_i} \times 100\% = \frac{\$20.46 - \$15.50}{\$15.50} \times 100\% = 32.0\%$$

which exceeds 10% + 20% = 30%. When each percent change acts on the amount *after* the preceding percent change, we are **compounding** the percent changes.

You can obtain the \$20.46 price directly from the beginning \$15.50 price as follows:

$$V_f = V_i(1 + c_1)(1 + c_2) = \$15.50(1 + 0.1)(1 + 0.2) = \$20.46$$

If you have a series of three, four, or more percent changes, you need a $(1 + c)$ factor for each percent change. In general, to compound a series of n percent changes,

COMPOUNDING PERCENT CHANGES

(2-3) $$V_f = V_i(1 + c_1)(1 + c_2)(1 + c_3)\ldots(1 + c_n)$$

TIP *Customizing Formula (2-3)*

1. If some of the percent changes are the same, their $(1 + c)$ factors may be combined in a power. (The factors need not be from consecutive periods.) For example, if the percent change or rate of return for any three periods is 8%, their $(1 + c)$ factors may be combined as 1.08^3.
2. When a quantity decreases, the percent change is negative. The corresponding negative value must be substituted for c.

Example 2.7A *Compounding Rates of Total Return on an Investment*

The Brazil Fund is a mutual fund that can be purchased on the New York Stock Exchange (trading symbol BZF). As its name suggests, the fund invests in the stocks of Brazilian companies. For individual years from 1994 to 1998, the rates of total return provided by the fund were 61.1%, −23.3%, 28.9%, 19.8%, and −25.4%, respectively. (As these rates of return indicate, the Brazilian stock market is notoriously volatile.)

a. If you had invested \$1000 in the fund at the beginning of 1994, what was your investment worth at the end of 1998?

b. What would have been the dollar amount of your total return in 1996?

Solution

a. We can directly substitute the given values into formula (2-3).

$$\begin{aligned} V_f &= V_i(1 + c_1)(1 + c_2)(1 + c_3)(1 + c_4)(1 + c_5) \\ &= \$1000(1 + 0.611)[1 + (-0.233)](1 + 0.289)(1 + 0.198)[1 + (-0.254)] \\ &= \$1000(1.611)(0.767)(1.289)(1.198)(0.746) \\ &= \$1423.44 \end{aligned}$$

b. In 1996 the rate of total return was 28.8%. The dollar amount of the total return was

$$\begin{aligned} &0.288 \times (\text{Value of the investment at the end of 1995}) \\ &= 0.288 \times \$1000(1.611)(0.767) \\ &= \$355.86 \end{aligned}$$

Example 2.7B *Comparing the Performance of a Mutual Fund to a Benchmark*

The following table presents the rates of total return on the Investors Canadian Equity mutual fund for each year from 1994 to 1998 inclusive. Corresponding figures are also given for the Toronto Stock Exchange's TSE Total Return Index.[4] What is the difference between the overall rate of total return on the mutual fund and on the benchmark portfolio represented by the TSE Index?

Fund name	Rate of total return (%)				
	1994	1995	1996	1997	1998
Investors Canadian Equity	0.2	10.6	24.9	9.0	−13.1
TSE Total Return Index	−0.2	14.5	28.3	15.0	−1.6

Solution

Suppose you invested an amount V_i in the Investors Canadian Equity Fund at the beginning of 1994. By the end of 1998, the investment would have grown to

$$\begin{aligned} V_f &= V_i(1 + c_1)(1 + c_2)(1 + c_3)(1 + c_4)(1 + c_5) \\ &= V_i(1 + 0.002)(1 + 0.106)(1 + 0.249)(1 + 0.09)(1 - 0.131) \\ &= V_i(1.311) \end{aligned}$$

Since the final value is 1.311 times the initial value, the investment in the mutual fund grew by a total of 31.1%.

For the same initial investment in the portfolio represented by the TSE Index,

$$\begin{aligned} V_f &= V_i(1 + c_1)(1 + c_2)(1 + c_3)(1 + c_4)(1 + c_5) \\ &= V_i(1 - 0.002)(1 + 0.145)(1 + 0.283)(1 + 0.15)(1 - 0.016) \\ &= V_i(1.659) \end{aligned}$$

This investment grew by 65.9%. Therefore, the unmanaged TSE Index portfolio grew

$$65.9\% - 31.1\% = 34.8\%$$

more than the professionally managed Investors Canadian Equity Fund.

[4] The TSE Total Return Index measures the performance of a portfolio of the common shares of 300 of the largest Canadian companies trading on the Toronto Stock Exchange. The index is often used as the benchmark for evaluating the performance of other portfolios of Canadian stocks.

Example 2.7C Calculating One of a Series of Percent Changes

Teri invested in a stock that doubled in the first year and rose another 50% in the second year. Now at the end of the third year, Teri is surprised to discover that the stock's price is up only 80% from her purchase price. By what percentage did the stock's price change in the third year?

Solution

The stock's price is up 80% over the entire three-year period. Therefore,

$$V_f = 1.80V_i$$

In terms of the capital gain yield in individual years,

$$\begin{aligned} V_f &= V_i(1 + c_1)(1 + c_2)(1 + c_3) \\ &= V_i(1 + 1.00)(1 + 0.50)(1 + c_3) \\ &= 3.0V_i(1 + c_3) \end{aligned}$$

For the same final value in both cases, we require

$$\begin{aligned} V_i(1.80) &= 3.0V_i(1 + c_3) \\ 1.80 &= 3.0(1 + c_3) \\ \frac{1.80}{3.0} &= 1 + c_3 \\ c_3 &= 0.60 - 1 = -0.40 = -40\% \end{aligned}$$

The stock's price declined 40% in Year 3.

POINT OF INTEREST

THE UPS AND DOWNS OF PERCENT RETURNS ON INVESTMENT

When positive and negative rates of return are compounded, the outcome can be surprising. As a rather extreme example, suppose an investment had a 100% gain one year followed by a 50% loss the next year. We might be tempted to estimate the overall two-year gain as 100% − 50% = 50%. On more careful thought, we note that the investment doubled in the first year and then "halved" in the second year. Consequently, the value of the investment was back at its initial value—the actual two-year return was 0%!

Consider other examples of the asymmetrical effects of positive and negative percent returns.

- A 50% gain one year can be wiped out by a 33.3% loss in the next year.
- To offset a 50% loss in one period, you need a 100% gain in the next period.
- To recover from a 25% loss, you would need a 33.3% gain.

These statements can be verified using formula (2-3). The general conclusion we can draw is that the negative impact of a loss of $x\%$ on the final value of an investment is more significant than the positive impact of a gain of $x\%$.

Question 1: An investment's rate of total return in each of two consecutive years was a positive $y\%$. In the third year, the investment lost $y\%$. At the end of the three years, the value of the investment was back at its original value. What is the value of $y\%$? (Hint: Try values between 50% and 70%.)

When you are presented with a series of annual returns on an investment (such as a mutual fund), there is the temptation to average the annual returns to measure the overall long-term performance of the investment. At best, this average is only a fair approximation. At worst, it is very misleading. We can illustrate this point dramatically using the rather extreme example from the beginning of this Point of Interest. The simple average of a 100% gain and a 50% loss is $[100\% + (-50\%)]/2 = 25\%$. An average gain of 25% per year for the two years has no relationship whatsoever to the actual two-year gain of 0%!

You must be very cautious about drawing conclusions based on a simple average of a series of annual rates of return. It will always overstate the actual performance. The more volatile the year-to-year rates of return, the greater the degree of overstatement. The calculation in Question 2 will illustrate this point.

Question 2: For the years 1995 to 1998, the Fidelity Latin American Growth Fund had rates of return of −22.3%, 28.9%, 35.7%, and −34.3%, respectively.

a. What was the average annual rate of return for the four years?

b. If a $1000 investment earns this average rate of return every year for four years, what is its final value?

c. What was the actual final value of $1000 invested in the Fidelity Latin American Growth Fund at the beginning of 1995?

Concept Questions

1. What is meant by "compounding a series of percent changes"?
2. If a series of compound percent changes are all positive, is the overall percent change larger or smaller than the sum of the individual changes? Justify your answer.
3. If a series of compound percent changes are all negative, is the overall percent decrease larger or smaller (in magnitude) than the sum of the individual changes? Justify your answer.
4. Does the combined effect of a 20% increase followed by a 20% decrease differ from the combined effect of a 20% decrease followed by a 20% increase? Justify your answer.

Exercise 2.7 *Answers to the odd-numbered problems are at the end of the book.*

1. A union agreed to a collective agreement providing for wage increases of 5%, 3%, and 1% in successive years of a three-year contract. What wage will an employee earning $15 per hour at the beginning be making at the end of the term of the contract?
2. Inflation rates as determined from the consumer price index (CPI) were 4.8%, 5.6%, 1.5%, 1.8%, and 0.3% in five successive years. A sample of goods and services representative of the CPI cost $1000 at the beginning of the period. What did the sample cost at the end of the period?
3. Inflation rates as determined from the consumer price index (CPI) were 10.2%, 12.4%, 10.9%, 5.7%, and 4.4% for the years 1980 to 1984, respectively. What was the percent increase in overall price levels during the entire five years?
4. The value of assets under the management of Canadian mutual funds increased by 27.3%, 5.5%, 41.4%, 43.7%, and 10.6% in successive years from 1994 to 1998, respectively.
   - **a.** What was the overall percent change in mutual fund assets during the five years?
   - **b.** If Canadian mutual fund assets totalled $102.5 billion at the end of 1993, what was the total at the end of 1998?
5. The price of Bionex Inc. shares rose by 25% in each of two successive years. If they began the two-year period at $12 per share, what was the percent increase in price over the entire two years?
6. The price of Biomed Corp. shares also began the same two-year period (as in Problem 5) at $12 but fell 25% in each year. What was their overall percent decline in price?
7. What rate of return in the second year of an investment will wipe out a 50% gain in the first year?
8. What rate of return in the second year of an investment will nullify a 25% return on investment in the first year?
9. What rate of return in the second year of an investment is required to break even after a 50% loss in the first year?
10. What rate of return in the second year of an investment is required to break even after a rate of total return of −20% in the first year?
11. After two consecutive years of 10% rates of return, what rate of return in the third year will produce a cumulative gain of 30%?
12. After two consecutive years of 10% losses, what rate of return in the third year will produce a cumulative loss of 30%?
13. Annual sales of microcomputers increased by 35%, 40%, 30% and 25% in four consecutive years. What was the cumulative percent increase in microcomputer sales over the four years?
14. A mining operation announced a three-year "downsizing" program whereby the number of employees will be reduced by 10%, 6%, and 5% in

Years 1, 2, and 3, respectively. How many of the current 6750 positions will be eliminated over the next three years?

15. A provincial government presented a budget that projects (compound) annual cuts in the provincial deficit of 20%, 40%, and 60%.

a. What will the deficit be after the third year if it starts the first year at $1 billion?

b. What is the dollar amount of the projected decrease in the third year?

16. The price of newsprint rose in four successive years from $400 per tonne to $740 per tonne. If the first three increases were 10%, 22%, and 18%, what was the fourth increase:

a. In percent?

b. In dollars?

17. Calculate and compare the cumulative percent increase for the following two cases:

a. 10 years of constant 10% annual increases

b. 5 years of 20% increases and 5 years of 0% decreases

Note that in both cases the average of the annual increases is 10%.

18. Victor cannot find the original record of his purchase four years ago of units of the Imperial Global Fund. The current statement from the fund shows that the total current value of the units is $47,567. From a mutual fund database, Victor found that the rates of return on investment in the fund for Years 1 to 4 have been 15.4%, 24.3%, 32.1%, and −3.3%, respectively.

a. What was Victor's original investment in the fund?

b. What was the dollar increase in the value of the fund in Year 3?

19. A company announced that it will make cuts of 9%, 7%, and 5% to its current work force of 18,750 over the next three years. If the cuts proceed as indicated,

a. How many employees will the company have at the end of the three years?

b. How many employees will be cut in the second year?

20. A town in a rural area of Saskatchewan reported population declines of 4.5%, 6.7%, and 10.5% for the three successive five-year periods 1984 to 1988, 1989 to 1993, and 1994 to 1998. If the population at the end of 1998 was 7450,

a. How many lived in the town at the beginning of 1984?

b. What was the population loss in each of the five-year periods?

•21. The number of jobs in the British Columbia forest industry fell by 22% from the beginning of 1990 to the end of 1992. If the decline was 5.3% in 1990 and 10.4% in 1991, what was the percent decrease in 1992?

•22. The TSE 300 Index rose 3.4%, dropped 1.4%, and then rose 2.1% in three successive months. The Index ended the three-month period at 7539.

a. What was the Index at the beginning of the three-month period?

b. How many points did the Index drop in the second month?

23. In three successive years the price of the common shares of Abysmal Resources Ltd. fell 35%, 55%, and 80%, ending the third year at 75 cents.

a. What was the share price at the beginning of the three-year skid?

b. How much (in dollars and cents) did the share price drop in the third year?

The following table lists the rates of total return during each of five years on each of five well-known Canadian equity mutual funds. Comparable figures are also given for the Toronto Stock Exchange's Total Return Index. For each fund, calculate:

- The percent increase (over the entire five years) in the value of an investment made at the beginning of 1994.
- The percentage differential by which the fund outperformed or underperformed the TSE Index during the five-year period.

Problem	Fund name	1994 return	1995 return	1996 return	1997 return	1998 return
24.	Altamira Equity	1.7%	14.8%	17.0%	4.1%	−9.0%
25.	AGF Growth Equity	−13.6	14.3	29.3	17.1	−17.5
26.	Industrial Growth	−1.4	5.8	20.5	−1.5	−19.3
27.	Royal Canadian Equity	−0.4	13.2	21.9	12.9	−0.6
28.	PH&N Canadian Equity	3.9	13.1	30.0	14.2	−2.7
	TSE Total Return Index	−0.2	14.5	28.3	15.0	−1.6

Appendix: Interpretation of Negative and Fractional Exponents

Interpretation of a^0

Clearly,

$$\frac{a^n}{a^n} = 1$$

But Rule 2 gives

$$\frac{a^n}{a^n} = a^{n-n} = a^0$$

Therefore, we must interpret $a^0 = 1$

Interpretation of a^{-n}

Using the previous result that $a^0 = 1$

we can write $$\frac{a^0}{a^n} = \frac{1}{a^n}$$

But Rule 2 gives $$\frac{a^0}{a^n} = a^{0-n} = a^{-n}$$

For consistency, we must define $$a^{-n} = \frac{1}{a^n}$$

INTERPRETATION OF $a^{1/n}$

Rule 1 gives

$$a^{1/2} \times a^{1/2} = a^{1/2+1/2} = a^1 = a$$

Similarly,

$$a^{1/3} \times a^{1/3} \times a^{1/3} = a^{1/3+1/3+1/3} = a^1 = a$$

However, we already know that

$$\sqrt{a} \times \sqrt{a} = a$$

and that

$$\sqrt[3]{a} \times \sqrt[3]{a} \times \sqrt[3]{a} = a$$

Therefore, consistency requires that

$$a^{1/2} = \sqrt{a}$$

and that

$$a^{1/3} = \sqrt[3]{a}$$

Generalizing from these particular results, we can conclude that

$$a^{1/n} = \sqrt[n]{a}$$

INTERPRETATION OF $a^{m/n}$

Building on Rule 3 and the interpretation of $a^{1/n}$, we can write

$$a^{m/n} = (a^{1/n})^m = (\sqrt[n]{a})^m$$

and also

$$a^{m/n} = (a^m)^{1/n} = \sqrt[n]{a^m}$$

These results for the interpretation of zero, negative, and fractional exponents are summarized below.

ZERO, NEGATIVE, AND FRACTIONAL EXPONENTS:

$$a^0 = 1 \qquad a^{-n} = \frac{1}{a^n} \qquad a^{1/n} = \sqrt[n]{a}$$

$$a^{m/n} = (\sqrt[n]{a})^m = \sqrt[n]{a^m}$$

Review Problems

Answers to the odd-numbered review problems are at the end of the book.

◆ **1.** Simplify and collect the like terms.

a. $\frac{9y-7}{3} - 2.3(y-2)$ **b.** $P\left(1 + 0.095 \times \frac{135}{365}\right) + \frac{2P}{1 + 0.095 \times \frac{75}{365}}$

2. Multiply and collect the like terms:

$$4(3a + 2b)(2b - a) - 5a(2a - b)$$

3. Evaluate each of the following expressions for the given values of the variables. The answer should be accurate to the cent.

a. $L(1 - d_1)(1 - d_2)(1 - d_3)$ for $L = \$340$, $d_1 = 0.15$, $d_2 = 0.08$, $d_3 = 0.05$

b. $\frac{R}{i}\left[1 - \frac{1}{(1+i)^n}\right]$ for $R = \$575$, $i = 0.085$, $n = 3$

◆ **4.** Simplify:

$$\left(-\frac{2x^2}{3}\right)^{-2}\left(\frac{5^2}{6x^3}\right)\left(-\frac{15}{x^5}\right)^{-1}$$

5. Evaluate the following expressions to six-figure accuracy.

a. $\frac{(1.00\overline{6})^{240} - 1}{0.00\overline{6}}$ **b.** $(1 + 0.025)^{1/3} - 1$

◆ **6.** Solve the following equations for x to five-figure accuracy and verify the solution.

a. $\frac{x}{1.08^3} + \frac{x}{2}(1.08)^4 = \$850$ **b.** $2x\left(1 + 0.085 \times \frac{77}{365}\right) + \frac{x}{1 + 0.085 \times \frac{132}{365}} = \$1565.70$

7. Solve each of the following:

a. What amount is 17.5% more than \$29.43?

b. What amount reduced by 80% leaves \$100?

c. What amount reduced by 15% equals \$100?

d. What is \$47.50 increased by 320%?

e. What amount when decreased by 62% equals \$213.56?

f. What amount when increased by 125% equals \$787.50?

g. What amount is 30% less than \$300?

8. Yellowknife Mining sold 34,300 oz of gold in 1992 at an average price of \$320 per ounce. Production was down to 23,750 oz in 1993 because of a strike by the miners, but the average price obtained was \$360 per ounce. What was the percent change from 1992 to 1993 in:

a. The amount of gold produced?

b. The average selling price per ounce?

c. The revenue from the sale of gold?

9. Two years ago the shares of Diamond Strike Resources traded at a price of \$3.40 per share. One year later the shares were at \$11.50, but then they declined in value by 35% during the subsequent year. Calculate:

a. The percent change in the share price during the first year.

b. The current share price.

10. Barry recently sold some stock after holding it for two years. The stock's price rose 150% during the first year, but fell 40% in the second year. At what price did he buy the stock if he sold it for $24 per share?

11. Christos bought 15 Government of Canada bonds in a new series issued at $1000 each. Each bond pays $40 interest six months after issue and every six months thereafter. One year later he sold the bonds for $980 each. For the entire year what was his:

a. Interest yield?

b. Capital gain yield?

c. Total return in dollars?

d. Rate of total return?

12. From the end of 1994 to the end of 1999, the number of cellular phones doubled. If during the first four years, the year-to-year increases were 18%, 17%, 14%, and 13%, what was the percent change in the last year?

13. A company's annual report states that the prices of its common shares had changes of 23%, 10%, −15%, and 5% during the past four fiscal years. If the shares were trading at $30.50 just after the 5% increase in the most recently completed year,

a. What was the price of the shares at the beginning of the four-year period?

b. How much (in dollars and cents) did the price decline in the third year?

◆ **14.** The profits from a partnership are to be distributed so that Grace receives 20% more than Marie, and Mary Anne receives five-eighths as much as Grace. How much should each receive from a total distribution of $36,000?

◆ **15.** Rory invested a total of $7800 in shares of ABC Ltd. and XYZ Inc. One year later the investment was worth $9310, after the shares of ABC had increased in value by 15% and the shares of XYZ were up 25%. How much did Rory invest in each company?

Self-Test Exercise

Answers to the self-test problems are at the end of the book.

1. Perform the indicated multiplication and division, and combine the like terms.

a. $6(4y - 3)(2 - 3y) - 3(5 - y)(1 + 4y)$

◆ **b.** $\dfrac{5b - 4}{4} - \dfrac{25 - b}{1.25} + \dfrac{7}{8}b$

◆ **c.** $\dfrac{x}{1 + 0.085 \times \frac{63}{365}} + 2x\left(1 + 0.085 \times \dfrac{151}{365}\right)$

d. $\dfrac{96nm^2 - 72n^2m^2}{48n^2m}$

◆ **2.** Evaluate:

$$P(1 + i)^n + \frac{S}{1 + rt}$$

accurate to the cent for $P = \$2500$, $i = 0.1025$, $n = 2$, $S = \$1500$, $r = 0.09$, and $t = \frac{93}{365}$.

3. Simplify:

a. $\dfrac{(-3x^2)^3(2x^{-2})}{6x^5}$

◆ **b.** $\dfrac{(-2a^3)^{-2}(4b^4)^{3/2}}{(-2b^3)(0.5a)^3}$

4. Evaluate the following expressions to six-figure accuracy.

a. $(1.0075)^{24}$

b. $(1.05)^{1/6} - 1$

c. $\dfrac{(1 + 0.0075)^{36} - 1}{0.0075}$

d. $\dfrac{1 - (1 + 0.045)^{-12}}{0.045}$

◆ **5.** Solve the following equations for x to five-figure accuracy.

a. $\dfrac{2x}{1 + 0.13 \times \frac{92}{365}} + x\left(1 + 0.13 \times \dfrac{59}{365}\right) = \$831$

b. $3x(1.03^5) + \dfrac{x}{1.03^3} + x = \dfrac{\$2500}{1.03^2}$

6. Albion Distributors' revenues and expenses for the fiscal year just completed were $2,347,000 and $2,189,000, respectively.

a. If in the current year revenues rise by 10% but expense increases are held to 5%, what will be the percent increase in operating profit?

b. If, instead, revenues decline by 10% and expenses are reduced by 5%, what will be the percent change in operating profit?

◆ **7.** Marsha and Steve bought a small house two years ago for $95,000, using $45,000 of personal savings and a $50,000 mortgage loan. They rented the house for $500 per month for the first year and, after a two-month vacancy, found new tenants who paid $525 per month. Both rental rates are net of all expenses except property taxes and mortgage interest. Property taxes were $1456 in the first year and $1515 in the second year. Mortgage interest totalled $5453 in the first year and $5387 in the second. What is the rate of total return on their $45,000 investment for the entire two-year holding period if they now sell the house for $112,000 less a selling commission of 5.5%?

8. Three years ago, General Avionics announced plans to triple its annual R&D spending over the next four years. If R&D spending was increased by 25%, 30%, and 35% in the first three years, what minimum percent increase is required in the fourth year to reach the target?

◆ **9.** One thousand shares of Gonzo Software were purchased at $6.50 per share. The share price rose 110% in the first year after purchase, dropped 55% in the second year, and then dropped another 55% in the third year.

a. What was the percent change in the price of the shares over the entire three-year period?

b. How much (in dollars and cents) did the share price drop in the second year?

10. The annual net income of the Todd Bros. partnership is distributed so that Ken receives $15,000 more than 80% of Hugh's share. How should a net income of $98,430 be divided between the partners?

Summary of Notation and Key Formulas

V_i = Initial (or beginning or original or old) value
V_f = Final (or ending or new) value
c = Percent change (or its decimal equivalent)

Formula (2-1) $c = \frac{V_f - V_i}{V_i} \times 100\%$ Finding the percent change in a quantity

Formula (2-2) $\text{Income yield} = \frac{\text{Income}}{V_i} \times 100\%$ Finding investment yields and rate of total return

$$\text{Capital gain yield} = \frac{\text{Capital gain}}{V_i} \times 100\% = \frac{V_f - V_i}{V_i} \times 100\%$$

$$\text{Rate of total return} = \text{Income yield} + \text{Capital gain yield}$$

$$= \frac{\text{Income} + \text{Capital gain}}{V_i} \times 100\%$$

Formula (2-3) $V_f = V_i(1 + c_1)(1 + c_2)(1 + c_3)\ldots(1 + c_n)$ Finding the final value after a series of compound percent changes

STEPS FOR SOLVING WORD PROBLEMS:

1. Read the entire problem.
2. Extract and label the data. Identify the unknown quantity and specify its symbol. Draw and label a diagram if appropriate.
3. Identify the principle, concept, or idea that can be used to construct a word equation. The word equation relates the given data to the unknown quantity.
4. Convert the word equation to an algebraic equation, and substitute the values extracted in Step 2.
5. Solve the equation.

List of Key Terms

Algebraic expression *(p. 44)*
Base *(p. 50)*
Binomial *(p. 44)*
Capital gain *(p. 69)*
Capital gain yield *(p. 70)*
Capital loss *(p. 70)*
Compounding *(p. 78)*
Equation *(p. 54)*
Exponent *(p. 50)*
Factors *(p. 44)*
Holding period *(p. 70)*
Income *(p. 69)*
Income yield *(p. 70)*
Like terms *(p. 45)*
Linear equation *(p. 54)*
Literal coefficient *(p. 44)*
Monomial *(p. 44)*
Nonlinear equation *(p. 54)*
Numerical coefficient *(p. 44)*
Polynomial *(p. 44)*
Power *(p. 50)*
Rate of total return *(p. 70)*
Root (of an equation) *(p. 54)*
Substitution *(p. 47)*
Terms *(p. 44)*
Total return *(p. 70)*
Trinomial *(p. 44)*

CHAPTER OUTLINE

LEARNING OBJECTIVES

After completing this chapter, you will be able to:

- Set up and manipulate ratios
- Set up and solve proportions
- Use proportions to allocate or prorate an amount on a proportionate basis
- Use quoted exchange rates to convert between currencies
- Relate currency exchange rate movement to currency appreciation or depreciation
- Interpret and use index numbers

3

Ratios and Proportions

RAW BUSINESS DATA CAN TAKE on greater meaning when comparisons are made between associated quantities. For example, a firm's profit for a year is an important figure in itself. However, profit relative to invested capital, profit relative to total sales, and current profit relative to last year's profit provide useful insights into the firm's profitability, efficiency, and profit growth. Ratios are widely used to make such comparisons. In accounting and finance, a primary technique for the detailed analysis and interpretation of financial statements is known as *ratio analysis.* Each financial statement ratio compares the size of one balance sheet or income statement figure to another. Each ratio provides an indication of a financial strength or weakness of the business.

Ratios and proportions are also employed when resources, costs, profits, etc., must be allocated on a pro rata or proportionate basis. For example, a partnership's profits are commonly distributed among the partners in proportion to each partner's capital investment. Many quantities we encounter in economics and finance are ratios in disguise. Late in the chapter, we will discuss two examples—currency exchange rates and index numbers.

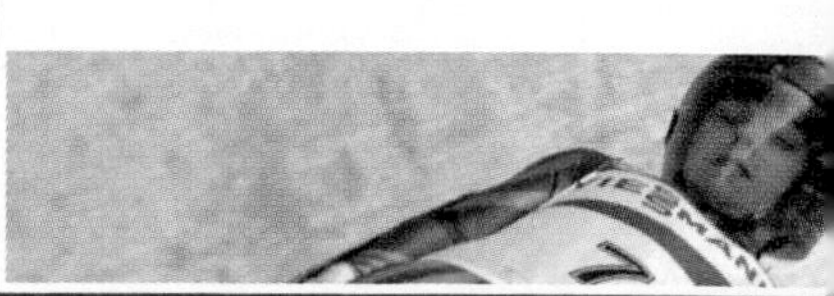

3.1 Ratios

A **ratio** is a comparison, by division, of two or more quantities. Suppose that a store sells \$2000 worth of Product X and \$1500 worth of Product Y in a particular month. The ratio of the sales of Product X to the sales of Product Y may be expressed in any of the following ways:

- Using a colon, as in "2000 : 1500" which is read "2000 to 1500."
- As a common fraction, $\frac{2000}{1500}$.
- As the decimal equivalent of the common fraction, $1.3\overline{3}$.
- As the percent equivalent of the common fraction, $133\frac{1}{3}\%$.

In the first two forms, the components of the ratio separated by division are called the **terms**. Each of the terms[1] in a ratio may be multiplied or divided by the same number to give an **equivalent ratio**. For example, both terms in the ratio 2000 : 1500 may be divided by 100 to give the equivalent ratio 20 : 15 or $\frac{20}{15}$.

Ratios may have as many terms as there are quantities being compared. If, in our example, the store sold \$2500 worth of Product Z in the same month, the ratio of the sales of Products X, Y, and Z is 2000 : 1500 : 2500.

Reducing a Ratio to Its Lowest Terms It is customary to express a ratio in its **lowest terms**, that is, as the equivalent ratio having the smallest integers possible for its terms. The relative size of the terms is then more apparent. Three cases require somewhat different procedures to reduce a ratio to its lowest terms.

1. If all terms in the given ratio are integers, divide every term by the common factors of all terms. For example, the terms in 2000 : 1500 : 2500 have 100 and 5 as common factors. After dividing by 100 and 5 (or by their product, 500), the ratio becomes 4 : 3 : 5.
2. If one or more terms are decimal numbers, shift the decimal point in every term to the right by the same number of positions until all of the terms are integers. Then reduce the ratio to its lowest terms as in the previous case.
3. If one or more terms contain a fraction, the terms should first be cleared of the fractions. Start by multiplying every term in the ratio by the denominator of one of the fractions. Repeat this process using the denominator of any fraction that remains. When the ratio contains only integers, reduce the ratio to its lowest terms as in the first case.

Example 3.1B includes an illustration of each case.

[1] It is unfortunate that the word *term* has two quite different uses in basic algebra. In Chapter 2, *term* referred to a component of an algebraic expression separated from other components by addition or subtraction signs. In this chapter, *term* refers to a component of a ratio set apart by division. The meaning of *term* must be inferred from the context in which it is used.

Example 3.1A Expressing a Ratio in Equivalent Forms

a. A hospital ward has 10 nurses caring for 60 patients. The ratio of nurses to patients can be expressed as:

$10 : 60$	Using the colon notation
$1 : 6$	Using the colon notation with the lowest terms
$\frac{1}{6}$	As a common fraction
$0.1\overline{6}$	As a decimal equivalent
$16.\overline{6}\%$	As a percent equivalent

b. A survey of cars in a parking lot indicated that two fifths of the cars were North American brands and one third were Japanese brands. The ratio of North American to Japanese cars was:

$\frac{2}{5} : \frac{1}{3}$	Ratio with given terms in the colon notation
$6 : 5$	As an equivalent ratio obtained by multiplying both terms by 5 and by 3 to clear the terms of fractions
$\frac{6}{5}$	As a common fraction
1.2	As a decimal equivalent
120%	As a percent equivalent

c. The costs of manufacturing an item are \$150 for materials and \$225 for labour. The ratio of labour to materials costs is:

$225 : 150$	Ratio with the given terms in the colon notation
$9 : 6$	Equivalent ratio (each term divided by 25)
$3 : 2$	Equivalent ratio with lowest terms (after division by 3)

d. A municipal development bylaw requires that a shopping centre provide four parking spots for each 100 m^2 of developed retail area. The ratio of parking spots to retail area is:

$4 : 100$	Ratio with the given terms in the colon notation
$1 : 25$	Equivalent ratio with lowest terms (after division by 4)

Even though the two values in a ratio can have differing units (parking spaces and square metres in this case), the units are often omitted when they are generally known from the context. In this case, one parking space is required for each 25 m^2 of retail area.

Example 3.1B Reducing a Ratio to Its Lowest Terms

Reduce the following ratios to their lowest terms.

a. $105 : 63 : 84$ **b.** $1.2 : 1.68 : 0.72$ **c.** $\frac{3}{8} : \frac{5}{6} : \frac{1}{3}$

Solution

a. $105 : 63 : 84$

$= 35 : 21 : 28$	Each term divided by 3
$= 5 : 3 : 4$	Each term divided by 7

b. $1.2 : 1.68 : 0.72$

$= 120 : 168 : 72$	Decimal point moved two positions to the right
$= 30 : 42 : 18$	Each term divided by 4
$= 5 : 7 : 3$	Each term divided by 6

c. $\frac{3}{8} : \frac{5}{6} : \frac{1}{3}$

$= \frac{9}{8} : \frac{5}{2} : 1$	Each term multiplied by 3
$= \frac{9}{4} : 5 : 2$	Each term multiplied by 2
$= 9 : 20 : 8$	Each term multiplied by 4

Converting a Ratio to an Equivalent Ratio Whose Smallest Term Is 1 The ratio 179 : 97 : 29 is already in its lowest terms but still contains rather large integers. In this situation, many people prefer to express the ratio as the equivalent ratio whose *smallest* term has the value 1. If we divide all terms by the smallest term, we obtain

$$\frac{179}{29} : \frac{97}{29} : \frac{29}{29} \quad \text{or} \quad 6.17 : 3.34 : 1$$

where the terms have been rounded to three figures. The relative size of the terms is more apparent in 6.17 : 3.34 : 1 than in 179 : 97 : 29.

Example 3.1C *Determining an Equivalent Ratio Having 1 as the Smallest Term*

Convert each of the following ratios to an equivalent ratio having 1 as the smallest term. Round the terms to three figures.

a. $117 : 79 : 167$ **b.** $1.05 : 8.1 : 2.2$ **c.** $\frac{18}{19} : 1\frac{13}{14}$

Solution

a. $117 : 79 : 167$

$= \frac{117}{79} : \frac{79}{79} : \frac{167}{79}$	Divide each term by the smallest term, 79.
$= 1.48 : 1 : 2.11$	

b. $1.05 : 8.1 : 2.2$

$= \frac{1.05}{1.05} : \frac{8.1}{1.05} : \frac{2.2}{1.05}$	Divide each term by the smallest term, 1.05.
$= 1 : 7.71 : 2.10$	

c. $\frac{18}{19} : 1\frac{13}{14}$

$= 0.947 : 1.929$	Convert the fractions to decimal equivalents.
$= 1 : 2.04$	Divide by the smaller term, 0.947.

POINT OF INTEREST

Ratios That Affect Your Eligibility for a Mortgage Loan

Most of us go through a similar experience for the purchase of our first home. We save for a few years to accumulate enough money for the down payment. For the balance of the purchase price, we obtain a mortgage loan close to the maximum amount for which we qualify. We then struggle financially for a few years to make our early-career income cover the monthly mortgage payments and other expenses of a young family.

Mortgage lenders must determine whether a mortgage loan is adequately secured by the property, and whether the borrower has the financial capacity to make the mortgage payments. To do this, they calculate and set upper limits on three ratios:

1. *Loan-to-Value Ratio* $= \dfrac{\text{Principal amount of the loan}}{\text{Lending value of the property}} \times 100\% \leq 75\%$

   The 75% maximum for this ratio means the borrower's minimum down payment is 25% of the "lending value." (The lending value is the lesser of the purchase price and the market value as determined by a certified appraiser.)

2. *Gross Debt Service Ratio* (GDS ratio):

$$\text{GDS ratio} = \frac{\left(\begin{array}{c}\text{Total monthly payments for}\\ \text{mortgage, property taxes, and heat}\end{array}\right)}{\text{Gross monthly income}} \times 100\% \leq 32\%$$

   The upper limit on this ratio means that the major costs of home ownership should not require more than 32% of the borrower's gross income.

3. *Total Debt Service Ratio* (TDS ratio):

$$\text{TDS ratio} = \frac{\left(\begin{array}{c}\text{Total monthly payments for mortgage,}\\ \text{property taxes, heat, and other debt}\end{array}\right)}{\text{Gross monthly income}} \times 100\% \leq 40\%$$

   The upper limit on this ratio means that payments related to home ownership *and all other debt* should not require more than 40% of the borrower's gross income.

The upper limits set for the GDS and TDS ratios differ slightly from one lender to another.

Questions

1. Marge and Homer Sampson have saved $50,000 toward the purchase of their first home. Allowing $5000 for legal and moving expenses, they

CAUGHT IN THE WEB

The Canadian Imperial Bank of Commerce has a calculator (Calculate What You Can Afford) on its Web site that allows you to enter data relevant to the three key ratios defined in the accompanying Point of Interest. Instead of entering the monthly mortgage payment, you enter the interest rate you will pay on a mortgage loan and the number of years over which the loan will be repaid. The calculator then determines the maximum price you can pay for a home and still satisfy CIBC's upper limits on the three ratios.

Go to the Web site at www.cibc.com/secure/mort_calc_home_own.html and enter the requested information.

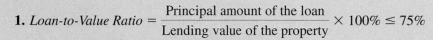

have \$45,000 available for a down payment. What is the maximum purchase price they can consider?

2. After thorough investigation, the Sampsons made a \$150,000 offer on a townhouse subject to arranging financing. They next met with their banker. If the Sampsons make a \$45,000 down payment, the monthly payment on a \$105,000 mortgage loan will be \$723. The banker gathered data for calculating the GDS and TDS ratios. Annual property taxes will be \$1800. Annual heating costs will be about \$1200. The Sampsons make monthly payments of \$400 on a car loan (\$7000 balance). Their gross monthly income is \$3300. Calculate the GDS and TDS ratios.
3. Note that the Sampsons meet the GDS requirement but exceed the TDS limit (40%). The item causing the problem is the \$400 per month car payment. Suppose the Sampsons use \$7000 of their savings to pay off the car loan. They will still have enough to make the minimum down payment ($0.25 \times \$150{,}000 = \$37{,}500$) but will have to increase the mortgage loan by \$7000 to \$112,000. The monthly mortgage payment will increase proportionately to \$771 per month. Re-calculate the GDS and TDS ratios. Do the Sampsons satisfy all three ratios by taking the second approach?

Exercise 3.1

Answers to the odd-numbered problems are at the end of the book.

Express each of the following ratios in its lowest terms.

1. $12 : 64$

2. $56 : 21$

3. $45 : 15 : 30$

4. $26 : 130 : 65$

5. $0.08 : 0.12$

6. $2.5 : 3.5 : 3$

7. $0.84 : 1.4 : 1.96$

8. $11.7 : 7.8 : 3.9$

9. $0.24 : 0.39 : 0.15$

10. $0.091 : 0.021 : 0.042$

11. $\frac{1}{8} : \frac{3}{4}$

12. $\frac{4}{3} : \frac{3}{2}$

13. $\frac{3}{5} : \frac{6}{7}$

14. $\frac{11}{3} : \frac{11}{7}$

15. $1\frac{1}{4} : 1\frac{2}{3}$

16. $2\frac{1}{2} : \frac{5}{8}$

17. $4\frac{1}{8} : 2\frac{1}{5}$

18. $\frac{2}{3} : \frac{3}{4} : \frac{5}{6}$

19. $\frac{1}{15} : \frac{1}{5} : \frac{1}{10}$

20. $10\frac{1}{2} : 7 : 4\frac{1}{5}$

Express each of the following ratios as an equivalent ratio whose smallest term is 1.

21. $7.6 : 3$

22. $1.41 : 8.22$

23. $0.177 : 0.81$

24. $0.0131 : 0.0086$

25. $\frac{3}{7} : \frac{19}{17}$

26. $4\frac{3}{13} : \frac{27}{17}$

27. 77 : 23 : 41

28. 11 : 38 : 27

29. 3.5 : 5.4 : 8

30. 0.47 : 0.15 : 0.26

31. $\frac{5}{8} : \frac{17}{11} : \frac{6}{7}$

32. $5\frac{1}{2} : 3\frac{3}{4} : 8\frac{1}{3}$

Set up a ratio for each of the following problems. If the ratio cannot be reduced to an equivalent ratio in terms of small integers, then express it as a ratio of decimal equivalents with the smallest term set at 1. Maintain three-figure accuracy.

33. During the last three months, Mako Distributing made 25% of its sales in Region A, 35% in Region B, and 40% in Region C. What is the ratio of the sales in Region A to the sales in Region B to the sales in Region C?

34. Don, Bob, and Ron Maloney's partnership interests in Maloney Bros. Contracting are in the ratio of their capital contributions of \$78,000, \$52,000, and \$65,000, respectively. What is the ratio of Bob's to Ron's to Don's partnership interest?

35. Victoria Developments has obtained \$3.6 million of total capital from three sources. Preferred shareholders contributed \$550,000 (preferred equity), common shareholders contributed \$1.2 million (common equity), and the remainder was borrowed (debt). What is the firm's ratio of debt to preferred equity to common equity?

36. The cost to manufacture a fibreglass boat consists of \$2240 for materials, \$3165 for direct labour, and \$1325 for overhead. Express the three cost components as a ratio.

37. A provincial government budget forecasts expenditures of \$1.04 billion on education, \$910 million on health services, and \$650 million on social services. Express the three budget items as a ratio.

3.2 Proportions

In Section 3.1 we introduced ratios using an example in which sales of Products X, Y, and Z in a month were \$2000, \$1500, and \$2500, respectively. We will extend the same example to illustrate proportions. Mathematics has a special notation for a compact version of the statement "the ratio of the sales of X to the sales of Y is 4 : 3." This notation is

$$\text{Sales of X} : \text{Sales of Y} = 4 : 3$$

If we let x represent "sales of Product X" and y represent "sales of Product Y," a still more compact statement is

$$x : y = 4 : 3$$

This equation is an example of a proportion. In general, a **proportion** is a statement of the equality of two ratios. The language we use to express this proportion is

"x is to y as 4 is to 3"

To carry out mathematical operations on a proportion, first convert each ratio to its equivalent fraction. In the current example, we can rewrite the proportion as the equation

$$\frac{x}{y} = \frac{4}{3}$$

The two ratios in this proportion contain a total of four terms. If three terms are known, you can calculate the fourth term. As an example, suppose that the sales of Product X in the next month are forecast to be \$1800. What will be the sales of Product Y if the sales of the two products maintain the same ratio? You can answer this question by substituting $x = \$1800$ and solving for y:

$$\frac{\$1800}{y} = \frac{4}{3}$$

We can clear the equation of fractions by multiplying both sides by $3y$. This gives

$$\frac{\$1800}{y} \times 3y = \frac{4}{3} \times 3y$$

After simplifying each side, we obtain

$$\$1800 \times 3 = 4y$$

TIP *Cross-Multiplication Short Cut*

We can obtain

$$\$1800 \times 3 = 4y \qquad \text{directly from} \qquad \frac{\$1800}{y} = \frac{4}{3}$$

using *cross-multiplication.* Simply multiply each numerator by the denominator from the other side, as indicated below.

$$\frac{\$1800}{y} \qquad \frac{4}{3}$$

It is legal to perform just one of the two cross-multiplications. For example, to solve for w in

$$\frac{w}{\$1400} = \frac{7}{5}$$

just cross-multiply \$1400 by 7 giving

$$w = \frac{7 \times \$1400}{5} = \$1960$$

Returning to the calculation of y,

$$y = \frac{\$1800 \times 3}{4} = \$1350$$

The projected sales of Product Y in the next month are \$1350.

Example 3.2A *Solving a Proportion*

Solve the proportions:

a. $3 : 5 = 9 : x$ **b.** $2.5 : y = 4 : 7$

Solution

a. $\frac{3}{5} = \frac{9}{x}$ Express each ratio as a fraction.

$3x = 45$ Cross-multiply.

$x = \frac{45}{3} = 15$ Divide both sides by the coefficient of x.

b. $\frac{2.5}{y} = \frac{4}{7}$ Express each ratio as a fraction.

$7(2.5) = 4y$ Cross-multiply.

$y = \frac{7(2.5)}{4} = 4.375$ Divide both sides by the coefficient of y.

Proportions With Three Variables From Section 3.1, the value of the ratio

Sales of X : Sales of Y : Sales of Z

was 4 : 3 : 5 in the base month. That is,

$$x : y : z = 4 : 3 : 5$$

where x, y, and z represent the monthly sales of products X, Y, and Z, respectively. Read the proportion as follows:

"x is to y is to z, as 4 is to 3 is to 5"

This proportion implies a separate proportion for each pair of terms. That is,

$$x : y = 4 : 3 \quad \text{and} \quad y : z = 3 : 5 \quad \text{and} \quad x : z = 4 : 5$$

We can construct the following three equations from them.

$$\frac{x}{y} = \frac{4}{3} \quad \text{and} \quad \frac{y}{z} = \frac{3}{5} \quad \text{and} \quad \frac{x}{z} = \frac{4}{5}$$

If we know just one of the three variables x, y, and z, these equations allow us to solve for the other two. Example 3.2B provides an illustration.

Example 3.2B *Solving a Proportion Having Two Unknowns*

Solving the following proportion for x and y.

$$2 : 5 : 3 = 7 : x : y$$

Solution

Based on the given proportion, we can write the following two equations.

$$\frac{2}{5} = \frac{7}{x} \quad \text{and} \quad \frac{5}{3} = \frac{x}{y}$$

After cross-multiplication, these equations become

$$2x = 35 \qquad \text{and} \qquad 5y = 3x$$

The first equation can immediately be solved for x:

$$x = \frac{35}{2} = 17.5$$

Then y may be obtained from the second equation after substituting $x = 17.5$:

$$5y = 3(17.5) = 52.5$$

$$y = \frac{52.5}{5} = 10.5$$

Example 3.2C Solving a Word Problem Using a Proportion

Betty and Lois have already invested \$8960 and \$6880, respectively, in their partnership. If Betty invests another \$5000, what amount should Lois contribute to maintain their investments in the original ratio?

Solution

Let Lois's additional investment be represented by x. In the colon notation, the proportion may be written

$$x : \$5000 = \$6880 : \$8960$$

Writing the ratios as fractions,

$$\frac{x}{\$5000} = \frac{\$6880}{\$8960}$$

Therefore,

$$x = \frac{\$6880 \times \$5000}{\$8960} = \$3839.29$$

Lois should contribute \$3839.29 to maintain the same ratio of investment in the partnership.

Example 3.2D Solving a Problem Using a Proportion

A 560-bed hospital operates with 232 registered nurses and 185 other support staff. The hospital is about to open a new 86-bed wing. Assuming the same proportionate staffing levels, how many more nurses and support staff will need to be hired?

Solution

Let n represent the number of additional nurses and s the number of additional staff. n and s must satisfy the proportion

$$560 : 232 : 185 = 86 : n : s$$

Therefore,

$$\frac{560}{86} = \frac{232}{n} \qquad \text{and} \qquad \frac{560}{86} = \frac{185}{s}$$

$$560n = 86 \times 232 \qquad 560s = 86 \times 185$$

$$n = \frac{86 \times 232}{560} \qquad s = \frac{86 \times 185}{560}$$

$$= 35.6 \qquad = 28.4$$

Rounding the calculated values to the nearest integer, the hospital should hire 36 nurses and 28 support staff for the new wing.

Example 3.2E *Solving a Proportion Where the Terms Are Fractions*

The profit of the BGK partnership is to be divided among Barry, Guiseppe, and Karla in the ratio $\frac{1}{2} : \frac{1}{4} : \frac{1}{3}$, respectively. How much should each partner receive from a profit of \$14,560 in the most recent quarter?

Solution

TRAP *INTERPRETING TERMS WHICH ARE FRACTIONS*

Do not interpret the given ratio to mean that Barry is to receive one half of the profit, Guiseppe one quarter, and Karla one third. Simply view the fractional terms as you would the terms in a ratio such as 5 : 7: 4—three numbers that establish the relative sizes of the three partners' shares of the profit.

Let the partners' initials represent their respective shares of the profit. Then

$$B : G : K = \frac{1}{2} : \frac{1}{4} : \frac{1}{3} = 6 : 3 : 4$$

where the ratio has been converted to its lowest terms by multiplying every term by 12. Now we can take the approach of breaking the profit into 13 parts (the sum of the terms). Barry should receive 6 of the 13 parts, Guiseppe should receive 3, and Karla should receive 4. That is,

$$\text{Barry should receive } \frac{6}{13} \times \$14{,}560 = \$6720$$

$$\text{Guiseppe should receive } \frac{3}{13} \times \$14{,}560 = \$3360$$

$$\text{Karla should receive } \frac{4}{13} = \$14{,}560 = \$4480$$

Example 3.2F Solving a Problem Involving Successive Partitioning of a Whole

Getty Oil and Gas has a 47% interest in an oil well. Paliser Energy owns a 29% interest in the same well. If Getty sells five eighths of its interest for \$470,000, what value does the transaction imply for Paliser's interest?

Solution

The following diagram helps to organize the data and show the composition of the ownership.

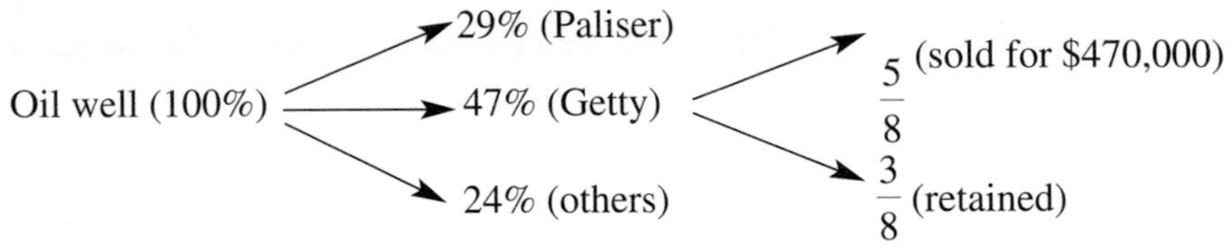

Let G represent the value of Getty's interest before the sale. Hence,

$$\frac{5}{8}G = \$470{,}000$$

and

$$G = \frac{8}{5} \times \$470{,}000 = \$752{,}000$$

If P represents the value of Paliser's interest, then

$$P : G = 29 : 47$$

and

$$\frac{P}{G} = \frac{29}{47}$$

Therefore,

$$P = \frac{29}{47} \times G = \frac{29}{47} \times \$752{,}000 = \$464{,}000$$

Assuming that each ownership interest has a market value proportional to the size of the interest, the transaction implies a value of \$464,000 for Paliser's interest.

Exercise 3.2

Answers to the odd-numbered problems are at the end of the book.

Solve the following proportions for the unknown quantities.

1. $9 : 7 = 54 : b$

2. $17 : q = 119 : 91$

3. $88 : 17 = a : 45$

4. $d : 13.2 = 16 : 31$

5. $1.89 : 0.31 = 175 : k$

6. $1.56 : h = 56.2 : 31.7$

7. $0.043 : y = 550 : 198$

8. $0.057 : 0.149 = z : 0.05$

9. $m : \frac{3}{4} = \frac{1}{2} : \frac{9}{8}$

10. $\frac{10}{3} : \frac{12}{7} = \frac{5}{18} : r$

•**11.** $6 : 7 : 5 = n : 105 : m$

•**12.** $3 : 4 : 13 = x : y : 6.5$

•**13.** $625 : f : 500 = g : 3 : 4$

•**14.** $a : 58 : 132 = 38 : 27 : b$

•**15.** $0.69 : 1.17 : 0.4 = r : s : 6.5$

•**16.** $8500 : x : y = \frac{1}{3} : \frac{1}{4} : \frac{5}{12}$

Solve the following problems using proportions.

17. Mr. Borelli has just received notice that the current year's property tax on his home, which has an assessed value of $210,000, is $2376. What will be the property taxes on his neighbour's house, assessed at $235,000, if the taxes are in the same ratio as the assessed values?

18. The West Essex School Board employs 348 teachers for the 7412 students registered in the district's schools in the current year. The enrollment forecast for next year is 7780 students. Assuming the same student–teacher ratio for the next year, how many additional teaching positions must the board fill?

19. An electrical generator will run for 1 hour and 30 minutes on 4 L of gasoline. For how many hours was the generator operated since it was last refueled, if 29.5 L are required to fill the fuel tank today?

20. Connie's neighbour sold 14.5 hectares of raw land for $128,000. If Connie were to sell her 23.25-hectare parcel at a proportionate price, what amount would she receive?

21. Based on past experience, a manufacturing process requires 2.3 hours of direct labour for each $87 worth of raw materials processed. If the company is planning to consume $39,150 worth of raw materials, what total amount should it budget for labour at $18.25 per hour?

22. Mr. Bartlett's will specified that, upon liquidation of any asset, the proceeds be divided among his wife, his son, and his sister in the ratio of $7 : 5 : 3$.

a. If the son received $9500 from the sale of securities, what amounts did Bartlett's wife and sister receive?

b. What amount would the sister receive from the sale of the deceased's boat for $27,000?

23. An international equity mutual fund includes American stocks, Japanese stocks, German stocks, and British stocks in the ratio $27 : 19 : 14 : 11$, respectively. If its current holdings of German stocks are valued at US$238 million, what are the values of its holdings in the securities of the other three countries?

24. Last year, the U.S. sales of Ford, General Motors, and Chrysler, respectively, were in the ratio $92 : 121 : 35$. GM has just announced sales of $10.8 billion for the first half of the current fiscal year. If the three companies have maintained the same market share as they had last year, what were the first-half sales of Ford and Chrysler?

•**25.** A punch recipe calls for fruit juice, ginger ale, and vodka to be mixed in the ratio $\frac{3}{2} : \frac{3}{5} : \frac{1}{4}$. How much fruit juice and ginger ale should be mixed with a 0.75-litre bottle of vodka?

26. Larry, Curley, and Moe formed a partnership. The partnership agreement requires them to provide capital when and as required by the partnership in the ratio of 1 : 1.35 : 0.85.

a. If the total required initial investment was $102,400, how much did each contribute?

b. One year later, Moe's share of another injection of capital was $6528. What was Curley's share?

27. A business consultant is analyzing the cost structure of two firms in the same retail business. On sales of $3.66 million, Thriftys had wholesale costs of $2.15 million and overhead expenses of $1.13 million. If Economart had the same proportionate costs on its sales of $5.03 million, what would its wholesale costs and overhead expenses have been?

28. A province's Ministry of Social Services has found that the number of people receiving social assistance and the province's expenditures on social assistance tend to be proportional to the rate of unemployment. Last August when the provincial unemployment rate was 11.6%, the province provided benefits to 89,300 individuals at a cost of $53.7 million. What are the expected number of claimants and the total cost next August if the forecast unemployment rate is 10.3%?

•29. The Ministry of Education reported that the average school district in the province has 13,450 students in "K to 12" programs, an annual budget of $66.3 million, and 635 full-time-equivalent teachers. The Middleton School District (MSD), with an annual budget of $52.1 million and 498 teachers, serves 10,320 students. What adjustments would have to be made to MSD's budget and staffing to have them in the same proportion to enrollment as the provincial average?

•30. Shirley had a three-sevenths interest in a partnership. She sold three-fifths of her interest for $27,000.

a. What is the implied value of Shirley's remaining partnership interest?

b. What is the implied value of the entire partnership?

•31. Regal Resources owns a 58% interest in a mineral claim. Yukon Explorations owns the remainder. If Regal sells one fifth of its interest for $1.2 million, what is the implied value of Yukon's interest?

•32. The statistics for a professional accounting program indicate that five sevenths of those who enter the program complete Level 1. Two ninths of Level-1 completers do not finish Level 2. If 587 students completed Level 2 last year, how many (including this group of 587) began Level 1?

•33. Executive Fashions sold four sevenths of its inventory at cost in a bankruptcy sale. The remainder was sold to liquidators for $6700, representing 45% of the cost of the goods.

a. What was the original cost of the inventory that was sold to the liquidators?

b. What were the proceeds from the bankruptcy sale?

*3.3 Application: Percent Change

We solved problems on percent change in Section 2.5 using an algebraic method. Such problems may also be solved by setting up a proportion—the choice is a matter of preference. A simple table helps organize the data and identify the appropriate proportion. In the accompanying table, an initial value of \$400 plus a change of \$100 gives a final value of \$500. In terms of percentages, the initial value (100%) undergoes a 25% increase, giving a final value of 125%. Note that any two numbers in the "\$" column have the same ratio as the corresponding numbers in the "%" column. For example,

	\$	%
Initial value	400	100
+ Change	+100	+25
= Final value	500	125

$$\frac{\text{Initial value (\$)}}{\text{Final value (\$)}} = \frac{\text{Initial value (\%)}}{\text{Final value (\%)}}$$

If two quantities in a column are unknown (and the other four are known), you can calculate either unknown by setting up and solving a proportion. (Initial value = 100% is always known.) Then the remaining unknown is simply the "plug" needed to complete the addition. To illustrate this approach, Examples 2.5C, 2.5D, and 2.5E will now be repeated as Examples 3.3A, 3.3B, and 3.3C.

Example 3.3A *Calculating Initial Value Given Final Value and Percent Change*

What amount when increased by 230% equals \$495?

Solution

Construct a table as described in the preceding exposition. We are given the final value in dollars (\$495) and the change in percent (230%). The initial value is always 100%. The "plug" in the % column is 330%. This leaves us with two unknowns (denoted by ? symbols in the table). Next, set up a proportion having the desired unknown (initial value) as the only unknown. That is,

	\$	%
Initial value	?	100
+ Change	+ ?	+230
= Final value	495	330

$$\frac{\text{Initial value (\$)}}{\$495} = \frac{100\%}{330\%}$$

Hence,

$$\text{Initial value} = \frac{110\%}{330\%} \times \$495 = \$150$$

\$150 is the amount which, when increased by 230%, equals \$495.

Example 3.3B *Calculating Final Value Given Initial Value and Percent Change*

How much is \$9550 after a decrease of 0.75%?

Solution

Again, construct a table as shown below. The proportion for calculating the final value is

$$\frac{\$9550}{\text{Final value}} = \frac{100\%}{99.25\%}$$

	\$	%
Initial value	9550	100.00
+ Change	+ ?	− 0.75
= Final value	?	99.25

Therefore,

$$99.25\% \times \$9550 = 100\% \times \text{Final value}$$

$$\text{Final value} = \frac{99.25\% \times \$9550}{100\%} = \$9478.38$$

In summary, \$9550 decreased by 0.75% is \$9478.38.

Example 3.3C *Calculating Initial Value Given Final Value and Percent Change*

For the fiscal year just completed, a company had sales of \$157,500. This represents a 5% increase over the prior year. What were the sales in the prior year?

Solution

Enter the known values in the customary table. Then,

$$\frac{\text{Initial value}}{\$157{,}500} = \frac{100\%}{105\%}$$

	\$	%
Initial value	?	100
+ Change	+ ?	+ 5
= Final value	157,500	105

$$\text{Initial value} = \frac{100}{105} \times \$157{,}500 = \$150{,}000$$

The sales in the prior year were \$150,000.

Exercise 3.3 *Use problems in Exercise 2.5 to practise the method presented in this section.*

3.4 Application: Proration

There are many instances in business where an amount of money must be allocated among people, departments, cost centres, etc. In a procedure called **proration**, the allocation is on a proportionate basis. Some examples are:

- When a partnership's profit is distributed among the partners, the most common arrangement is to prorate the profit based on each partner's investment.
- Lease agreements for retail space in malls and shopping centres usually require that tenants pay common-area costs such as property taxes, janitorial services, landscape maintenance, and snow removal. Typically, these common-area costs are prorated on the basis of the floor area leased by each tenant.

- When insurance coverage is cancelled, the premium is partially refunded. The refund is usually a prorated amount based on the unexpired portion of the period of coverage.
- For accounting purposes, general administration and overhead expenses of a business are often prorated among departmental or divisional cost centres. The basis chosen for the pro rata allocation usually reflects the relative benefit each cost centre derives from these expenses. For example, the proration might be based on sales volume, number of employees, or floor area.

TIP *AN IMPLIED TERM IN PRORATION PROBLEMS*

Students sometimes overlook a term when writing a proportion for a proration problem. We will use an example to illustrate. Suppose \$700 is to be divided between Kristen and Connor in the ratio of 4 : 7. Let K = Kristen's share and C = Connor's share. Then

$$K : C = 4 : 7$$

This proportion by itself does not allow us to solve for K or C. We must somehow use the additional information that the total amount to be allocated is \$700. If we make \$700 a third term in the ratio for the dollar amounts on the left side, what should be the corresponding third term on the right side? That is, what number should be at "?" in

$$K : C : \$700 = 4 : 7 : ?$$

Since \$700 is the sum of K and C, then "?" should be the sum of 4 and 7. Hence,

$$K : C : \$700 = 4 : 7 : 11$$

Now we construct equations to solve for K and C. That is,

$$\frac{K}{\$700} = \frac{4}{11} \quad \text{and} \quad \frac{C}{\$700} = \frac{7}{11}$$

Example 3.4A *Prorating a Refund Based on the Unused Time Period*

Franco paid \$1058 for his automobile insurance coverage for the period July 1 to June 30. He sold his car and cancelled the insurance on March 8. The insurer's procedure is to calculate a refund prorated to the exact number of days remaining in the period of coverage. (March 8 is not included in the refundable days.) A \$20 service charge is then deducted. What refund will Franco receive?

Solution

The basis for calculating the refund (before the service charge) is:

$$\frac{\text{Refund}}{\text{Annual premium}} = \frac{\text{Number of remaining days of coverage}}{365 \text{ days}}$$

The "unused" days in the July 1 to June 30 period are the 23 days remaining in March plus all of April, May, and June. (See the appendix to Chapter 6 for a method of determining the number of days in each month.) Hence,

$$\frac{\text{Refund}}{\$1058} = \frac{23 + 30 + 31 + 30}{365}$$

$$\text{Refund} = \frac{114 \times \$1058}{365}$$

$$= \$330.44$$

After deduction of the service charge, the net refund will be $310.44.

Example 3.4B Allocating Profits Based on the Amount Invested by Each Owner

The partnership of Mr. X, Mr. Y, and Ms. Z has agreed to distribute profits in the same proportion as their respective capital investments in the partnership. How will the recent period's profit of $28,780 be allocated if Mr. X's capital account shows a balance of $34,000, Mr. Y's shows $49,000, and Ms. Z's shows $54,500?

Solution

The ratio of a partner's share of the profit to the total profit will equal the ratio of that partner's capital investment to the total investment.

$$\text{Total investment} = \$34{,}000 + \$49{,}000 + \$54{,}500 = \$137{,}500$$

$$\frac{\text{Mr. X's share}}{\text{Total profit}} = \frac{\text{Mr. X's investment}}{\text{Total investment}}$$

$$\frac{\text{Mr. X's share}}{\$28{,}780} = \frac{\$34{,}000}{\$137{,}500}$$

$$\text{Mr. X's share} = \frac{\$34{,}000}{\$137{,}500} \times \$28{,}780 = \$7116.51$$

Similarly,

$$\text{Mr. Y's share} = \frac{\$49{,}000}{\$137{,}500} \times \$28{,}780 = \$10{,}256.15$$

Either of two approaches may now be employed to calculate Ms. Z's share. The longer approach has the advantage of providing a means of checking the answers. In it we calculate Ms. Z's share in the same manner as the other two shares:

$$\text{Ms. Z's share} = \frac{\$54{,}500}{\$137{,}500} \times \$28{,}780 = \$11{,}407.35$$

The allocations can be checked by verifying that their total is $28,780:

$$\$7116.51 + \$10{,}256.15 + \$11{,}407.35 = \$28{,}780.01$$

The shorter method for calculating Ms. Z's share is to calculate the balance left from the $28,780 after Mr. X's and Mr. Y's shares have been paid out:

$$\begin{aligned}\text{Ms. Z's share} &= \$28{,}780.00 - \$7116.51 - \$10{,}256.15\\ &= \$11{,}407.34\end{aligned}$$

However, we do not have a means of checking the calculations since, in effect, we have forced Ms. Z's share to be the balance of the $28,780 (whether Mr. X's and Mr. Y's shares were correctly calculated or not).

Example 3.4C *Allocating a Firm's Overhead Costs*

The Quebec plant of a manufacturing company produced 10,000 units of a product during the last fiscal quarter using 5000 hours of direct labour. In the same period, the Ontario plant produced 20,000 units using 9000 hours of direct labour. How will overhead costs of $49,000 for the period be allocated between the two plants if the allocation is based on:

a. Direct labour hours?

b. Units of output?

Solution

a.

$$\frac{\text{Quebec's share}}{\text{Total overhead}} = \frac{\text{Quebec's labour hours}}{\text{Total labour hours}}$$

$$\text{Quebec's share} = \frac{5000}{14{,}000} \times \$49{,}000 = \$17{,}500$$

Similarly,

$$\text{Ontario's share} = \frac{9000}{14{,}000} \times \$49{,}000 = \$31{,}500$$

b.

$$\frac{\text{Quebec's share}}{\text{Total overhead}} = \frac{\text{Quebec's output}}{\text{Total output}}$$

$$\text{Quebec's share} = \frac{10{,}000}{30{,}000} \times \$49{,}000 = \$16{,}333$$

Similarly,

$$\text{Ontario's share} = \frac{20{,}000}{30{,}000} \times \$49{,}000 = \$32{,}667$$

Example 3.4D *Maintaining Proportionate Ownership in a Buyout*

The ownership interests of the four partners in a marina are 20% for Mr. P, 30% for Mr. Q, 15% for Mr. R, and 35% for Mr. S. The partners have agreed on an arrangement to buy out Mr. P for $100,000. Mr. Q, Mr. R, and Mr. S are to split the 20% interest and contribute to the $100,000 price in proportions that will leave them with the same relative ownership interests as they now possess.

a. What will their ownership interests be after the sale?

b. How much should each partner contribute toward the $100,000 purchase price?

Solution

a. Before the sale, the ownership ratio for the three continuing partners is

$$Q : R : S = \frac{30}{100} : \frac{15}{100} : \frac{35}{100} = 30 : 15 : 35$$

After the sale, 100% ownership is to be allocated to Mr. Q, Mr. R, and Mr. S in the ratio 30 : 15 : 35. Since

$$30 + 15 + 35 = 80$$

we can allocate the 100% ownership in the required ratio by assigning

$$\frac{30}{80} \times 100\% = 37.5\% \qquad \text{to Mr. Q}$$

$$\frac{15}{80} \times 100\% = 18.75\% \qquad \text{to Mr. R}$$

$$\frac{35}{80} \times 100\% = 43.75\% \qquad \text{to Mr. S}$$

After the sale of Mr. P's interest in the marina, Mr. Q, Mr. R, and Mr. S will own 37.5%, 18.75%, and 43.75%, respectively, of the partnership.

b. The partners' allocation of the $100,000 purchase price should be in the same ratio as their ownership interests. Therefore,

Mr. Q should contribute 0.375 × $100,000 = $37,500,
Mr. R should contribute 0.1875 × $100,000 = $18,750,
Mr. S should contribute 0.4375 × $100,000 = $43,750.

Exercise 3.4

Answers to the odd-numbered problems are at the end of the book.

1. A three-year magazine subscription costing $136 may be cancelled at any time, and a prorated refund will be made for the remaining weekly issues. If Juanita cancels her subscription after receiving 17 issues in the second year, what refund should she get? Assume there are exactly 52 weeks in a year.
2. When real estate is sold, the year's property taxes are allocated to the vendor and the purchaser in proportion to the number of days that each party owns the property during the year. If the purchaser took possession of a property effective August 8 (of a 365-day year), how will the year's property taxes of $2849 be allocated to the vendor and purchaser?
3. On May 3, Mary Ann bought a two-year membership in a fitness club for $495, on a special promotion. Cancellation is allowed at any time. A

prorated refund will be paid based upon the number of days remaining in the membership period. If she cancelled the membership on the following September 9, what refund should she receive? (Count both May 3 and September 9 as days used.)

4. In some instances Revenue Canada allows an individual to deduct from income a portion of the annual operating expenses for a personally owned automobile that is used to earn employment income. If an individual qualifies for the deduction, the deductible portion is based on the ratio of the distance travelled on business to the total distance travelled in the year.

Harold spent a total of $5674 during the last year on gas, oil, insurance, licence and registration fees, and repairs and maintenance for his automobile. From his travel log he has determined that 14,488 km were driven for business use and 8329 km were driven for personal use during the year. What automobile expense can he deduct from income?

5. An individual who operates a business primarily from his or her personal residence may deduct certain "office-in-home" expenses in the calculation of taxable income. The proportion of the annual costs of heat, insurance, electricity, property taxes, and mortgage interest that may be deducted must be determined on a basis that Revenue Canada finds "reasonable under the circumstances."

Rose uses two of the 11 rooms in her home for a real estate appraisal business that she operates with one assistant. The combined area of the two rooms is 360 square feet, and the remainder of the house has an area of 1470 square feet. The total of the eligible expenses for the taxation year is $8756. What amount will be deductible if the expenses are prorated based on:

a. The number of rooms used for the business?

b. The floor area devoted to business use?

6. The leases in multiple-unit commercial developments commonly permit the landlord to allocate to the tenants various common area and general costs such as property taxes, janitorial services, security services, and snow removal. These costs are usually prorated on the basis of the floor area leased to each tenant. Granny's Chicken, Toys 'n Novelties, and Pine Tree Pharmacy are the three tenants in Pine Tree Square. They lease 172 square metres, 136 square metres, and 420 square metres, respectively. How should common costs totaling $9872 for the past year be allocated?

7. Three insurance companies agree to jointly insure a cargo ship for $38.6 million. If insurers A, B, and C allocate premiums received and accept the risk in the ratio 3 : 8 : 5, respectively:

a. How will the annual premium of $900,000 be distributed?

b. What is the maximum claim exposure of each insurer?

•8. Kevin, Lyle, and Marnie operate Food Country as a partnership. Their agreement provides that half the profit in each calendar quarter be distributed in proportion to each partner's investment in the partnership, and that the other half be distributed in proportion to the total number of hours that each partner works in the business. How should the most recent quarter's profit of $56,230 be allocated if their respective investments are $65,000, $43,000, and $14,500, and their hours of work for the quarter were 210, 365, and 632, respectively?

•**9.** The following table shows National Paper Products' capital investment in each of its three divisions, and the most recent year's gross sales for each division. The operating costs of the head office for the year were $839,000. These costs are allocated to the divisions before each division's profit is determined. How much should be allocated to each division if the costs are prorated on the basis of:

a. The capital investment in each division?

b. The sales of each division?

Division	Investment	Gross sales
Industrial products	$25,300,000	$21,200,000
Fine paper	17,250,000	8,350,000
Containers and packaging	11,900,000	7,450,000

•**10.** Last year, Reliable Securities established a sales achievement bonus fund of $10,000 to be distributed at the year's end among its four-person mutual fund sales force. The distribution is to be made in the same proportion as the amounts by which each person's sales exceed the basic quota of $500,000. How much will each salesperson receive from the fund if the sales figures for the year were $910,000 for Mr. A, $755,000 for Ms. B, $460,000 for Mr. C, and $615,000 for Ms. D?

•**11.** Geological Consultants Ltd. is a private company with four shareholders—W, X, Y, and Z—owning 300, 500, 350, and 400 shares, respectively. X is retiring and has come to an agreement with the other three shareholders to sell his shares for $175,000. The agreement calls for the 500 shares to be purchased and allocated to W, Y, and Z in the same ratio as their present shareholdings. The shares are indivisible, and consequently the share allocation must be rounded to integer values.

a. What implied value does the transaction place on the entire company?

b. How many shares will W, Y, and Z each own after the buyout?

c. What amount will each of the continuing shareholders contribute toward the $175,000 purchase price? Prorate the $175,000 on the basis of the allocation of the shares in part (b).

••**12.** Canadian Can Co. operates a profit-sharing plan wherein half the annual profits are distributed to employees. By agreement, the amounts received by *individual* executives, supervisors, and production workers are to be in the ratio of 10 : 7 : 5, respectively. During the last fiscal year, there were four executives, eight supervisors, and 45 production personnel. What profit-sharing amount will each executive, supervisor, and production worker receive if the year's profit was $265,000?

*3.5 Application: Exchange Rates and Currency Conversion

International trade and travel constitute an increasing component of commercial activity in Canada. Also, Canadians are increasingly investing in foreign securities. The vast majority of these transactions involve a conversion from Canadian dollars to a foreign currency, or vice versa. In this section, we will study the mathematics of currency conversion.

Suppose that

$$\$1.00 \text{ Canadian} = \$0.67 \text{ American}$$

In finance, this is usually written

$$\text{C\$1.00} = \text{US\$0.67}$$

To get the C$ equivalent of US$1.00, divide both sides of the equation by 0.67 giving

$$\text{C\$1.4925} = \text{US\$1.00}$$

The **exchange rate** between two currencies is defined as the amount of one currency required to purchase one unit of the other currency. Consequently, the exchange rate for a pair of currencies has two equivalent forms, depending on which currency is being purchased. For the C$ and US$, the exchange rate may be quoted as either

$$\frac{\text{US\$0.67}}{\text{C\$1.00}} \quad \text{or} \quad \frac{\text{C\$1.4925}}{\text{US\$1.00}}$$

You should employ a formal approach for currency conversion in order to handle cases where you do not have a feel for the relative values of two currencies. Using the preceding exchange rates, let us calculate the cost in C$ to purchase[2] US$600. It does not matter which version of the two exchange rates you pick. Suppose you choose $\frac{\text{US\$0.67}}{\text{C\$1.00}}$. Set up an equation stating that the ratio of the actual amounts of money in the exchange transaction equals the exchange rate. That is,

$$\frac{\text{US\$600}}{\text{C\$}x} = \frac{\text{US\$0.67}}{\text{C\$1.00}}$$

Note that the currencies must be in the *same order* in both ratios. Now solve for the unknown amount of money, C$*x*. In this case, cross-multiplication gives

$$\text{C\$1.00} \times \text{US\$600} = \text{US\$0.67} \times \text{C\$}x$$

Then

$$\text{C\$}x = \frac{\text{C\$1.00} \times \text{US\$600}}{\text{US\$0.67}} = \text{C\$895.52}$$

---

[2] Financial institutions usually charge for currency exchange services. They either charge a commission or they use a different exchange rate for buying a currency than for selling the same currency. In effect, they "mark up" the currency so that, like any retailer, they sell the product for more than they pay for it. *Unless otherwise stated,* we will simplify matters by assuming that a foreign currency may be bought or sold at the same exchange rate.

Example 3.5A *Currency Conversion Including a Commission*

After spending a week in France, you are travelling on to Portugal. Before departure from Marseilles Airport, you convert your remaining 287 French francs (Fr fr) to Portuguese escudos (Es) at the exchange rate Fr fr0.0328 per Es (that is, $\frac{\text{Fr fr0.0328}}{\text{Es1.00}}$). How many Escudos will you receive if the currency shop charges a 5% commission on transactions of this small size?

Solution

Before any commission, equivalent currency amounts have a ratio equal to the exchange rate. Let Esp represent the amount of Portuguese currency before deduction of commission. Then,

$$\frac{\text{Fr fr287}}{\text{Es}p} = \frac{\text{Fr fr0.0328}}{\text{Es1.00}}$$

Hence,

$$(\text{Es1.00}) \times (\text{Fr fr287}) = (\text{Fr fr0.0328}) \times (\text{Es}p)$$

$$\text{Es}p = \frac{(\text{Es1.00}) \times (\text{Fr fr287})}{\text{Fr fr0.0328}} = \text{Es8750}$$

The commission charge is

$$0.05 \times \text{Es8750} = \text{Es438}$$

The net amount of Portuguese currency is

$$\text{Es8750} - \text{Es438} = \text{Es8312}$$

Using Exchange Rate Tables Each day, the financial pages of major Canadian daily newspapers present tables of currency exchange rates. Since most exchange rates change from hour to hour in foreign exchange markets, a table of exchange rates usually specifies the time on the preceding day when the quotations were obtained.

Exchange rates are normally presented in two formats. The less commonly traded currencies are listed in a table similar to Table 3.1. Exchange rates are reported for over 40 currencies in terms of "C$ per unit of foreign currency" and "US$ per unit of foreign currency." A few of them are presented in Table 3.1.

The major currencies of international trade are usually presented in a Currency Cross Rate table such as Table 3.2. The figure in any cell of the table is the number of units of the currency in the *row* heading per unit of the currency in the *column* heading. For example, in the top row we see that it required C$1.5020 to purchase US$1.00, C$2.4136 to purchase £1.00, C$0.8282 to purchase DM1.00, and so on. These exchange rates expressed as ratios are

$$\frac{\text{C\$1.5020}}{\text{US\$1.00}}, \quad \frac{\text{C\$2.4136}}{\text{£1.00}}, \quad \text{and} \quad \frac{\text{C\$0.8282}}{\text{DM1.00}}$$

Along the diagonal of the table, the obvious value 1.00000 has been omitted to avoid needless clutter. Note that each exchange rate below the diagonal is the reciprocal of its counterpart above the diagonal. For example,

$$\text{US\$0.6658 per C\$} = \text{US\$}\frac{1}{1.5020} \text{ per C\$}$$

CAUGHT IN THE WEB

One-day-old currency exchange rates may be obtained through the comprehensive financial Web site www.canoe.ca. A table corresponding to Table 3.1 is at www.canoe.ca/MoneyRates/foreign.html. A table corresponding to Table 3.2 is at www.canoe.ca/MoneyRates/cross.html.

Table 3.1 *Foreign Exchange Rates (noon, Toronto, April 9, 1999)*

Country	Currency	C$ per unit	US$ per unit
Australia	Dollar	0.9470	0.6305
Brazil	Real	0.8809	0.5865
Hong Kong	Dollar	0.1939	0.1291
India	Rupee	0.03523	0.02346
Indonesia	Rupiah	0.000173	0.000115
Italy	Lira	0.000837	0.000557
Mexico	N Peso	0.1568	0.1044
Netherlands	Guilder	0.7351	0.4894
New Zealand	Dollar	0.8054	0.5362
Philippines	Peso	0.03911	0.02604
Portugal	Escudo	0.00808	0.00538
Russia	Ruble	0.0575234	0.0382979
Singapore	Dollar	0.8672	0.5774
South Korea	Won	0.001235	0.000822
Spain	Peseta	0.00974	0.00648
Taiwan	Dollar	0.04558	0.0303

Table 3.2 *Currency Cross Rates (noon, April 9, 1999 Toronto)*

	Per C$	Per US$	Per £	Per DM	Per ¥	Per Sw fr	Per Fr fr	Per €
Canadian dollar (C$)	•	1.5020	2.4136	0.8282	0.012410	1.0129	0.2470	1.6199
US dollar (US$)	0.6658	•	1.6069	0.5514	0.008262	0.6744	0.1644	1.0785
British pound (£)	0.4143	0.6223	•	0.3431	0.005142	0.4197	0.1023	0.6712
German mark (DM)	1.2074	1.8136	2.9143	•	0.014984	1.2230	0.2982	1.9559
Japanese yen (¥)	80.58	121.03	194.49	66.74	•	81.62	19.90	130.53
Swiss franc (Sw fr)	0.9873	1.4829	2.3829	0.8177	0.012252	•	0.2439	1.5993
French franc (Fr fr)	4.0486	6.0810	9.7717	3.3530	0.050243	4.1008	•	6.5583
Euro (€)	0.6173	0.9272	1.4900	0.5113	0.007661	0.6253	0.1525	•

and

$$\text{DM}1.9559 \text{ per } € = \text{DM}\frac{1}{0.5113} \text{ per } €$$

Consequently, half of the values in the table are not really needed. It would be sufficient to have just the values above the diagonal or just the values below the diagonal.

Example 3.5B *Currency Conversion Using a Currency Cross Rate Table*

Using an exchange rate from Table 3.2, calculate the number of yen that C$650 could purchase at noon (Toronto time) on April 9, 1999.

Solution

Let the number of yen be ¥y. From Table 3.2, we can work with either

$$\frac{\text{C}\$0.01241}{¥1.00} \quad \text{or} \quad \frac{¥80.58}{\text{C}\$1.00}$$

If we choose the second version, then

$$\frac{¥y}{C\$650} = \frac{¥80.58}{C\$1.00}$$

and

$$¥y = \frac{¥80.58}{C\$1.00} \times C\$650 = ¥52{,}377$$

C$650 could purchase ¥52,377 at noon (Toronto time) on April 9, 1999.

Example 3.5C *Two Successive Currency Conversions*

Suppose C$650 were first converted to German marks and then the German marks were converted to yen at the exchange rates in Table 3.2. Show that the same number of yen was purchased as in Example 3.5B. (Assume that no charges are imposed by the institutions providing the currency exchange services.)

Solution

Let DMg represent the number of German marks obtained from converting C$650. Then

$$\frac{DMg}{C\$650} = \frac{DM1.2074}{C\$1.00}$$

and

$$DMg = \frac{DM1.2074}{C\$1.00} \times C\$650 = DM784.81$$

Converting the marks to ¥y, we obtain

$$\frac{¥y}{DM784.81} = \frac{¥66.74}{DM1.00}$$

and

$$¥y = \frac{¥66.74}{DM1.00} \times DM784.81 = ¥52{,}378$$

The ¥1 difference between this result and the answer in Example 3.5B arises because the exchange rate is given with only four-figure accuracy. (We need six figures in the exchange rate to ensure five-figure accuracy in the answer.)

Example 3.5D *Comparing Prices Quoted in Two Currencies*

Gasoline sold for C$0.609 per litre in Vancouver and US$1.39 per gallon in Seattle on April 9, 1999. By what percentage (based on the Vancouver price) was gas cheaper in Seattle? (1 US gallon = 3.785 litres)

Solution

The solution requires three steps. We will calculate the price in Canada of a volume of gas equal to 1 US gallon, then convert US\$1.39 to C\$, and finally calculate the percent difference between the two prices.

Step 1: Calculate the cost in Canada of 3.785 litres (= 1 US gallon) of gasoline.

$$3.785 \text{ litres} \times \text{C\$}0.609 \text{ per litre} = \text{C\$}2.305$$

Step 2: Convert US\$1.39 to C\$. Let C\$$x$ represent the Canadian dollar equivalent of the Seattle price (US\$1.39) of 1 US gallon. Then

$$\frac{\text{C\$}x}{\text{US\$}1.39} = \frac{\text{C\$}1.5020}{\text{US\$}1.00}$$

and

$$\text{C\$}x = \frac{\text{C\$}1.5020 \times \text{US\$}1.39}{\text{US\$}1.00} = \text{C\$}2.088$$

Step 3: Calculate the percent difference between the Step 1 and Step 2 results. A US gallon was C\$2.305 − C\$2.088 = C\$0.217 cheaper in Seattle. The percent difference was

$$\frac{\text{C\$}0.217}{\text{C\$}2.305} \times 100\% = 9.4\%$$

Gasoline was 9.4% cheaper in Seattle.

Appreciation and Depreciation of Currencies If Currency A *appreciates* (or strengthens) relative to Currency B, it means that a unit of Currency A now buys *more* of Currency B. Consequently, the exchange rate in terms of the amount of Currency B per unit of Currency A *increases.* On the other hand, the exchange rate in terms of the amount of Currency A per unit of Currency B *decreases.*

Consider this example. Suppose the exchange between the US\$ and the C\$ changed from US\$0.67 per C\$ to US\$0.68 per C\$ over a period of one month. Which currency strengthened (appreciated) relative to the other during the month?

At the end of the month, a Canadian dollar purchased US\$0.01 more than at the beginning of the month. Therefore, the Canadian dollar strengthened (appreciated) relative to the US dollar. The flip side of the coin, so to speak, is that the US dollar weakened (depreciated) relative to the Canadian dollar. In this circumstance, Canadians importing goods from the US or travelling in the US will benefit from the stronger "Canuck buck." It requires fewer C\$ (than it did one month earlier) to purchase American goods and services. On the other hand, Americans importing goods from Canada or travelling in Canada require more US\$ (than needed one month earlier) to pay prices denominated in C\$.

Example 3.5E *Interpreting Changes in Exchange Rates*

The exchange rate between the Swiss franc and British pound changed from Sw fr2.38 per £1.00 to Sw fr2.36 per £1.00.

a. Which currency depreciated (weakened) relative to the other?

b. What were the beginning and ending exchange rates in terms of £ per Sw fr?

Solution

a. £1.00 purchased fewer Sw fr after the change. Therefore the £ depreciated and the Sw fr appreciated.

b. The two versions of an exchange rate are reciprocals of each other. Hence, the exchange rate went from

$$£\frac{1}{2.38} \text{ per Sw fr} \qquad \text{to} \qquad £\frac{1}{2.36} \text{ per Sw fr}$$

That is, from

$$£0.4202 \text{ per Sw fr} \qquad \text{to} \qquad £0.4237 \text{ per Sw fr}$$

Example 3.5F *Consequences of Exchange Rate Shifts*

Many commodities produced by Canadian oil, mining, and forest product companies are priced in US$ in international markets. Suppose a Canadian producer sells newsprint for US$800 per tonne. What is the consequence for the C$ revenue per tonne if the exchange rate goes from US$0.67 per C$ to US$0.68 per C$?

Solution

Let C$$x$ represent the C$ revenue per tonne. At the first exchange rate,

$$\frac{\text{US\$800}}{\text{C\$}x} = \frac{\text{US\$0.67}}{\text{C\$1.00}}$$

After rearranging to isolate C$$x$, we obtain

$$\text{C\$}x = \frac{\text{C\$1.00}}{\text{US\$0.67}} \times \text{US\$800} = \text{C\$1194.03 per tonne}$$

Similarly, at the second exchange rate,

$$\text{C\$}x = \frac{\text{C\$1.00}}{\text{US\$0.68}} \times \text{US\$800} = \text{C\$1176.47 per tonne}$$

The weakening of the US$ (strengthening of the C$) causes the producer's revenue to decrease by C$17.56 per tonne.

Concept Questions

1. If the exchange rate in terms of units of Currency N per unit of Currency M decreases, which currency strengthened? Explain.
2. If the exchange rate in terms of units of Currency P per unit of Currency Q increases, which currency weakened? Explain.

3. If Currency G weakens relative to Currency H, will the exchange rate in terms of units of G per unit of H increase or decrease? Explain.
4. If Currency R strengthens relative to Currency S, will the exchange rate in terms of units of S per unit of R increase or decrease? Explain.

Exercise 3.5

Answers to the odd-numbered problems are at the end of the book.

For Problems 1 through 12, use the currency exchange rates in Table 3.2 to calculate the amount of the currency in the third column of the following table that is equivalent to the amount in the second column.

Problem	Given amount	Equivalent amount
1.	US$1856	C$?
2.	£123.50	DM ?
3.	C$14,500	¥ ?
4.	¥3,225,000	£ ?
5.	DM3251	C$?
6.	£56,700	US$?
7.	¥756,000	C$?
8.	DM159,500	US$?
9.	C$94,350	£ ?
10.	DM37,650	¥ ?
11.	C$49,900	DM ?
12.	£8950	¥?

13. Calculate the exchange rates in the third column in the following table using the exchange rates given in the second column.

	Given exchange rate	Desired exchange rate
a.	Fr fr3.954 = C$1.00	Fr fr1.00 = C$?
b.	Sw fr2.3649 = £1.00	Sw fr1.00 = £?
c.	Australian$1.00 = ¥77.16	Australian$? = ¥1.00
d.	C$1.00 = Australian$1.0327	C$? = Australian$1.00

If the necessary exchange rates are not given in the following problems, use the exchange rates in Table 3.2.

14. How much will it cost in Canadian dollars to purchase US$200 of currency at a bank that charges a 1.5% commission on the transaction?
15. Simon returns from a weekend in the United States with US$48 of currency. How much will he receive from the bank when he converts the currency back to Canadian dollars? (Assume that the bank charges a 1.5% commission on the transaction.)
16. How much will it cost (in Canadian funds) to purchase £2000 worth of traveller's cheques if the commission rate for this quantity of cheques is 0.5%?

17. Lois returned from a holiday in Britain with £350 of uncashed traveller's cheques. How much will she receive in Canadian funds if the bank charges a fee of 0.75% to convert the traveller's cheques to Canadian funds?

18. If Canadian auto workers earn an average of C$30 per hour and their American counterparts earn US$23 per hour, which country has a cost of labour advantage after adjusting for the currency exchange rate? What is the size of the advantage in C$?

19. If cheese costs C$5.50 per pound in Canada and US$3.85 per pound in the United States, in which country is cheese less expensive? How much cheaper is it in C$ per pound?

•20. If the number of £ per C$1.00 increases by 0.054 from the value in Table 3.2, which currency has depreciated and by what percentage?

•21. If the number of C$ per ¥1.00 decreases by 0.00054 from the value in Table 3.2, which currency has appreciated and by what percentage?

•22. If the C$ weakens by 0.5% relative to the DM in Table 3.2, what will be the new values for DM per C$1.00 and C$ per DM1.00?

•23. If the C$ strengthens by 1.2% relative to the US$ in Table 3.2, what will be the new values for US$ per C$1.00 and C$ per US$1.00?

•24. If the C$ appreciates (from the value in Table 3.2) by C$0.0017 relative to the £, what will be the new value for £ per C$1.00?

•25. If the C$ weakens (from the value in Table 3.2) by C$0.0033 relative to the US$, what will be the new value for US$ per C$1.00?

•26. If the C$ strengthens by £0.0021 from the value in Table 3.2, what will be the new value of C$ per £1.00?

•27. If the C$ weakens by DM0.021 from the value in Table 3.2, what will be the new value of C$ per DM1.00?

•28. If the number of US$ per C$1.00 rises from 0.6823 to 0.6966, what will be the change in the C$ price to an importer of a US$1500 item?

•29. If the number of ¥ per C$1.00 declines from 83.26 to 81.39, what will be the change in the C$ price to an importer of a ¥195,000 item?

•30. If the number of £ per C$1.00 rises from 0.4218 to 0.4335, what will be the change in the C$ revenue from a foreign contract fixed at £23,000?

•31. If the number of US$ per C$1.00 declines from 0.6941 to 0.6788, what will be the change in the C$ price per ounce of gold which a Canadian gold mine sells at the international price of US$295 per ounce?

•32. Using the exchange rates in Table 3.2, show that you will receive as many German marks for C$1150 by first converting the dollars to pounds and then converting the pounds to German marks, as you would by converting the dollars directly to German marks.

•33. Using the exchange rates in Table 3.2, show that you will receive as many pounds for US$2560 by first converting the dollars to yen and then converting the yen to pounds, as you would by converting the dollars directly to pounds.

•**34.** A cross-border shopping trip reveals that milk sells for US\$0.85 per quart versus C\$1.37 per litre in Canada. Calculate the percent difference (using the Canadian price as the base) in the exchange rate-adjusted price of milk between Canada and the United States. (1 U.S. quart = 0.94635 litres).

•**35.** If pork chops cost US\$3.25 per pound in the United States and C\$8.50 per kilogram in Canada, in which country are the chops more expensive? (1 kg = 2.2 pounds) How much more expensive are they in US\$ per pound?

*3.6 Application: Index Numbers

If you read the business section of a newspaper, you soon encounter index numbers such as the Consumer Price Index and the Toronto Stock Exchange 300 composite index (TSE 300 Index). In economics and finance, index numbers are used to compare prices on different dates of a group of related items. For example, the Consumer Price Index is used to compare prices on different days of goods and services purchased by a typical urban Canadian family. The TSE 300 Index is used to compare the general price levels on different dates of shares on the Toronto Stock Exchange.

We will use the Consumer Price Index (CPI) to illustrate the construction of an index. Statistics Canada tracks the prices of about 500 consumer goods and services (the CPI "basket"). The Consumer Price Index for a selected date is calculated from the proportion[3]:

$$\frac{\text{CPI}}{100} = \frac{\text{Price of CPI basket on the selected date}}{\text{Price of CPI basket on the base date}}$$

The *base date* now used for the CPI is mid-1992. The *base value* chosen by Statistics Canada for the index on the base date is the "100" in the denominator on the left side. Multiplying both sides by 100 gives

$$\text{CPI} = \frac{\text{Price of CPI basket on the selected date}}{\text{Price of CPI basket on the base date}} \times 100$$

Because of rising price levels, CPI values are greater than 100 for any date since the base date. In mid-1999 the CPI reached 110. This means that prices were, on average, 10% higher in mid-1999 than on the base date (in mid-1992).

In general, an index number for a selected date is calculated from

$$\text{Index number} = \frac{\text{Price or value on the selected date}}{\text{Price or value on the base date}} \times \text{Base value}$$

[3] The price of the CPI "basket" is a weighted-average price. The weighting factor for each item reflects the percentage of consumer expenditures on each item.

The TSE 300 Index reflects the share prices of 300 large companies trading on the Toronto Stock Exchange. The price ratio in the index is calculated in terms of the value of a portfolio of the 300 stocks.[4] A base value of 1000 was chosen for the base date in 1975. Hence,

$$\text{TSE 300 Index} = \frac{\text{Value of TSE 300 portfolio on the selected date}}{\text{Value of TSE 300 portfolio on the base date}} \times 1000$$

In late February of 1998, the TSE 300 Index reached 7000. On that date, the value of the TSE 300 portfolio was seven times the portfolio's value on the base date in 1975. In other words, the portfolio's value increased by 600% during the approximately 23-year period.

Example 3.6A *Calculating an Index Number*

Suppose the TSE 300 portfolio cost \$168,400 in 1975 (when the base value of the index was set at 1000). What value was quoted for the TSE 300 Index on a later date when the same portfolio had a value of \$1,000,000?

Solution

$$\begin{aligned}\text{TSE 300 Index} &= \frac{\text{Value of TSE 300 portfolio on the selected date}}{\text{Value of TSE 300 portfolio on the base date}} \times 1000 \\ &= \frac{\$1{,}000{,}000}{\$168{,}400} \times 1000 \\ &= 5938.2\end{aligned}$$

The index stood at 5938.2 on the date the portfolio was worth \$1,000,000.

Example 3.6B *Using CPI Data*

The mid-year Consumer Price Index was 84.8 in 1988, 101.8 in 1993, and 108.6 in 1998.

a. What amount in 1988 had the same purchasing power as \$1000 in 1993?

b. What was the overall percent inflation from 1988 to 1998?

c. Kay earned \$30,000 in 1993. What amount must she earn in 1998 to keep pace with inflation?

Solution

a. Amounts having the same purchasing power will have the same ratio as the respective CPIs. That is,

---

[4] The number of shares of each stock is chosen so that larger companies affect the portfolio and the index more than smaller companies. We need not be concerned with the details in this section.

$$\frac{\text{1988 amount}}{\text{1993 amount}} = \frac{\text{1988 CPI}}{\text{1993 CPI}}$$

$$\frac{\text{1988 amount}}{\$1000} = \frac{84.8}{101.8}$$

$$\text{1988 amount} = 0.83301 \times \$1000 = \$833.01$$

b. The usual measure of inflation is the percent increase in the CPI. Hence,

$$\text{Percent inflation} = \frac{\text{1998 CPI} - \text{1988 CPI}}{\text{1988 CPI}} \times 100\% = \frac{108.6 - 84.8}{84.8} \times 100\% = 28.1\%$$

1998 consumer prices were, on average, 28.1% higher than 1988 prices.

c. To keep pace with inflation, salaries must be in the same ratio as the corresponding CPIs.

$$\frac{\text{1998 salary}}{\text{1993 salary}} = \frac{\text{1998 CPI}}{\text{1993 CPI}}$$

$$\frac{\text{1998 salary}}{\$30{,}000} = \frac{108.6}{101.8}$$

$$\text{1998 salary} = 1.0668 \times \$30{,}000 = \$32{,}004$$

Kay must earn $32,004 in 1998 to keep pace with inflation.

Exercise 3.6

Answers to the odd-numbered problems are at the end of the book.
Calculate the missing quantities in Problems 1 through 8 to four-figure accuracy.

Problem	Value on base date	Base value	Current value	Current index number
1.	$3278	100	$4961	?
2.	$3278	1000	$4961	?
3.	$7532	100	?	119.5
4.	$189.50	?	$431.70	2278
5.	$735	10	$689	?
6.	$8950	100	?	89.50
7.	?	1000	$7729	2120
8.	$451.10	?	$398.60	441.8

9. The basket of goods and services included in the Consumer Price Index cost $21,350 on the base date. Eight years later, the same basket cost $26,090. What was the CPI on the latter date?

10. A basket of goods and services representative of the CPI cost $2750 when the CPI stood at 118.3.

a. What did the basket of goods cost 10 years earlier, when the CPI was at 93.1?

b. What was the overall percent inflation experienced by consumers for the entire 10-year period?

11. In one year, the CPI increased from 106.3 to 108.9. How much money was required at the end of the year in order to have the same purchasing power as $1000 at the beginning?

12. A college student wants to check whether tuition fee increases over the last five years have exceeded the general increase in the cost of living. Tuition increased from $205 per course to $255 per course while the CPI rose from 102.5 to 109.7. What would be the current tuition per course if tuition had merely kept pace with inflation?

13. Statistics Canada calculates separate subindexes of the CPI for goods and for services. The goods index rose from 96.8 to 112.0 over a 10-year period. During the same period, the services index rose from 95.2 to 115.1.

a. How much did representative goods worth $1000 at the beginning cost at the end of the 10-year period?

b. How much did representative services worth $1000 at the beginning cost at the end of the 10-year period?

c. By what percentage did the increase in the price level of services exceed the increase in the price level of goods during the decade?

14. From the end of 1988 until the end of 1998, the TSE 300 Index rose from 3390 to 6486. If an investor had invested $50,000 in a portfolio of the shares of these 300 companies at the end of 1988, what would the value of those shares have been at the end of 1998? (This calculation considers only the price appreciation of the original shares. It does not include the portion of the growth in the portfolio's value resulting from the receipt and reinvestment of dividends.)

•15. Did the share prices in Problem 14 increase more or less than prices experienced by consumers if the CPI rose from 86.8 at the end of 1988 to 109.0 at the end of 1998? Expressed as a percentage of 1988 price levels, how much more or less did the share prices increase than consumer prices?

16. From the end of 1988 until the end of 1998, the American Standard & Poor's 500 (S&P 500) stock index rose from 319.1 to 1229.2. If an investor had invested $50,000 in a portfolio of the shares of these 500 companies at the end of 1988, what would the value of those shares have been at the end of 1998? (This calculation considers only the price appreciation of the original shares. It does not include the portion of the growth in the portfolio's value resulting from the receipt and reinvestment of dividends.)

17. The late 1970s and early 1980s were years of historically high rates of inflation in Canada. The CPI was at 70.8, 77.1, 84.5, 94.6, 105.4, and 114.1 at the beginning of 1978, 1979, 1980, 1981, 1982, and 1983, respectively. These price index numbers are quoted in terms of a base value of 100 in mid-1981.

a. What amount was required at the beginning of 1983 in order to have the same purchasing power as $100 just five years earlier?

b. What were the inflation rates for each of the years 1978 to 1982 inclusive?

*Appendix: Linkages Among Exchange Rates

Suppose you first convert C$1000 to US$, then convert the US$ to £, and finally convert the £ back to C$. Assume there are no service charges or commissions. Suppose you end up with C$1010 after the three conversions. In that event, you have stumbled onto a "money-making machine"! If you put the C$1010 through the cycle again, you will end up with another 1% gain. By repeating the process often enough, you can become rich. This scenario seems highly unlikely since it violates the "no-free-lunch" principle of finance.

Suppose, instead, you end up with only C$990 after the three successive conversions. This seems much more plausible than the preceding scenario. But hold it! If you are a conniving sort of person, it might occur to you that C$990 can be turned into C$1000 by reversing the sequence of the three conversions. Therefore, this scenario also presents us with a "free lunch."

For there to be no "free lunch," the three successive currency conversions must leave us with the original C$1000. In foreign exchange markets, market forces keep exchange rates aligned so that no significant profit can be made from a series of currency conversions ending at the initial currency. Let us verify this point by carrying out the C$→US$→£→C$ conversions using the exchange rates in Table 3.2.

$$\text{C\$1000} \times \frac{\text{US\$0.6658}}{\text{C\$1.00}} \times \frac{\text{£0.6223}}{\text{US\$1.00}} \times \frac{\text{C\$2.4136}}{\text{£1.00}} = \text{C\$1000.02}$$

Since we begin and end with C$1000, the product of the three exchange rates is 1.000. Should the exchange rates drift away from this alignment, a "free lunch" opportunity arises. Arbitrageurs will move huge amounts of money through the conversion cycle. This movement creates supply and demand forces that reduce the value of currencies being sold relative to the value of currencies being purchased. Exchange rates then adjust until the equilibrium alignment is re-established.

Review Problems

Answers to the odd-numbered review problems are at the end of the book.

1. Express each of the following ratios in its lowest terms.

   a. $0.18 : 0.60 : 0.45$ **b.** $\frac{9}{8} : \frac{3}{4} : \frac{3}{2}$

   c. $\frac{1}{6} : \frac{1}{3} : \frac{1}{9}$ **d.** $6\frac{1}{4} : 5 : 8\frac{3}{4}$

2. Solve the following proportions for the unknown quantities.

   a. $t : 26 : 10 = 24 : 39 : s$

   b. $x : 3600 : y = \frac{4}{5} : \frac{2}{3} : \frac{7}{4}$

3. Mark, Ben, and Tanya own 4250, 2550, and 5950 shares, respectively, of MBT Inc. What is the ratio of their share holdings?

4. Coral paid a total of $4845, including a 2% brokerage commission, for 200 shares of Terra Corp.

   a. What dollar amount of commission did she pay on the transaction?

   b. What (before-commission) price per share did she pay for the stock?

5. The new University Hospital is scheduled to have 436 beds. The ratio of nurses to beds to nurses' aides for staffing the hospital is 4 : 9 : 2. How many nurses and aides will need to be hired?

6. For the last five years the sales of Departments D, E, and F have maintained a relatively stable ratio of 13: 17: 21. Department E is forecasting sales of $478,000 for next year. Based on the past sales ratio, what sales would be expected for Departments D and F?

7. Bart purchased 60% of a three-eighths interest in a ski chalet for $25,000. What was the implied value of the chalet?

8. Wendy, Simone, and Leif share the costs of their coffee fund in the ratio $\frac{3}{2} : \frac{2}{3} : \frac{5}{3}$. How will $50 be allocated among them?

9. How should common area costs totalling $28,575 be allocated among commercial tenants A, B, C, and D if the costs are prorated based on leased areas of 1260, 3800, 1550, and 2930 sq ft, respectively?

10. A bartenders' handbook recommends that one bottle of spirits be provided per 10 guests at a New Year's Eve party. Furthermore, the relative consumption of scotch, rye, and rum is in the ratio of 3 : 5 : 4. How many bottles of each liquor should be stocked for a party expecting 480 guests?

11. A partnership agreement provides that half of the annual profit be distributed in proportion to each partner's investment in the partnership, and that the other half be distributed in proportion to the total number of hours that each partner worked in the business during the year. How should the most recent year's profit of $84,780 be allocated if the amounts invested by Huey, Dewey, and Louie are $70,000, $30,000, and $45,000, and their hours of work for the year were 425, 1680, and 1440, respectively?

12. Before Mr. and Mrs. Percival left for Great Britain, they purchased British pounds at an exchange rate of C$2.395 = £1.00. When they returned to Canada eight weeks later they converted the £242 they had left over back to Canadian currency at the rate of C$2.437 = £1.00. How much did they gain or lose in Canadian dollars on the round-trip transaction involving the £242?

◆ 13. The exchange rate between Currencies X and Y is currently Y0.05614 = X1.00. If X weakens by 1.5% relative to Y, what will be the new values for the exchange rates per unit of X and per unit of Y?

◆ **14.** The exchange rate between the US$ and the C$ declines from US$0.7013 to US$0.6827 per C$. What will be the change in the C$ price to an importer of a US$2000 item?

15. The CPI stood at 96.4, 98.6, 101.2, 103.3, 105.7, and 108.9 on the same date in successive years.

a. What was the inflation rate:

i. in the fourth one-year interval?

ii. in the fifth one-year interval?

b. What amount was required at the end in order to have the same purchasing power as $100 five years earlier?

Self-Test Exercise

Answers to the self-test problems are at the end of the book.

1. Solve the following proportions.

a. $65 : 43 = 27.3 : x$

b $1410 : 2330 : 870 = a : 550 : b$

2. Milan, Stephen, and Fred started their partnership with a total investment of $135,000 contributed in the ratio of 3 : 4 : 2. If each partner contributes another $10,000, what will be the ratio of their total contributions?

3. A test-marketing of a newly released video in a representative Canadian city, with a population of 120,000, resulted in sales of 543 units in a three-month period. If the video sells at the same rate in the rest of the country, where 21,000,000 Canadians have access to retail outlets, what three-month sales may be forecast for the video?

4. A provincial government allocates 29% of its budget to education, 31% to health care, and 21% to social services. If the dollar amount budgeted for education is $3.17 billion, how much is budgeted for health care and for social services?

5. The total cost, including the 7% Goods and Services tax (GST), for a business lunch was $23.22. What was the dollar amount of the GST?

6. A profit-sharing bonus was divided among four employees—Ms. L, Mr. M, Ms. N, and Mr. P—in the ratio of 1.5 : 1 : 0.75 : 0.5, respectively. If Ms. N received $2000, how much did each of the others receive?

7. Mr. Nolan's will specifies that the proceeds from his estate be divided among his wife, son, and stepson in the ratio of $\frac{7}{5} : 1 : \frac{5}{7}$, respectively. How much will each receive from the distribution of his $331,000 estate?

8. If Italian lira 1.00 = C$0.0008526, how many lira can be purchased with C$1500?

9. Three years ago, when the CPI was at 102.6, the members of a union were earning $22.25 per hour. Now, with the current CPI at 108.4, they are negotiating for a new hourly rate that will restore their former purchasing power. What hourly rate are they seeking?

◆ **10.** If C$1.00 rises from ¥78.11 to ¥80.89, what will be the change in the C$ price to an importer of a ¥2,965,000 car?

◆ **11.** A steel company in Hamilton can purchase Alberta coal at C$39.50 per metric tonne (1000 kg) or Virginia coal at US$27.25 per ton (2000 lb) (1 kg = 2.205 lb). How much cheaper in C$ per metric tonne is the less expensive source if US$0.7028 = C$1.00?

CHAPTER OUTLINE

LEARNING OBJECTIVES

After completing this chapter, you will be able to:

- Calculate the net price of an item after single or multiple trade discounts
- Calculate a single discount rate that is equivalent to a series of multiple discounts
- Understand the ordinary dating notation for the terms of payment of an invoice
- Calculate the amount of the cash discount for which a payment qualifies
- Solve merchandise pricing problems involving markup and markdown

4

Mathematics of Merchandising

MATHEMATICS TOUCHES ALMOST EVERY STAGE of product distribution and merchandising. Consider a retailer who buys goods from her suppliers, marks up the price, and sells the goods to her customers. The cost of the goods to the retailer is usually determined by deducting a "trade discount" from the supplier's "list price." The invoice she receives may offer a "cash discount" for prompt payment of the invoice. The amount of "markup" the retailer adds to the cost price must cover an appropriate amount of her overhead costs, and also generate a suitable profit. For a sale or special promotion, the retailer may offer a discount or "markdown" from the regular selling price.

In this chapter, we will learn the terminology and procedures for these calculations. We will also explore the relationships among certain variables to better understand the effects a change in one variable has on the others.

4.1 Trade Discounts

Goods move from a manufacturer to the ultimate consumer through the *distribution chain* or *merchandising chain.* In the chain illustrated in Figure 4.1, a product is first sold by a *manufacturer* to a *distributor.* The agreement between a manufacturer and a distributor usually gives the distributor the *exclusive* right to distribute the product in a fairly large geographic region, but prohibits the distributor from handling competing products. Typically, a distributor also has marketing responsibilities in the region. The distributor then resells the goods to a number of *wholesalers.* A wholesaler carries a wider range of products within a general category or theme. The majority of a wholesaler's product lines are complementary, but some will be competing. All are for resale to *retailers* within a smaller geographic area. Retailers sell mainly to the ultimate consumers of the goods.

Figure 4.1 *The Distribution Chain*

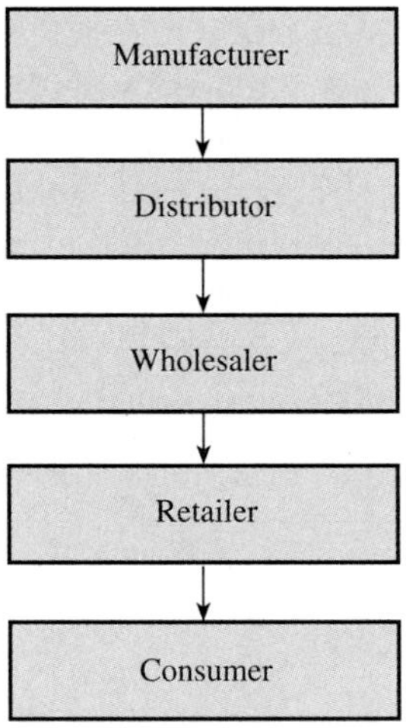

In many cases, one or more of the intermediate links may be absent. Large national retailers and *buying groups* of smaller retailers often have enough buying power to purchase directly from manufacturers.

To understand how prices are usually established within the merchandising chain, imagine that you are a wholesaler buying from a distributor. The distributor is likely to have a catalogue of **list prices**. List prices at any level in the chain are commonly chosen to approximate the ultimate retail selling price. (No doubt you have noticed terms such as "manufacturer's suggested retail price," "suggested list price," or "recommended selling price" on the packaging or in advertisements for certain products.) The distributor will offer you a percent discount from the list price[1] called the **trade discount** rate. The word "trade" signifies that the discount applies only to a transaction within the "trade," that is, within the

[1] The use of trade discounts in conjunction with fixed list prices makes it easier for the seller to set different prices for various categories of customers. For example, a manufacturer might offer one discount rate to a distributor in one part of the country, another discount rate to "big-box" retailers, and yet another rate to smaller buying groups. Every customer sees the same "up front" list price. Price flexibility is achieved in the setting of the trade discount rate.

TRAP *WATCH FOR IMPRECISE LANGUAGE IN "EVERYDAY" USAGE*

In everyday usage, "trade discount" can refer to either the *percent* amount or the *dollar* amount of the discount. The intended meaning is sometimes obvious from the units quoted (% or $). Where there is a possibility of confusion, we will use "*rate* of trade discount" or "trade discount *rate*" for the trade discount quoted as a percentage of the list price. The "*amount* of the trade discount" will refer to the trade discount measured in dollars. For example, if a trade discount *rate* of 35% applies to a $200 list price item, the *amount* of the trade discount is 0.35 ($200) = $70.

merchandising chain. There may be some negotiating room for setting the rate of trade discount.

The resulting price after deducting the amount of the trade discount from the list price is called the **net price**. That is,

$$\begin{aligned}\text{Net price} &= \text{List price} - \text{Amount of trade discount}\\ &= \text{List price} - (\text{Discount rate} \times \text{List price})\end{aligned}$$

The following symbols will be used to convert the preceding word equation to an algebraic equation.

$$\begin{aligned}N &= \text{Net price}\\ L &= \text{List price}\\ d &= \text{Rate of trade discount}\end{aligned}$$

Replacing the quantities in the word equation by these symbols, we obtain

$$N = L - dL$$

Since L is a common factor on the right side, we can write the basic discounting formula as:

NET PRICE AFTER A DISCOUNT

(4-1) $$N = L(1 - d)$$

Multiple Discounts (or a Discount Series) In the past, it was common for a seller/vendor in the merchandising chain to offer more than one discount. For example, in addition to the basic trade discount offered to all customers, the seller might also offer additional small discounts for large volume purchases, special promotions and cooperative advertising, and early orders of seasonal items.

If a purchaser qualifies for more than one discount, the understanding is that the discounts should be compounded rather than added. This means that we use a formula similar to formula (4-1) but with a $(1 - d)$ factor for each discount. If there are three discounts, d_1, d_2, and d_3, then the net price is

NET PRICE AFTER THREE DISCOUNTS

(4-2) $$N = L(1 - d_1)(1 - d_2)(1 - d_3)$$

The granting of separate multiple discounts has been largely abandoned. It is now much more typical for buyers and sellers to negotiate a single discount rate that can be adjusted over time as the business relationship evolves. Rather than offering a volume discount on individual orders, vendors increasingly pay end-of-year rebates (in the 2% to 5% range) based on the total volume of a customer's purchases during the year.

Other Applications Although formula (4-1) was derived in the context of trade discounts, it may be used in any discount or "% off" calculation. Indeed, formula (4-1)

applies to any situation in which an amount (L) is reduced by d percent. Such applications include the calculation of the "sale" price after a percentage markdown, sales revenue net of commission, security prices after a percentage loss in value, and budget amounts after a percentage cut.

Similarly, formula (4-2) may be employed in any situation where a beginning amount, L, undergoes a series of compound percent decreases. N represents the amount left after the decreases. For example, suppose a product's sales are forecast to decline from the past year's sales of \$200,000 by 10%, 20%, and 15% in successive years. Then sales in the third year are forecast to be

$$N = \$200{,}000(1-0.10)(1-0.20)(1-0.15) = \$200{,}000(0.90)(0.80)(0.85) = \$122{,}400$$

Note that the combined effect of the three percent decreases is less than a single decrease of 10% + 20% + 15% = 45%.

Example 4.1A *Calculating the Discount Amount and Net Price*

A wholesaler lists an item at \$117 less 20%. What is the amount of the discount and the net price to a retailer?

Solution

Given: $L = \$117$, $d = 0.20$.

$$\begin{aligned} \text{Amount of discount} &= dL = (0.20)(\$117) = \$23.40 \\ \text{Net price} &= \text{List price} - \text{Amount of discount} \\ &= \$117 - \$23.40 \\ &= \$93.60 \end{aligned}$$

Example 4.1B *Calculating the List Price*

After a trade discount of 30%, a garage is able to purchase windshield wiper blades for a net price of \$9.73. What is the list price of the blades?

Solution

Given: $d = 0.30$, $N = \$9.73$.

If formula (4–1) is rearranged to isolate L, we obtain

$$L = \frac{N}{1-d} = \frac{\$9.73}{1-0.30} = \frac{\$9.73}{0.7} = \$13.90$$

The list price of the blades is \$13.90.

Example 4.1C *Calculating the Trade Discount Rate*

A clothing store is able to purchase men's leather coats at a net price of \$173.40 after a discount of \$115.60. What rate of trade discount was obtained?

Solution

Given: Net price = \$173.40, Amount of discount = \$115.60.

$$\begin{aligned}\text{List price} &= \text{Net price} + \text{Amount of discount}\\ &= \$173.40 + \$115.60\\ &= \$289.00\\ d &= \frac{\text{Amount of discount}}{\text{List price}}\\ &= \frac{\$115.60}{\$289.00}\\ &= 0.40\end{aligned}$$

The trade discount rate is 40%.

Example **4.1D** *Calculating the Net Price after Multiple Discounts*

WGW Manufacturing and Ace Clothing both produce basic work shirts that are very similar in quality and popularity. Both manufacturers quote a list price of \$29.90 for the shirt. WGW offers a regular trade discount of 25% plus an additional volume discount of 10% on orders of at least 1000 shirts. Ace offers a standard discount of 30% and a further 5% discount on orders exceeding 500 shirts. Which source will give the lower net price on an order for 1000 shirts?

Solution

The net price per shirt from WGW is

$$\begin{aligned}N = L(1-d_1)(1-d_2) &= \$29.90(1-0.25)(1-0.10)\\ &= \$29.90(0.75)(0.90)\\ &= \$20.18\end{aligned}$$

The net price per shirt from Ace Clothing is

$$\begin{aligned}N = L(1-d_1)(1-d_2) &= \$29.90(1-0.30)(1-0.05)\\ &= \$29.90(0.70)(0.95)\\ &= \$19.88\end{aligned}$$

Therefore, Ace's net price is 30 cents per shirt lower. (Note that the sum of the two discount rates in each case is 35%. However, they do not have the same effect.)

Example **4.1E** *Calculating the Single Discount Rate that is Equivalent to Two Series Discounts*

What single discount rate is equivalent to series (or compound) discounts of 20% and 10%?

Solution

Let us apply the two discounts to a beginning value of 100. When we get the "net" amount, we can simply inspect the answer to determine the single equivalent discount. (For example, if the amount after the discounts is 74, the reduction of 100 − 74 = 26 is 26% of the initial value.)

$$\begin{aligned} N = L(1 - d_1)(1 - d_2) &= 100(1 - 0.20)(1 - 0.10) \\ &= 100(0.80)(0.90) \\ &= 72.0 \end{aligned}$$

Since the two discounts reduce 100 to 72.0, they are equivalent to a single discount of 28.0%.

Example 4.1F Calculating One of a Series of Discounts

A provincial government recently tabled a budget in which agricultural subsidies will be reduced by 10% in each of the next three years. Subsidies in the current fiscal year total \$11,500,000. What will be the amount of the reduction in the third year?

Solution

The third 10% reduction will apply to the amount left after the first two reductions. The subsidies paid in the second year will be

$$\begin{aligned} N = L(1 - d_1)(1 - d_2) &= \$11{,}000{,}000(1 - 0.10)(1 - 0.10) \\ &= \$11{,}000{,}000(0.90)(0.90) \\ &= \$8{,}910{,}000 \end{aligned}$$

Reduction in the third year $= d_3 \times \$8{,}910{,}000 = 0.10(\$8{,}910{,}000) = \$891{,}000$

Exercise 4.1

Answers to the odd-numbered problems are at the end of the book.

Calculate the missing values in Problems 1 through 10.

Problem	List price (\$)	Discount rate (%)	Discount amount (\$)	Net price (\$)
1.	249.00	$33\frac{1}{3}$	?	?
2.	995.00	$16\frac{2}{3}$	?	?
3.	127.98	?	?	106.65
4.	49.95	?	?	34.97
5.	?	35	612.50	?
6.	?	40	7.99	?
7.	?	?	12.33	15.07
8.	?	?	258.75	891.25
•9.	?	12.5	?	2849.00
•10.	?	$16\frac{2}{3}$	?	413.05

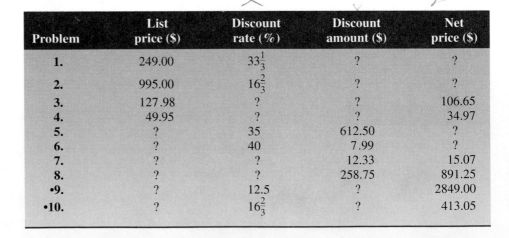

Calculate the missing values in Problems 11 through 14.

Problem	List price ($)	Discount rate (%)	Discount amount ($)	Net price ($)
11.	99.00	30, $16\frac{2}{3}$	?	?
12.	595.00	20, $12\frac{1}{2}$, $8\frac{1}{3}$	?	?
13.	?	25, 10, $7\frac{1}{2}$	?	93.03
14.	?	20, 10, $8\frac{1}{3}$	?	989.00

15. The distributor of Nikita power tools is offering a trade discount of 38% to hardware stores. What will be their cost to purchase a rotary saw listed at $135?

16. SuperSave stores can purchase Annapolis Gold apple juice for $11.50 per case less a trade discount of 30%. They can also obtain No-Name apple juice at a discount of 22% from the suggested retail price of $10.50 per case. Which juice will have the lower cost to SuperSave?

17. A 37.5% trade discount on a camera represents a discount of $111.57 from the suggested retail price. What is the net price to the buyer?

18. The net price of a product after a discount of 15% is $845.75. What is the (dollar) amount of the discount?

19. The net price on an item listed for $369 is $287.82. What trade discount rate is being given?

20. Green Thumb Nursery sells spreading junipers to the gardening departments of local grocery and building supply stores. The net price per tree is $27.06 after a trade discount of $22.14. What rate of trade discount is the nursery giving to retailers?

21. Niagara Dairies gives convenience stores a discount of 24% on butter listed at $72.00 per case. What rate of discount will Silverwood Milk Products have to give on its list price of $74.50 per case to match Niagara's price to convenience stores?

22. A grocery store is offering an in-store special of 15% off the sticker price of all cheese. What will a customer pay for a pound of cheese listed at $5.23?

23. The net proceeds to the vendor of a house after payment of a 5.5% real estate commission were $160,555.50. At what price did the house sell?

24. A merchant pays a 3.5% fee to the Bank of Montreal on all MasterCard sales.

a. What amount will she pay on sales of $17,564 for a month?

b. What were her gross sales for a month in which the bank charged total fees of $732.88?

25. Cynthia and Byron sell mutual funds for Syndicated Investors. Purchasers of mutual funds from agents of Syndicated Investors pay a front-end commission of 5.5%. The commission is paid on the total amount placed with Syndicated Investors, not on just the net amount actually invested in mutual funds.

a. Mr. and Mrs. Stevens placed $5500 through Cynthia. What (net) amount was actually invested in mutual funds after the commission was paid?

b. If the net amount invested in mutual funds as a result of Byron's sale to Mrs. Stocker was \$6426, what (dollar) amount of commission was paid on the sale?

26. **a.** Lauren's income tax rate on additional income is 42%. She has just received a wage increase of \$1.25 per hour. What is her after-tax increase in hourly pay?

b. Marvin's tax rate on additional income is 47%. How much extra must he earn to keep an additional \$1000 after tax?

27. The evening news reports that the TSE 300 index dropped 1.3% on the day to close at 3561 points. How many points did the index fall on the day?

28. At its current price of \$0.80 per share, Golden Egg Resources stock is down 73% from its price one year ago. What was that price?

•29. **a.** In a budget speech the federal government announced a \$132 million cut in defense spending. This represents 11.4% of the previous year's defense budget. What is the new budgeted amount?

b. The number of military personnel is to be reduced by 8.8% to 76,500. How many people are to be cut from the military?

30. A manufacturer of snowmobiles sells through distributors in some regions of the country, through wholesalers in other regions, and directly to retailers in its home province. The manufacturer gives a 25% trade discount to retailers, an additional 10% discount to wholesalers, and a further 7.5% discount to distributors. What net price does the manufacturer receive from each buying level on a snowmobile listed at \$5800?

•31. A retailer is offered a regular discount of 25%, a further discount of 7.5% if she places an order exceeding \$10,000 (at list prices), and another 5% discount for participating in a joint promotion with the distributor.

a. If the retailer is eligible for all three discounts, what will be the net price of an order totalling \$11,500?

b. What is the dollar amount of the saving from the quantity discount (assuming that she does not participate in the joint promotion)?

c. What is the dollar amount of the discount received for participating in the joint promotion?

32. An invoice shows a net price of \$176.72 after discounts of 30%, 10%, and 2% have been deducted.

a. What was the list price of the goods?

b. What single discount would be equivalent to the discount series?

33. A wholesaler lists an item for \$48.75 less 20%. What additional "special promotion" discount must be offered to retailers to get the net price down to \$36.66?

•34. The representative for a European ski manufacturer offers Snow 'n Surf Sporting Goods a regular discount of 25%, a volume discount of 10% for an order of at least 100 pairs of skis, and an early booking discount of 5% for orders placed before July 1.

a. If Snow 'n Surf is eligible for all three discounts on skis listed at a suggested retail price of \$445, what is the net price per pair of skis?

b. Assuming that Snow 'n Surf qualifies for the volume discount, what is the dollar amount of the early-order discount per pair of skis?

c. The net price after all three discounts on a less expensive model of skis is $205.20. What is the suggested retail price?

d. What single trade discount rate would be equivalent to the three trade discounts?

•35. In addition to the basic trade discount of 20%, an outboard motor manufacturer gives a boat dealer an additional discount of 12.5% for providing follow-up warranty service, and a 5% discount for cooperative advertising and boat show promotions.

a. After the basic discount, what further price reduction (in dollars) does the 12.5% discount represent on a $1000 list price motor?

b. After the first two discounts, what price reduction does the 5% discount give on the $1000 motor?

•36. Everest sells its mattresses for $480 less 25%. Posture-Perfect mattresses are listed at $440 less 20% and 5%. What second discount would Everest need to offer to match Posture-Perfect's net price?

4.2 Cash Discounts and Terms of Payment

For most transactions within the merchandising chain, the vendor does not require payment for the purchased goods for a period that can range from 15 days to a few weeks. No interest is charged during this interval. This arrangement is referred to as "trade credit." Following a transaction, the vendor sends an invoice to the buyer. A sample sales invoice is shown in Figure 4.2. The invoice presents details of the items purchased, unit prices, sales taxes, and any shipping costs charged to the purchaser.

Figure 4.2 *A Sample Sales Invoice*

ATLANTIC ATHLETIC WHOLESALE LTD.
177 Main Avenue
Halifax, Nova Scotia B3M 1B4

Sold to:
McGarrigle Sports
725 Kings Road
Sydney, N.S. B1S 1C2

Date: July 17, 2000
Terms: 2/10, n30

Invoice No: 3498
Via: Beatty Trucking

Quantity	Product number	Description	Unit list price	Trade discount	Amount
5	W-32	Universal Gymnasium	$1150	30%	$5750.00
150	S-4	Soccer balls	$28.00	25%, 15%	4200.00
1000	H-8a	Hockey pucks	$1.10	35%, 10%, 7%	1100.00
				Invoice total:	$11,050.00
				HST:	1657.50
				Shipping charges:	346.00
				Total amount due:	$13,053.50

1.5% per month on overdue accounts

Terms of Payment The sample invoice includes the entry "Terms: 2/10, n30." This is code or shorthand for the **terms of payment** which embody the following information.

- The length of the **credit period**. The credit period or *net period* is the length of time for which trade credit is granted. The invoice amount is due at the end of the credit period. Normally, interest is not charged for the credit period. It is common practice to charge a penalty on overdue amounts. The "1.5% per month" indicated on the sample invoice means that any portion of the invoice amount that goes overdue (anywhere from one day to one month) is liable for a 1.5% penalty. How strictly a vendor enforces the penalty is a judgment call.
- The **cash discount** rate offered (if any) and the length of the **discount period**. A cash discount is a deduction allowed for prompt payment[2] of the invoice amount (or any portion thereof). The time period within which a payment qualifies for the cash discount is called the discount period.
- The date on which the credit and discount periods begin.

Shorthand notations have evolved for quoting the terms of payment on an invoice. The most common (by far) is known as **ordinary dating** or *invoice dating.* Two other notations are presented in this chapter's appendix. The credit period and the discount period both begin on the date of the invoice. Figure 4.3 illustrates the interpretation of a particular example of ordinary dating—2/10, n/30 (read as "two ten, net thirty"). This notation means that a 2% cash discount is allowed for *full or partial* payments made within the 10-day discount period. The balance is due by the end of the 30-day credit period.

Figure 4.3 *Interpreting the Terms of Payment in Ordinary Dating*

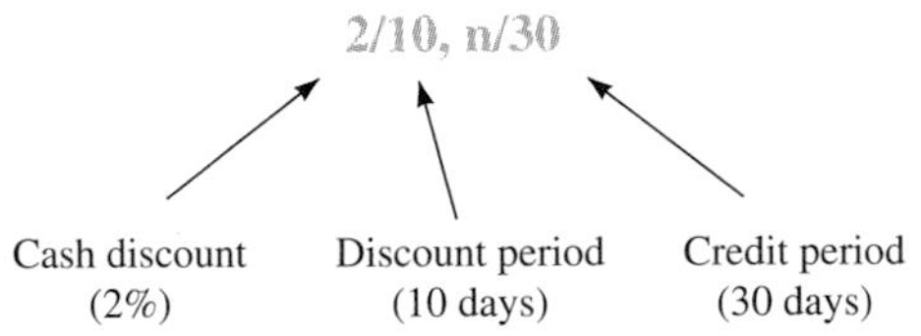

Figure 4.4 shows the invoice date, the discount period, and the credit period plotted on a time axis for the ordinary dating example 2/10, n/30. Note that the day *following* the invoice date is the first day of the credit and discount periods.

A variation of the ordinary dating notation is "2/10, 1/30, n/60." In this case, a reduced cash discount of 1% is offered on payments made any time from the eleventh to the thirtieth day after the invoice date.

The following are common practices with ordinary dating (and with the two other notations described in the appendix).

---

[2] It is generally advisable for the purchaser to take advantage of a cash discount. Forgoing the discount is usually equivalent to paying a high interest rate for trade credit during the remainder of the credit period. Therefore, failure of a customer to take advantage of a cash discount provides an early warning signal that the customer may, at least temporarily, be in a weak financial condition.

In recent years, there has been a trend of fewer vendors offering cash discounts. They find that many customers pay after the discount period but still deduct the cash discount from their remittance. Enforcement of the discount period cut-off gives rise to too many hassles with customers.

Figure 4.4 *Discount and Credit Periods for the Ordinary Dating Case 2/10, n/30*

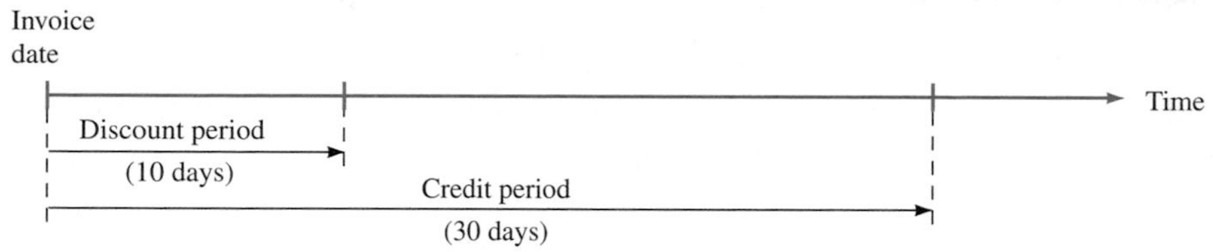

- If the last day of the discount period or the credit period falls on a non-business day, the period is extended to the next business day.
- If no cash discount is offered, only the "net" figure for the credit period is given (for example, n/15 or n/30).
- If a net figure for the credit period is not stated, it is understood that the credit period ends 20 days after the end of the discount period.

Formula (4-1), $N = L(1 - d)$, may be used to calculate the amount required to settle an invoice if the cash discount is taken. Substitute the invoiced amount for L and the cash discount rate for d. The value calculated for N is the payment that will settle the invoice within the discount period.

Partial Payments Unless otherwise indicated on the invoice, **partial payments** made within the discount period are eligible for the cash discount. The basic discount formula (4-1) may be used to calculate the amount credited to the customer's account. But you must be careful how you use it. See the Trap box below. In general,

$$\text{Amount credited, } L = \frac{\text{Amount paid, } N}{1 - d}$$

TRAP *THIS ONE CATCHES A MAJORITY OF STUDENTS!*

A very common error is to calculate the cash discount allowed on a *partial* payment as ($d \times$ payment). To understand why this is incorrect, think about how you calculate the cash discount when you pay an invoice *in full*. Suppose you receive an invoice for \$1000 and you are eligible for a 2% cash discount. Therefore a payment of

$$N = L(1 - d) = \$1000(1 - 0.02) = \$980$$

will settle the account if you pay within the discount period. The vendor will credit your account for \$1000 consisting of the \$980 payment and a \$20 cash discount. Notice that the \$20 discount is 2% of the amount credited ($L = \$1000$), not 2% of the amount paid ($N = \$980$). Similarly, if you make a partial payment of $N = \$500$ within the discount period, the cash discount will be 2% of the amount credited (L) which is initially unknown. Do not take 2% of \$500 to obtain the cash discount in this case (just as you did not take 2% of \$980 in the former case). The amount credited will be

$$L = \frac{N}{1 - d} = \frac{\$500}{1 - 0.02} = \$510.20$$

The cash discount allowed on the \$500 payment is therefore \$10.20 (which is 2% of the \$510.20 credited).

Example 4.2A Invoice Settlement with Ordinary Dating

An invoice for \$1079.80 with terms 2/10, n/30 is dated November 25. It was received in the mail on November 27. What payment will settle the invoice if payment is made on:

a. December 1?

b. December 5?

c. December 7?

Solution

a., b. The discount period ends at the end of the tenth day after the invoice date (November 25). November has 30 days. Therefore, payments made on or before December 5 are eligible for the 2% cash discount. The payment required to settle the invoice is:

$$N = L(1 - d) = \$1079.80(1 - 0.02) = \$1058.20$$

c. The full amount of the invoice must be paid after December 5. The payment required is \$1079.80.

Example 4.2B Partial Payments with Ordinary Dating

Roland Electric received an invoice for \$3845 dated March 25 with terms 3/10, 1/20, n/60. Roland paid \$1500 on April 4, \$500 on April 12, and \$500 on April 30. What balance was still owed after April 30?

Solution

The \$1500 payment qualifies for the 3% discount, and the first \$500 payment qualifies for the 1% discount. Since

$$\text{Amount credited} = \frac{\text{Amount paid}}{1 - d}$$

the total amount credited for the three payments is

$$\frac{\$1500}{1 - 0.03} + \frac{\$500}{1 - 0.01} + \$500 = \$1546.39 + \$505.05 + \$500$$

$$= \$2551.44$$

$$\text{Balance owed} = \$3845 - \$2551.44 = \$1293.56$$

POINT OF INTEREST

When Late-Payment Penalties Really Are "Criminal"

In late October of 1998, the Supreme Court of Canada made a ruling that meant certain late-payment penalties used by many utilities and large corporations were in violation of Section 347 of the Criminal Code. This section makes it a criminal offence to charge interest at a rate exceeding an annual rate of 60%. For purposes of this section, "interest" is a broad term which expressly includes charges or expenses "in the form of a penalty."

The particular case (Garland vs. Consumers' Gas Co.) before the Supreme Court was a class action brought by Gordon Garland on behalf of over 500,000 Ontario customers of Consumers' Gas Co. (now Enbridge Consumers' Gas). Consumers' Gas billed its customers on a monthly basis. The monthly statement specified a "due date" for the payment of current charges. The due date was normally 10 days after the statement date for commercial customers, and 16 days after the statement date for residential customers. Customers who failed to pay by the due date were charged a late-payment penalty (LPP) of 5% of the current amount billed. The LPP was an all-or-nothing penalty—it was the same whether the customer paid 1 day or 20 days beyond the due date.

After you peel away the actuaries, Garland's argument before the Court was essentially this. If a customer paid 10 days after the due date, the customer was, in effect, charged 5% interest for a term of just 10 days. This was like being charged $5\% \times \frac{365}{10} = 182.5\%$ per year! (If compounding is included, the rate is even higher.) This exceeds the upper limit of 60% set by the Criminal Code. The Court ruled six to one in favour of Garland.

As of April 1999, a few ancillary issues remained to be settled in lower courts. But it appeared that the gas company would be responsible for refunding about $130 million (including interest) that it had charged in LPPs since 1981.

The Supreme Court's ruling throws into doubt the status of cash discounts for prompt payment. For example, the distinction between "adding a 2% penalty for payments after 10 days" versus "deducting a 2% discount for payments before 10 days" is more in the wording than in the effect. The likelihood is that companies will move away from these flat one-time penalties or discounts, and instead charge simple interest (Chapter 6).

Mr. Garland now has a similar class-action suit under way against Ontario Hydro.

SOURCE: "Late-fee Penalty Ruled Usurious" by Kirk Makin, *The Globe and Mail*, October 31, 1998. Data extracted with permission from *The Globe and Mail*.
Also, thanks to Michael McGowan of McGowan & Associates.

Exercise 4.2

Answers to the odd-numbered problems are at the end of the book.

For Problems 1 through 4, determine the payment required to settle the invoice on the indicated payment date.

Problem	Invoice amount	Credit terms	Invoice date	Payment date
1.	$2365.00	2/10, n/30	Sept 25	Oct 5
2.	2365.00	$1\frac{1}{2}$/15, n/45	Oct 25	Nov 10
3.	815.49	2/10, 1/20, n/60	June 27	July 7
4.	5445.00	3/10, $1\frac{1}{2}$/20, n/60	March 23	April 13

Calculate the missing values in Problems 5 through 8. Assume in each case that the payment is made within the discount period.

Problem	Invoice amount	Credit terms	Payment	Amount credited	Balance owed
5.	$2365.00	2/10, n/30	?	$1365.00	?
6.	5445.00	3/10, n/90	$3000	?	?
7.	3765.25	$1\frac{1}{3}$/15, n/45	?	?	$2042.28
8.	775.50	$1\frac{1}{4}$/15, n/60	?	?	293.98

9. What total amount must be paid on July 4 to settle invoices dated June 20 for $485, June 24 for $367, and June 30 for $722, all with terms $1\frac{1}{2}$/10, n/30?

10. The Simcoe School Board has three invoices from Johnston Transport, all with terms 2/10, 1/20, n/60. Invoice 277, dated October 22, is for $14,200; Invoice 327, dated November 2, is for $8600; and Invoice 341, dated November 3, is for $11,500. What total payment to Johnston on November 12 will settle all three invoices?

11. Ballard Jewellers received an invoice dated August 22 from Safeguard Security Systems for $2856.57 with terms $2\frac{1}{2}$/10, 1/20, n/45. Ballard made payments of $900 on September 1, $850 on September 10, and $700 on September 30. What amount was still owed on October 1?

12. Peak Roofing sent Jensen Builders an invoice dated July 12 for $5400 with terms 3/10, $1\frac{1}{2}$/20, n/45. Jensen made a payment of $2000 on July 20, and a second payment on August 1 that reduced the balance owed to $1000. What was the size of the second payment?

•13. On August 6, A&B Construction received a progress payment from one of its projects that will enable it to apply $10,000 to three outstanding invoices payable to A-1 Builders Supply. Invoice 535, dated July 16, is for $3228.56; Invoice 598, dated July 24, is for $2945.31; and Invoice 678, dated August 3, is for $6217.69. All invoices have terms 4/10, 2/20, n/60. If A&B makes a $10,000 payment to A-1 on August 6, what further payment on August 15 will settle the account? Note that A-1 applies payments to the oldest invoices first.

••**14.** Sutton Trucking made two equal payments, on June 25 and July 15, on an invoice for \$6350 dated June 15 with terms 3/10, 1/30, n/60. The payments reduced the balance owed on the invoice to \$1043.33. What was the amount of each payment?

••**15.** An invoice for \$2956.60, dated February 2, has terms 2/15, 1/30, n/90. What three equal payments on February 17, March 2, and May 2 will settle the account?

4.3 Markup

The amount a merchandising operation adds to the unit cost of an item to arrive at the selling price is known as the **markup** or **gross profit**. Thus,

Selling price = Unit cost + Markup

The markup must be large enough to cover a portion of the overall operating expenses (such as wages, rent, and utilities) and make a suitable contribution to the overall operating profit. Expressing this idea as a word equation,

Markup = Overhead expenses per unit + Operating profit[3] per unit

Let us define the following symbols:

$$\begin{aligned} SP &= \text{Unit selling price} \\ C &= \text{Unit cost} \\ M &= \text{(Amount of) Markup} \\ OE &= \text{Overhead or operating expenses per unit} \\ OP &= \text{Operating profit per unit} \end{aligned}$$

The algebraic counterparts of the preceding two word equations are

SELLING PRICE **(4-3)**

$$SP = C + M$$

MARKUP **(4-4)**

$$M = OE + OP$$

If we replace M in formula (4-3) by $OE + OP$, we obtain

SELLING PRICE **(4-5)**[4]

$$SP = C + OE + OP$$

Figure 4.5 is a pictorial representation of formulas (4-3), (4-4), and (4-5). It shows that SP may be viewed as being composed of C and M, or of C, OE, and OP.

---

[3] In accounting, the "operating profit" on a Statement of Earnings is the profit from normal business operations. Unusual revenues from the sale of capital assets or other nonrecurring events are not included. The "operating profit" in our discussion of markup corresponds to the operating profit from a Statement of Earnings, but calculated on a per-unit basis.

[4] In applications of formulas (4-3), (4-4), and (4-5) in this chapter, we will assume that OE and OP are constant over the range of sales being considered. In practice, economies of scale usually result in the operating expenses per unit decreasing as the sales volume rises.

Figure 4.5 *Relationships among SP, C, M, OE, and OP*

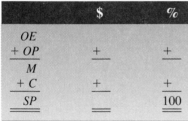

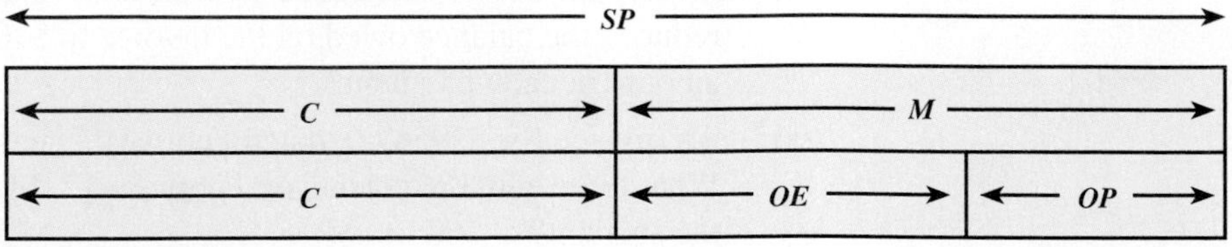

If a retailer is prepared to break even ($OP = 0$) to clear out old stock, then the reduced price in a clearance sale need cover only the unit cost and the unit overhead expense. That is,

$$SP(\text{break even}) = C + OE \qquad \text{and} \qquad M(\text{break even}) = OE$$

Managers in merchandising tend to think of an item's markup as a percentage of its cost and as a percentage of its selling price. In the "real world," the terminology is inconsistent and confusing in this area. We will use

$$\textbf{Rate of markup} = \frac{M}{C} \times 100\%$$

and

$$\textbf{Gross profit margin} = \frac{M}{SP} \times 100\%$$

When pricing merchandise, retailers tend to first decide upon the rate of markup for each product line. Then they calculate the corresponding dollar amount of the markup for each product and add it to the unit's cost.

	$	%
OE		
$+\ OP$	+	+
M		
$+\ C$	+	+
SP		100

The accompanying table is a useful aid for setting up and solving problems involving the pricing variables. Note that the first column impounds formulas (4-3), (4-4), and (4-5). Markup is the subtotal of OE plus OP. Selling price is the sum of M and C, which also makes it the sum of OE, OP, and C. Known dollar values of SP and its components may be entered in the centre column. In the third column, each component may be expressed as a percentage of SP. We can see that the first benefit of the table is in helping us to organize the given information.

The main advantage of working with the table is that, in comparison to working directly with formulas (4-3), (4-4), and (4-5), it is more apparent *which* quantity can be calculated next *and how* it can be calculated. Not only does the table "build in" the additive relationships of formulas (4-3), (4-4), and (4-5), it also assists us in setting up proportions. The ratio of any two items from the \$ column is equal to the ratio of the corresponding two items from the % column. The following examples will illustrate the utility of this table.

Example 4.3A Using Relationships Among Pricing Variables

Cal-Tire retails its regular tires at \$80 each and its high-performance tires at \$120 each. Cal-Tire purchases the tires from the factory for \$55 and \$85, respectively. Overhead expenses are 20% of the selling price. For each line of tires, determine:

a. The amount of markup.

b. The rate of markup.

c. The gross profit margin.

d. The operating profit per tire.

Solution

Enter the given information for each tire in its own table. The quantities to be determined in parts (a), (c), and (d) are indicated in the tables by the letters *a, c,* and *d,* respectively.

Regular tire

	$	%
OE	0.2*SP*	20
+ *OP*	+ *d*	+
M	*a*	*c*
+ *C*	+ 55	+
SP	80	100

High-performance tire

	$	%
OE	0.2*SP*	20
+ *OP*	+ *d*	+
M	*a*	*c*
+ *C*	+ 85	+
SP	120	100

An inspection of the tables reveals that *M* may be calculated immediately as the "plug" needed in the lower section of the $ column.

Regular tire:

a.
$$M + \$55 = \$80$$
$$M = \$80 - \$55 = \$25$$

b.
$$\text{Rate of markup} = \frac{M}{C} \times 100\% = \frac{\$25}{\$55} \times 100\% = 45.45\%$$

c.
$$\text{Gross profit margin} = \frac{M}{SP} \times 100\% = \frac{\$25}{\$80} \times 100\% = 31.25\%$$

High-performance tire:

$$M + \$85 = \$120$$
$$M = \$120 - \$85 = \$35$$

$$\text{Rate of markup} = \frac{M}{C} \times 100\% = \frac{\$35}{\$85} \times 100\% = 41.18\%$$

$$\text{Gross profit margin} = \frac{M}{SP} \times 100\% = \frac{\$35}{\$120} \times 100\% = 29.17\%$$

d. As values are calculated, they should be entered in the appropriate cells of the tables. After part (c), the tables appear as follows:

Regular tire

	$	%
OE	$0.2SP$	20
$+OP$	$+\quad d$	$+$
M	25	31.25
$+\ C$	$+\quad 55$	$+$
SP	80	100

High-performance tire

	$	%
OE	$0.2SP$	20
$+OP$	$+\quad d$	$+$
M	35	29.17
$+\ C$	$+\quad 85$	$+$
SP	120	100

From the % column of the table on the left, it is evident that

$$OP = (31.25\% - 20\%) \text{ of } SP = 11.25\% \text{ of } SP = 0.1125 \times \$80 = \$9.00$$

for the regular tire. Similarly, for the high-performance tire,

$$OP = (29.17\% - 20\%) \text{ of } SP = 9.17\% \text{ of } SP = 0.0917 \times \$120 = \$11.00$$

Example 4.3B *Using Relationships Among Pricing Variables*

The cost of a gas barbecue to a retailer is $245. If the retailer wants a gross profit margin of 30%, determine the amount of the markup and the selling price.

Solution

	$	%
OE		
$+OP$	$+$	$+$
M	$0.3SP$	30
$+\ C$	$+\quad 245$	$+70$
SP		100

Tabulate the given information. The 70% "plug" for C in the % column is then apparent. The table at this stage is as shown at the left. Do not expect to be able to determine a requested quantity directly. Instead, just start calculating any items you can until you obtain the one the question wants. If we construct a proportion equating the $ and % values for the ratio C/SP, the dollar amount of SP will be the only unknown. That is,

$$\frac{\$245}{SP} = \frac{70}{100}$$

After cross-multiplying and dividing both sides by 70, we obtain

$$SP = \frac{100 \times \$245}{70} = \$350$$

Finally,

$$M = 0.3 \times SP = 0.3(\$350) = \$105$$

The selling price after a markup of $105 is $350.

Example 4.3C *Using Relationships Among Pricing Variables*

A sporting goods store sets the selling price of baseball gloves to include overhead expenses of 25% of the selling price and a profit of 20% of the selling price. Determine the selling price and the rate of markup for a glove that costs the store $56.50.

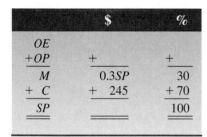

Solution

	$	%
OE	0.25SP	25
+ OP	+0.20SP	+ 20
M	0.45SP	45
+ C	+ 56.50	+
SP		100

Tabulate the given information. You may then add OE and OP to give values for M in both columns. The contents of the table at this stage are shown at the left. From the lower section of the middle column it is apparent that

$$0.45SP + \$56.50 = SP$$
$$\$56.50 = SP - 0.45\ SP$$
$$\$56.50 = 0.55SP$$
$$SP = \frac{\$56.50}{0.55} = \$102.73$$

Then

$$\text{Rate of markup} = \frac{M}{C} \times 100\% = \frac{0.45(\$102.73)}{\$56.50} \times 100\% = 81.8\%$$

The selling price of the glove is $102.73 after a markup of 81.8%.

The Connection Between the Net Price, *N*, and the Unit Cost, *C* In Section 4.1, we calculated the net price, N, after one or more trade discounts. In this section we have been using C to represent an item's unit cost. In most cases that we will encounter, C will be equal to N calculated for one unit.

There are two common situations in which C will not be equal to N. Since *cash discounts* for prompt payment are credited toward N, any cash discounts taken on the purchase of an item will make C less than N. Any *shipping charges* included in the invoiced amount are added to the net price after trade discounts. Therefore, shipping charges on purchases to inventory will make C greater than N. Unless a cash discount or shipping charges apply in a problem, assume that the net price (per unit) after trade discounts will also be the unit cost.

Concept Questions

1. Which will be the larger number: the rate of markup or the gross profit margin? Explain.
2. Is it possible for the gross profit margin to exceed 100%? Explain.
3. Is it possible for the rate of markup to exceed 100%? Explain.
4. Under what unusual circumstance will the rate of markup equal the gross profit margin?
5. Does a retailer break even if an item is sold "at cost"?
6. What sort of items in a grocery store will tend to have the highest markup rates?

Exercise 4.3

Answers to the odd-numbered problems are at the end of the book.

For Problems 1 through 6, determine:

- **a.** The amount of markup.
- **b.** The amount of operating (overhead) expenses.
- **c.** The operating profit or loss.
- **d.** The rate of markup.
- **e.** The gross profit margin.

Problem	Cost, C	Selling price, SP	Operating expenses, OE
1.	$30.00	$50.00	40% of cost
2.	64.00	96.00	25% of selling price
3.	55.65	79.50	30% of selling price
4.	17.50	29.75	50% of cost
5.	53.90	77.00	35% of selling price
6.	23.00	29.90	45% of cost

Calculate the missing values in Problems 7 through 14.

Problem	Cost, C	Overhead, OE	Profit, OP	Markup, M	Selling price, SP	Rate of markup	Gross profit margin
7.	$152.50	?	$15.35	$47.45	?	?	?
8.	51.30	$18.65	?	?	79.90	?	?
9.	?	308.00	?	435.00	1990.00	?	?
10.	?	?	2.45	?	19.90	?	50%
11.	?	11.25	3.75	?	?	?	38%
12.	8.89	?	1.37	?	?	90%	?
•13.	6.60	3.15	?	?	?	?	40%
•14.	?	?	0.14	?	0.95	150%	?

15. Computer Warehouse buys a printer for $380 less trade discounts of 20% and 10%. If the operating expenses are $57 per printer:

a. What should be the selling price to generate a profit of $33 per printer?

b. What is the rate of markup?

c. What is the gross profit margin?

d. What would be the break-even selling price for an inventory clearance sale?

16. Young Damsels orders a line of jeans at a suggested retail price of $58 less trade discounts of 30% and 7%. The manager intends to sell the jeans at the suggested retail price. If overhead expenses are 25% of the selling price:

a. What will be the unit operating profit?

b. What is the rate of markup?

c. What is the gross profit margin?

d. What would be the break-even selling price for an inventory clearance sale?

17. The rate of markup on a toaster selling at $54.95 is 45%.

a. What was the cost of the toaster to the retailer?

b. What is the gross profit margin?

18. Cuddly Pets purchased a litter of six puppies for $38.50 each. If the markup is 45% of the selling price:

a. What is the selling price of each puppy?

b. What is the rate of markup?

•**19.** If the markup on lettuce in a grocery store is 60% of the selling price, what is the rate of markup?

•**20.** The rate of markup on fresh peaches in a grocery store is 125% because of the large losses from spoilage and bruising while the peaches are in storage and on display. What is the gross profit margin?

21. The rate of markup on a line of cosmetics is 85%. If the markup on an eye shadow kit is $14:

a. What is the retail selling price of the kit?

b. What is the gross profit margin?

22. A hardware store's gross profit margin on a line of electric power tools is 27%. If the markup on a drill is $12.50:

a. What is the cost of the drill to the store?

b. What is the rate of markup on the drill?

•**23.** No-Nonsense Liquidators bought 250 pairs of gum boots at $15 per pair. In the first month, 165 pairs sold at the regular price of $29.50 per pair. Another 43 pairs sold in the second month at a "one-third-off" sale price. The remaining boots, consisting primarily of odd sizes, were cleared out in the third month at $14.95. The store's overhead is 40% of cost.

a. What was the break-even price on a pair of the boots?

b. What was the average rate of markup?

c. What was the total operating profit or loss on the sale of all of the boots?

•**24.** A florist buys potted poinsettias from a nursery at $15 each less 40% and 10%. The florist prices her stock to allow for overhead of 55% of cost and an operating profit of 20% of the selling price. At what price should she sell the poinsettias?

•**25.** Beaver Building Supply obtains 4- by 8-ft sheets of half-inch plywood from Macmillan Forest Products at $18 per sheet less 30% and 5%. The price is to be set to cover Beaver's overhead of 20% of the selling price and to provide an operating profit of 12% of the selling price. What should be the retail price per sheet?

4.4 Markdown

A **markdown** is a reduction in the selling price of an item. Retailers use markdowns for many reasons: to reduce excess inventory, to clear out damaged or discontinued items, or to increase sales volume during special "sale" events. Sometimes retailers will mark down a few popular items to or even below break-even just to attract additional customers who may also purchase other items. Grocery stores do this on a regular basis.

$$\text{Amount of markdown} = \text{Regular selling price} - \text{Reduced selling price}$$

In terms of the symbols

$$D = \text{Amount of markdown}$$
$$SP = \text{(Regular) selling price}$$
$$RSP = \text{Reduced selling price}$$

the word equation becomes

$$D = SP - RSP$$

The rate of markdown is the markdown calculated as a percentage of the regular selling price. That is,

$$\textbf{Rate of markdown} = \frac{D}{SP} \times 100\%$$

If the regular selling price and rate of markdown are given, you can calculate the reduced selling price using the basic discounting formula $N = L(1 - d)$ with

$$L = \text{Regular selling price, } SP$$
$$d = \text{Rate of markdown}$$
$$N = \text{Reduced selling price, } RSP$$

Example 4.4A *Using Relationships Among Pricing Variables*

Toby's Cycle Shop advertises a 20% markdown on an Alpine mountain bike regularly priced at \$445. Cycle City's regular selling price for the same model of bike is \$429.

a. What is the reduced price at Toby's?

b. What rate of markdown would Cycle City have to offer to match Toby's reduced price?

Solution

a. The reduced or marked-down price may be calculated using formula (4-1):

$$\begin{aligned} N &= L(1 - d) \\ &= \$445(1 - 0.20) \\ &= \$356 \end{aligned}$$

The reduced price is \$356.

b. In order to match Toby's reduced price, Cycle City must mark down its price by

$$\begin{aligned} D &= SP - RSP \\ &= \$429 - \$356 \\ &= \$73 \end{aligned}$$

The necessary rate of markdown is

$$\frac{D}{SP} \times 100\% = \frac{\$73}{\$429} \times 100\% = 17.0\%$$

A markdown of 17.0% will enable Cycle City to match Toby's reduced price.

Example 4.4B *Using Relationships Among Pricing Variables*

An item costing \$150 was marked up by 40% of the selling price. During the store's Tenth Anniversary Sale, the selling price was reduced to \$175. What was the regular selling price, and what was the rate of markdown during the sale?

Solution

	$	%
M		40
$+\ C$	+150	+
SP		100
$-\ D$	−	−
RSP	175	

For the more difficult problems, a table similar to that used in the example problems in Section 4.3 is very helpful. In this problem, OE and OP are not involved but D and RSP must be included. The table at left has omitted $OE + OP = M$ from the top of the first column but included $SP - D = RSP$ at the bottom. All figures in the % column are still expressed as a percentage of SP. The information given in the statement of the problem has been entered in the table.

In the % column, we can see that 60% is the "plug" in the addition. In other words, unit cost is 60% of selling price. After entering 60% for C, it becomes apparent that a proportion equating the \$ and % values of the ratio $\frac{C}{SP}$ may be constructed to solve for SP. That is,

$$\frac{\$150}{SP} = \frac{60}{100}$$

Hence,

$$SP = \frac{100}{60} \times \$150 = \$250$$

After entering $SP = \$250$ in the middle column, we quickly see that D is the amount which when subtracted from \$250 gives \$175. Therefore, $D = \$75$ and

$$\text{Rate of markdown} = \frac{D}{SP} \times 100\% = \frac{\$75}{\$250} \times 100\% = 30\%$$

The regular selling price was \$250 and the rate of markdown was 30%.

Concept Questions

1. Suppose an item that originally had a 40% rate of markup is marked down 40%. Is its reduced selling price equal to C? Explain.
2. If an item is marked down by the same percentage as the gross profit margin, will the reduced operating profit be positive, negative, or zero? Explain.

Exercise 4.4

Answers to the odd-numbered problems are at the end of the book.
Calculate the missing values in Problems 1 through 8.

Problem	Cost, C	Rate of markup	Gross profit margin	Selling price, SP	Markdown, D	Rate of markdown	Reduced price, RSP
1.	$185.00	50%	?	?	$60	?	?
2.	58.50	?	?	$ 95.00	?	30%	?
3.	?	?	50%	49.95	?	25	?
4.	580.00	30	?	?	?	30	?
5.	19.25	?	35	?	?	25	?
6.	249.00	?	25	?	?	?	$249.00
7.	?	75	?	395.00	?	40	?
8.	?	40	?	?	?	20	100.00

9. Patti's Lingerie marked up an article from its \$37.50 cost to \$59.98.

a. What is the rate of markup?

b. What is the gross profit margin?

c. What rate of markdown can be advertised if, at a later date, the price is reduced to the cost price for a clearance sale?

10. a. Merchant A operates on a rate of markup of 45%. If she later marks the price of a few items down to their cost price in order to attract additional customers to the store, what rate of markdown can she advertise?

b. Merchant B operates on a gross profit margin of 45%. If he later marks the price of a few items down to their cost price in order to attract additional customers to the store, what rate of markdown can he advertise?

11. The Ski Hut purchased Lampinen cross-country skis for \$96.80 per pair and marked them up to give a gross profit margin of 45%. When the skis were discontinued, the Ski Hut marked down its remaining stock by 35%. What was the sale price after the markdown?

12. The sign on a rack of sport coats reads: "All prices marked down 30%!" What is the regular selling price of a coat marked at:

a. \$100? **b.** \$196.49?

13. Merchants C and D sell the same article at \$69.95 and \$64.95, respectively. They both advertise that they will match the price offered by any other store on any product that they stock.

a. What discount rate must C give to match D's price marked down by 20% during a sale?

b. What discount rate must D give to match C's price marked down by 20% during a sale?

•14. A pharmacy marks up its springtime shipment of sunglasses to provide for overhead expenses of 40% of cost and a profit of 70% of cost. At the end of the summer, what rate of markdown can the pharmacy apply to the remaining inventory of sunglasses and still break even on sales at this level?

*4.5 Integrated Applications

The problems in this section bring together elements from two or more sections of the chapter. Consequently, their solution usually requires several steps and has a higher degree of difficulty.

For these more complex problems, the use of an extended version of the tables introduced in the preceding two sections pays even greater dividends. In Figure 4.6, the first five rows are just the table we used in Section 4.3. The next two rows (taking us from *SP* to *RSP*) were introduced in Section 4.4. The new feature added in Figure 4.6 is the last three rows for calculating the reduced operating profit, *ROP,* arising from the markdown. Since the unit cost, *C,* and the overhead expenses per unit, *OE,* do not change when a retailer marks down the price, then

$$ROP = RSP - C - OE$$

Figure 4.6 *Table Model for Solutions*

	$	%
OE		
$+\ OP$	+	+
M		
$+\ C$	+	+
SP		100
$-\ D$	−	−
RSP		
$-\ C$	−	−
$-\ OE$	−	−
ROP		

SP remains the base (100%) for all percentages in the % column. Examples 4.5A and 4.5B demonstrate the use of this model in solving more complex problems.

Example 4.5A *Using Relationships Among Pricing Variables*

Standard Appliances obtains Frigid-Air refrigerators for $1460 less 30% and 5%. Standard's overhead works out to 18% of the regular selling price of $1495. A scratched demonstrator unit from their floor display was cleared out for $1195.

a. What is the regular rate of markup?

b. What was the rate of markdown?

c. What was the operating profit or loss on the demonstrator unit?

d. What rate of markup was actually realized?

Solution

Standard Appliances' cost for one refrigerator was

$$C = N = L(1 - d_1)(1 - d_2)$$
$$= \$1460(1 - 0.30)(1 - 0.05)$$
$$= \$970.90$$

	$	%
OE		18
$+\ OP$	+	+
M		
$+\ C$	+ 970.90	+
SP	1495.00	100
$-\ D$	−	− b
RSP	1195.00	
$-\ C$	− 970.90	−
$-\ OE$	−	− 18
ROP	c	

Now construct a table similar to Figure 4.6. Enter all given values and the value calculated above for *C*. Parts (b) and (c) require us to calculate the quantities at locations occupied by *b* and *c* in the table.

a. The question is asking for $\frac{M}{C} \times 100\%$. We can see in the middle column how to obtain *M*.

$$M + \$970.90 = \$1495.00$$

Therefore,

$$M = \$1495 - \$970.90 = \$524.10$$

and

$$\text{Rate of markup} = \frac{\$524.10}{\$970.90} \times 100\% = 54.0\%$$

The regular markup rate is 54.0%.

b. In the middle column we observe that

$$\$1495.00 - D = \$1195.00$$

Isolating D on the left side of the equation gives

$$D = \$1495.00 - \$1195.00 = \$300.00$$

Hence

$$\text{Rate of markdown} = \frac{D}{SP} \times 100\% = \frac{\$300}{\$1495} \times 100\% = 20.1\%$$

The rate of markdown is 20.1%.

	$	%
OE		18
$+\ OP$	+	+
M	524.10	
$+\ C$	+ 970.90	+
SP	1495.00	100
$-\ D$	− 300.00	− 20.1
RSP	1195.00	79.9
$-\ C$	− 970.90	−
$-\ OE$	−	− 18
ROP		

c. The values determined as of the end of part (b) are included in the table. This part asks for the value of ROP. We need to fill in the value of OE in the lower part of the middle column before ROP can be calculated. In the % column, we are reminded that OE is 18% of SP. Therefore,

$$OE = 0.18 \times \$1495 = \$269.10$$

and

$$ROP = \$1195.00 - \$970.90 - \$269.10 = -\$45.00$$

The negative sign means that the store suffered a loss of $45.00 on the demonstrator unit.

d. The actual amount of markup at the reduced price was

$$M = OE + ROP = \$269.10 + (-\$45.00) = \$224.10$$

The rate of markup actually realized was

$$\frac{M}{C} \times 100\% = \frac{\$224.10}{\$970.90} \times 100\% = 23.1\% \text{ of cost}$$

Sales, Sales, and More Sales! Some merchants seem to have a sale of some sort going on almost all the time. A few "SALE!" signs around the premises help to induce curious shoppers to investigate potential bargains. Once in the store, the shopper may make other purchases. Some retailers initially price certain lines of merchandise in order to provide "room" for a substantial planned markdown in a future sale event. Some merchandise may sell at the high "regular" price, but the merchant fully expects the bulk of the sales volume to occur at the reduced price.[5] In such cases, the merchant may regard the ultimate marked-down price as the primary selling price that provides the "normal" unit operating profit.

Example 4.5B *Using Relationships Among Pricing Variables*

Fromme's Jewellers purchased sterling silver tea services for $960 each, less 35% and 15%. The "regular" selling price was set so that, in a "30% off" sale, overhead

[5] Mattresses are an example of a product line for which the majority of sales occur at a significant markdown from the "regular" price. The following footnote appeared in a display advertisement placed in a Victoria newspaper by one of Vancouver Island's largest furniture stores: "The reference to our 'regular selling price' is to a price at which goods are regularly offered for sale in our store and is not a representation that this is the price at which most of a product is actually sold."

expenses represent 25% of the sale price and the operating profit is 15% of the sale price.

a. At what price will a tea service sell in a "30% off" sale?

b. What was the "regular" price before the markdown?

c. If the last set in inventory is cleared out at 50% off the regular price, what will the operating profit be on that set?

Solution

Fromme's cost of a silver tea service was

$$\begin{aligned} C = N &= L(1 - d_1)(1 - d_2) \\ &= \$960(1 - 0.35)(1 - 0.15) \\ &= \$530.40 \end{aligned}$$

Construct a table similar to Figure 4.6. Enter all given values and the value for C.

	\$	%
OE		
$+\ OP$	+	+
M		
$+\ C$	+ 530.40	+
SP		100
$-\ D$	−	− 30
RSP		70
$-\ C$	− 530.40	−
$-\ OE$	$-0.25RSP$	−
ROP	$0.15RSP$	

a. The question is asking for RSP. We note from the lower part of the middle column that

$$RSP - \$530.40 - 0.25(RSP) = 0.15(RSP)$$

Solving for RSP,

$$RSP - 0.40(RSP) = \$530.40$$

$$RSP = \frac{\$530.40}{0.60} = \$884.00$$

b. We now want to calculate SP. We can use the proportion

$$\frac{SP}{\$884} = \frac{100}{70}$$

Then

$$SP = \frac{100}{70} \times \$884 = \$1262.85$$

The "regular" price of the tea service was \$1262.85.

	\$	%
SP	1262.85	100
$-\ D$	−	− 50
RSP		50
$-\ C$	− 530.40	−
$-\ OE$	− 221.00	−
ROP		

c. This part presents a new scenario—a markdown of 50%. We want the ROP at this markdown. We should start a new table as shown. The upper rows are not needed. The dollar amount of OE does not change if a discount is offered. Therefore, OE remains at

$$OE = 0.25(RSP \text{ in (b)}) = 0.25(\$884) = \$221.00$$

The "clear-out" price will be

$$RSP = 0.50(SP) = 0.50(\$1262.85) = \$631.43$$

As the middle column indicates,

$$ROP = \$631.43 - \$530.40 - \$221.00 = -\$119.97$$

Fromme's will lose \$119.97 on the last set.

POINT OF INTEREST

Misleading Price Representation

A few categories of consumer goods (expensive jewellery, for example) seem to be "ON SALE" so frequently or for so long that the consumer may wonder whether any significant volume of sales takes place at the "regular price."

Price representations usually fall under Section 52(1)(d) of the federal Competition Act. In layman's terms, the section states that any materially misleading representation as to the price at which a product is ordinarily sold is prohibited. The courts have interpreted "ordinary selling price" to include words and phrases (such as "Compare to . . ." or "x% off") used to give the impression that the implied comparison price is the price at which the product is ordinarily sold.

Section 52(1)(d) states that the quoted or implied ordinary selling price should be one of the following:

- The price at which the product ordinarily sells in the market area.
- The advertiser's own regular selling price, clearly identified by such words as "our regular price."

The comparison price should be sufficiently recent to have relevance. The "ordinary selling price" implied or quoted for comparison should be one at which the product has had significant sales, not merely a price at which it was offered for sale. The volume needed in order to be regarded as "significant" depends on the product and the market. However, the volume should have been large enough to justify a consumer believing that the markdown represented a genuine bargain or true savings. On the other hand, if the price of a product had been raised for a few weeks during which very few sales took place, then the merchant should not state or imply that the inflated price was the regular or ordinary selling price. Furthermore, the use of a "Manufacturer's Suggested Retail Price" or "Suggested List Price" can constitute deceptive pricing if this price was not the product's ordinary selling price.

Exercise 4.5

Answers to the odd-numbered problems are at the end of the book.

Calculate the missing values in Problems 1 through 6.

Problem	Cost, *C* ($)	Overhead, *OE*	Markup, *M*	Regular price, *SP* ($)	Rate of markdown	Sale price, *RSP* ($)	Reduced profit, *ROP* ($)
1.	115.70	20% of *SP*	35% of *SP*	?	25%	?	?
2.	?	18% of *SP*	$33\frac{1}{3}$% of *SP*	147.00	$16\frac{2}{3}$%	?	?
3.	37.25	? % of *C*	? % of *C*	59.60	?	41.72	− 2.98
4.	?	70% of *C*	150% of *C*	19.80	?	?	2.38
5.	?	50% of *C*	50% of *SP*	?	$33\frac{1}{3}$%	111.80	?
6.	420.00	? % of *SP*	? % of *C*	575.40	15%	?	11.55

•**7.** Hi-Lites Inc. purchased a ceiling fixture for \$480 less 40% and 25%, and marked it up 120% of cost. For its Fifth Anniversary Sale, Hi-Lites offered the fixture at 40% off.

a. What was the sale price?

b. At the sale price, what was the rate of markup?

•**8.** Long Lake Nursery bought fertilizer in bulk in March at \$18.60 less $33\frac{1}{3}\%$, $12\frac{1}{2}\%$, and 5% per 20 kg bag. The fertilizer is normally priced to give a gross profit margin of 55%. The fertilizer was marked down 45% for an inventory reduction sale in late July.

a. What was the sale price?

b. What was the (reduced) gross profit margin?

•**9.** Water Sports Ltd. pays \$360 less 25% for a backyard above-ground pool kit. Overhead expenses are $16\frac{2}{3}\%$ of the regular selling price, and the operating profit is 15% of the selling price.

a. What is the maximum rate of markdown the store can offer and still break even?

b. What is the profit or loss per unit if Water Sports clears out its remaining stock at 20% off in a Hot August Bargains sale?

•**10.** A lawn mower retails for \$349. The dealer's overhead is 25% of cost, and normal operating profit is $16\frac{2}{3}\%$ of cost.

a. What is the largest amount of markdown that will allow the dealer to break even?

b. What rate of markdown will price the lawn mower at cost?

•**11.** Rainbow Paints is discontinuing a line of paint that it purchased at \$30 less 45% and 10% per 4-litre pail. The store's overhead is 50% of cost, and normal operating profit is 30% of cost. If the manager of the store is prepared to accept a loss of one-quarter of the overhead expenses, what markdown rate can the store offer in order to clear out the paint?

•**12.** United Furniture buys reclining rocking chairs at \$550 less 40% and 10%. The price is marked up to allow for overhead of 50% of cost and profit of 35% of cost. The unit on display in the store acquired a stain. What rate of markdown from the regular price can the store offer if it is to recover only half of the unit overhead costs?

•**13.** Fashion Master purchased men's sweaters for \$72 less 40% and 15%. The normal gross profit margin is 40%, and overhead is 25% of the selling price. The sweaters were reduced to \$45.90 for the store's Boxing Day Blowout.

a. What was the rate of markdown for the sale?

b. What was the profit or loss on each sweater at the sale price?

c. At the sale price, what was the rate of markup?

•**14.** Mr. Vacuum obtains vacuum cleaners for \$360 less $33\frac{1}{3}\%$ and 15%. A demonstration unit regularly priced at \$375 was sold for \$225. The shop's overhead is 12% of the regular selling price.

a. What was the markdown rate on the vacuum cleaner?

b. What was the profit or loss on the sale of the demonstrator?

c. What rate of markup was realized at the reduced price?

•15. A discount furniture store bought a waterbed at the wholesale price of $665. The "regular price" of the waterbed is set so that, in a "20% off" sale, the gross profit margin is 30%.

a. What is the price of the waterbed in a "20% off" sale?

b. What is the "regular price" of the waterbed?

•16. A jewellery store purchased a diamond ring for $2500 less 40% and 5%. The "regular price" of the ring is established so that, if it is sold in a "20% off" sale, overhead expenses amounting to 20% of the sale price and unit operating profit amounting to 12.5% of the sale price will be covered.

a. What is the reduced price of the ring in a "20% off" sale?

b. What is the "regular price" of the ring?

••17. Sonic Boom obtained a stereo system for $2400 less 30% and 15%. The system was originally priced so that, when sold in a "20% off" sale, the store's overhead and operating profit represent 25% and 15%, respectively, of the sale price. In a Midnight Madness Special, the system was sold at a "$\frac{1}{3}$ off" special price.

a. What was the original "regular price"?

b. What was the profit or loss at the special price?

••18. Furniture Warehouse bought upright freezers for $1800 less $33\frac{1}{3}$% and 5%. The store's overhead works out to 30% of cost and its profit requirement to $16\frac{2}{3}$% of cost. The freezers are initially priced so that the required amount of markup is realized when a freezer is sold at a "15% off" price.

a. What is the initial rate of markup?

b. During its Scratch-and-Save sale, customers qualify for an extra discount of either 5%, 7%, or 10%. This extra discount appears when the customer scratches a ticket at the time of a purchase. It is added to the basic 15% discount, making the combined discount 20%, 22%, or 25%, respectively. What is the store's profit or loss per freezer at each of these discounts?

Appendix: Other Notations for Terms of Payment

END-OF-MONTH (EOM) DATING

In end-of-month dating, the discount and credit periods both begin at the end of the month in the invoice date. Figure 4.7 shows the invoice date, the end-of-month date, the discount period, and the credit period plotted on a time axis for the example 2/10 n/30, EOM. In this case the 2% cash discount may be taken in the first 10 days of the next month. If no credit period is explicitly stated, it is understood that the credit period ends 20 days after the discount period. Therefore, n/30 is implied in the notation 2/10, EOM.

Figure 4.7 *Discount and Credit Periods for the EOM Dating Case 2/10, n/30, EOM*

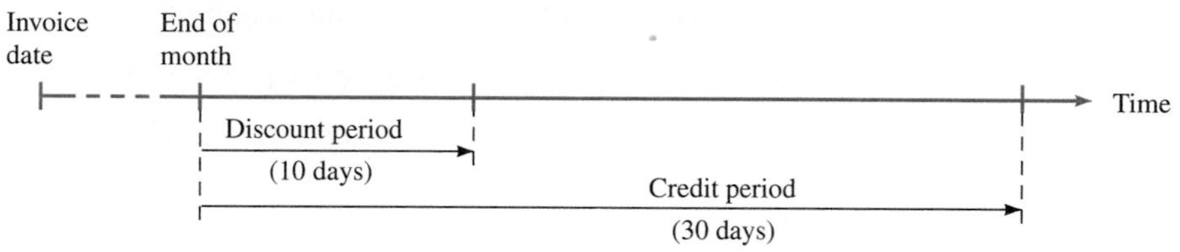

Example 4AA *Invoice Settlement with EOM Dating*

An invoice for $650.48 with terms $1\frac{1}{2}/10$, EOM is dated November 25. What payment will settle the invoice on:

a. November 28?

b. December 6?

c. December 10?

d. December 11?

Solution

a., b., c. The discount period ends at the end of the tenth day after the month's end. Payments made on or before December 10 qualify for the $1\frac{1}{2}\%$ cash discount. The payment required to settle the invoice is

$$\begin{aligned} N &= L(1 - d) \\ &= \$650.48(1 - 0.015) \\ &= \$640.72 \end{aligned}$$

d. Payment of the full $650.48 is required.

Receipt-of-Goods (ROG) Dating

When the goods being purchased are to be shipped over a long distance with an uncertain delivery date, receipt-of-goods (ROG) dating is sometimes used. Payment terms quoted in the form "2/10, n/30, ROG" mean that the discount and credit periods start on the date of receipt of the goods. Figure 4.8 shows the invoice date, the date of receipt of the goods, the discount period, and the credit period plotted on a time axis for the ROG dating example 2/10, n/30, ROG.

Figure 4.8 *Discount and Credit Periods for the ROG Dating Case 2/10, n/30, ROG*

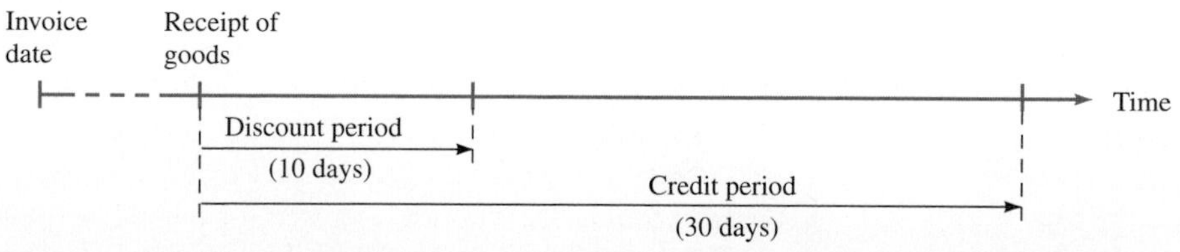

Example 4AB ROG Dating

An invoice dated November 25 for \$5340 with terms 1/15, ROG was received on December 1. The merchandise was shipped from Vancouver on December 15 and was received by the purchaser on January 8.

a. What is the last day of the discount period?

b. What is the last day of the credit period?

Solution

a. The discount period ends at the end of the fifteenth day after the date of receipt of the goods. January 23 is the last day of the discount period.

b. When a net period is not stated, the understanding is that the credit period ends 20 days after the end of the discount period. This makes February 12 the last day of the credit period. Any unpaid balance is due on that date.

Example 4AC Partial Payments with EOM Dating

Counter Culture Microbiological Labs received an invoice for \$3000 dated October 20 with terms 2/10, EOM.

a. What amount must Counter Culture pay on November 10 to reduce the balance owed by \$1000?

b. What will be the balance owed if Counter Culture pays \$1000 on November 10?

Solution

a. November 10 is the last day of the discount period. Any partial payment within the discount period qualifies for the cash discount. Using the adaptation of formula (4-1),

$$\begin{aligned}\text{Amount paid, } N &= \text{Amount credited, } L \times (1 - d)\\ &= \$1000(1 - 0.02)\\ &= \$980.00\end{aligned}$$

b.
$$\begin{aligned}\text{Amount paid} &= \text{Amount credited} \times (1 - d)\\ \$1000 &= \text{Amount credited} \times (1 - 0.02)\end{aligned}$$

$$\text{Amount credited} = \frac{\$1000}{1 - 0.02} = \frac{\$1000}{0.98} = \$1020.41$$

$$\text{Balance owed} = \$3000 - \$1020.41 = \$1979.59$$

Review Problems

Answers to the odd-numbered review problems are at the end of the book.

1. A 28% trade discount on a VCR represents a discount of $136.92 from the suggested retail price. What is the net price to the buyer?

2. The net price of an item after a discount of 22% is $155.61. What is the (dollar) amount of the discount?

◆ 3. Chicken Little Farms gives convenience stores a discount of 25% on eggs listed at $43.00 per case. What discount will Sunnyside Farms have to give on its list price of $44.50 per case to match Chicken Little's price to convenience stores?

4. The net proceeds to the vendor of a house after payment of a 4.5% real estate commission were $275,995. At what price did the house sell?

5. A merchant pays a 2.9% fee to the Royal Bank on all Visa sales.

   a. What amount will he pay on sales of $28,476 for a month?

   b. What were his gross sales for a month in which the bank charged fees totalling $981.71?

◆ 6. The evening news reports that the Vancouver Stock Exchange index dropped 0.9% on the day to close at 1098.6 points. How many points did the index fall?

7. At its current price of $1.10 per share, the price of Apex Resources stock is down 78% from its price one year ago. What was that price?

8. An invoice shows a net price of $199.16 after discounts of 22%, 7%, and 5% are deducted.

   a. What was the list price of the goods?

   b. What single discount would be equivalent to the discount series?

9. A uranium mining town reported population declines of 3.2%, 5.2%, and 4.7% for the three successive five-year periods 1980–84, 1985–89, and 1990–94. If the population at the end of 1994 was 9320:

   a. How many lived in the town at the beginning of 1980?

   b. What was the population loss in each of the five-year periods?

10. What total amount must be paid on May 4 to settle invoices dated April 20 for $650, April 24 for $790, and April 30 for $465, all with terms $1\frac{1}{2}$/10, n/30?

11. Omega Restaurant received an invoice dated July 22 from Industrial Kitchen Equipment for $3691, with terms 2/10, 1/20, n/45. Omega made payments of $1100 on August 1, $900 on August 10, and $800 on August 31. What amount was still owed on September 1?

12. Nelson Hardware ordered a shipment of gas barbecues at a suggested retail price of $459 less trade discounts of 25% and 10%. The manager intends to sell the barbecues at the suggested retail price. If overhead expenses are 20% of the selling price:

    a. What will be the unit operating profit?

    b. What is the rate of markup?

    c. What is the gross profit margin?

    d. What would be the break-even selling price for an inventory clearance sale?

◆ 13. If a grocery store's gross profit margin on tomatoes is 55%, what is the rate of markup on the tomatoes?

◆ **14.** Sunrise Building Supply obtains 4- by 8-ft sheets of wallboard from Canadian Gypsum at $15 per sheet less 30% and 10%. The price is to be set to cover Sunrise's overhead of 20% of the selling price and to provide an operating profit of 18% of the selling price. What should be the retail price per sheet?

◆ **15.** Ski 'n Cycle purchased Elan 200 skis for $246 per pair and priced them to give a gross profit margin of 40%. When this model was discontinued, the store marked down its remaining stock by 30%. What was the sale price after the markdown?

◆ **16.** A pharmacy marked up its sunscreen to provide for overhead expenses of 40% of cost and a profit of 45% of cost. At the end of the summer, what rate of markdown can the pharmacy apply to the remaining inventory of sunscreen and still break even on sales at the reduced price?

◆ **17.** A snowblower retails for $489. The dealer's overhead is 20% of cost, and normal operating profit is $16\frac{2}{3}$% of cost.

a. What is the largest amount of markdown that will allow the dealer to break even?

b. What rate of markdown will price the snowblower at cost?

Self-Test Exercise

Answers to the self-test problems are at the end of the book.

1. Specialty Builders Supply has two sources for the same power saw. Source A sells the saw at $196.00 less 20%, and Source B offers it at $186.60 less $16\frac{2}{3}$%. Which source is less expensive for the purchaser?

2. A trade discount of 22.5% from the suggested selling price for a line of personal computers translates to a $337.05 discount. What net price will a retailer pay?

3. Mr. and Mrs. Ogrodnik want to list their house at a price that will net them a minimum of $160,000 after a real estate commission of 5.5% of the selling price. Rounded to the nearest $100, what is the lowest offer they could accept on their home?

4. In addition to the regular trade discount of 25% and a volume purchase discount of $8\frac{1}{3}$% from a major manufacturer, Appliance Warehouse is offered a further 5% discount for orders placed in January.

a. What is the net price after all three discounts on refrigerators listed at $1195?

b. What is the list price on an electric range whose net price works out to be $470.25?

c. What single discount is equivalent to the three trade discounts?

d. What dollar amount of savings does the extra discount for January orders represent on a $1000 list price item?

5. In three successive years the price of the common shares of Bedrock Resources Ltd. fell 40%, 60%, and 70%, ending the third year at 50 cents.

a. What was the share price at the beginning of the three-year skid?

b. How much (in dollars and cents) did the share price drop in the second year?

6. Custom Kitchens received an invoice dated November 17 from Idea Cabinets Ltd. for $7260 with terms 3/15, $1\frac{1}{2}$/30, n/60. If Custom Kitchens made a payment of $4000 on December 2, what further payment on December 16 will settle the account?

7. A payment of \$500 on an invoice for \$887 reduced the balance owed to \$378.09. What cash discount rate was allowed on the \$500 payment?

8. What is the cost of an item that sells for \$87.49 if:

a. The rate of markup is 30%?

b. The gross profit margin is 30%?

9. Bosley's Pet Foods buys dog kibble for \$19.50 per bag less 40%. The store's overhead is $33\frac{1}{3}\%$ of the selling price, and the desired profit is 10% of the selling price.

a. At what price per bag should the dog food be sold?

b. At this price, what is the rate of markup?

c. What is the break-even price?

◆ **10.** The Pro Shop at Sunny Lake Golf and Country Club prices its golf club sets to allow for overhead of $33\frac{1}{3}\%$ of cost and profit of 20% of cost.

a. What is the regular selling price as a percentage of cost?

b. What discount rate can the Pro Shop offer to club members if it will accept half of the normal profit on member purchases?

◆ **11.** Central Ski and Cycle purchased 50 pairs of ski boots for \$360 per pair less $33\frac{1}{3}\%$ and 10%. The regular gross profit margin on the boots is 40%. The store's overhead is 22% of the selling price. During a January clearance sale, the price was reduced to \$270 per pair.

a. What was the rate of markdown for the sale?

b. What was the profit or loss on each pair of boots at the sale price?

c. At the sale price, what was the rate of markup?

Summary of Notation and Key Formulas

L = List price
d = Rate of trade discount
N = Net price

In the broader context of calculating the final amount after a percentage reduction to a beginning amount:

L = Beginning amount
d = Decimal equivalent of percentage reduction
N = Final amount after the reduction

The variables used in pricing and profit calculations are:

SP = Unit selling price
C = Unit cost
M = Amount of markup
OE = Overhead or operating expenses per unit
OP = Operating profit per unit
D = (Amount of) Markdown
RSP = Reduced selling price
ROP = Reduced operating profit per unit

Formula (4-1)	$N = L(1 - d)$	Finding the net amount or net price after applying a single rate of discount to the original amount or list price.
Formula (4-2)	$N = L(1 - d_1)(1 - d_2)(1 - d_3)$	Finding the net price after a series of three compound discount rates.
Formula (4-3)	$SP = C + M$	Selling price is the sum of the unit cost and the markup.
Formula (4-4)	$M = OE + OP$	Markup is the sum of the unit overhead expenses and the unit operating profit.
Formula (4-5)	$SP = C + OE + OP$	Selling price is the sum of the unit cost plus overhead expenses plus operating profit.

List of Key Terms

Cash discount *(p. 139)*
Credit period *(p. 139)*
Discount period *(p. 139)*
Gross profit *(p. 145)*
Gross profit margin *(p. 146)*
List price *(p. 132)*
Markdown *(p. 151)*
Markup *(p. 145)*
Net price *(p. 133)*
Ordinary dating *(p. 140)*
Partial payments *(p. 141)*
Rate of markdown *(p. 152)*
Rate of markup *(p. 146)*
Terms of payment *(p. 139)*
Trade discount *(p. 132)*

CHAPTER OUTLINE

LEARNING OBJECTIVES

After completing this chapter, you will be able to:

- Solve two linear equations in two variables
- Solve problems that require setting up two linear equations in two variables
- Graph a linear equation in two variables
- Perform linear cost-volume-profit and break-even analysis employing:
  - The contribution margin approach
  - The algebraic approach of solving the cost and revenue functions
  - A break-even chart

5

Applications of Linear Equations

A LARGE NUMBER OF QUANTITATIVE problems encountered in business may be described or simulated by linear equations. These range from one- and two-variable problems of the kind included in this book to applications in production, transportation, scheduling, and distribution involving dozens of variables. The procedure for solving linear equations in one variable was discussed in Chapter 2. In this chapter we move on to solving linear equations in two variables. An important application of linear equations is estimating the sales needed for a business to break even during a period of operations. We will examine this application (known as cost-volume-profit analysis) in considerable detail.

5.1 Solving Two Equations in Two Unknowns

Recall from Section 2.3 that there is only one numerical value that satisfies a linear equation in one variable. That value is called the *solution* to the equation. In contrast, a linear equation in two variables has an *infinite* number of solutions. For example, the equation $y = x + 2$ has solutions $(x, y) = (0, 2), (1, 3), (2, 4)$, and so on.

If, however, two linear equations in two unknowns must be satisfied *at the same time,* there is *only one solution.* In other words, only one pair of values of the two variables will satisfy *both* equations.

Algebraic Method for Solving Two Equations in Two Unknowns The goal is to combine the two equations in a way that will eliminate one of the two variables, leaving a single linear equation in one variable. We will illustrate a technique using the following pair of equations. The equations are numbered for ease of reference.

$$2x - 3y = -6 \qquad ①$$
$$x + y = 2 \qquad ②$$

It is legitimate to add the respective sides of two equations or to subtract the respective sides of two equations. For example, if we add equations ① and ②, we obtain $3x - 2y = -4$. Equation ① minus equation ② gives $x - 4y = -8$. Although legal, neither the addition nor the subtraction of the two equations has moved us closer to a solution—we have merely produced more equations containing two unknowns.

The insight that suggests a technique for solving the equations is that, if the numerical coefficient of x in equation ② had been 2, the subtraction ① − ② would produce an equation without a term in x. Furthermore, you can achieve this outcome if you multiply both sides of equation ② by 2 *before* the subtraction. Then the equations before subtraction are

$$\begin{aligned} ① \qquad & 2x - 3y = -6 \\ ② \times 2: \qquad & \underline{2x + 2y = 4} \\ \text{Subtraction gives:} \qquad & -5y = -10 \\ & y = \frac{-10}{-5} = 2 \end{aligned}$$

You can now obtain the solution for the other variable by substituting $y = 2$ into either of the original equations. Substitution into equation ① gives

$$\begin{aligned} 2x - 3(2) &= -6 \\ 2x &= -6 + 6 \\ x &= 0 \end{aligned}$$

The solution is $x = 0$, $y = 2$ or $(x, y) = (0, 2)$. You may verify this solution by substituting $(x, y) = (0, 2)$ into the equation that was not used in the preceding step. That is, substitute $x = 0$ and $y = 2$ into the left side of equation ② giving:

$$x + y = 0 + 2 = 2$$

Since the value obtained for the left side of equation ② equals the value of the right side, we have verified that $(x, y) = (0, 2)$ is the solution to the pair of equations.

Alternatively, you can solve the two equations by eliminating y instead of x. To eliminate y, multiply equation ② by 3, and then *add* it to the existing equation ①.

In general, it may be necessary to multiply *each* equation by a different number to set up the elimination of one variable. Suppose the objective is to eliminate x. You can always obtain identical coefficients for x in both equations by:

1. Multiplying the first equation by the coefficient of x from the second equation.
2. Multiplying the second equation by the coefficient of x from the first equation (in its original form).
3. Subtracting one equation from the other (with both in their new forms).

The following examples demonstrate the technique.

Example 5.1A Solving Two Equations Having "Nice" Coefficients

Solve the following pair of equations to three-figure accuracy. Check the solution.

$$7x - 5y = 3 \qquad ①$$
$$5x + 2y = 9 \qquad ②$$

Solution

To eliminate y, first make the numerical coefficients of y the same in both equations:

$$① \times 2: \qquad 14x - 10y = 6$$
$$② \times -5: \qquad -25x - 10y = -45$$

Subtracting the second equation from the first eliminates the variable y:

$$14x - (-25x) = 6 - (-45)$$
$$39x = 51$$
$$x = \frac{51}{39} = 1.308$$

Substitute this value for x into equation ② and solve for y:

$$5(1.308) + 2y = 9$$
$$2y = 9 - 6.538$$
$$y = 1.231$$

To three figures, the solution is $x = 1.31$, $y = 1.23$.

Check:
Substitute $x = 1.308$ and $y = 1.231$ into equation ①:

$$\text{LHS of ①} = 7(1.308) - 5(1.231)$$
$$= 3.002$$
$$= \text{RHS of ① to three figures.}$$

Example 5.1B Solving Two Equations Having "Nasty" Coefficients

Solve the following pair of equations to three figures. Check the solution.

$$1.9a + 3.8b = 85.5 \quad ①$$
$$3.4a - 5.1b = -49.3 \quad ②$$

Solution

$$\begin{aligned} ① \times 3.4: &\quad 6.46a + 12.92b = 290.7 \\ ② \times 1.9: &\quad 6.46a - 9.69b = -93.67 \\ \text{Subtract:} &\quad 22.61b = 384.27 \\ &\quad b = 17.00 \end{aligned}$$

Substitute $b = 17.00$ into equation ①:

$$1.9a + 3.8(17.00) = 85.5$$
$$a = \frac{85.5 - 3.8(17.00)}{1.9}$$
$$= 11.00$$

The solution is $a = 11.00$, $b = 17.00$.

Check:
Substitute $a = 11.00$ and $b = 17.00$ into equation ②:

$$\begin{aligned} \text{LHS of ②} &= 3.4(11.00) - 5.1(17.00) \\ &= 37.40 - 86.70 \\ &= -49.30 \\ &= \text{RHS of ②} \end{aligned}$$

Example 5.1C Creating and Solving Two Equations from a Word Problem

Whistling Mountain sells downhill skiing day passes at \$29 and cross-country skiing passes at \$8.50. If a day's total revenue from the sale of 760 passes was \$17,366, how many of each type of pass were sold?

Solution

Let d and c represent the respective numbers of downhill and cross-country passes sold.[1]

$$d + c = 760 \quad ①$$

[1] The solution to this problem can also be developed in terms of a single variable, say d for the number of downhill passes sold. Then the number of cross-country passes sold is $760 - d$. In the present context of solving two equations in two variables, we are choosing the two-variable approach.

The total revenue from the sale of both types of passes was

$$\begin{aligned} 29.0d + 8.5c &= 17{,}366 \quad ② \\ ① \times 8.5{:}\ \ 8.5d + 8.5c &= 6{,}460 \\ \text{Subtract: } 20.5d &= 10{,}906 \\ d &= 532 \end{aligned}$$

Substitute $d = 532$ into equation ①:

$$c = 760 - 532 = 228$$

On this particular day, 532 downhill skiing passes and 228 cross-country skiing passes were sold:

Check:
Substitute $c = 228$ and $d = 532$ into equation ②:

$$\begin{aligned} \text{LHS of ②} &= \$29(532) + \$8.50(228) \\ &= \$15{,}428 + \$1938 \\ &= \$17{,}366 \\ &= \text{RHS of ②} \end{aligned}$$

Example 5.1D *A Word Problem Giving Two Equations with Large Coefficients*

Westwood Orchard received \$1921.95 for its first shipment of 1530 kg of Macintosh apples and 945 kg of Delicious apples to the processing plant. Its second shipment, consisting of 2485 kg of Macintosh and 2370 kg of Delicious, resulted in a payment of \$3697.85. What was Westwood Orchard paid per kilogram for each variety of apple?

Solution

Shipment	Macintosh (kg)	Delicious (kg)	Total revenue ($)
1	1530	945	1921.95
2	2485	2370	3697.85

The details of each shipment are summarized in the table. Let M and D represent the price per kilogram that Westwood received for Macintosh and Delicious apples, respectively. The idea in words that provides the basis for constructing algebraic equations in terms of M and D is:

Revenue from Macintosh apples + Revenue from Delicious apples = Total revenue

Expressing this idea in algebraic terms for each shipment gives

$$\begin{aligned} 1530M + 945D &= \$1921.95 \quad ① \\ 2485M + 2370D &= \$3697.85 \quad ② \end{aligned}$$

Since multiplication by the numerical coefficient of either M or D will result in large unwieldy numbers, divide each equation by its own coefficient of M. This will make the coefficient of M equal to 1 in both equations and permit the elimination of M by subtraction.

$$\begin{aligned}
\text{①} \div 1530: &\quad M + 0.6176D = \$1.2562\\
\text{②} \div 2485: &\quad M + 0.9537D = \$1.4881\\
\text{Subtract:} &\quad -0.3361D = -\$0.2319\\
&\quad D = \frac{\$0.2319}{0.3361} = \$0.6900
\end{aligned}$$

To solve for M with the least amount of work, substitute $D = \$0.69$ into one of the modified equations.

$$M = \$1.2562 - 0.6176 \times \$0.69 = \$0.8301$$

Westwood Orchard receives 69 cents per kilogram for Delicious apples and 83 cents per kilogram for Macintosh apples.

Check:
Substitute $D = \$0.69$ and $M = \$0.83$ into equation ②:

$$\begin{aligned}
\text{LHS of ②} &= 2485(\$0.83) + 2370(\$0.69)\\
&= \$2062.55 + \$1635.30\\
&= \$3697.85
\end{aligned}$$

Example 5.1E A More Difficult Word Problem Involving Two Unknowns

An automotive supply store sells motor oil at \$3.20 per litre. In a one-day special promotion, it offers five litres for the price of four litres. At the end of the day, the revenue from the sale of 1171 litres of oil was \$3052.80. How many litres were sold at the regular price and how many were sold at the special promotional price?

Solution

Let

$$\begin{aligned}
r &= \text{Number sold at the regular price}\\
s &= \text{Number sold at the special price}
\end{aligned}$$

Then

$$r + s = 1171 \quad \text{①}$$

We can construct a second equation by expressing the idea that the total revenue from the sale of r litres at the regular price plus the sale of s litres at the reduced price is \$3052.80. That is,

$$(\text{Regular price}) \times r + (\text{Special price}) \times s = \$3052.80$$

In effect, the price per litre in the promotion was

$$\frac{4}{5} \times \$3.20 = \$2.56$$

Hence,

$$\$3.20\,r + \$2.56\,s = \$3052.80$$

Dividing both sides by \$3.20 will give r the same coefficient (1) that r has in equation ①. (This will set up a subtraction to eliminate the variable r.)

$$r + 0.8s = 954 \quad ②$$

If equation ② is now subtracted from equation ①, we obtain

$$s - 0.8s = 1171 - 954$$
$$0.2s = 217$$
$$s = 1085$$

Substitution of this value for s into equation ① gives

$$r + 1085 = 1171$$
$$r = 1171 - 1085$$
$$= 86$$

Therefore, the store sold 86 litres at the regular price and 1085 litres at the promotional price.

Exercise 5.1

Answers to the odd-numbered problems are at the end of the book.

Solve each of the following pairs of equations. Verify your solution in each case.

1. $x - y = 2$
$3x + 4y = 20$

2. $y - 3x = 11$
$5x + 30 = 4y$

3. $4a - 3b = -3$
$5a - b = 10$

4. $7p - 3q = 23$
$-2p - 3q = 5$

5. $y = 2x$
$7x - y = 35$

6. $g - h = 17$
$\frac{4}{3}g + \frac{3}{2}h = 0$

Solve each of the following pairs of equations to three-figure accuracy. Verify your solution in each case.

7. $d = 3c - 500$
$0.7c + 0.2d = 550$

8. $0.03x + 0.05y = 51$
$0.8x - 0.7y = 140$

9. $2v + 6w = 1$
$-9w + 10v = 18$

10. $2.5a + 2b = 11$
$8a + 3.5b = 13$

11. $37x - 63y = 235$
$18x + 26y = 468$

12. $68.9n - 38.5m = 57$
$45.1n - 79.4m = -658$

13. $0.33e + 1.67f = 292$
$1.2e + 0.61f = 377$

14. $318j - 451k = 7.22$
$-249j + 193k = -18.79$

15. The annual dues for the Southern Pines Golf Club are \$1070 for regular members and \$428 for student members. If the total revenue from the dues of 583 members for the past year was \$471,014, how many members did the club have in each category?

16. Product X requires 30 minutes of machining on a lathe, and Product Y requires 45 minutes of machining. If the lathe was operated for 60.5 hours last week for machining a combined total of 93 units of Products X and Y, how many units of each product were produced?

17. Marion bought five litres of milk and four dozen eggs for $13.97. Lonnie purchased nine litres of milk and three dozen eggs for $16.83. What were the prices for a litre of milk and a dozen eggs?

18. Tiny-Tot School purchases the same amount of milk and orange juice each week. After price increases from $1.10 to $1.15 per litre of milk and from $0.98 to $1.14 per can of frozen orange juice, the weekly bill rose from $42.20 to $45.85. How many litres of milk and cans of orange juice are purchased every week?

•19. Marcel and Maurice agree to invest a total of $83,000 in the M&M Appliance Repair partnership. If the partnership agreement requires Marcel to invest $8000 less than four-thirds of Maurice's investment, how much should each partner invest?

•20. Morton Office Supplies sent First United Church an invoice in the amount of $113.30 for three boxes of large envelopes and seven boxes of small envelopes. If a box of large envelopes sells for 50 cents more than twice the price of a box of small envelopes, what is the price of a box of large envelopes?

•21. In the first week of July a beer and wine store sold 871 cases of beer and paid refunds on 637 cases of empty bottles, for a net revenue of $12,632.10. For the following week the net revenue was $13,331.70 from the sale of 932 cases and the return of 805 cases of empties. What refund did the store pay per case of empty bottles?

•22. As a fund-raiser, a local charity sold raffle tickets on a trip to Disney World at $2 each or three for $5. In all, 3884 tickets were sold for a total of $6925. How many people bought tickets at the three-for-$5 discount?

•23. A convenience store sells canned soft drinks at $4.35 for a six-pack or 90 cents for a single can. If revenue from the sale of 225 cans of soft drinks on a weekend was $178.35, how many six-packs and how many single cans were sold?

•24. A partnership in a public accounting practice has seven partners and 12 accounting technicians. Each partner draws the same salary, and each technician is paid the same salary. The partners calculate that if they give the technicians a raise of 8% and if they increase their own salaries by 5%, the gross annual salaries for all accounting personnel will rise from the current $1,086,000 to $1,156,500. What are the current annual salaries of a partner and an accounting technician?

•25. A manufacturing firm pays monthly salaries of $3400 to each production worker and $2800 to each assembly worker. As the economy drops into a recession, the firm decides to reduce its total monthly manufacturing payroll from $253,800 to $198,000 by laying off 20% of its production workers and 25% of its assembly workers. How many layoffs will there be from each of the assembly and production divisions?

5.2 Cost-Volume-Profit and Break-Even Analysis

Cost-volume-profit analysis is a basic planning tool in business. It is a technique for estimating a firm's operating *profit* or net income at any sales *volume* given the firm's *cost* structure. The terms "operating profit" and "net income" will be used interchangeably in this chapter to refer to:

Total revenue − Operating expenses

Examples of "operating expenses" are cost of goods sold and overhead expenses.

Cost-volume-profit (CVP) analysis helps managers answer questions such as:

How will total costs, revenues, and operating profit be affected:

- If the firm sells 100 more units in the next operating period?
- If prices are raised by10%, resulting in the sale of 150 fewer units each month?
- If the occupancy rate in a hotel is increased by 5%?
- If the acquisition of a new machine reduces unit manufacturing costs but increases fixed costs?

A key component of CVP analysis is **break-even analysis**, to determine the break-even point where a firm's net income will be zero. In other words, the **break-even point** is the volume of sales at which the business will just manage to cover all costs.

Definitions and Assumptions

Basic cost-volume-profit analysis assumes that costs may be treated as either fixed or variable. A **fixed cost** does not change if sales increase or decrease. Examples include rent, management salaries, some forms of depreciation expense, and property taxes. **Variable costs** grow in direct proportion to the volume of sales. This means that, if unit sales increase by 10%, total *variable* costs will increase by 10%. (Total *fixed* costs will not change in this example.) Variable costs typically include materials costs and direct labour costs in manufacturing, or the wholesale cost of goods in retailing.

The definitions of fixed costs and variable costs have important implications for the cost of producing an additional unit. To illustrate, consider a case where the number of units sold by a business doubles from one year to the next. By definition, *total fixed* costs do not change but *total variable* costs in the second year are double the total variable costs in the first year. Therefore, each *additional* unit produced in the second year adds *no* fixed costs, but each *additional* unit adds the *same* amount of variable costs. We call this amount the **unit variable cost.** It can be calculated by dividing the total variable costs by the total units produced. To produce one more unit, the only additional cost is just the unit variable cost.

The initial assumption that costs may be classified as either fixed or variable appears at first to be unrealistic—we can readily identify costs that are neither strictly fixed nor purely variable. The compensation of sales personnel by a salary plus commission is an example of a *mixed cost* that has fixed and variable cost components. Some costs, referred to as *semivariable costs,* rise as sales volume increases but not in a proportional way. This pattern usually results from achieving economies of scale as the volume of production or sales increases.

Our simplified approach[2] to cost-volume-profit analysis may still provide useful insights in situations where these other types of costs are significant. The fixed and variable components of a mixed cost should be assigned to the respective fixed cost and variable cost categories. Semivariable costs may be approximated reasonably well by variable costs.

Other assumptions of CVP analysis are:

- The unit selling price remains the same regardless of sales volume. (The basic CVP analysis does not, therefore, accommodate volume discounts or price reductions during a sale or promotion.)
- Production volume equals sales volume. (Consequently, the business neither builds up nor runs down its inventory during the time frame of the analysis.)

In the following example, we describe a proposed business, analyze its costs, and begin to organize the given information in a form appropriate for CVP analysis. The symbols we need at this point are:

$$SP = \text{Selling price or revenue per unit}$$
$$VC = \text{Variable costs per unit}$$
$$FC = \text{(Total) fixed costs}$$

Example 5.2A *Determining SP, VC, and FC in Preparation for CVP Analysis*

Chuck is conducting a financial analysis for a neighbourhood pub that he is planning to open in a small shopping centre. The landlord is prepared to pay for the leasehold improvements, fixtures, and furniture, and to recover this extra investment through higher rent. The total rent will be \$4300 per month.

Three full-time cooks, each earning \$2200 per month, can cover the hours of operation. Six full-time-equivalent (FTE) servers will be sufficient to handle the expected 1500 to 3000 customers per month. They will receive the minimum wage, which works out to \$1200/month/FTE. If the number of customers exceeds 3000 per month, three more FTE staff will be required. Chuck will manage the pub but does not need to draw a salary for several months.

Other monthly expenses are \$150 for electricity, \$200 for natural gas, \$100 for telephone, \$900 for janitorial service, \$250 for the lease of a computer and cashier terminal, and \$200 for licences and miscellaneous fixed expenses. The annual insurance premium is \$1200.

Chuck's previous experience at another pub in the city indicates that, on average, each customer will buy 2.5 drinks at an average price of \$3.60, and will also spend \$6 on food. Drinks and food will be priced at three times the cost of the ingredients to the pub.

a. Classify the various costs as fixed or variable.

b. Determine values for

P, the revenue per customer
VC, the variable costs per customer
FC, the (monthly) fixed costs

if the number of customers is between 1500 and 3000 per month.

[2] A more thorough analysis of costs and a more rigorous treatment of CVP relationships is presented in a course in managerial accounting.

Solution

a. Fixed costs are those costs that remain the same, regardless of the number of customers per month. They include rent, salaries of the cooks, electricity, gas,[3] telephone, janitorial service, computer lease, licences and miscellaneous fixed expenses, and insurance. Over the range of 1500 to 3000 customers per month, the wages paid to the servers are also fixed costs.

Variable costs are costs that vary in direct proportion to the number of customers. In this example, the only variable costs are the expenditures by the pub on the ingredients for the drinks and food it serves.

b. Since each customer buys, on average, \$6.00 worth of food and 2.5 drinks at \$3.60 each,

$$SP = 2.5(\$3.60) + \$6.00 = \$15.00 \text{ per customer}$$

Since food and beverages are priced at three times the cost of ingredients,

$$VC = \frac{SP}{3} = \frac{\$15.00}{3} = \$5.00 \text{ per customer}$$

Monthly fixed costs are as follows:

Rent	\$ 4300
Salaries of cooks	6600
Wages of servers	7200
Electricity and gas	350
Telephone	100
Janitorial service	900
Computer lease	250
Licence and misc.	200
Insurance	100
Fixed costs (*FC*)	\$20,000

Contribution Margin Approach to CVP Analysis

Most managers use this approach for cost-volume-profit analysis. When variable costs were defined earlier in this section, we pointed out that variable costs *per unit, VC,* are the *same* for every unit. If one more unit is produced, *total* variable costs increase by *VC*. If one less unit is produced, *total* variable costs decrease by *VC*. In either case, total fixed costs remain at *FC*.

Imagine that you are doing a feasibility study for a new business. Based on your investigation, you have estimated values for *FC, VC,* and *SP*. Every unit produced adds *VC* to the total costs. (Clearly, *SP* must exceed *VC*—otherwise the business proposal is a "non-starter.") Next you want to examine the profitability of the business at various

[3] Arguably, electricity and gas are semivariable costs since more customers will mean more cooking, dishwashing, and so forth. However, the dependence on the number of customers is so weak that a fixed-cost assumption for these relatively small costs is reasonable.

levels of sales. Entrepreneurs and potential investors/lenders commonly begin by calculating the break-even point. This is the number of units that must be sold just to cover all costs. For the business proposal to merit further consideration, the volume of sales needed to break even should be attainable within a reasonable time frame.

Most managers find the following approach for break-even and profitability analysis to be the most insightful. Think of the revenue *SP* from each unit as having two components. One is the amount required to cover *VC,* the extra variable costs incurred to produce and sell that particular unit. The remaining part, $SP - VC$, is the amount available from *SP* to pay fixed costs and generate a profit. The name given to this component of *SP* is the **contribution margin,** *CM.* The contribution margin expressed as a percentage of the unit selling price is called the **contribution rate,** *CR.* That is,

CONTRIBUTION MARGIN

CONTRIBUTION RATE

(5-1)
$$CM = SP - VC$$
$$CR = \frac{CM}{SP} \times 100\%$$

In Figure 5.1, the small rectangle of size *SP* represents the revenue from selling a single unit. Its two components are *VC* and *CM.* The large rectangle represents the total fixed costs, *FC,* for the period of operations.

Figure 5.1 *Key Variables in Cost-Volume-Profit Analysis*

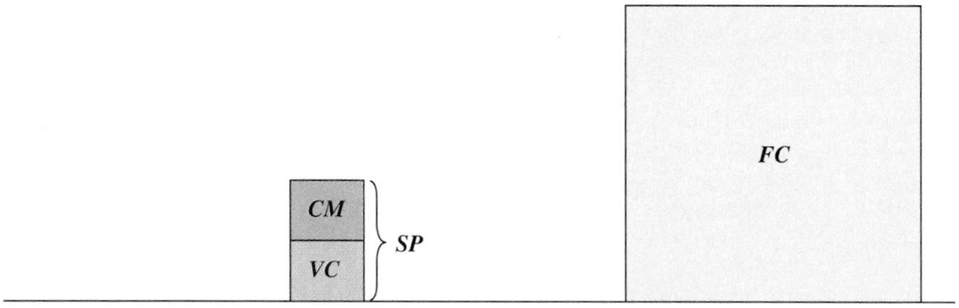

All fixed costs must be paid in order to break even. The amount available from each unit to pay fixed costs is *CM* only. In Figure 5.2, the *CM* from each unit is shown being applied to pay fixed costs. How many units must be sold to accumulate enough *CM*s to cover the entire *FC?* In other words, what is the break-even point?

Figure 5.2 *Using the Contribution Margin to Pay Fixed Costs*

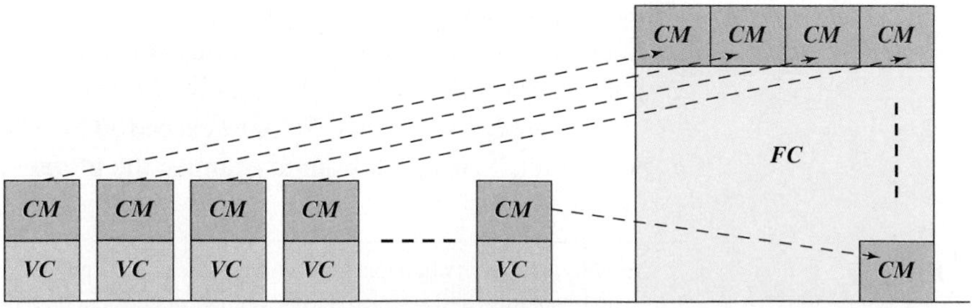

With each unit contributing CM toward the payment of fixed costs, FC, the number of units that must be sold just to break even is

$$\text{Unit sales at the break-even point} = \frac{FC}{CM}$$

For each unit sold beyond the break-even point, its entire CM goes toward profit (net income). To obtain an algebraic expression for the net income, let

X = Total number of units sold in the period
NI = Net income (or operating profit) for the period

Then

$$\begin{aligned} NI &= \text{Total contribution margin collected} - \text{Fixed costs} \\ &= (CM)X - FC \end{aligned}$$

NET INCOME **(5-2)** $$NI = (CM)X - FC$$

POINT OF INTEREST

Break-Even Analysis as Part of a Business Plan

The Royal Bank of Canada has published a series of booklets titled *Your Business Matters* to help entrepreneurs achieve their business goals. *Starting Out Right,* the first book in the series, emphasizes the importance of a thorough business plan.

> *"Completing a business plan requires that you compile information on yourself and other principals, the industry you're in and its key success factors, the market and competition, the history of your business, types and sources of financing, and its future prospects."*

Borrowing Money, the second book in the series, is aimed at entrepreneurs who are considering applying for a bank loan. It points out that:

> *"When you apply for a small business loan, you'll be asked for a great deal of information, most of which should be contained in one key document—your business plan. Not only does a plan show lenders that you have a firm grasp of your business, it's also your own road map for planning and running your enterprise on an ongoing basis."*

However, the book complains that:

> *"Fewer than one-half of small-business loan applicants approach their bank with a business plan in hand."*

One of the key elements recommended for the financial section of the business plan is:

> *". . . a break-even calculation indicating your variable costs, your fixed costs, and what you will be charging for each unit of your product or service. Only by calculating the level of sales at which your revenues equal your expenses will you know at what point your business is likely to be profitable."*

Example 5.2B CVP Analysis Using the Contribution Margin Approach

In Example 5.2A concerning the neighbourhood pub proposal, we found that

$$SP = \$15.00 \text{ per customer}$$
$$VC = \$5.00 \text{ per customer}$$
$$FC = \$20{,}000 \text{ per month}$$

for the range of 1500 to 3000 customers per month.

a. Calculate and interpret the unit contribution margin.

b. What is the break-even point in:
(i) customers per month? (ii) revenue per month?

c. What will be the monthly net income if there are:
(i) 1600 customers per month? (ii) 2300 customers per month?

d. How many customers per month are required for a net income of \$5000 per month?

e. If the average revenue turns out to be only \$13.50 per customer, how many customers per month will be needed to break even?

f. If the customer volume exceeds 3000 per month, the owner/manager intends to start drawing a salary of \$4000 per month and to hire three more servers at \$1200 per month. With these additional costs and an average revenue of \$15.00 per customer, what would be the monthly net income from 3500 customers per month?

Solution

a. The contribution margin per customer is:

$$CM = SP - VC = \$15.00 - \$5.00 = \$10.00$$

This means that, after covering unit variable costs (of \$5.00), each customer contributes \$10.00 toward the payment of fixed costs. Once the cumulative total of contribution margins reaches the fixed costs for the month (\$20,000), each *additional* customer will contribute \$10.00 to the net income (operating profit) for the month.

b. (i) With each customer contributing \$10.00 toward fixed costs totalling \$20,000, the break-even point is at

$$\frac{FC}{CM} = \frac{\$20{,}000}{\$10} = 2000 \text{ customers per month}$$

(ii) Since each customer generates an average revenue of \$15.00 per visit, the break-even revenue is 2000(\$15.00) = \$30,000 per month.

c. In general, $NI = (CM)X - FC$

(i) If $X = 1600$ customers per month,

$$NI = (\$10.00)1600 - \$20{,}000 = -\$4000$$

That is, the pub will lose \$4000 per month.

Note: A more intuitive approach to answering this part is to begin with the break-even volume of 2000 customers per month from part (a). For each

customer short of 2000, the pub will lose $CM = \$10.00$. If the pub falls 400 customers short of the break-even point, it will lose (\$10.00)400 = \$4000.
(ii) If $X = 2300$ customers per month,

$$NI = (\$10.00)2300 - \$20{,}000 = \$3000$$

Note: We can arrive at the same figure by noting that each of the 300 customers beyond the break-even point contributes \$10 to the net income. Hence the net income is \$3000 per month.

d. A net income of \$5000 must come from the \$10.00 contribution margins from customers above the break-even point (2000 per month). This requires

$$\frac{\$5000}{\$10} = 500 \text{ customers above break-even}$$

or a total of 2500 customers per month.
(Alternatively, the answer may be obtained by rearranging formula (5-2) to solve for *X*.)

e. Recall from the information given in Example 5.2A that the variable costs are the food and drink ingredients which amount to one third of the selling prices. Under the new scenario, $SP = \$13.50$ and $VC = \$13.50/3 = \$4.50$. The fixed costs remain at \$20,000. The contribution margin will be

$$CM = SP - VC = \$13.50 - \$4.50 = \$9.00$$

Now the break-even point is

$$\frac{FC}{CM} = \frac{\$20{,}000}{\$9} = 2223 \text{ customers per month}^4$$

f. In this scenario, *SP* and *VC* are at their original estimates but fixed costs are increased by \$4000 + 3(\$1200) = \$7600 to a total of \$27,600. In this case formula (5-2) gives

$$NI = \$10.00(3500) - \$27{,}600 = \$7400$$

With 3500 customers per month and the increased payroll, the net income will be \$7400 per month.

Example 5.2C *CVP Analysis Using the Contribution Margin Approach*

A manufacturing company is studying the feasibility of producing a new product. A new production line could manufacture up to 800 units per month at a cost of \$50 per unit. Fixed costs would be \$22,400 per month. Variable selling and

[4] The usual rules for rounding the mathematical result of 2222.22 would have us round down to 2222 customers per month. That number would actually leave us with a loss of about \$2. Because of the imperative to "pay the bills," we have rounded up to 2223 customers per month for the break-even point.

e. Recall from the information given in Example 5.2A that the variable costs are the food and drink ingredients, and that they amount to one-third of the selling prices. Under the new scenario, $SP = \$13.50$ and $VC = \$13.50/3 = \$4.50$. The fixed costs remain at \$20,000 per month. The net income equation becomes

$$NI = (\$13.50 - \$4.50)X - \$20{,}000 = \$9X - \$20{,}000$$

The break-even point where $NI = 0$ is at

$$X = \frac{\$20{,}000}{\$9} = 2223 \text{ customers per month}$$

f. In this scenario, SP and VC are at their original estimates but fixed costs are increased by $\$4000 + 3(\$1200) = \$7600$ to \$27,600 per month. In this case, the third equation gives

$$NI = (\$10)3500 - \$27{,}600 = \$7400$$

With 3500 customers per month and the increased payroll, the net income will be \$7400 per month.

Example 5.2G *CVP Analysis Using the Revenue and Cost Function Approach*

A manufacturing company is studying the feasibility of producing a new product. A new production line could manufacture up to 800 units per month at a cost of \$50 per unit. Fixed costs would be \$22,400 per month. Variable selling and shipping costs are estimated to be \$20 per unit. Market research indicates that a unit price of \$110 would be competitive.

a. What is the break-even point as a percent of capacity?

b. What would be the net income at 90% of capacity?

c. What would unit sales have to be to attain a net income of \$9000 per month?

d. In a serious recession sales might fall to 55% of capacity. What would be the resulting net income?

e. What dollar amount of sales would result in a loss of \$2000 per month?

f. In the highest cost scenario, fixed costs might be \$25,000, production costs might be \$55 per unit, and selling and shipping costs might be \$22 per unit. What would the break-even point be in these circumstances?

Solution

In the expected scenario, $SP = \$110$, $VC = \$50 + \$20 = \$70$, and $FC = \$22{,}400$. Hence,

$$TR = \$110X$$
$$TC = \$70X + \$22{,}400$$
$$NI = \$40X - \$22{,}400$$

a. Using formula (5-3a),

$$\text{Break-even volume} = \frac{FC}{SP - VC} = \frac{\$22{,}400}{\$110 - \$70} = 560 \text{ units}$$

This represents

$$\frac{560}{800} \times 100\% = 70\% \text{ of capacity}$$

b. At 90% of capacity, production would be 0.9 × 800 = 720 units per month. Using the third equation,

$$NI = \$40(720) - \$22{,}400 = \$6400 \text{ per month}$$

c. Setting NI = \$9000 in the third equation, we obtain

$$\$9000 = \$40X - \$22{,}400$$

Unit sales would have to be $X = \dfrac{\$9000 + \$22{,}400}{\$40} = 785$ per month.

d. In the recession scenario, unit sales would be 0.55 × 800 = 440 per month. Then

$$NI = (\$40)440 - \$22{,}400 = -\$4800$$

The company would lose \$4800 per month in the recession.

e. Substituting NI = −\$2000 per month in the third equation,

$$-\$2000 = \$40X - \$22{,}400$$

$$X = \frac{-\$2000 + \$22{,}400}{\$40} = 510 \text{ units per month}$$

The dollar amount of sales would be

$$TR = (\$110)X = (\$110)510 = \$56{,}100$$

f. In the highest cost scenario, FC = \$25,000 and VC = \$77 per unit. Then

$$\text{Break-even volume} = \frac{FC}{SP - VC} = \frac{\$25{,}000}{\$110 - \$77} = 758 \text{ units}$$

The break-even point in this scenario would be at 758 units per month (94.75% of capacity).

Example 5.2H CVP Analysis with Sales Volume in Dollars Instead of Units

Last year Marconi Printing had total sales of \$375,000 while operating at 75% of capacity. The total of its variable costs was \$150,000. Fixed costs were \$180,000.

a. What is Marconi's break-even point expressed:
(i) in dollars of sales? (ii) as a percent of capacity?

b. If the current prices, cost structure, and product mix are the same as last year's, what net income can be expected from sales of \$450,000 in the current year?

Solution

In this situation, we let $SP = \$1$ and then X represents the number of \$1 units sold. The revenue function is simply

$$TR = \$1X$$

In the cost function, $TC = (VC)X + FC$, VC must be interpreted as the variable cost per \$1 of sales. In the present case,

$$VC = \frac{\text{Total variable costs}}{\text{Total unit sales}} = \frac{\$150{,}000}{375{,}000} = \$0.40$$

Then

$$TC = \$0.40X + \$180{,}000$$

and

$$NI = (\$1.00 - \$0.40)X - \$180{,}000 = \$0.60X - \$180{,}000$$

a. (i) Setting $NI = 0$ in the net income equation, we obtain

$$\text{Break-even point} = \frac{\$180{,}000}{\$0.60} = 300{,}000 \text{ units}$$

Since each unit is deemed to sell at \$1, Marconi will break even on sales of \$300,000.

(ii) If sales of \$375,000 represents 75% of capacity, then

$$\text{Full capacity} = \frac{\$375{,}000}{0.75} = \$500{,}000 \text{ of sales}$$

The break-even point of \$300,000 of sales represents

$$\frac{\$300{,}000}{\$500{,}000} \times 100\% = 60\% \text{ of capacity}$$

b. Substitute $X = 450{,}000$ in the net income equation.

$$NI = \$0.60(450{,}000) - \$180{,}000 = \$90{,}000$$

Sales of \$450,000 in the current year should produce a net income of \$90,000.

Concept Questions

1. A company's sales revenue decreased by 15% from one operating period to the next. Assuming no change in the prices of its inputs and outputs, by what percentage did:

   a. Fixed costs change? **b.** Total variable costs change?

2. What effect will each of the following have on a product's unit contribution margin? In each case, assume that all other variables remain unchanged.

   a. The business raises the selling price of the product.

   b. The prices of some raw materials used in manufacturing decrease.

c. The local regional government increases the business's property tax.

d. The company's president is given a raise.

e. The production workers receive a raise in their hourly rate.

3. Once a business is operating beyond the break-even point, why doesn't each additional dollar of revenue add a dollar to net income?

Exercise 5.2

Answers to the odd-numbered problems are at the end of the book.

1. A small manufacturing operation can produce up to 250 units per week of a product that it sells for \$20 per unit. The variable cost per unit is \$12, and the fixed cost per week is \$1200.

a. What is the contribution margin per unit?

b. How many units must it sell per week to break even?

c. Determine the firm's weekly profit or loss if it sells:

(i) 120 units per week (ii) 250 units per week

d. At what level of sales will the net income be \$400 per week?

2. Valley Peat Ltd. sells peat moss for \$10 per bag. Variable costs are \$7.50 per bag and annual fixed costs are \$100,000.

a. What are the contribution margin and the contribution ratio?

b. How many bags of peat must be sold to break even?

c. What will be the net income for a year in which 60,000 bags of peat are sold?

d. How many bags must be sold for a net income of \$60,000 in a year?

e. What annual sales in terms of bags and in terms of dollars would produce a loss of \$10,000?

f. How much do the break-even unit sales and break-even revenue increase per \$1000 increase in annual fixed costs?

3. Reflex Manufacturing Corp. manufactures borgels at a unit variable cost of \$43. It sells them for \$70 each. It can produce a maximum of 3200 borgels per month. Annual fixed costs total \$648,000.

a. What is the contribution margin per unit?

b. What is the break-even volume?

c. What is the monthly net income at a volume of 2500 borgels per month?

d. What is the monthly net income if Reflex operates at 50% of capacity during a recession?

e. At what percent utilization would the annual net income be \$226,800?

f. If fixed and variable costs remain the same, how much do the monthly break-even unit sales change for a \$1 increase in the selling price?

4. Bentley Plastics Ltd. has annual fixed costs of \$450,000, variable costs of \$15 per unit, and a contribution rate of 40%.

a. What annual revenue is required to break even?

b. What annual unit sales are required to break even?

c. What will be the annual net income at annual sales of:

(i) 50,000 units? (ii) $1,000,000?

d. What minimum annual unit sales are required to limit the annual loss to $50,000?

e. If the unit selling price and fixed costs remain the same, what are the changes in break-even unit sales and break-even revenue for a $1 increase in variable costs?

•**5.** Calculate the missing quantities:

Part	Sales ($)	Variable costs ($)	Contribution margin ($)	Fixed costs ($)	Net income ($)	Unit sales
a.	400,000	?	20	100,000	60,000	?
b.	?	60,000	10	?	12,500	4000
c.	360,000	?	?	90,000	60,000	5000

•**6.** Calculate the missing quantities:

Part	Sales ($)	Variable costs ($)	Contribution rate (%)	Fixed costs ($)	Net income ($)
a.	800,000	?	40	?	100,000
b.	450,000	360,000	?	?	47,500
c.	?	?	30	180,000	120,000

•**7.** A college ski club is planning a weekend package for its members. The members will each be charged $135. For a group of 15 or more, the club can purchase a two-day downhill pass and two nights' accommodation for $110 per person. A 36-passenger capacity bus can be chartered for $700.

a. How many must sign up for the package for all costs to be covered?

b. If the bus is filled, how much profit will the club make?

c. If the student government agrees to cover any loss up to $200, what is the minimum number of participants required?

•**8.** Genifax reported the following information for September:

Sales	$180,000
Fixed manufacturing costs	22,000
Fixed marketing and overhead costs	14,000
Total variable costs	120,000
Unit price	9

a. Determine the unit sales required to break even.

b. What unit sales would generate a net income of $30,000?

c. What unit sales would generate a profit of 20% of the sales dollars?

d. What sales dollars are required to produce a profit of $20,000?

e. If unit variable costs are reduced by 10% with no change in the fixed costs, what will the break-even point become?

•**9.** The social committee of a college's student government is planning the annual graduation dinner and dance. The preferred band can be signed for \$500 plus 10% of ticket revenues. A hall can be rented for \$2200. Fire regulations limit the hall to 400 guests plus the band and caterers. A food caterer has quoted a price of \$12 per person for the dinner.

The committee thinks that the event will be a sellout if ticket prices are set at \$23 per person. Some on the committee are in favour of less crowding at the dance and argue for a ticket price of \$28. They estimate that 300 will attend at the higher price.

a. Calculate the number of tickets that need to be sold at each price to break even.

b. What will the profit be at the predicted sales at each ticket price?

•**10.** This problem is designed to illustrate how the relative proportions of fixed and variable costs affect a firm's net income when the sales volume changes.

Two hypothetical firms, A and B, manufacture and sell the same product at the same price of \$50. Firm A is highly mechanized with monthly fixed costs of \$4000 and unit variable costs of \$10. Firm B is labour-intensive and can readily lay off or take on more workers as production requirements warrant. B's monthly fixed costs are \$1000, and its unit variable costs are \$40.

a. Calculate the break-even volume for both firms.

b. At each firm's break-even point, calculate the proportion of the firm's total costs that are fixed and the proportion that are variable.

c. For a 10% increase in sales above the break-even point, calculate the dollar increase in each firm's net income. Explain the differing results.

d. For a 10% decrease in sales below the break-even point, calculate the dollar decrease in each firm's net income. Explain the differing results.

e. What is each firm's net income at sales of 150 units per month and each firm's loss at sales of 50 units per month?

•**11.** In the year just ended, a small appliance manufacturer sold its griddle at the wholesale price of \$37.50. The unit variable costs were \$13.25, and the monthly fixed costs were \$5600.

a. If unit variable costs are expected to rise to \$15.00 and fixed costs to \$6000 per month for the next year, at what amount should the griddle be priced in order to have the same break-even volume as last year?

b. What should be the griddle's price in order to have the same profit as last year on sales of 300 griddles per month in both years?

•**12.** Mickey's Restaurant had a net income last year of \$40,000 after fixed costs of \$130,000 and total variable costs of \$80,000.

a. What was the restaurant's break-even point in sales dollars?

b. If fixed costs in the current year rise to \$140,000 and variable costs remain at the same percentage of sales as for last year, what will be the break-even point?

c. What sales in the current year will result in a profit of \$50,000?

•**13.** A farmer is trying to decide whether to rent his neighbour's land to grow additional hay for sale to feedlots at \$90 per delivered tonne. The land can be rented at \$200 per hectare for the season. Cultivation and planting will cost \$300 per hectare; spraying and fertilizer will cost \$225 per hectare. It will cost \$21 per tonne to cut, condition, and bale the hay, and \$12 per tonne to transport it to the feedlots.

a. How many tonnes per hectare must be produced to break even?

b. How much is the break-even tonnage lowered if the selling price is \$5 per tonne higher?

c. What is the profit or loss at the \$90 per tonne price if the crop yield is:

(i) 15 tonnes per hectare?

(ii) 10 tonnes per hectare?

•**14.** A sporting goods manufacturer lost \$400,000 on sales of \$3 million in a year during the last recession. The production lines operated at only 60% of capacity during the year. Variable costs represent one-third of the sales dollars.

a. At what percent of capacity must the firm operate in order to break even?

b. What would its net income be at 80% of capacity?

c. What dollar sales would generate a net income of \$700,000?

d. How much does each additional dollar of sales increase the net income?

e. How much does a \$1 increase in fixed costs raise the break-even sales?

*5.3 Introduction to Graphical Techniques

The relationship between two variables may be presented in a variety of ways. Three common methods are:

- A table listing pairs of values of the two variables.
- An algebraic equation involving the two variables.
- A graph depicting the relationship between the two variables.

The graphical presentation is best for quickly giving an impression of the nature of the relationship between the two variables. It also allows a user to *quickly estimate* the value of one variable that corresponds to any selected value of the other variable.

An algebraic equation has the advantage of expressing the relationship with the greatest degree of precision. Graphical analysis is usually limited to three-figure precision.

Graphing a Linear Equation in Two Unknowns

The notation used to indicate that a mathematical relationship exists between two variables is

$$y = f(x)$$

which is read "y is a function of x." A pair of numerical values of the variables, customarily written in the order (x, y), is said to *satisfy* the equation if the two sides of the equation are equal after substitution of the values.

A single pair of (x, y) values gives a point when plotted on graph paper. In the context of graphing, this pair of values is called the *coordinates* of the point. A graph of the equation $y = f(x)$ is a plot of all pairs of (x, y) values within a certain range that satisfy the equation. Conversely, if the x-coordinate and the y-coordinate of *any* point on a plotted curve are substituted into the corresponding algebraic equation, both sides of the equation will have the same numerical value.

In practice, we obtain the graph of an equation through the following steps:

1. Construct a *table of values* consisting of pairs of (x, y) values that satisfy the equation. Each pair is obtained by assigning a value to one variable and then solving the resulting equation in one unknown for the other variable.
2. Construct and label the x-axis and the y-axis to accommodate the range of values in the table.
3. Plot the (x, y) pairs from the table as the (x, y) coordinates of points on the graph.
4. Connect the plotted points with a *smooth* curve.

Example 5.3A *Graphing a Linear Equation in Two Variables*

Graph the equation $2x - 3y = -6$ over the range $x = -6$ to $x = 6$.

Solution

The first step listed above is to construct a table of values. Since the range over which the graph is to be plotted is specified in terms of x, it is natural to assign to x a series of values covering the range. Since we will be repeatedly solving the equation for y, we should rearrange the equation so that y is isolated on one side.

Transposing $2x$ to the right side and dividing both sides by -3, we obtain

$$y = \frac{2}{3}x + 2$$

Now substitute a few values for x over the range $x = -6$ to $x = 6$:

$$x = -6: \quad y = \frac{2}{3}(-6) + 2 = -2$$

$$x = -3: \quad y = \frac{2}{3}(-3) + 2 = 0$$

$$x = 0: \quad y = \frac{2}{3}(0) + 2 = 2$$

$$x = 3: \quad y = \frac{2}{3}(3) + 2 = 4$$

$$x = 6: \quad y = \frac{2}{3}(6) + 2 = 6$$

The table of values summarizing these (x, y) pairs is:

x:	−6	−3	0	3	6	← Assigned x value
y:	−2	0	2	4	6	← Calculated y value

The next step is to draw axes, with the x-axis including the range from -6 to $+6$ and the y-axis encompassing the range from -2 to $+6$. The five points can then be plotted and a smooth curve drawn to connect the points.

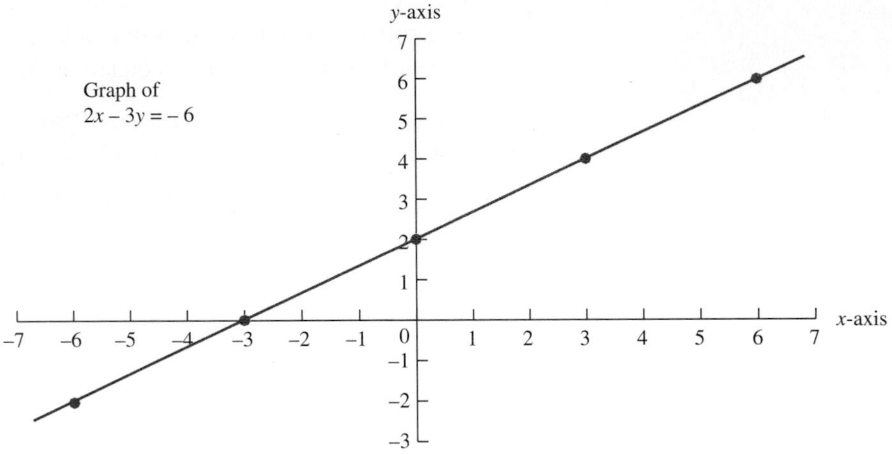

The most notable feature about the graph is that the plotted points fall on a straight line. This is a general outcome for linear equations in two variables and, of course, is the reason they are called *linear* equations.

TIPS

- To construct the graph of a *linear* equation, it is sufficient to have just two (x, y) pairs in the table of values.
- For the best precision in constructing the graph of a linear equation, the two points used should be near the ends of the range over which the graph is to be drawn.
- The easiest (x, y) pair to determine comes from assigning the value 0 to x.
- If x has a fractional coefficient, assign values to x that are a multiple of the coefficient's denominator. This makes the calculations easier and is likely to yield "nicer" values to plot for y. In the preceding example, we used values for x that were multiples of 3.

Example 5.3B *Graphing a Linear Equation in Two Variables*

Graph the equation $3y - 150x = 24{,}000$ over the range $x = 0$ to $x = 200$.

Solution

$$3y = 150x + 24{,}000$$

Divide both sides by 3 to isolate y on the left side of the equation:

$$y = 50x + 8000$$

Construct a table of values[5] for the range of x:

$$x = 0: \quad y = 50(0) + 8000 = 8000$$
$$x = 100: \quad y = 50(100) + 8000 = 13{,}000$$
$$x = 200: \quad y = 50(200) + 8000 = 18{,}000$$

x:	0	100	200
y:	8000	13,000	18,000

Construct and label the axes. Then plot the points.

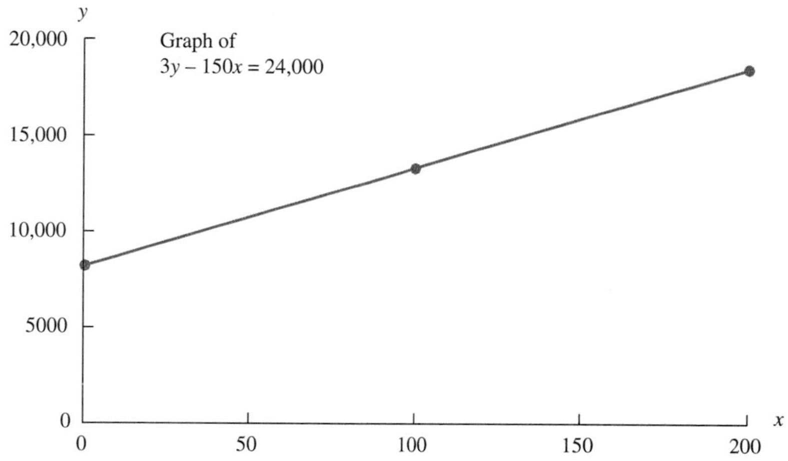

Graphical Approach to Cost-Volume-Profit Analysis

This approach requires that both the cost function and the revenue function be plotted on the same graph as in Figure 5.3. Such a graph is called a **break-even chart** because the sales volume at which the business will break even is immediately apparent.

The intersection of the *TR* and *TC* lines is the only point at which total revenue equals total costs, and the firm breaks even. This intersection is therefore called the *break-even point.* The coordinates of the point give the sales volume and total revenue required for the firm to break even. At higher sales, the business will show a profit because the revenue line is above the total cost line. The profit equals the vertical separation of the lines. At any sales volume to the left of the break-even point, total costs exceed total revenue. The size of the loss is determined by the vertical separation of the two lines. At zero sales volume, there are no revenues or variable costs, but the business still incurs the fixed costs.

[5] Although two points are sufficient to define the line, plotting a third point provides a check of the calculation. If the three points do not all fall on a straight line, then at least one mistake has been made in calculating the coordinates of the points or in plotting the points.

Figure 5.3 *Break-Even Chart*

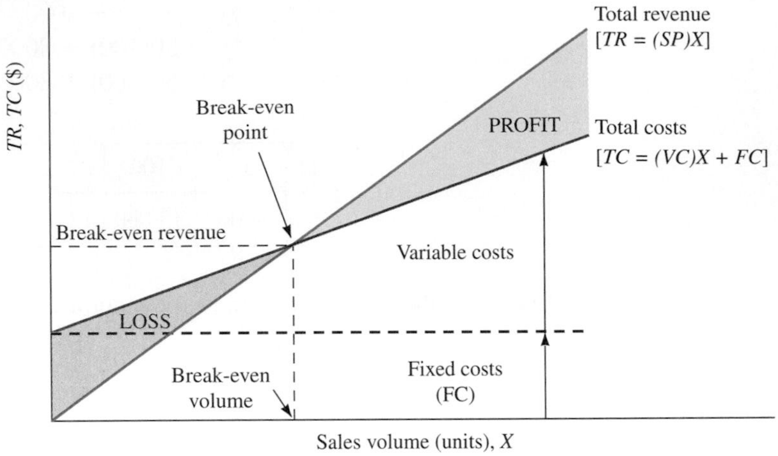

Example 5.3C *Graphical CVP Analysis of the Business Described in Example 5.2A*

We will use the data presented in Example 5.2A for the neighbourhood pub proposal. There it was determined that $SP = \$15$, $VC = \$5$, and $FC = \$20{,}000$.

a. What are the revenue and cost functions for this business?

b. Construct a break-even chart for the range of 1500 to 3000 customers per month.

c. What is the break-even point in:
(i) customers per month? (ii) revenue per month?

d. What will be the monthly net income if there are:
(i) 1600 customers per month? (ii) 2300 customers per month?

e. How many customers per month are required for a net income of \$5000 per month?

Note: Parts (c), (d), and (e) were answered in Example 5.2B using the contribution margin approach and in Example 5.2F by solving the revenue and cost functions algebraically. The three sets of solutions to the identical questions may be used to compare the three approaches to CVP analysis.

Solution

a. Using formula (5-3), we obtain

$$\text{Revenue function:} \quad TR = (SP)X = \$15X$$
$$\text{Cost function:} \quad TC = (VC)X + FC = \$5X + \$20{,}000$$

b. Construct a table of values for both the revenue function and the cost function. The two endpoints of the range for X are good choices to plot.

X:	1500	3000
TR:	\$22,500	\$45,000
TC:	\$27,500	\$35,000

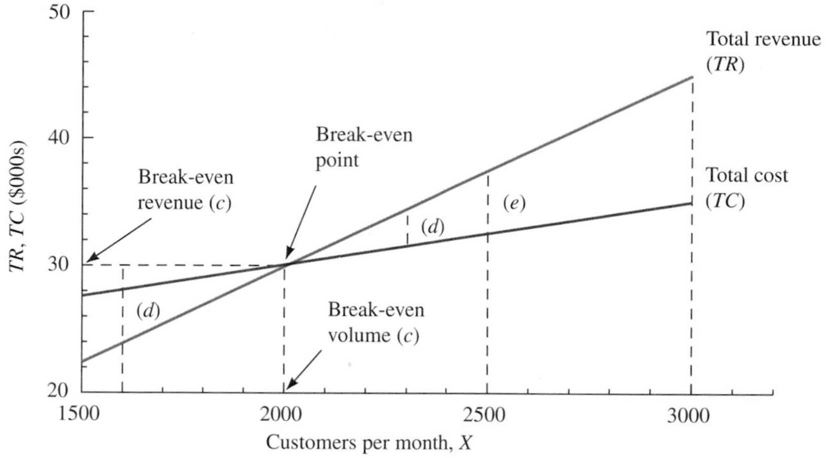

c. (i) At the break-even point, the pub requires 2000 customers per month.
(ii) The revenue is then \$30,000 per month.

d. (i) At $X = 1600$ customers per month, the TC line is \$4000 above the TR line. The pub will lose \$4000 per month if it has only 1600 customers per month.
(ii) At $X = 2300$ customers per month, the TR line is \$3000 above the TC line. The pub will have a profit of \$3000 per month if it has 2300 customers per month.

e. The answer will be the value for X at which the TR line is \$5000 above the TC line. This occurs at $X = 2500$ customers per month.[6]

Example 5.3D *Graphical Cost-Volume-Profit and Break-Even Analysis*

The board of directors of a Tier 2 Junior A hockey team is preparing financial projections for the next season's operations. The team rents the city's 4000-seat arena for the entire season for \$100,000 plus 25% of revenue from ticket sales. The city operates the food concessions at the games and pays the team one third of the gross revenue.

The team will pay \$100,000 for uniforms and equipment, \$100,000 for travel costs, \$50,000 for the coach's salary, \$50,000 for housing subsidies for team members not living at home, and \$20,000 for insurance. The average ticket price will be \$8, and past experience shows that each fan spends an average of \$3 on food and beverages at the games.

[6] The graphical approach to CVP analysis has the disadvantage of limited accuracy. The error in plotting or reading the coordinates of a point can be in the 2% to 4% range. The cumulative effects of limited precision in each of a few successive steps can easily lead to a 10% error in the answer to a question such as this one.

Use a break-even chart to answer the following questions.

a. What must the aggregate attendance for the 30 home games be for the team to just cover all of its costs for the season?

b. What will the profit or loss be if the attendance averages 75% of capacity?

c. The team has \$140,000 in a contingency fund to absorb losses. What season attendance would just wipe out this fund?

Solution

a. The total of the fixed costs is

$$FC = \$100{,}000 + \$100{,}000 + \$100{,}000 + \$50{,}000 + \$50{,}000 + \$20{,}000$$
$$= \$420{,}000$$

The unit variable cost is the 25% of the price of each ticket that the team must pay to the city as part of the rent.

$$VC = 0.25 \times \$8 = \$2$$

The cost function for the analysis is

$$TC = FC + (VC)X$$
$$= \$420{,}000 + \$2X$$

Each ticket sold generates revenue for the team of \$8 from the admission price and \$1 from the team's share (one third) of the concession revenue (\$3 per fan). The revenue function is

$$TR = (\$8 + \$1)X$$
$$= \$9X$$

The cost and revenue functions should be plotted for the range from $X = 0$ to $X = 120{,}000$, which is full capacity (30×4000) for the season.

X:	0	120,000
TR:	\$0	\$1,080,000
TC:	\$420,000	\$660,000

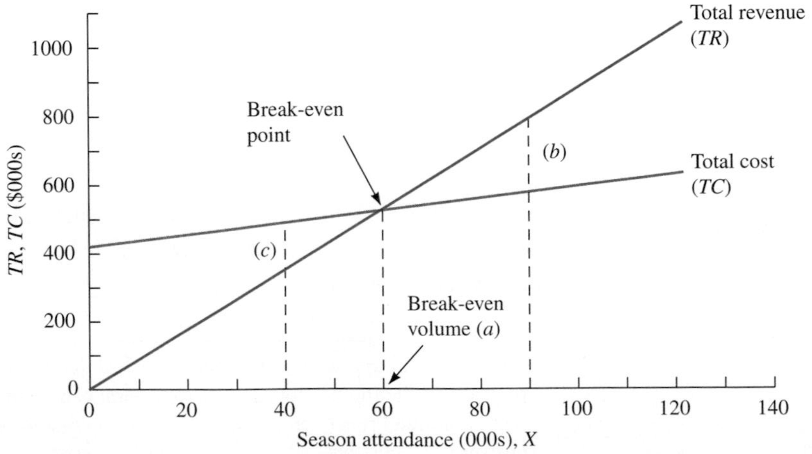

For the team to cover its costs, it must have the attendance figure at the break-even point. Therefore, the team will just cover all its expenses if the total season attendance is 60,000.

b. The season attendance at 75% of capacity is

$$0.75 \times 120{,}000 = 90{,}000$$

At an attendance of 90,000, the *TR* line is \$210,000 above the *TC* line. The team will then have a profit of \$210,000.

c. The answer will be the attendance at which the *TC* line is \$140,000 above the *TR* line. This separation occurs at an attendance of 40,000.

Exercise 5.3

Answers to the odd-numbered problems are at the end of the book.

Graph each of the following equations.

1. $-2x + y = 0$ over the range $x = -3$ to $x = 6$

2. $-2x + y = 4$ over the range $x = -3$ to $x = 6$

3. $2x + y = 4$ over the range $x = -3$ to $x = 6$

4. $y = 4$ over the range $x = -3$ to $x = 6$

5. $3x - 4y + 12 = 0$ over the range $x = -8$ to $x = 12$

6. $y = 60x + 6000$ over the range $x = 0$ to $x = 50$

7. $y = 4.5x + 5000$ over the range $x = 0$ to $x = 6000$

The graphical approach to CVP analysis may be used to solve Problems 1, 2, 3, 7, 8, and 13 in the Exercise at the end of Section 5.2.

Review Problems

Answers to the odd-numbered review problems are at the back of the book.

1. Solve each of the following pairs of equations to three-figure accuracy.

a. $4a - 5b = 30$
$2a - 6b = 22$

b. $76x - 29y = 1050$
$-13x - 63y = 250$

2. Deanna is paid a base salary plus commission. On sales of $27,000 and $35,500 in two successive months, her gross pay was $2815.00 and $3197.50, respectively. What are her base salary and commission rate (in percent)?

3. Nguyen fishes for red snapper and ling cod off the coast of British Columbia and delivers his catch each week to a fish buyer. On one delivery, he received $2454.20 for 370 kg of red snapper and 264 kg of ling cod. On another occasion he was paid $2124.70 for 304 kg of ling cod and 255 kg of red snapper. What price per kilogram was Nguyen paid for each type of fish?

◆**4.** Durable Toys Inc. wants to calculate from recent production data the monthly fixed costs and unit variable costs on its Mountain Trike product line. In the most recent month, it produced 530 Trikes at a total cost of $24,190. In the previous month, it produced 365 Trikes at a total cost of $18,745. What are the fixed costs per month and the unit variable costs? *Hint:* Recall from Section 5.2 that

$$\text{Total costs} = \text{Fixed costs} + (\text{Unit variable costs}) \times (\text{Number of units produced})$$

5. Calculate the missing quantities:

	Unit selling price ($)	Variable cost per unit ($)	Unit sales	Total contribution margin ($)	Total fixed costs ($)	Net income ($)
a.	?	10	150,000	300,000	220,000	?
b.	25	?	180,000	900,000	800,000	?
c.	20	14	?	120,000	?	12,000

6. The Armour Company had the following revenue and costs in the most recently completed fiscal year:

Total revenue	$10,000,000
Total fixed costs	$2,000,000
Total variable costs	$6,000,000
Total units produced and sold	1,000,000

a. What is the contribution margin per unit?

b. What is the sales volume at the break-even point?

c. How many units must be produced and sold for the company to have a net income of $1,000,000 for the year?

7. During an economic slowdown, an automobile plant lost $6,000,000 on the production and sale of 9000 cars. Total revenue for the year was $135,000,000. If the break-even volume for the plant is 10,000 cars per year, calculate:

a. The contribution margin per car.

b. The plant's total fixed costs for a year.

c. The net income if unit sales for the year had been equal to the five-year average of 12,000.

8. Fisher Publishing Inc. is doing a financial feasibility analysis for a new book. Editing and preproduction costs are estimated at $45,000. The printing costs are a flat $7000 for setup plus $8.00 per book. The author's royalty is 8% of the publisher's net price to bookstores. Advertising and promotion costs are budgeted at $8000.

a. If the price to bookstores is set at $35, how many books must be sold to break even?

b. In a highest cost scenario, fixed costs might be $5000 higher and the printing costs might be $9.00 per book. By how many books would the break-even volume be raised?

c. The marketing department is forecasting sales of 4800 books at the $35 price. What will be the net income from the project at this volume of sales?

d. The marketing department is also forecasting that, if the price is reduced by 10%, unit sales will be 15% higher. Which price should be selected? (Show calculations that support your recommendation.)

◆9. Norwood Industries has annual fixed costs of $1.8 million and a contribution rate of 45%.

a. What annual revenue is required to break even?

b. What revenue would result in a loss of $100,000 in a year?

c. What annual revenue would produce an operating profit of $300,000?

d. If the firm raises all its selling prices by 10% but variable costs are unchanged, what will be the new contribution rate?

e. Market research indicates that if prices are increased by 10%, total revenue will remain at the part (c) amount because the higher prices will be offset by reduced sales volume. Will the operating profit remain at $300,000? Present calculations to justify your answer.

◆10. Cambridge Manufacturing is evaluating the introduction of a new product that would have a unit selling price of $100. The total annual fixed costs are estimated to be $200,000, and the unit variable costs are projected at $60. Forecast sales volume for the first year is 8000 units.

a. What sales volume (in units) is required to break even?

b. What volume is required to generate a net income of $100,000?

c. What would be the net income at the forecast sales volume?

d. At the forecast sales volume, what will be the change in the net income if fixed costs are:

(i) 5% higher than expected? (ii) 10% lower than expected?

e. At the forecast sales volume, what will be the change in the net income if unit variable costs are:

(i) 10% higher than expected? (ii) 5% lower than expected?

f. At the forecast sales volume, what will be the change in the net income if the unit selling price is:

(i) 5% higher? (ii) 10% lower?

g. At the forecast sales volume, what will be the change in the net income if unit variable costs are 10% higher than expected and fixed costs are simultaneously 10% lower than expected?

Self-Test Exercise

Answers to the self-test problems are at the end of the book.

1. Solve the following equations.

$$3x + 5y = 11$$

$$2x - y = 16$$

2. During a one-day special, a grocery store sells cucumbers at 49 cents each or four for the price of three. At the end of the day, the store's computer reports that revenue from the sale of 541 cucumbers was \$209.23. How many cucumbers were sold on the four-for-three promotion?

◆3. A hockey arena has 2500 seats in the preferred blue sections near centre ice and 4500 seats in the less desirable red sections. At regular season prices, a sellout would generate ticket revenue of \$50,250 for a single game. Ticket prices are raised by 20% in the "reds" and 30% in the "blues" for the playoffs. Ticket revenue from a playoff sellout would be \$62,400. What are the ticket prices for the playoffs?

◆4. To raise funds for its community activities, a Lions' Club chapter is negotiating with International Carnivals to bring its midway rides and games to town for a three-day opening. The event will be held on part of the parking lot of a local shopping centre, which is to receive 10% of the gross revenue. The Lions' Club members will sell the ride and game tickets at the site. International Carnivals requires either \$15,000 plus 30% of revenue or \$10,000 plus 50% of revenue. Contacts in other towns that have held the event indicate that customers spend an average of \$10 per person on rides and games.

a. What is the break-even attendance under each basis for remunerating International Carnivals?

b. For each alternative, what will be the club's profit or loss if the attendance is:

(i) 3000? (ii) 2200?

c. How would you briefly explain the advantages and disadvantages of the two alternatives to a club member?

◆5. The monthly fixed costs of operating a 30-unit motel are \$14,000. The price per unit per night for next year is set at \$55. Costs arising from rentals on a per-unit per-day basis are \$6 for maid service, \$3 for supplies and laundry, and \$3 for heat and utilities.

a. Based on a 30-day month, at what average occupancy rate will the motel break even?

b. What will the motel's net income be at an occupancy rate of:

(i) 40%? (ii) 30%?

c. Should the owner reduce the price from \$55 to \$47 per unit per night if it will result in an increase in the average occupancy rate from 40% to 50%? Present calculations that justify your answer.

CASE

ESTIMATING THE CONTRIBUTION RATE IN A MULTI-PRODUCT BUSINESS

Classifying individual costs as either purely fixed or purely variable can be problematic, especially when a firm produces more than one product. Rather than determining *FC* and *VC* by analyzing each cost, you can use an income statement approach for estimating a firm's *FC* and average contribution rate, *CR*.

We will use two familiar formulas to develop an equation that will enable us to estimate *FC* and *CR* from a business's income statements. Recall that

$$CR = \frac{CM}{SP} \times 100\% \quad (5\text{-}1) \qquad \text{and} \qquad NI = (CM)X - FC \quad (5\text{-}2)$$

From (5-1), $CM = CR \times SP$. Substitute this product for *CM* in (5-2) giving

$$NI = (CR \times SP)X - FC$$

But NI is the net income or "bottom line" of an income statement and the product $(SP)X$ is the total revenue or "top line" of an income statement. Therefore,

$$\text{Net income} = CR \times (\text{Total revenue}) - FC$$

If the average CR for all products does not change significantly from one year to the next, we can use the income statements for the two years to construct two equations in two unknowns (CR and FC).

Suppose the income statements for Miscellaneous Manufacturing Ltd. (MML) showed the following results for Years 1 and 2.

Year	Total revenue	Net income
1	\$750,000	\$105,000
2	\$825,000	\$127,500

QUESTIONS:

1. What are MML's total annual fixed costs and contribution rate?
2. What total revenue does MML require to break even?
3. What will be next year's net income based on revenue forecast to be \$875,000?

Summary of Notation and Key Formulas

The following notation was introduced for cost-volume-profit analysis:

SP = Selling price or revenue per unit
VC = Variable costs per unit
FC = Fixed costs
CM = Contribution margin per unit
CR = Contribution rate
X = Total number of units sold in the period
NI = Net income (or operating profit) for the period
TC = Total revenue (from the sale of X units)

Formula (5-1) $CM = SP - VC$

$$CR = \frac{CM}{SP} \times 100\%$$

Finding the contribution margin and the contribution rate

Formula (5-2) $NI = (CM)X - FC$

Finding net income from the sale of X units

Formula (5-3) $TR = (SP)X$

$$TC = (VC)X + FC$$

$$NI = (SP - VC)X - FC$$

Finding the total revenue, total costs, and net income from the sale of X units

List of Key Terms

Break-even analysis *(p. 177)*
Break-even chart *(p. 199)*
Break-even point *(p. 177)*
Contribution margin *(p. 180)*
Contribution rate *(p. 180)*
Cost function *(p. 188)*
Cost-volume-profit analysis *(p. 177)*
Fixed costs *(p. 177)*
Revenue function *(p. 188)*
Unit variable cost *(p. 177)*
Variable costs *(p. 177)*

CHAPTER OUTLINE

LEARNING OBJECTIVES

After completing this chapter, you will be able to:

- Calculate interest, maturity value, future value, and present value in a simple interest environment
- Present details of the amount and timing of payments in a time diagram
- Calculate the equivalent value on any date of a single payment or a stream of payments

6

Simple Interest

EVERY DAY MONEY IS BORROWED and loaned in tens of thousands of transactions. The transaction amounts range from a few dollars on credit-card purchases to billion-dollar refinancings of federal government debt.

Interest is the fee or rent that lenders charge for the use of their money. For many individuals and corporations, and for most provincial and federal governments, interest on debt is one of the largest expenditures in their annual budgets.

Clearly, debt plays a key role in our personal finances and our economic system. As a fundamental skill, you must be able to calculate interest on debt. But to be a truly effective participant in financial decision-making, you must be able to analyze broader effects that prevailing interest rates have on the value of personal investments and business assets. The remainder of the text is devoted to developing these skills and techniques.

In this chapter you will first learn how to calculate interest in the simple-interest system. We will then take the first step toward answering a central question in finance: "What is an investment worth?" This step is the concept of "equivalent value." It is a far-reaching concept that will carry forward to the compound-interest system in later chapters.

6.1 Basic Concepts

Borrowing and lending are two sides of the same transaction. The amount borrowed/loaned is called the **principal**. To the borrower, the principal is a *debt*; to the lender, the principal represents an *investment.*

The interest paid by the borrower is the lender's investment income. There are two systems[1] for calculating interest.

- *Simple* interest is used mainly for short-term loans and investments. (By "short-term," we mean durations of up to one year.) Chapters 6 and 7 cover the mathematics and applications of simple interest.
- *Compound* interest is used mainly for durations longer than one year. Chapters 8 and beyond cover the mathematics and applications of compound interest.

The **rate of interest** is the interest amount expressed as a percentage of the principal. **Simple interest** rates are usually calculated and quoted on a *per annum* (pa) basis. That is,

$$\text{Interest rate (per annum)} = \frac{\text{Annual interest}}{\text{Principal}} \times 100\%$$

Unless otherwise stated, assume that a quoted rate of interest is an annual rate.

The rate of interest charged on a loan is the lender's rate of return on investment. (It seems more natural for us to take the borrower's point of view because we usually become borrowers before we become lenders.)

If you "go with your intuition," you will probably correctly calculate the amount of simple interest. For example, how much interest will \$1000 earn in six months if it earns an 8% pa rate of interest? Your thinking probably goes as follows: "In one year, \$1000 will earn \$80 (8% of \$1000). In six months ($\frac{1}{2}$ year), \$1000 will earn only \$40 ($\frac{1}{2}$ of \$80)."

Now write an equation for the preceding steps, but in terms of the following symbols:

I = Amount of interest paid or received
P = Principal amount of the loan or investment
r = Annual rate of simple interest
t = Time period (term), in years, of the loan or investment

To obtain the \$40 (I) amount, you multiplied \$1000 (P) by 0.08 (r) and by $\frac{1}{2}$ year (t). In general,

AMOUNT OF SIMPLE INTEREST

(6-1) $$I = Prt$$

TIP *USE DECIMAL EQUIVALENTS OF INTEREST RATES IN ALGEBRAIC FORMULAS*
When substituting the numerical value for an interest rate into any equation or formula, you must use the decimal equivalent of the interest rate.

[1] We are *not* referring to two methods for obtaining the same answer to an interest calculation. Rather, the two "systems" usually result in different amounts of interest being calculated.

If any three of the four variables I, P, r, and t in formula (6-1) are known, the formula may easily be rearranged to solve for the unknown variable. Other versions of formula (6-1) are:

$$P = \frac{I}{rt} \qquad r = \frac{I}{Pt} \qquad \text{and} \qquad t = \frac{I}{Pr}$$

TIP *AVOID "FORMULA CLUTTER"*

You should not attempt to remember different versions of the same fundamental formula. Instead, learn how to quickly rearrange the fundamental formula to obtain the equivalent versions.

Example 6.1A *Calculation of the Amount of Interest*

What amount of interest will be charged on \$6500 borrowed for five months at a simple interest rate of 11% per annum (abbreviated 11% pa)?

Solution

Given: $P = \$6500$, $t = \frac{5}{12}$ year, $r = 11\%$ pa
The amount of interest payable at the end of the loan period is

$$I = Prt = \$6500(0.11)\left(\frac{5}{12}\right) = \$297.92$$

Example 6.1B *Calculation of the Principal Amount*

If a three-month term deposit at a bank pays a simple interest rate of 4.5% pa, how much will have to be deposited to earn \$100 of interest?

Solution

Given: $t = \frac{3}{12}$ year, $r = 4.5\%$ pa, $I = \$100$
Divide both sides of formula (6-1) by rt to isolate P:

$$P = \frac{I}{rt} = \frac{\$100}{(0.045)\left(\frac{3}{12}\right)} = \$8888.89$$

\$8888.89 must be placed in the three-month term deposit to earn \$100 of interest.

Example 6.1C *Calculation of the Interest Rate*

Interest of \$429.48 was charged on a loan of \$9500 for seven months. What simple annual rate of interest was charged on the loan?

Solution

Given: $I = \$429.48$, $P = \$9500$, $t = \frac{7}{12}$ year
Rearrange formula (6-1) to isolate r:

$$r = \frac{I}{Pt} = \frac{\$429.48}{(\$9500)\frac{7}{12}} = \frac{\$429.48}{\$5541.66} = 0.0775 = 7.75\%$$

An interest rate of 7.75% pa was charged on the loan.

Example 6.1D Calculation of the Time Period

The interest earned on a $6000 investment was $240. What was the term in months if the interest rate was 6% pa?

Solution

Given: $P = \$6000$, $I = \$240$, $r = 6\%$ pa
Rearrange formula (6-1) to solve for t:

$$t = \frac{I}{Pr} = \frac{\$240}{(\$6000)(0.06)} = 0.66667 \text{ year} = 8 \text{ months}$$

The term of the investment was eight months.

Example 6.1E Using Months as the Unit of Time

The simple interest rate being charged on a $5000 loan is three-quarters of 1% per month. If the principal and interest are to be paid in nine months, how much interest will be charged?

Solution

Given: $P = \$5000$, loan term = 9 months, interest rate = 0.75% per month
We normally use formula (6-1) with r representing the annual rate of interest and t representing the term in years. However, we can substitute the monthly interest rate for r if the term t is measured in months. We will present both approaches.

Method 1: With time expressed in years,

$$t = \frac{9}{12} = 0.75 \text{ year} \qquad \text{and} \qquad r = 12(0.75\%) = 9\% \text{ pa}$$
$$I = Prt = \$5000 \times 0.09 \times 0.75 = \$337.50$$

Method 2: With time expressed in months,

$$t = 9 \text{ months} \qquad \text{and} \qquad r = 0.75\% \text{ per month}$$
$$I = Prt = \$5000 \times 0.0075 \times 9 = \$337.50$$

The interest that will be charged on the loan is $337.50.

Exercise 6.1

Answers to the odd-numbered problems are at the end of the book.

Calculate the missing values in Problems 1 through 8.

Problem	Principal ($)	Rate	Time (months)	Interest ($)
1.	1500	9.5% pa	7	?
2.	?	$10\frac{1}{4}$% pa	11	328.85
3.	4850	$11\frac{1}{2}$% pa	?	371.83
4.	15,000	?% pa	5	546.88
5.	6800	7.7% pa	13	?
6.	25,000	1.1% per month	3	?
7.	9125	0.8% per month	?	511.00
8.	8900	?% per month	8	890.00

9. How much interest will be earned on $5000 in five months if the interest rate is 5.5% pa?

10. An invoice states that interest will be charged on overdue accounts at the rate of $1\frac{1}{2}$% per month. What will be the interest charges on a $3760 billing that is three months overdue?

11. The interest owed on a loan after five months was $292.50. If the simple interest rate charged on the loan was 0.9% per month, what was the amount borrowed?

12. How much must be placed in a five-month term deposit earning 8.3% pa simple interest in order to earn $500 interest?

13. Carl has forgotten the rate of simple interest he earned on a three-month term deposit at the Bank of Montreal. At the end of the three-month period, he received interest of $214.65 on his $10,600 deposit. What annual rate of simple interest did his deposit earn?

14. Daniella paid interest charges of $169.05 on a $4830 invoice that was two months overdue. What monthly rate of simple interest was she charged?

15. Ken's calculations show that the total interest owed to Barbara on his $2700 loan is $315.90. If he pays simple interest at the rate of 0.9% per month, for how long did Ken borrow the money?

16. Trevor cashed in a one-year term deposit after only five months had elapsed. In order to do so, he accepted an interest rate penalty—a reduction from the scheduled 7.5% per annum rate of simple interest. If he was paid $187.50 interest on the $10,000 term deposit, what reduction was made in the per-annum rate of simple interest?

•17. Evelyn put $10,000 in a three-month term deposit at Canada Trust, earning a simple interest rate of 7.8% pa. After the three months, she invested the entire amount of the principal and interest from the first term deposit in a new three-month term deposit earning the same rate of interest. How much interest did she earn on each term deposit? Why are the two interest amounts not equal?

••18. Randall has $5000 to invest for six months. The rates offered on three-month and six-month term deposits at his bank are 5.5% pa and 5.8% pa, respectively. He is trying to choose between the six-month term deposit and two consecutive three-month term deposits. What would the simple interest rate on three-month term deposits have to be, three months from now, for Randall to end up in the same financial position with either alternative? Assume that he would place both the principal and the interest from the first three-month term deposit in the second three-month term deposit.

6.2 Determining the Time Period (Term)

Whenever possible, the time period t should be determined using the *exact* number of days involved. For example, if the only information provided is that a loan is made for three months, the best that can be done is to use $t = \frac{3}{12} = 0.25$ year. But if it is known that the three-month loan was advanced on September 21, the exact number of days to the December 21 repayment date can be determined. *The most common practice among Canadian financial institutions is to count the starting date* (September 21 in this case) *but not the ending date* (December 21).[2] The numbers of days in each month are listed in Table 6.1. The three-month loan period from September 21 to December 21 includes 10 days in September (September 21 to 30 inclusive), 31 days in October, 30 days in November, and 20 days in December (December 1 to 20 inclusive), for a total of 91 days. The value that should be used for t is 91/365 = 0.24932 year.

Table 6.1 *The Number of Days in Each Month*

Month	Days	Month	Days	Month	Days
January	31	May	31	September	30
February	28	June	30	October	31
March	31	July	31	November	30
April	30	August	31	December	31

Figure 6.7 in the appendix to this chapter presents a technique for determining which months have 31 days.

Years that are divisible by four are leap years. Therefore, 2000 and 2004 are leap years, with February having 29 days. When the term of a short-term loan or investment includes part of a leap year, there is no uniform practice across financial institutions for adjusting the length of the year in the denominator of t. The majority of them continue to use 365 days as the length of the year. In this text we will follow the majority and always use 365 days in the denominator.[3] If a loan period includes February 29, that day should be counted in the numerator of t.

CAUGHT IN THE WEB

There are hundreds of financial calculators available on the Web, but it is rare to find one that will handle simple interest calculations. Pine Grove Software has a versatile user-friendly calculator (Loan*Calculator! Plus for Windows) that you can download free from its Web site at www.pine-grove.com. *PC Computing* magazine named it the best download in the Loan/Lease category. The software contains five calculators—at this point you want to choose the Compound and Simple Interest Calculator and select "Simple" for the compounding period. The calculator automatically computes the number of days in the term if you enter the start and end dates. Or, if you enter the start date and number of days in the term, it will determine the end date.

---

[2] There is a good business rationale for not counting *both* the start and the end dates. Consider that if you borrow money today and repay it at the same time tomorrow, you have had the use of the money for a time *interval* of just one day, not two days. Agreement on whether to count the first or the last day of the interval matters only in cases where the interest rate changes part way through the interval. An example later in the section will illustrate this point.

[3] The United States and some other countries compute simple interest based on a 360-day year in what they call the "ordinary interest method."

Instead of using Table 6.1, another method for calculating the number of days in a loan period employs Table 6.2, in which the days of the year are consecutively numbered. Both methods are illustrated in Example 6.2A.

Table 6.2 *The Serial Number of Each Day of the Year*

Day of Month	Jan	Feb	Mar	Apr	May	Jun	Jul	Aug	Sep	Oct	Nov	Dec	Day of Month
1	1	32	60	91	121	152	182	213	244	274	305	335	1
2	2	33	61	92	122	153	183	214	245	275	306	336	2
3	3	34	62	93	123	154	184	215	246	276	307	337	3
4	4	35	63	94	124	155	185	216	247	277	308	338	4
5	5	36	64	95	125	156	186	217	248	278	309	339	5
6	6	37	65	96	126	157	187	218	249	279	310	340	6
7	7	38	66	97	127	158	188	219	250	280	311	341	7
8	8	39	67	98	128	159	189	220	251	281	312	342	8
9	9	40	68	99	129	160	190	221	252	282	313	343	9
10	10	41	69	100	130	161	191	222	253	283	314	344	10
11	11	42	70	101	131	162	192	223	254	284	315	345	11
12	12	43	71	102	132	163	193	224	255	285	316	346	12
13	13	44	72	103	133	164	194	225	256	286	317	347	13
14	14	45	73	104	134	165	195	226	257	287	318	348	14
15	15	46	74	105	135	166	196	227	258	288	319	349	15
16	16	47	75	106	136	167	197	228	259	289	320	350	16
17	17	48	76	107	137	168	198	229	260	290	321	351	17
18	18	49	77	108	138	169	199	230	261	291	322	352	18
19	19	50	78	109	139	170	200	231	262	292	323	353	19
20	20	51	79	110	140	171	201	232	263	293	324	354	20
21	21	52	80	111	141	172	202	233	264	294	325	355	21
22	22	53	81	112	142	173	203	234	265	295	326	356	22
23	23	54	82	113	143	174	204	235	266	296	327	357	23
24	24	55	83	114	144	175	205	236	267	297	328	358	24
25	25	56	84	115	145	176	206	237	268	298	329	359	25
26	26	57	85	116	146	177	207	238	269	299	330	360	26
27	27	58	86	117	147	178	208	239	270	300	331	361	27
28	28	59	87	118	148	179	209	240	271	301	332	362	28
29	29	*	88	119	149	180	210	241	272	302	333	363	29
30	30		89	120	150	181	211	242	273	303	334	364	30
31	31		90		151		212	243		304		365	31

Note: For leap years, February 29 becomes day number 60 and the serial number for each subsequent day in the table must be increased by 1.

Example 6.2A Calculating and Using the Exact Number of Days

a. Calculate the term for each of the following loans.

b. Calculate the interest due on the repayment date for each loan.

	Loan principal	Date advanced	Date repaid	Interest rate pa
(i)	\$3000	March 31, 1999	September 4, 1999	$7\frac{3}{4}\%$
(ii)	\$14,600	January 11, 2000	June 4, 2000	$9\frac{1}{4}\%$
(iii)	\$23,000	November 29, 2000	April 1, 2001	6.9%

Solution

a. The term will be calculated by two methods:

Method 1: Counting the number of days of each partial and full month within the interval (using Table 6.1).

Method 2: Using the serial numbers of the beginning date and the ending date (from Table 6.2).

Method 1: (using Table 6.1)

(i) Month	(i) Days	(ii) Month	(ii) Days	(iii) Month	(iii) Days
March	1	January	21	November	2
April	30	February	29	December	31
May	31	March	31	January	31
June	30	April	30	February	28
July	31	May	31	March	31
August	31	June	3	April	0
September	3				
Total	157	Total	145	Total	123

Method 2: (using Table 6.2) Particularly when the term of the loan includes a year-end, it is helpful to draw a time line showing the dates on which the loan was advanced and repaid. Look up the serial numbers for these dates in Table 6.2, and write them on the time line.

(i)

	March 31, 1999	September 4, 1999
Date	March 31, 1999	September 4, 1999
Day number	90	247

$247 - 90 = 157$ days

The term of the loan is 157 days.

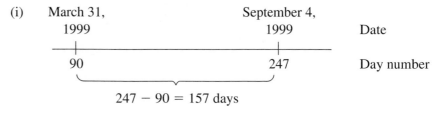

(ii) When a date falls after February 29 of a leap year, you must add one day to the serial number obtained from Table 6.2.

January 11, 2000	June 4, 2000	Date
11	$155 + 1 = 156$	Day number

$156 - 11 = 145$ days

The term of the loan is 145 days.

(iii)

Nov. 29, 2000	Dec. 31, 2000	April 1, 2001	Date
$333 + 1 = 334$	$365 + 1 = 366$	91	Day number

$366 - 334 = 32$ days   91 days

The term of the loan is $32 + 91 = 123$ days.

b. Each loan's term should be expressed as a fraction of a year when substituted in formula (6-1).

(i) $$I = Prt = \$3000(0.0775)\left(\frac{157}{365}\right) = \$100.01$$

(ii) $$I = Prt = \$14{,}600(0.0925)\left(\frac{145}{365}\right) = \$536.50$$

(iii) $$I = Prt = \$23{,}000(0.069)\left(\frac{123}{365}\right) = \$534.80$$

Variable or Floating Interest Rates The interest rate on short-term loans is often linked to the "prime rate" charged by the chartered banks. The **prime rate of interest** is the banks' lowest lending rate—it is available only on the most secure loans. Less secure loans are charged between $\frac{1}{2}\%$ and 5% above the prime rate. The chartered banks change the prime rate from time to time in response to interest rate movements in the financial markets. When a loan's interest rate is linked to the prime rate (for example, prime + 2%), it is described as a *variable* interest rate or a *floating* interest rate.

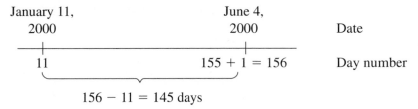

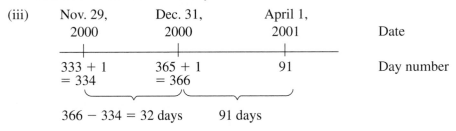

Example 6.2B Floating Interest Rates

Winston borrowed \$5000 on April 7 at prime + 1%. The prime rate was initially $5\frac{1}{2}\%$ pa. It increased to 6% pa effective May 23, and $6\frac{1}{4}\%$ pa effective July 13. What amount was required to repay the loan on August 2?

Solution

The statement that the interest rate "increased to 6% pa effective May 23" means that interest was charged for May 23 (and subsequent days) at the new 6% rate. We need to break the overall loan period into intervals within which the interest rate is constant.

In the following table, the beginning and ending dates have been given for each interval. Since we count the first day but not the last day in an interval, May 23 is counted only in the second interval and July 13 is counted only in the third interval. This is consistent with the new interest rates taking effect on May 23 and July 13.

Interval	Number of days	Interest rate	Interest
April 7 to May 23	24 + 22 = 46	5.5 + 1 = 6.5%	\$ 40.96①
May 23 to July 13	9 + 30 + 12 = 51	6.0 + 1 = 7.0%	48.90②
July 13 to August 2	19 + 1 = 20	6.25 + 1 = 7.25%	19.86
Total:			\$109.72

① Interest = $Prt = \$5000(0.065)\frac{46}{365} = \$40.96$

② Interest = $Prt = \$5000(0.07)\frac{51}{365} = \$48.90$

The amount required to repay the loan on August 7 was \$5000 + \$109.72 = \$5109.72.

TIP *Counting Days When the Interest Rate is Floating*

With a variable interest rate, it matters whether you count "the first day but not the last day" (our practice) or "the last day but not the first day." Suppose we count the last day but not the first day in Example 6.2B (that is, count August 2 but not April 7). We then count 45 days (instead of 46 days) at the 6.5% interest rate and 21 days (instead of 20 days) at the 7.25% rate.

Exercise 6.2

Answers to the odd-numbered problems are at the end of the book.

Calculate the amount of interest owed on the repayment date in Problems 1 through 6.

Problem	Loan principal (\$)	Date advanced	Date repaid	Interest rate pa (%)
1.	3800	June 17, 1997	Oct. 1, 1997	$10\frac{3}{4}$
2.	7350	Nov. 30, 1997	Mar. 4, 1998	7.5
3.	85,000	Dec. 1, 1996	May 30, 1997	9.9
4.	850	Jan. 7, 1996	July 1, 1996	14
5.	27,000	Oct. 16, 1995	Apr. 15, 1996	8.7
6.	14,400	May 21, 1996	July 19, 1997	$11\frac{1}{4}$

Calculate the missing values in Problems 7 through 12.

Problem	Principal ($)	Start date	End date	Interest rate pa (%)	Interest ($)
7.	1000	Jan. 15, 1996	July 7, 1996	?	40.52
8.	?	Oct. 28, 1997	Apr. 14, 1998	$9\frac{1}{2}$	67.78
•9.	1000	?	Nov. 16, 1997	$7\frac{1}{4}$	50.05
•10.	1000	?	Mar. 13, 1999	11	49.42
•11.	1000	June 26, 1996	?	$10\frac{3}{4}$	63.91
•12.	1000	Apr. 18, 1997	?	7.7	32.28

13. On June 26 Laura put $2750 into a term deposit until September 3, when she needs the money for tuition, books, and other expenses to return to college. For term deposits in the 60–89-day range, her credit union pays an interest rate of $4\frac{1}{4}$% per annum. How much interest will she earn on the term deposit?

14. Raimo borrowed $750 from Chris on October 30 and agreed to repay the debt with simple interest at the rate of 12.3% pa on May 10. How much interest was owed on May 10? Assume that February has 28 days.

15. Joyce had $2146 in her daily interest savings account for the entire month of June. Her account was credited with interest of $9.70 on June 30 (for the exact number of days in June). What annual rate of simple interest did her balance earn?

16. Tony's chequing account was $329 overdrawn beginning on September 24. On October 9 he made a deposit that restored a credit balance. If he was charged overdraft interest of $2.50, what annual rate of simple interest was charged?

17. In addition to a $2163 refund of his income tax overpayment, Revenue Canada paid Roy $23.08 of interest on the overpayment. If the simple interest rate paid by Revenue Canada was $9\frac{1}{2}$% pa, how many days' interest was paid?

18. Megan was charged $124.83 interest on her bank loan for the period September 18 to October 18. If the rate of interest on her loan was 8.25% pa, what was the outstanding principal balance on the loan during the month?

•19. Bruce borrowed $6000 from Darryl on November 23. When Bruce repaid the loan, Darryl charged $203.22 interest. If the rate of simple interest on the loan was $10\frac{3}{4}$%, on what date did Bruce repay the loan? Assume that February has 28 days.

•20. Sharon's $9000 term deposit matured on March 16, 2000. Based on a simple interest rate of 7.5% pa, she received $221.92 in interest. On what date did she originally make the term deposit?

•21. Mario borrowed $6000 on March 1 at a variable rate of interest. The interest rate began at 7.5% pa, increased to 8% effective April 17, and then fell by 0.25% effective June 30. How much interest will be owed on the August 1 repayment date?

•22. Penny invested $4500 on October 28 at a floating rate of interest that initially stood at 6.3% pa. Effective December 2, the rate dropped by $\frac{1}{2}$%, and then it declined another $\frac{1}{4}$% effective February 27. What total amount of principal plus interest will Penny receive when the investment matures on March 15? Assume that the new year is a leap year.

•**23.** How much will be required on February 1 to pay off a \$3000 loan advanced on the previous September 30 if the variable interest rate began the interval at 10.7% pa, rose to 11.2% effective November 2, and then dropped back to 11% effective January 1?

•**24.** The total accrued interest owed as of August 31 on a loan advanced the preceding June 3 was \$169.66. If the variable interest rate started at $8\frac{3}{4}\%$ pa, rose to 9% effective July 1, and increased another $\frac{1}{2}\%$ effective July 31, what was the principal amount of the loan?

6.3 Maturity Value (Future Value) of a Loan or Investment

When a loan or investment reaches the end of its term, we say it "matures." The last day of the term is called the **maturity date**. The **maturity value** (or **future value**) is the total of the original principal plus interest due on the maturity date. Using the symbol S to represent the maturity value (or future value), we have

$$S = P + I$$

Substituting $I = Prt$, we obtain

$$S = P + Prt$$

Extracting the common factor P yields:

MATURITY VALUE (FUTURE VALUE)

(6-2) $$S = P(1 + rt)$$

Example 6.3A *Calculating the Maturity Value*

Celia invests \$1500 by lending it to Chuck for eight months at an interest rate of $9\frac{1}{4}\%$ pa. What is the maturity value of the investment/loan?

Solution

This problem reminds us that, when an interest-bearing debt is created, the lender has made an interest-earning investment.

Given: $P = \$1500$, $t = \frac{8}{12}$ year, $r = 9.25\%$

The maturity value of the investment/loan is:

$$\begin{aligned} S &= P(1 + rt) \\ &= \$1500\left[1 + 0.0925\left(\frac{8}{12}\right)\right] \\ &= \$1500(1.061667) \\ &= \$1592.50 \end{aligned}$$

Note that this answer can be obtained just as easily by first calculating the interest due at maturity using $I = Prt$. Then simply add the principal to obtain the maturity value ($S = P + I$). The choice of method is a matter of personal preference.

The maturity value that Chuck must pay to Celia at the end of the eight months is \$1592.50.

Example 6.3B Calculating the Principal

What amount of money would have to be invested at $10\frac{3}{4}\%$ pa to grow to \$10,000 after 91 days?

Solution

Given: $r = 10.75\%$, $S = \$10,000$, $t = \frac{91}{365}$ year

Substitute the known values into formula (6-2) and then solve for P.

$$S = P(1 + rt)$$

$$\$10{,}000 = P\left[1 + 0.1075\left(\frac{91}{365}\right)\right]$$

$$= P(1.026801)$$

The value for P will be a few hundred dollars less than \$10,000. To have P accurate to the cent (six figures), seven-figure accuracy should be maintained in intermediate steps. Solving for P,

$$P = \frac{\$10{,}000}{1.026801} = \$9738.98$$

The required investment is \$9738.98

TIP *Solving for "r" or "t"*

If any three of the four variables S, P, r, and t are known, formula (6-2) can be used to solve for the remaining variable. However, the manipulations required to solve for r or t are not trivial. It is usually simpler to first calculate $I = S - P$ and then solve $I = Prt$ for r or t. The following example illustrates the latter approach.

Example 6.3C Calculating the Interest Rate

Liam put \$9500 in a term deposit with Canada Trust on May 22. It matured on September 4 at \$9588.82. What interest rate (per annum) did he earn on his term deposit?

Solution

Given: $P = \$9500$; $S = \$9588.82$; the term runs from May 22 to September 4

Hence,

$$I = S - P = \$9588.82 - \$9500 = \$88.82$$

and, using Table 6.2,

$$t = 247 \text{ (September 4)} - 142 \text{ (May 22)} = 105 \text{ days}$$

The annual rate of simple interest is

$$r = \frac{I}{Pt} = \frac{\$88.82}{\$9500 \times \frac{105}{365}} = 0.03250 = 3.25\%$$

Liam earned 3.25% pa on his term deposit.

Example 6.3D *Reinvesting Simple Interest Proceeds*

Kyle has a 90-day $5000 term deposit about to mature at the Bank of Nova Scotia. The interest rate on the term deposit is 3% pa. Since he does not need the money for at least another 90 days, Kyle instructs the bank to "roll over" the proceeds of the maturing term deposit into a new 90-day term deposit. The prevailing rate for 90-day deposits is now 2.75% pa. What will be the maturity value of the second term deposit?

Solution

The maturity value of the first term deposit is

$$S = P(1 + rt) = \$5000\left(1 + 0.03 \times \frac{90}{365}\right) = \$5036.99$$

The entire maturity value of the maturing deposit becomes the beginning principal for the second term deposit. The maturity value of Kyle's second term deposit will be

$$S = P(1 + rt) = \$5036.99\left(1 + 0.0275 \times \frac{90}{365}\right) = \$5071.14$$

Exercise 6.3 *Answers to the odd-numbered problems are at the end of the book.*
Calculate the missing values in Problems 1 through 14.

Problem	Principal ($)	Interest rate pa (%)	Time	Maturity value ($)
1.	2950.00	$13\frac{1}{2}$	7 months	?
2.	12,800.00	$11\frac{3}{4}$	237 days	?
3.	?	$10\frac{1}{2}$	23 days	785.16
4.	?	7.7	360 days	2291.01
5.	?	9.9	11 months	15,379.58
6.	?	$8\frac{1}{4}$	14 months	7348.25
7.	1750.00	?	5 months	1828.02
8.	2875.40	?	8 months	3000.00
9.	780.82	?	45 days	798.63
10.	680.00	?	300 days	730.30
11.	9625.63	7.8	? days	10,000.00
12.	3500.00	8.4	? days	3646.60
13.	7760.00	$6\frac{1}{4}$	? months	8083.33
14.	859.50	$10\frac{1}{4}$	? months	907.22

15. What will be the maturity value in 15 months of a $4500 loan at a simple interest rate of 11.9% pa?

16. Ian placed $17,000 in a 270-day term deposit earning $7\frac{1}{4}\%$ pa. How much will the bank pay Ian on the maturity date?

17. Sharon received the proceeds from an inheritance on March 25. She wants to set aside enough on March 26 so that she will have $20,000 available on October 1 to purchase a car when the new models are introduced. If the current interest rate on 181- to 270-day deposits is $6\frac{3}{4}\%$ pa, what amount should she place in the term deposit?

18. The bookkeeper for Durham's Garage is trying to allocate to principal and interest the payment that was made to settle a loan. The cheque stub has the note "$3701.56 for principal and 7 months' interest at 12.5% pa." What are the principal and interest components of the payment?

19. The annual membership fee at the Oak Meadows Golf Club is $1800 payable at the beginning of the year. A member may delay payment of half the annual membership fee for five months if she pays a surcharge of $60 with the second $900 payment. In effect, what annual rate of simple interest is the golf club charging on the $900 owed?

20. The snow tires that you are planning to buy next October 1 at the regular price of $107.50 each are advertised at $89.95 in a spring clearance special that will end on the preceding March 25. What annual rate of simple interest will you earn if you "invest" in the new snow tires at the sale price on March 25 instead of waiting until October 1 to buy them at the regular price?

21. A&B Appliances sells a washer–dryer combination for $1535 cash. C&D Appliances offers the same combination for $1595 with no payments and no interest for six months. Therefore, you can pay $1535 now or invest the $1535 for six months and then pay $1595. Above what annual rate of interest would the latter alternative be to your advantage?

22. How many days will it take $2500 to grow to $2614.47 at 8.75% pa?

•23. Karen borrowed $2000 at $10\frac{1}{4}\%$ pa on July 13. On what date would the amount owed first exceed $2100?

•24. On what date did a corporation borrow $350,000 at 7.5% from its bank if the debt was settled by a payment of $356,041 on February 28?

•25. Village Finance Co. advanced three loans to Kamiko—$2200 on June 23, $1800 on August 5, and $1300 on October 31. Simple interest at 14.5% pa was charged on all three loans, and all were repaid on December 31 when some bonds that she owned matured. What total amount was required to pay off the loans?

•26. The cash balance in Roger's account with his stockbroker earns interest on the daily balance at 4% per annum payable on June 30 and December 31. His cash balance on January 1 was $3347. As a result of the purchase or sale of securities from time to time, the balance changed to $8687 on March 4, to $2568 on May 24, and to $5923 on June 17. What interest was credited to Roger's account on June 30? The brokerage firm includes interest for both January 1 and June 30 in the June 30 payment. Assume that February had 28 days.

•**27.** Dominion Contracting invested surplus funds in term deposits all chosen to mature on April 1, when the firm intends to purchase a new grader. If $7400 was invested at 6.3% on the previous November 16, $6600 was invested at 5.9% on December 30, and $9200 was invested at 5.1% on February 8, what total amount will be available from the maturing term deposits on April 1 (of a leap year)?

TIP *NOW HEAR THIS . . .*

The concepts that will be developed in Sections 6.4 and 6.5 are fundamental to many other topics and applications in later chapters. If you invest extra effort at this stage to gain a thorough understanding of these concepts, it will pay substantial dividends later.

6.4 Equivalent Payments

Which amount would you prefer to receive: $100 today, or $105 paid one year from now? Make your decision from the point of view of a rational investor. A rational investor should pick the alternative that results in the greater wealth (that is, the greater number of dollars) at a future date.

If you can invest money to earn 5% pa, $100 invested today will grow to $105 after one year. In this case, $100 paid today is *economically equivalent* to $105 paid one year from now. You should be indifferent between them because, either way, you will end up with $105 after one year. Alternative payments that yield the same dollar amounts at a later date are called **equivalent payments**.

If you can invest money to earn more than 5%, the maturity value after one year of a $100 investment will exceed $105. Therefore, $100 paid today has a greater economic value than $105 paid in one year. But if money earns less than 5%, $100 paid today has a smaller economic value than the alternative.

The general question is: How do we compare the economic values of different payments occurring on different dates? In Figure 6.1, X and Y are alternative payments separated by a time interval, t. The diagram indicates the same approach as we used earlier to compare the $100 and $105 payments. That is, first use formula (6-2) to calculate the future value of the payment (X) on the date of the second payment. This gives the amount at the second date that is equivalent to X. Then compare this amount to Y.

Figure 6.1 *Comparing Alternative Payments Using Future Value*

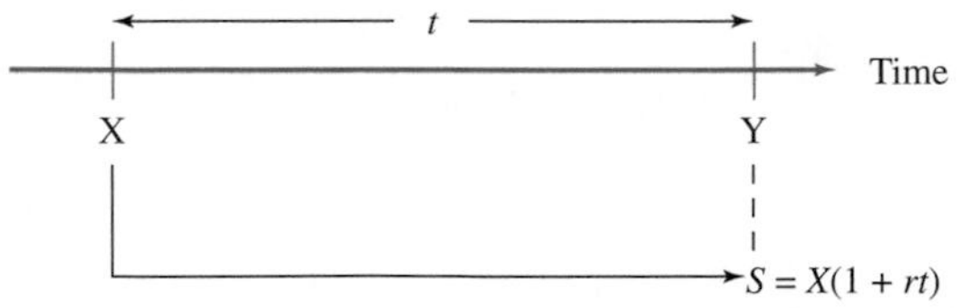

At this point we know how to calculate an equivalent payment at a *subsequent* date. We also need to know how to calculate an equivalent payment at an *earlier*

date. For example, what amount paid today is equivalent to \$100 paid one year from now if money can earn 5% pa? The equivalent payment is the principal that, invested at 5% pa, will have a maturity value of \$100 in one year. That is,

$$P = \frac{S}{1 + rt} = \frac{\$100}{1 + 0.05 \times 1} = \$95.24$$

We use the term **present value** to mean an equivalent payment at a *prior* date. In our example, the present value of \$100 one year earlier is \$95.24.

In Figure 6.2, we return to the comparison of Payments X and Y occurring at different dates. We made the comparison in Figure 6.1 using a future value calculation. You can make the comparison equally well using a present value calculation. First calculate the present value of the second payment (Y) on the date of the first payment. This gives the amount at the earlier date that is equivalent to Y. Then compare this amount to X.

Figure 6.2 *Comparing Alternative Payments Using Present Value*

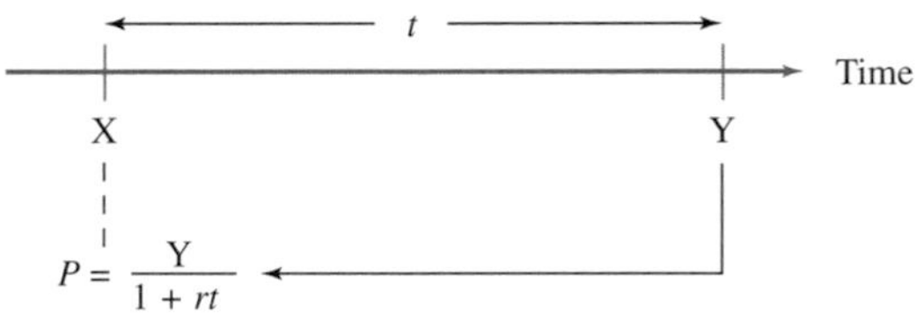

The techniques we have just learned for comparing two payments may be extended to compare any number of payments. Suppose you are asked to compare the economic values of the four payments W, X, Y, and Z shown in Figure 6.3. First calculate the equivalent value of every payment at the *same* date. The term **focal date** is often used for the date at which equivalent values are calculated. The focal date need not coincide with any particular payment date. For the focal date chosen in the diagram, we calculate the present value of Y a time interval t_Y earlier, the future value of X a time interval t_X later, and so on. Then the four equivalent values, P_Y, S_X, P_Z, and S_W may be directly compared.

Figure 6.3 *Comparing Several Payments*

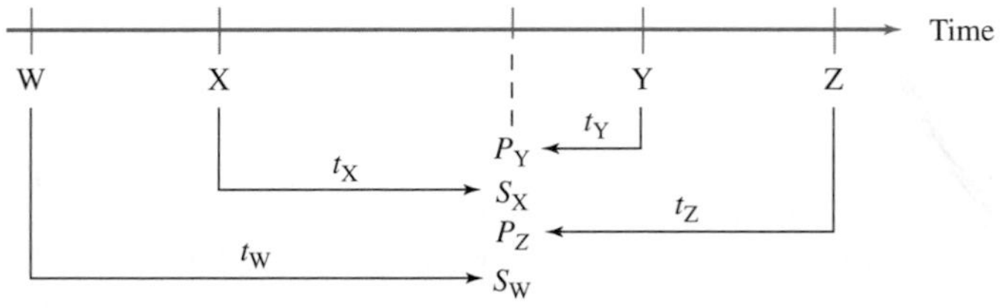

The selection of the interest rate that should be used in an equivalent payment calculation involves the "opportunity cost" concept from economics and the "risk–return" relationship from finance. In this text, we are primarily concerned with the mathematics of calculating equivalent values *given* the appropriate interest rate. Words such as "money can earn . . .", "money is worth . . .", or "money can be invested at . . ." will be used to indicate the interest rate for calculating equivalent payments. At this point, you can think of it as the rate of return that can be earned on a low-risk investment.[4]

Figure 6.4 presents a graph of equivalent values (present value and future value) of \$100. Numerical values are indicated at two-month intervals before and after the scheduled payment date (zero on the time axis). We have chosen a simple interest rate of 12% per annum because it is easy to work with 1% per month. The future value increases by \$1 every month in a straight-line pattern. The present value decreases for longer time periods in advance of the scheduled payment. However, the rate of decrease is less than linear. This is evident from the widening gap between the present-value curve and the straight line extending backward from the future-value region (to the \$88.00 figure).

Figure 6.4 *Graph of Present and Future Values of \$100*

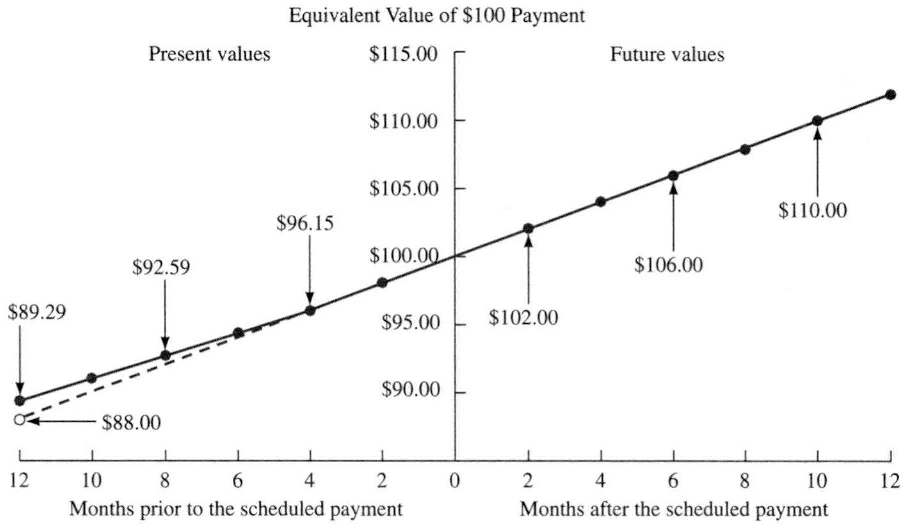

TIP

EFFICIENT USE OF YOUR CALCULATOR

Note that the present value version of formula (6-2) is

$$P = \frac{S}{1 + rt} \qquad \text{which may be written} \qquad P = S \times \left(\frac{1}{1 + rt}\right)$$

The most efficient procedure for using a calculator to evaluate the right side of this formula is to:

1. Calculate the denominator, $1 + rt$.

2. With the value of $1 + rt$ in the calculator's display, press the reciprocal function key, 1/x . The value of $\frac{1}{1+rt}$ then appears in the display.

3. Multiply the number in the display by the value of S.

[4] The lowest risk short-term investment is a Government of Canada treasury bill (Section 7.3). For time frames exceeding one year, the lowest risk investment is a Government of Canada bond (Section 15.1).

Example 6.4A *Calculating a Future Value*

What is the equivalent value on September 15 of a $1000 payment on July 6, if money can earn 7% pa?

Solution

Since we want the equivalent value at a later date, we should calculate the future value on September 15.

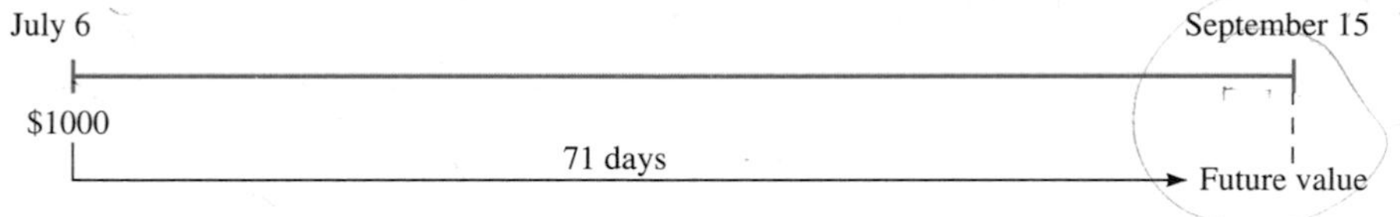

The number of days in the interval is

$$26 + 31 + 14 = 71$$

Substitute $P = \$1000$, $r = 7\%$, and $t = \frac{71}{365}$ into formula (6-2) to obtain the future value:

$$\begin{aligned} S &= P(1 + rt) \\ &= \$1000\left[1 + 0.07\left(\frac{71}{365}\right)\right] \\ &= \$1013.62 \end{aligned}$$

$1000 on July 6 has the equivalent value of $1013.62 on the following September 15.

Example 6.4B *Calculating a Present Value*

What is the equivalent value on March 12 of a $1000 payment on the following July 6 if money is worth 6.8% pa?

Solution

Since we want the equivalent value at an earlier date, we should calculate the present value on March 12.

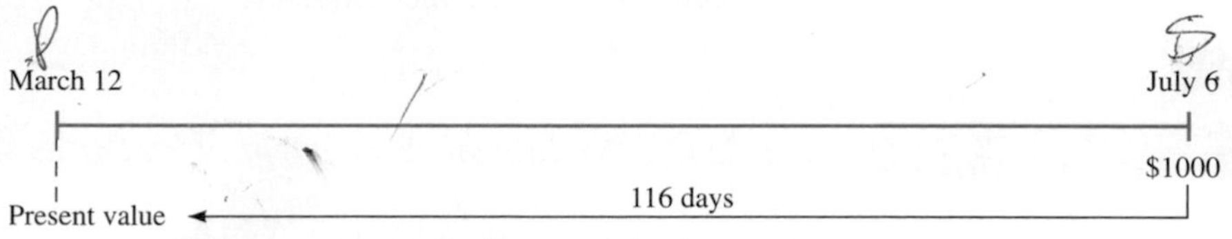

The number of days in the interval is

$$20 + 30 + 31 + 30 + 5 = 116$$

Substituting $S = \$1000$, $r = 6.8\%$, and $t = \frac{116}{365}$ into formula (6-2), we obtain

$$P = \frac{S}{1 + rt} = \frac{\$1000}{1 + 0.068\left(\frac{116}{365}\right)} = \$978.85$$

\$1000 on July 6 has the equivalent value of \$978.85 on the preceding March 12.

Example 6.4C Calculating the Equivalent Payment at a Later Date

Herb is supposed to pay \$1500 to Ranjit on September 20. Herb wishes to delay payment until December 1.

a. What amount should Herb expect to pay on December 1 if Ranjit can earn 8.25% pa on a low-risk investment?

b. Show that Ranjit should not care whether he receives the scheduled payment or the delayed payment.

Solution

a. Herb is seeking a postponement of

$$11 + 31 + 30 = 72 \text{ days}$$

He should expect to pay an amount that is equivalent to \$1500, 72 days later, allowing for an $8\frac{1}{4}\%$ pa time value of money. That is, he should expect to pay the future value of \$1500, 72 days later.

Substituting $P = \$1500$, $t = \frac{72}{365}$, and $r = 8.25\%$ into formula (6-2), the future value is

$$S = P(1 + rt) = \$1500\left[1 + 0.0825\left(\frac{72}{365}\right)\right] = \$1524.41$$

Herb should expect to pay \$1524.41 on December 1 instead of \$1500 on September 20.

b. Suppose that Herb makes the \$1500 payment as scheduled on September 20. Since Ranjit can earn an $8\frac{1}{4}\%$ rate of interest, by December 1 the \$1500 will grow to

$$S = P(1 + rt) = \$1500\left[1 + 0.0825\left(\frac{72}{365}\right)\right] = \$1524.41$$

Ranjit should therefore be indifferent between receiving \$1500 on September 20 or \$1524.41 on December 1 because he will end up with \$1524.41 on December 1 under either alternative.

Example 6.4D Calculating the Equivalent Payment at an Earlier Date

Tanis owes Lola \$1000 payable on December 10. If money can earn $7\frac{1}{2}\%$ pa, what amount should Lola accept in settlement of the debt:

a. 30 days before the scheduled payment date?

b. 60 days before the scheduled payment date?

Solution

a. Lola should accept the amount that is equivalent to \$1000, 30 days earlier, allowing for a $7\frac{1}{2}\%$ pa time value of money. This amount is the present value of the \$1000 at a point 30 days earlier. Using formula (6-2),

$$P = \frac{S}{1 + rt} = \frac{\$1000}{1 + 0.075\left(\frac{30}{365}\right)} = \$993.87$$

Lola should accept \$993.87, 30 days before the scheduled payment of \$1000.

b. The present value of \$1000, 60 days earlier is

$$P = \frac{\$1000}{1 + 0.075\left(\frac{60}{365}\right)} = \$987.82$$

Lola should accept \$987.82, 60 days before the scheduled payment date.

This example also demonstrates that the further back you go before the scheduled payment date, the smaller the equivalent payment will be.

Example 6.4E Comparing the Economic Values of Alternative Payments

Marcus can purchase an airplane ticket now on the airline's Early Bird Sale for \$459, or he can wait and pay \$479 in three months. If he can earn 9% pa on his money, which option should he choose?

Solution

Marcus should choose the price having the smaller economic value. To compare the economic values, first calculate the future value three months from now of the Early Bird price of \$459. Then compare the future value with the regular price of \$479. Select the option having the smaller value.

$$S = P(1 + rt) = \$459\left[1 + 0.09\left(\frac{3}{12}\right)\right] = \$469.33$$

Marcus should buy the ticket at the Early Bird price. However, his true saving is not \$20 but \$479.00 − \$469.33 = \$9.67.

Example 6.4F Finding the Interest Rate That Makes Two Payments Equivalent

Extending the problem in Example 6.4E, what rate of interest would Marcus have to earn in order to be indifferent between the two prices?

Solution

He will be indifferent between the two prices if \$459 invested for three months will grow to \$479. In other words, he will be indifferent if \$459 can earn

$479 − $459 = $20 interest in three months. The interest rate that would cause this to occur is

$$r = \frac{I}{Pt} = \frac{\$20}{\$459 \times \frac{3}{12}} = 0.174 = 17.4\%$$

If Marcus could earn a 17.4% rate of interest, he could invest the $459 for three months and it would mature at $479, providing exactly the right amount to buy the ticket. (If Marcus could earn more than 17.4% pa, it would be to his advantage to invest the $459 now and buy the ticket three months later.)

Example 6.4G *Calculating a Prior Equivalent Payment*

A furniture store advertises a dining table and chairs for $1495 with nothing down, no payments, and no interest for six months. What cash price should the store be willing to accept if, on a six-month investment, it can earn

a. 11% pa?

b. 13% pa?

Solution

The store faces the choice between the cash offer and $1495 to be received six months from now (if a customer takes the credit terms). The store should be willing to accept a cash amount that is today's equivalent of $1495. In other words, the store should accept the present value of $1495.

a. If money can earn 11% pa,

$$P = \frac{S}{1 + rt} = \frac{\$1495}{1 + 0.11\left(\frac{6}{12}\right)} = \frac{\$1495}{1.055} = \$1417.06$$

The store should accept a cash offer of $1417.06

b. If money can earn 13% pa,

$$P = \frac{\$1495}{1 + 0.13\left(\frac{6}{12}\right)} = \$1403.76$$

The store should accept $1403.76 cash.

Concept Questions

1. What is meant by "equivalent payments"?
2. Under what circumstance is $100 paid today equivalent to $110 paid one year from now?
3. How can you determine whether two payments are equivalent to each other?
4. What is meant by the "present value" of a payment that is scheduled for a future date?

5. How can you determine which of three payments has the largest economic value?

6. If the interest rate money can earn is revised upward, will a scheduled payment's present value be higher or lower? Explain.

Exercise 6.4

Answers to the odd-numbered problems are at the end of the book.

Calculate the missing values in Problems 1 through 10.

Problem	Scheduled payment ($)	Interest rate (%)	Equivalent payment ($)
1.	560	$10\frac{3}{4}$	?; 5 months earlier
2.	1215	$8\frac{1}{2}$	?; 7 months later
3.	5230	9.25	?; 174 days later
4.	1480	6.75	?; 60 days earlier
5.	1975	?	1936.53; 100 days earlier
6.	2370	?	2508.79; 190 days later
7.	830	9.9	850.26; ? days ?
8.	3500	$12\frac{1}{4}$	3362.69; ? months ?
9.	4850	$8\frac{3}{4}$	4574.73; ? days ?
10.	2740	$13\frac{1}{2}$	2785.60; ? days ?

In Problems 11 through 14 determine:

a. Whether the earlier or the later payment has the greater economic value at the given interest rate.

b. The interest rate at which the two payments would be equivalent.

Problem	Earlier payment ($)	Later payment ($)	Time interval	Interest rate
11.	560	570	60 days	$10\frac{3}{4}$% pa
12.	1215	1280	11 months	$8\frac{1}{2}$% pa
13.	5230	5500	5 months	0.6% per month
14.	1480	1515	150 days	6.75% pa

15. What amount on September 24 is equivalent to $1000 on the following December 1 if money can earn 14% pa?

16. What amount on January 13 is equivalent to $1000 on the preceding August 12 if money can earn 9.5% pa?

17. Victor wishes to postpone for 90 days the payment of $450 that he owes to Roxanne. If money now earns 6.75% pa, what amount can he reasonably expect to pay at the later date?

18. Allan owes Value Furniture $1600, which is scheduled to be paid on August 15. Allan has surplus funds on June 15 and will settle the debt early if Value Furniture will make an adjustment reflecting the current short-term interest rate of 7.25%. What amount should be acceptable to both parties?

19. On September 10 Duncan Stereo and TV advertised that any TV set may be purchased with nothing down, no interest, and nothing to pay until next year (January 2). What cash price should Duncan accept on a TV set listed at $1195 if Duncan can use cash to pay off debt on which it pays a 13.5% rate of interest?

20. A $5000 payment is scheduled for 120 days from now. If money is worth 7.25% pa, calculate the payment's equivalent value at each of nine different dates—today and every 30 days for the next 240 days.

21. A $3000 payment is scheduled for six months from now. If money is worth 6.75% pa, calculate the payment's equivalent values at two-month intervals beginning today and ending one year from now.

22. During its 50-50 Sale, Marpole Furniture will sell its merchandise for 50% down, with the balance payable in six months. No interest is charged for the first six months. What 100% cash price should Marpole accept on a $1845 chesterfield and chair set if Marpole can earn a return of 10.75% pa on its funds?

23. Jody received a $2000 college entrance scholarship. Nine months later Brian was awarded a $2100 academic proficiency scholarship for his outstanding grades in the first year of studies. Which scholarship had the greater economic value if money can earn 8.25% pa?

•24. Mr. and Mrs. Chan are considering two offers on a building lot that they own in a nearby town. One is for $49,000, consisting of $10,000 down and the balance to be paid in a lump payment in eight months. The second is for $50,000, with $10,000 down and the balance to be paid in one year. Which offer has the greater economic value if money can earn 7.5% pa? (Use today as the focal date.)

•25. What rate of return must money earn for Mr. and Mrs. Chan to be indifferent between the two offers in Problem 24?

•26. What interest rate must money earn for a payment of $1389 on August 20 to be equivalent to a payment of $1348 on the previous March 29?

6.5 The Equivalent Value of a Payment Stream

A **payment stream** is a series of two or more payments required by a single transaction or contract. To get their combined value, you might be inclined to add the payments. Then every dollar, regardless of when it is paid, has an equal influence on the sum. In other words, the simple addition of payments occurring on different dates implies that a dollar on one date has the same economic value as a dollar on any other date. But we have seen that the economic value of a dollar depends on when it is paid. This property of money is often referred to as the **time value of money.** The simple addition of the payments ignores the time value of money. To determine the equivalent value of a payment stream, we must take into account the time value of money.

In Section 6.4, you learned how to calculate the equivalent value, on any date, of a *single* payment. A logical extension of this basic idea allows us to determine the equivalent value of a payment *stream.* We simply add the equivalent values (at the chosen focal date) of the individual payments. The following example illustrates the procedure.

Consider a payment stream consisting of three payments: \$1000, \$2000, and \$3000, scheduled for March 1, May 1, and December 1 of the same year. Let us calculate the single payment on August 1 that is equivalent to the three scheduled payments. (This is the same problem as calculating the economic value of the three payments on August 1.) Suppose money can earn a simple interest rate of 8% pa.

For problems involving multiple payments, a **time diagram** is virtually essential. It consists of a time axis or *time line* showing the dollar amounts and the dates of the payments. Figure 6.5 presents a time diagram for the problem at hand. The first benefit of a timeline is that it helps us organize the data. Indicate the payment dates above the time line and the amounts of the corresponding payments below the line. Do not make your diagram too small—use the full width of your page. Attempt to draw reasonably proportionate time intervals between the dates.

Figure 6.5 *Entering Given Data on a Time Diagram*

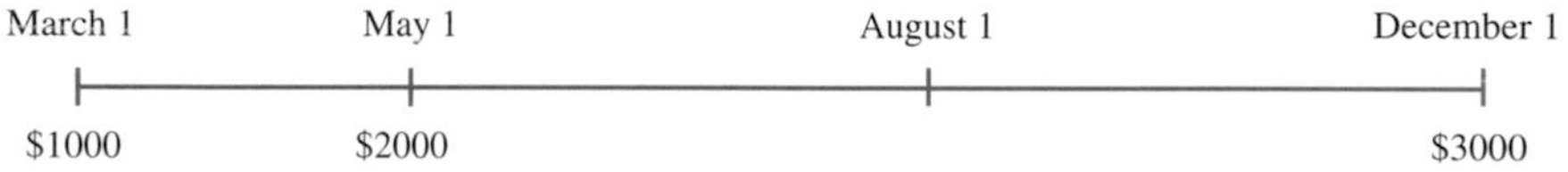

The solution idea for this problem is:

$$\begin{pmatrix}\text{The equivalent payment}\\ \text{on August 1}\end{pmatrix} = \begin{pmatrix}\text{The sum of the equivalent values of the}\\ \text{individual payments on August 1}\end{pmatrix}$$

The second benefit of a time diagram is that it allows us to indicate the steps needed to implement the solution idea. In Figure 6.6, an arrow is drawn from each payment to the August 1 date (on which we want the equivalent value). On each arrow we can write the number of days in the time interval. An appropriate symbol (*S* for future value, *P* for present value) is entered for each equivalent value. Finally,

Figure 6.6 *Showing the Solution Steps on a Time Diagram*

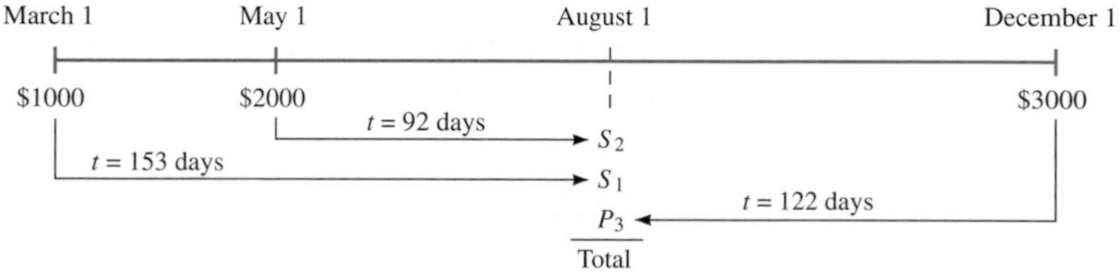

we can indicate on the diagram that the three equivalent values are to be added. The written solution is now a matter of following the steps outlined in the diagram.

$$S_1 = \text{Future value on August 1 of the \$1000 payment}$$
$$= \$1000\left(1 + 0.08 \times \frac{153}{365}\right)$$
$$= \$1033.53$$
$$S_2 = \text{Future value on August 1 of the \$2000 payment}$$
$$= \$2000\left(1 + 0.08 \times \frac{92}{365}\right)$$
$$= \$2040.33$$
$$P_3 = \text{Present value on August 1 of the \$3000 payment}$$
$$= \frac{\$3000}{1 + 0.08 \times \frac{122}{365}}$$
$$= \$2921.87$$

The equivalent value on August 1 of the payment stream is

$$S_1 + S_2 + P_3 = \$1033.53 + \$2040.33 + \$2921.87 = \$5995.73$$

The significance of this equivalent value is that a payment of \$5995.73 on August 1 is economically equivalent to the three scheduled payments. The recipient will be in the same economic position whether he accepts \$5995.73 on August 1 or he receives the three payments as scheduled.

Example 6.5A *Calculating a Payment Equivalent to Three Scheduled Payments*

A financial obligation was supposed to be settled by payments of \$1000 on a date two months ago, \$2000 today, and \$3000 on a date six months from now. The creditor has agreed to accept a single equivalent payment two months from now instead of the scheduled payments. If money can earn 12% pa, what will be the size of the equivalent payment?

Solution

Construct a time diagram indicating the scheduled payments and their equivalent values on the date of the replacement payment.

Note: In the absence of specific calendar dates, we will represent today as time 0 on the time axis. Dates prior to today will have negative labels. However, time intervals to be substituted for t in $S = P(1 + rt)$ will always be positive.

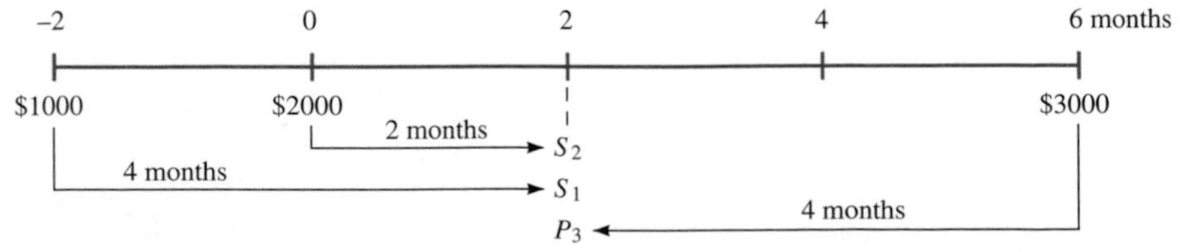

The size of the single replacement payment two months from now will be

$$S_1 + S_2 + P_3$$

where

$$\begin{aligned} S_1 &= \text{Future value of } \$1000 \\ &= \$1000\left[1 + 0.06\left(\frac{4}{12}\right)\right] \\ &= \$1020 \\ S_2 &= \text{Future value of } \$2000 \\ &= \$2000\left[1 + 0.06\left(\frac{2}{12}\right)\right] \\ &= \$2020 \\ P_3 &= \text{Present value of } \$3000 \\ &= \frac{\$3000}{1 + 0.06\left(\frac{4}{12}\right)} \\ &= \$2941.18 \end{aligned}$$

Then

$$S_1 + S_2 + P_3 = \$1020 + \$2020 + \$2941.18 = \$5981.18$$

The single equivalent payment two months from now is \$5981.18.

Example 6.5B Calculating a Payment Equivalent to Interest-Earning Obligations

Four months ago Darren borrowed \$1000 from Sean and agreed to repay the loan in two payments to be made five and ten months after the date of the agreement. Each payment is to consist of \$500 of principal, and interest at the rate of 9% pa on that \$500 from the date of the agreement. Today Darren is asking Sean to accept instead a single payment three months from now to settle the debt. What payment should Sean require if money can now earn 7% pa?

Solution

In this problem we do not initially know the dollar amounts of the scheduled payments because we do not know how much interest must be paid along with each \$500 of principal. The first step, then, is to calculate the maturity value of each \$500 payment on its scheduled payment date.

The maturity values are represented by S_1 and S_2 in the following time diagram.

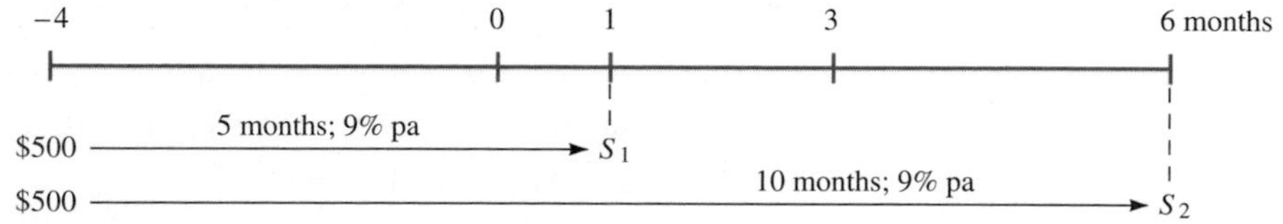

$$S_1 = \$500\left[1 + 0.09\left(\frac{5}{12}\right)\right] = \$518.75$$

$$S_2 = \$500\left[1 + 0.09\left(\frac{10}{12}\right)\right] = \$537.50$$

Now we can construct a time diagram presenting the scheduled payments and their equivalent values, S and P, on the date of the replacement payment.

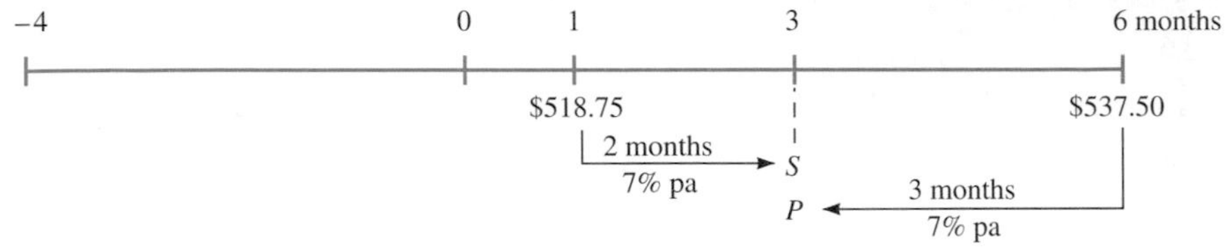

The *current* rate of interest, 7%, is used to calculate the equivalent values of the scheduled payments.

$$\begin{aligned} S &= \text{Future value of \$518.75 on a date two months later} \\ &= \$518.75\left[1 + 0.07\left(\frac{2}{12}\right)\right] \\ &= \$524.80 \\ P &= \text{Present value of \$537.50 on a date three months earlier} \\ &= \frac{\$537.50}{1 + 0.07\left(\frac{3}{12}\right)} \\ &= \$528.26 \end{aligned}$$

The single equivalent payment is

$$S + P = \$524.80 + \$528.26 = \$1053.06$$

Sean should require a payment of \$1053.06 on a date three months from now.

Example 6.5C Comparing the Economic Value of Two Payment Streams

Which of the following two payment streams has the greater economic value today if money can earn 6.5%: \$500 in two months plus \$500 in five months, or \$700 in three months plus \$300 in four months?

Solution

Construct a time line for each payment stream, indicating the scheduled payments and their equivalent values today. The stream with the larger total equivalent value today has the greater economic value.

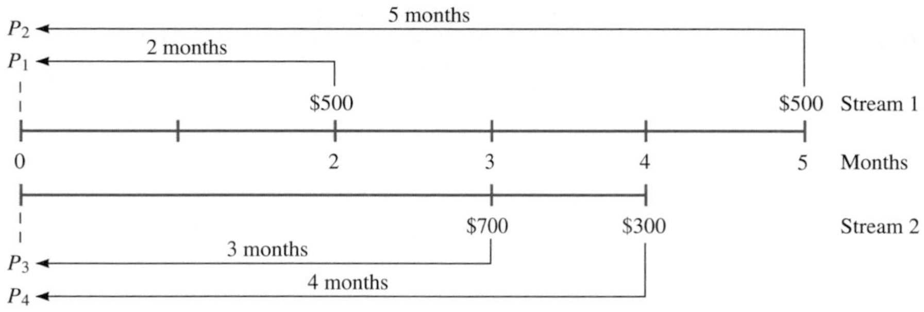

$$
\begin{aligned}
\text{Equivalent value of Stream 1} &= P_1 + P_2 \\
&= \frac{\$500}{1 + 0.065\left(\frac{2}{12}\right)} + \frac{\$500}{1 + 0.065\left(\frac{5}{12}\right)} \\
&= \$494.641 + \$486.815 \\
&= \$981.46
\end{aligned}
$$

$$
\begin{aligned}
\text{Equivalent value of Stream 2} &= P_3 + P_4 \\
&= \frac{\$700}{1 + 0.065\left(\frac{3}{12}\right)} + \frac{\$300}{1 + 0.065\left(\frac{4}{12}\right)} \\
&= \$688.807 + \$293.638 \\
&= \$982.45
\end{aligned}
$$

Even though the sum of the nominal payments in each stream is $1000, the second stream's economic value today is 99 cents greater than the first stream's value. This happens because, on average, the money in the second stream is received sooner (3.3 months for Stream 2 versus 3.5 months for Stream 1).

POINT OF INTEREST

Consumers Often Defy Common Sense

Imagine two refrigerators in the appliance section of a department store. One sells for $700 and uses $85 worth of electricity a year. The other is $100 more expensive but costs only $25 a year to run, saving the owner $60 per year. Given that either refrigerator should last at least 10 years without repair, consumers would overwhelmingly buy the second model, right?

Well, not exactly. Many studies by economists have shown that in a wide range of decisions about money—from paying taxes to buying major appliances—consumers consistently make decisions that defy common sense.

In some cases—as in the refrigerator example—this means that people are generally unwilling to pay a little more money up front to save a lot of money in the long run. At times, psychological studies have shown, consumers appear to assign entirely whimsical values to money, values that change depending on time and circumstances.

In recent years, these apparently irrational patterns of human behaviour have become a subject of intense interest among economists and psychologists, both for what they say about the way the human mind works and because of their implications for public policy. How, for example, can we move toward a more efficient use of electricity if so many consumers refuse to buy energy-efficient appliances even when such a move is in their own best interest?

At the heart of research into the economic behaviour of consumers is a concept known as the *discount rate.* It is a measure of how consumers compare the value of a dollar received today with one received tomorrow.

Suppose, for example, you win \$1000 in a lottery. How much more money would officials have to give you before you would agree to postpone cashing the cheque for a year? Some people might insist on at least another \$100, or 10%, since that is roughly how much it would take to make up for the combined effects of a year's worth of inflation and lost interest.

But the studies show that someone who wants immediate gratification might not be willing to postpone receiving the \$1000 for 20% or 30% or even 40% more money. In the language of economists, this type of person has a high discount rate: He or she discounts the value of \$1000 so much over a year that it would take hundreds of extra dollars to make waiting as attractive as getting the money immediately.

Of the two alternatives, waiting a year for more money is clearly more rational than taking the \$1000 now. Why would people turn down \$1400 next year in favour of \$1000 today? Even if they need the \$1000 immediately, they would be better off borrowing it from a bank, even at 20% or even 30% interest. Then, a year later, they could pay off the loan—including the interest—with the \$1400 and pocket the difference.

The fact is, however, that economists found numerous examples of such high discount rates implicit in consumer behaviour. While consumers were very much aware of savings to be made at the point of purchase, they so heavily discounted the value of monthly electrical costs they would pay over the lifetime of their dryer or freezer that they were oblivious of the potential for greater savings.

Gas water heaters, for example, were found to carry an implicit discount rate of 100 percent. This means that in deciding which model was cheapest over the long run, consumers acted as if today's value of a \$100 gas bill for the first year was only

$$P = \frac{S}{1 + rt} = \frac{\$100}{1 + 1.00 \times 1} = \frac{\$100}{2} = \$50$$

The next \$100 gas bill in the second year was worth \$25 (\$100 cut in half for each of two years), and so on through the life of the appliance. Few consumers actually make this formal calculation, of course. But, on average, they behave this way.

Some experiments, for example, have shown that the way in which consumers make decisions about money depends a great deal on how much is at stake. Few people are willing to give up \$10 now for \$15 next year. But most will give up \$100 now for \$150 next year, a fact that helps explain why consumers appear to care less about many small electricity and gas bills—even if they add up to a lot—than one big initial outlay.

SOURCE: "Consumers Often Defy Common Sense" by Malcolm Gladwell from *The Washington Post.*

Concept Questions

1. What is meant by the "time value of money"?
2. We frequently hear a news item that goes something like: "Joe Superstar signed a five-year deal worth $25 million. Under the contract he will be paid $3 million, $4 million, $5 million, $6 million and $7 million in successive years." In what respect is the statement incorrect? How should the value of the contract be calculated?
3. How do you determine the economic value on a particular date of a series of payments?
4. How can you determine whether two payment streams are equivalent to each other?
5. If the interest rate money can earn is revised upward, is today's economic value of a stream of future payments higher or lower? Explain.

Exercise 6.5

Answers to the odd-numbered problems are at the end of the book.

In Problems 1 through 6, calculate the equivalent value of the scheduled payments if money can earn the rate of return specified in the last column. Assume that any payments due before today have been missed.

Problem	Scheduled payments	Equivalent value as of:	Interest rate (%)
1.	$500 6 months ago, $300 in 3 months	Today	$9\frac{1}{2}$
2.	$1000 today, $1500 in 5 months	2 months from now	$10\frac{1}{4}$
3.	$900 150 days ago, $1000 in 30 days	90 days from now	$7\frac{3}{4}$
4.	$2500 in 70 days, $4000 in 200 days	30 days from now	12
5.	$1000 60 days ago, $1500 in 10 days, $2000 in 150 days	Today	$8\frac{1}{2}$
6.	$1750 75 days ago, $1750 today, $1750 in 75 days	45 days from now	9.9

7. Payments of $850 and $1140 were scheduled to be paid five months ago and four months from now, respectively. If the first payment was not made, what payment three months from now would place the payee in the same financial position as the scheduled payments? Money can earn $8\frac{1}{4}\%$ pa.
8. For the scheduled payments in Problem 7, determine the equivalent payment today.

9. Two payments of $2000 each are to be received six and 12 months from now. If money is worth 10% pa, what is the total equivalent value of the payments:

a. Today?

b. Six months from today?

c. Explain why the answer in part (b) is larger.

10. Two payments of $3000 each are due in 50 and 100 days. What is their combined economic value today if money can earn:

a. 9% pa?

b. 11% pa?

c. Explain why the answer in part (b) is smaller.

11. If money earns 9.5% pa, calculate and compare the economic value today of the following payment streams:

a. Payments of $900 and $1400 due 150 and 80 days ago, respectively.

b. Payments of $800, $600, and $1000 due 30, 75, and 125 days from now, respectively.

12. What is the economic value today of each of the following payment streams if money is worth 7.5% pa? (Note that the two streams have the same total nominal value.)

a. $1000, $3000, and $2000 due in one, three, and five months, respectively.

b. Two $3000 payments due two and four months from now.

•13. Eight months ago, Louise agreed to pay Thelma $750 and $950 six and 12 months, respectively, from the date of the agreement. With each payment, Louise agreed to pay interest at the rate of 9.5% pa from the date of the agreement. Louise failed to make the first payment and now wishes to settle her obligations with a single payment four months from now. What payment should Thelma be willing to accept if money can earn 7.75%?

•14. Ninety days ago Stella signed an agreement with Ed requiring her to make three payments of $400 plus interest 90, 150, and 210 days, respectively, from the date of the agreement. Each payment was to include interest on the $400 principal at the rate of 13.5% from the date of the agreement. Stella now wants Ed to renegotiate the agreement and accept a single payment 30 days from now, instead of the three scheduled payments. What payment should Ed require in the new agreement if money is worth 8.5%?

*6.6 Loans: A Principle About Principal

In Section 8.3, we will develop (in the context of compound interest) an important relationship between the principal amount of a loan and the payments required to pay off the loan. The relationship applies to *all* compound interest loans and to *some* loans[5] at simple interest. Since Section 8.3 is covered in virtually all business math curricula but this section is frequently omitted, we will simply state the relationship at this point and demonstrate its use.

> *A General Principle Concerning Loans*
> The original principal amount of a loan is equal to the sum of the present values of all the payments required to pay off a loan. The interest rate used for the present-value calculations is the interest rate charged on the loan.

Example 6.6A *Calculating the Size of the Final Loan Payment*

A \$5000 loan advanced on April 1 at $10\frac{1}{2}\%$ pa requires payments of \$1800 on each of June 1 and August 1, and a final payment on October 1. What must the final payment be to satisfy the loan in full?

Solution

Let x represent the amount of the final payment. The payments and their equivalent (present) values, P_1, P_2, and P_3, are shown in the following time diagram.

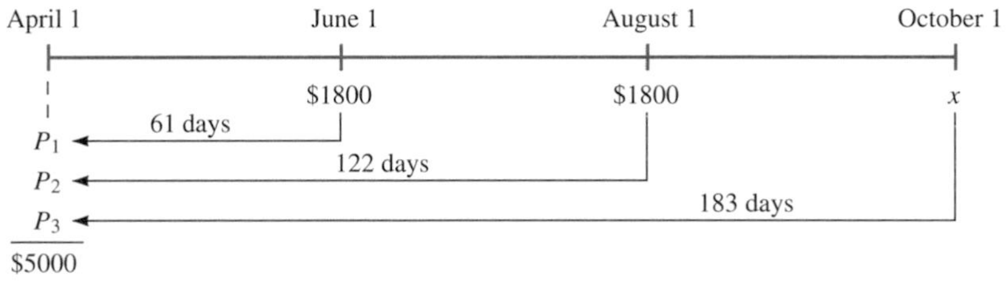

Since the original loan equals the present value of all of the payments, then

$$\$5000 = P_1 + P_2 + P_3$$

where

$$P_1 = \frac{\$1800}{1 + 0.105\left(\frac{61}{365}\right)} = \frac{\$1800}{1.0175479} = \$1768.96$$

$$P_2 = \frac{\$1800}{1 + 0.105\left(\frac{122}{365}\right)} = \frac{\$1800}{1.0350959} = \$1738.97$$

$$P_3 = \frac{x}{1 + 0.105\left(\frac{183}{365}\right)} = \frac{x}{1.0526438} = 0.9499889x$$

---

[5] In general, a loan payment consists of a principal portion and an interest portion. Most loans are structured so that the interest portion of a payment is the accrued interest on the *entire* principal balance still outstanding. However, for the relationship presented in this section to apply precisely to a simple interest loan, the following condition must be met. The interest portion of a simple interest loan payment must be the accrued interest on *only the principal portion of the payment.* Accrued interest on other outstanding principal must be paid only when that principal is repaid. Instances of loans meeting this condition are rare.

Thus

$$\$5000 = \$1768.96 + \$1738.97 + 0.9499889x$$
$$\$1492.07 = 0.9499889x$$
$$x = \frac{\$1492.07}{0.9499889} = \$1570.62$$

The final payment on October 1 must be \$1570.62.

Example 6.6B *Calculating the Size of Equal Loan Payments*

A \$4000 loan made at 11.75% pa is to be repaid in three equal payments due 30, 90, and 150 days, respectively, after the date of the loan. Determine the size of the payments.

Solution

Let the amount of each payment be represented by x. The payments and their equivalent (present) values are presented in the following time diagram.

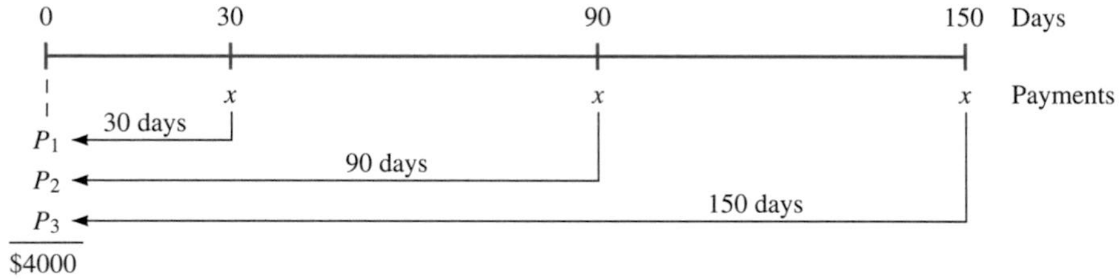

The original loan is equal to the present value of all of the payments:

$$\$4000 = P_1 + P_2 + P_3$$

where

$$P_1 = \frac{x}{1 + 0.1175\left(\frac{30}{365}\right)} = \frac{x}{1.0096575} = 0.9904348x$$

$$P_2 = \frac{x}{1 + 0.1175\left(\frac{90}{365}\right)} = \frac{x}{1.0289726} = 0.9718432x$$

$$P_3 = \frac{x}{1 + 0.1175\left(\frac{150}{365}\right)} = \frac{x}{1.0482877} = 0.9539366x$$

Thus,

$$\$4000 = 0.9904348x + 0.9718432x + 0.9539366x$$
$$= 2.916215x$$
$$x = \frac{\$4000}{2.916215} = \$1371.64$$

Each payment should be \$1371.64.

Exercise 6.6

Answers to the odd-numbered problems are at the end of the book.

For each of Problems 1 through 4, the original \$3000 loan was advanced on March 1. The loan is to be repaid by three payments whose dates (in the same year) are indicated in the column following the respective payment. Calculate the unknown payment in each case. Use the loan date as the focal date.

Problem	Payment (\$)	Date	Payment (\$)	Date	Payment (\$)	Date	Interest rate (%)
•1.	1000	May 1	1000	June 1	?	July 1	11
•2.	1000	April 1	?	June 1	1000	August 1	$9\frac{1}{2}$
•3.	?	April 13	1100	May 27	1100	July 13	10.2
•4.	500	March 31	1000	June 15	?	August 31	$8\frac{1}{4}$

Calculate the size of the equal payments for Problems 5 through 10. Use the loan date as the focal date.

Problem	Original loan (\$)	Interest rate (%)	Number of payments	Dates of payments (after the date of the loan)
5.	1000	9	2	30 and 60 days
6.	3000	$10\frac{1}{4}$	2	50 and 150 days
•7.	2500	$8\frac{3}{4}$	3	2, 4, and 7 months
•8.	8000	$11\frac{1}{2}$	3	30, 90, and 150 days
•9.	5000	12	4	100, 150, 200, and 250 days
•10.	7500	9.9	4	2, 5, 9, and 12 months

•11. Payments of \$2600, due 50 days ago, and \$3100, due in 40 days, are to be replaced by \$3000 today and another payment in 30 days. What must the second payment be if the payee is to end up in an equivalent financial position? Money now earns 8.25% pa. Use 30 days from now as the focal date.

•12. A loan of \$10,000 is to be repaid by three payments of \$2500 due in two, four, and six months, and a fourth payment due in eight months. What should be the size of the fourth payment if an interest rate of 11% is charged on the loan? Use today as the focal date.

•13. A loan of \$4000 at 13% pa is to be repaid by three equal payments due four, six, and eight months after the date on which the money was advanced. Calculate the amount of each payment.

•14. Anthony borrowed \$7500 on September 15 and agreed to repay the loan by three equal payments on the following November 10, December 30, and February 28. Calculate the payment size if the interest rate on the loan was $11\frac{3}{4}$% pa.

•15. Maurice borrowed \$6000 from Heidi on April 23 and agreed to make payments of \$2000 on June 1 and \$2000 on August 1, and to pay the balance on October 1. If simple interest at the rate of 10% pa was charged on the loan, what is the amount of the third payment?

*Appendix: An Aid for Determining the Number of Days in Each Month

Figure 6.7 presents a method for determining which months have 31 days. The knuckles and the spaces between them are consecutively given the names of the months as shown in the figure. Then each knuckle corresponds to a month with 31 days and each space corresponds to a short month.

Figure 6.7 *"Knuckle Months" Have 31 Days*

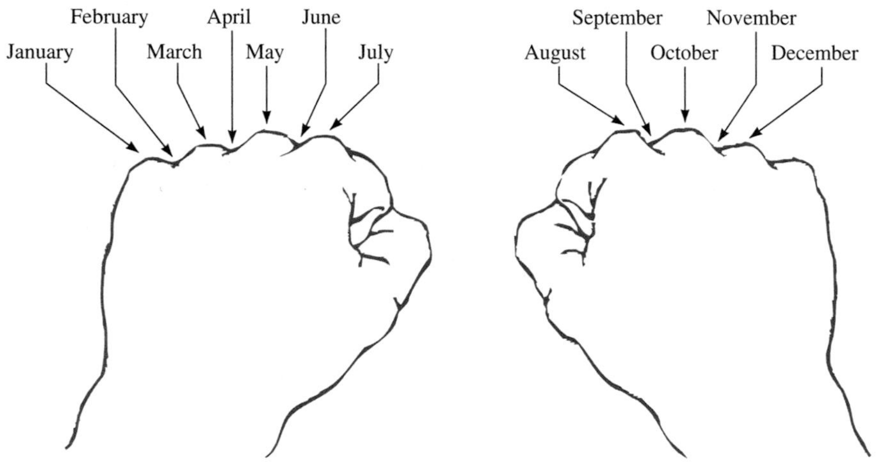

Review Problems

Answers to the odd-numbered review problems are at the end of the book.

1. Peter has forgotten the rate of simple interest he earned on a 120-day term deposit at the Bank of Nova Scotia. At the end of the 120 days, he received interest of \$327.95 on his \$21,000 deposit. What rate of simple interest was his deposit earning?

◆ 2. Evelyn put \$15,000 into a 90-day term deposit at Montreal Trust paying a simple interest rate of 5.2% pa. When the term deposit matured, she invested the entire amount of the principal and interest from the first term deposit into a new 90-day term deposit earning the same rate of interest. What total amount of interest did she earn on both term deposits?

3. Mary borrowed \$1750 from Jason on November 15, 1998, and agreed to repay the debt with simple interest at the rate of 7.4% pa on June 3, 1999. How much interest was owed on June 3?

◆ 4. Bert borrowed \$7500 from Delores on November 7, 1997. When Bert repaid the loan, Delores charged \$190.02 interest. If the rate of simple interest on the loan was $6\frac{3}{4}\%$, on what date did Bert repay the loan?

5. Jack received the proceeds from an inheritance on March 15. He wants to set aside, in a term deposit on March 16, an amount sufficient to provide a \$45,000 down payment for the purchase of a home on November 1. If the current interest rate on 181-day to 270-day deposits is $5\frac{3}{4}\%$, what amount should he place in the term deposit?

6. A rototiller that you are planning to buy next April 1 is advertised at \$499.95 in a fall clearance special that will end on the preceding September 15. What annual rate of simple interest will you earn if you "invest" in the rototiller at the sale price on September 15 instead of waiting until the following April 1 to purchase it at the regular price of \$579.00? (Assume that the intervening February has 28 days.)

7. What amount on January 23 is equivalent to \$1000 on the preceding August 18 if money can earn $6\frac{1}{2}\%$ pa?

8. Mr. and Mrs. Parsons are considering two offers to purchase their summer cottage. One is for \$100,000, consisting of \$20,000 down and the balance to be paid in a lump payment in one year. The second is for \$96,000, with \$48,000 down and the balance to be paid in six months. Compare the current economic values of the two offers if money can earn:

   a. 6% pa **b.** 9% pa

9. Payments of \$1000 and \$7500 were originally scheduled to be paid five months ago and four months from now, respectively. What payment two months from now would place the payee in an equivalent financial position if money can earn $6\frac{1}{4}\%$ pa?

10. If money earns 7.5% pa, calculate and compare the economic value today of the following payment streams:

    a. Payments of \$1800 and \$2800 due 150 and 90 days ago, respectively.

    b. Payments of \$1600, \$1200, and \$2000 due 30, 75, and 120 days from now, respectively.

◆ 11. Nine months ago, Muriel agreed to pay Tanya \$1200 and \$800 on dates six and 12 months, respectively, from the date of the agreement. With each payment Muriel agreed to pay interest at the rate of $8\frac{1}{2}\%$ pa from the date of the agreement. Muriel failed to make the first payment and now wishes to settle her obligations with a single payment four months from now. What payment should Tanya be willing to accept if money can earn $6\frac{3}{4}\%$?

12. A \$9000 loan is to be repaid in three equal payments occurring 60, 180, and 300 days, respectively, after the date of the loan. Calculate the size of these payments if the interest rate on the loan is $7\frac{1}{4}\%$ pa. Use the loan date as the focal date.

Self-Test Exercise

Answers to the self-test problems are at the end of the book.

1. If \$3702.40 earned \$212.45 interest from September 17, 1999, to March 11, 2001, what rate of interest was earned?
2. A loan of \$3300 at $9\frac{1}{4}\%$ pa simple interest was made on March 27. On what date was it repaid if the interest cost was \$137.99?
3. What amount invested at $9\frac{1}{2}\%$ on November 19, 1997, had a maturity value of \$10,000 on March 3, 1998?
4. Sheldrick Contracting owes Western Equipment \$60,000 payable on June 14. In late April, Sheldrick has surplus cash and wants to settle its debt to Western Equipment, if Western will agree to a fair reduction reflecting the current 7.6% interest rate that short-term funds can earn. What amount on April 29 should Sheldrick propose to pay to Western?
5. Peter and Reesa can book their Horizon Holiday package at the early-booking price of \$3850, or wait four months and pay the full price of \$3995.
   a. Which option should they select if money can earn 9.25% pa?
   b. At what interest rate would they be indifferent between the two prices?
6. The first two of the following three payments were not made as scheduled. \$1200 was due seven months ago, \$900 was due two months ago, and \$1500 is due in one month. The three payments are to be replaced by a single equivalent payment due three months from now. What should the payment be if money is worth 9.9% pa? Use three months from now as the focal date.
7. Two payments of \$5000 are to be received four and eight months from now.
   a. What is the combined equivalent value of the two payments today if money can earn 9% pa?
   b. If the rate of interest money can earn is 7% pa, what is the payments' combined equivalent value today?

Summary of Notation and Key Formulas

P = Principal amount of the loan or investment; Present value
r = Annual rate of simple interest
t = Time period (term), in years, of the loan or investment
I = Amount of interest paid or received
S = Maturity value of a loan or investment; Future value

Formula (6-1)	$I = Prt$	Finding the amount of simple interest earned
Formula (6-2)	$S = P(1 + rt)$	Finding the maturity value or future value of a lump amount

A GENERAL PRINCIPLE CONCERNING LOANS

The sum of the present values of all of the payments required to pay off a loan equals the original principal of the loan. The interest rate used in the present-value calculation is the rate of interest charged on the loan.

List of Key Terms

CHAPTER OUTLINE

LEARNING OBJECTIVES

After completing this chapter, you will be able to:

- Calculate the interest paid on savings accounts, term deposits, and short-term guaranteed investment certificates
- State the Valuation Principle and apply it to the calculation of the fair market value of an investment providing specified future cash flows
- Calculate the market price and rate of return for Treasury bills and commercial paper
- Describe typical terms, conditions, and repayment arrangements for revolving (demand) loans, fixed-payment (demand) loans, and Canada Student Loans
- Prepare loan repayment schedules for revolving loans, fixed-payment loans, and Canada Student Loans

CHAPTER

7

Applications of Simple Interest

HAVE YOU HEARD OF TERM deposits, short-term Guaranteed Investment Certificates (GICs), and Treasury bills? Perhaps not, because these short-term simple-interest investments do not get the media attention received by more volatile and exciting long-term investments such as stocks and bonds. But short-term (or "money market") investments represent a much larger part of the investment "picture" than their low profile suggests. For example, the average size of Canadian money market mutual funds (that hold short-term investments) is similar to the average size of mutual funds that invest in stocks and bonds. When a "bear" market hits stocks, many investors move their money from stocks to these low-risk short-term investments.

Our discussion of short-term investments raises the question: "How much should you pay for an investment?" Answering the question leads us to the Valuation Principle—a very important concept having broad application.

Most businesses and many individuals have a line of credit or other demand loan from a financial institution. Over half of post-secondary graduates face repayment of student loans. We conclude the chapter by describing the features and the calculation of interest on such loans.

*7.1 Savings Accounts, Term Deposits, and Short-Term GICs

Banks, trust companies, and credit unions use $I = Prt$ for calculating the interest they pay depositors and investors on a variety of savings accounts and short-term investment products. Interest on most **savings accounts** is calculated on the daily closing balance and paid monthly. This means that you earn one day's interest on each day's closing balance, but the interest is not credited to your account until the last day of the month. Some savings accounts have a tiered scale of interest rates, with higher rates paid when the account's balance reaches certain higher levels. The interest rates on savings accounts are floating; they are adjusted to follow the trend of short-term rates in the financial markets. Interest on a few savings and chequing accounts is calculated on only the *minimum monthly* balance and paid monthly or semiannually.

CAUGHT IN THE WEB

Most financial institutions post on their Web sites the current interest rates they pay on savings and investment products. For example, visit the Royal Bank Financial Group page at www.royalbank.com/rates/index.html. This page is an index that links to detailed rate schedules for each category of deposit account, investment product, and loan.

Banks, trust companies, and credit unions also offer two types of short-term investments paying a *fixed rate* of simple interest for the *fixed term* of the investment. **Term deposits** (also known as *certificates of deposit* and *redeemable GICs*) may be obtained for terms of 30 days to one year. Generally speaking, higher interest rates are paid for longer maturities and for larger deposits. Interest is paid on the maturity date of the term deposit. The investor may redeem or "cash in" the term deposit before maturity. There will, however, be a penalty in the form of a reduced interest rate for the partial term.

The second type of short-term investment is the **Guaranteed Investment Certificate,** usually referred to as a "GIC." Typically, a GIC is issued by a mortgage-lending subsidiary of a bank or trust company and is *unconditionally guaranteed* by the parent company. The Canada Deposit Insurance Corporation also guarantees up to $60,000 per investor. The main difference between term deposits and short-term GICs from an investor's point of view is that GICs are *nonredeemable*[1]—the investor cannot cash-in a GIC before its maturity date. Since the financial institution is assured of the use of the funds for the full term, a GIC pays a higher rate of interest than a term deposit having the same principal and term.

Example 7.1A *Savings Account Interest Based on a Tiered Interest Rate*

Mr. and Mrs. Hernandez have a Performance 55 bank account that pays a slightly higher rate to depositors age 55 or older. Interest is calculated on the daily closing balance and paid monthly as follows:

Portion of balance	Interest rate
From 0 to $1000.00	3.50%
From $1000.01 to $3000.00	3.75
Over $3000.00	4.50

[1] In recent years, there has been a proliferation of special features or "wrinkles" attached to basic investments. A few examples of redeemable GICs may now be found.

On April 1, their balance was \$1416.32. They withdrew \$500 on April 9, deposited \$1200 on April 15, and deposited another \$1200 on April 29. Calculate the interest that they will be paid for the month of April.

Solution

The following table organizes the given information in preparation for the interest calculation:

Period	Number of days	Balance	Amount subject to a rate of: 3.5%	3.75%	4.5%
April 1–8	8	\$1416.32	\$1000.00	\$ 416.32	—
April 9–14	6	916.32	916.32	—	—
April 15–28	14	2116.32	1000.00	1116.32	—
April 29–30	2	3316.32	1000.00	2000.00	\$316.32

The interest earned for the period April 1 to 8 inclusive is

$$\begin{aligned} I(\text{April 1–8}) &= P_1r_1t + P_2r_2t \\ &= (P_1r_1 + P_2r_2)t \\ &= [\$1000.00(0.035) + \$416.32(0.0375)]\left(\frac{8}{365}\right) \\ &= (\$35.00 + \$15.61)(0.021918) \\ &= \$1.109 \end{aligned}$$

Similarly,

$$I(\text{April 9–14}) = \$916.32(0.035)\left(\frac{6}{365}\right) = \$0.527$$

$$\begin{aligned} I(\text{April 15–28}) &= [\$1,000.00(0.035) + \$1116.32(0.0375)]\left(\frac{14}{365}\right) \\ &= (\$35.00 + \$41.86)(0.038356) \\ &= \$2.948 \end{aligned}$$

$$\begin{aligned} I(\text{April 29–30}) &= [\$1000(0.035) + \$2000(0.0375) + \$316.32(0.045)]\left(\frac{2}{365}\right) \\ &= (\$35.00 + \$75.00 + \$14.23)(0.005479) \\ &= \$0.681 \end{aligned}$$

Total interest for April = \$1.109 + \$0.527 + \$2.948 + \$0.681 = \$5.27

Mr. and Mrs. Hernandez will earn \$5.27 interest in April.

Example 7.1B *Calculation of Interest on a Term Deposit*

A credit union pays an interest rate of 4.25% pa on term deposits of \$5000 to \$99,999 with terms of 30 to 179 days. If the term deposit is redeemed before maturity, the interest rate is reduced to 3%. Edith made a term deposit of \$25,000 for 150 days.

a. How much will she be paid at the maturity date?
b. How much will she receive if she redeems the deposit after 95 days?

Solution

a. Maturity value, $S = P(1 + rt)$

$$= \$25{,}000\left[1 + 0.0425\left(\frac{150}{365}\right)\right]$$

$$= \$25{,}436.64$$

Edith will receive $25,436.64 on the maturity date of the term deposit.

b. She will receive the principal plus 95 days' interest at 3.0% pa.

$$\text{Redemption amount} = \$25{,}000\left[1 + 0.03\left(\frac{95}{365}\right)\right] = \$25{,}195.21$$

Upon early redemption after 95 days, Edith will be paid $25,195.21.

Exercise 7.1

Answers to the odd-numbered problems are at the end of the book.

1. **a.** What will be the maturity value of $15,000 placed in a 120-day term deposit paying an interest rate of 5.25% pa?

   b. If on the maturity date the proceeds are "rolled over" into a 90-day term deposit paying 4.75% pa, what amount will the depositor receive when the second term deposit matures?

2. For amounts between $10,000 and $24,999, a credit union pays a rate of 5% pa on term deposits with maturities in the 91- to 120-day range. However, early redemption will result in a rate of 3.25% pa being applied. How much more interest will a 91-day $20,000 term deposit earn if it is held until maturity than if it is redeemed after 80 days?

3. For 90- to 365-day GICs, the Toronto-Dominion Bank offered a rate of 6.000% on investments of $25,000 to $59,999 and a rate of 6.375% on investments of $60,000 to $99,999. How much more will an investor earn from a single $60,000, 270-day GIC than from two $30,000, 270-day GICs?

4. On the same date, a bank offered interest rates of 6.75% on a $10,000, one-year GIC and 6.000% on a $10,000, 180- to 269-day GIC. How much more will an investor earn from the one-year GIC than from consecutive 183-day and 182-day GICs? (Assume that interest rates on 180- to 269-day GICs are the same at the renewal date as they are today. Remember that interest earned from the first, 183-day GIC can be invested in the second, 182-day GIC.)

5. For investments of $5000 to $24,999, a bank quotes interest rates of 5.75% on 90-day GICs and 6.00% on 180-day GICs. How much more interest will an investor earn by placing $15,000 in a 180-day GIC than by purchasing two consecutive 90-day GICs? (Assume that interest rates do not change over the next 90 days. Remember that interest earned from the first 90-day GIC can be invested in the second 90-day GIC.)

•6. Suppose that the current rates on 90- and 180-day GICs are 6.25% and 6.50%, respectively. An investor is weighing the alternatives of purchasing a 180-day GIC versus purchasing a 90-day GIC and then reinvesting its maturity value in a second 90-day GIC. What would the interest rate on 90-day GICs have to be 90 days from now for the investor to end up in the same financial position with either alternative?

•7. Joan has savings of $12,000 on June 1. Since she may need some of the savings during the next three months, she is considering two options at her bank. An Investment Builder savings account earns a 4.00% rate of interest on the entire balance for balances between $10,000 and $24,999. The interest is calculated on the daily closing balance and paid on the first day of the following month. A redeemable 90- to 179-day term deposit of the same amount earns interest at the rate of 4.2%, paid at maturity. If the interest rate on the savings account does not change during the next three months and Joan does not withdraw any of the funds, how much more interest will she earn from the term deposit up to September 1? (Keep in mind that savings account interest paid on the first day of the month will itself subsequently earn interest.)

8. A savings account pays interest of 3.5% pa. Interest is calculated on the daily closing balance and paid at the close of business on the last day of the month. A depositor had a $2239 opening balance on September 1, deposited $734 on September 7 and $627 on September 21, and withdrew $300 on both September 10 and September 21. What interest will be credited to the account at the month's end?

•9. An Investment Savings account offered by a trust company pays a rate of 3.25% on the first $1000 of daily closing balance, 4% on the portion of the balance between $1000 and $3000, and 4.5% on any balance in excess of $3000. What interest will be paid for the month of April if the opening balance was $2439, $950 was deposited on April 10, and $500 was withdrawn on April 23?

10. The Moneybuilder account offered by a chartered bank calculates interest daily based on the daily closing balance as follows:

Interest rate (%)	Amount to which the rate applies
0.00	Balance when it is below $1000
3.25	Entire balance when it is between $1000 and $3000
4.00	Portion of balance above $3000

The balance at the beginning of March was $1678. On March 5, $700 was withdrawn. Then $2500 was deposited on March 15, and $900 was withdrawn on March 23. What interest will be credited to the account for the month of March?

•**11.** The Super Savings account offered by a trust company calculates interest daily based on the *lesser* of each day's opening or closing balance as follows:

Interest rate (%)	Amount to which the rate applies
3.00	Entire balance when it is between $0 and $2999.99
3.75	Entire balance when it is between $3000 and $4999.99
3.90	Entire balance when it is between $5000 and $9999.99
4.02	Entire balance when it is between $10,000 and $24,999.99
5.09	Entire balance when it is between $25,000 and $49,999.99
5.50	Entire balance when it is $50,000 or more

September's opening balance was $8572. The transactions in the account for the month were a $9500 deposit on September 6, a deposit of $8600 on September 14, and a withdrawal of $25,000 on September 23. What interest will be credited to the account at the end of September?

•**12.** On the same day, a bank advertised the following interest rates for investments of $5000 to $25,000 with 120- to 179-day maturities:

(i) 3.50% on fully redeemable term deposits.

(ii) 4.0% on term deposits that pay only 3.0% upon early redemption.

(iii) 5.75% on nonredeemable guaranteed investment certificates.

For a $20,000 investment with a 150-day term:

a. What is the dollar differential between alternatives (i) and (ii) if redemption occurs on day 120?

b. What is the dollar differential between alternatives (i) and (ii) if early redemption does not occur?

c. What dollar amount of interest is sacrificed over the full 150-day term by maintaining full redemption privileges in alternative (i) versus no redemption privileges in alternative (iii)?

7.2 The Valuation Principle

Consider an investment that will deliver a single payment of $110 one year from today. What is the most you should pay to buy the investment if you require a minimum rate of return of 10% pa? (In other words, what is the value of the investment to you?) After a little thought, you probably answer "$100" for the following reason. The $10 difference between the amount you pay ($100) and the $110 you will receive represents a 10% pa return on your $100 investment.

But how would you calculate the price to pay if the given numbers are not so "nice"? For example, what maximum price should you pay for an investment that will pay you $129 after 247 days, if you require a rate of return of 5.5% pa? Let us think about where the $100 came from in the first example. Note that $100 invested for one year at 10% pa will grow to $110. Since $110 is the *future* value of $100, then $100 is the *present* value of $110. That is,

$$P = \frac{S}{1 + rt} = \frac{\$110}{1 + 0.10 \times 1} = \$100$$

This demonstrates that the present value calculation gives a price that "builds in" or "impounds" the required 10% rate of return. If your minimum required rate of return is only 8% pa, then you should be willing to pay up to

$$P = \frac{S}{1 + rt} = \frac{\$110}{1 + 0.08 \times 1} = \$101.85$$

The \$8.15 (\$110.00 − \$101.85) you will earn during the next year provides a rate of return (on your \$101.85 investment) of

$$\frac{\$8.15}{\$101.85} \times 100\% = 8.00\% \text{ pa}$$

The lower the rate of return you are prepared to accept, the higher the price you can pay now for a given future payment.

In the language of finance, the process of calculating a payment's present value is often called "**discounting** the payment." (When you calculate the present value of a payment, you get a smaller number than the payment.) The interest rate used in the present value calculation is then called the **discount rate**.

To determine the price to pay for an investment that promises two or more future payments, we simply extend our basic idea. That is, first calculate the present value of each of the payments (using the required rate of return as the discount rate). Then add the present values.

For investments purchased privately, you have some flexibility to negotiate a *higher* rate of return by bargaining *down* the price. But for various types of investments available to the general public, the rates of return are determined by market forces of supply and demand. When an investment's price is established by competitive bidding among many buyers and sellers, we refer to the price as the **fair market value**. A particular fair market value implies a specific value for the rate of return used to discount the future cash flows from the investment. This rate of return is what we mean by the *market-determined rate of return*. For publicly traded investments, your only decision is whether to accept or reject the prevailing price and market-determined rate of return.

These ideas are so important and of such wide application in finance that they are formally embodied in the Valuation Principle.

VALUATION PRINCIPLE

The fair market value of an investment is the sum of the present values of the expected cash flows. The discount rate used in the present value calculations should be the market-determined rate of return required for this type of investment.

If the expected cash flows are received as forecast, the investor's actual rate of return on the amount invested will be precisely the discount rate used in the fair market value calculation.

Example 7.2A Valuation of a Non-Interest-Bearing Obligation

An investment contract calls for a payment of $1000 five months from now and another payment, 10 months from now, of $1500.

a. What price will an investor be prepared to pay for the investment today if the required rate of return is 12% pa?

b. Demonstrate that the investor will realize a 12% rate of return on the purchase price if the payments are received as expected.

Solution

a. According to the Valuation Principle,

$$\begin{aligned}\text{Price} &= \text{Present value of } \$1000 + \text{Present value of } \$1500\\ &= \frac{\$1000}{1 + 0.12\left(\frac{5}{12}\right)} + \frac{\$1500}{1 + 0.12\left(\frac{10}{12}\right)}\\ &= \$952.38 + \$1363.64\\ &= \$2316.02\end{aligned}$$

An investor requiring a 12% rate of return should be willing to pay $2316.02 today for the contract.

b. Think of the $952.38 and $1363.64 components of the $2316.02 price as separately buying the future cash flows of $1000 and $1500, respectively.

The sum of $952.38 invested for five months at 12% will grow to

$$S = P(1 + rt) = \$952.38\left[1 + 0.12\left(\frac{5}{12}\right)\right] = \$1000.00$$

Therefore, the $1000 payment received after five months returns the $952.38 investment along with five months' interest on $952.38 at 12%.

Similarly, it can be shown that the $1500 payment received after 10 months returns the $1363.64 component of the initial investment plus 10 months' interest on $1363.64 at 12%.

Example 7.2B Valuation of an Interest-Earning Obligation

On March 1, Murray signed a contract to pay Anton or his designate $2000 plus interest at 8% pa on June 1, and $3000 plus interest at 8% pa on September 1. Anton sold the contract on May 1 at a price that will yield the buyer a 10% rate of return. What was the price?

Solution

According to the Valuation Principle, the price paid by the buyer is the present value on May 1 of the two scheduled payments discounted at 10% pa. Unlike Example 7.2A, we do not know at the outset the dollar amounts of the scheduled payments. As indicated in the time diagram, we must first calculate the maturity value of each obligation using the contract's 8% interest rate. Then we can determine the present value of each scheduled payment using a discount rate of 10% (to "impound" a 10% rate of return to the buyer).

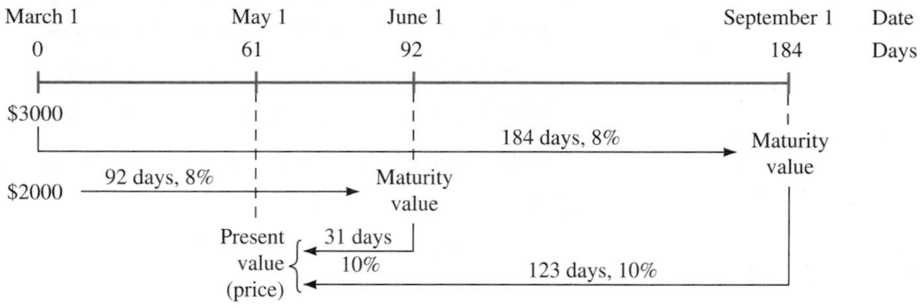

$$\begin{aligned}
\text{Payment due on June 1} &= \text{Maturity value of } \$2000 \\
&= \$2000\left[1 + 0.08\left(\frac{92}{365}\right)\right] \\
&= \$2040.33 \\
\text{Payment due on September 1} &= \text{Maturity value of } \$3000 \\
&= \$3000\left[1 + 0.08\left(\frac{184}{365}\right)\right] \\
&= \$3120.99
\end{aligned}$$

$$\begin{aligned}
\text{Price} &= \text{Present value of scheduled payments} \\
&= \frac{\$2040.33}{1 + 0.10\left(\frac{31}{365}\right)} + \frac{\$3120.99}{1 + 0.10\left(\frac{123}{365}\right)} \\
&= \$2023.15 + \$3019.25 \\
&= \$5042.40
\end{aligned}$$

The buyer paid $5042.40 for the contract.

Concept Questions

1. What do you need to know to be able to calculate the fair market value of an investment that will deliver two future payments?
2. If the market-determined rate of return on an investment declines, what happens to the investment's fair market value? Explain. (Assume the expected cash flows from the investment do not change.)
3. If you purchase an investment privately, how do you determine the maximum price you are prepared to pay?
4. Assume that the expected cash flows from an investment and the market-determined rate of return do not change as time passes.
   a. What will happen to the investment's fair market value leading up to the first scheduled payment? Explain.
   b. If the first scheduled payment is $500, what will happen to the fair market value of the investment just after the payment is made? Explain.

Exercise 7.2

Answers to the odd-numbered problems are at the end of the book.

1. An investment promises two payments of $500, on dates three and six months from today. If the required return on investment is 9% pa:
   a. What is the price of the investment today?
   b. What will its price be in one month if the required return remains at 9%?
   c. Give an explanation for the change in price as time passes.
2. An investment promises two payments of $1000, on dates 60 and 90 days from today. What price will an investor pay today:
   a. If her required return is 10% pa?
   b. If her required return is 11% pa?
   c. Give an explanation for the lower price at the higher required return.
3. Certificate A pays $1000 in four months and another $1000 in eight months. Certificate B pays $1000 in five months and another $1000 in nine months. If the current rate of return required on this type of investment certificate is 5.75% pa, determine the current value of each of the certificates. Give an explanation for the lower price of B.
4. A contract requires payments of $1500, $2000, and $1000 in 100, 150, and 200 days, respectively, from today. What is the value of the contract today if the payments are discounted to yield a 10.5% pa rate of return.
5. An agreement stipulates payments of $4000, $2500, and $5000 in three, six, and nine months, respectively, from today. What is the highest price an investor will offer today to purchase the agreement if he requires a minimum rate of return of 9.25% pa?

•6. An assignable loan contract executed three months ago requires two payments of $1800 plus interest at 10% pa on each $1800 from the date of the contract, to be paid five and 10 months after the contract date. The payee is offering to sell the contract to a finance company in order to raise cash. If the finance company requires a return of 15% pa, what price will it be prepared to pay today for the contract?

•7. Claude Scales, a commercial fisherman, bought a new navigation system for $10,000 from Coast Marine Electronics on March 20. He paid $2000 in cash and signed a conditional sales contract requiring a payment on July 1 of $3000 plus interest on the $3000 at 11% pa, and another payment on September 1 of $5000 plus interest at 11% pa from the date of the sale. The vendor immediately sold the contract to a finance company, which discounted the payments at its required return of 16% pa. What proceeds did Coast Marine receive from the sale of the contract?

7.3 Treasury Bills and Commercial Paper

Treasury bills (T-bills) are paper contracts issued to lenders by the federal government and several provincial governments when they borrow money for terms of less than one year. In early 1999, slightly over 20% of the Government of Canada's market-financed debt of $450 billion was borrowed through T-bills. The lenders in the first instance are chartered banks and investment dealers. The lending transaction is usually described as "buying T-bills"; the borrowing governments are said to be "selling T-bills." A few billion dollars' worth of new 98-day, 168-day, and 364-day maturity Government of Canada Treasury bills are sold by auction to the institutional dealers every second Tuesday. The auction is administered by the Bank of Canada, acting as the agent for the federal government. Through a financial institution, individual investors may purchase T-bills in multiples of $1000.

In everyday loan transactions, we normally stipulate the principal and then calculate the payment or payments required to repay the principal with interest. With T-bills, the arrangement is different. When selling a $1 million **face value** 168-day T-bill, the borrowing government is, in effect, asking the following question: "What amount will you lend to the government today on the government's promise to pay you $1 million (*including interest*) 168 days from now?" Of course, you will lend less than $1 million, and the difference represents the interest on your loan. In investment language, T-bills are "issued (or sold) at a discount to their face value."

CAUGHT IN THE WEB

Current rates of return (or "yields") on T-bills and commercial paper are also posted on the Bank of Canada's Web site at www.bank-banque-canada.ca/english/monmrt.htm.

How do financial institutions decide how much to pay (lend) for the right to receive a T-bill's face value on a known future date? This is the same type of question you were asked at the beginning of Section 7.2. The institutions calculate the present value of the T-bill's face value, using their required rate of return[2] as the discount rate.

The purchaser of a T-bill is not obligated to hold it until it matures. There is an active market for the sale/purchase of T-bills that are partway through their terms. On any day, the price at which a T-bill may be sold or bought is the present value of the face value, discounted at the *current* market-determined interest rate over the *time remaining* until maturity. Typical market rates for a few maturities are listed in the financial pages of major newspapers each day. An example of T-bill quotations is presented in Table 7.1.

Table 7.1 *Treasury Bill and Commercial Paper Rates (April 27, 1999)*

Time remaining until maturity	Rate of return (pa) on on Treasury bills	Rate of return (pa) on commercial paper
1 month	4.66%	4.83%
2 months	4.64%	4.83%
3 months	4.62%	4.83%
6 months	4.68%	na
1 year	4.74%	na

[2] These financial institutions submit price bids just prior to the auction. The institutions use their own required rate of return as the discount rate when determining the present value of the face value. An institution arrives at its required rate of return based on prevailing short-term interest rates in financial markets and on the expected demand for T-bills from its clients. The Bank of Canada accepts bids in order of decreasing prices until the government's borrowing requirements for the week are met. Reserve bids submitted by the Bank of Canada itself serve to influence minimum prices (and maximum discount rates).

Some large corporations also borrow money for short periods by selling contracts called **commercial paper.** Commercial paper is essentially a corporation's version of T-bills. Common maturities are 30, 60, and 90 days (usually referred to as one-month, two-month, and three-month maturities). The minimum face value is usually \$100,000. Like Treasury bills, commercial paper is priced at its discounted present value. The required rate of return (discount rate) on commercial paper is usually 0.1% to 0.2% higher than that on T-bills. (See Table 7.1.) The higher rate of return is required because of the small risk that the corporation might be unable to pay the face value on the due date.

Example 7.3A *Valuation of a T-Bill on Its Issue Date*

Suppose the average rate of return or yield on 168-day Government of Canada Treasury bills sold at a Tuesday auction was 4.68% pa. At this yield, what price was paid for a \$100,000 face value T-bill?

Solution

$$\begin{aligned}\text{Price} &= \text{Present value of \$100,000 discounted at 4.68\% for 168 days}\\ &= \frac{\$100{,}000}{1 + 0.0468 \times \frac{168}{365}}\\ &= \$97{,}891.34\end{aligned}$$

To obtain a yield of 4.68% pa, \$97,891.34 was paid for the 168-day, \$100,000 face value T-bill.

Example 7.3B *Valuation of a T-Bill*

The institutional purchaser of the T-bill in Example 7.3A sells it to a client at a higher price that represents a (lower) yield to the client of 4.48% pa. What profit did the institution make on the transaction?

Solution

$$\text{Selling price to the client} = \frac{\$100{,}000}{1 + 0.0448 \times \frac{168}{365}} = \$97{,}979.63$$

$$\begin{aligned}\text{Profit} &= \text{Price charged to the client} - \text{Acquisition price}\\ &= \$97{,}979.63 - \$97{,}891.34\\ &= \$88.29\end{aligned}$$

The institution's profit on the resale of the T-bill was \$88.29.

Example 7.3C Calculation of the Rate of Return on a T-Bill Sold before Maturity

Suppose the client who purchased the 168-day, $100,000 T-bill in Example 7.3B for $97,979.63, sold the T-bill after 73 days in order to invest the proceeds elsewhere.

a. What price would she receive if the short-term interest rate for this maturity had risen to 4.92% by the date of sale?

b. What rate of return (per annum) did the client realize while holding the T-bill?

Solution

a. Days remaining to maturity = 168 − 73 = 95

Selling price = Present value of $100,000 discounted at 4.92% for 95 days

$$= \frac{\$100{,}000}{1 + 0.0492 \times \frac{95}{365}}$$

$$= \$98{,}735.64$$

The client sold the T-bill for $98,735.64.

b. We want the rate of return when $97,979.63 grows to $98,735.64 in 73 days. In effect, the initial investment of $97,979.63 earned interest amounting to

$$I = \$98{,}735.64 - \$97{,}979.63 = \$756.01$$

Formula (6-1) may now be used to obtain the corresponding rate of return.

$$r = \frac{I}{Pt} = \frac{\$756.01}{\$97{,}979.63\left(\frac{73}{365}\right)} = 0.03858 = 3.858\%$$

The client's rate of return *during the 73-day holding period* was only 3.858% pa. This is lower than the yield she would earn (4.48% in Example 7.3B) if she held the T-bill until its maturity. To enable the new purchaser to realize a rate of return (4.92% pa) that is greater than 4.48% pa during the remaining 95 days, the first investor must accept a rate lower than 4.48% pa for the first 73 days.

Example 7.3D Calculation of the Rate of Return on Commercial Paper

Sixty-day commercial paper with face value $100,000 was issued by Suncor Inc. for $98,940. What rate of return will be realized if the paper is held until maturity?

Solution

In effect, the interest earned on an investment of $98,940 for 60 days is

$$\$100{,}000 - \$98{,}940 = \$1060$$

Using formula (6-1) rearranged to solve for r, we have

$$r = \frac{I}{Pt} = \frac{\$1060}{\$98{,}940\left(\frac{60}{365}\right)} = 0.06517 = 6.517\%$$

A 6.517% pa rate of return will be realized if the paper is held until it matures.

Concept Questions

1. Is the price of a 98-day $100,000 T-bill higher or lower than the price of a 168-day $100,000 T-bill? Why?
2. If short-term interest rates have increased during the past week, will investors pay more this week (than last week) for T-bills of the same maturity and face value? Explain.
3. If short-term interest rates do not change, what happens to a T-bill's fair market value as time passes?

Exercise 7.3

Answers to the odd-numbered problems are at the end of the book.
Calculate T-bill prices accurate to the nearest dollar and rates of return accurate to the nearest 0.001%.

Note: A few problems in this and later exercises have been taken (with permission) from professional courses offered by the **Canadian Institute of Financial Planning** and the **Institute of Canadian Bankers**. These problems are indicated by the organization's logo in the margin next to the problems.

1. Calculate the price of a $25,000, 91-day Province of British Columbia Treasury bill on its issue date if the current market rate of return is 5.672% pa.
2. Calculate the price on its issue date of $100,000 face value, 90-day commercial paper issued by Northern Telecom Limited if the prevailing market rate of return is 6.560% pa.
3. A money market mutual fund purchased Montreal Trustco Inc. 90-day commercial paper with $1 million face value 28 days after its issue. What price was paid if the paper was discounted at 6.10% pa?
4. A $100,000, 91-day Province of Ontario Treasury bill was issued 37 days ago. What will it sell at today in order to yield the purchaser 5.52% pa?
5. Calculate and compare the issue-date prices of $100,000 face value commercial paper investments with 30-, 60-, and 90-day maturities, all priced to yield 8% pa.
6. Calculate and compare the market values of a $100,000 face value Government of Canada Treasury bill on dates that are 91 days, 61 days, 31 days, and one day before maturity. Assume that the return required in the market stays constant at 5% pa over the lifetime of the T-bill.
7. A $100,000, 364-day T-bill was purchased on its issue date to yield 4.5% pa. What can it be sold for 60 days later if prevailing interest rates have increased to 4.9% pa? (Taken from CIFP course on Strategic Investment Planning.)
8. A $100,000, 90-day commercial paper certificate issued by Noranda Inc. was sold on its issue date for $98,750. What rate of return will it yield to the buyer?
9. A $50,000, 168-day T-bill was purchased on its issue date for $48,880. What was the annual yield (rate of return) on the T-bill? (Taken from CIFP course on Strategic Investment Planning.)

10. An investor purchased a 168-day, $100,000 face value T-bill for $98,000 and sold it 90 days later for $99,000. What was the yield rate (per annum) during the holding period? (Taken from ICB course on Wealth Valuation.)

•11. A 168-day, $100,000 T-bill was initially issued at a price that would yield the buyer 5.2% pa. If the yield required by the market remains at 5.2%, how many days before its maturity date will the T-bill's market price first exceed $99,000?

•12. An investor purchased a 168-day, $25,000 Province of Alberta Treasury bill on its date of issue for $24,310 and sold it 60 days later for $24,520.

a. What rate of return was implied in the original price?

b. What rate of return did the market require on the sale date?

c. What rate of return did the original investor actually realize during the 60-day holding period?

•13. A $100,000, 168-day Government of Canada Treasury bill was purchased on its date of issue to yield 5.1% pa.

a. What price did the investor pay?

b. Calculate the market value of the T-bill 85 days later if the rate of return then required by the market has:

(i) risen to 5.4%. **(ii)** remained at 5.1%. **(iii)** fallen to 4.8%.

c. Calculate the rate of return actually realized by the investor if the T-bill is sold at each of the three prices calculated in part (b).

7.4 Demand Loans

Most businesses have demand loans or lines of credit to meet short-term financing requirements. Many individuals obtain personal lines of credit, set up on a demand basis, to meet their short-term borrowing needs.

Common Terms and Conditions

The name **demand loan** comes from the lender's right to demand full repayment of the loan at any time without notice. This rarely happens if the borrower fulfills the terms of the loan (unless the lender has reason to believe the borrower's financial condition is deteriorating). The borrower may repay any portion of the loan at any time without penalty.

The interest rate charged on demand loans is usually "floating." This means that the rate is linked to the prime rate of interest in the banking system. Interest rates are then quoted as "prime plus" some additional amount. For example, if a small business is viewed by the lender as a moderate risk, the business might be charged a rate of prime plus 2% or prime plus 3%.

Interest on a demand loan is calculated on the same "statement date" each month. The daily-interest method is employed—the interest rate in effect each day is applied to the daily closing loan balance. Some lenders calculate interest up to *and including* the statement date; others calculate interest up to *but not including* the statement date. The latter approach will be used in this text. (It is consistent with the count-the-first-day-but-not-the-last-day rule for determining the length of the time interval in interest calculations.)

Arrangements for repaying the loan principal are negotiated between the borrower and lender. Acceptable terms will depend upon the purpose of the loan, the nature of the security given, and the seasonality of the borrower's income. The two most common demand loan arrangements are:

- A revolving loan.
- A fixed-payment loan.

Revolving Loans

Revolving loans are preferred by businesses and individuals whose short-term borrowing requirements vary over the year. These loans give borrowers the flexibility to borrow additional funds at their discretion and to reduce their debt whenever extra funds are available. Most *lines of credit* and business *operating loans* are set up as revolving loans.

The borrower and the lending institution negotiate the terms and conditions of the loan—the credit limit, the security required, the interest rate, and so on. Subject to the credit limit and a few general guidelines, draws (or advances) of principal and repayments of principal are at the borrower's discretion.

For *fully-secured* revolving loans, the minimum monthly payment may be only the accrued interest on the outstanding loan balance. In most other cases, the minimum monthly payment is something like "the greater of \$100 or 3% of the *current* balance." The "current balance" in this context means the combination of principal and accrued interest. The lender usually requires the borrower to have a chequing account (sometimes called a *current account* for a business) with the lending institution. The required monthly payment is then automatically withdrawn from the account on the due date (which is usually the statement date).

Example 7.4A *Calculation of Interest on a Revolving Loan*

On March 20, Hank's Cycle Shop received an initial advance of \$10,000 on its revolving demand loan. On the fifteenth of each month, interest is calculated (up to but not including the fifteenth) and deducted from Hank's bank account. The floating rate of interest started at 9.75%, and dropped to 9.5% on April 5. On April 19, another \$10,000 was drawn on the line of credit. What interest was charged to the bank account on April 15 and May 15?

Solution

The one-month period ending on an interest calculation date (April 15 and May 15) must be broken into intervals within which the balance on the loan and the interest rate are constant. In the following table, we should count the first day but not the last day in each interval. This will cause April 5 (the first day at the 9.5% interest rate) to be included in the second interval but not in the first interval.

Interval	Principal	Rate	Amount of Interest
March 20–April 5	\$10,000	9.75%	$\$10{,}000(0.0975)\left(\frac{16}{365}\right) = \$\ 42.74$
April 5–April 15	10,000	9.5	$\$10{,}000(0.095)\left(\frac{10}{365}\right) = 26.03$
			Interest charged on April 15: \$ 68.77
April 15–April 19	10,000	9.5	$\$10{,}000(0.095)\left(\frac{4}{365}\right) = \$\ 10.41$
April 19–May 15	20,000	9.5	$\$20{,}000(0.095)\left(\frac{26}{365}\right) = 135.34$
			Interest charged on May 15: \$145.75

The interest charged to Hank's bank account on April 15 was \$68.77 and on May 15 was \$145.75.

Repayment Schedule For a Revolving Loan A **loan repayment schedule** is a table in which interest charges, loan draws and payments, and outstanding balances are recorded. The schedule helps us organize our calculations and properly allocate payments to interest and principal.

Figure 7.1 presents a format for a demand loan repayment schedule. A row is entered in the schedule when any of the following three events takes place:

- A principal amount is advanced or repaid.
- The interest rate changes.
- Interest (and possibly principal) is paid on a statement date.

The columns in the table are used as follows. (Each item refers to a numbered column in Figure 7.1.)

1. In chronological order, enter the dates on which payments are made, the interest rate changes, and principal amounts are advanced to the borrower.
2. Enter the number of days in the interval *ending* on the date in Column (1). This is the number of days from (and including) the *previous* row's date to (but not including) the *current* row's date.

Figure 7.1 *Demand Loan Repayment Schedule*

(1) Date	(2) Number of days	(3) Interest rate	(4) Interest	(5) Accrued interest	(6) Payment (Advance)	(7) Principal portion	(8) Balance

3. Enter the interest rate that applies to the interval in Column (2). When the date in Column (1) is the date on which a new interest rate takes effect, the interest rate in Column (3) is still the *previous rate* because the days in Column (2) refer to the period *up to but not including* the date in Column (1).
4. Enter the interest charges ($I = Prt$) for the number of days (t) in Column (2) at the interest rate (r) in Column (3) on the balance (P) in Column (8) of the *preceding* line.
5. Enter the cumulative total of unpaid or accrued interest as of the current date. This amount is the interest just calculated in Column (4) plus any previously accrued but unpaid interest [from Column (5) in the *preceding* line].
6. Enter the amount of any payment (of principal and/or interest). A loan advance is enclosed in brackets to distinguish it from a loan payment.
7. On a statement date, the accrued interest in Column (5) is deducted from the payment to obtain the principal portion of the payment. Put a single stroke through the accrued interest in Column (5) as a reminder that it has been paid and should not be carried forward to the next period.

   If an *unscheduled* payment is entered in Column (6), the entire amount is usually applied to principal. Enter it again in Column (7). Similarly, duplicate in Column (7) the amount of any loan advance in Column (6).
8. The new loan balance is the previous line's balance *less* any principal repaid or *plus* any principal advanced [the amount in Column (7)].

Example 7.4B *Repayment Schedule for a Revolving Operating Loan*

The Bank of Montreal approved a $50,000 line of credit on a demand basis to Tanya's Wardrobes to finance the store's inventory. Interest at the rate of prime plus 3% is calculated and charged to Tanya's chequing account at the bank on the twenty-third of each month. The initial advance was $25,000 on September 23 when the prime rate stood at 8.25%. There were further advances of $8000 on October 30 and $10,000 on November 15. Payments of $7000 and $14,000 were applied against the principal on December 15 and January 15, respectively. The prime rate rose to 8.75% effective December 5. What was the total interest paid on the loan for the period September 23 to January 23?

Solution

A large amount of information is given in the statement of the problem. The best way to organize the data is to construct a repayment schedule using the format in Figure 7.1. In the date column, list in chronological order all of the dates on which a transaction or event affecting the loan occurs. These are the dates of advances, payments of principal or interest, and interest rate changes. Next, enter the information that is given for each transaction or event. At this point the schedule has the following entries:

Date	Number of days	Interest rate	Interest	Accrued interest	Payment (Advance)	Principal portion	Balance
Sept 23	—	—	—	—	($25,000)	($25,000)	$25,000
Oct 23		11.25%				0	
Oct 30		11.25			(8000)	(8000)	
Nov 15		11.25			(10,000)	(10,000)	
Nov 23		11.25				0	
Dec 5		11.25				0	
Dec 15		11.75			7000	7000	
Dec 23		11.75				0	
Jan 15		11.75			14,000	14,000	
Jan 23		11.75				0	

Note that 11.25% (8.25% + 3%) has been entered on the December 5 line. Although the interest rate changes to 11.75% *effective* December 5, the "Number of days" column of this line is the number of days from (and including) November 23 to (but not including) December 5. These 13 days are still charged interest at the 11.25% rate. The 11.75% rate will first apply to the December 5 to December 15 period, which is handled on the December 15 line.

The "Number of days" column may be completed next. Then the calculations can proceed row by row to obtain the full schedule. The circled numbers (①, ②, etc.) in the following schedule refer to sample calculations listed below the schedule. A stroke is drawn through an accrued interest figure when the interest is paid.

Date	Number of days	Interest rate	Interest	Accrued interest	Payment (Advance)	Principal portion	Balance
Sept 23	—	—	—	—	($25,000)	($25,000)	$25,000
Oct 23	30	11.25%	$231.16 ①	~~$231.16~~	231.16	0	25,000
Oct 30	7	11.25	53.94	53.94	(8000)	(8000)	33,000
Nov 15	16	11.25	162.74 ②	216.68 ③	(10,000)	(10,000)	43,000
Nov 23	8	11.25	106.03 ④	~~322.71~~ ⑤	322.71	0	43,000
Dec 5	12	11.25	159.04	159.04		0	43,000
Dec 15	10	11.75	138.42	297.46	7000	7000	36,000
Dec 23	8	11.75	92.71	~~390.17~~	390.17	0	36,000
Jan 15	23	11.75	266.55	266.55	14,000	14,000	22,000
Jan 23	8	11.75	56.66	~~323.21~~	323.21	0	22,000

① $I = Prt = \$25{,}000(0.1125)\left(\frac{30}{365}\right) = \$231.16$

② $I = \$33{,}000(0.1125)\left(\frac{16}{365}\right) = \$162.74$

③ Accrued interest = $53.94 + $162.74 = $216.68

④ $I = \$43{,}000(0.1125)\left(\frac{8}{365}\right) = \$106.03$

⑤ Accrued interest = $216.68 + $106.03 = $322.71

The total interest paid on the loan for the period September 23 to January 23 was

$$\$231.16 + \$322.71 + \$390.17 + \$323.21 = \$1267.25$$

Example 7.4C Repayment Schedule for a Revolving Personal Line of Credit

Warren Bitenko has a \$20,000 personal line of credit with the Royal Bank. The interest rate is prime + 2.5%. On the last day of each month, a payment equal to the greater of \$100 or 3% of the current balance (including the current month's accrued interest) is deducted from his chequing account.

On July 6, he took his first advance of \$2000. On August 15, he took another draw of \$7500. The prime rate started at 6%, and rose to 6.25% on September 9. Prepare a loan repayment schedule up to and including September 30.

CAUGHT IN THE WEB

An example of a personal line of credit is TD Bank's Select Line described at www.tdbank.ca/lending/tdsel.html. From this site you can link to the Select Line Calculator which calculates the minimum payment (the greater of \$50 or 3% of the outstanding balance) on a principal amount that you enter. Do a manual calculation to confirm TD's calculated payment (for a 30-day month).

Solution

Begin a schedule by entering, in chronological order, the dates of advances, interest rate changes, and payments. Information known about these events should also be entered. At this point, the schedule has the following entries and you are ready to begin the calculations.

Date	Number of days	Interest rate	Interest	Accrued interest	Payment (Advance)	Principal portion	Balance
July 6	—	8.5%	—	—	(\$2000)	(\$2000)	\$2000
July 31		8.5					
Aug 15		8.5			(7500)	(7500)	
Aug 31		8.5					
Sept 9		8.5					
Sept 30		8.75					

Now proceed row by row to construct the loan schedule. The circled numbers (①, ②, etc.) in the following schedule refer to the sample calculations listed immediately after the schedule.

Date	Number of days	Interest rate	Interest	Accrued interest	Payment (Advance)	Principal portion	Balance
July 6	—	8.5%	—	—	(\$2000.00)	(\$2000.00)	\$2000.00
July 31	25	8.5	\$11.64 ①	~~\$11.64~~	100.00 ②	88.36 ③	1911.64
Aug 15	15	8.5	6.68	6.68	(7500.00)	(7500.00)	9411.64
Aug 31	16	8.5	35.07	~~41.75~~	283.60 ④	241.85 ⑤	9169.79
Sept 9	9	8.5	19.22	19.22			9169.79
Sept 30	21	8.75	46.16	~~65.39~~	65.38	211.68	8958.11

① Interest $= Prt = \$2000(0.085)\frac{25}{365} = \$11.64$

② The payment is the greater of \$100 or $0.03 \times \$2011.64 = \$60.35$. The larger amount is \$100.

③ Principal repaid $= \$100 - \$11.64 = \$88.36$

④ Required payment $= 0.03 \times$ Current balance $= 0.03 \times (\$9411.64 + \$41.75) = \$283.60$

⑤ Principal repaid $= \$283.60 - \$41.75 = \$241.85$

Fixed-Payment Loans

A fixed-payment loan requires *equal* monthly payments. The interest component of each payment is the interest that has accrued on the outstanding principal balance since the preceding payment. As the outstanding loan balance declines, each successive payment has a smaller interest component and a larger principal component.

Example 7.4D *Repayment Schedule for a Fixed-Payment Loan*

Bailey & Co. borrowed \$4000 at prime plus $1\frac{1}{2}\%$ from its bank on May 29 to purchase a new computer. The floating-rate demand loan requires fixed monthly payments of \$800 on the first day of each month, beginning July 1. The prime rate was at 7.25% on May 29 and increased to 7.5% effective August 4. Construct a full repayment schedule showing details of the allocation of each payment to interest and principal.

Solution

On a loan repayment schedule, enter the dates of payments and interest rate changes in chronological order. Information known about these events can also be entered. At this point, the schedule has the following entries:

Date	Number of days	Interest rate	Interest	Accrued interest	Payment (Advance)	Principal portion	Balance
May 29	—	8.75%	—	—	—	—	\$4000.00
July 1		8.75			\$800		
Aug 1		8.75			800		
Aug 4		8.75					
Sept 1		9			800		
Oct 1		9			800		
Nov 1		9			800		
Dec 1		9					

The calculations then proceed row by row to complete the schedule. The circled numbers (①, ②, etc.) in the following schedule refer to sample calculations listed below the schedule. A stroke is drawn through an accrued interest figure when the interest is paid.

Date	Number of days	Interest rate	Interest	Accrued interest	Payment (Advance)	Principal portion	Balance
May 29	—	8.75%	—	—	—	—	$4000.00
July 1	33	8.75	$31.64 ①	~~$31.64~~	$800	$768.36 ②	3231.64
Aug 1	31	8.75	24.02	~~24.02~~	800	775.98	2455.66
Aug 4	3	8.75	1.77	1.77			
Sept 1	28	9	16.95	~~18.72~~	800	781.28	1674.38
Oct 1	30	9	12.39	~~12.39~~	800	787.61	886.77
Nov 1	31	9	6.78	~~6.78~~	800	793.22	93.55
Dec 1	30	9	0.69	~~0.69~~	94.24 ③	93.55	0

① $I = Prt = \$4000(0.0875)\left(\frac{33}{365}\right) = \$31.64$

② Principal portion $= \$800 - \$31.64 = \$768.36$

③ Final payment $= \$93.35 + \$0.69 = \$94.24$

Exercise 7.4

Answers to the odd-numbered problems are at the end of the book.
Some problems in this and later Exercises have spreadsheet icons in the left margin. Formatted spreadsheet templates (Excel 97) are available for these problems on the diskette accompanying this text.

Revolving Demand Loans

•**1.** Dr. Robillard obtained a $75,000 operating line of credit at prime plus 1%. Accrued interest up to but not including the last day of the month is deducted from his bank account on the last day of each month. On February 5 (of a leap year) he received the first draw of $15,000. He made a payment of $10,000 toward principal on March 15, but took another draw of $7000 on May 1. Prepare a loan repayment schedule showing the amount of interest charged to his bank account on the last days of February, March, April, and May. Assume that the prime rate remained at 7.5% through to the end of May.

•**2.** Mr. Michaluk has a $50,000 personal (revolving) line of credit with the Canadian Imperial Bank of Commerce (CIBC). The loan is on a demand basis at a floating rate of prime plus 1.5%. On the fifteenth of each month, a payment equal to the greater of $100 or 3% of the combined principal and accrued interest is deducted from his chequing account. The principal balance after a payment on September 15 stood at $23,465.72. Prepare the loan repayment schedule from September 15 up to and including the payment on January 15. Assume that he makes the minimum payments and the prime rate remains at 8.25%.

•**3.** McKenzie Wood Products negotiated a $200,000 revolving line of credit with the Bank of Montreal at prime plus 2%. On the twentieth of each month, interest is calculated (up to but not including the twentieth) and deducted from the company's chequing account. If the initial loan advance of $25,000 on July 3 was followed by a further advance of $30,000 on

July 29, how much interest was charged on July 20 and August 20? The prime rate was at 8% on July 3 and fell to 7.75% on August 5.

•**4.** On the June 12 interest payment date, the outstanding balance on Delta Nurseries' revolving loan was $65,000. The floating interest rate on the loan stood at 9.25% on June 12, but rose to 9.5% on July 3, and to 10% on July 29. If Delta made principal payments of $10,000 on June 30 and July 31, what were the interest charges to its bank account on July 12 and August 12? Present a repayment schedule supporting the calculations.

•**5.** The Bank of Nova Scotia approved a $75,000 line of credit for Curved Comfort Furniture on the security of its accounts receivable. Curved Comfort drew down $30,000 on October 7, $15,000 on November 24, and $20,000 on December 23. The bank debited interest at the rate of prime plus 1.5% from the business's bank account on the fifteenth of each month. The prime rate was 10.25% on October 7, and dropped by 0.25% on December 17. Present a loan repayment schedule showing details of transactions up to and including January 15.

•**6.** Shoreline Yachts has a $1 million line of credit with the Royal Bank secured by its inventory of sailboats. Interest is charged at the floating (naturally!) rate of prime plus 2% on the tenth of each month (for days up to but not including the tenth). On February 10 (of a non-leap year), the loan balance stood at $770,000 and the prime rate at 9.5%. Shoreline took an additional $100,000 draw on March 1. Spring sales enabled Shoreline to make payments of $125,000 and $150,000 against the principal on March 30 and April 28. The prime rate rose by 0.5% on April 8. What total interest was Shoreline charged for the three months from February 10 to May 10? Present a repayment schedule showing how this interest figure was determined.

•**7.** Hercules Sports obtained a $60,000 operating line of credit on March 26. Interest charges at the rate of prime plus 2.5% were deducted from its chequing account on the eighteenth of each month. Hercules took an initial draw of $30,000 on March 31, when the prime rate was 8.25%. Further advances of $10,000 and $15,000 were taken on April 28 and June 1. Payments of $5000 and $10,000 were applied against the principal on June 18 and July 3. The prime rate rose to 8.5% effective May 14. Present a repayment schedule showing details of transactions up to and including July 18.

•**8.** Benjamin has a $20,000 personal line of credit at prime plus 2% with his credit union. His minimum end-of-month payment is the greater of $100 or 3% of the combined principal and accrued interest. After his payment on April 30, his balance was $3046.33. On May 23, he used his income tax refund to make a principal payment of $1000. On July 17, he took a $7000 advance to purchase a car. The prime rate began at 6% pa, rose 0.25% on June 25, and jumped another 0.25% on July 18. Prepare a loan repayment schedule showing details of payments on May 31, June 30, and July 31.

•**9.** Bronwyn's $15,000 line of credit is at prime plus 2.5%. The minimum payment (the greater of $100 or 3% of the combined principal and accrued interest) is automatically deducted from her chequing account on the fifteenth of each month. After the payment on August 15, her balance was $3589.80. To reduce the loan faster, she makes an additional discretionary payment of $300 on the last day of each month. Each $300 payment is applied entirely to principal. Prepare a repayment schedule for the August 15 to November 15 period. The prime rate was at 6.25% on August 15 but dropped 0.25% effective October 11.

Fixed-Payment Demand Loans

10. A $5000 demand loan was advanced on June 3. Fixed monthly payments of $1000 were required on the first day of each month beginning July 1. Prepare the full repayment schedule for the loan. Assume that the interest rate remained at 12.5% for the life of the loan.

•11. Giovando, Lindstrom & Co. obtained a $6000 demand loan at prime plus 1.5% on April 1 to purchase new office furniture. The company agreed to fixed monthly payments of $1000 on the first of each month, beginning May 1. Calculate the total interest charges over the life of the loan if the prime rate started at 9.75% on April 1, decreased to 9.5% effective June 7, and returned to 9.75% on August 27. Present a repayment schedule in support of your answer.

•12. Dwayne borrowed $3500 from his credit union on a demand loan on July 20 to purchase a motorcycle. The terms of the loan require fixed monthly payments of $700 on the first day of each month, beginning September 1. The floating rate on the loan is prime plus 3%. The prime rate started at 8.25%, but rose 0.5% on August 19, and another 0.25% effective November 2. Prepare a loan repayment schedule presenting the amount of each payment and the allocation of each payment to interest and principal.

•13. Beth borrowed $2500 on demand from Canada Trust on February 23 for a Registered Retirement Savings Plan (RRSP) contribution. Because she used the loan proceeds to purchase Canada Trust's mutual funds for her RRSP, she received a special interest rate of prime plus 0.5%. Beth was required to make fixed monthly payments of $500 on the fifteenth of each month, beginning April 15. The prime rate was initially 8.5%, but it jumped to 9% effective June 15 and increased another 0.25% on July 31. (It was not a leap year.) Construct a repayment schedule showing the amount of each payment and the allocation of each payment to interest and principal.

•14. Dr. Chan obtained a $15,000 demand loan at prime plus 1.5% on September 13 from the Toronto-Dominion Bank to purchase a new dental X-ray machine. Fixed payments of $700 will be deducted from the dentist's chequing account on the twentieth of each month, beginning October 20. The prime rate was 9.5% at the outset, dropped to 9.25% on the subsequent November 26, and rose to 9.75% on January 29. Prepare a loan repayment schedule showing the details of the first five payments.

*7.5 Canada Student Loans

The first significant debt incurred by many who pursue post-secondary education is a student loan. All provincial governments and the federal government offer student loan programs. Only the federal Canada Student Loan Program is discussed in this section. Currently over 400,000 students (representing about 30% of post-secondary enrolment) borrow over $600 million per year under the program.

As long as you are eligible for interest-free status, the Government of Canada pays the interest charges on your Canada Student Loans from banks, trust companies, and other approved lenders. Six months after you cease to be a student, you must begin to make monthly loan payments. For example, if final examinations end on May 17 and you do not return to college the following September, the six-month grace period runs from June 1 to November 30. Interest accrues at the floating rate of prime plus $2\frac{1}{2}\%$ during this six-month grace period. You may pay the accrued interest at the end of the grace period or have it *capitalized* (that is, converted to principal).

Before December 1, you must arrange with your lender to consolidate all Canada Student Loans into a single loan. The first payment on a consolidated loan is due one month after the end of the grace period. In the preceding example, the first payment is due December 31.[3]

The terms of repayment are usually negotiated at the time of consolidation. Depending on the amount of the student loan, fixed monthly payments may be spread over as long as 15 years. The borrower can choose either a *floating* interest rate of prime plus $2\frac{1}{2}\%$, or a *fixed* rate of prime plus 5%. In the latter case, the rate used is the prime rate in effect at the time repayment is negotiated. The borrower cannot subsequently switch from fixed to floating or from floating to fixed during the term of the loan.

The interest portion of each monthly payment is calculated using the daily-interest method with the exact number of days since the previous payment. A loan repayment schedule can be constructed using the same format as for demand loans in Section 7.4. (Canada Student Loans are not demand loans from the lender's point of view. However, the borrower may prepay additional principal at any time without penalty.)

POINT OF INTEREST

Repaying Student Loans is a Must

Have you got plans to travel, buy a car, rent an apartment? They all have to be measured against repaying your student loan. Paying off student loans is the most pressing financial matter for a graduate, ahead of even as harmless a move as starting a Registered Retirement Savings Plan.

This isn't just propaganda spread by people eager to get their loan money back. If you let your student debt get away from you, it could ruin your credit rating and make it difficult to get a mortgage or car loan in the future. On the other hand, smooth repayment of your student debts will help establish you as a good lending risk.

---

[3] Most lenders schedule end-of-month payments but a few arrange beginning-of-month payments.

The maximum payback period for government loans is 15 years. The average student ends up with a 10-year payback period. Revenue Canada provides a small amount of relief for students paying back government student loans. You can claim a 17% federal tax credit on the amount of loan interest you pay. You can use the credit immediately, or carry it forward for five years.

It may happen that you can't pay back the loan right away, possibly because you don't have a job or have a position with a low salary. Interest rate relief is possible on government loans. Essentially, the government pays the interest on the debt until you're able.

Don't ignore the need to repay your student loans. Delinquent loans sponsored by the federal and some provincial governments are reported to credit bureaus and therefore will affect your credit rating. The debt may also be referred to a collection agency—another blotch on your credit record. If your loan is in arrears, you may also find Revenue Canada deducting what's owed the government from your tax refund.

SOURCE: "Repaying Student Loans is a Must" by Rob Carrick, *The Globe and Mail,* April 10, 1999. Reprinted with permission from *The Globe and Mail.*

Example 7.5A *Constructing a Repayment Schedule for a Canada Student Loan*

Heidi had Canada Student Loans totalling \$5300 when she graduated from college. Her six-month grace period ended on November 30, and she chose to have the grace period's accrued interest converted to principal. Heidi selected the floating interest rate option (prime plus 2.5%) when the prime rate was at 7.5%. Monthly payments beginning December 31 were set at \$76.

Prepare a loan repayment schedule up to and including the payment on the following March 31. The intervening February had 29 days. The prime rate increased from 7.25% to 7.5% per annum effective August 3, and rose another 0.5% effective January 14.

Solution

The period from June 1 to August 3 has 215 − 152 = 63 days, and the period from August 3 to (and including) November 30 has 334 + 1 − 215 = 120 days. The accrued interest at the end of the grace period was

$$\begin{aligned} I &= Pr_1t_1 + Pr_2t_2 \\ &= \$5300(0.0975)\frac{63}{365} + \$5300(0.10)\frac{120}{365} \\ &= \$89.19 + \$174.25 \\ &= \$263.44 \end{aligned}$$

The consolidated loan balance at the end of November was

$$\$5300.00 + \$263.44 = \$5563.44.$$

Date	Number of Days	Interest rate	Interest	Accrued interest	Payment Advance	Principal portion	Balance
Dec 1	—	—	—	—	—	—	$5563.44
Dec 31	30	10.0%	$45.73 ①	~~$45.73~~	$76	$30.27	5533.17
Jan 14	14	10.0	21.22	21.22			
Jan 31	17	10.5	27.06	~~48.28~~	76	27.72	5505.45
Feb 29	29	10.5	45.93	~~45.93~~	76	30.07	5475.38
Mar 31	31	10.5	48.83	~~48.83~~	76	27.17	5448.21

① Interest $= Prt = 5563.40(0.10)\left(\frac{30}{365}\right) = \$45.73$

Exercise 7.5

Answers to the odd-numbered problems are at the end of the book.

•**1.** Sarah's Canada Student Loans totalled $9400 by the time she graduated from college in May. She arranged to capitalize the interest on November 30 and to begin monthly payments of $135 on December 31. Sarah elected the floating rate interest option (prime plus 2.5%). The prime rate stood at 6.75% on June 1, dropped to 6.5% effective September 3, and then increased by 0.25% on January 17. Prepare a repayment schedule presenting details of the first three payments. February has 28 days.

•**2.** Harjap completed his college program in December. On June 30, he paid all of the interest that had accrued (at prime plus 2.5%) on his $5800 Canada Student Loan during the six-month grace period. He selected the fixed rate option (prime plus 5%) and agreed to make end-of-month payments of $95 beginning July 31. The prime rate began the grace period at 8% and rose by 0.5% effective March 29. On August 13, the prime rate rose another 0.5%. The relevant February had 28 days.

a. What amount of interest accrued during the grace period?

b. Calculate the total interest paid in the first three regular payments, and the balance owed after the third payment.

•**3.** Monica finished college on June 3 with Canada Student Loans totalling $6800. She decided to capitalize the interest that accrued (at prime plus 2.5%) during the grace period. In addition to regular end-of-month payments of $200, she made an extra $500 lump payment on March 25 that was applied entirely to principal. The prime rate dropped from 9% to 8.75% effective September 22, and declined another 0.5% effective March 2. Calculate the balance owed on the floating rate option after the regular March 31 payment. The relevant February had 28 days.

•**4.** Kari had Canada Student Loans totalling $3800 when she completed her program at St. Lawrence College in December. She had enough savings at the end of June to pay the interest that had accrued during the six-month grace period. Kari made arrangements with her credit union to start end-of-month payments of $60 in July. She chose the fixed interest rate option (at prime plus 5%) when the prime rate was at 5.5%. Prepare a loan repayment schedule up to and including the September 30 payment.

•**5.** Seth had accumulated Canada Student Loans totalling $5200 by the time he graduated from Mount Royal College in May. He arranged with the Bank of Nova Scotia to select the floating-rate option (at prime plus $2\frac{1}{2}\%$) and to begin monthly payments of $110 on December 31. Prepare a loan repayment schedule up to and including the February 28 payment. The prime rate was initially at 7.25%. It dropped by 0.25% effective January 31. Seth made an additional principal payment of $300 on February 14.

*Appendix: Promissory Notes

Promissory notes are like abominable snowmen—they are often referred to but seldom seen. Because they have become an endangered species of financial instrument, promissory notes are relegated to this appendix. Furthermore, the author has made no personal sightings in recent years of the particular behaviour known as "discounting (private) promissory notes." Unless other observers report occurrences, this behaviour will not be mentioned in the next edition.

Concepts and Definitions

A **promissory note** is a written promise by one party to pay an amount of money to another party on a specific date, or on demand.

The required elements and the general rules of law that apply to promissory notes are set out in the federal Bills of Exchange Act. The basic information required in a promissory note is illustrated in Figure 7.2. A *demand* promissory note that might be used by a financial institution in connection with a demand loan is shown in Figure 7.3. The bracketed numbers in Figures 7.2 and 7.3 refer to the following terms.

1. The **maker** of the note is the debtor promising the payment.
2. The **payee** is the creditor to whom the payment is to be made.
3. The **face value** is the principal amount of the debt.
4. The **issue date** is the date on which the note was written or "made" and the date from which interest, if any, is computed.
5. The term of the note is the length of the loan period. (A demand note is payable at any time the payee chooses.)
6. The Bills of Exchange Act provides that, unless otherwise specified[4], an extra **three days of grace** are added at the end of a note's term to determine the note's legal due date. The maker is not in default until after the **legal due date**. No days of grace are allowed in the case of demand notes.
7. If interest is to be charged on the face value, the interest rate must be specified on the note. This makes it an interest-bearing promissory note.

---

[4] To extinguish the normal three days of grace, "NO DAYS OF GRACE" should be indicated on the note by the payee.

Figure 7.2 *Term Promissory Note*

PROMISSORY NOTE

(3) *$7200.00* — *Edmonton, Alberta* — (4) *November 30, 1997*

(5) *Three months* after date *I* promise to pay to the order of

(2) *Western Builders Supply Ltd.*

the sum of *seventy-two hundred and* ------------- *00* /100 Dollars

at (8) *Royal Bank, Terminal Plaza Branch*

for value received, with interest at (7) *12%* per annum.

Due: (6) *March 3, 1998* Signed: (1) *J. Anderson*

Figure 7.3 *Demand Promissory Note*

(3) *$5000.00* — *Hamilton, Ontario* — (4) *April 30, 1997*

ON DEMAND after date for value received, *I* promise to pay to the order of

(2) *Acme Distributing Ltd.* at

(8) the Royal Bank of Canada, Limeridge Mall Branch the sum of

(3) *five thousand* ------------------------ *00* /100 Dollars

(7) with interest thereon calculated and payable monthly at a rate equal to the Royal Bank of Canada's prime interest rate per annum in effect from time to time plus 2 % per annum as well after as before maturity, default and judgment. At the date of this note, such prime interest rate is 8 % per annum.

Prime interest rate is the annual rate of interest announced from time to time by the Royal Bank of Canada as a reference rate then in effect for determining interest rates on Canadian dollar commercial loans in Canada.

Signed: (1) *R. A. Matthews*

The days of grace are included in the interest period for calculating the maturity value (face value plus interest) of the note on the legal due date[5]. For terms of one year or less, it is understood that the simple-interest method should be used. The maturity value of a non-interest-bearing note is just its face value.

8. The note can specify the location at which the maker is to make the payment to the payee's account.

Example 7AA Determining the Legal Due Date

Show how the due date of the promissory note in Figure 7.2 is obtained.

[5] The Bills of Exchange Act provides that, whenever the last day of grace falls on a Saturday, Sunday, or legal holiday, the next following business day becomes the last day of grace. Technically, any extra calendar days added as a consequence of this provision should be included in the interest period. We will ignore this fine point of law to avoid the extra complication. The dollar amount involved (in relation to the maturity value otherwise calculated) is not material.

Solution

When the term of the note is specified in months, the end of the term is normally on the same numbered day in the expiry month as the date of issue. This particular instance is different, as there is no February 30. In such cases the last day of the expiry month is used as the end of the term. The legal due date is then three days later.

For the note in Figure 7.2, the term expires on February 28, 1998, and the legal due date is March 3, 1998.

Example 7AB *Calculating an Interest-Bearing Note's Maturity Value*

What is the maturity value of the note in Figure 7.2?

Solution

Even though the term is specified in months, the interest is calculated to the exact number of days, including the three days of grace.

Month	Days of interest
November	1
December	31
January	31
February	28
March	2
	93

$$\text{Maturity value} = P(1 + rt)$$
$$= \$7200\left[1 + 0.12\left(\frac{93}{365}\right)\right]$$
$$= \$7420.14$$

The maturity value required to settle the note on March 3, 1998 is $7420.14.

Example 7AC *Legal Due Date and Maturity Value of an Interest-Bearing Note*

What would be the legal due date of the promissory note in Figure 7.2 if the term were 120 days instead of three months? What would be the maturity value of the note?

Solution

The legal due date will occur 123 days after the issue date.

Interval	Number of days of interest in the interval	Remaining days of interest in the term
Nov 30 to Dec 31	32	123 − 32 = 91
Jan 1 to Jan 31	31	91 − 31 = 60
Feb 1 to Feb 28	28	60 − 28 = 32
March 1 to Mar 31	31	32 − 31 = 1
April 1 to Apr 2	1①	0

① We have counted the first day (Nov 30) of the term but not the last day (Apr 2).

The legal due date falls on April 2, 1998.

$$\text{Maturity value} = \$7200\left[1 + 0.12\left(\frac{123}{365}\right)\right] = \$7491.16$$

The maturity value on the legal due date is $7491.16.

Discounting Promissory Notes

Promissory notes are *negotiable.* This means that the payee can transfer ownership of the note by *endorsing* it—that is, by signing his name on the back of the note. The payee will do this if he sells the note to an investor at any time before the note's legal due date. The maker is then obliged to pay the maturity value to the holder of the endorsed note on its due date.

The usual reason for selling a note is that the payee needs cash before the due date of the note. The price received for the note is often referred to as the **proceeds** of the note. The general case is presented in Figure 7.4. The face value P of an interest-bearing note earns interest at the rate r_1 (specified in the note) for the time period t_1 until its legal due date. That maturity value will be

$$S = P(1 + r_1t_1)$$

We want to calculate the selling/purchase price of the note on the date of sale, a time period t_2 prior to the due date.

Figure 7.4 *Calculating the Proceeds of a Promissory Note*

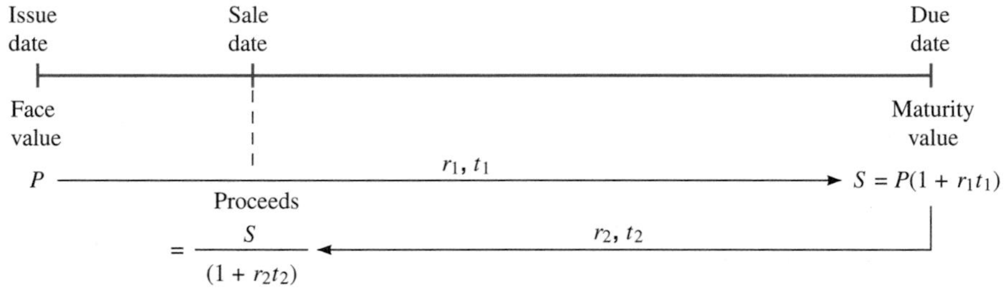

According to the Valuation Principle, the purchase price should be the present value of the maturity value discounted at the buyer's required rate of return. That is,

$$\text{Purchase price (Proceeds)} = \frac{S}{1 + r_2t_2}$$

In summary, the calculation of the purchase price or proceeds of a promissory note is a two-step procedure.

1. Calculate the maturity value on the due date using the interest rate *specified in the note.* If the note does not bear interest, its maturity value is just its face value.
2. Calculate the present value, on the date of sale, of the maturity value using the discount rate agreed upon by the buyer and the seller.

Example 7AD Calculating the Proceeds of a Non-Interest-Bearing Note

A 150-day non-interest-bearing note for $2500 was made on June 15. The note was sold on August 21 at a price reflecting a discount rate of 12.5% pa. What were the proceeds of the note?

Solution

There are 153 days from the issue date until the legal due date. By August 21, $16 + 31 + 20 = 67$ of the days have passed and $153 - 67 = 86$ days remain.

This information and the solution approach are presented in the following time diagram.

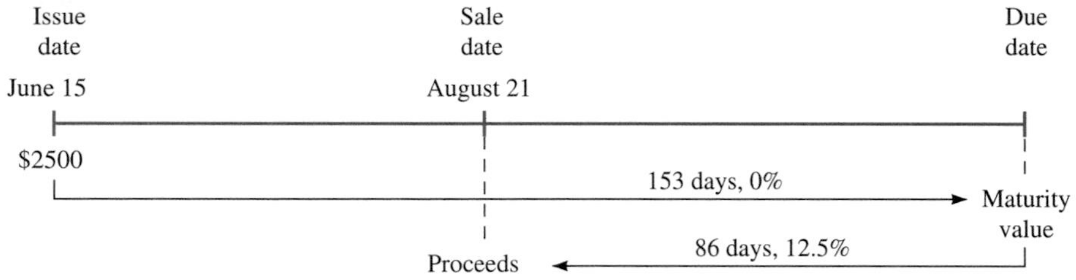

Since the face value does not earn interest, the maturity value will equal the face value of $2500.

The proceeds of the note will be the present value, 86 days earlier, of the maturity value discounted at the rate of 12.5% pa.

$$\text{Proceeds} = \frac{S}{1 + rt} = \frac{\$2500}{1 + 0.125\left(\frac{86}{365}\right)} = \$2428.48$$

Note: By paying this price, the extra

$$\$2500 - \$2428.48 = \$71.52$$

received on the note's legal due date provides a 12.5% rate of return for 86 days on the investment of $2428.48. To verify this, calculate

$$r = \frac{I}{Pt} = \frac{\$71.52}{\$2428.48\left(\frac{86}{365}\right)} = 0.125 = 12.5\%$$

Example 7AE Calculating the Proceeds of an Interest-Bearing Note

Old Country Antiques accepted a six-month promissory note from a customer for the $2850 balance owed on the purchase of a dining room suite. The note was dated November 8, 1999, and charged interest at 13% pa. The store's proprietor sold the promissory note 38 days later to a finance company at a price that would yield the finance company 18% pa on its purchase price. What price did the finance company pay?

Solution

The note's legal due date was May 11, 2000 (May 8 + 3 days). The total number of days from the issue date to the due date was

$$23 + 31 + 31 + 29 + 31 + 30 + 10 = 185 \text{ days}$$

When the note was sold, 185 − 38 = 147 days remained until the due date. The given information and the steps in the solution can be presented in a time diagram.

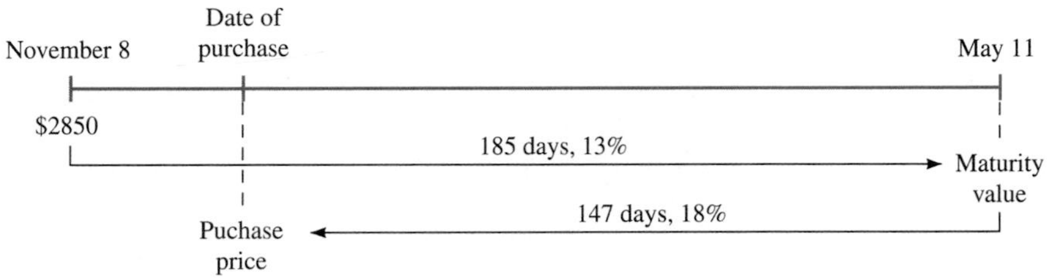

$$\text{Maturity value of note} = \$2850\left[1 + 0.13\left(\frac{185}{365}\right)\right] = \$3037.79$$

The price paid by the finance company was the present value, 147 days earlier, of the maturity value discounted at 18% pa.

$$\text{Price} = \frac{\$3037.79}{1 + 0.18\left(\frac{147}{365}\right)} = \$2832.46$$

The finance company paid $2832.46 for the promissory note.

Exercise 7A

Answers to the odd-numbered problems are at the end of the book.

Calculate the missing values for the promissory notes described in Problems 1 through 22.

Problem	Issue date	Term	Legal due date
1.	May 19	120 days	?
2.	June 30	90 days	?
3.	July 6	? days	Oct 17
4.	Nov 14	? days	Jan 31
5.	?	4 months	Feb 28
6.	?	9 months	Oct 3
7.	?	180 days	Sept 2
8.	?	60 days	March 1(leap year)

Problem	Issue date	Face value ($)	Term	Interest rate (%)	Maturity value ($)
9.	April 30	1000	4 months	9.50	?
10.	Feb 15	3300	60 days	8.75	?
11.	July 3	?	90 days	10.20	2667.57
12.	Aug 31	?	3 months	7.50	7644.86
13.	Jan 22	6200	120 days	?	6388.04
14.	Nov 5	4350	75 days	?	4445.28
15.	Dec 31	5200	? days	11.00	5275.22
16.	March 30	9400	? days	9.90	9560.62

Problem	Face value ($)	Issue date	Interest rate (%)	Term	Date of sale	Discount rate (%)	Proceeds ($)
17.	1000	March 30	0	50 days	April 8	10	?
18.	6000	May 17	0	3 months	June 17	9	?
19.	2700	Sept 4	10	182 days	Dec 14	12	?
20.	3500	Oct 25	10	120 days	Dec 14	8	?
21.	9000	July 28	8	91 days	Sept 1	?	9075.40
22.	4000	Nov 30	8	75 days	Jan 1	?	4015.25

23. Determine the legal due date for:

a. A five-month note dated September 29, 1997.

b. A 150-day note issued September 29, 1997.

24. Determine the legal due date for:

a. A four-month note dated April 30, 1994.

b. A 120-day note issued April 30, 1994.

25. Calculate the maturity value of a 120-day, $1000 face value note dated November 30, 1997, and earning interest at 10.75% pa.

26. Calculate the maturity value of a $1000 face value, five-month note dated December 31, 1997, and bearing interest at 9.5% pa.

27. A 90-day non-interest-bearing note for $3300 is dated August 1. What would be a fair selling price of the note on September 1 if money can earn 7.75% pa?

28. A six-month non-interest-bearing note issued on September 30, 1997 for $3300 was discounted at 11.25% on December 1. What were the proceeds of the note?

29. A 100-day $750 note with interest at 12.5% was written on July 15. The maker approaches the payee on August 10 to propose an early settlement. What amount should the payee be willing to accept on August 10 if short-term investments can earn 8.25% pa?

30. The payee on a three-month \$2700 note earning interest at 8% wishes to sell the note to raise some cash. What price should she be prepared to accept for the note (dated May 19) on June 5 in order to yield the purchaser an 11% rate of return?

31. A six-month note dated June 30 for \$2900 bears interest at 13.5%. Determine the proceeds of the note if it is discounted at 9.75% on September 1.

32. An investor is prepared to buy short-term promissory notes at a price that will provide him with a return on investment of 12%. What amount would he pay on August 9 for a 120-day note dated July 18 for \$4100 with interest at 10.25% pa?

Review Problems

Answers to the odd-numbered review problems are at the end of the book.

1. An agreement stipulates payments of \$4500, \$3000, and \$5500 in four, eight, and 12 months, respectively, from today. What is the highest price an investor will offer today to purchase the agreement if he requires a minimum return of 10.5% pa?

◆ **2.** An assignable loan contract executed three months ago requires two payments of \$3200 with interest at 9% from the date of the contract, to be paid four and eight months after the contract date. The payee is offering to sell the contract to a finance company in order to raise urgently needed cash. If the finance company requires a return of 16% pa, what price will it be prepared to pay today for the contract?

3. Calculate the price of a \$50,000, 91-day Province of Nova Scotia Treasury bill on its issue date if the current market rate of return is 6.773% pa.

4. A \$100,000, 182-day Province of New Brunswick Treasury bill was issued 66 days ago. What will it sell at today to yield the purchaser 7.48%?

5. A \$100,000, 90-day commercial paper certificate issued by Bell Canada was sold on its issue date for \$98,450. What annual rate of return (to the nearest 0.001%) will it yield to the buyer?

◆ **6.** A \$100,000, 168-day Government of Canada Treasury bill was purchased on its date of issue to yield 6.5% pa.

a. What price did the investor pay?

b. Calculate the market value of the T-bill 85 days later if the annual rate of return then required by the market has:

(i) risen to 7%. **(ii)** remained at 6.5%. **(iii)** fallen to 6%.

c. Calculate the rate of return actually realized by the investor if the T-bill is sold at each of the three prices calculated in part (b).

7. A chartered bank offers a rate of 5.500% on investments of \$25,000 to \$59,999 and a rate of 5.750% on investments of \$60,000 to \$99,999 in 90- to 365-day GICs. How much more will an investor earn from a single \$80,000, 180-day GIC than from two \$40,000, 180-day GICs?

◆ **8.** Suppose that the current rates on 60- and 120-day GICs are 5.50% and 5.75%, respectively. An investor is weighing the alternatives of purchasing a 120-day GIC versus purchasing a 60-day GIC and then reinvesting its maturity value in a second 60-day GIC. What would the interest rate on 60-day GICs have to be 60 days from now for the investor to end up in the same financial position with either alternative?

9. An Investment Savings account offered by a trust company pays a rate of 3.00% on the first \$1000 of daily closing balance, 3.75% on the portion of the balance between \$1000 and \$3000, and 4.25% on any balance in excess of \$3000. What interest will be paid for the month of January if the opening balance was \$3678, \$2800 was withdrawn on the fourteenth of the month, and \$950 was deposited on the twenty-fifth of the month?

SPATS ◆ **10.** George borrowed \$4000 on demand from the Royal Bank on January 28 for an RRSP contribution. Because he used the loan proceeds to purchase the Royal Bank's mutual funds for his RRSP, the interest rate on the loan was set at the bank's prime rate. George agreed to make monthly payments of \$600 (except for a smaller final payment) on the twenty-first of each month, beginning February 21. The prime rate was initially 6.75%, dropped to 6.5% effective May 15, and decreased another 0.25% on July 5. It was not a leap year. Construct a repayment schedule showing the amount of each payment and the allocation of each payment to interest and principal.

◆ **11.** Mayfair Fashions has a $90,000 line of credit from the Bank of Montreal. Interest at prime plus 2% is deducted from Mayfair's chequing account on the twenty-fourth of each month. Mayfair initially drew down $40,000 on March 8 and another $15,000 on April 2. On June 5, $25,000 of principal was repaid. If the prime rate was 8.25% on March 8 and rose by 0.25% effective May 13, what were the first four interest deductions charged to the store's account?

12. Roxanne's Canada Student Loans totalled $7200 by the time she finished college in April. The accrued interest at prime plus 2.5% for the grace period was converted to principal on October 31. She chose the floating interest rate option and began monthly payments of $120 on November 30. The prime rate of interest was 8% on May 1, 7.75% effective July 9, and 7.5% effective December 13. Prepare a repayment schedule presenting details of the first three payments.

Self-Test Exercise

Answers to the self-test problems are at the end of the book.

◆ **1.** A conditional sale contract requires two payments three and six months after the date of the contract. Each payment consists of $1900 principal plus interest at 12.5% on $1900 from the date of the contract. One month into the contract, what price would a finance company pay for the contract if it requires an 18% rate of return on its purchases?

◆ **2.** A $25,000, 91-day Province of Newfoundland Treasury bill was originally purchased at a price that would yield the investor a 5.438% pa rate of return if the T-bill is held until maturity. Thirty-four days later, the investor sold the T-bill through his broker for $24,775.

a. What price did the original investor pay for the T-bill?

b. What rate of return will the second investor realize if she holds the T-bill until maturity?

c. What rate of return did the first investor realize during his holding period?

3. Paul has $20,000 to invest for six months. For this amount, his bank pays 6.3% on a 90-day GIC and 6.5% on a 180-day GIC. If the interest rate on a 90-day GIC is the same three months from now, how much more interest will Paul earn by purchasing the 180-day GIC than by buying a 90-day GIC and then reinvesting its maturity value in a second 90-day GIC?

◆ **4.** Duncan Developments Ltd. obtained a $120,000 line of credit from its bank to subdivide a parcel of land it owned into four residential lots and to install water, sewer, and underground electrical services. Amounts advanced from time to time are payable on demand to its bank. Interest at prime plus 4% on the daily principal balance is charged to the developer's bank account on the twenty-sixth of each month. The developer must apply at least $30,000 from the proceeds of the sale of each lot against the loan principal. Duncan drew down $50,000 on June 3, $40,000 on June 30, and $25,000 on July 17. Two lots quickly sold, and Duncan repaid $30,000 on July 31 and $35,000 on August 18. The initial prime rate of 8% changed to 8.25% effective July 5 and 8.5% effective July 26. Prepare a repayment schedule showing loan activity and interest charges up to and including the interest payment on August 26.

◆ **5.** Ms. Wadeson obtained a $15,000 demand loan from the Canadian Imperial Bank of Commerce on May 23 to purchase a car. The interest rate on the loan was prime plus 2%. The loan required payments of $700 on the fifteenth of each month, beginning June 15. The prime rate was 7.5% at the outset, dropped to 7.25% on July 26, and then jumped by 0.5% on September 14. Prepare a loan repayment schedule showing the details of the first five payments.

CASE

DEBT CONSOLIDATION

Graham and Stacy are having difficulty stretching their salaries to pay the bills. Before their marriage three months ago, they purchased new furnishings for their apartment. Then they paid for their honeymoon with "plastic." Now the bills are all in. The following table lists their debts.

Debt	Balance	Interest rate	Monthly payment Minimum	Monthly payment Fixed
Car loan	$6000	9.5%	—	$300
Canada Student Loan	6800	Prime + 2.5%	—	100
Visa	4700	17.5%	5%	—
MasterCard	3900	15.9%	5%	—
Sears	3850	28.8%	4%	—
Canadian Tire	1250	28.8%	5%	—

The minimum monthly payment on each credit card is the indicated percentage of the *combined* principal balance plus accrued interest. The prime rate of interest is 6.5%.

With a view to consolidating their debts, Stacy and Graham have discussed their personal financial position with the Personal Banking Representative (PBR) at the bank close to their new apartment. The PBR is prepared to approve a $20,000 joint line of credit at prime plus 3% on the condition that $6000 be used immediately to pay off the car loan (obtained from another bank). The minimum monthly payment would be 3% of the combined principal balance plus accrued interest.

QUESTIONS

1. Assuming 30 days' interest on the indicated (principal) balances, what is the next minimum payment on each of the four credit cards?
2. If all the debt balances except the Canada Student Loan are consolidated in the new line of credit, what will be the first minimum payment? (Again assume a full 30 days' accrued interest on the principal for the fairest comparison with the "status quo.")
3. Based on the preceding results, what is the reduction in the first month's total debt service payments?
4. With respect to credit card debt only, what is the reduction in the first month's interest charges?
5. What (weighted) average interest rate are Graham and Stacy currently paying? What (weighted) average interest rate will they be paying after loan consolidation? (Include the Canada Student Loan in both calculations.)
6. Give two reasons why the PBR set the condition that Graham and Stacy use part of the line of credit to pay off the car loan.
7. Give two reasons why the PBR did not suggest a $27,000 line of credit and require that Graham and Stacy use the extra $7000 to pay off the Canada Student Loan. (The student loan is with another bank.)

www.Exercise.com

THE PRICE OF REDEEMABILITY From the Royal Bank Financial Group page at www.royalbank.com/rates/index.html, link to the rate pages for "Redeemable GICs" and "Non-Redeemable GICs." For each type of simple interest investment, how much interest will you earn on $10,000 invested for 100 days? How much interest will you earn on the Redeemable GIC if you redeem it after:

(i) 29 days? (ii) 31 days?

Summary of Notation and Key Formulas

VALUATION PRINCIPLE:

The fair market value of an investment is the sum of the present values of the expected cash flows. The discount rate used in the present value calculations should be the market-determined rate of return required for this type of investment.

List of Key Terms

Commercial paper *(p. 260)*
Demand loan *(p. 263)*
Discounting a payment *(p. 255)*
Discount rate *(p. 255)*
Face value *(p. 259)*
Fair market value *(p. 255)*
Guaranteed Investment Certificate (GIC) *(p. 250)*
Loan repayment schedule *(p. 265)*
Savings account *(p. 250)*
Term deposit *(p. 250)*
Treasury bill *(p. 258)*

CHAPTER OUTLINE

LEARNING OBJECTIVES

After completing this chapter, you will be able to:

- Calculate maturity value, future value, and present value in compound interest applications, by both the algebraic method and the preprogrammed financial calculator method
- Calculate the maturity value of compound interest Guaranteed Investment Certificates (GICs)
- Calculate the price of strip bonds
- Calculate the redemption value of a compound interest Canada Savings Bond
- Adapt the concepts and equations of compound interest to cases of compound growth
- Calculate the payment on any date that is equivalent to one or more payments on other dates
- Calculate the economic value of a payment stream

8

Compound Interest: Future Value and Present Value

EXAMPLES OF COMPOUND INTEREST ARE easy to find. If you obtain a loan to purchase a car, interest will be compounded monthly. The advertised interest rates on mortgage loans are semiannually compounded rates. Interest is always compounded in long-term financial planning. So if you wish to take control of your personal financial affairs or to be involved in the financial side of a business, you must thoroughly understand compound interest and its applications. The remainder of this textbook is devoted to the mathematics and applications of compound interest.

You will be able to hit the ground running! In Chapters 6 and 7, you learned the concepts of maturity value, time value of money, future value, and present value for the case of simple interest. These ideas transfer to compound interest. We need only to develop new mathematics for calculating future value and present value when interest is compounded. And there is good news in this regard! Most compound interest formulas are permanently programmed into financial calculators. After you become competent in the algebraic method for solving compound interest problems, your instructor may allow you to use a financial calculator to automate the computations. Before long, you will be impressed at the types of financial calculations you can handle!

8.1 Basic Concepts

The simple interest method discussed in Chapter 6 is restricted primarily to loans and investments having terms of less than one year. The compound interest method is employed in virtually all instances where the term exceeds one year. It is also used in a few cases where the duration is less than one year.

In the **compound interest method**, interest is *periodically* calculated and *converted* to principal. "Converting interest to principal" means that the interest is added to principal and thereafter treated as principal. Consequently, interest earned in one period will itself earn interest in all subsequent periods. The time interval between successive interest conversion dates is called the **compounding period**. Suppose, for example, you invest \$1000 at 10% compounded annually. "Compounded annually" means that "interest is compounded once per year." Therefore, the compounding period is one year. On each anniversary of the investment, interest will be calculated and converted to principal. The process is indicated in Figure 8.1. The original \$1000 investment is represented by the column located at "0" on the time axis. During the first year, you will earn \$100 interest (10% of \$1000). At the end of the first year, this \$100 will be converted to principal. The new principal (\$1100) will earn \$110 interest (10% of \$1100) in the second year. Note that you earn \$10 more interest in the second year than in the first year because you have \$100 more principal invested at 10%. How much interest will be earned in the third year? Do you see the pattern developing? Each year you will earn more interest than in the preceding year—\$100 in the first year, \$110 in the second year, \$121 in the third year, and so on. Consequently, the growth in value of the investment will accelerate as the years pass. In contrast, if the \$1000 earns 10% per annum *simple* interest, only the *original* principal will earn interest (\$100) each year. A \$1000 investment will grow by just \$100 each year. After two years, your investment will be worth only \$1200 (compared to \$1210 with annual compounding).

Figure 8.1 *Converting Interest to Principal at the End of Each Compounding Period*

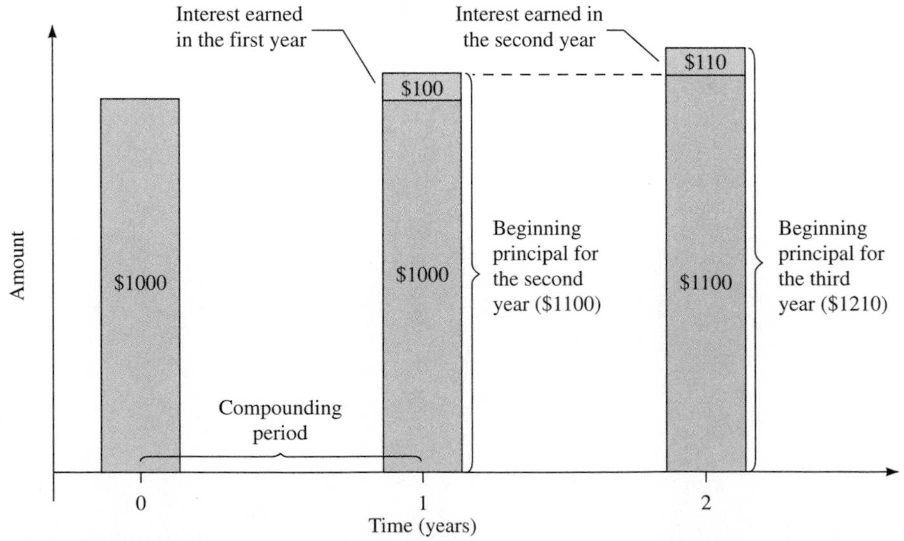

In many circumstances, interest is compounded more frequently than once per year. The number of compoundings per year is called the **compounding frequency**. The commonly used frequencies and their corresponding compounding periods are listed in Table 8.1.

Table 8.1 *Compounding Frequencies and Periods*

Compounding frequency	Number of compoundings per year	Compounding period
Annual	1	1 year
Semiannual	2	6 months
Quarterly	4	3 months
Monthly	12	1 month

A compound interest rate is normally quoted with two components:

- A number for the annual interest rate (called the **nominal[1] interest rate**).
- Words stating the compounding frequency.

For example, an interest rate of 8% compounded semiannually means that half of the 8% nominal annual rate is earned and compounded each six-month compounding period. A rate of 9% compounded monthly means that 0.75% (one-twelfth of 9%) is earned and compounded each month. We use the term **periodic interest rate** for the interest rate per compounding interval. In the two examples at hand, the periodic interest rates are 4% and 0.75%, respectively. In general,

$$\text{Periodic interest rate} = \frac{\text{Nominal interest rate}}{\text{Number of compoundings per year}}$$

If we define the following symbols:

j = ~~Nominal~~ compound. interest rate
m = Number of compoundings per year
i = Periodic interest rate

the simple relationship between the periodic interest rate and the nominal interest rate is:

PERIODIC INTEREST RATE

(8-1) $$i = \frac{j}{m}$$

TRAP *VALUE OF "m" FOR QUARTERLY COMPOUNDING*

What is the value of m for quarterly compounding? Sometimes students incorrectly use $m = 3$ with quarterly compounding because $\frac{1}{4}$ year = 3 months. But m represents the number of compoundings per year (4), not the length of the compounding period.

[1] As you shall soon understand, you cannot conclude that $100 invested for one year at 8% compounded semiannually will earn exactly $8.00 of interest. Therefore, we use the word "nominal," meaning "in name only," to describe the numerical part of a quoted rate.

TIP

GIVE THE COMPLETE DESCRIPTION OF AN INTEREST RATE

Whenever you are asked to calculate or state a nominal interest rate, it is understood that you should also include the compounding frequency in your response. For example, an answer of just "8%" is incomplete. Rather, you must state "8% compounded quarterly" if interest is compounded four times per year.

Example 8.1A *Calculating the Periodic Interest Rate*

Calculate the periodic interest rate corresponding to:

a. 10.5% compounded annually.

b. 9.75% compounded semiannually.

c. 9.0% compounded quarterly.

d. 9.5% compounded monthly.

Solution

Employing formula (8-1), we obtain:

a. $i = \frac{j}{m} = \frac{10.5\%}{1} = 10.5\%$ (per year)

b. $i = \frac{9.75\%}{2} = 4.875\%$ (per half year)

c. $i = \frac{9.0\%}{4} = 2.25\%$ (per quarter)

d. $i = \frac{9.5\%}{12} = 0.791\overline{6}\%$ (per month)

Example 8.1B *Calculating the Compounding Frequency*

For a nominal interest rate of 8.4%, what is the compounding frequency if the periodic interest rate is:

a. 4.2%? **b.** 8.4%? **c.** 2.1%? **d.** 0.70%?

Solution

The number of compoundings or conversions in a year is given by the value of m in formula (8-1). Rearranging this formula to solve for m, we obtain

$$m = \frac{j}{i}$$

a. $m = \frac{8.4\%}{4.2\%} = 2$ which corresponds to semiannual compounding.

b. $m = \frac{8.4\%}{8.4\%} = 1$ which corresponds to annual compounding.

c. $m = \dfrac{8.4\%}{2.1\%} = 4$ which corresponds to quarterly compounding.

d. $m = \dfrac{8.4\%}{0.7\%} = 12$ which corresponds to monthly compounding.

Example 8.1C *Calculating the Nominal Interest Rate*

Determine the nominal rate of interest if:

a. The periodic rate is 1.75% with quarterly compounding.

b. The periodic rate is $0.8\overline{3}\%$ with monthly compounding.

Solution

Rearranging formula (8-1) to solve for *j*, the nominal interest rate, we obtain

$$j = mi$$

a. $j = 4(1.75\%) = 7.0\%$

b. $j = 12(0.8\overline{3}\%) = 10.0\%$

The nominal interest rates are 7.0% compounded quarterly and 10.0% compounded monthly, respectively.

Concept Questions

1. What does it mean to compound interest?
2. Explain the difference between "compounding period" and "compounding frequency."
3. Explain the difference between "nominal rate of interest" and "periodic rate of interest."

Exercise 8.1

Answers to the odd-numbered problems are at the end of the book.
Calculate the missing values in Problems 1 through 9.

Problem	Nominal interest rate (%)	Compounding frequency	Periodic interest rate (%)
1.	10.8	Quarterly	?
2.	11.75	Semiannually	?
3.	10.5	Monthly	?
4.	?	Semiannually	4.95
5.	?	Monthly	0.91667
6.	?	Quarterly	2.9375
7.	9.5	?	2.375
8.	8.25	?	4.125
9.	13.5	?	1.125

8.2 Future Value (or Maturity Value)

Calculating Future Value

Remember from our study of simple interest in Chapter 6 that the **maturity value** or **future value** is the combined principal and interest due at the maturity date of a loan or investment. We used $S = P(1 + rt)$ to calculate future value in the simple interest case. Now our first task is to develop the corresponding formula for use with compound interest. The general question we want to answer is:

> "What is the future value, S, of an initial principal, P, earning a periodic interest rate, i, in each of n compounding periods?"

Before we answer this question, let's be sure we understand the distinction between the new variable

$$n = \text{Total number of compoundings}$$

and the variable (from Section 8.1)

$$m = \text{Number of compoundings per year}$$

Our intuition usually works better if we put numbers to the variables. Suppose a \$1000 investment earns 8% compounded semiannually for three years. From this given information, we can "attach" numbers to variables as follows:

$$P = \$1000 \qquad j = 8\% \text{ compounded semiannually} \qquad \text{Term} = 3 \text{ years}$$

$$m = 2 \text{ compoundings per year} \qquad i = \frac{j}{m} = \frac{8\%}{2} = 4\% \text{ per half year}$$

"n" represents the total number of compoundings *in the entire* ***term*** of the investment. In our example, n is the number of compoundings in three years. Since there are two compoundings per year, then $n = 2 \times 3 = 6$. In general,

TOTAL NUMBER OF COMPOUNDING PERIODS

(8-3) $$n = m \times (\textit{Number of years in the term})$$

How can we calculate the future value of the \$1000 investment? Think of the periodic interest rate as the *percentage change* in the principal in each compounding period. To calculate the future value of the initial \$1000, we must compound a series of six percentage changes of 4% each. Do you remember encountering this sort of question before?

In Section 2.7, we learned how to compound a series of percentage changes. If an initial value, V_i, undergoes a series of n percentage changes, $c_1, c_2, c_3, \ldots, c_n$, the final value, V_f, is:

$$\begin{array}{cccccc} V_f = & V_i(1 + c_1) & (1 + c_2) & (1 + c_3) & \cdots & (1 + c_n) \\ \uparrow & \uparrow & \uparrow & \uparrow & & \uparrow \\ S & P \quad i & i & i & & i \end{array} \qquad (2\text{-}3)$$

The corresponding compound interest variables are indicated under formula (2-3). Making the substitutions, we obtain

$$S = P(1 + i)(1 + i)(1 + i)\ldots(1 + i)$$

Since the factor $(1 + i)$ occurs n times, then

FUTURE VALUE OR MATURITY VALUE (COMPOUND INTEREST)

$$S = P(1 + i)^n \tag{8-2}$$

Example 8.2A *Calculating the Maturity Value of a Lump Investment*

What will be the maturity value of \$10,000 invested for five years at 9.75% compounded semiannually?

Solution

Given: $P = \$10,000$, Term of investment = 5 years, $j = 9.75\%$, $m = 2$
The interest rate per six-month compounding period is

$$i = \frac{j}{m} = \frac{9.75\%}{2} = 4.875\% \text{ (per half year)}$$

$$n = m \times \text{Term (in years)} = 2(5) = 10$$

The maturity value will be

$$\begin{aligned} S &= P(1 + i)^n \\ &= \$10,000(1 + 0.04875)^{10} \\ &= \$10,000(1.6096066) \\ &= \$16,096.07 \end{aligned}$$

The investment will grow to \$16,096.07 after five years.

Example 8.2B *Comparing Two Nominal Rates of Interest*

Other things being equal, would an investor prefer an interest rate of 10.5% compounded monthly or 11% compounded annually for a two-year investment?

Solution

The preferred rate will be the one that results in the higher maturity value. Pick an arbitrary initial investment, say \$1000, and calculate the maturity value at each rate.

For $i = \frac{10.5\%}{12} = 0.875\%$ and $n = 12(2) = 24$,

$$S = \$1000(1.00875)^{24} = \$1232.55$$

For $i = \frac{11\%}{1} = 11\%$ and $n = 1(2) = 2$,

$$S = \$1000(1.11)^2 = \$1232.10$$

The rate of 10.5% compounded monthly is slightly better. The more frequent compounding more than offsets the lower nominal rate.

Example 8.2C Calculating the Maturity Value When the Interest Rate Changes

George invested \$5000 at 9.25% compounded quarterly. After 18 months, the rate changed to 9.75% compounded semiannually. What amount will George have three years after the initial investment?

Solution

The periodic rate of interest is

$$i = \frac{j}{m} = \frac{9.25\%}{4} = 2.3125\% \text{ (per quarter)}$$

for the first 18 months and

$$i = \frac{9.75\%}{2} = 4.875\% \text{ (per half year)}$$

for the next 18 months. Because of the interest rate change, the solution should be done in two steps, as indicated by the following diagram.

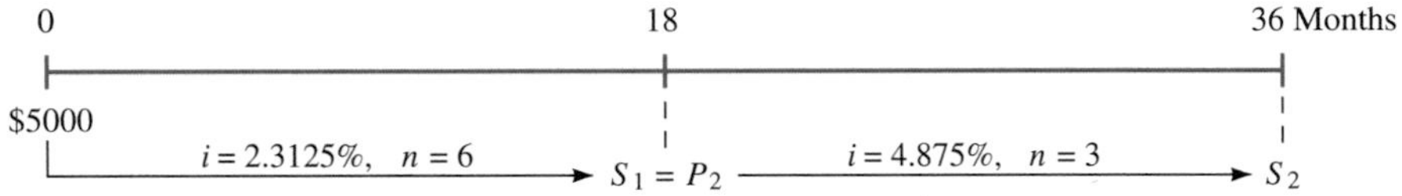

The "maturity value" S_1 after 18 months becomes the beginning "principal" P_2 for the remainder of the three years.

Step 1: Calculate the amount S_1 after 18 months.

$$S_1 = P(1 + i)^n = \$5000(1.023125)^6 = \$5735.12$$

Step 2: Calculate the amount S_2 at the end of the three years.

$$S_2 = P_2(1 + i)^n = \$5735.12(1.04875)^3 = \$6615.44$$

George will have \$6615.44 after three years.

Example 8.2D The Balance Owed after Payments on a Compound Interest Loan

Fay borrowed \$5000 at an interest rate of 11% compounded quarterly. On the first, second, and third anniversaries of the loan, she made payments of \$1500. What payment made on the fourth anniversary will extinguish the debt?

Solution

At each anniversary we will first calculate the amount owed (S) and then deduct the payment to obtain the principal balance (P) at the beginning of the next year. The periodic interest rate is

$$i = \frac{j}{m} = \frac{11\%}{4} = 2.75\%$$

The sequence of steps is indicated by the following time diagram.

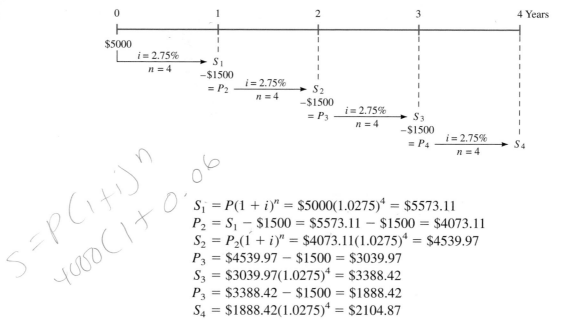

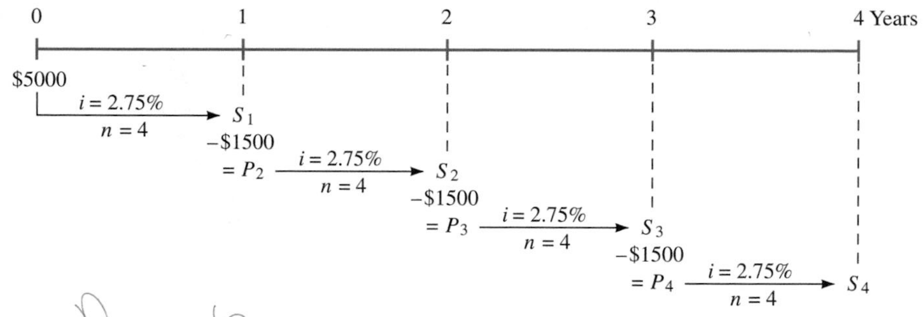

$$
\begin{aligned}
S_1 &= P(1+i)^n = \$5000(1.0275)^4 = \$5573.11 \\
P_2 &= S_1 - \$1500 = \$5573.11 - \$1500 = \$4073.11 \\
S_2 &= P_2(1+i)^n = \$4073.11(1.0275)^4 = \$4539.97 \\
P_3 &= \$4539.97 - \$1500 = \$3039.97 \\
S_3 &= \$3039.97(1.0275)^4 = \$3388.42 \\
P_3 &= \$3388.42 - \$1500 = \$1888.42 \\
S_4 &= \$1888.42(1.0275)^4 = \$2104.87
\end{aligned}
$$

A payment of $2104.87 on the fourth anniversary will pay off the debt.

Graphs of Future Value versus Time

A picture is worth a thousand words, but a graph can be worth more. The best way to develop our understanding of the nature of compounding and the roles of key variables is through the study of graphs.

The Components of Future Value Let us investigate in greater detail (than we did in Section 8.1) the consequences of earning "interest on interest" through compounding. In Figure 8.2, we compare the growth of two investments:

- $100 invested at 10% compounded annually (the upper curve)
- $100 invested at 10% per annum simple interest (the inclined straight line)

For the compound interest investment,

$$S = P(1+i)^n = \$100(1+0.10)^n = \$100(1.10)^n$$

The upper curve was obtained by plotting values of S for n ranging from 0 to 10 compounding periods (years).

For the simple interest investment,

$$S = P(1+rt) = \$100(1+0.10t)$$

This gives an upward sloping straight line when we plot values of S for t ranging from 0 to 10 years. In this case, the future value increases $10 per year because only

Figure 8.2 *The Components of the Future Value of $100*

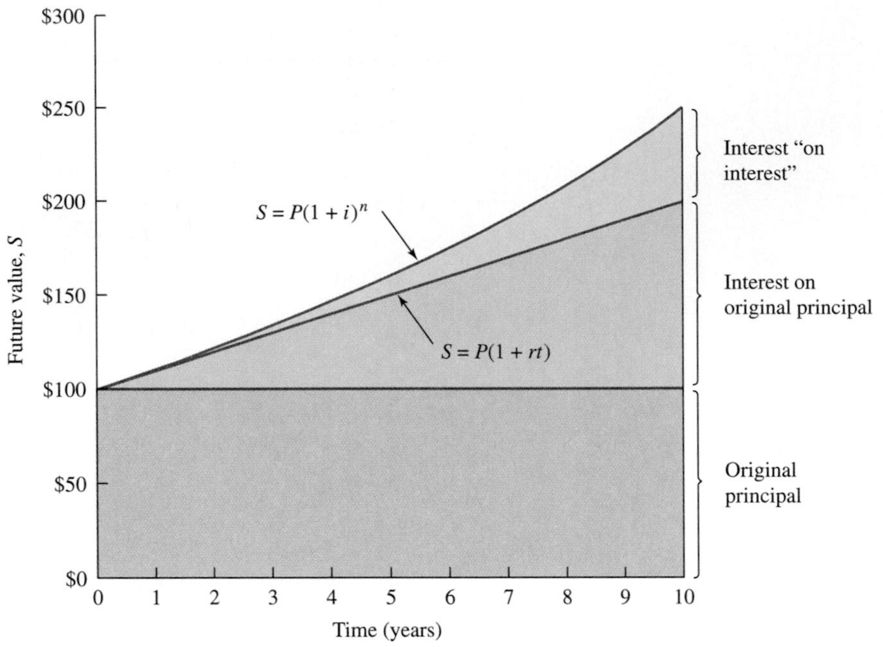

the original principal of $100 earns 10% interest each year. At any point, the future value of the simple interest investment has *two* components:

1. The original principal ($100)
2. The interest earned on the original principal. In the graph, this component is the vertical distance from the line (at $100) to the sloping simple interest line.

Returning to the compound interest investment, we can think of its future value at any point as having *three* components: the same two listed above for the simple interest investment plus

3. "Interest earned on interest"—really interest earned on interest previously converted to principal. In the graph, this component is the vertical distance from the inclined simple interest line to the upper compound interest curve. Note that this component increases at an accelerating rate as time passes. Eventually, "interest on interest" will exceed the interest earned on the original principal! How long do you think this will take to happen for the case plotted in Figure 8.2?

The Effect of the Nominal Interest Rate on the Future Value Suppose Investment A earns 10% compounded annually, while Investment B earns 12% compounded annually. B's rate of return (12%) is one-fifth larger than A's (10%). You might think that if $100 is invested in each investment for say, 25 years, the investment in B will grow one-fifth or 20% more than the investment in A. Wrong! Let's look into the outcome more carefully. It has very important implications for long-term financial planning.

In Figure 8.3, the future value of a \$100 investment is plotted over a 25-year period for four *annually* compounded rates of interest. The four rates are at 2% increments, and include the rates earned by Investments A (10%) and B (12%). We expect the separation of the curves to increase as time passes—that would happen without compounding. The most important observation you should make is the *disproportionate* effect each 2% increase in interest rate has on the long-term growth of the future value. Compare the future values after 25 years at the 10% and 12% rates. You can see that the future value at 12% compounded annually (Investment B) is about 1.5 times the future value at 10% compounded annually (Investment A). In comparison, the ratio of the two interest rates is only $\frac{12\%}{10\%} = 1.2$!

Figure 8.3 *Future Values of \$100 at Various Compound Rates of Interest*

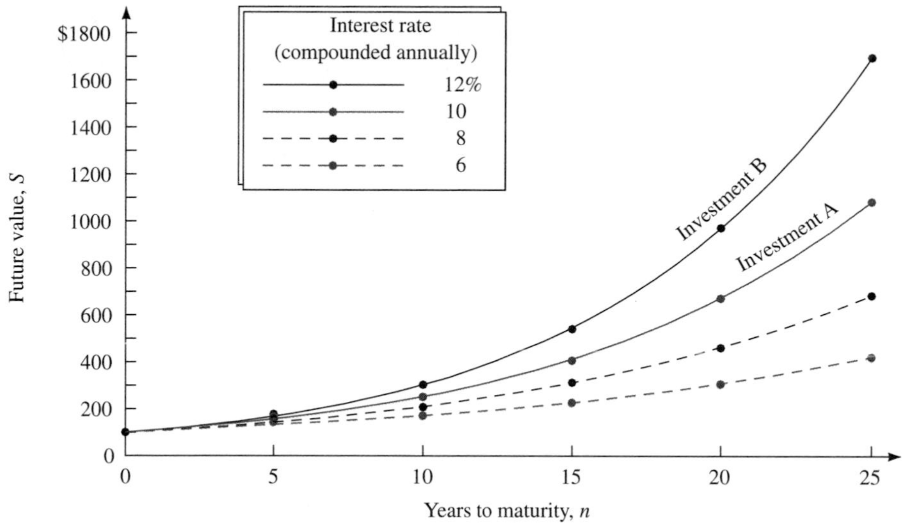

The contrast between long-term performances of A and B is more dramatic if we compare their *growth* instead of their future values. Over the full 25 years, B grows by

$$S - P = P(1 + i)^n - P = \$100(1.12)^{25} - \$100 = \$1600.01$$

while A grows by

$$S - P = P(1 + i)^n - P = \$100(1.10)^{25} - \$100 = \$983.47$$

In summary, B's growth is 1.63 times A's growth, even though the interest rate earned by B is only 1.2 times the rate earned by A. What a difference the extra 2% per year makes, especially over longer time periods! The implications for planning and managing your personal financial affairs are:

- You should begin an investment plan early in life in order to realize the dramatic effects of compounding beyond a 20-year time horizon.
- You should try to obtain the best available rate of return (at your acceptable level of risk). An extra 0.5% or 1% annual rate of return has a disproportionate effect on investment growth, particularly in the long run.

The Effect of the Compounding Frequency on the Future Value What difference will it make if we invest $100 at 12% compounded *monthly* instead of 12% compounded *annually?* In the first case, the $1 interest (1% of $100) earned in the first month gets converted to principal at the end of the month. We will then have $101 earning interest in the second month, and so on. With annual compounding, the $1 interest earned in the first month is not paid out or converted to principal. Just the original principal ($100) will earn interest in the second through to the twelfth month. Only then will the $12 interest earned during the year be converted to principal. Therefore, the original $100 will grow faster with monthly compounding.

The long-run effect of more frequent compounding is shown in Figure 8.4. As time passes, the higher compounding frequency produces a surprisingly large and ever-increasing difference between the future values. After 15 years, the future value with monthly compounding is about 10% larger than with annual compounding. Thereafter, the gap continues to widen in both dollar and percentage terms. After 20 years, it is almost 13% and after 25 years, it is 16.4%!

Where do you think the curves for semiannual and quarterly compounding would lie if they were added to the graph?

Figure 8.4 *Future Values of $100 at the Same Nominal Rate but Different Compounding Frequencies*

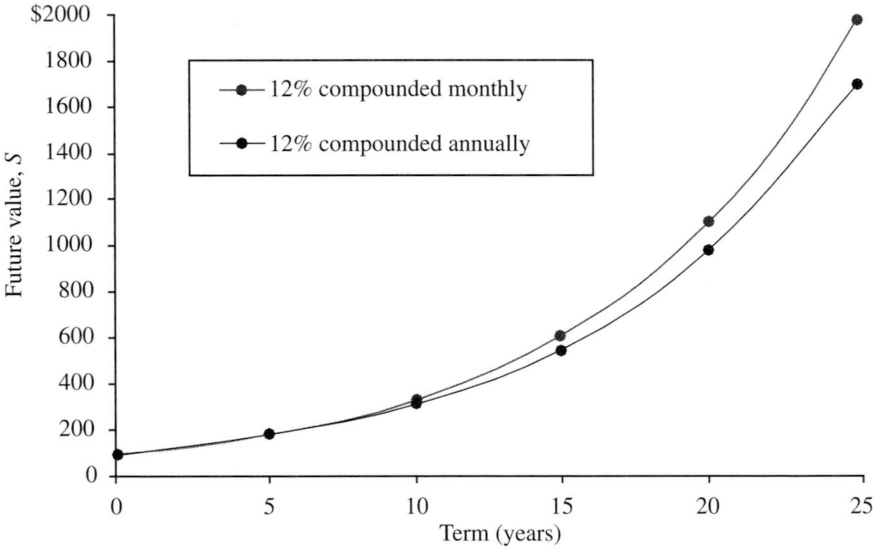

Equivalent Payments

What amount would you accept five years from now instead of $100 paid today? When we ask this question, we have in mind the notion of *economic* equivalence. Economically equivalent amounts may be *substituted* for one another even though they are paid on different dates. Regardless of which alternative you select, you will end up with the same number of dollars (including interest earnings) at a future date.

We encountered this sort of question (with a shorter time horizon) in Section 6.4. The same logic applies with a longer time frame. You should calculate the amount you could have five years from now if you were to receive and invest \$100 today. This is just the future value of the \$100. For the rate of return, you should use an interest rate you can expect from a low-risk investment. The current rate of return on five-year Government of Canada bonds[2] would be suitable in this case.

Let's push our thinking a little further. What single amount paid five years from now is economically equivalent to the combination of two payments: \$100 due today, and a \$100 payment due one year from now? There are no surprises here—follow your instincts. Calculate the future value of each \$100 payment at the focal date five years from now and add the two future values.

Example 8.2E *Calculating the Economic Value of Two Payments*

A small claims court has ruled in favour of Mrs. Peacock. She claimed that Professor Plum defaulted on two payments of \$1000 each. One payment was due 18 months ago, and the other 11 months ago. What is the appropriate amount for the court to order Plum to pay immediately if the court uses 6% compounded monthly as the time value of money?

Solution

The appropriate award is the combined future value of the two payments brought forward from their due dates to today. The periodic rate of interest is

$$i = \frac{6\%}{12} = 0.5\%$$

The solution plan is presented in the diagram below.

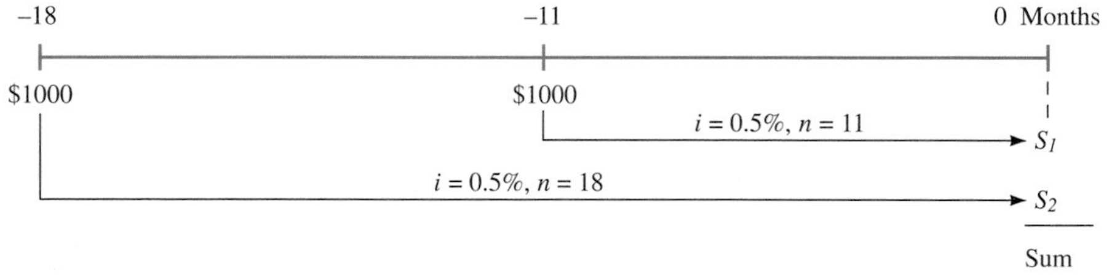

The amount today that is equivalent to the payment due 11 months ago is

$$S_1 = P(1+i)^n = \$1000(1.005)^{11} = \$1056.396$$

Similarly,

$$S_2 = \$1000(1.005)^{18} = \$1093.929$$
$$S_1 + S_2 = \$1056.396 + \$1093.929 = \$2150.33$$

The appropriate amount for Plum to pay is \$2150.33.

2 This rate can be found any day of the week in the financial pages of major newspapers. Bonds will be covered in detail in Chapter 15.

POINT OF INTEREST

THE "MAGIC" OF COMPOUND INTEREST

"I don't know the names of the Seven Wonders of the World, but I do know the Eighth Wonder: ***Compound Interest.****"* *Baron Rothschild*

Many books and articles on personal financial planning write with similar awe about the "miracle" or "magic" of compound interest. The authors make it appear that mysterious forces are involved. *The Wealthy Barber,* a Canadian bestseller, says that "it's a real tragedy that most people don't understand compound interest and its wondrous powers." Another book states that "one of the greatest gifts that you can give your children is a compound interest table" (which you will be able to construct by the end of this chapter).

These books do have a legitimate point, even if it seems overstated once you become familiar with the mathematics of compound interest. Most people really do underestimate the long-term growth of compound-interest investments. Also, they do not take seriously enough the advice to start saving and investing early in life. As we noted in Figure 8.3, compound growth accelerates rapidly beyond the 20-year horizon.

The reason most people underestimate the long-term effects of compounding is that they tend to think in terms of proportional relationships. For example, most would estimate that an investment will earn about twice as much over 20 years as it will earn over 10 years at the same rate of return. Let's check your intuition in this regard.

Questions

1. How do you think the growth of a $100 investment over 20 years compares to its growth over 10 years? Assume a return of 8% compounded annually. Will the former be twice as large? Two-and-a-half times as large? Make your best educated guess and then work out the actual ratio. Remember, we want the ratio for the *growth,* not the *future value.*
2. Will the growth ratio be larger, smaller, or the same if we invest $1000 instead of $100 at the start? After making your choice, calculate the ratio.
3. Will the growth ratio be larger, smaller, or the same if the rate of return is 10% compounded annually instead of 8% compounded annually? After making your choice, calculate the ratio.

Concept Questions

1. What is meant by the future value of an investment?
2. For a given nominal interest rate (say 10%) on a loan, would the borrower prefer it to be compounded annually or compounded monthly? Which compounding frequency would the lender prefer? Give a brief explanation.

3. For a six-month investment, rank the following interest rates (number one being "most preferred"): 6% per annum simple interest, 6% compounded semiannually, 6% compounded quarterly. Explain your ranking.
4. From a *simple inspection,* rank the four interest rates in each of parts (a) and (b). Take an investor's point of view. Give a brief explanation to justify your answer.
   a. 9.0% compounded monthly, 9.1% compounded quarterly, 9.2% compounded semiannually, 9.3% compounded annually.
   b. 9.0% compounded annually, 9.1% compounded semiannually, 9.2% compounded quarterly, 9.3% compounded monthly.
5. If an investment doubles in nine years, how long will it take to quadruple (at the same rate of return)? (This problem does not require any detailed calculations.)
6. Suppose it took x years for an investment to grow from \$100 to \$200 at a fixed compound rate of return. How many more years will it take to earn an additional
   a. \$100? **b.** \$200? **c.** \$300?
   In each case, pick an answer from:
   (i) more than x years, (ii) less than x years, (iii) exactly x years.
7. John and Mary both invest \$1000 on the same date and at the same compound interest rate. If the term of Mary's investment is 10% longer than John's, will Mary's maturity value be (pick one):
   (i) 10% larger (ii) less than 10% larger (iii) more than 10% larger?
   Explain.
8. John and Mary both invest \$1000 on the same date for the same term to maturity. John earns a nominal interest rate that is 1.1 times the rate earned by Mary (but both have the same compounding frequency). Will John's interest earnings be (pick one):
   (i) 1.1 times (ii) less than 1.1 times (iii) more than 1.1 times
   Mary's earnings? Explain.
9. Why is \$100 paid today worth more than \$100 paid at a future date? Is inflation the fundamental reason?

Exercise 8.2

Answers to the odd-numbered problems are at the end of the book.

Note: In Section 8.4, you will learn how to use special functions on a financial calculator to solve compound-interest problems. Exercise 8.4 will suggest that you return to this Exercise to practise the financial calculator method.

Calculate the maturity value in Problems 1 through 4.

Problem	Principal (\$)	Term	Nominal rate (%)	Compounding frequency
1.	5000	7 years	10	Semiannually
2.	8500	$5\frac{1}{2}$ years	9.5	Quarterly
3.	12,100	$3\frac{1}{4}$ years	7.5	Monthly
4.	4400	$6\frac{3}{4}$ years	11	Monthly

5. Calculate the maturity amount of a $1000 RRSP[3] contribution after 25 years if it earns an interest rate of 9% compounded:

   a. Annually. b. Semiannually. c. Quarterly. d. Monthly.

6. Calculate the maturity amount of a $1000 RRSP contribution after five years if it earns an interest rate of 9% compounded:

   a. Annually. b. Semiannually. c. Quarterly. d. Monthly.

7. By calculating the maturity value of $100 invested for one year at each rate, determine which rate of return an investor would prefer.

   a. 8.0% compounded monthly.

   b. 8.1% compounded quarterly.

   c. 8.2% compounded semiannually.

   d. 8.3% compounded annually.

8. By calculating the maturity value of $100 invested for one year at each rate, determine which rate of return an investor would prefer.

   a. 12.0% compounded monthly.

   b. 12.1% compounded quarterly.

   c. 12.2% compounded semiannually.

   d. 12.3% compounded annually.

9. What is the maturity value of a $3000 loan for 18 months at 9.5% compounded semiannually? How much interest is charged on the loan?

10. What total amount of interest will be earned by $5000 invested at 7.5% compounded monthly for $3\frac{1}{2}$ years?

11. How much more will an investment of $1000 be worth after 25 years if it earns 11% compounded annually instead of 10% compounded annually? Calculate the difference in dollars and as a percentage of the smaller maturity value.

12. How much more will an investment of $1000 be worth after 25 years if it earns 6% compounded annually instead of 5% compounded annually? Calculate the difference in dollars and as a percentage of the smaller maturity value.

13. How much more will an investment of $1000 earning 9% compounded annually be worth after 25 years than after 20 years? Calculate the difference in dollars and as a percentage of the smaller maturity value.

14. How much more will an investment of $1000 earning 9% compounded annually be worth after 15 years than after 10 years? Calculate the difference in dollars and as a percentage of the smaller maturity value.

---

[3] Some features of Registered Retirement Savings Plans (RRSPs) will be discussed in Section 8.5. At this point, simply view an RRSP contribution as an investment.

15. A $1000 investment is made today. Calculate its maturity values for the six combinations of terms and annually compounded interest rates in the following table.

Interest rate (%)	Term 20 years	25 years	30 years
8	?	?	?
10	?	?	?

16. Suppose an individual invests $1000 at the beginning of each year for the next 30 years. Thirty years from now, how much more will the first $1000 investment be worth than the sixteenth $1000 investment if both earn 8.5% compounded annually?

In Problems 17 through 20, calculate the combined equivalent value of the scheduled payments on the indicated dates. The rate of return that money can earn is given in the fourth column. Assume that payments due in the past have not yet been made.

Problem	Scheduled payments	Date of equivalent value	Money can earn (%)	Compounding frequency
17.	$5000 due $1\frac{1}{2}$ years ago	$2\frac{1}{2}$ years from now	8.25	Annually
18.	$3000 due in 5 months	3 years from now	7.5	Monthly
19.	$1300 due today, $1800 due in $1\frac{3}{4}$ years	4 years from now	6	Quarterly
20.	$2000 due 3 years ago, $1000 due $1\frac{1}{2}$ years ago	$1\frac{1}{2}$ years from now	6.8	Semiannually

21. What amount today is equivalent to $2000 four years ago, if money earned 10.5% compounded semiannually over the last four years?

22. What amount two years from now will be equivalent to $2300 $1\frac{1}{2}$ years ago, if money earns 9.25% compounded semiannually during the intervening time?

•**23.** Jeff borrowed $3000, $3500, and $4000 from his father on January 1 of three successive years at college. Jeff and his father agreed that interest would accumulate on each amount at the rate of 5% compounded semiannually. Jeff is to start repaying the loan on the January 1 following graduation. What consolidated amount will he owe at that time?

•**24.** You project that you will be able to invest $1000 this year, $1500 one year from now, and $2000 two years from today. You hope to use the accumulated funds six years from now to cover the $10,000 down payment on a house. Will you achieve your objectives, if the investments earn 8% compounded semiannually? (Taken from ICB course on Wealth Valuation.)

•25. Mrs. Vanderberg has just deposited $5000 in each of three savings plans for her grandchildren. They will have access to the accumulated funds on their nineteenth birthdays. Their current ages are 12 years, seven months (Donna); 10 years, three months (Tim); and seven years, 11 months (Gary). If the plans earn 8% compounded monthly, what amount will each grandchild receive at age 19?

•26. Nelson borrowed $5000 for $4\frac{1}{2}$ years. For the first $2\frac{1}{2}$ years, the interest rate on the loan was 8.4% compounded monthly. Then the rate became 7.5% compounded semiannually. What total amount was required to pay off the loan if no payments were made before the expiry of the $4\frac{1}{2}$-year term?

•27. Scott has just invested $60,000 in a five-year Guaranteed Investment Certificate (GIC) earning 6% compounded semiannually. When the GIC matures, he will reinvest its entire maturity value in a new five-year GIC. What will be the maturity value of the second GIC if it yields:

a. The same rate as the current GIC?

b. 7% compounded semiannually?

c. 5% compounded semiannually?

•28. An investment of $2500 earned interest at 7.5% compounded quarterly for $1\frac{1}{2}$ years, and then 6.8% compounded monthly for two years. How much interest did the investment earn in the $3\frac{1}{2}$ years?

•29. A debt of $7000 accumulated interest at 9.5% compounded quarterly for 15 months, after which the rate changed to 8.5% compounded semiannually for the next six months. What was the total amount owed at the end of the entire 21-month period?

•30. Megan borrowed $1900 $3\frac{1}{2}$ years ago at 11% compounded semiannually. Two years ago she made a payment of $1000. What amount is required today to pay off the remaining principal and the accrued interest?

•31. Duane borrowed $3000 from his grandmother five years ago. The interest on the loan was to be 5% compounded semiannually for the first three years, and 9% compounded monthly thereafter. If he made a $1000 payment $2\frac{1}{2}$ years ago, what is the amount now owed on the loan?

•32. A loan of $4000 at 12% compounded monthly requires three payments of $1000 at six, 12, and 18 months after the date of the loan, and a final payment of the full balance after two years. What is the amount of the final payment?

••33. Dr. Sawicki obtained a variable-rate loan of $10,000. The lender required payment of at least $2000 each year. After nine months the doctor paid $2500, and another nine months later she paid $3000. What amount was owed on the loan after two years if the interest rate was 11.25% compounded monthly for the first year, and 11.5% compounded quarterly for the second year?

8.3 Present Value

What amount must you invest today at 6% compounded annually for it to grow to \$1000 in five years? In other words, what initial principal will have a future value of \$1000 after five years? To answer the question, we need only rearrange $S = P(1 + i)^n$ to isolate P, and then substitute the values for S, i, and n. Division of both sides by $(1 + i)^n$ will leave P by itself on the right side. We thereby obtain a second version of formula (8-2):

$$P = \frac{S}{(1 + i)^n} = S(1 + i)^{-n}$$

TIP

Efficient Use of Your Calculator

Calculating P using $S(1 + i)^{-n}$ leads to a more efficient calculation than using $\frac{S}{(1 + i)^n}$. To illustrate, we will evaluate $S(1 + i)^{-n}$ for the values $S = \$1000$, $n = 5$, and $i = 6\%$ (from the question posed at the beginning of this section). Then $P = \$1000(1.06)^{-5}$. The number of keystrokes is minimized if we reverse the order of multiplication and evaluate $(1.06)^{-5} \times \$1000$. Enter the following keystroke sequence.

1.06 (2nd F) y^x 5 +/- × 1000 =

The 2nd F keystroke is in brackets because it is required *only* if the power function, y^x, is the "second function" of a key on your calculator. The +/- key must be pressed immediately after entering the number whose sign is to be reversed. When the × key is pressed, the value of $(1.06)^{-5}$ appears in the display. Pressing = completes the multiplication, giving \$747.26 in the display.

Consider a second question. If money can earn 6% compounded annually, what amount *today* is equivalent to \$1000 paid five years from now? This is an example of determining a payment's **present value**—an economically equivalent amount at an *earlier* date. In this instance, the present value is the (principal) amount you would have to invest today in order to end up with \$1000 after five years. We see that $P = S(1 + i)^{-n}$ applies to two types of problems:

- Calculating the initial principal, and
- Calculating the present value.

The present value of a future payment will, of course, always be a smaller number than the payment. This is why the process of calculating a payment's present value is sometimes described as **discounting a payment**. The interest rate used in the present value calculation is then referred to as the **discount rate**.

The longer the time period before a scheduled payment, the smaller will be the present value. Figure 8.5 shows the pattern of decreasing present value for longer periods before the payment date. The decline is rapid at first but steadily tapers off. With a discount rate of 10% compounded annually, the present value seven years before the payment is about half the *numerical* value of the payment. Twenty-five years prior to the payment, the present value is less than one-tenth of the payment's size! In practical terms, payments that will be received more than 25 years in the future have little *economic* value today.

How would Figure 8.5 change for a discount rate of 8% compounded annually? And how would it differ for a discount rate of 12% compounded annually?

Figure 8.5 *The Present Value Of $1000 (Discounted at 10% Compounded Annually)*

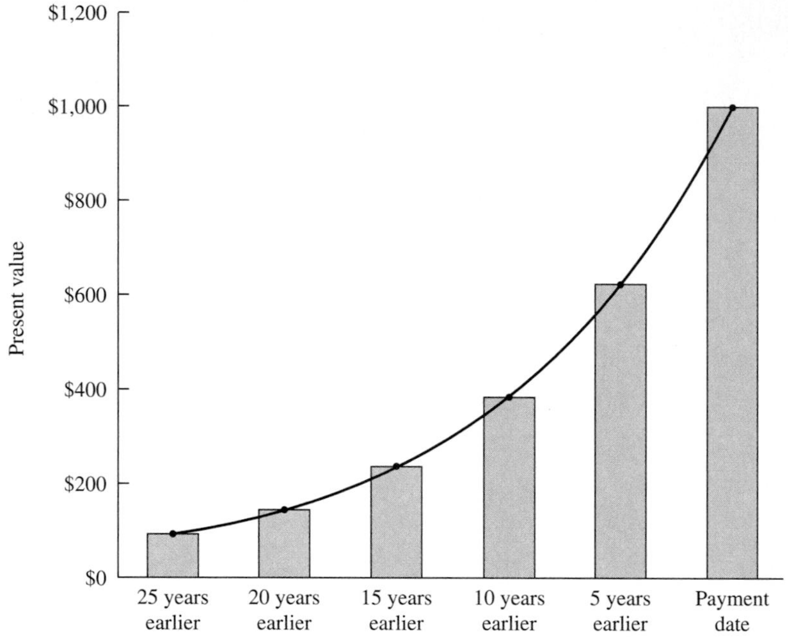

TIP *Making Comparisons*

When comparing a payment to its present value or to its future value, notice whether *numerical* values or *economic* values are being discussed. In terms of numerical values, present value is smaller than the payment, and future value is larger than the payment. However, these *numerically* different amounts all have the *same* economic value. For example, suppose a $100 payment is due one year from now, and money can earn 10% compounded annually. Today's present value is $\$100(1.10)^{-1} = \$91.91$. The future value two years from now is $110.00. The three amounts all have the same economic value, namely the value of $91.91 *current* dollars.

Example 8.3A *The Principal Needed to Produce a Specified Maturity Value*

What amount must be invested now in a savings account earning 8% compounded monthly to accumulate a total of $10,000 after $2\frac{1}{2}$ years?

Solution

Given: $j = 8\%$, $m = 12$, $S = \$10{,}000$, Term $= 3\frac{1}{2}$ years

$$i = \frac{8\%}{12} = 0.\overline{6}\% \text{ (per month)}$$

$$n = m \times \text{Term} = 12(3.5) = 42$$

Rearranging formula (8-2) to solve for *P*,

$$P = S(1+i)^{-n} = \$10{,}000(1+0.00\overline{6})^{-42} = \$7564.86$$

A total of \$7564.86 must be invested now in order to have \$10,000 after $3\frac{1}{2}$ years.

Example 8.3B *Calculating an Equivalent Payment*

Mr. and Mrs. Espedido's property taxes, amounting to \$2450, are due on July 1. What amount should the city accept if the taxes are paid eight months in advance and the city can earn 6% compounded monthly on surplus funds?

Solution

The city should accept an amount that is equivalent, eight months earlier, to \$2450, allowing for the rate of interest that the city can earn on its surplus cash. This equivalent amount is the present value of \$2450, eight months earlier.
Given: $S = \$2450$, $j = 6\%$ compounded monthly, $m = 12$, $n = 8$

$$i = \frac{j}{m} = \frac{6\%}{12} = 0.5\% \text{ (per month)}$$

$$\text{Present value, } P = S(1+i)^{-n} = \$2450(1.005)^{-8} = \$2354.17$$

The city should be willing to accept \$2354.17 on a date eight months before the scheduled due date.

Example 8.3C *Calculating the Equivalent Value of Two Payments*

Two payments of \$10,000 each must be made one year and four years from now. If money can earn 9% compounded monthly, what single payment two years from now would be equivalent to the two scheduled payments?

Solution

When more than one payment is involved in a problem, it is helpful to present the given information in a time diagram. Some of the necessary calculations may be indicated on the diagram. In this case, the calculation of the equivalent values, two years from now, of the scheduled payments is indicated by constructing arrows from the scheduled payments to the date of the replacement payment.

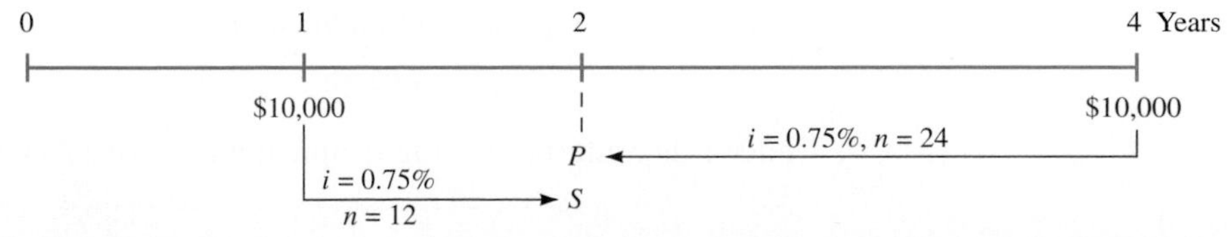

The single equivalent payment will be $P + S$.

$$S = \text{Future value of } \$10{,}000, \text{ 12 months later}$$
$$= \$10{,}000(1.0075)^{12}$$
$$= \$10{,}938.07$$
$$P = \text{Present value of } \$10{,}000, \text{ 24 months earlier}$$
$$= \$10{,}000(1.0075)^{-24}$$
$$= \$8358.31$$

The equivalent single payment is

$$\$10{,}938.07 + \$8358.31 = \$19{,}296.38$$

Example 8.3D Demonstrating Economic Equivalence

Show why the recipient of the payments in Example 8.3C should be indifferent between receiving the scheduled payments and receiving the replacement payment.

Solution

If the recipient ends up in the same economic position under either alternative, then he should not care which alternative is used.

We will calculate how much money the recipient will have under each alternative at the end of four years, assuming that any amounts received are invested at 9% compounded monthly.

The alternatives are presented in the two following time diagrams.

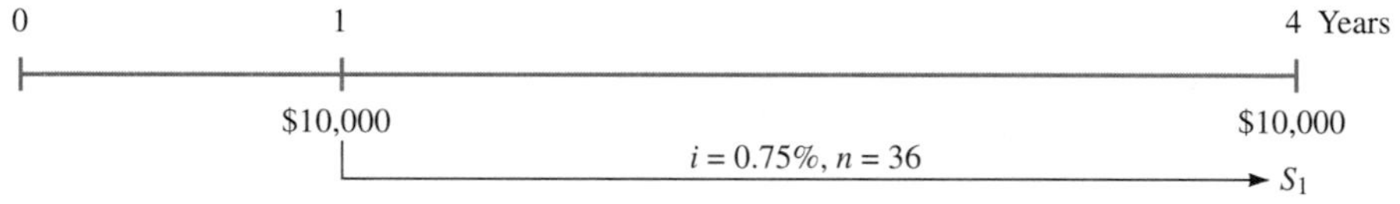

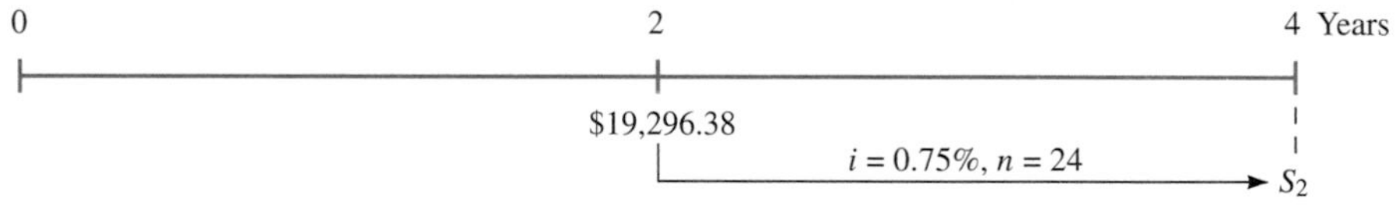

With the scheduled payments, the total amount that the recipient will have after four years is

$$S_1 + \$10{,}000 = \$10{,}000(1.0075)^{36} + \$10{,}000$$
$$= \$13{,}086.45 + \$10{,}000$$
$$= \$23{,}086.45$$

With the single replacement payment, the recipient will have

$$S_2 = \$19{,}296.38(1.0075)^{24} = \$23{,}086.45$$

Under either alternative, the recipient will have \$23,086.45 after four years.

A General Principle Regarding the Present Value of Loan Payments Let us work through a problem that will illustrate a very important principle. We will use the data and results from Example 8.2D. In that example, we were told that three payments of \$1500 each were made on a \$5000 loan at one-year intervals after the date of the loan. The interest rate on the loan was 11% compounded quarterly. The problem was to determine the additional payment needed to pay off the loan at the end of the fourth year. The answer was \$2104.87.

We will now calculate the sum of the present values of all four payments at the date on which the loan was granted. Use the interest rate on the loan as the discount rate. The calculation of each payment's present value is given in the following table.

Payment	Amount, S	n	i	$P = S(1+i)^{-n}$
First	\$1500.00	4	2.75%	$P_1 = \$1500(1.0275)^{-4} = \$1345.75$
Second	\$1500.00	8	2.75%	$P_2 = \$1500(1.0275)^{-8} = \$1207.36$
Third	\$1500.00	12	2.75%	$P_3 = \$1500(1.0275)^{-12} = \$1083.20$
Fourth	\$2104.87	16	2.75%	$P_4 = \$2104.87(1.0275)^{-16} = \$1363.69$
				Total: \$5000.00

Note that the sum of the present values is \$5000.00, precisely the original principal amount of the loan. *This outcome will occur for all loans.* The payments do not need to be equal in size or to be at regular intervals. The fundamental principle is highlighted below because we will use it repeatedly in later work.

PRESENT VALUE OF LOAN PAYMENTS

The sum of the present values of all of the payments required to pay off a loan is equal to the original principal of the loan. The discount rate for the present-value calculations is the rate of interest charged on the loan.

Example 8.3E *Calculating Two Unknown Loan Payments*

Kramer borrowed \$4000 from George at an interest rate of 7% compounded semiannually. The loan is to be repaid by three payments. The first payment, \$1000, is due two years after the date of the loan. The second and third payments are due three and five years, respectively, after the initial loan. Calculate the amounts of the second and third payments if the second payment is to be twice the size of the third payment.

Solution

In Example 8.2D, we solved a similar problem but only the last of four loan payments was unknown. In this problem, two payments are unknown and it would be difficult to use the Example 8.2D approach. However, the fundamental principle developed in this section may be used to solve a wide range of loan problems (including Example 8.2D). Applying this principle to the problem at hand, we have

Sum of the present values of the three payments = \$4000

The given data are presented on the time line below. If we let x represent the third payment, then the second payment must be $2x$. Notice how the idea expressed by the preceding word equation can (and should) be indicated on the diagram.

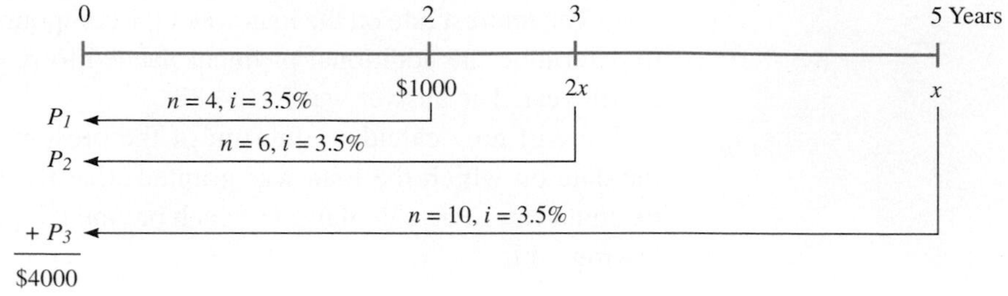

The second and third payments must be of sizes that will make

$$P_1 + P_2 + P_3 = \$4000 \quad ①$$

We can obtain a numerical value for P_1, but the best we can do for P_2 and P_3 is to express them in terms of x. That is just fine—after we substitute these values into equation ①, we will be able to solve for x.

$$\begin{aligned} P_1 &= S(1+i)^{-n} = \$1000(1.035)^{-4} = \$871.44 \\ P_2 &= 2x(1.035)^{-6} = 1.6270013x \\ P_3 &= x(1.035)^{-10} = 0.7089188x \end{aligned}$$

Now substitute these values into equation ① and solve for x.

$$\begin{aligned} \$871.44 + 1.6270013x + 0.7089188x &= \$4000 \\ 2.3359201x &= \$3128.56 \\ x &= \$1339.33 \end{aligned}$$

Kramer's second payment will be 2($1339.33) = $2678.66, and the third payment will be $1339.33.

Concept Questions

1. What is the meaning of the term *discount rate*?
2. Does a smaller discount rate result in a larger or a smaller present value? Explain.
3. The process of discounting is the opposite of doing what?
4. Why does $100 have less economic value one year from now than $100 has today? What do you need to know before you can determine the difference between the economic values of the two payments?
5. If the present value of $X due eight years from now is 0.5$X, what is the present value of $X due 16 years from now? Answer without using formula (8-2).
6. Suppose the future value of $1 after x years is $5. What is the present value of $1 x years before its scheduled payment date? (Assume the same interest rate in both cases.)

Exercise 8.3

Answers to the odd-numbered problems are at the end of the book.

Note: In Section 8.4, you will learn how to use special functions on a financial calculator to solve compound-interest problems. Exercise 8.4 will invite you to return to this Exercise to practise the financial calculator method.

In Problems 1 through 4, calculate the original principal that has the given maturity value.

Problem	Maturity value ($)	Term	Nominal rate (%)	Compounding frequency
1.	10,000	10 years	9.9	Annual
2.	5437.52	27 months	8.5	Quarterly
3.	9704.61	42 months	7.5	Semiannually
4.	8000	18 months	13	Monthly

5. What amount must be invested for eight years at 7.5% compounded semiannually to reach a maturity value of $10,000?

6. Ross has just been notified that the combined principal and interest on an amount that he borrowed 27 months ago at 11% compounded quarterly is now $2297.78. How much of this amount is principal and how much is interest?

7. What amount today is equivalent to $3500 $3\frac{1}{2}$ years from now, if money can earn 9% compounded quarterly?

8. What amount 15 months ago is equivalent to $2600 $1\frac{1}{2}$ years from now, if money earns 9% compounded monthly during the intervening time?

9. If you owe $4000 at the end of five years, what amount should your creditor accept in payment immediately, if she could earn 6% compounded semiannually on her money? (Source: ICB course on Wealth Valuation.)

10. Gordon can receive a $77 discount if he pays his property taxes early. Alternatively, he can pay the full amount of $2250 when payment is due in nine months. Which alternative is to his advantage if he can earn 6% compounded monthly on short-term investments? In current dollars, how much is the advantage?

11. Gwen is considering two offers on a residential building lot that she wishes to sell. Mr. Araki's offer is $58,000 payable immediately. Ms. Jorgensen's offer is for $10,000 down and $51,000 payable in one year. Which offer has the greater economic value if Gwen can earn 6.5% compounded semiannually on funds during the next year? In current dollars, how much more is this offer worth?

12. A lottery winner is offered the choice between $20,000 paid now, or $12,000 now and another $12,000 in five years. Which option should the winner choose, if money can now earn 10% compounded semiannually over a five-year term? How much more is the preferred choice worth in current dollars?

13. You have been offered \$100 one year from now, \$600 two years from now, and \$400 three years from now. The price you are asked to pay in today's dollars for these cash flows is \$964. If the rate of interest you are using to evaluate this deal is 10% compounded annually, should you take it? (Source: ICB course on Wealth Valuation.)

In Problems 14 through 21, calculate the combined equivalent value of the scheduled payments on the indicated dates. The rate of return that money can earn is given in the fourth column. Assume that payments due in the past have not yet been made.

Problem	Scheduled payments	Date of equivalent value	Money can earn (%)	Compounding frequency
14.	\$7000 due in 8 years	$1\frac{1}{2}$ years from now	9.9	Semiannually
15.	\$1300 due in $3\frac{1}{2}$ years	9 months from now	10.5	Quarterly
16.	\$1400 due 3 years ago, \$1800 due in 2 years	Today	12	Quarterly
17.	\$900 due 15 months ago, \$500 due in 7 months	3 months from now	10	Monthly
18.	\$1000 due in $3\frac{1}{2}$ years, \$2000 due in $5\frac{1}{2}$ years	1 year from now	7.75	Semiannually
19.	\$1500 due 9 months ago, \$2500 due in $4\frac{1}{2}$ years	$2\frac{1}{4}$ years from now	9	Quarterly
20.	\$2100 due $1\frac{1}{2}$ years ago, \$1300 due today, \$800 due in 2 years	6 months from now	10.5	Monthly
21.	\$750 today, \$1000 due in 2 years, \$1250 due in 4 years	18 months from now	9.5	Semiannually

22. What single payment six months from now would be equivalent to payments of \$500 due (but not paid) four months ago, and \$800 due in 12 months? Assume money can earn 7.5% compounded monthly.

23. What single payment one year from now would be equivalent to \$2500 due in three months, and another \$2500 due in two years? Money is worth 7% compounded quarterly.

24. To motivate individuals to start saving at an early age, financial planners will sometimes present the results of the following type of calculation. How much must a 25-year-old individual invest five years from now to have the same maturity value at age 55 as an immediate investment of \$1000? Assume that both investments earn 8% compounded annually.

•25. Michelle has just received an inheritance from her grandfather's estate. She will be entering college in $3\frac{1}{2}$ years, and wants to immediately purchase three compound-interest investment certificates having the following maturity values and dates: \$4000 at the beginning of her first academic year, \$5000 at the start of her second year, and \$6000 at the beginning of her third year. She can obtain interest rates of 7.75% compounded semiannually for any terms between three and five years, and 8% compounded quarterly for terms between five and seven years. What principal amount should she invest in each certificate?

26. Daniel makes annual payments of $2000 to the former owner of a residential lot that he purchased a few years ago. At the time of the fourth from last payment, Daniel asks for a payout figure that would immediately settle the debt. What amount should the payee be willing to accept instead of the last three payments, if money can earn 8.5% compounded semiannually?

•27. Commercial Finance Co. buys conditional sale contracts from furniture retailers at discounts that provide a 16.5% compounded monthly rate of return on the purchase price. What total price should Commercial Finance pay for the following three contracts: $950 due in four months, $780 due in six months, and $1270 due in five months?

•28. Teresita has three financial obligations to the same person: $2700 due in one year, $1900 due in $1\frac{1}{2}$ years, and $1100 due in three years. She wishes to settle the obligations with a single payment in $2\frac{1}{4}$ years, when her inheritance will be released from her mother's estate. What amount should the creditor accept if money can earn 10.5% compounded quarterly?

•29. A $15,000 loan at 11.5% compounded semiannually is advanced today. Two payments of $4000 are to be made one and three years from now. The balance is to be paid in five years. What will the third payment be?

•30. A $4000 loan at 10% compounded monthly is to be repaid by three equal payments due five, 10, and 15 months from the date of the loan. What is the size of the payments?

•31. A $10,000 loan at 8% compounded semiannually is to be repaid by three equal payments due $2\frac{1}{2}$, four, and seven years after the date of the loan. What is the size of each payment?

•32. A $6000 loan at 9% compounded quarterly is to be settled by two payments. The first payment is due after nine months and the second payment, half the amount of the first payment, is due after $1\frac{1}{2}$ years. Determine the size of each payment.

•33. A $7500 loan at 9% compounded monthly requires three payments at five-month intervals after the date of the loan. The second payment is to be twice the size of the first payment, and the third payment is to be double the amount of the second payment. Calculate the size of the second payment.

•34. Three equal payments were made two, four, and six years after the date on which a $9000 loan was granted at 10% compounded quarterly. If the balance immediately after the third payment was $5169.81, what was the amount of each payment?

••35. Repeat Problem 27 with the change that each contract accrues interest from today at the rate of 12% compounded monthly.

••36. Repeat Problem 28 with the change that each obligation accrues interest at the rate of 12% compounded monthly from a date nine months ago when the obligations were incurred.

••**37.** If the total interest earned on an investment at 8.2% compounded semiannually for $8\frac{1}{2}$ years was $1175.98, what was the original investment?

••**38.** Peggy has never made any payments on a five-year-old loan from her mother at 6% compounded annually. The total interest owed is now $845.56. How much did she borrow from her mother?

8.4 Using Financial Calculators

The formulas for many compound interest calculations are permanently programmed into financial calculators. These calculators allow you to enter the numerical values for the variables into memory. Then you select the appropriate financial function to automatically perform the calculation.

Ideally, you should be able to solve compound-interest problems using both the algebraic method and the financial functions on a calculator. The algebraic approach strengthens your mathematical skills and provides more flexibility for handling non-standard cases. It helps prepare you to create spreadsheets for specific applications. Financial calculators make routine calculations more efficient and reduce the likelihood of making arithmetic errors. Most of the example problems from this point onward will present both algebraic and financial calculator solutions.

Key Definitions and Calculator Operation

Any financial calculator may be used in conjunction with this text. The key labels and the operating procedures can differ from one model to another. Example problems in the text will employ the labels and procedures used by Sharp financial calculators . There are two reasons for this choice:

- The key labels on Sharp calculators directly correspond to our algebraic variables.
- We can set other financial calculators to simulate the Sharp operation, but not vice versa.

Appendices to Chapters 8 and 13 present some instructions for operating five types of calculators in their financial mode. One part of the Chapter 8 appendix is devoted to the Texas Instruments BA II PLUS calculator.

We will use five basic financial keys. Each will be represented by a box containing the key's label. At this point, you can probably correctly guess the meaning of the labels on four of the five keys. Each corresponds to a variable in formula (8-2), $S = P(1 + i)^n$.

[n] represents the number of compounding periods

[i] represents the periodic interest rate

[PV] represents the principal or present value

(PMT) represents the periodic annuity payment (not used until Chapter 10)

(FV) represents the maturity value or future value

Each of the five keys has two uses:

1. Saving a numerical value of the variable in memory.
2. Computing the value of the variable (using the values saved in memory for all other variables).

As an illustration, let us compute the future value of $1000 invested at 8% compounded semiannually for three years. We must first enter values for (n), (i), (PV), and (PMT). They may be entered in any order. (If the instructions given below do not seem to work, your calculator may need to be set to its *financial mode*. Refer to "Setting the Calculator in the Financial Mode" in the Appendix.) To save $1000 in the (PV) memory, just enter the digits for 1000 and press (PV). Even though 1000 remains in the display, it will also be stored in the memory. Next, enter values for the other variables in the same manner. The *periodic interest rate must be entered in percent form* rather than in its decimal equivalent form. For all compound interest problems in Chapters 8 and 9, the value "0" must be stored in the (PMT) memory. This tells the calculator that there is no regular annuity payment. In summary, the keystrokes for entering all of the data are:

1000 (PV) 6 (n) 4 (i) 0 (PMT)

We are now ready to compute the future value of the $1000 investment. Most calculators have a "compute" key labelled (COMP) or (CPT). To obtain the future value, press

(COMP) (FV)

The future value (−1265.32) appears in the display[4]. The significance of the negative sign will be discussed in the next subsection.

TIP *EFFICIENT USE OF YOUR CALCULATOR*

You can operate your calculator more efficiently if you take advantage of the following features.

1. After any computation, the values previously saved in the memories still remain. Therefore, you do not need to re-enter a variable's value if it is unchanged in a subsequent calculation. (However, any time you accidentally press one of the five financial keys, the number in the display at the time will be saved as the value for that variable.)
2. At any time you can check the value stored in any memory by pressing (RCL) followed by the key for the particular memory.
3. When turned off, most calculators will retain their settings and the values in memory. (When the calculator's battery becomes weak, this feature and other calculator operations are unreliable.)

---

[4] The Texas Instruments BA 35 does not display a negative sign at this point.

Cash-Flow Sign Convention

Cash flow is a term frequently used in finance and accounting to refer to a cash payment. A cash inflow is a cash receipt; a cash outflow is a cash disbursement. A cash *inflow* should be saved in a financial calculator's memory as a *positive* value. A cash *outflow* should be entered as a *negative* number. These two simple rules have a rather overblown name in finance—the **cash-flow sign convention.**

CASH-FLOW SIGN CONVENTION
Cash inflows (receipts) are positive.
Cash outflows (disbursements) are negative.

All financial calculators use the cash-flow convention[5]. Finance courses and finance textbooks use it. The financial functions in Microsoft's Excel and Corel's Quattro Pro spreadsheet software employ it. The benefits from using the sign convention come in later chapters. However, we will introduce it now to become familiar with it before moving on to more complex cases.

To implement the cash-flow sign convention, you must treat a compound interest problem as either an investment or a loan. The directions of the cash flows for these two cases are compared in the following table. When you invest money, you pay it (cash outflow) to some institution or individual. Subsequently, you receive cash inflows from investment income and from the sale or redemption of the investment. In contrast, when you receive a loan, it is a cash inflow for you. The subsequent cash flows in the loan transaction are the loan payments (cash outflows).

Transaction	Initial cash flow	Subsequent cash flows
Investment	Outflow (negative)	Inflows (positive)
Loan	Inflow (positive)	Outflows (negative)

Now you can understand why your calculator gave a negative future value earlier in this section. Because we entered 1000 as a positive number in the PV memory, the calculator interpreted the $1000 as a loan. The computed future value represents the single payment required to pay off the loan. Since it is a cash outflow, the calculator displayed it as a negative number. To properly employ the sign convention for the initial $1000 investment, we should have entered 1000 in PV as a negative number. The calculator would then compute a positive future value—the cash inflow we will receive when the investment matures.

To illustrate the use of financial calculators, Example problems 8.3A, 8.3C, and 8.3E will now be repeated as Examples 8.4A, 8.4B, and 8.4C, respectively.

[5] The Texas Instruments BA 35 calculator employs a modified version of this sign convention. Users of the BA 35 are referred to the Appendix of this chapter for details.

Example 8.4A *The Investment Needed to Reach a Target Future Value*

What amount must you invest now at 8% compounded monthly to accumulate \$10,000 after $3\frac{1}{2}$ years?

Solution

Given: $j = 8\%$, $m = 12$, $S = \$10{,}000$, Term = 3.5 years

Then $i = \frac{8\%}{12} = 0.\overline{6}\%$ and $n = m \times \text{Term} = 12(3.5) = 42$

Enter the known variables and then compute the present value.

42 (n) 0.666666667 (i) 10000 (FV) 0 (PMT) (COMP) (PV) [−7564.86]

The initial investment required is \$7564.86.

TIP *Efficient Use of Your Calculator*

For fewer keystrokes and maximum accuracy in your answer, press (i) immediately after calculating i and (n) immediately after calculating n. That is, the keystrokes

8 (÷) 12 (=) (i) and 12 (×) 3.5 (=) (n)

are sufficient to calculate and save values for both i and n in the preceding example. Furthermore, the value for i is saved with more than the nine decimal places you see in the display (or are able to enter manually). In subsequent Example problems, this procedure will be assumed but not be shown.

Example 8.4B *Calculating the Equivalent Value of Two Payments*

Two payments of \$10,000 each must be made one year and four years from now. If money can earn 9% compounded monthly, what single payment two years from now would be equivalent to the two scheduled payments?

Solution

The data and solution strategy are shown on the time line below. S_1 represents the future value of the first scheduled payment and P_2 represents the present value of the second payment.

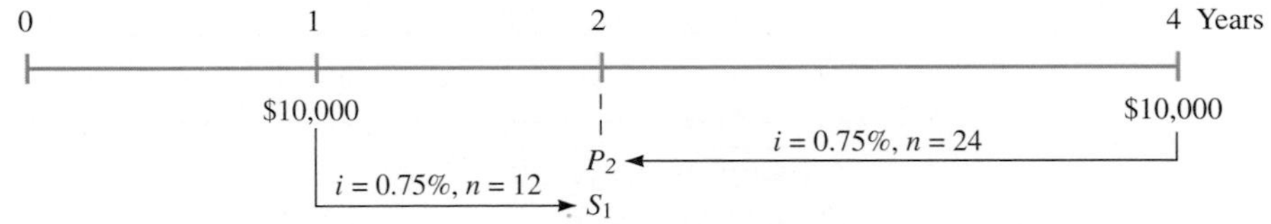

The single equivalent payment is $S_1 + P_2$. Before we start crunching numbers, let's exercise your intuition. Do you think the equivalent payment will be greater or smaller than \$20,000? It is clear that S_1 is greater than \$10,000 and that P_2 is less than \$10,000. When the two amounts are added, will the sum be more or less than

\$20,000? We can answer this question by comparing the time intervals through which we "shift" each of the \$10,000 payments. The first payment will have one year's interest added, but the second payment will be discounted for two years' interest.[6] Therefore, P_2 is farther below \$10,000 than S_1 is above \$10,000. Therefore, the equivalent payment will be less than \$20,000. In the event your equivalent payment turns out to be more than \$20,000, you would know that your solution has an error. Returning to the calculations,

S_1: 10000 (PV) 0.75 (i) 12 (n) 0 (PMT) (COMP) (FV) | −10,938.07 |

P_2: 10000 (FV) 24 (n) (COMP) (PV) | −8358.31 |

The equivalent payment two years from now is \$10,938.07 + \$8358.31 = \$19,296.38.

Note: An equivalent payment problem is neither a loan nor an investment situation. Loans and investments always involve at least one cash flow in each direction.[7] An equivalent payment is a payment that can *substitute for* one or more other payments. The substitute payment will flow in the *same* direction as the payment(s) it replaces. So how should you apply the cash-flow sign convention to equivalent payment calculations? Just enter the scheduled payments as positive numbers and ignore the opposite sign on the calculated equivalent value.

Example 8.4C Calculating Two Unknown Loan Payments

Kramer borrowed \$4000 from George at an interest rate of 7% compounded semiannually. The loan is to be repaid by three payments. The first payment, \$1000, is due two years after the date of the loan. The second and third payments are due three and five years, respectively, after the initial loan. Calculate the amounts of the second and third payments if the second payment is to be twice the size of the third payment.

Solution

Let x represent the third payment. Then the second payment must be $2x$. As indicated in the following diagram, P_1, P_2, and P_3 represent the present values of the first, second, and third payments.

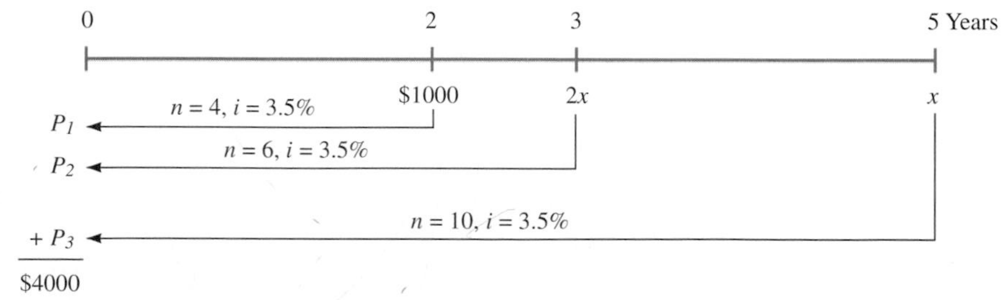

[6] You cannot conclude that the difference between \$10,000 and P_2 will be twice the difference between S_1 and \$10,000. The simplest illustration of this sort of effect is that, at 10% compounded annually, the future value of \$100 one year later is \$110 (an increase of \$10). On the other hand, the present value one year earlier is \$90.91 (a reduction of \$9.09).

[7] At least, this is what lenders and investors hope.

Since the sum of the present values of all payments equals the original loan, then

$$P_1 + P_2 + P_3 = \$4000 \quad ①$$

P_1: 1000 (FV) 4 (n) 3.5 (i) 0 (PMT) (COMP) (PV) [−871.41]

At first, we are stumped as to how to proceed for P_2 and P_3. Let's think about the third payment of x dollars. Your intuition tells you that it will be several hundred dollars. Compute the present value of just one of those dollars.

1 (FV) 10 (n) (COMP) (PV) [−0.7089188]

The present value of \$1 paid five years from now is \$0.7089188 (almost \$0.71). Consider the following questions (Q) and their answers (A).

Q: What is the present value of \$2?	A: It is about $2 \times \$0.71 = \$1.42$.
Q: What is the present value of \$5?	A: It is about $5 \times \$0.71 = \$3.55$.
Q: What is the present value of \$$x$?	A: Extending the preceding pattern, the present value of \$$x$ is about $x \times \$0.71 = \$0.71x$. Precisely, it is $P_3 = \$0.7089188x$.

Similarly, calculate the present value of one of the dollars in the second payment \$$2x$. The only variable that changes from the previous calculation is (n).

6 (n) (COMP) (PV) [−0.8135006]

Hence, the present value of \$$2x$ is $P_2 = 2x(\$0.8135006) = \$1.6270013x$
Now substitute the values for P_1, P_2, and P_3 into equation ① and solve for x.

$$\$871.44 + 1.6270013x + 0.7089188x = \$4000$$
$$2.3359201x = \$3128.56$$
$$x = \$1339.33$$

Kramer's second payment will be 2(\$1339.33) = \$2678.66, and the third payment will be \$1339.33.

Exercise 8.4 *Solve problems in Exercises 8.2 and 8.3 using the financial functions on a calculator.*

8.5 Other Applications of Compounding

Change of Notation

Recall that each variable in $S = P(1+i)^n$ has a corresponding financial calculator key.

$S \Leftrightarrow$ (FV) $\quad P \Leftrightarrow$ (PV) $\quad i \Leftrightarrow$ (i) $\quad n \Leftrightarrow$ (n)

Spreadsheet software such as Excel, Quattro Pro, and 1-2-3 have "built-in" financial functions similar to those on financial calculators. The spreadsheet financial functions use

FV instead of *S* as the symbol for future value, and
PV instead of *P* as the symbol for present value and principal.

Furthermore, FV and PV are much more commonly used in finance texts to represent future value and present value than S and P. No doubt this is because FV and PV clearly suggest the quantities they represent, and because FV and PV match both the key labels on calculators and the variables used in spreadsheet financial functions. For these reasons, we will switch to using FV and PV instead of S and P in algebraic formulations.[8] Hereafter, formula (8-2) will be written as

FUTURE VALUE OR MATURITY VALUE (COMPOUND INTEREST)

(8-2) $$FV = PV(1 + i)^n$$

Rearranged to calculate present value, formula (8-2) becomes $PV = FV(1 + i)^{-n}$.

Compound-Interest Investments

The two most common types of compound interest investments owned by Canadians are Guaranteed Investment Certificates and Canada Savings Bonds.[9]

Guaranteed Investment Certificates (GICs) GICs may be purchased from banks, credit unions, trust companies, and caisses populaires (mostly in Quebec). When you buy a GIC from a financial institution, you are in effect lending money to it or to one of its subsidiaries. The financial institution uses the funds raised from selling GICs to make loans—most commonly, mortgage loans. The interest rate charged on mortgage loans is typically 1.5% to 2% higher than the interest rate paid to GIC investors. The word "Guaranteed" in the name of this investment refers to the *unconditional guarantee* of principal and interest by the parent financial institution. In addition to this guarantee, there is invariably some form of government-regulated deposit insurance.

Most Guaranteed Investment Certificates are purchased with maturities in the range of one to five years. Longer maturities (up to 10 years) are available, but are not covered by deposit insurance. Most GICs are not redeemable before maturity. The following diagrams present alternative arrangements for structuring interest rates and for paying interest on conventional GICs.

Structure of interest rates

- **Fixed rate:** The interest rate does not change over the term of the GIC.
- **Step-up rate:** The interest rate is increased every six months or every year according to a *predetermined* schedule.
- **Variable Rate:** The interest rate is adjusted every year or every six months to reflect prevailing market rates. There may be a minimum "floor" below which rates cannot drop.

CAUGHT IN THE WEB

Information about the GICs offered by a financial institution is usually available on its Web site. At any one time, a chartered bank may have 10 or 12 varieties of GICs in its repertoire. In recent years, "financial engineers" have created more exotic forms of GICs. The rate of return on some is linked to the performance of a stock market. Here are the Home Page URLs of our largest financial institutions:

Royal Bank (www.royalbank.com)
Bank of Montreal (www.bmo.com)
CIBC (www.cibc.com)
Canada Trust (www.canadatrust.com)
Scotiabank (www.scotiabank.ca)
TD Bank (www.tdbank.ca)

---

8 The choice of this point in the text for the notation change was based on the following considerations. The FV and PV notation was not used for simple interest cases because students might later infer that the FV and PV functions of a calculator or spreadsheet can be used in a simple interest context. We continued to use S and P in Sections 8.1, 8.2, and 8.3 to draw certain parallels between compound interest and simple interest, and to await the introduction of calculator financial functions in Section 8.4.

9 In recent years provincial savings bonds have been issued by the governments of Alberta, British Columbia, Manitoba, Ontario, and Saskatchewan. Purchase of provincial bonds is usually restricted to residents of the issuing province.

Payment of interest

Regular interest version:	Compound interest version:
Interest is paid to the investor every year or every six months.	Interest is periodically converted to principal and paid at maturity.

The regular interest versions of GICs are not mathematically interesting since periodic interest is paid out to the investor instead of being converted to principal. For compound interest versions, there are two mathematically distinct cases.

1. If the interest rate is *fixed,* use $FV = PV(1 + i)^n$ to calculate the maturity value.
2. If the interest rate is either a *variable rate* or a *step-up rate,* you must multiply the individual $(1+i)$ factors for all compounding periods. That is, use

FUTURE VALUE (VARIABLE AND STEP-UP INTEREST RATES)

(8-4) $$FV = PV(1 + i_1)(1 + i_2)(1 + i_3)\cdots(1 + i_n)$$

Example 8.5A Calculating the Payment from a Periodic-Payment GIC

What regular payment will an investor receive from a \$9000, four-year, monthly payment GIC earning a nominal rate of 8.25% compounded monthly?

Solution

The interest rate per payment interval is

$$i = \frac{j}{m} = \frac{8.25\%}{12} = 0.6875\%$$

The monthly payment will be

$$PV \times i = \$9000 \times 0.006875 = \$61.88$$

Example 8.5B Comparing GICs Having Different Nominal Rates

Suppose a bank quotes nominal annual interest rates of 8.6%, 8.5%, and 8.4% on five-year GICs with annual, semiannual, and monthly compounding, respectively. Which rate should an investor choose?

Solution

An investor should choose the rate that results in the highest maturity value.

j	m	i	n
8.6%	1	8.6%	5
8.5	2	4.25	10
8.4	12	0.7	60

Choose an amount to invest, say \$1000, and calculate the maturity values for the three alternatives.

Algebraic Solution

$$\begin{aligned} FV &= PV(1+i)^n \\ &= \$1000(1.086)^5 = \$1510.60 \quad \text{for } m = 1 \\ &= \$1000(1.0425)^{10} = \$1516.21 \quad \text{for } m = 2 \\ &= \$1000(1.007)^{60} = \$1519.74 \quad \text{for } m = 12 \end{aligned}$$

The investor should choose 8.4% compounded monthly. The high compounding frequency more than compensates for the low nominal rate in this instance.

Financial Calculator Solution

For annual compounding,

1000 (+/−) (PV) 5 (n) 8.6 (i) 0 (PMT) (COMP) (FV) [1510.60]

For semiannual compounding,

10 (n) 4.25 (i) (COMP) (FV) [1516.21]

For monthly compounding,

60 (n) 0.7 (i) (COMP) (FV) [1519.74]

The investor should choose 8.4% compounded monthly. The high compounding frequency more than compensates for the low nominal rate in this instance.

Example 8.5C *Maturity Value Of a Variable-Rate GIC*

A chartered bank offers a five-year "Escalator Guaranteed Investment Certificate." In successive years it pays annual interest rates of 4%, 4.5%, 5%, 5.5%, and 6%, respectively, *compounded* at the end of each year. The bank also offers regular five-year GICs paying a fixed rate of 5% compounded annually. Calculate and compare the maturity values of \$1000 invested in each type of GIC. (Note that 5% is the average of the five successive one-year rates paid on the Escalator GIC.)

Solution

Using formula (8-4), the maturity value of the Escalator GIC is

$$FV = \$1000(1.04)(1.045)(1.05)(1.055)(1.06) = \$1276.14$$

Using formula (8-2), the maturity value of the regular GIC is

$$FV = \$1000(1.05)^5 = \$1276.28$$

The Escalator GIC will mature at \$1276.14, but the regular GIC will mature at \$1276.28 (\$0.14 more). We can also conclude from this example that a series of compound interest rates does not produce the same future value as the *average* rate compounded over the same period.

CAUGHT IN THE WEB

Canada Investment and Savings is an agency of the federal Department of Finance. It maintains a Web site (www.cis-pec.gc.ca) providing information on Canada Savings Bonds, Canada Premium Bonds, and answers to frequently asked questions. Interest rates on all unmatured issues are available on the site. Calculators are provided that allow you to determine the amount you will receive if you redeem a particular CSB on a specific date.

***Canada Savings Bonds (CSBs)** Although you may purchase CSBs from the same financial institutions that issue GICs, your money goes to the federal government to help finance its debt.[10] The financial institution is merely an agent in the transaction.

Canada Savings Bonds sold in recent years have terms of 10 or 12 years. The batch of bonds sold on a particular date is assigned a series number. For example, the CSBs issued on November 1, 1998 are referred to as Series 54 (S54). All CSBs have variable interest rates—the interest rate is changed on each anniversary to keep it in line with prevailing rates. When the Finance Department announces the new rate for the next year, it usually also announces guaranteed *minimum* rates for the subsequent two years. The annually compounded rates (effective November 1 each year) for recent issues are presented in Table 8.2.

Canada Savings Bonds are issued in regular interest versions (that pay out the interest on each anniversary date) and compound interest versions (that convert interest to principal on each anniversary). They may be redeemed at any time.[11] The following rules apply to calculating the interest for the *partial* year since the most recent anniversary date.

- Interest is accrued to the first day of the month in which redemption occurs. (If you redeem a CSB part way through a month, you receive no interest for the partial month.)

Table 8.2 *Interest Rates (%) on Canada Savings Bonds*

Interest rate effective Nov. 1 of:	S44 (issued Nov. 1, 1989)	S45 (issued Nov. 1, 1990)	S46 (issued Nov. 1, 1991)	S47 (issued Nov. 1, 1992)	S48 (issued Nov. 1, 1993)	S49 (issued Nov. 1, 1994)	S50 (issued Nov. 1, 1995)	S51 (issued Nov. 1, 1996)	S52 (issued Nov. 1, 1997)	S54 (issued Nov. 1, 1998)
1989	10.91									
1990	10.75	10.75								
1991	7.50	7.50	7.50							
1992	6.00	6.00	6.00	6.00						
1993	5.125	5.125	5.125	5.125	5.125					
1994	6.375	6.375	6.375	6.375	6.375	6.375				
1995	6.75	6.75	6.75	6.75	6.75	6.75	5.25			
1996	7.50	7.50	7.50	7.50	7.50	7.50	6.00	3.00		
1997	3.56	3.56	3.56	3.56	3.56	3.56	6.75	4.00	3.42	
1998	4.25	4.25	4.25	4.25	4.25	4.25	4.00	5.00	4.00	4.00
*1999	5.25	5.25	5.25	5.25	5.25	5.25		6.00	5.00	
*2000	5.50	5.50	5.50	5.50	5.50	5.50		6.50	5.25	
Matures Nov. 1 of:	2001	2002	2003	2004	2005	2006	2007	2008	2007	2008

*These are guaranteed minimum rates. They can be raised if prevailing rates warrant.

[10] In early 1999, the total outstanding amount of CSBs was over $28 billion. This represented 6.25% of all Government of Canada market-financed debt.

[11] In 1997, the Government of Canada started to issue a new type of savings bond called Canada Premium Bonds. They may be redeemed but only on an anniversary date. Because of this restriction on redemption, Canada Premium Bonds pay a higher interest rate than Canada Savings Bonds.

- Interest is calculated on a simple interest basis. That is, the additional interest for the partial year is $I = Prt$ where

P = The principal (including converted interest on compound interest bonds) at the preceding anniversary date
r = The prescribed annual interest rate for the current year
t = The number of months (from the preceding anniversary date up to the first day of the month in which redemption occurs) divided by 12

Example 8.5D *Calculating the Redemption Value of a Compound Interest Canada Savings Bond*

A $1000 face value Series S48 compound interest Canada Savings Bond (CSB) was presented to a credit union branch for redemption. What amount did the owner receive if the redemption was requested on:

a. November 1, 1998? **b.** January 17, 1999?

Solution

a. In Table 8.2, we note that Series S48 CSBs were issued on November 1, 1993. November 1, 1998 falls on the fifth anniversary of the issue date. Substituting the annual interest rates for S48 bonds from Table 8.2 into formula (8-4), we have

$$\begin{aligned} FV &= PV(1 + i_1)(1 + i_2)(1 + i_3)(1 + i_4(1 + i_5) \\ &= \$1000(1.05125)(1.06375)(1.0675)(1.075)(1.0356) \\ &= \$1328.97 \end{aligned}$$

The owner received $1328.97 on November 1, 1998.

b. For a redemption that took place on January 17, 1999, the bond's owner would have been paid extra interest at the rate of 4.25% pa for November 1998 and December 1998. The amount of the extra interest was

$$I = Prt = \$1328.97(0.0425)\frac{2}{12} = \$9.41$$

Therefore, the total amount the owner received on January 17, 1999 was

$$\$1328.97 + \$9.41 = \$1338.38$$

Valuation of Investments

With many types of investments, the owner can sell the investment to another investor. Such investments are said to be transferable.[12] The key question is: What is the appropriate price at which the investment should be sold/purchased? We encountered the same question in Chapter 7 for investments earning simple interest.

[12] Guaranteed Investment Certificates are generally not transferable. Canada Savings Bonds are not transferable but, unlike GICs, they may be redeemed at any time.

There we discussed the thinking behind the Valuation Principle (repeated below for ease of reference).

> ***Valuation Principle***
> The fair market value of an investment is the sum of the present values of the expected cash flows. The discount rate used should be the prevailing market-determined rate of return required on this type of investment.

For an investment with cash inflows extending beyond one year, the market-determined rate of return is almost always a compound rate of return. In this section, we will apply the Valuation Principle to two types of investments.

Strip Bonds Many investors hold strip bonds in their Registered Retirement Savings Plans (RRSPs). We will often refer to RRSPs in Examples and Exercises. Therefore, let us digress for a moment to discuss the bare essentials of Registered Retirement Savings Plans. An RRSP is not a type of investment. Instead, think of an RRSP as a type of account to which you can contribute money and then purchase certain investments. The Income Tax Act sets out strict rules covering the amount of money you may contribute and the type of investments you may hold within an RRSP. There are two main advantages of using an RRSP to accumulate savings for retirement.

- A contribution to an RRSP is deductible from the contributor's taxable income. The individual's income tax is thereby reduced.
- Earnings on investments held within an RRSP are not subject to income tax until they are withdrawn from the RRSP.

The essential feature of a **strip bond** is that its owner will receive a *single* payment (called the face value of the bond) on the bond's maturity date. The maturity date could be as much as 30 years in the future. No interest will be received in the interim. Suppose, for example, a \$1000 face value strip bond matures 18 years from now. The owner of this bond will receive a payment of \$1000 in 18 years. What is the appropriate price to pay for the bond today? Clearly, it will be substantially less than \$1000. The difference between the \$1000 you will receive at maturity and the price you pay today represents the earnings on your initial investment (the purchase price). The situation is similar to the pricing of T-bills in Chapter 7.

According to the Valuation Principle, the fair market price is the present value of the bond's face value. The discount rate you should use for i in $PV = FV(1 + i)^{-n}$ is the prevailing rate of return in the financial market for bonds of similar risk and maturity. The nominal rates quoted for strip bonds are understood to be *semiannually* compounded.

Example 8.5E *Calculating the Price of a Strip Bond*

A \$10,000 face value strip bond has $15\frac{1}{2}$ years remaining until maturity. If the prevailing market rate of return is 8.75% compounded semiannually, what is the fair market value of the strip bond?

Solution

Given: $FV = \$10{,}000$ $j = 8.75\%$ $m = 2$ Term $= 15\frac{1}{2}$ years

Therefore

$$i = \frac{j}{m} = \frac{8.75\%}{2} = 4.375\% \quad \text{and} \quad n = 2(15.5) = 31$$

Fair market value = Present value of the face value

Algebraic Solution

$$PV = FV(1 + i)^{-n} = \$10{,}000(1.04375)^{-31} = \$2651.61$$

Financial Calculator Solution

10000 (FV) 31 (n) 4.375 (i) 0 (PMT) (COMP) (PV) | −2651.61 |

The price of the bond will be \$2651.61.

***Long-Term Promissory Notes** A promissory note is a simple contract between a debtor and creditor setting out the amount of the debt (face value), the interest rate thereon, and the terms of repayment. A long-term promissory note is a note whose term is longer than one year. Such notes usually accrue compound interest on the face value.

The payee (creditor) on a promissory note may sell the note to an investor before maturity. The debtor is then obligated to make the remaining payments to the new owner of the note. To determine the note's selling/purchase price, we need to apply the Valuation Principle to the note's maturity value. The two steps are:

1. Determine the note's maturity value based on the contractual rate of interest on the note.
2. Discount (that is, calculate the present value of) the Step 1 result back to the date of sale/purchase. Since there is no "market" for private promissory notes, the seller and purchaser must negotiate the discount rate.

Example 8.5F Calculating the Proceeds of a Long-Term Promissory Note

A five-year promissory note with a face value of \$3500, bearing interest at 11% compounded semiannually, was sold 21 months after its issue date to yield the buyer 10% compounded quarterly. What amount was paid for the note?

Solution

We should find the maturity value of the note and then discount the maturity value (at the required yield) to the date of the sale.

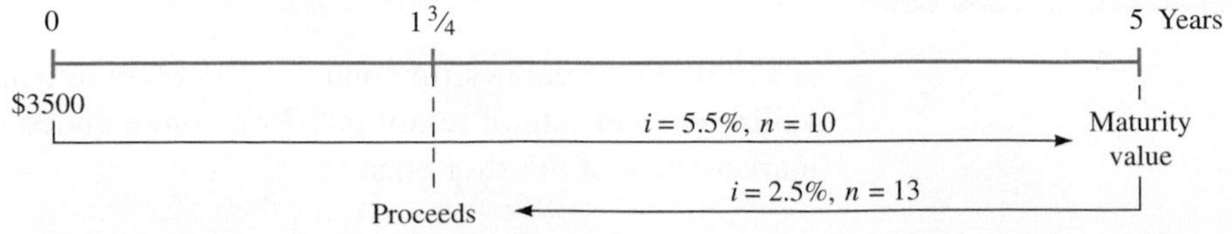

Algebraic Solution

Step 1: Maturity value $= \$3500(1.055)^{10} = \$5978.51$

Step 2: Price paid $= \$5978.51(1.025)^{-13} = \$4336.93$

Financial Calculator Solution

Step 1: Calculate the maturity value.

3500 (+/-) (PV) 10 (n) 5.5 (i) 0 (PMT) (COMP) (FV) [5978.51]

Step 2: Discount the maturity value (still in (FV)) at 10% compounded quarterly.

13 (n) 2.5 (i) (COMP) (PV) [−4336.93]

The amount paid for the note was \$4336.93.

Compound Growth

The topic of compounding percent changes was introduced in Chapter 2. We revisit the topic here to point out that $FV = PV(1 + i)^n$ may be used in problems involving compound growth at a fixed periodic rate. Furthermore, you can use the financial functions of your calculator in such cases. Simply place the following interpretations on the variables.

Variable	General interpretation
PV	Beginning value, size, or quantity
FV	Ending value, size, or quantity
i	Fixed periodic rate of growth
n	Number of periods with growth rate i

If a quantity shrinks or contracts at a fixed periodic rate, it can be handled mathematically by treating it as *negative growth.* For example, suppose a firm's annual sales volume is projected to decline for the next four years by 5% per year from last year's level of 100,000 units. The expected sales volume in the fourth year may be obtained using $FV = PV(1 + i)^n$ with $n = 4$ and $i = (-5\%) = (-0.05)$. That is,

$$\begin{aligned}\text{Sales (in Year 4)} &= 100{,}000[1 + (-0.05)]^4 \\ &= 100{,}000(0.95)^4 \\ &= 81{,}450 \text{ units}\end{aligned}$$

In the financial calculator approach, you would save "−5" in the (i) memory. The answer represents an overall decline of 18.55% in the annual volume of sales. Note that the overall decline is less than 20%, an answer you might be tempted to reach by simply adding the percentage changes.

Inflation and Purchasing Power A useful application of compound growth in financial planning is using forecast rates of inflation to estimate future prices and the purchasing power of money. As discussed in Chapter 3, the rate of inflation measures the annual percent change in the price level of goods and services. By compounding the forecast rate of inflation over a number of years, we can estimate the level of prices at the end of the period.

When prices rise, money loses its purchasing power—these are "two sides of the same (depreciating) coin." If price levels double, a given nominal amount of money will purchase only half as much. We then say that the money has half its former purchasing power. Similarly, if price levels triple, money retains only one-third of its former purchasing power. These examples demonstrate that price levels and purchasing power have an inverse relationship. That is,

$$\frac{\text{Ending purchasing power}}{\text{Beginning purchasing power}} = \frac{\text{Beginning price level}}{\text{Ending price level}}$$

Let us push the reasoning one step further to answer this question: If price levels rise 50% over a number of years, what will be the percent *loss* in purchasing power? This gets a little tricky—the answer is *not* 50%. With an overall price increase of 50%, the ratio of price levels (on the right side of the preceding proportion) is

$$\frac{100}{150} \quad \text{or} \quad \frac{2}{3}$$

Therefore, money will *retain* $\frac{2}{3}$ of its purchasing power and *lose* the other $\frac{1}{3}$ or $33\frac{1}{3}\%$ of its purchasing power.

Example 8.5G *The Long-term Effect of Inflation on Purchasing Power*

If the rate of inflation for the next 20 years is 2.5% per year, what annual income will be needed 20 years from now to have the same purchasing power as a $30,000 annual income today?

Solution

The required income will be $30,000 compounded at 2.5% per year for 20 years.

Given: $PV = \$230{,}000 \qquad i = \frac{2.5\%}{1} = 2.5\% \qquad n = 4(5) = 20$

Algebraic Solution

$$FV = PV(1 + i)^n = \$30{,}000(1.025)^{20} = \$49{,}158.49$$

Financial Calculator Solution

30000 (+/–) (PV) 2.5 (i) 20 (n) 0 (PMT) (COMP) (FV) [49,158.49]

After 20 years of 2.5% annual inflation, an annual income of $49,158 will be needed to have the same purchasing power as $30,000 today.

Example 8.5H *Compound Annual Decrease in Population*

The population of a rural region is expected to fall by 2% per year for the next 10 years. If the region's current population is 100,000, what is the expected population 10 years from now?

Solution

The 2% "negative growth" should be compounded for 10 years.

Given: $PV = 100{,}000$ $i = -2\%$ $n = 10$

Algebraic Solution

$$FV = PV(1 + i)^n = 100{,}000[1 + (-0.02)]^{10} = 100{,}000(0.98)^{10} = 81{,}707$$

Financial Calculator Solution

100000 (PV) 2 (+/–) (i) 10 (n) 0 (PMT) (COMP) (FV) | −81,707 |

The region's population is expected to drop to about 81,707 during the next 10 years.

Concept Questions

1. How, if at all, will the future value of a three-year variable-rate GIC differ if it earns 4%, 5%, and 6% in successive years instead of 6%, 5%, and 4% in successive years?
2. In general, do you think the interest rate on a new three-year fixed-rate GIC will be more or less than the rate on a new five-year fixed-rate GIC? Why?
3. Why must the Finance Department keep the interest rates on existing CSBs at least as high as the rate on a new CSB issue?
4. Should we conclude that the owner of a strip bond earns nothing until the full face value is received at maturity? Explain.
5. If a quantity declines by $x\%$ per year (compounded) for two years, will the overall percent decrease be more or less than $2x\%$? Explain.

Exercise 8.5

Answers to the odd-numbered problems are at the end of the book.

Note: A few problems in this and later exercises have been taken (with permission) from professional courses offered by the **Canadian Institute of Financial Planning** and the **Institute of Canadian Bankers.** These problems are indicated by the organization's logo in the margin next to the problems.

1. Krista invested $18,000 in a three-year regular-interest GIC earning 7.5% compounded semiannually. What is each interest payment?
2. Eric invested $22,000 in a five-year regular-interest GIC earning 7.25% compounded monthly. What is each interest payment?
3. Mr. Dickson purchased a seven-year, $30,000 compound-interest GIC with funds in his RRSP. If the interest rate on the GIC is 8.25% compounded semiannually, what is the GIC's maturity value?
4. Mrs. Sandhu placed $11,500 in a four-year compound-interest GIC earning 6.75% compounded monthly. What is the GIC's maturity value?
5. A trust company offers three-year compound-interest GICs paying 7.2% compounded monthly or 7.5% compounded semiannually. Which rate should an investor choose?

6. If an investor has the choice between rates of 5.4% compounded semiannually and 5.5% compounded annually for a six-year GIC, which rate should be chosen?

•7. For a given term of compound-interest GIC, the nominal interest rate with annual compounding is typically 0.125% higher than the rate with semiannual compounding and 0.25% higher than the rate with monthly compounding. Suppose that the rates for five-year GICs are 5.00%, 4.875%, and 4.75% for annual, semiannual, and monthly compounding, respectively. How much more will an investor earn over five years on a $10,000 GIC at the most favourable rate than at the least favourable rate?

8. A new issue of compound-interest Canada Savings Bonds guaranteed minimum annual rates of 5.25%, 6%, and 6.75% in the first three years. At the same time, a new issue of compound interest British Columbia Savings Bonds guaranteed minimum annual rates of 6.75%, 6%, and 6% in the first three years. Assuming that the rates remain at the guaranteed minima, how much more will $10,000 earn in the first three years if invested in BC Savings Bonds instead of Canada Savings Bonds?

•9. Using the information given in Problem 8, calculate the interest earned in the third year from a $10,000 investment in each savings bond.

10. Stan purchased a $15,000 compound-interest Canada Savings Bond on November 1, 1996. The interest rate in the first year was 3.0% and in the second year was 4.0%. What interest did he receive when he redeemed the CSB on April 1, 1998?

11. What amount did the owner of a $5000 face value compound-interest series S49 Canada Savings Bond receive when she redeemed the bond on:

a. November 1, 1998? **b.** August 21, 1999?

12. What amount did the owner of a $10,000 face value compound-interest series S50 CSB receive when he redeemed the bond on:

a. November 1, 1998? **b.** May 19, 1999?

13. What was the redemption value of a $300 face value compound-interest series S48 CSB on March 8, 1999?

14. What was the redemption value of a $500 face value compound-interest series S47 CSB on June 12, 1998?

In each of Problems 15 through 22, calculate the maturity value of the five-year compound interest GIC whose interest rate for each year is given. Also calculate the dollar amount of interest earned in the fourth year.

Problem	Amount invested ($)	Year 1(%)	Year 2(%)	Interest rate Year 3(%)	Year 4(%)	Year 5(%)
15.	2000	7.5	7.5	7.5	7.5	7.5
16.	3000	7	7	8	8	8
17.	8000	4	4.5	5	5.5	6
18.	7500	4.125	4.25	4.5	4.875	5

19. A chartered bank advertised rates of 5.5%, 6.125%, 6.75%, 7.375%, and 8% in successive years of its five-year compound-interest RateRiser GIC. At the same time, the bank was selling fixed-rate five-year compound-interest GICs yielding 6.75% compounded annually. What total interest would be earned during the five-year term on a $5000 investment in each type of GIC?

20. A bank advertised rates of 4%, 4.5%, 5%, 5.5%, 6%, 6.5%, and 7% in successive years of its seven-year compound-interest RateRiser GIC. The bank also offered 5.5% compounded annually on its seven-year fixed-rate GIC. How much more will a $10,000 investment in the preferred alternative be worth at maturity?

21. Using the information given in Problem 20, calculate the interest earned in the fourth year from a $10,000 investment in each GIC.

22. Using the information given in Problem 20, how much would have to be initially invested in each GIC to have a maturity value of $20,000?

23. How much will you need 20 years from now to have the purchasing power of $100 today if the (compound annual) rate of inflation during the period is:

a. 2%? **b.** 3%? **c.** 4%?

24. How much money was needed 15 years ago to have the purchasing power of $1000 today if the average (compound annual) rate of inflation has been:

a. 2%? **b.** 4%? **c.** 6%?

25. If the inflation rate for the next 10 years is 3.5% per year, what hourly rate of pay in 10 years will be equivalent to $15/hour today?

26. A city's population stood at 120,000 after five years of 3% annual growth. What was the population five years previously?

27. Mr. and Mrs. Stephens would like to retire in 15 years at an annual income level that would be equivalent to $35,000 today. What is their retirement income goal if, in the meantime, the annual rate of inflation is:

a. 2%? **b.** 3%? **c.** 5%?

28. In 1992 the number of workers in the forest industry was forecast to decline by 3% per year, reaching 80,000 in 2002. How many were employed in the industry in 1992?

•29. A pharmaceutical company had sales of $28,600,000 in the year just completed. Sales are expected to decline by 4% per year for the next three years until new drugs, now under development, receive regulatory approval. Then sales should grow at 8% per year for the next four years. What are the expected sales for the final year of the seven-year period?

•30. A 1989 study predicted that the rural population of Saskatchewan would decline by 2% per year during the next decade. If this occurred, what fraction of the rural population was lost during the 1990s?

31. A $1000 face value strip bond has 22 years remaining until maturity. What is its price if the market rate of return on such bonds is 6.5% compounded semiannually?

32. What price should be paid for a $5000 face value strip bond with 19.5 years remaining to maturity if it is to yield the buyer 8.25% compounded semiannually?

33. A client wants to buy a five-year Ontario Hydro strip bond yielding 7.5% with a maturity value of $10,000. What is the current market value of the bond? (Taken from ICB course on Wealth Valuation.)

34. If the current discount rate on 15-year strip bonds is 5.75% compounded semiannually, how many $1000 face value strips can be purchased with $10,000?

35. Mrs. Janzen wishes to purchase 13-year-maturity strip bonds with $12,830 cash she now has in her RRSP. If these strip bonds are currently priced to yield 6.25% compounded semiannually, how many $1000 denomination bonds can she purchase?

36. Liz purchased a $100,000 face value strip bond with five years remaining until maturity. If the bond was discounted to yield 8% compounded semiannually, how much total interest will she earn over the five years? (Taken from CIFP course on Strategic Investment Planning.)

•37. A four-year $8000 promissory note bearing interest at 13.5% compounded monthly was discounted 21 months after issue to yield 12% compounded quarterly. What were the proceeds from the sale of the note?

•38. An eight-year note for $3800 with interest at 11% compounded semiannually was sold after three years and three months to yield the buyer 14% compounded quarterly. What price did the buyer pay?

•39. A loan contract requires a payment after two years of $2000 plus interest (on this $2000) at 9% compounded quarterly and, one year later, a second payment of $1500 plus interest (on this $1500) at 9% compounded quarterly. What would be the appropriate price to pay for the contract six months after the contract date to yield the buyer 10% compounded semiannually?

•40. A loan contract requires two payments three and five years after the contract date. Each payment is to include a principal amount of $2500 plus interest at 10% compounded annually on that $2500. What would an investor pay for the contract 20 months after the contract date if the investor requires a rate of return of 9% compounded monthly?

*8.6 Equivalent Payment Streams

Sometimes a scheduled payment stream is replaced by another payment stream. This can happen, for example, in re-scheduling payments on a loan. In this section we will learn how to make the new stream of payments economically equivalent to the stream it replaces. In this way, neither the payer nor the payee gains any financial advantage.

The general principle we will develop is an extension of ideas from Sections 8.2 and 8.3. In those sections you learned how to obtain the equivalent value of a multiple-payment stream at a particular focal date. It was a two-step procedure:

1. Calculate the equivalent value of each payment at the focal date.
2. Add up the equivalent values to obtain the stream's equivalent value.

How, then, would you compare the economic values of two payment streams? Your intuition should be a good guide here. First calculate the equivalent value of each stream at the *same* focal date. Then compare the two equivalent values to rank them. For two payment streams to be economically equivalent, they must meet the following condition.

CRITERION FOR THE EQUIVALENCE OF TWO PAYMENT STREAMS
A payment stream's equivalent value (at a focal date) is the sum of the equivalent values of all of its payments. Two payment streams are economically equivalent if they have the *same* equivalent value at the *same* focal date.

You must impose this requirement when designing a payment stream that is to be economically equivalent to a given payment stream. The criterion becomes the basis for an equation that enables us to solve for an unknown payment in the new stream.

TIP *CHOOSING A FOCAL DATE*
Any interest conversion date may be chosen for the focal date in an equivalent-payment stream problem. If two payment streams are equivalent at one conversion date, they will be equivalent at any other conversion date. Therefore, problems will generally not specify a particular focal date to be used in the solution. Calculations will usually be simplified if you locate the focal date at one of the unknown payments in the new stream. Then that payment's equivalent value on the focal date is simply its nominal value. But be careful to use the *same* focal date for *both* payment streams.

Example 8.6A *Calculating an Unknown Payment in a Two-Payment Replacement Stream*

Payments of \$2000 and \$1000 were originally scheduled to be paid one year and five years, respectively, from today. They are to be replaced by a \$1500 payment due four years from today, and another payment due two years from today. The replacement stream must be economically equivalent to the scheduled stream. What is the unknown payment, if money can earn 7% compounded semiannually?

Solution

The diagram at the top of the next page presents just the given information. Each payment stream has its own time line. The unknown payment is represented by x. We must calculate a value for x such that the two streams satisfy the Criterion for Equivalence.

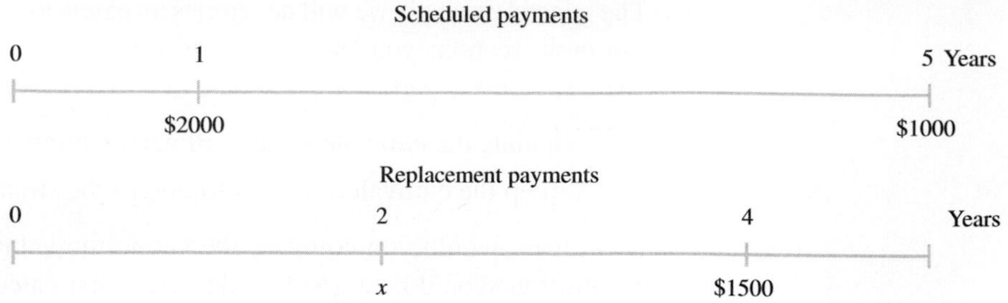

In the next diagram, the date of the unknown payment has been chosen as the focal date. Consequently, the unknown payment's equivalent value on the focal date is just x. The equivalent values of the other payments are represented by FV_1, PV_2, and PV_3.

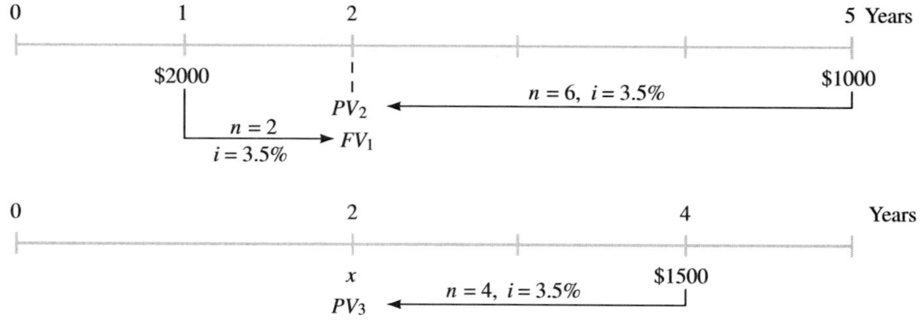

To satisfy the Criterion for Equivalence, we require

$$FV_1 + PV_2 = x + PV_3 \qquad ①$$

Algebraic Solution

The equivalent values of the individual payments are calculated in the usual way.

$$\begin{aligned}
FV_1 &= \text{Future value of \$2000 one year later} \\
&= \$2000(1.035)^2 \\
&= \$2142.45 \\
PV_2 &= \text{Present value of \$1000 three years earlier} \\
&= \$1000(1.035)^{-6} \\
&= \$813.50 \\
PV_3 &= \text{Present value of \$1500 two years earlier} \\
&= \$1500(1.035)^{-4} \\
&= \$1307.16
\end{aligned}$$

Substituting these amounts into equation ①, we have

$$\begin{aligned}
\$2142.45 + \$813.50 &= x + \$1307.16 \\
\$2955.95 - \$1307.16 &= x \\
x &= \$1648.79
\end{aligned}$$

The first payment in the replacement stream must be $1648.79.

Financial Calculator Solution

Calculate FV_1:

2000 (PV) 3.5 (i) 2 (n) 0 (PMT) (COMP) (FV) [−2142.45]

Calculate PV_2:

1000 (FV) 6 (n) (COMP) (PV) [−813.50]

Calculate PV_3 for \$1500:

1500 (FV) 4 (n) (COMP) (PV) [−1307.16]

Substituting these amounts into equation ①, we have

$$\$2142.45 + \$813.50 = x + \$1307.16$$
$$\$2955.95 - \$1307.16 = x$$
$$x = \$1648.79$$

The first payment in the replacement stream must be \$1648.79.

Example 8.6B Calculating Two Payments in a Three-Payment Replacement Stream

A financial obligation was to be settled by a payment of \$1500 on a date one year ago, and a second payment of \$2500 on a date four years after the first payment. The debtor missed the first payment and now wishes to pay \$1000 today and to make two more payments in $1\frac{1}{2}$ and three years. The payment due in three years is to be twice as large as the payment due in $1\frac{1}{2}$ years. What should these payments be if the creditor can earn 8% compounded semiannually on any payments received?

Solution

Let the payment due in $1\frac{1}{2}$ years be x. The scheduled and replacement streams are presented in the following time diagrams. The date of the first unknown payment has been chosen as the focal date, and the symbols for equivalent values on the focal date are indicated.

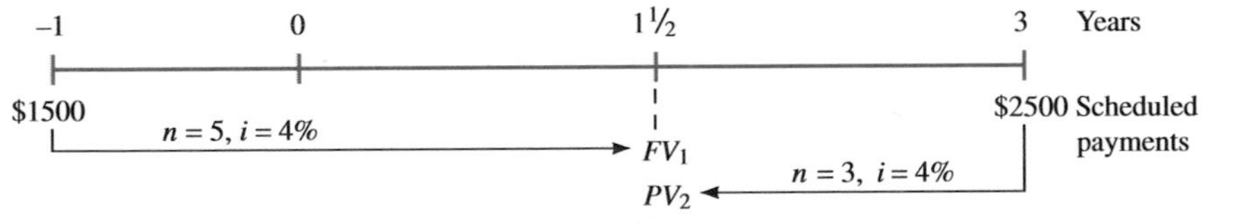

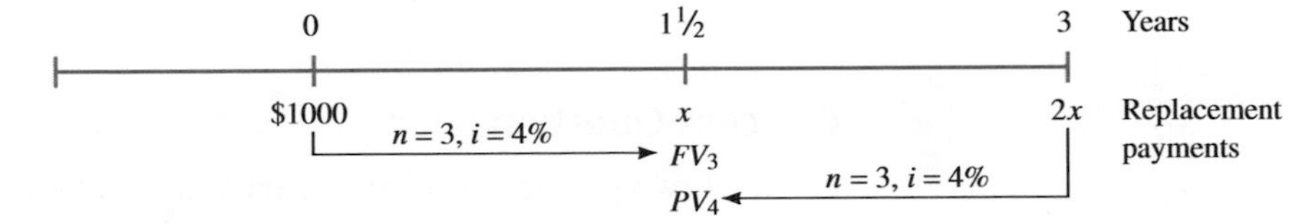

For equivalence of the two payment streams,

$$FV_1 + PV_2 = x + FV_3 + PV_4 \quad ①$$

Algebraic Solution

$$\begin{aligned}
FV_1 &= \text{Future value of \$1500, } 2\tfrac{1}{2} \text{ years later} \\
&= \$1500(1.04)^5 \\
&= \$1824.98 \\
PV_2 &= \text{Present value of \$2500, } 1\tfrac{1}{2} \text{ years earlier} \\
&= \$2500(1.04)^{-3} \\
&= \$2222.49 \\
FV_3 &= \text{Future value of \$1000, } 1\tfrac{1}{2} \text{ years later} \\
&= \$1000(1.04)^3 \\
&= \$1124.86 \\
PV_4 &= \text{Present value of } 2x,\ 1\tfrac{1}{2} \text{ years earlier} \\
&= 2x(1.04)^{-3} \\
&= 1.777993x
\end{aligned}$$

Substituting these values into equation ①, we obtain

$$\begin{aligned}
\$1824.98 + \$2222.49 &= x + \$1124.86 + \$1.777993x \\
\$4047.47 &= 2.777993x + \$1124.86 \\
x &= \frac{\$4047.47 - \$1124.86}{2.777993} \\
&= \$1052.06
\end{aligned}$$

The payments should be \$1052.06 in $1\frac{1}{2}$ years and \$2104.12 in three years.

Financial Calculator Solution

Calculate FV_1:

1500 (PV) 4 (*i*) 5 (*n*) 0 (PMT) (COMP) (FV) [−1824.98]

Calculate PV_2:

2500 (FV) 3 (*n*) (COMP) (PV) [−2222.49]

Calculate FV_3:

1000 (PV) 3 (*n*) (COMP) (FV) [−1124.86]

Calculate the present value of \$1 of the \$2*x*:

1 (FV) 3 (*n*) (COMP) (PV) [−0.88899636]

The present value of \$2x is $2x(\$0.88899636) = \$1.777993x$

Now substitute these values into equation (1). Then solve for x as in the preceding algebraic solution.

Concept Questions

1. If two payment streams are equivalent at one interest rate, will they be equivalent at another interest rate?
2. List three examples of advertisements or news items that routinely ignore the time value of money.
3. What would be the most convincing way to demonstrate that the replacement stream in Example 8.6A is economically equivalent to the given stream?

4. Are two equal payments of size x equivalent to a single payment of $2x$ made midway between the two scheduled payments? If not, is the equivalent payment larger or smaller than $2x$? Explain.

Exercise 8.6

Answers to the odd-numbered problems are at the end of the book.

In Problems 1 through 8, calculate the replacement payment(s) if money can earn the rate of return indicated in the last two columns. Assume that payments scheduled for dates before today have not been made.

Problem	Scheduled payments	Replacement payments	Interest rate (%)	Compounding frequency
1.	\$3000 15 months ago, \$2000 today	\$1500 today, and a payment in 9 months	6	Quarterly
2.	\$1750 7 months ago, \$2900 in 11 months	A payment in 2 months, \$3000 in 12 months	9	Monthly
•3.	\$1400 in 3 months, \$2300 in 21 months	Two equal payments in 9 and 27 months	13	Semiannually
•4.	\$850 2 years ago, \$1760 6 months ago	Two equal payments in 3 months and in 9 months	11	Quarterly
•5.	\$400 8 months ago, \$650 3 months ago	A payment in 2 months and another, twice as large, in 7 months	10.5	Monthly
•6.	\$2000 in 6 months, \$2000 in 2 years	A payment in 1 year and another, half as large, in 3 years	12.5	Semiannually
•7.	\$4500 today	Three equal payments today, in 4 months, and in 9 months	7.2	Monthly
•8.	\$5000 today; \$10,000 in 5 years	Three equal payments in 1, 3, and 5 years	10.75	Annually

•9. Repeat Problem 3 with the change that the scheduled payments consist of \$1400 and \$2300 principal portions *plus interest* on these respective principal amounts at the rate of 10.5% compounded quarterly starting today.

•10. The owner of a residential building lot has received two purchase offers. Mrs. A is offering a \$20,000 down payment plus \$40,000 payable in one year. Mr. B's offer is \$15,000 down plus two \$25,000 payments due one and two years from now. Which offer has the greater economic value if money can earn 9.5% compounded quarterly? How much more is it worth in current dollars?

•11. During its January sale, Furniture City is offering terms of 25% down with no further payments and no interest charges for six months when the balance is due. Furniture City sells the conditional sale contracts from these credit sales to a finance company. The finance company discounts the contracts to yield 18% compounded monthly. What cash amount should Furniture City accept on a \$1595 item in order to end up in the same financial position as if the item were sold under the terms of the January sale?

•12. Henri has decided to purchase a \$25,000 car. He can either liquidate some of his investments and pay cash, or accept the dealer's proposal that Henri pay \$5000 down and \$8000 at the end of each of the next three years.

a. Which choice should Henri make if he can earn 7% compounded semi-annually on his investments? In current dollars, what is the economic advantage of the preferred alternative?

b. Which choice should Henri make if he can earn 11% compounded semi-annually on his investments? In current dollars, what is the economic advantage of the preferred alternative?

(*Hint:* When choosing among alternative streams of cash inflows, we should select the one with the greatest economic value. When choosing among alternative streams of cash outflows, we should select the one with the least economic value.)

•13. A lottery prize gives the winner a choice between (1) $10,000 now and another $10,000 in five years, or (2) four $7000 payments—now and in five, 10, and 15 years.

a. Which alternative should the winner choose if money can earn 7% compounded annually? In current dollars, what is the economic advantage of the preferred alternative?

b. Which alternative should the winner choose if money can earn 11% compounded annually? In current dollars, what is the economic advantage of the preferred alternative?

•14. CompuSystems was supposed to pay a manufacturer $19,000 on a date four months ago and another $14,000 on a date two months from now. CompuSystems is proposing to pay $10,000 today and the balance in five months, when it will receive payment on a major sale to the provincial government. What will the second payment be if the manufacturer requires 18% compounded monthly on overdue accounts?

•15. Payments of $5000 and $7000 are due three and five years from today. They are to be replaced by two payments due $1\frac{1}{2}$ and four years from today. The first payment is to be half the amount of the second payment. What should the payments be if money can earn 7.5% compounded semiannually?

•16. Two payments of $3000 are due today and five years from today. The creditor has agreed to accept three equal payments due one, three, and five years from now if the payments are based on the recognition that money can earn 7.5% compounded monthly. What payments will the creditor accept?

•17. Payments of $8000 due 15 months ago and $6000 due in six months are to be replaced by a payment of $4000 today, a second payment in nine months, and a third payment, three times as large as the second, in $1\frac{1}{2}$ years. What should the last two payments be if money is worth 11% compounded quarterly?

•18. The principal plus interest at 14% compounded quarterly on a $15,000 loan made $2\frac{1}{2}$ years ago is due in two years. The debtor is proposing to settle the debt by a payment of $5000 today and a second payment in one year that will place the lender in an equivalent financial position, given that money can now earn only 10% compounded semiannually.

a. What should be the amount of the second payment?

b. Demonstrate that the lender will be in the same financial position two years from now with either repayment alternative.

••19. Three years ago, Andrea loaned $2000 to Heather. The principal with interest at 13% compounded semiannually is to be repaid four years from the date of the loan. Eighteen months ago, Heather borrowed another $1000 for $3\frac{1}{2}$ years at 11% compounded semiannually. Heather is now proposing to settle both debts with two equal payments to be made one and three years from now. What should the payments be if money now earns 10% compounded quarterly?

Appendix: Instructions for Specific Models of Financial Calculators

Setting the Calculator in the Financial Mode

SHARP EL-733A	SHARP EL-735	Texas Instruments BA-35 Solar	Texas Instruments BA II PLUS	Hewlett Packard 10B
Press 2nd F MODE repeatedly until the "FIN" indicator appears in the upper right corner of the display.	Pressing 2nd F STAT switches between the "statistics" mode (" STAT " indicator in the display) and the financial mode (no indicator displayed).	Press MODE repeatedly until the "FIN" indicator appears in the lower left corner of the display.	Calculator is "ready to go" for financial calculations.	Calculator is "ready to go" for financial calculations.

Setting the Number of Decimal Places Displayed at 9

SHARP EL-733A	SHARP EL-735	Texas Instruments BA-35 Solar	Texas Instruments BA II PLUS	Hewlett Packard 10B
2nd F TAB 9	2nd F TAB 9	2nd Fix 9	2nd Format 9 ENTER 2nd QUIT	DISP 9

Setting a Floating Point Decimal[13]

SHARP EL-733A	SHARP EL-735	Texas Instruments BA-35 Solar	Texas Instruments BA II PLUS	Hewlett Packard 10B
2nd F TAB •	2nd F TAB •	2nd Fix •	Set for 9 decimal places as in the preceding table.	DISP •

[13] With this setting, the calculator will show all of the digits but no trailing zeros for a terminating decimal. Non-terminating decimals will be displayed with 10 digits.

Checking the Contents of A Financial Key's Memory (using the PV key as an example)

SHARP EL-733A	SHARP EL-735	Texas Instruments BA-35 Solar	Texas Instruments BA II PLUS	Hewlett Packard 10B
2nd F	RCL	RCL	RCL	RCL
RCL	PV	PV	PV	PV
PV				

The Financial Functions of the Texas Instruments BA II PLUS

Key Definitions

Key label	Definition
N	1. Number of compoundings (for lump payments) 2. Number of payments (for annuities)
I/Y	The nominal (annual) interest rate. (**I**nterest/**Y**ear).
PV	Present value or initial lump payment.
PMT	Periodic annuity payment.
FV	Future value or terminal lump payment.

Setting P/Y and C/Y None of the values for the preceding keys gives the calculator information about the compounding frequency (that is, the value for m in our algebraic approach). The following table leads you through the procedure for making two further settings.

Keystrokes	Explanation
2nd P/Y	These keystrokes provide access to a particular "settings" worksheet. In your display you will see "P/Y = 12". (You may see a number other than 12; 12 is the default setting.) "P/Y" stands for "payments per year." Although this "label" has annuities in mind, we must still set an appropriate value for "lump" payment problems (in Chapters 8 and 9). We will show you how to do this a little later.
↓	Pressing the "down arrow" key scrolls you down to a second setting. Your display shows "C/Y = 12". (Again the number you see may be different.) "C/Y" stands for "compoundings per year." This is the value the calculator uses for m. For lump payment problems, you must set *both* P/Y and C/Y equal to m. We will now show you the most efficient way to do this.

Keystrokes	Explanation
↑	Press the "up arrow" to return to the P/Y setting.
4 ENTER	Suppose your problem requires quarterly compounding. These two keystrokes change the P/Y setting to four. *The C/Y setting automatically changes to the same value.* (Only in some annuity problems will the two settings differ.)
2nd QUIT	These keystrokes cause you to exit the settings area. Enter any remaining values and complete the calculation. The settings you made will remain in memory until you change them. (They are retained even when the calculator is shut off.)

Simulating the SHARP Operation At many colleges, no recommendation is made for a particular model of financial calculator. Students using a Texas Instruments BA II PLUS in that circumstance may prefer to set their BA II PLUS so that the I/Y key operates like the SHARP's *i* key. Then classroom (and textbook) instructions may be followed literally. If you wish do this, follow the instructions in the centre column of the following table.

Setting the Calculator to Operate per the Instructions in the Text

(that is, setting the calculator to simulate the SHARP operation)

Texas Instruments BA-35 Solar	Texas Instruments BA II Plus	HEWLETT PACKARD 10B
The BA 35 employs the standard cash-flow sign convention for the FV and PMT values but *reverses* the rule[14] for the value of PV ! In other words, for the PV function only, cash inflows are negative and cash outflows are positive. When following the instructions in the text, *remember to reverse the sign used in the text for the value of* PV .	The following six keystrokes will set the calculator so that the I/Y key behaves like the *i* key in the text. 2nd P/Y 1 ENTER 2nd QUIT The setting will not change even when you turn the calculator OFF. (It is likely to be lost when the battery becomes weak. It must be reset after the battery is replaced.)	The following three keystrokes will set the calculator so that the I/YR key behaves like the *i* key in the text. 1 [ ] P/YR The setting will not change even when you turn the calculator OFF. (It is likely to be lost when the battery becomes weak. It must be reset after the battery is replaced.)

[14] The reason Texas Instruments has chosen to use an *inconsistent sign convention* with the BA 35 is that, for a limited range of basic problems, the user can get away with not using (or even being aware of) a cash-flow sign convention. However, there are several cases where, if you do not employ the BA 35's awkward sign convention, you will get an incorrect answer or an "Error" message.

Review Problems

Answers to the odd-numbered review problems are at the end of the book.

1. At the same time as compound-interest Canada Savings Bonds were being sold with guaranteed minimum annual rates of 5.25%, 6%, and 6.75% in the first three years of their 12-year term, a trust company offered three-year "Bond-Beater" GICs paying 5.75%, 6.5%, and 7.25% compounded annually in the three successive years. If the CSBs earn their minimum interest rates, how much more will $4000 earn over the three years if invested in the GIC?

2. A trust company offers a "step-up" GIC that pays an increasing rate of interest in each successive year of its term. The compound interest version of the GIC with a four-year term pays 5.25%, 5.75%, 6.25%, and 6.75% compounded annually in Years 1 to 4, respectively.

   a. What is the maturity value of $8000 invested in a step-up GIC?

   b. How much interest will this GIC earn in the third year?

   c. How much more or less interest will it earn over the entire four-year term than the trust company's standard four-year GIC paying 6% compounded annually?

3. A credit union's "Move-up" GIC pays rates of 6%, 7%, and 8% compounded semiannually in successive years of a three-year term.

   a. What will be the maturity value of $12,000 invested in this GIC?

   b. How much interest will be earned in the second year?

4. Use the data in Table 8.2 to determine the redemption value of a $500 face value compound-interest series S48 Canada Savings Bond on:

   a. November 1, 1998. **b.** April 15, 1999.

5. Jacques has just been notified that the combined principal and interest on an amount he borrowed 19 months ago at 8.4% compounded monthly is now $2297.78. How much of this amount is principal and how much is interest?

◆ 6. Marilyn borrowed $3000, $3500, and $4000 from her grandmother on December 1 in each of three successive years at college. They agreed that interest would accumulate at the rate of 4% compounded semiannually. Marilyn is to start repaying the loan on June 1 following the third loan. What consolidated amount will she owe at that time?

7. Accurate Accounting obtained a private loan of $25,000 for five years. No payments were required, but the loan accrued interest at the rate of 9% compounded monthly for the first $2\frac{1}{2}$ years and then at 8.25% compounded semiannually for the remainder of the term. What total amount was required to pay off the loan?

8. Isaac borrowed $3000 at 10.5% compounded quarterly $3\frac{1}{2}$ years ago. One year ago he made a payment of $1200. What amount will extinguish the loan today?

9. What amount three years ago is equivalent to $4800 on a date $1\frac{1}{2}$ years from now if money earns 8% compounded semiannually during the intervening time?

◆ 10. If the total interest earned on an investment at 6.6% compounded monthly for $3\frac{1}{2}$ years was $1683.90, what was the original investment?

◆ 11. Payments of $2400, $1200, and $3000 were originally scheduled to be paid $1\frac{1}{2}$ years ago, today, and 15 months from today, respectively. Using 6% compounded quarterly as the rate of return money can earn, what payment six months from now would be equivalent to the three scheduled payments?

◆ 12. A furniture store is advertising television sets for 25% down and no interest on the balance, which is payable in a lump amount six months after the date of sale. When asked what discount would be given for cash payment on an $1195 set, the salesclerk offered $40. If you can earn 8% compounded monthly on short-term funds:

a. Should you pay cash and take the discount, or purchase the set on the advertised terms?

b. What is the economic advantage, in today's dollars, of the preferred alternative?

13. If an investor has the choice between rates of 7.5% compounded semiannually and 7.75% compounded annually for a six-year GIC, which rate should be chosen?

◆ **14.** A five-year, compound-interest GIC purchased for $1000 earns 6% compounded annually.

a. How much interest will the GIC earn in the fifth year?

b. If the rate of inflation during the five-year term is 4% per year, what will be the percent increase in the purchasing power of the invested funds over the entire five years?

◆ **15.** A $1000 face value strip bond has 19 years remaining until maturity. What is its price if the market rate of return on such bonds is 7.9% compounded semiannually? At this market rate of return, what will be the increase in the value of the strip bond during the fifth year of ownership?

16. A four-year $7000 promissory note bearing interest at 10.5% compounded monthly was discounted 18 months after issue to yield 9.5% compounded quarterly. What were the proceeds from the sale of the note?

◆ **17.** A loan contract called for a payment after two years of $1500 plus interest (on this $1500 only) at 8% compounded quarterly, and a second payment after four years of $2500 plus interest (on this $2500) at 8% compounded quarterly. What would you pay to purchase the contract 18 months after the contract date if you require a return of 10.5% compounded semiannually?

18. If the inflation rate for the next 10 years is 4.5% per year, what hourly rate of pay in 10 years will be equivalent to $15 per hour today?

19. A 1995 study predicted that employment in base metal mining would decline by 3.5% per year for the next five years. What percentage of total base metal mining jobs was expected to be lost during the five-year period?

◆ **20.** Two payments of $5000 were scheduled 18 months ago and one year from now. They are to be replaced by a payment of $3000 today, a second payment in 18 months, and a third payment, twice as large as the second, in three years. What should the last two payments be if money is worth 9% compounded semiannually?

◆ **21.** Three equal payments were made one, two, and three years after the date on which a $10,000 loan was granted at 10.5% compounded monthly. If the balance immediately after the third payment was $5326.94, what was the amount of each payment?

◆ **22.** Carla has decided to purchase a $30,000 car. She can either liquidate some of her investments and pay cash, or accept the dealer's terms of $7000 down and successive payments of $10,000, $9000, and $8000 at the end of each of the next three years.

a. Which choice should Carla make if she can earn 7% compounded semiannually on her investments? In current dollars, how much is the economic advantage of the preferred alternative?

b. Which choice should Carla make if she can earn 10% compounded semiannually on her investments? In current dollars, how much is the economic advantage of the preferred alternative?

◆◆ **23.** Four years ago John borrowed $3000 from Arlette. The principal with interest at 10% compounded semiannually is to be repaid six years from the date of the loan. Fifteen months ago, John borrowed another $1500 for $3\frac{1}{2}$ years at 9% compounded quarterly. John is now proposing to settle both debts with two equal payments to be made two and $3\frac{1}{2}$ years from now. What should the payments be if money now earns 8% compounded quarterly?

Self-Test Exercise

Answers to the self-test problems are at the end of the book.

1. On the same date that the Bank of Montreal was advertising rates of 6.5%, 7%, 7.5%, 8%, and 8.5% in successive years of its five-year compound interest "RateRiser GIC," it offered 7.5% compounded annually on its five-year fixed-rate GIC.

   a. What will be the maturity values of $10,000 invested in each GIC?

   b. How much interest will each GIC earn in the third year?

2. For the 20 years ended December 31, 1998, the annually compounded rate of return on the portfolio of stocks represented by the TSE 300 Index was 11.92%. For the same period, the compound annual rate of inflation (as measured by the increase in the Consumer Price Index) was 4.50%.

   a. What was $1000 invested in the TSE 300 stock portfolio on December 31, 1978, worth 20 years later?

   b. What amount of money was needed on December 31, 1998, to have the same purchasing power as $1000 on December 31, 1978?

   c. For an investment in the TSE 300 stock portfolio, what was the percent increase in purchasing power of the original $1000?

3. A $1000 face value compound-interest series S49 Canada Savings Bond was redeemed on March 14, 1999. What amount did the bond's owner receive? (Obtain the issue date and the interest rates paid on the bond from Table 8.2.)

4. Maynard Appliances is holding a "Fifty-Fifty Sale." Major appliances may be purchased for nothing down and no interest to pay if the customer pays 50% of the purchase price in six months and the remaining 50% in 12 months. Maynard then sells the conditional sale contracts at a discount to Consumers Finance Co. What will the finance company pay Maynard for a conditional sale contract in the amount of $1085 if it requires a return of 14% compounded quarterly?

◆ 5. On February 1 of three successive years, Roger contributed $3000, $4000, and $3500, respectively, to his RRSP. The funds in his plan earned 9% compounded monthly for the first year, 8.5% compounded quarterly for the second year, and 7.75% compounded semiannually for the third year. What was the value of his RRSP three years after the first contribution?

◆ 6. Payments of $1800 and $2400 were made on a $10,000 variable-rate loan 18 and 30 months after the date of the loan. The interest rate was 11.5% compounded semiannually for the first two years and 10.74% compounded monthly thereafter. What amount was owed on the loan after three years?

7. Donnelly Excavating has received two offers on a used backhoe that Donnelly is advertising for sale. Offer 1 is for $10,000 down, $15,000 in six months, and $15,000 in 18 months. Offer 2 is for $8000 down plus two $17,500 payments one and two years from now. What is the economic value of each offer today if money is worth 10.25% compounded semiannually? Which offer should be accepted?

8. A bank is advertising a Five-Year Escalator GIC. It can be purchased in a compound-interest version paying annually compounded rates of 6%, 6.5%, 7.5%, 8.5%, and 9.5% in successive years. At the same time, the bank's regular five-year compound-interest GIC yields 7.5% compounded annually for the full term. Which GIC will have the higher maturity value? How much more would be earned on $10,000 invested in the preferred GIC for five years?

9. To satisfy more stringent restrictions on toxic waste discharge, a pulp mill will have to reduce toxic wastes by 10% from the previous year's level every year for the next five years. What fraction of the current discharge level is the target level?

◆ 10. Payments of $2300 due 18 months ago and $3100 due in three years are to be replaced by an equivalent stream of payments consisting of $2000 today and two equal payments due two and four years from now. If money can earn 9.75% compounded semiannually, what should be the amount of each of these two payments?

◆ 11. A $6500 loan at 11.25% compounded monthly is to be repaid by three equal payments due three, six, and 12 months after the date of the loan. Calculate the size of each payment.

www.Exercise.com

1. REDEMPTION VALUE OF A CANADA SAVINGS BOND Go to the Canada Investment and Savings Web site (www.cis-pec.gc.ca) and link to the interest rate table for Canada Savings Bonds. Update your textbook's Table 8.2 for the Series 50 CSB. If you own a $1000 face value S50 compound-interest CSB, for what amount could you redeem it at the beginning of next month? Do the calculation mathematically and then check your answer using the calculator available on the Web site.

2. SHOPPING FOR GICs Visit www.canoe.ca/MoneyRates/gics.html for a comprehensive comparison of current rates available on GICs. How much more would you earn on $10,000 invested for five years at the highest available rate than at the lowest rate?

Summary of Notation and Key Formulas

j = Nominal annual interest rate
m = Number of compoundings per year
i = Periodic rate of interest
PV or P = Principal amount of the loan or investment; Present value
FV or S = Maturity value of the loan or investment; Future value
n = Number of compounding periods

Formula (8-1)	$i = \frac{j}{m}$	Finding the periodic interest rate from the nominal annual rate
Formula (8-2)	$FV = PV(1+i)^n$ or $S = P(1+i)^n$	Finding the maturity or future value
	$PV = FV(1+i)^{-n}$ or $P = S(1+i)^{-n}$	Finding the principal or present value
Formula (8-3)	$n = m \times$ (Number of years in the term)	Finding the number of compounding periods
Formula (8-4)	$FV = PV(1+i_1)(1+i_2)(1+i_3)\cdots(1+i_n)$	Finding the maturity value with compounding at a variable interest rate

CASH-FLOW SIGN CONVENTION
Cash inflows (receipts) are positive.
Cash outflows (disbursements) are negative.

PRESENT VALUE OF LOAN PAYMENTS
The sum of the present values of all of the payments required to pay off a loan is equal to the original principal of the loan. The discount rate for the present-value calculations is the rate of interest charged on the loan.

Criterion for the Equivalence of Two Payment Streams

A payment stream's equivalent value (at a focal date) is the sum of the equivalent values of all of its payments. Two payment streams are economically equivalent if they have the *same* equivalent value at the *same* focal date.

List of Key Terms

Cash flow *(p. 318)*
Cash-flow sign convention *(p. 318)*
Compounding frequency *(p. 291)*
Compounding period *(p. 290)*
Compound interest method *(p. 290)*
Discounting a payment *(p. 307)*
Discount rate *(p. 307)*
Future value *(p. 294)*
Maturity value *(p. 294)*
Nominal interest rate *(p. 291)*
Periodic interest rate *(p. 291)*
Present value *(p. 307)*
Strip bond *(p. 327)*
Term *(p. 294)*

CHAPTER OUTLINE

LEARNING OBJECTIVES

After completing this chapter, you will be able to:

- Calculate the interest rate and term in compound interest applications
- Given a nominal interest rate, calculate its effective interest rate
- Given a nominal interest rate, calculate its equivalent interest rate at another compounding frequency

9

Compound Interest: Further Topics and Applications

IN ALL COMPOUND INTEREST PROBLEMS in Chapter 8, the interest rate and the time interval were known. With a little reflection, we can think of many situations requiring the calculation of the interest rate or the rate of return. For example, what was the rate of return on the home your parents recently sold after owning it for 14 years? What rate of return has been earned on a mutual fund investment made $3\frac{1}{2}$ years ago? If you invest \$1000 in a mutual fund, what rate of return must it earn to grow to \$5000 over a 12-year period?

In other circumstances, we want to know the time required for an amount to grow from a beginning value to a target value. How long, for example, will it take an investment to double if it earns 10% compounded annually? By the end of Section 9.2, you will readily answer such questions.

Compound interest rates on loans and investments may be quoted with differing compounding frequencies. This gives rise to questions such as: "How do we compare 7.9% compounded semiannually to 8% compounded annually? What semiannually compounded rate is equivalent to 6% compounded monthly?" The techniques you will learn in Sections 9.3 and 9.4 will enable you to answer these questions. Later on, in Chapters 10 through 14, this ability will be used routinely in calculations involving annuities.

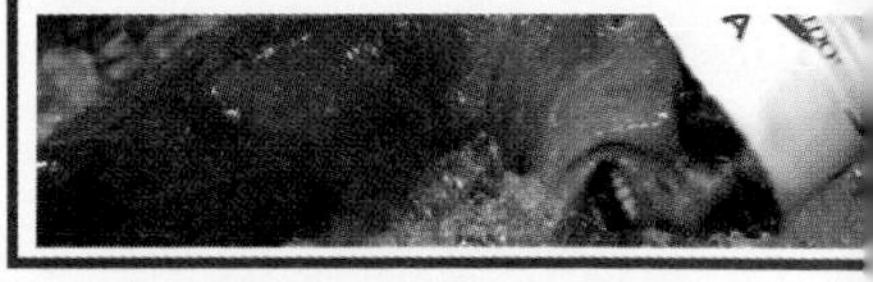

9.1 Calculating the Periodic Interest Rate, *i*

In cases where we know values for *PV*, *FV*, and *n*, the periodic and nominal rates of interest may be calculated.

Algebraic Method Rearranging the basic equation $FV = PV(1 + i)^n$ to isolate i is more difficult than isolating *PV*. First divide both sides of the equation by *PV* and then interchange the two sides, giving

$$(1 + i)^n = \frac{FV}{PV}$$

Next take the *n*th root[1] of both sides of the equation. This makes the left side simply $(1 + i)$ and we have

$$1 + i = \sqrt[n]{\frac{FV}{PV}}$$

Therefore,

PERIODIC RATE OF INTEREST

$$i = \sqrt[n]{\frac{FV}{PV}} - 1 = \left(\frac{FV}{PV}\right)^{1/n} - 1 \qquad \textbf{(9-1)}$$

Financial Calculator Method Enter values for the three known variables—*PV*, *FV*, and *n*—into the appropriate memories. Then press (COMP) (*i*) in sequence to execute the calculation.

TRAP *THE SIGN CONVENTION IS NOW MANDATORY*

When you enter values for *FV* and *PV*, it is imperative that you employ the cash-flow sign convention. If you fail to use it, an error message will appear in your calculator's display.

Example 9.1A *Calculating the Periodic and Nominal Rates of Interest*

The maturity value of a three-year, $5000 compound-interest GIC was $6193.60. To three-figure accuracy, calculate the nominal rate of interest paid on the GIC if interest was compounded:

a. Annually. **b.** Quarterly.

Solution

Given: $PV = \$5000$ and $FV = \$6193.60$.
In part (a), $m = 1$, $n = m(\text{Term}) = 1(3) = 3$ compounding periods.
In part (b), $m = 4$, $n = m(\text{Term}) = 4(3) = 12$ compounding periods.

---

[1] It was shown in the Appendix to Chapter 2 that the *n*th root of a quantity is equivalent to raising it to the exponent $1/n$.

Algebraic Solution

Formula (9-1) enables us to calculate the interest rate for one compounding period.

a.
$$i = \left(\frac{FV}{PV}\right)^{1/n} - 1$$
$$= \left(\frac{\$6193.60}{\$5000.00}\right)^{1/3} - 1$$
$$= (1.23872)^{0.\overline{3}} - 1$$
$$= 0.073967$$
$$= 7.397\%$$

The nominal rate of interest on the GIC was $j = mi = 1(7.40\%) = 7.40\%$ compounded annually.

b.
$$i = \left(\frac{FV}{PV}\right)^{1/n} - 1$$
$$= \left(\frac{\$6193.60}{\$5000.00}\right)^{1/12} - 1$$
$$= (1.23872)^{0.08\overline{3}} - 1$$
$$= 0.018000$$
$$= 1.800\%$$

The nominal rate of interest on the GIC was $j = mi = 4(1.80\%) = 7.20\%$ compounded quarterly.

Financial Calculator Solution

a. 5000 (+/–) (PV) 6193.60 (FV) 3 (n) 0 (PMT) (COMP) (i) [7.396738]

The nominal rate of interest on the GIC was

$$j = mi = 1(7.40\%) = 7.40\% \text{ compounded annually}$$

b. Remember that you need enter only those values that change.

12 (n) (COMP) (i) [1.799996]

The nominal rate of interest on the GIC was

$$j = mi = 4(1.80\%) = 7.20\% \text{ compounded quarterly}$$

TRAP *DON'T LEAVE OUT THE FINAL STEP*

The calculation of i is usually not the last step in a problem. Typically you are asked to determine either the nominal interest rate or the effective interest rate (to be discussed in Section 9.3). Do not forget to complete the extra step needed to directly answer the question.

Example 9.1B *Calculating a Semiannually Compounded Rate of Return*

Mr. Dunbar paid \$10,000 for a \$50,000 face value strip bond having $19\frac{1}{2}$ years remaining until maturity. (Recall that a strip bond is an investment that returns just one payment, the face value, at maturity.) What semiannually compounded rate of return will Mr. Dunbar earn on his investment?

Solution

Given: $PV = \$10,000$ $FV = \$50,000$ Term $= 19\frac{1}{2}$ years $m = 2$

Then $n = m(\text{Term}) = 2(19.5) = 39$

Algebraic Solution

$$i = \left(\frac{FV}{PV}\right)^{1/n} - 1 = \left(\frac{\$50{,}000}{\$10{,}000}\right)^{1/39} - 1 = 5^{0.0256410} - 1 = 0.04213 = 4.213\%$$

$$j = mi = 2(4.213\%) = 8.43\% \text{ compounded semiannually}$$

Mr. Dunbar will earn 8.43% compounded semiannually on his strip bond investment.

Financial Calculator Solution

10000 (+/–) (PV) 50000 (FV) 39 (n) 0 (PMT) (COMP) (i) [4.2131]

$$j = 2i = 2(4.213\%) = 8.43\% \text{ compounded semiannually}$$

Mr. Dunbar will earn 8.43% compounded semiannually on his strip bond investment.

Example 9.1C Calculating an Annually Compounded Rate of Return that is Equivalent to a Series of Individual Annual Returns

For the years 1996, 1997, and 1998, the Investors Canadian Equity mutual fund earned returns of 24.9%, 9.0%, and −13.1%, respectively. Calculate the fund's equivalent annually compounded rate of return for the three years. (This is the fixed annual rate of return that would produce the same overall growth.)

Solution

The equivalent annually compounded rate of return for the three-year period cannot be obtained by simply averaging the three individual annual returns. Instead, we must use a two-step procedure:

Step 1: Use $FV = PV(1 + i_1)(1 + i_2)(1 + i_3) \ldots (1 + i_n)$ to calculate how much an investment on December 31, 1995 was worth on December 31, 1998.

Step 2: Calculate the annually compounded rate of return that will produce the *same* growth in three years.

Step 1: For the initial investment, choose a "nice, round" amount such as \$100 or \$1000.

$$\begin{aligned} FV &= PV(1 + i_{1996})(1 + i_{1997})(1 + i_{1998}) \\ &= \$1000(1 + 0.249)(1 + 0.09)(1 - 0.131) \\ &= \$1183.07 \end{aligned}$$

Step 2: This step can be done algebraically or using the financial functions on a calculator.

Algebraic Solution

$$i = \left(\frac{FV}{PV}\right)^{1/n} - 1 = \left(\frac{\$1183.07}{\$1000}\right)^{1/3} - 1 = 1.18307^{0.333333} - 1 = 0.05764 = 5.764\%$$

Financial Calculator Solution

1000 (+/–) (PV) 1183.07 (FV) 3 (n) 0 (PMT) (COMP) (i) 5.764

The mutual fund's equivalent annually compounded rate of return for the three-year period ended December 31, 1998 was

$$j = mi = 1(5.76\%) = 5.76\% \text{ compounded annually.}$$

CAUGHT IN THE WEB

One of the most popular Web sites for mutual fund information and analysis is www.globefund.com. If you visit this site and choose "Fund Filter," you can set criteria on which a comprehensive Canadian mutual fund database will be searched. For example, you can easily obtain a listing of all Canadian Equity funds whose equivalent annually compounded rate of return for the past 10 years has been greater than 10%.

If you want to obtain detailed information about a fund whose name you know, choose the "Fund Selector" option on the home page.

Postscript: At the end of every month, the type of calculation in Example 9.1C is done for most of the 1200 (and increasing) mutual funds available in Canada. The equivalent compound annual rates of return are calculated for three-year, five-year, and 10-year periods terminating at the month-end. These returns are then published in monthly mutual fund supplements to major newspapers. They are also available on investment Web sites that specialize in mutual funds. (In fact, these equivalent rates of return are more easily found than the year-by-year returns on which they are based.) You may have noticed that mutual fund advertisements commonly quote mutual fund performance in terms of the three-year, five-year, and 10-year compound annual returns. Now you know how they are obtained and how to interpret them.

Example 9.1D *Calculating an Inflation-Adjusted (Real) Rate of Return*

Over a 10-year period, Brook's investment in Suncor stock grew in value from \$9480 to \$17,580. During the same period, the Consumer Price Index (CPI) rose from 93.6 to 126.1. What was her *real* compound annual rate of return on the stock during the decade? (The real rate of return is the rate of return net of inflation. It represents the rate of increase in purchasing power.)

Solution

With the CPI up from 93.6 to 126.1, Brook needed $\frac{126.1}{93.6}$ times as many dollars at the end of the decade to purchase the same goods and services as at the beginning. The \$9480 value of the stock at the beginning had to grow to

$$\$9480 \times \frac{126.1}{93.6} = \$12,772$$

just to maintain her purchasing power. In fact, it grew to \$17,580. In terms of end-of-decade dollars, her purchasing power rose from \$12,772 to \$17,580. Hence, to obtain the real rate of return, use $PV = \$12,772$, $FV = \$17,580$, and $n = 10$.

Algebraic Solution

$$i = \left(\frac{FV}{PV}\right)^{1/n} - 1 = \left(\frac{\$17,580}{\$12,772}\right)^{1/10} - 1 = 1.37645^{0.1} - 1 = 0.03247 = 3.25\%$$

The real rate of return on the Suncor stock was

$$j = mi = 1(3.25\%) = 3.25\% \text{ compounded annually}$$

Financial Calculator Solution

12772 (+/–) (PV) 17580 (FV) 10 (n) 0 (PMT) (COMP) (i) 3.247

The real rate of return on the Suncor stock was

$$j = mi = 1(3.25\%) = 3.25\% \text{ compounded annually}$$

Postscript: Two points should be mentioned.

1. The same answer will be obtained if you choose to adjust for inflation by expressing $17,580 in terms of beginning-of-decade dollars.
2. An entirely different approach may have occurred to you. Suppose you separately calculate the (usual) rate of return on the stock, and the rate of inflation from the CPI data. (You would obtain 6.37% and 3.03% compounded annually, respectively.) You might think that:

$$\begin{aligned}\text{Real rate of return} &= \text{Actual rate of return} - \text{Rate of inflation}\\ &= 6.37\% - 3.03\%\\ &= 3.35\%\end{aligned}$$

This is a slightly larger value (by 0.10%) than the strictly correct answer we obtained in the "official solution." The reason for the small difference is quite subtle and technical—we will spare you the details. However, real rates of return are, more often than not, calculated this way.[2] Since nominal rates of return and inflation rates are easily obtained from published data, the approximation is a distinctly easier approach and is good enough for most purposes.

Concept Questions

1. If FV is less than PV, what can you predict about the value for i?
2. Is FV negative if you lose money on an investment?
3. Which scenario had the higher periodic rate of return: "$1 grew to $2" or "$3 grew to $5"? Both investments were for the same length of time at the same compounding frequency. Justify your choice.

Exercise 9.1

Answers to the odd-numbered problems are at the end of the book.

Calculate interest rates accurate to the nearest 0.01%.

Calculate the nominal rate of interest in Problems 1 through 6.

Problem	Principal ($)	Maturity amount ($)	Compounding frequency	Nominal rate (%)	Term
1.	3400	4297.91	Annually	?	3 years
2.	1000	4016.94	Annually	?	20 years
3.	1800	2299.16	Quarterly	?	2 years, 9 months
4.	6100	13,048.66	Semiannually	?	7 years, 6 months
5.	950	1165.79	Monthly	?	2 years, 5 months
6.	4300	10,440.32	Annually	?	8 years, 6 months

[2] You could say that the real rates of return usually calculated in the real world are not really real.

7. When he died in 1790, Benjamin Franklin left $4600 to the city of Boston, with the stipulation that the money and its earnings could not be used for 100 years. The bequest grew to $332,000 by 1890. What equivalent compound annual rate of return did the bequest earn?

8. The Templeton Growth Fund, an international equity mutual fund, presented a graph in a December 1998 advertisement showing that a $10,000 investment in the fund at the end of November 1954 would have grown to over $4,930,000 by November 30, 1998. What (equivalent) compound annual rate of return did the fund realize over this period?

9. Anders discovered an old pay statement from 11 years ago. His monthly salary at the time was $2550 versus his current salary of $4475 per month. At what (equivalent) compound annual rate has his salary grown during the period?

10. Bank of Canada data show that aggregate consumer credit in Canada rose from $115.6 billion in December 1994 to $158 billion in December 1998. What was the compound annual rate of increase in consumer credit during the period?

11. Mr. and Mrs. Markovich note that the home they purchased 17 years ago for $70,000 is now appraised at $260,000. What was the (equivalent) annual rate of appreciation in the value of their home during the 17-year period?

12. If the population of a city grew from 53,500 at the beginning of 1993 to 64,300 at the end of 2000, what was the city's (equivalent) annual rate of growth during the period?

13. The total amount of money invested in Canadian mutual funds grew from $35.0 billion at the end of 1990 to $394 billion at the end of 1998. What was the compound annual rate of increase in mutual fund assets during the period?

14. The number of mutual funds in Canada grew from 483 at the end of 1992 to 2016 at the end of 1998. What was the compound annual rate of increase in the number of mutual funds during the period?

15. If the number of workers in the forest industry in Canada declined by 30% from the end of 1993 to the beginning of 2000, what was the compound annual rate of attrition in the industry?

16. The Canadian Consumer Price Index (based on a value of 100 in 1971) rose from 97.2 in 1970 to 210.6 in 1980. What was the (equivalent) annual rate of inflation in the decade of the 1970s?

17. The Consumer Price Index (based on a value of 100 in 1986) rose from 67.2 in 1980 to 119.5 in 1990. What was the (equivalent) annual rate of inflation in the decade of the 1980s?

18. The Consumer Price Index (based on a value of 100 in 1992) rose from 93.3 in 1990 to 110.3 in 1999. What was the (equivalent) annual rate of inflation during the period?

•19. Using the data given in Problems 16 and 17, calculate the average rate of inflation for the 1970–1990 period. (Note: Simply averaging the two answers to Problems 16 and 17 will give only an approximation of the correct result.)

20. Aldo purchased a $13,000 strip bond on October 1, 1997 for $11,352.56. The bond matured on October 1, 2000. What was his semiannually compounded rate of return on the bond? (Source: CIFP course on Strategic Investment Planning.)

•21. A four-year promissory note for $3800 plus interest at 9.5% compounded semiannually was sold 18 months before maturity for $4481. What quarterly compounded (annual) rate of return will the buyer realize on her investment?

•22. A $6000, three-year promissory note bearing interest at 11% compounded semiannually was purchased 15 months into its term for $6854.12. What monthly compounded discount rate was used in pricing the note?

•23. In recent years Canadian stocks as a group have significantly underperformed U.S. stocks. Consider that, at the end of 1987, the TSE 300 Stock Price Index was at 3160 at the same time as the S&P 500 Stock Price Index in the United States stood at 278.1. By the end of 1998, the S&P 500 Stock Price Index had risen to 1229 and the TSE Stock Price Index to 6486.

a. Calculate the compound annual change in the price of each group of stocks during the period.

b. Suppose that, at the end of 1987, you invested $10,000 in each of two stock portfolios that tracked the respective indexes precisely. How much more would your U.S. portfolio be worth at the end of 1998? (Ignore currency exchange effects.)

•24. During the 1987 to 1998 period (for which TSE 300 Stock Price Index data and S&P 500 Stock Price Index data are given in Problem 23), the Consumer Price Index rose from 81.5 to 108.6. What was the real compound annual rate of growth in the two market indices during the 11-year period?

•25. An investor's portfolio increased in value by 93% over a seven-year period in which the Consumer Price Index rose from 95.6 to 115.3. What was the compound annual real rate of return on the portfolio during the period?

•26. An investment grew in value from $5630 to $8485 during a five-year period. The annual rate of inflation for the five years was 2.3%. What was the compound annual real rate of return during the five years?

•27. An investment earned 12% compounded semiannually for two years and 10% compounded annually for the next three years. What was the equivalent annually compounded rate of return for the entire five-year period?

•28. A portfolio earned 20%, −20%, 0%, 20%, and −20% in five successive years. What was the portfolio's five-year equivalent annually compounded rate of return?

•29. A portfolio earned 20%, 15%, −10%, 25%, and −5% in five successive years. What was the portfolio's five-year equivalent annually compounded rate of return?

•30. At the end of 1998, the Templeton Growth Fund was the largest mutual fund in Canada. This fund invests primarily in common stocks of foreign companies. The aggregate market value of its holdings at the end of 1998 was over $9 billion (Canadian). The fund's annual returns in successive years from 1989 to 1998 inclusive were 21.1%, −13.6%, 30.3%, 15.2%, 36.3%, 3.8%, 14.1%, 18.4%, 17.1%, and 0.7%, respectively. For three-year, five-year, and 10-year periods ending December 31, 1998, what were the fund's equivalent annually compounded returns?

•31. At the end of 1998, the AIC Advantage Fund had the best 10-year compound annual return of any mutual fund based in Canada. During the 10-year period, this fund had a disproportionate weighting in stocks of banks and other financial companies. The fund's annual returns in successive years from 1989 to 1998 inclusive were 20.3%, −18.6%, 39.8%, 9.1%, 65.2%, −12.6%, 30.7%, 66.5%, 43.3%, and 6.3%, respectively. For three-year, five-year, and 10-year periods ending December 31, 1998, what were the fund's equivalent annually compounded returns?

•32. At the end of 1998, the Investors Japanese Growth fund had one of the worst 10-year compound annual returns of any mutual fund based in Canada. The fund's annual returns in successive years from 1989 to 1998 inclusive were 6.3%, −27.1%, 7.1%, −5.9%, 35.3%, 21.2%, −6.7%, −15.6%, −20.5%, and 12.1%, respectively. For three-year, five-year, and 10-year periods ending December 31, 1998, what were the fund's equivalent annually compounded returns?

9.2 Calculating the Number of Compounding Periods, *n*

In cases where we know values for *PV*, *FV*, and *i*, the number of compounding periods and the total term may be calculated.

Algebraic Method Manipulation of $FV = PV(1 + i)^n$ to isolate *n* requires the use of logarithms. Logarithms are briefly mentioned in Appendix A. Example 9AB in this appendix derives the following formula for the number of compounding periods.

NUMBER OF COMPOUNDING PERIODS

(9-2)
$$n = \frac{\ln\left(\frac{FV}{PV}\right)}{\ln(1 + i)}$$

TIP *YOU HARDLY RECOGNIZE THEM WHEN THEY'RE ALL DRESSED UP!*

Remember that formulas (9-1) and (9-2) are merely alternative versions of $FV = PV(1 + i)^n$ with different variables isolated. Each formula contains the same information. Any one of them may be derived from any of the others by strictly algebraic manipulations.

Financial Calculator Method Enter values for the three known variables—*PV*, *FV*, and *i*—into the appropriate memories. Then press (COMP) (*n*) in sequence to execute the calculation.

investor for $4327.70. The sale price was based on a discount rate of 8.5% compounded semiannually. How long before the maturity date did the sale take place?

Solution

The selling price represents the present value on the date of sale of the loan's maturity value. In other words, $4327.70 was the present value of the maturity value discounted at 8.5% compounded semiannually. Therefore, the solution requires two steps as indicated in the following time diagram.

1. Calculate the maturity value of the debt.
2. Determine the length of time over which the maturity value was discounted to yield the $4327.70 present value.

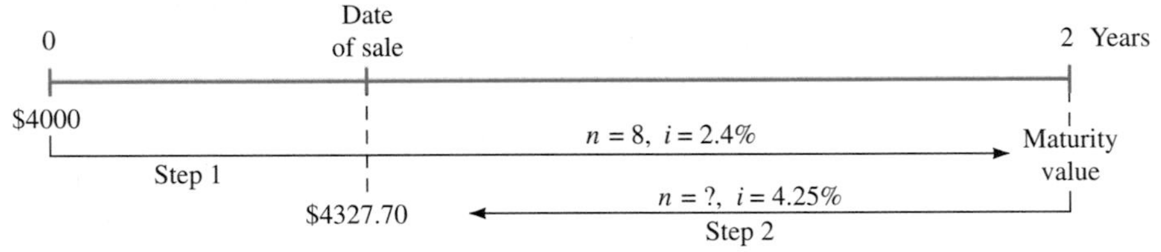

Step 1: For the maturity value calculation, $n = m(\text{Term}) = 4(2) = 8$ and

$$i = \frac{j}{m} = \frac{9.6\%}{4} = 2.4\%$$

Step 2: For discounting the maturity value, $i = \dfrac{8.5\%}{2} = 4.25\%$

Algebraic Solution

Step 1: The maturity value of the contract is

$$FV = PV(1+i)^n = \$4000(1.024)^8 = \$4835.70$$

Step 2: The number of compounding periods between the date of sale and the maturity date is

$$n = \frac{\ln\left(\frac{FV}{PV}\right)}{\ln(1+i)} = \frac{\ln\left(\frac{\$4835.70}{\$4327.70}\right)}{\ln(1.0425)} = \frac{0.110990}{0.0416217} = 2.6666$$

Each compounding period is six months long. Therefore, the date of sale was

2.6666×6 months $= 16.00$ months before the maturity date.

Financial Calculator Solution

Step 1: Maturity value of the contract (sign convention from the lender's point of view):

4000 (+/−) (PV) 8 (n) 2.4 (i) 0 (PMT) (COMP) (FV) | 4835.70 |

Step 2: Number of compounding periods between the date of sale and the maturity date (sign convention from the new investor's point of view):

4327.70 (+/−) (PV) 4.25 (i) (COMP) (n) [2.6666]

Since each compounding period is six months long, the settlement date was

$$2.6666 \times 6 \text{ months} = 16.00 \text{ months before the maturity date.}$$

Concept Questions

1. Under what circumstance does the value calculated for n equal the number of years in the term of the loan or investment?
2. Which investment scenario requires more time: "\$1 growing to \$2" or "\$3 growing to \$5"? Both investments earn the same rate of return. Justify your choice.

Exercise 9.2

Answers to the odd-numbered problems are at the end of the book.

Calculate the term of each loan or investment in Problems 1 through 6.

Problem	Principal (\$)	Maturity amount (\$)	Compounding frequency	Nominal rate (%)	Term
1.	1100	4483.92	Annually	6.3	? years, ? months
2.	4625	8481.61	Annually	7.875	? years, ? months
3.	5670	10,365.39	Semiannually	9.5	? years, ? months
4.	2000	3172.42	Annually	8.75	? years, ? months
5.	2870	3837.30	Monthly	10	? years, ? months
6.	3250	4456.90	Quarterly	7.5	? years, ? months

7. How long before a scheduled payment of \$3252 will a payment of \$2150 be equivalent? Money is worth 12% compounded quarterly.
8. Marilyn was supposed to pay \$1450 to Bernice on March 1. Some time later Marilyn paid Bernice an equivalent payment of \$1609.90, allowing for a time value of money of 9% compounded monthly. When did Marilyn make the payment?
9. What is the remaining time until the maturity date of a \$10,000 strip bond if it is purchased for \$2603.35 to yield 9.5% compounded semiannually until maturity?
10. Rounded to the nearest month, how long will it take a town's population to:
    a. Grow from 32,500 to 40,000 if the annual growth rate is 3%?
    b. Shrink from 40,000 to 32,500 if the annual rate of decline is 3%?
11. Rounded to the nearest month, how long will it take an investment to double if it earns:
    a. 8.4% compounded annually? **b.** 10.5% compounded semiannually?
12. Rounded to the nearest month, how long will it take an investment to triple if it earns:
    a. 9% compounded annually? **b.** 8% compounded quarterly?

13. Rounded to the nearest quarter year, how long will it take an investment to quadruple if it earns:

    a. 8% compounded annually? b. 9% compounded semiannually?

•14. Rounded to the nearest month, how long will it take money to lose half of its purchasing power if the annual inflation rate is:

    a. 3% b. 6%

•15. Rounded to the nearest month, how long will it take money to lose 25% of its purchasing power if the annual rate of inflation is:

    a. 2% b. 4%

16. A few years ago, John Ellis invested $3000 at 9% compounded annually. If the investment is now worth $5484, how long ago was the investment made? (Source: CIFP course on Personal Financial Planning.)

•17. When discounted to yield 10.5% compounded monthly, a $2600 three-year promissory note bearing interest at 12.25% compounded annually was priced at $3283.57. How long after the issue date did the discounting take place?

•18. The proceeds from the sale of a $4500 five-year promissory note bearing interest at 9% compounded quarterly were $6055.62. How long before its maturity date was the note sold if it was discounted to yield 10.5% compounded monthly?

•19. A $4000 loan at 7.5% compounded monthly was settled by a single payment of $5000. How many days after the initial loan was the $5000 payment made? For the purpose of determining the number of days in a partial month, assume that a full month has 30 days.

•20. If money is worth 8% compounded quarterly, how long (to the nearest day) before a scheduled payment of $6000 is $5000 an equivalent payment? For the purpose of determining the number of days in a partial calendar quarter, assume that a full quarter has 91 days.

•21. Wilf paid $416.71 for a $1000 face value strip bond. At this price the investment will yield a return of 7.86% compounded semiannually. How long (to the nearest day) before its maturity date did Wilf purchase the bond? Assume that each half-year has exactly 182 days.

•22. A $5000 face value strip bond may be purchased today for $1073.36 yielding the purchaser 7.27% compounded semiannually. How much time (to the nearest day) remains until the maturity date? Assume that each half-year has exactly 182 days.

•23. $7500 was borrowed for a four-year term at 9% compounded quarterly. The terms of the loan allow prepayment of the loan based on discounting the loan's maturity value at 7% compounded quarterly. How long (to the day) before the maturity date was the loan prepaid if the payout amount was $9380.24? For the purpose of determining the number of days in a partial calendar quarter, assume that a full quarter has 91 days.

9.3 Effective Interest Rate

Would you choose a mortgage loan at 6% compounded monthly or a loan at 6.1% compounded semiannually? You want the *lower* interest cost. (A tiny difference in interest rates can represent hundreds of dollars in interest costs over the life of a mortgage loan.) The lower nominal rate favours the first alternative but the lower compounding frequency favours the second loan.

How much better is a rate of return of 8% compounded monthly than 8% compounded semiannually? These questions invite a comparison of nominal interest rates. But nominal interest rates may be directly compared *only if* they have the *same* compounding frequency.

There is a natural preference in business for comparing interest rates on the basis of annual compounding. This is because an *annually* compounded rate of return represents the *actual* percentage increase in a year. For example, at a return of 10% compounded annually, you can immediately say that \$100 will grow by 10% (\$10) in the next year. But at a return of 10% compounded monthly, you cannot say how much \$100 will grow in a year without a short calculation. In the second case, the *actual* percentage increase will be more than 10%.

The standard approach for comparing two nominal interest rates is to convert each to its **effective interest rate.** This is the *annually* compounded rate that produces the *same* future value or present value as the given nominal rate. We use the symbol "f" to represent the effective rate of interest. After converting nominal rates to effective rates, you can directly compare and rank the effective rates.

It is not difficult to derive a formula for the effective interest rate, f. Suppose you invest \$100 for one year at the effective rate f (compounded annually) and another \$100 for one year at the nominal rate $j = mi$. Their future values are calculated in parallel columns below.

The first \$100 will undergo just one compounding of the effective rate f.

$$FV = PV(1 + i)^n$$
$$= \$100(1 + f)^1$$

The second \$100 will undergo m compoundings of the periodic rate i.

$$FV = PV(1 + i)^n$$
$$= \$100(1 + i)^m$$

If f is equivalent to the nominal rate j, then these two future values must be equal. That is,

$$\$100(1 + f) = \$100(1 + i)^m$$
$$1 + f = (1 + i)^m$$

EFFECTIVE INTEREST RATE

(9-3)
$$f = (1 + i)^m - 1$$

With a financial calculator, we can take a more intuitive approach [than just substituting values into formula (9-3)]. Suppose you calculate the future value of \$100 invested *for one year* at the given nominal rate. For the sake of discussion, let's say you get \$107.64 for the future value. What annually compounded rate would give the same growth (\$7.64) in one year? Clearly it is 7.64% compounded annually. Therefore, the effective rate is 7.64%.

When an effective interest rate is quoted or calculated, the compounding frequency does not need to be specified. Everyone understands from the definition of effective interest rate that "effective" implies "annual compounding."

Example 9.3A Calculating the Effective Rate Given a Nominal Interest Rate

What is the effective rate of interest corresponding to 10.5% compounded monthly?

Solution

For $j = 10.5\%$ and $m = 12$,

$$i = \frac{10.5\%}{12} = 0.875\% \text{ per month.}$$

Algebraic Solution

$$\begin{aligned} f &= (1 + i)^m - 1 \\ &= 1.00875^{12} - 1 \\ &= 1.11020 - 1 \\ &= 0.11020 \\ &= 11.02\% \end{aligned}$$

The effective interest rate is 11.02% (compounded annually).

Financial Calculator Solution

Invest $100 for one year at the given nominal rate.

100 (+/–) (PV) 12 (n) 0.875 (i) 0 (PMT) (COMP) (FV) **111.020**

An interest rate of 11.02% compounded annually would produce the same interest earnings ($11.02). Therefore, the effective interest rate is 11.02% (compounded annually).

Example 9.3B Comparing Alternative Nominal Interest Rates

Which is the most attractive of the following interest rates offered on five-year GICs?

a. 5.70% compounded annually **b.** 5.68% compounded semiannually

c. 5.66% compounded quarterly **d.** 5.64% compounded monthly

Solution

The preferred rate is the one having the highest effective rate. The calculations of the effective rates are presented in the table below.

Algebraic Solution

j	m	i	$f = (1 + i)^m - 1$
a. 5.70%	1	0.057	$f = j$ when $m = 1$; $f = 5.700\%$
b. 5.68%	2	0.0284	$f = (1.0284)^2 - 1 = 0.05761 = 5.761\%$
c. 5.66%	4	0.01415	$f = (1.01415)^4 - 1 = 0.05781 = 5.781\%$
d. 5.64%	12	0.0047	$f = (1.0047)^{12} - 1 = 0.05788 = 5.788\%$

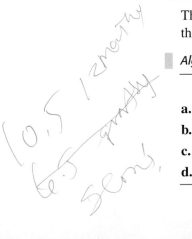

The most attractive rate is 5.64% compounded monthly since it has the highest effective rate. For the alternative rates in this example, the ranking in terms of effective rates is in the reverse order of the nominal rates.

Financial Calculator Solution

a: $f = j$ when $m = 1$; $f = 5.700\%$

b: 100 (+/−) (PV) 2 (n) 2.84 (i) 0 (PMT) (COMP) (FV) [105.761]

Hence, $f = 5.761\%$.

c: 4 (n) 1.415 (i) (COMP) (FV) [105.781]

Hence, $f = 5.781\%$.

d: 12 (n) 0.47 (i) (COMP) (FV) [105.788]

Hence, $f = 5.788\%$.

The most attractive nominal rate is 5.64% compounded monthly since it has the highest effective rate. For the alternative rates in this example, the ranking based on effective rates turns out to be the reverse order of the nominal rates.

POINT OF INTEREST

NOT IN YOUR BEST INTEREST

Revenue Canada charges interest on overdue income tax, Canada Pension Plan contributions, and Employment Insurance Premiums. The prescribed rate is adjusted by Revenue Canada every three months based on changes in the Bank of Canada rate. For the first quarter of 1999, the prescribed nominal rate was 9%.

You now know that the compounding frequency matters. The more frequently a given nominal rate is compounded, the higher the effective rate of interest. Considering who is setting the rate in this case, you would probably guess that the prescribed rate is compounded monthly (the highest compounding frequency encountered in normal commerce). Not so! But before you start thinking Revenue Canada has some compassion after all, now hear this—the prescribed rate is compounded daily!

Questions

1. Calculate the effective rate of interest corresponding to 9% compounded daily.
2. How much more interest would accrue on a \$1000 debt in a year at 9% compounded daily than at 9% compounded monthly?

Example 9.3C *Finding the Effective Rate Given the Principal and Maturity Value*

Calculate the effective rate of interest if \$100 grew to \$150 in $3\frac{1}{2}$ years with quarterly compounding.

Solution

The problem could be solved by first finding the quarterly compounded nominal rate that produces the given maturity value. Then the corresponding effective rate could be calculated. But this two-step solution is unnecessarily long.

The essential question (which may be answered in one step) is: At what annually compounded rate will \$100 grow to \$150 after $3\frac{1}{2}$ years?

Algebraic Solution

The annually compounded rate can be obtained by substituting $PV = \$100$, $FV = \$150$, and $n = 3.5$ in formula (9-1).

$$i = \left(\frac{FV}{PV}\right)^{1/n} - 1 = \left(\frac{\$150}{\$100}\right)^{1/3.5} - 1 = 1.5^{0.28571} - 1 = 0.1228$$

Financial Calculator Solution

Compute the annually compounded rate that causes a \$100 investment to grow to \$150 in $3\frac{1}{2}$ years.

100 (+/–) (PV) 3.5 (n) 150 (FV) 0 (PMT) (COMP) (i) **12.28**

Since \$100 will grow to \$150 in $3\frac{1}{2}$ years at 12.28% compounded annually, the effective interest rate is 12.28%.

Example 9.3D Calculating the Effective Rate on a Charge Card

The monthly statement for a bank charge card quotes an annual interest rate of 18% and a daily interest rate of 0.049315% $\left(=\frac{18\%}{365}\right)$. Calculate the effective interest rate if the interest charges must be paid each month.

Solution

Since the accrued interest is paid each month, we have monthly compounding with

$$i = \frac{18\%}{12} = 1.5\% \qquad \text{and} \qquad m = 12$$

Algebraic Solution

$$f = (1 + i)^m - 1 = 1.015^{12} - 1 = 0.19562$$

That is, the effective rate is 19.56%.

Financial Calculator Solution

Compute the future value of \$100 invested at 18% compounded monthly for one year. The interest earned is numerically equal to the effective interest rate.

100 (+/–) (PV) 12 (n) 1.5 (i) 0 (PMT) (COMP) (FV) **119.562**

Therefore, the effective rate is 19.56%.

Example 9.3E Calculating a Nominal Interest Rate Given the Effective Rate

What monthly compounded (nominal) rate of interest has an effective rate of 10%?

Solution

Given: $f = 10\%$ $m = 12$

At $f = 10\%$, \$100 (PV) will grow to \$110 (FV) in one year. Find the periodic interest rate, i, that gives the same maturity value after one year.

Algebraic Solution

$$i = \left(\frac{FV}{PV}\right)^{1/n} - 1 = \left(\frac{\$110}{\$100}\right)^{1/12} - 1 = 1.1^{0.08333} - 1 = 0.007974 = 0.7974\%$$

Then $j = mi = 12(0.7974\%) = 9.57\%$ compounded monthly

Financial Calculator Solution

100 (+/−) (PV) 12 (n) 110 (FV) 0 (PMT) (COMP) (i) 0.7974

Then $j = mi = 12(0.7974\%) = 9.57\%$ compounded monthly

POINT OF INTEREST

REDEFINING "EFFECTIVE" TO MAKE IT MORE EFFECTIVE

The following description of an "Investment Option Term Deposit" was extracted from the Web site of a credit union in March 1999. The escalating interest rates quoted for each year are compounded at the end of the year. The "average rate" and "effective annual rate" are also given.

Take a careful look at the quoted effective rate. It is very close to 4.8%. Does it not seem odd that a single year at 5% can pull up the low rates for the other two years all the way to an overall of effective rate 4.8%? Let's see what is going on.

Investment Option Term Deposit

Annual escalating rates. Option to convert on 1st or 2nd anniversary to another NCU non-redeemable term for the remaining term or longer, at no penalty. Non-redeemable.

36 month term	Year 1	4.250%
	Year 2	4.500%
	Year 3	5.000%
	Effective Annual Rate	4.796%

Questions

1. Calculate the maturity value of a \$100 investment in this type of term deposit.
2. Calculate the effective interest rate over the three years. Is your value more reasonable than the quoted effective rate? (With annual compounding at rates that do not change much from year to year, the effective rate will not differ much from the average rate.)

3. Let us try to figure out whether the person who did the calculation just made a mechanical error or whether he or she really doesn't know what "effective rate" means.
   a. How much total interest will the $100 investment earn in Question 1?
   b. On average, how much interest will be earned per year? Observe that this amount is numerically equal to the quoted "effective annual rate."
   c. How could the quoted "effective annual rate" be used to obtain the future value you calculated in Question 1? (Hint: How would you calculate future value at a *simple* rate of interest?)
4. Put on your "marketing hat" for a moment. Is there any reason to suspect that the credit union had an ulterior motive in promoting its notion of effective rate instead of the true effective rate?

Concept Questions

1. What is meant by the effective rate of interest?
2. Is the effective rate of interest ever smaller than the nominal interest rate?
3. Is the effective rate of interest ever equal to the nominal interest rate?
4. A semiannually compounded nominal rate and a monthly compounded nominal rate have the same effective rate. Which has the larger nominal rate? Explain.
5. From a lender's point of view, would you rather disclose to borrowers the nominal interest rate or the effective interest rate?

Exercise 9.3

Answers to the odd-numbered problems are at the end of the book.
Calculate interest rates and growth rates accurate to the nearest 0.01%.
Calculate the missing interest rates in Problems 1 through 20.

Problem	Nominal rate and compounding frequency	Effective rate (%)
1.	10.5% compounded semiannually	?
2.	10.5% compounded quarterly	?
3.	10.5% compounded monthly	?
4.	7.5% compounded semiannually	?
5.	7.5% compounded quarterly	?
6.	7.5% compounded monthly	?
7.	?% compounded semiannually	10.5
8.	?% compounded quarterly	10.5
9.	?% compounded monthly	10.5
10.	?% compounded semiannually	7.5

Problem	Nominal rate and compounding frequency	Effective rate (%)
11.	?% compounded quarterly	7.5
12.	?% compounded monthly	7.5
13.	12% compounded monthly	?
14.	18% compounded monthly	?
15.	11.5% compounded quarterly	?
16.	9.9% compounded semiannually	?
17.	?% compounded semiannually	10.25
18.	?% compounded quarterly	14
19.	?% compounded monthly	10
20.	?% compounded monthly	8

21. What is the effective rate of interest on a credit card that calculates interest at the rate of 1.8% per month?

22. What is the effective rate of interest corresponding to a nominal rate of:

a. 8% compounded semiannually? **b.** 12% compounded quarterly?

(Source: ICB course on Wealth Valuation.)

23. If an invoice indicates that interest at the rate of 2% per month will be charged on overdue amounts, what effective rate of interest will be charged?

24. If the nominal rate of interest paid on a savings account is 4% per annum paid monthly, what is the effective rate of interest?

25. If an interest rate of 8.9% compounded semiannually is charged on a car loan, what effective rate of interest should be disclosed to the borrower?

26. A company reports that its sales have grown 3% per quarter for the last eight fiscal quarters. What annual growth rate has the company been experiencing for the last two years?

27. If a \$5000 investment grew to \$6450 in 30 months of monthly compounding, what effective rate of return was the investment earning?

28. After 27 months of quarterly compounding, a \$3000 debt had grown to \$3810. What effective rate of interest was being charged on the debt?

29. Lisa is offered a loan from a bank at 12.25% compounded monthly. A credit union offers similar terms but a rate of 12.5% compounded semiannually. Which loan should she accept? Present calculations that support your answer.

30. Craig can buy a three-year compound-interest GIC paying 7.5% compounded semiannually or 7.4% compounded monthly. Which option should he choose? Present calculations that support your answer.

31. Camille can obtain a residential mortgage loan from a bank at 6.5% compounded semiannually, or from an independent mortgage broker at 6.4% compounded monthly. Which source should she pick if other terms and conditions of the loan are the same? Present calculations that support your answer.

32. ABC Ltd. reports that its sales are growing at the rate of 1.3% per month. DEF Inc. reports sales increasing by 4% each quarter. What is each company's effective annual rate of sales growth?

33. Columbia Trust wants its annually, semiannually, and monthly compounded five-year GICs all to have an effective interest rate of 5.75%. What nominal annual rates should it quote for the three compounding options?

34. Belleville Credit Union has established interest rates on its three-year GICs so that the effective rate of interest is 7% on all three compounding options. What are the monthly, semiannually, and annually compounded rates?

•35. A department store chain currently charges 18% compounded monthly on its credit card. To what amount should it set the monthly compounded annual rate if it wants to add 2% to the effective interest rate?

•36. An oil company wants to drop the effective rate of interest on its credit card by 3%. If it currently charges a periodic rate of 1.7% per month, at what amount should it set the periodic rate?

9.4 Equivalent Interest Rates

Preamble The main purpose of this section is to prepare you for a routine calculation that you will carry out for a broad category of annuities in Chapters 10, 11, 13, and 14. The concept behind the calculation is developed here because it is an extension of ideas from Section 9.3.

Equivalent interest rates are interest rates that produce the *same* future value after one year. For example, 8% compounded quarterly and 8.08% compounded semiannually are equivalent *nominal* interest rates. If you calculate the future value of \$100 invested at either rate for one year, you will obtain \$108.24. You can see that equivalent interest rates have *different numerical values* but produce the *same effect.*

If *nominal* rates are equivalent, so also are their respective *periodic* rates. From the preceding example, we can conclude that:

$$i = \frac{8\%}{4} = 2\% \text{ per quarter} \quad \text{is } \textit{equivalent} \text{ to} \quad i = \frac{8.08\%}{2} = 4.04\% \text{ per half year}$$

They will both produce the same future value when compounded over a one-year term.

TIP

Clarifying Terminology

Be clear on the distinction between the descriptions "compounded quarterly" and "per quarter." The former refers to the compounding *frequency.* The latter refers to the compounding *period.* For example, if you hear or read "6% compounded semiannually," you are being given the value for j. Then $i = \frac{j}{2} = 3\%$ (per half year). On the other hand, if an interest rate is described as "6% per half year," you are being given the value for i and the period to which it applies. Then $j = 2i = 12\%$ compounded semiannually.

Here is the kind of question we wish to answer.

"What six-month periodic rate, i, is equivalent to 2.5% per quarter?"

For equivalence, \$100 invested for one year at either rate must have the same future value. Using $FV = PV(1 + i)^n$ with $n = 2$ for the six-month periodic rate and $n = 4$, $i = 2.5\%$ for the three-month periodic rate, the equivalence requirement is

$$\$100(1 + i)^2 = \$100(1.025)^4$$

Solving for i,

$$(1 + i)^2 = (1 + 0.025)^4$$
$$1 + i = (1 + 0.025)^{4/2}$$
$$i = (1 + 0.025)^{4/2} - 1 \qquad (1)$$

The result of the calculation is 0.050625 = 5.0625% per half year.

In order to streamline the procedure, let us infer a general formula from our particular example. We have two m variables and two i variables involved. We will distinguish between them using subscripts. Let

i_1 and m_1 represent the *given* values of i and m
i_2 and m_2 represent the *equivalent* values of i and m

To obtain the general formula, replace the particular values in equation (1) by the corresponding symbol. That is, replace 0.025 by i_1, 4 by m_1, 2 by m_2, and i by i_2. We get

EQUIVALENT PERIODIC RATE

(9-4) $$i_2 = (1 + i_1)^{m_1/m_2} - 1$$

Financial Calculator Method We can use an intuitive approach instead of formula (9-4). It goes right to the definition of "equivalent interest rates." We will require the equivalent periodic rate to produce the same future value of \$100 after one year as the given periodic rate.

Step 1: Calculate the future value of \$100 invested for one year at the given i_1 and m_1. That is,

100 (+/–) (PV) i_1 (i) m_1 (n) 0 (PMT) (COMP) (FV)

Step 2: Compute the value of i_2 that also makes \$100 grow to the same FV in m_2 compoundings. Leaving the current values for PV and FV in the memories,

m_2 (n) (COMP) (i)

Example 9.4A *Calculation of Three Equivalent Interest Rates*

For a given interest rate of 10% compounded quarterly, what is the equivalent nominal rate of interest with:

a. Annual compounding? **b.** Semiannual compounding?
c. Monthly compounding?

Solution

The given rate is $j_1 = 10\%$ with $m_1 = 4$. Therefore, $i_1 = 2.5\%$ per quarter.

Algebraic Solution

In the following columns, we substitute the given values for m_1, m_2, and i_1 into formula (9-4). To save space in our solution, we use the abbreviations[4]: "ca" for "compounded annually," "csa" for "compounded semiannually," and "cm" for "compounded monthly."

a. $m_2 = 1$

$$i_2 = (1.025)^{4/1} - 1 = 0.1038 = 10.38\% \text{ per year}$$

$$j_2 = m_2 \times i_2 = 1 \times 10.38\% = 10.38\% \text{ ca}$$

b. $m_2 = 2$

$$i_2 = (1.025)^{4/2} - 1 = 0.050625 = 5.0625\% \text{ per half-year}$$

$$j_2 = m_2 \times i_2 = 2 \times 5.0625\% = 10.125\% \text{ csa}$$

c. $m_2 = 12$

$$i_2 = (1.025)^{4/12} - 1 = 0.0082648 = 0.82648\% \text{ per month}$$

$$j_2 = m_2 \times i_2 = 12 \times 0.82648\% = 9.918\% \text{ cm}$$

Financial Calculator Solution

a. 100 (+/-) (PV) 2.5 (i) 4 (n) 0 (PMT) (COMP) (FV) [110.381]
1 (n) (COMP) (i) [10.381] % per year.
$j_2 = m_2 \times i_2 = 1 \times 10.381\% = 10.381\%$ compounded annually.

b. We need not repeat the first step—we already have the *PV* and *FV* we want.
2 (n) (COMP) (i) [5.0625] % per half-year.
$j_2 = m_2 \times i_2 = 2 \times 5.0625\% = 10.125\%$ compounded semiannually.

c. 12 (n) (COMP) (i) [0.82648] % per month.
$j_2 = m_2 \times i_2 = 12 \times 0.82648\% = 9.918\%$ compounded monthly.

Concept Questions

1. What is the significance of two nominal interest rates being equivalent?
2. Suppose the periodic rate for six months is 4%. Is the equivalent periodic rate for three months (pick one):
(i) equal to $4\% \times \frac{3}{6} = 2\%$? (ii) less than 2%? (iii) greater than 2%?
Answer the question without doing any calculations. Explain your choice.
3. Suppose the periodic rate for one month is 0.5%. Is the equivalent periodic rate for six months (pick one):
(i) equal to $6(0.5\%) = 3\%$? (ii) less than 3%? (iii) greater than 3%?
Answer the question without doing calculations. Explain your choice.

[4] Whose idea was it to have such a long word for "abbreviation"?

Exercise 9.4

Answers to the odd-numbered problems are at the end of the book.

Throughout this Exercise, calculate interest rates accurate to the nearest 0.01%.

Calculate the equivalent interest rates in Problems 1 through 12.

Problem	Given interest rate	Equivalent interest rate
1.	10% compounded annually	?% compounded semiannually
2.	10% compounded annually	?% compounded quarterly
3.	10% compounded annually	?% compounded monthly
4.	10% compounded semiannually	?% compounded annually
5.	10% compounded semiannually	?% compounded quarterly
6.	10% compounded semiannually	?% compounded monthly
7.	10% compounded quarterly	?% compounded annually
8.	10% compounded quarterly	?% compounded semiannually
9.	10% compounded quarterly	?% compounded monthly
10.	10% compounded monthly	?% compounded annually
11.	10% compounded monthly	?% compounded semiannually
12.	10% compounded monthly	?% compounded quarterly

Calculate the equivalent interest rates in Problems 13 through 20.

Problem	Given interest rate	Equivalent interest rate
13.	9% compounded semiannually	?% compounded annually
14.	10% compounded quarterly	?% compounded annually
15.	8.25% compounded annually	?% compounded monthly
16.	12% compounded monthly	?% compounded semiannually
17.	7.5% compounded semiannually	?% compounded quarterly
18.	11.5% compounded quarterly	?% compounded monthly
19.	8.5% compounded quarterly	?% compounded semiannually
20.	10.5% compounded monthly	?% compounded quarterly

21. What annually compounded interest rate is equivalent to:

a. 9% compounded semiannually?

b. 9% compounded quarterly?

c. 9% compounded monthly?

22. What monthly compounded interest rate is equivalent to:

a. 9% compounded annually?

b. 9% compounded semiannually?

c. 9% compounded quarterly?

23. For a three-year GIC investment, what nominal rate compounded monthly would put you in the same financial position as 7.5% compounded semiannually?

24. A trust company pays 7.5% compounded semiannually on its three-year GICs. Above what nominal rate of interest would you choose an annually compounded GIC of the same maturity?

25. You are offered a loan at a rate of 12% compounded monthly. Below what nominal rate of interest would you choose semiannual compounding instead?

26. Banks usually quote residential mortgage interest rates on the basis of semiannual compounding. An independent mortgage broker is quoting rates with monthly compounding. What rate would the broker have to give to match 9.5% compounded semiannually available from a bank?

27. A credit union pays 8.25% compounded annually on five-year compound-interest GICs. It wants to set the rates on its semiannually and monthly compounded GICs of the same maturity so that investors will earn the same total interest. What should be the rates on the GICs with the higher compounding frequencies?

28. A bank offers a rate of 7.5% compounded semiannually on its four-year GICs. What monthly and annually compounded rates should it quote in order to have the same interest costs with all three nominal rates?

*Appendix A: Logarithms

A strictly algebraic approach to the solution of certain compound interest problems involves the use of logarithms. However, if the financial functions of a calculator are employed, logarithms are not needed.

Financial calculators all have a function labelled (ln) or (ln *x*). This denotes the "natural logarithm" function.

Example 9AA *Calculating Natural Logarithms*

a. $\ln 1 = 0$

b. $\ln 10 = 2.30258$

c. $\ln 1.1 = 0.09531$

d. $\ln 100 = 4.60517$

e. $\ln (1+ 0.01) = \ln 1.01 = 0.009950$

f. $\ln (1 + 0.06) = \ln 1.06 = 0.05827$

g. $\ln \left(\frac{\$5000}{\$2000}\right) = \ln 2.5 = 0.91629$

h. $\ln \left(\frac{\$3491.67}{\$1820.19}\right) = \ln 1.91830 = 0.65144$

Rules of Logarithms The Rules of Logarithms show how the logarithm of a product, quotient, or power may be expanded in terms of the logarithms of the individual factors. Their derivation is straightforward and can be found in any algebra text that introduces logarithms.

RULES OF LOGARITHMS:

1. The Product Rule:	$\ln (ab) = \ln a + \ln b$
2. The Quotient Rule:	$\ln (a/b) = \ln a - \ln b$
3. The Power Rule:	$\ln (a^k) = k(\ln a)$

TRAP *IT'S TEMPTING BUT . . .*

The following expansions are illegal.

$\ln(a + b) \neq \ln a + \ln b$ $\qquad$ $\ln(ab) \neq (\ln a)(\ln b)$

$\ln(a - b) \neq \ln a - \ln b$ $\qquad$ $\ln(a/b) \neq \ln a / \ln b$

Example 9AB *Derivation of Formula (9-2)*

Solve $FV = PV(1 + i)^n$ for n.

Solution

First divide both sides of the equation by PV and then interchange the two sides, giving

$$(1 + i)^n = \frac{FV}{PV}$$

Next take logarithms of both sides. Use the Power Rule to expand $\ln(1+i)^n$. We obtain

$$n \times \ln(1 + i) = \ln\left(\frac{FV}{PV}\right)$$

Finally, division of both sides by $\ln(1+i)$ yields

$$n = \frac{\ln\left(\frac{FV}{PV}\right)}{\ln(1 + i)}$$

*Appendix B: Annualized Rates of Return and Growth

Suppose that Investment A provided a total return of 3.1% during a four-month holding period, and Investment B's total return over a seven-month period was 5.25%. Although B produced the larger total return, it took a significantly longer time to do so. For a proper comparison of the performance of the two investments, we should compare their rates of return for the same time interval.

One possibility would be to compare the percent return per month from each investment. However, there is a general preference in business for quoting and comparing percent returns *per year* (even when the actual holding period is much less than one year). An **annualized rate of return** is the percent return that would result if a short-term rate of return continues for an entire year. In economics and business, other short-term rates of change are also usually quoted as annualized rates.

Two methods are used to annualize short-term returns. They make different assumptions regarding compounding.

Simple Annualized Rate This approach simply extends the short-term percent return, on a proportionate basis, to a full year. For example, a return of 2.5% for a three-month holding period would be multiplied by four to give an annualized rate of 10%. This calculation is the reverse of the procedure used in Chapters 6 and 7 to calculate a short-term interest rate from a *simple* per annum rate. Therefore, the annualized rate of return obtained by this approach is a *simple* rate of return—it assumes that the short-term rate does *not compound* when extended to a full year. For the general case, the basic proportion is

$$\frac{\text{Simple annualized rate}}{\text{Short-term percent return}} = \frac{\text{Full year}}{\text{Holding period (partial year)}}$$

Multiplying both sides by "Short-term percent return," we obtain

$$\text{Simple annualized rate} = \frac{\text{Full year}}{\text{Holding period}} \times \text{Short-term percent return}$$

Effective Annualized Rate By definition, the duration or term of a short-term investment is less than one year. Therefore, the proceeds from a short-term investment become available for reinvestment in less than one year. A rigorous method for annualizing a short-term rate of return should recognize this opportunity for compounding. The usual assumption is that the full maturity value is immediately reinvested in an identical short-term investment. This has the effect of:

1. Making the compounding period equal to one term of the investment

$$\left(\text{and } m = \frac{1 \text{ year}}{\text{Term of the investment}}\right).$$

2. Making the periodic rate of return, i, equal to the percent return during one term of the short-term investment.

To obtain the effective annualized rate of return, substitute these values for m and i into $f = (1 + i)^m - 1$. Note that m is not likely to be an integer. For example, the proceeds from a 60-day investment can, in principle, be reinvested or compounded $\frac{365}{60} = 6.083$ times during a year.

The inclusion of compounding makes the effective annualized rate *larger* than the corresponding simple annualized rate.

Example 9BA *Calculating Annualized Rates of Inflation*

If Statistics Canada reported that the Consumer Price Index (CPI) rose from 136.2 to 136.7 in the previous month, what was:

a. The simple annualized rate of inflation for the month?

b. The effective annualized rate of inflation for the month?

Solution

The percent increase in the CPI during the month was

$$i = \frac{\text{CPI(final)} - \text{CPI(initial)}}{\text{CPI(initial)}} \times 100\% = \frac{136.7 - 136.2}{136.2} \times 100\% = 0.3671\%$$

a. Simple annualized rate $= \dfrac{\text{Full year}}{\text{Partial year}} \times \text{Short-term percent change}$

$$= \frac{12 \text{ months}}{1 \text{ month}} \times 0.3671\%$$

$$= 4.41\% \text{ per annum}$$

b. Now calculate the annual rate of inflation on the assumption that the inflation rate for the previous month ($i = 0.3671\%$) will be repeated *and* compounded every month for one year ($m = 12$).

Algebraic Solution

$$f = (1 + i)^m - 1 = 1.003671^{12} - 1 = 0.0450 = 4.50\%$$

Financial Calculator Solution

Choose a beginning price level of 100 and compute the price level after 12 months of compound increase at 0.3671% per month.

100 (PV) 12 (n) 0.3671 (i) 0 (PMT) (COMP) (FV) [−104.495]

Price levels will be at 104.50 (up from 100) after one year at this inflation rate. The effective annualized inflation rate is therefore 4.50%.

Example 9BB Annualizing a Short-Term Rate of Economic Growth

Canada's gross domestic product (GDP), in constant 1992 dollars, rose from $861.99 billion in the second quarter to $872.22 billion in the third quarter of 1997. During the third quarter of 1997, what was:

a. The simple annualized rate of economic growth (as measured by the GDP)?

b. The effective annualized rate of economic growth (as measured by the GDP)?

Calculate the rates accurate to the nearest 0.01%.

Solution

The percent change in the GDP during the quarter was

$$i = \frac{\text{GDP(final)} - \text{GDP(initial)}}{\text{GDP(initial)}} \times 100\% = \frac{872.22 - 861.99}{861.99} \times 100\% = 1.187\%$$

a. Simple annualized rate $= \dfrac{\text{Full year}}{\text{Partial year}} \times \text{Short-term percent change}$

$$= \frac{12 \text{ months}}{3 \text{ months}} \times (1.187\%)$$

$$= 4.75\% \text{ per annum}$$

The economy grew at the simple annual rate of 4.75% during the third quarter of 1997.

b. Now calculate the annual rate of change on the assumption that the rate of GDP growth will be repeated and compounded for four successive quarters.

Algebraic Solution

$$f = (1 + i)^m - 1 = (1 + 0.01187)^4 - 1 = 1.0483 - 1 = 4.83\%$$

The GDP grew at an effective annual rate of 4.83% during the third quarter of 1997.

Financial Calculator Solution

Choose a beginning GDP level of 100 and compute the GDP level after one year of compound growth at 1.187% per quarter.

100 (+/−) (PV) 4 (n) 1.187 (i) 0 (PMT) (COMP) (FV) [104.83]

The GDP grew at an effective annualized rate of 4.83% during the third quarter of 1997.

Example 9BC Converting a Simple Annualized Rate to an Effective Annualized Rate

A $10,000 face value Treasury bill, with 42 days remaining to maturity, was purchased to yield 5% per annum simple interest. What effective annualized rate of return was earned on the T-bill?

Solution

We can calculate the 42-day holding-period return from the given simple annualized rate of return (5% pa). Then use $f = (1 + i)^m - 1$ or the functions on a financial calculator to obtain the effective annualized rate.

$$\text{Holding-period return, } i = \frac{42}{365} \times 5\% = 0.57534\%$$

$$\text{Number of compounding periods in a year, } m = \frac{365}{42} = 8.6905$$

Algebraic Solution

The effective annualized rate is

$$f = (1 + i)^m - 1 = (1.0057534)^{8.6905} - 1 = 0.0511 = 5.11\%$$

Financial Calculator Solution

100 (+/−) (PV) 8.6905 (n) 0.57534 (i) 0 (PMT) (COMP) (FV) [105.11]

Since $100 will grow to $105.11 in one year, the effective annualized rate of return was 5.11%.

Example 9BD Converting a Cash Discount to an Annualized Rate of Return

Cash discounts offered on invoices usually represent an opportunity to earn a large annualized rate of return on "investment." Consider the case where Sonya receives an invoice for \$100 with terms 2/10, net 30. The two natural alternatives[5] facing Sonya are:

1. Pay \$98 after 10 days; or
2. Pay \$100 20 days later (at the end of the 30-day credit period).

Investment was placed within quotation marks in the first sentence because the choice can be viewed as an investment decision. To put money to a better use than taking the cash discount, Sonya would need to be able to earn more than \$2 on an investment of \$98 for 20 days.

At what simple and effective annualized rates of return on investment would Sonya be indifferent between taking the cash discount after 10 days versus investing \$98 for 20 days (and then paying the full price on the last day of the credit period)?

Solution

Sonya will be indifferent if \$98 can earn exactly \$2 in 20 days. The percent return for the 20 days would have to be

$$i = \frac{\$2}{\$98} \times 100\% = 2.041\%$$

The corresponding simple annualized rate of return would be

$$\frac{365}{20} \times 2.041\% = 37.25\%$$

and the effective annualized rate would be

$$f = (1 + i)^m - 1 = (1.02041)^{365/20} - 1 = 0.4459 = 44.59\%$$

The cash discount represents a simple annualized return on "investment" of 37.25% and an effective annualized return on "investment" of 44.59%.[6]

Example 9BE *Annualized Returns on Money Market Mutual Funds*

A money market mutual fund invests in Treasury Bills and other short-term debt investments. The rate of return on the portfolio changes from day to day as "old" investments (earning "old" rates) mature and are replaced by new investments (earning current rates). Each day, major newspapers report the "current yield" and the "effective yield" for each of approximately 100 money market mutual funds. The "current yield" is the simple annualized rate of return; the "effective yield" is the effective annualized rate of return. In both cases, the fund's percent return for the previous seven days is annualized.

[5] It is a fundamental tenet of managing accounts payable to use "free" credit to its limit. If you choose to take the cash discount, you should pay on the last day of the discount period. Otherwise, you should pay on the last day of the credit period.

[6] Here is another interpretation of the numbers. Suppose the purchaser does not have the cash on hand to take advantage of the cash discount. An option is to borrow \$98 for 20 days to pay the bill. It would be to Sonya's advantage to borrow at any effective interest rate below 44.59% rather than forgo the discount and pay \$100 on the last day of the 30-day credit period.

Suppose that ABC Money Market fund had a return of 0.089% for the most recent seven days. What current yield and effective yield would be reported for the fund in the financial pages?

Solution

$$\begin{aligned}\text{Current yield} &= \text{Simple annualized rate}\\ &= \frac{\text{Full year}}{\text{Holding period}} \times \text{Short-term percent return}\\ &= \frac{365 \text{ days}}{7 \text{ days}} \times 0.089\%\\ &= 4.64\% \text{ per annum}\end{aligned}$$

Algebraic Solution

$$\begin{aligned}\text{Effective yield} &= \text{Effective annualized return}\\ &= (1 + i)^m - 1\\ &= (1.00089)^{365/7} - 1\\ &= 1.00089^{52.143} - 1\\ &= 0.0475\\ &= 4.75\%\end{aligned}$$

Financial Calculator Solution

100 (+/-) (PV) 365 (÷) 7 (=) (n) 0.089 (i) (COMP) (FV) 104.75

Since $100 will grow to $104.75 in one year, the effective annualized return is 4.75%. The financial pages would report a current yield of 4.64% and an effective yield of 4.75%.

Exercise 9B

Answers to the odd-numbered problems are at the end of the book.
Calculate percentages accurate to the nearest 0.01%.

1. If the Consumer Price Index rose by 1% over a two-month period, what were the simple and effective annualized rates of inflation during the two-month period?
2. The Consumer Price Index rose from 131.2 to 132.1 during the second quarter of a year. What was the effective annualized rate of inflation during the quarter?
3. If the money supply increased from $331.12 billion to $333.81 billion in a single month, what were the simple and effective annualized rates of increase in the money supply during the month?
4. If the TSE 300 stock price index declined from 7155 to 7023 over a 50-day period, what were the simple and effective annualized rates of decline in the index during the period?

5. The Calgary Real Estate Board reports that house prices increased by 8% during the first seven months of the year. If prices continue to rise at the same rate for the subsequent five months, what will be the (compound) increase for the entire year?

6. A bank pays a simple interest rate of 6.7% pa on 30- to 179-day GICs of at least $100,000. What is the effective annualized rate of return:

a. On a 40-day GIC? **b.** On a 160-day GIC?

7. A T-bill with 125 days remaining to maturity is discounted to yield 4.6% pa simple interest. What is the effective annualized rate of return on the T-bill?

8. Neil's common stock portfolio increased in value over a two-month period from $78,900 to $84,300. What were the simple and effective annualized rates of total return over the period?

9. Danielle's shares in the Industrial Growth Fund (an equity mutual fund) dropped in price from $12.86 to $12.56 over a three-month period. What were the simple and effective annualized rates of return during the period?

10. If the holding-period return on a money market mutual fund for the most recent seven days is 0.111%, what current (simple) yield and effective annualized yield will be quoted for the fund in the financial press?

11. If the holding-period return on a money market mutual fund for the most recent seven days is 0.097%, what current (simple) and effective annualized yields will be quoted for the fund in the financial pages?

12. The current (simple annualized) yield on a money market mutual fund, based on the return for the most recent seven days, is 5.62%. What effective (annualized) yield will be reported for the fund?

13. The current (simple annualized) yield, based on the holding-period return for the most recent seven days, is reported for a money market mutual fund as 6.17%. What is the fund's corresponding effective (annualized) yield?

•14. The terms of payment on an invoice are 3/10, n/90. What are the simple and effective annualized rates of return earned by taking the cash discount on the last day of the discount period instead of paying the full price on the last day of the credit period?

•15. An income tax preparation service discounts income tax refunds at the statutory maximum amount of 15% on the first $300. For example, a taxpayer eligible for a $200 tax refund can sell the refund to the discounter for immediate payment of $170. What is the discounter's effective annualized rate of return if the time taken by Revenue Canada to process the tax return and refund the tax is

a. 25 days? **b.** 50 days?

(*Note:* With Revenue Canada's EFILE electronic tax return filing system, the turnaround time should be less than three weeks.)

Review Problems

Answers to the odd-numbered review problems are at the end of the book.

Calculate percentages accurate to the nearest 0.01%.

1. A sum of $10,000 invested in the Greenline Science and Technology Fund at the end of 1993 would have grown to $34,995 by the end of 1998. What compound annual rate of return did the fund realize during this period?
2. Maxine found an old pay statement from nine years ago. Her hourly wage at the time was $13.50 versus her current wage of $20.80 per hour. At what equivalent (compound) annual rate has her wage grown over the period?
3. If a company's annual sales grew from $165,000 to $485,000 in a period of eight years, what has been the compound annual rate of growth of sales during the period?
4. ◆ An investor's portfolio increased in value by 53% over a five-year period while the Consumer Price Index rose from 121.6 to 135.3. What was the annually compounded real rate of return on the portfolio for the five years?
5. ◆ A portfolio earned −13%, 18%, 5%, 24%, and −5% in five successive years. What was the portfolio's five-year compound annual return?
6. ◆ The MD U.S. Equity fund was the top-performing fund in Canada for the five years ending December 31, 1998. What three-year and five-year compound annual returns, to December 31, 1998, did the fund report if its annual returns in successive years from 1994 to 1998 inclusive were 2%, 31.6%, 20.5%, 42.4%, and 56.3%, respectively?
7. Terry was supposed to pay $800 to Becky on March 1. At a later date, Terry paid Becky an equivalent payment in the amount of $895.67. If they provided for a time value of money of 8% compounded monthly, when did Terry make the payment?
8. What is the time remaining until the maturity date of a $100,000 strip bond if it has just been purchased for $19,725.75 to yield 8.5% compounded semiannually until maturity?
9. ◆ When discounted to yield 9.5% compounded quarterly, a $4500 four-year promissory note bearing interest at 11.5% compounded semiannually was priced at $5697.84. How long after the issue date did the discounting take place?
10. ◆ The population of a mining town declined from 17,500 to 14,500 in a five-year period. If the population continues to decrease at the same compound annual rate, how long, to the nearest month, will it take for the population to drop by another 3000?
11. To the nearest day, how long will it take a $10,000 investment to grow to $12,000 if it earns 8% compounded semiannually? Assume that a half-year has 182 days.
12. What monthly compounded nominal rate would put you in the same financial position as 6.5% compounded quarterly?
13. You are offered a loan at a rate of 10.5% compounded monthly. What would a semiannually compounded nominal rate have to be to make it more attractive?
14. A bank offers a rate of 7% compounded semiannually on its four-year GICs. What monthly and annually compounded rates should it quote in order to have the same effective interest rate at all three nominal rates?
15. If an invoice indicates that interest at the rate of 1.5% per month will be charged on overdue amounts, what effective rate of interest will be charged?
16. If the nominal rate of interest paid on a savings account is 3% per annum paid monthly, what is the effective rate of interest paid?

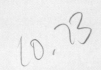

17. If an interest rate of 6.9% compounded semiannually is charged on a car loan, what effective rate of interest should be disclosed to the borrower?

18. If a $15,000 investment grew to $21,805 in $4\frac{1}{2}$ years of quarterly compounding, what effective rate of return was the investment earning?

19. Camille can obtain a residential mortgage loan from a bank at 8.75% compounded semiannually or from an independent mortgage broker at 8.6% compounded monthly. Which source should she pick if other terms and conditions of the loan are the same? Present calculations that support your answer.

Self-Test Exercise

Answers to the self-test problems are at the end of the book.

Calculate percentages accurate to the nearest 0.01%.

1. The home the Bensons purchased 13 years ago for $85,000 is now appraised at $215,000. What has been the annual rate of appreciation of the value of their home during the 13-year period?

2. If the Consumer Price Index rose from 109.6 to 133.8 over an $8\frac{1}{2}$-year period, what was the equivalent compound annual inflation rate during the period?

◆ **3.** A company's sales dropped 10% per year for five years.

a. What annual rate of sales growth for the subsequent five years would return the sales to the original level?

b. To the nearest month, how long would it take for sales to return to the original level if they increased at 10% per year?

◆ **4.** An investor's portfolio increased in value from $35,645 to $54,230 over a six-year period. At the same time, the Consumer Price Index rose by 26.5%. What was the portfolio's annually compounded real rate of return?

◆ **5.** One of the more volatile mutual funds in recent years has been the Fidelity Far East fund which invests primarily in common stocks of companies in southeast Asia. The fund's annual returns in successive years from 1992 to 1998 inclusive were 28.6%, 86.4%, −16.7%, 19.9%, 21.7%, −22.6%, and 7.9%, respectively. What was the fund's equivalent compound annual return for the seven years ended December 31, 1998?

6. To the nearest month, how long will it take an investment to increase in value by 150% if it earns 9% compounded quarterly?

◆ **7.** Rounded to the nearest month, how long will it take money to lose one-third of its purchasing power if the annual inflation rate is 3%?

◆ **8.** An investor paid $3658.46 to purchase a $10,000 face value strip bond for her RRSP. At this price the investment will provide a return of 7.67% compounded semiannually. How long (to the nearest day) after the date of purchase will the bond mature? Assume that each half-year is exactly 182 days long.

9. A trust company pays 5.375% compounded annually on its five-year GICs. What semiannually compounded nominal interest rate would have to be offered for investors to prefer it?

10. Which of the following rates would you prefer for a loan: 7.6% compounded quarterly, 7.5% compounded monthly, or 7.7% compounded semiannually?

11. A $6000 investment grew to $7900 after 33 months of semiannual compounding. What effective rate of return was the investment earning?

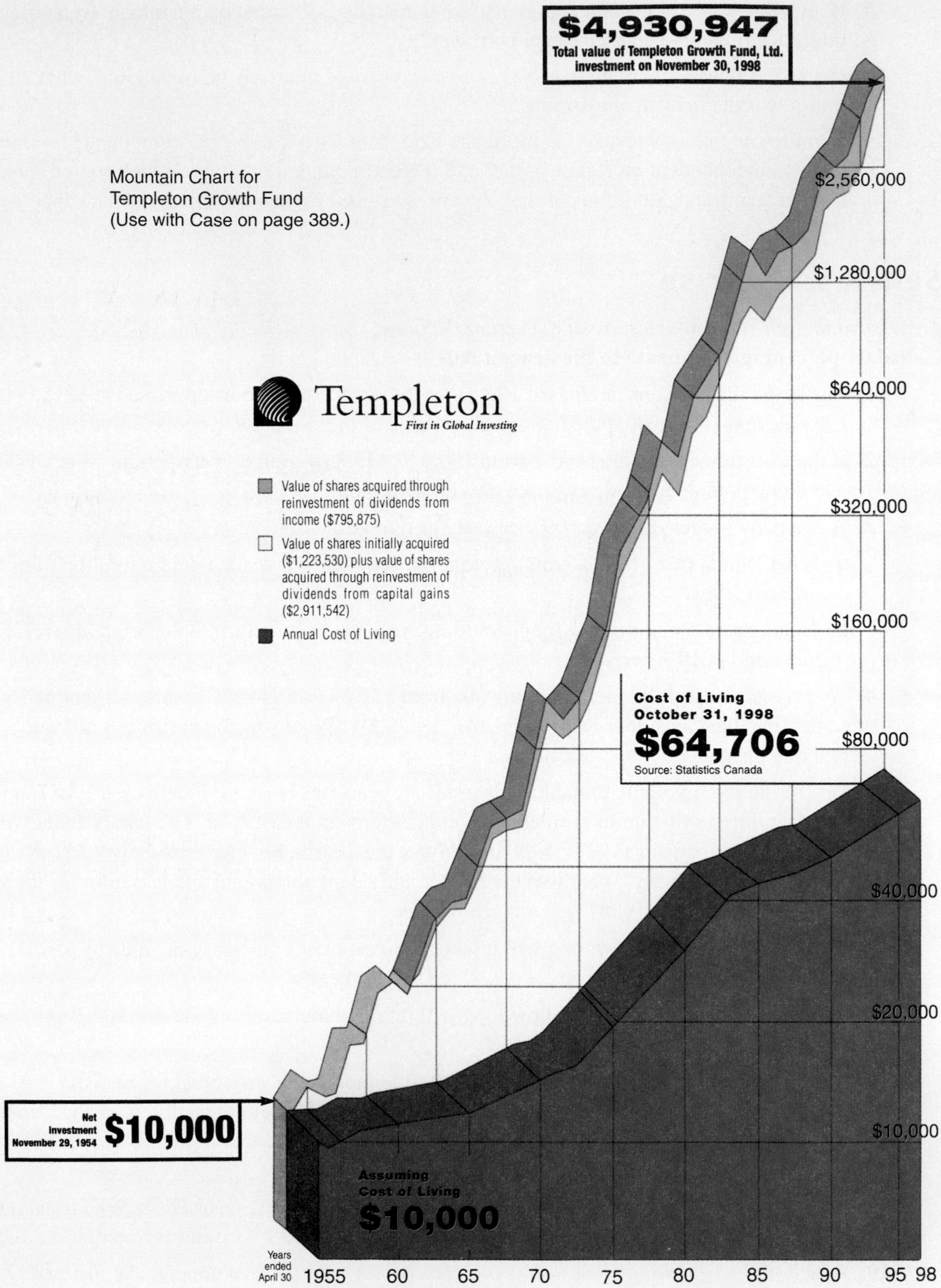

$4,930,947
Total value of Templeton Growth Fund, Ltd. investment on November 30, 1998
Mountain Chart for
Templeton Growth Fund
(Use with Case on page 389.)
Templeton
First in Global Investing
Value of shares acquired through reinvestment of dividends from income ($795,875)
Value of shares initially acquired ($1,223,530) plus value of shares acquired through reinvestment of dividends from capital gains ($2,911,542)
Annual Cost of Living
$2,560,000
$1,280,000
$640,000
$320,000
$160,000
$80,000
$40,000
$20,000
$10,000
Cost of Living
October 31, 1998
$64,706
Source: Statistics Canada
Net Investment November 29, 1954
$10,000
Assuming Cost of Living
$10,000
Years ended April 30
1955
60
65
70
75
80
85
90
95
98

Source: Reproduced with permission of Templeton Management Ltd.

CASE

MOUNTAINS OF MONEY

One of the oldest mutual funds in Canada is the Templeton Growth Fund, Ltd. Shares in the fund were first sold at the end of November 1954. A common graphic for dramatically illustrating the long-term performance of a mutual fund is known as a "mountain chart." The most recent version of the accompanying mountain chart for Templeton Growth may be seen on Templeton's Web site (*www.templeton.ca/TGFMountChart.html*). Note that the vertical scale is what is known as a logarithmic scale. With this scale, each doubling of the investment produces the same increment on the vertical scale.

The time axis covers 44 years (from November 29, 1954 to November 30, 1998). The chart indicates that an investment of $10,000 at the end of November 1954 was worth $4,930,947 on November 30, 1998. (This assumes that all dividends were reinvested in more shares of the fund.)

The chart also indicates, based on increases in the Consumer Price Index, that you needed $64,706 in November 1998 to have the same purchasing power as $10,000 in November 1954.

QUESTIONS

1. What was the fund's equivalent compound annual rate of return over the entire 44 years?
2. What was the equivalent compound annual rate of inflation during the entire period?
3. What was the fund's *real* compound annual rate of return over the entire period?
4. From the chart, you can estimate that the original investment was worth about $320,000 in November 1979. Compare the fund's performance before this date to its performance after this date. (That is, compare the fund's compound annual rates of return before and after November 1979.)

www.Exercise.com

1. SEARCHING A MUTUAL FUND DATABASE Go to the GLOBEfund Web site (www.globefund.com) and obtain the 10-year equivalent compound annual returns for the following Canadian Equity mutual funds: Bissett Canadian Equity, Industrial Growth, and Trimark Canadian. How much would $10,000 invested in each fund 10 years ago be worth today?

Summary of Notation and Key Formulas

f = Effective rate of interest

Formula (9-1) $i = \sqrt[n]{\frac{FV}{PV}} - 1 = \left(\frac{FV}{PV}\right)^{1/n} - 1$ Finding the periodic interest rate (or periodic rate of return)

Formula (9-2) $n = \frac{\ln\left(\frac{FV}{PV}\right)}{\ln(1+i)}$ Finding the number of compounding periods

Formula (9-3) $f = (1+i)^m - 1$ Finding the effective rate of interest (or effective rate of return)

Formula (9-4) $i_2 = (1+i_1)^{m_1/m_2} - 1$ Finding an equivalent periodic interest rate

List of Key Terms

Effective interest rate *(p. 367)* Equivalent interest rates *(p. 374)* Rule of 72 *(p. 362)*

CHAPTER OUTLINE	
	10.1 Terminology
	10.2 Future Value of an Ordinary Simple Annuity
	10.3 Present Value of an Ordinary Simple Annuity
	10.4 Deferred Annuities
	10.5 Ordinary General Annuities

LEARNING OBJECTIVES

After completing this chapter, you will be able to:

- Define and distinguish between ordinary simple annuities and ordinary general annuities
- Calculate the future value and present value of both ordinary simple annuities and ordinary general annuities
- Calculate the fair market value of a cash flow stream that includes an annuity
- Calculate the principal balance owed on a loan immediately after any payment
- Calculate the present value and period of deferral of a deferred annuity
- Calculate the interest rate per payment interval in a general annuity

10

Ordinary Annuities: Future Value and Present Value

A LARGE NUMBER OF PERSONAL and business transactions involve an annuity—a series of equal regular payments. Examples are loan payments, wages, pensions, rent, instalment savings plans, insurance premiums, mortgage payments, leases, bond interest, and preferred share dividends.

There is a variety of circumstances requiring the calculation of the future value or present value of an annuity. For example, how much (future value) will you accumulate after 20 years if you invest $100 per month? What is the balance (present value) you owe on a loan that has 23 remaining monthly payments of $227?

In this chapter, you will learn the language of annuities and how to answer these questions. This chapter is also the foundation we will build upon throughout Chapters 11 to 15. If you master the content of Chapter 10, you will be in an excellent position to comfortably handle later chapters.

10.1 Terminology

An **annuity** is a series of equal payments at regular intervals. We will use the symbols

$$PMT = \text{Amount of each payment in an annuity}$$
$$n = \text{Number of payments in the annuity}$$

In Figure 10.1, the n payments are shown on a time line. The time between successive payments in an annuity is called the **payment interval**. Chapters 10, 11, and 12 are concerned with **ordinary annuities** in which payments are made at the *end* of each payment interval.[1] The total time from the beginning of the first payment interval to the end of the last payment interval is the **term of the annuity**. To illustrate the use of these new terms, suppose you obtain a personal loan to be repaid by 48 equal monthly payments. The *payment interval* is one month and the *term of the annuity* is 48 months or four years. The first payment will be due one month after you receive the loan—that is, at the *end* of the first payment interval. Therefore, the payments form an *ordinary annuity.*

TRAP

"WHERE DO WE BEGIN?"

Don't confuse "the beginning of an annuity" with "the beginning of payments" or "the date of the first payment." The "beginning of an annuity" means "the beginning of the annuity's term" or "the beginning of the first payment interval." It occurs one payment interval *before* the first payment in an *ordinary* annuity.

Similarly, the *end of an annuity* refers to "the end of the annuity's term" or "the end of the last payment interval." It does coincide with the last payment in an ordinary annuity.

The following diagram presents the defining characteristics for two types of ordinary annuities. If the interest rate on the previously mentioned monthly-payment loan

Ordinary Annuities

Ordinary Simple Annuities:
The payment interval equals the compounding interval.

Ordinary General Annuities:
The payment interval differs from the compounding interval.

Figure 10.1 *Time Diagram for an n-Payment Ordinary Annuity*

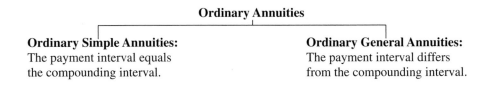

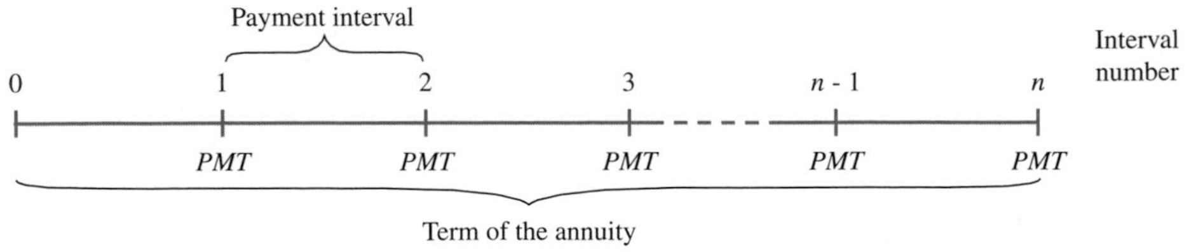

[1] Chapter 13 will cover annuities in which payments are made at the *beginning* of each payment interval.

is compounded monthly, then the payment interval (one month) equals the compounding interval (one month). Therefore, the payments form an ordinary *simple* annuity. But if the interest rate is compounded semiannually or compounded annually, the payments constitute an ordinary *general* annuity. In Sections 10.2, 10.3, and 10.4, we shall be concerned with ordinary simple annuities. Then in Section 10.5, we will learn the extra step needed to handle ordinary general annuities.

Concept Questions

1. What distinguishes an ordinary simple annuity from an ordinary general annuity?
2. What is meant by the "term" of an annuity?
3. If you pay automobile insurance premiums by monthly pre-authorized chequing, do the payments form an ordinary annuity?
4. If an ordinary annuity with quarterly payments and a $5\frac{1}{2}$-year term began June 1, 2000, what are the dates of the first and last payments?

10.2 Future Value of an Ordinary Simple Annuity

The **future value of an annuity** is the sum of the future values of all of the payments (evaluated at the end of the last payment interval). We will introduce the techniques for calculating an annuity's future value by considering a specific case.

Future Value Using the Algebraic Method

Figure 10.2 is a time diagram showing the investment of \$1000 at the *end* of every six months for two years. Suppose the invested money earns 8% compounded semiannually. Since we have semiannual payments and semiannual compounding, the four \$1000 payments form an ordinary *simple* annuity. The only way we can calculate the annuity's future value at this stage is to use $FV = PV(1 + i)^n$ to calculate the future value of each payment, one at a time. Then, as indicated in the time diagram, these future values should be added to obtain the future value of the annuity.

$$\begin{aligned} FV \text{ of annuity} &= \$1000 + \$1000(1.04) + \$1000(1.04)^2 + \$1000(1.04)^3 \\ &= \$1000 + \$1040 + \$1081.60 + \$1124.86 \\ &= \$4246.46 \end{aligned}$$

The investments, including earnings, will amount to \$4246.46 by the end of the annuity.

Figure 10.2 *The Future Value of a Four-Payment Ordinary Simple Annuity*

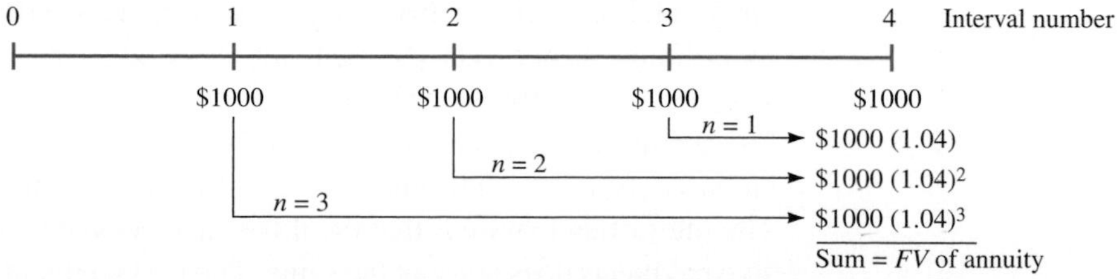

If an annuity consists of many payments, this "brute force" approach to the future value calculation can become very time-consuming and laborious. Fortunately, there is a relatively compact formula for the future value of an ordinary simple annuity.

FUTURE VALUE OF AN ORDINARY SIMPLE ANNUITY

(10-1) $$FV = PMT\left[\frac{(1+i)^n - 1}{i}\right]$$

Let us now use formula (10-1) to determine the future value of the annuity shown in Figure 10.2. We are given $PMT = \$1000$, $i = 4\% = 0.04$ per half year, and $n = 4$. Substituting these values into formula (10-1), we have

$$FV = \$1000\left[\frac{(1+0.04)^4 - 1}{0.04}\right] = \$1000\left(\frac{1.1698586 - 1}{0.04}\right) = \$4246.46$$

This is the same result obtained previously by the "brute force" approach. As the number of payments in an annuity increases, the time saved by employing formula (10-1) increases proportionately.

Future Value Using the Financial Calculator Functions

Save the known values for *n, i,* and *PMT* in the (n), (i), and (PMT) memories. Remember to obey the cash-flow sign convention for the dollar amount entered in (PMT). Zero should be entered in the (PV) memory. Then the (COMP) (FV) keystrokes instruct the calculator to compute the annuity's future value.

TIP *USE OF THE (PV) MEMORY WITH ANNUITIES*

If you do not have zero in the (PV) memory when you perform an annuity calculation, the calculator interprets the amount in (PV) as an *additional single* cash flow occurring at the *beginning* of the annuity. Then at the (COMP) (FV) command, the calculator will compute the *combined* future value of the annuity *and* the amount in (PV). This feature is useful in cases where, in a single calculation, we actually do want the combined future value of an annuity and an initial "lump" amount.

To calculate the future value of the annuity in Figure 10.2,

100 (+/−) (PMT) 4 (n) 4 (i) 0 (PV) (COMP) (FV) | 4246.46 |

Contribution of Each Payment to an Annuity's Future Value

When you use formula (10-1) or a calculator's financial functions to calculate an annuity's future value, the amount each payment contributes to the future value is not apparent. Figure 10.3 helps us see the pattern. Five \$10 investments are represented by columns at one-year payment intervals along the time axis. Assuming the investments earn 10% compounded annually, each payment's contribution to the \$61.05 future value is indicated at the right side of the diagram. It is no surprise that an early payment contributes more to future value than any subsequent payment. The interesting feature is that the difference between the contributions from successive payments does not stay the same. The first payment contributes \$1.33 more than

Figure 10.3 *Contribution of Each Payment to an Annuity's Future Value*

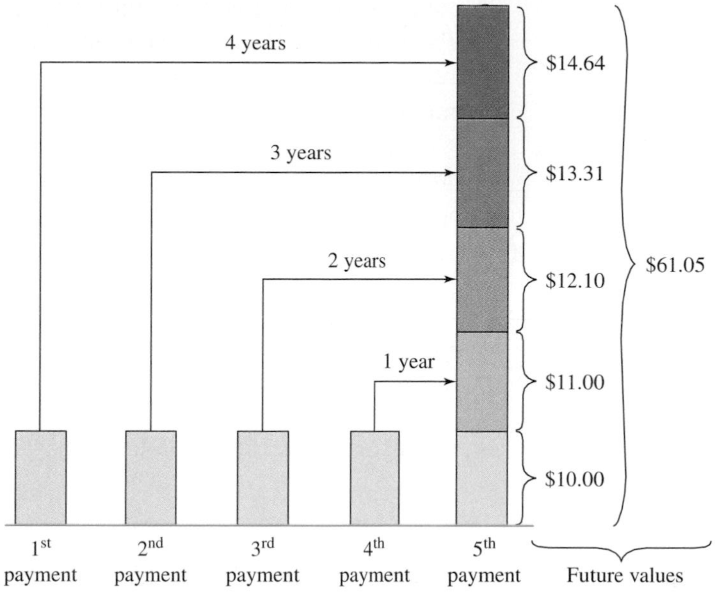

the second payment, the second payment contributes $1.21 more than the third payment, and so on. Putting it another way, each payment's contribution to future value increases in an *accelerating* manner as we look at earlier payments. This reinforces the point made in Chapter 8 concerning the advantages of starting a savings plan as early in life as possible. Consider the following remarkable illustration of the relative impact of earlier versus later payments. Suppose you construct Figure 10.3 to include 30 annual investments of $10.00. You would find that the first seven payments (in combination) contribute *more* to the future value than the remaining 23 payments (in combination)! Can you think how to verify this outcome?

Applications of the Future Value of an Annuity

Most applications of the future-value calculation fall into two categories (with the first being much more common):

- Determining the total amount of principal plus interest that will be accumulated at the end of a series of equal regular investments.
- Determining the single payment at the end of an annuity that is economically equivalent to the annuity. The interest rate that should be used in this case is the time value of money. (A suitable value is the rate of return currently available on Government of Canada bonds whose time remaining until maturity is similar to the term of the annuity.)

Example 10.2A *The Future Value of Regular Investments*

Heinz has been contributing $300 at the end of each month for the past 15 months to a savings plan that earns 6% compounded monthly. What amount will he have one year from now if he continues with the plan?

Solution

The total amount will be the future value of $n = 15 + 12 = 27$ contributions of $PMT = \$300$ each. Payments and compounding both occur at one-month intervals. Therefore, the payments form an ordinary simple annuity having $i = \frac{6\%}{12} = 0.5\%$ per month.

Algebraic Solution

$$FV = PMT\left[\frac{(1+i)^n - 1}{i}\right] = \$300\left[\frac{(1.005)^{27} - 1}{0.005}\right] = \$300\left[\frac{1.1441518 - 1}{0.005}\right] = \$8649.11$$

Financial Calculator Solution

300 (+/−) (PMT) 0 (PV) 27 (n) 0.5 (i) (COMP) (FV) | 8649.11 |

One year from now, Heinz will have \$8649.11 in the plan.

Example 10.2B Calculating the Future Value When the Interest Rate Changes During the Term of the Annuity

Calculate the future value of an ordinary annuity with payments of \$600 every six months for 16 years. The interest rate will be 8% compounded semiannually for the first $5\frac{1}{2}$ years and 9% compounded semiannually for the subsequent $10\frac{1}{2}$ years.

Solution

Because the compounding interval and the payment interval are both six months, we have an ordinary simple annuity with

$$i = \frac{8\%}{2} = 4\% \text{ for the first } 5\tfrac{1}{2} \text{ years and } i = \frac{9\%}{2} = 4.5\% \text{ for the subsequent } 10\tfrac{1}{2} \text{ years.}$$

Since the interest rate changes during the term of the annuity, we must consider the first $5\frac{1}{2}$ years separately from the subsequent $10\frac{1}{2}$ years. The algebraic solution has three steps indicated in the following time diagram.

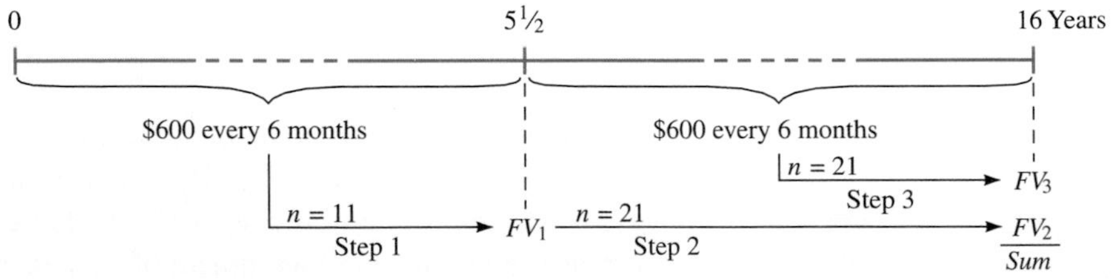

Algebraic Solution

Step 1: Calculate the future value, FV_1, of the first 11 payments.

$$FV_1 = PMT\left[\frac{(1+i)^n - 1}{i}\right] = \$600\left[\frac{(1.04)^{11} - 1}{0.04}\right] = \$600\left[\frac{1.539454 - 1}{0.04}\right] = \$8091.81$$

Step 2: Determine the future value, FV_2, of the Step 1 result an additional $10\frac{1}{2}$ years later.

$$FV_2 = \$8091.81(1.045)^{21} = \$8091.81(2.5202412) = \$20,393.32$$

Step 3: Calculate the future value, FV_3, of the last 21 annuity payments. Add FV_2 and FV_3.

$$FV_3 = \$600\left[\frac{(1.045)^{21}-1}{0.045}\right] = \$600\left[\frac{2.5202412 - 1}{0.045}\right] = \$20,269.88$$

$$FV_2 + FV_3 = \$40,663.20$$

The future value of the annuity is \$40,663.20.

Financial Calculator Solution

Step 1: Calculate the future value, FV_1, of the first 11 payments.

600 (+/-) (PMT) 0 (PV) 11 (n) 4 (i) (COMP) (FV) | 8091.81 |

Steps 2 & 3: The second and third steps may be combined because the calculator can compute the *combined* future value of an initial lump amount in (PV) and an annuity. The \$8091.81 future value after the first $5\frac{1}{2}$ years must be treated as an initial lump investment (cash outflow) at the beginning of the next $10\frac{1}{2}$ years. You need not re-enter \$8091.81 if, with \$8091.81 still in the display from Step 1, you press (+/-) (PV). This changes the sign of \$8091.81 and saves it in the (PV) memory as an initial lump investment.

(+/-) (PV) 21 (n) 4.5 (i) (COMP) (FV) | 40,663.20 |

The future value of the annuity is \$40,663.20.

Example 10.2C Calculating the Future Value after an Interruption of Payments

Mr. Cloutier, just turned 43, has already accumulated \$34,500 in his Registered Retirement Savings Plan. He makes monthly contributions of \$300 to the plan and intends to do so until age 60. He intends to retire then and cease further contributions. The RRSP will be allowed to continue to accumulate earnings until he reaches age 65. If the RRSP earns 8% compounded monthly for the next 22 years, what amount will his RRSP contain when he reaches age 65?

Solution

The amount in the RRSP will be the combined future value of the \$34,500 already accumulated and the future contributions. Mr. Cloutier will make 12(17) = 204 more \$300 contributions to his RRSP. The time diagram on the next page indicates the three steps in the algebraic solution. With the financial functions on a calculator, the solution may be reduced to two steps. For both approaches, $i = \frac{8\%}{12} = 0.\overline{6}\%$.

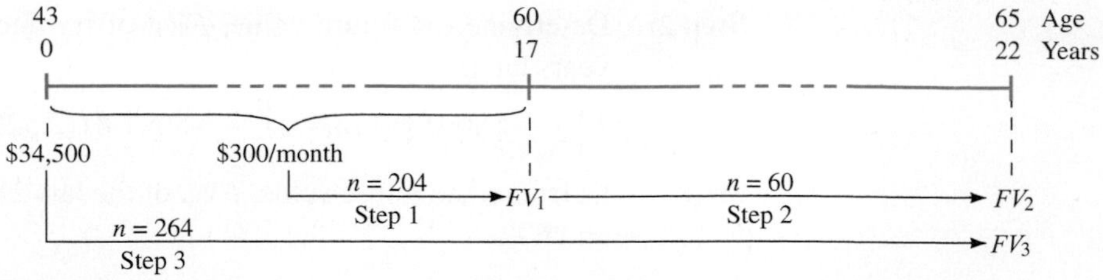

Algebraic Solution

Step 1: Calculate the future value at age 60 of the $300 per month annuity.

$$FV_1 = \$300\left[\frac{(1.00\overline{6})^{204} - 1}{0.00\overline{6}}\right] = \$300\left[\frac{3.87864829 - 1}{0.00\overline{6}}\right] = \$129{,}539.17$$

Step 2: Calculate the future value at age 65 of the Step 1 amount.

$$FV_2 = \$129{,}539.17(1.00\overline{6})^{60} = \$129{,}539.17(1.48984571) = \$192{,}933.38$$

Step 3: Calculate the future value at age 65 of the initial $34,500.

$$FV_3 = \$34{,}500(1.00\overline{6})^{264} = \$34{,}500(5.77858750) = \$199{,}361.27$$

The total amount in the RRSP when Mr. Cloutier reaches age 65 will be

$$FV_2 + FV_3 = \$192{,}993.38 + \$199{,}361.27 = \$392{,}354.65$$

Financial Calculator Solution

Steps 1 & 2: Compute the combined future value at age 60 of the initial $34,500 and the contribution annuity. The amount in the RRSP at age 60 will be:

34500 (+/−) (PV) 300 (+/−) (PMT) 0.666666667 (*i*) 204 (*n*)
(COMP) (FV) [263,352.54]

Step 3: Calculate the future value of the preceding amount an additional five years later:

(+/−) (PV) 0 (PMT) 60 (*n*) (COMP) (FV) [392,354.65]

The total amount in the RRSP when Mr. Cloutier reaches age 65 will be $392,354.65.

TIP *Improving the Accuracy of Algebraic Solutions*

To achieve accuracy to the penny (eight-figure accuracy) in the preceding algebraic solution, we should maintain at least nine significant figures in intermediate numbers. Consequently, if we use 0.006666667 (seven figures) as the value for *i*, the answer will have six-figure accuracy at best.[2]

Accuracy will be optimized if the value for *i* is obtained by dividing 0.08 by 12 instead of manually entering 0.006666667. Then the value used internally by the calculator will have at least two more figures than are shown in the display. If *i* will be needed elsewhere in the solution, save it in the calculator's memory for subsequent recall.

[2] The calculation of a power having a large exponent can have a *larger* rounding error than anticipated by our rule to keep one more figure than the number of figures required in the answer.

Example 10.2D *Comparing the Economic Values of Alternative Payment Streams*

You have received two offers on a residential building lot that you want to sell. Mr. Walcott has offered \$10,000 down plus \$5000 every three months for four years. Ms. Tang's offer is \$15,000 down and \$85,000 in a lump payment four years from now. Compare the economic values of the two offers if money can earn 8% compounded quarterly?

Solution

To make the comparison, you must first determine the equivalent value of each payment stream on the *same* focal date. Since you know how to calculate the future value of an ordinary simple annuity, the natural choice for the focal date is at the end of the annuity, four years from now. The solution strategy is indicated on the following diagram. For the annuity, $PMT = \$5000$, $n = 16$, and $i = \frac{8\%}{4} = 2\%$.

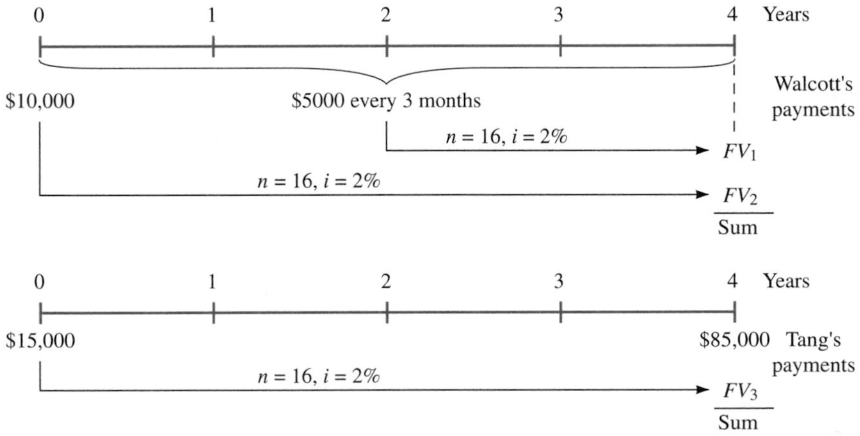

Algebraic Solution

Walcott offer:

$$FV_1 = \$10{,}000(1.02)^{16} = \$13{,}727.86$$

$$FV_2 = \$5000\left[\frac{(1.02)^{16} - 1}{0.02}\right] = \$5000\left[\frac{1.3727857 - 1}{0.02}\right] = \$93{,}196.43$$

$$FV_1 + FV_2 = \$13{,}727.86 + \$93{,}196.43 = \$106{,}924.29$$

The economic value, four years from now, of Mr. Walcott's offer is \$106,924.29.

Tang offer:

$$\$85{,}000 + FV_3 = \$85{,}000 + \$15{,}000(1.02)^{16} = \$105{,}591.79$$

The economic value, four years from now, of Ms. Tang's offer is \$105,591.79.

Hence, Mr. Walcott's offer is worth

$$\$106{,}924.29 - \$105{,}591.79 = \$1332.50 \text{ more}$$

(even though the nominal total of his payments is only \$90,000, compared to a total of \$100,000 for Ms. Tang's payments).

Financial Calculator Solution

Walcott offer:

$FV_1 + FV_2$: 10000 (PV) 5000 (PMT) 2 (i) 16 (n)

(COMP) (FV) $-106,924.28$

The economic value, four years from now, of Mr. Walcott's offer is \$106,924.28.

Tang offer:

FV_3: 15000 (PV) 0 (PMT) (COMP) (FV) $-20,591.79$

The economic value, four years from now, of Ms. Tang's offer is

$$\$85,000 + \$20,591.79 = \$105,591.79$$

Hence, Mr. Walcott's offer is worth

$$\$106,924.28 - \$105,591.79 = \$1332.49 \text{ more}$$

(even though the nominal total of his payments is only \$90,000 compared to a total of \$100,000 for Ms. Tang's payments).

POINT OF INTEREST

THE "MAGIC" OF COMPOUND INTEREST—THE SEQUEL

In Chapter 8, we mentioned the human tendency to underestimate long-term growth through compounding. The following type of illustration is often used to dramatically demonstrate the long-term payoff of earning an extra 1% or 2% return each year on your investment portfolio.

Bob and Rebecca have each contributed \$5000 to their RRSPs at the end of each year for the past 30 years. Bob's portfolio earned the equivalent of 10% compounded annually while Rebecca's earned 8% compounded annually. In estimating how much more Bob has in his RRSP than Rebecca has after 30 years, most people tend to think along the following line.

> *"Bob's rate of return was $\frac{2}{8} \times 100\% = 25\%$ higher than Rebecca's. Therefore, he has about 25% more growth than Rebecca. Compounding will make the difference higher—maybe another 5% or so."*

It turns out the difference in the growth of their portfolios is over 60%!

Questions

1. Calculate the amount in each portfolio after 30 years.
2. In percentage terms, how much more is Bob's portfolio worth?
3. It is more relevant to compare the growth of their investments. What are the dollar amounts of growth in each portfolio?
4. By what percentage does Bob's overall growth exceed Rebecca's growth?

Concept Questions

1. How would you determine how much of an annuity's future value is interest earned over the term of the annuity?
2. Annuity A has the same n and i as Annuity B. A's *PMT* is double B's *PMT.* Will A's future value be (pick one): (i) double, (ii) more than double, or (iii) less than double the amount of B's future value? Give the reason for your choice.
3. Annuity G has the same i and *PMT* as Annuity H. G has twice as many payments as H. Will G's future value be (pick one): (i) double, (ii) more than double, or (iii) less than double the amount of H's future value? Give the reason for your choice.

Exercise 10.2

Answers to the odd-numbered problems are at the end of the book.

Determine the future value of each of the ordinary annuities in Problems 1 through 8.

Problem	Periodic payment ($)	Payment interval	Term	Interest rate (%)	Compounding frequency
1.	500	1 year	13 years	11.5	Annually
2.	100	3 months	$5\frac{1}{2}$ years	10	Quarterly
3.	75	1 month	$2\frac{1}{2}$ years	8	Monthly
4.	2000	6 months	$12\frac{1}{2}$ years	7.5	Semiannually
5.	175	1 month	$8\frac{1}{4}$ years	11	Monthly
6.	700	1 quarter	7 years, 9 months	9	Quarterly
7.	3500	6 months	19 years	9.25	Semiannually
8.	435	1 month	6 years, 7 months	8.5	Monthly

9. What is the future value of a series of 10 annual payments of $300 starting in one year at 8% compounded annually? (Source: ICB course on Wealth Valuation.)
10. Mary and Steve Farmer plan to invest $2000 at the end of each year in an individual retirement account earning a rate of return of 10% compounded annually. What will be the value of the account in 12 years? (Source: CIFP course on Personal Financial Planning.)
11. Jeremy Griffen has systematically invested $3000 at the end of each year for the past 18 years. If his investments have earned 11.75% compounded annually, what is the value of his investments today? (Source: CIFP course on Personal Financial Planning.)

12. Tim and Laura plan to contribute $2000 at the end of every six months to an RRSP. What will be the value of the plan after 12 years if it earns 11.875% compounded semiannually? (Source: CIFP course on Personal Financial Planning.)

13. Josie spends $60 at the end of each month on cigarettes. If she stops smoking and invests the same amount in an investment plan paying 6% compounded monthly, how much will she have after five years?

14. Pascal has just agreed with his financial planner to begin a voluntary accumulation plan. He will invest $500 at the end of every three months in a balanced mutual fund. How much will the plan be worth after 20 years if the mutual fund earns:

a. 8% compounded quarterly? **b.** 10% compounded quarterly?

15. This problem demonstrates the dependence of the future value of an annuity on the number of payments. Suppose $1000 is invested at the end of each year. Assume the investments earn 10% compounded annually. Calculate the future value of the investments after each of the following numbers of payments:

a. 5 **b.** 10 **c.** 15 **d.** 20 **e.** 25 **f.** 30

Note that the future value increases proportionately more than n as n is increased.

16. This problem demonstrates the dependence of the future value of an annuity on the interest rate. Suppose $1000 is invested at the end of each year for 20 years. Calculate the future value if the investments earn an annually compounded rate of return of:

a. 9% **b.** 10% **c.** 11% **d.** 12%

Note that the future value increases proportionately more than the interest rate.

•17. Calculate and rank the economic values eight years from now of the following cash flow streams.

(i) A single payment of $5000 today.

(ii) An ordinary annuity starting today with eight annual payments of $910.

(iii) An ordinary annuity starting in three years with five annual payments of $1675.

Do the calculations and ranking for each of the following two cases:

a. Money can earn 8% compounded annually for the next eight years.

b. Money can earn 10% compounded annually for the next eight years.

18. Dave Bidini has saved $20,000 for a down payment on a home and plans to save another $5000 at the end of each year for the next five years. He expects to earn 7.25% compounded annually on his savings. How much will he have in five years' time? (Source: CIFP course on Personal Financial Planning.)

•19. Calculate the future value of an ordinary annuity consisting of quarterly payments of $1200 for five years, if the rate of interest is 10% compounded quarterly for the first two years, and 9% compounded quarterly for the last three years.

•20. Herb has made contributions of $2000 to his RRSP at the end of every six months for the past eight years. The plan has earned 9.5% compounded semiannually. He has just moved the funds to another plan, paying 8% compounded quarterly. He will now contribute $1500 at the end of every three months. What total amount will he have in the plan seven years from now?

•21. Marika has already accumulated $18,000 in her RRSP. If she contributes $2000 at the end of every six months for the next 10 years, and $300 per month for the subsequent five years, what amount will she have in her plan at the end of the 15 years? Assume that her plan will earn 9% compounded semiannually for the first 10 years, and 9% compounded monthly for the next five years.

•22. You work for a company that provides a pension plan for which the company contributes 50 percent of the amount you contribute. For example, if you specify that $1000 of your annual salary is to go into the plan, the company will add $500 to make the total contribution $1500 per year. The plan guarantees an annual interest rate of 6%. If you believe you can safely earn 8% per year by investing the money yourself, is it worthwhile belonging to the company plan? Assume that you plan to retire in 30 years and that you will set aside $1000 per year at the end of each of the next 30 years regardless of the plan you choose. (Source: ICB course on Wealth Valuation.)

The strong dependence of an annuity's future value on n (as demonstrated in Problem 15) means that it is important to start a savings plan as early as possible in order to accumulate a substantial retirement fund. Problems 23 to 26 reinforce this point in different ways.

23. How much more will you have in your RRSP 30 years from now if you start to contribute $1000 per year at the end of this year, instead of waiting five years to begin contributing $1000 at each year-end? Assume that the funds earn 8% compounded annually in the RRSP.

24. How much more will you have in your RRSP at age 65 if you begin annual $1000 contributions to your plan on your twenty-sixth birthday instead of on your twenty-seventh birthday? Assume that the RRSP earns 8% compounded annually, and that the last contribution is on your sixty-fifth birthday.

25. How much more will you have in your RRSP 30 years from now if you make fixed contributions of $3000 at the end of each of the next 30 years, instead of waiting 15 years and making annual contributions that are twice as large for half as many years? Assume that the RRSP earns 8% compounded annually.

•26. Leona contributed $3000 per year to her RRSP on every birthday from age 21 to age 30 inclusive. She stopped employment to raise a family and made no further contributions. Her husband, John, started to make annual contributions of $3000 to his RRSP on his thirty-first birthday and plans to continue up to and including his sixty-fifth birthday. Assuming that both of their plans earn 8% compounded annually over the years, calculate and compare the amounts in their RRSPs at age 65.

10.3 Present Value of an Ordinary Simple Annuity

The **present value of an annuity** is the sum of the present values of all of the payments (evaluated at the beginning of the first payment interval). To illustrate the techniques for calculating an annuity's present value, we will consider a specific case.

Present Value Using the Algebraic Method

Figure 10.4 shows an ordinary annuity consisting of four semiannual payments of \$1000. Suppose we want to find the present value of the annuity using a discount rate of 8% compounded semiannually. Since we have semiannual payments and semiannual compounding, the payments form an ordinary *simple* annuity. A "brute force" approach for determining the annuity's present value is shown in the diagram. In this approach, the present value of each payment is calculated using $PV = FV(1+i)^{-n}$. Then the four present values are added to obtain the present value of the annuity.

The present value of the annuity is

$$\begin{aligned} PV &= \$1000(1.04)^{-1} + \$1000(1.04)^{-2} + \$1000(1.04)^{-3} + \$1000(1.04)^{-4} \\ &= \$961.54 + \$924.56 + \$889.00 + \$854.80 \\ &= \$3629.90 \end{aligned}$$

As in the case of the future-value calculation, there is a formula that makes the present-value calculation more efficient.

PRESENT VALUE OF AN ORDINARY SIMPLE ANNUITY

(10-2)
$$PV = PMT\left[\frac{1-(1+i)^{-n}}{i}\right]$$

Substitute $PMT = \$1000$, $n = 4$, and $i = 0.04$ into formula (10-2) to obtain the present value of the preceding four-payment annuity.

$$\begin{aligned} PV &= \$1000\left[\frac{1-(1+0.04)^{-4}}{0.04}\right] \\ &= \$1000\left(\frac{1-0.8548042}{0.04}\right) \\ &= \$3629.90 \end{aligned}$$

Figure 10.4 *The Present Value of a Four-Payment Ordinary Simple Annuity*

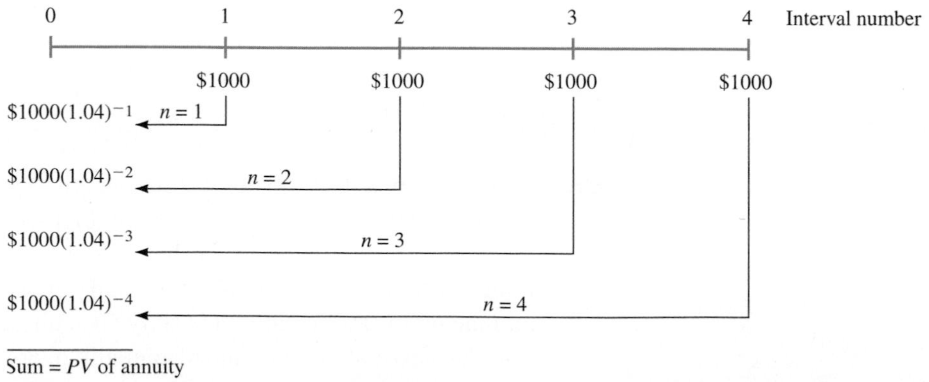

This is the same result as previously obtained by the "brute force" approach. As the number of payments in an annuity increases, the time saved by employing formula (10-2) increases proportionately.

Present Value Using the Financial Calculator Functions

Save the known values for *n, i,* and *PMT* in the (*n*), (*i*), and (PMT) memories. Remember to obey the cash-flow sign convention for the dollar amount entered in (PMT). Zero should be entered in the (FV) memory. Then the (COMP) (PV) keystrokes instruct the calculator to compute the annuity's future value.

TIP *Use of the (FV) Memory with Annuities*

If you do not have zero in the (FV) memory when you perform an annuity calculation, the calculator interprets the amount in (FV) as an *additional single* cash flow occurring at the *end* of the annuity. Then at the (COMP) (PV) command, the calculator will compute the *combined* present value of the annuity *and* the amount in (FV). This feature is useful in cases where, in a single calculation, we actually do want the combined present value of an annuity and a terminal "lump" amount.

To calculate the present value of the annuity in Figure 10.4,

1000 (PMT) 4 (*n*) 4 (*i*) 0 (FV) (COMP) (PV) [−3629.90]

Comment Regarding the Signs of the Cash Flows It is not clear from the given information whether the $1000 payments are cash inflows or outflows. In that case, arbitrarily pick a sign. When we entered 1000 into (PMT) as a *positive* number, we told the calculator that the payments are cash *inflows*. In its narrow view of the world, the calculator thinks that the inflows must come from a series of four $1000 loans. When it computes the future value, it calculates the single amount including interest needed to repay the four loans. Therefore, the future value is displayed as a negative number (cash outflow).

Example 10.3A *The Present Value of an Ordinary Simple Annuity*

Determine the present value of $500 paid at the end of each calendar quarter for $6\frac{1}{2}$ years. Use a discount rate of 6% compounded quarterly.

Solution

Given: $PMT = \$500$, Term $= 6\frac{1}{2}$ years, $j = 6\%$ compounded quarterly
Therefore,

$$i = \frac{6\%}{4} = 1.5\% \qquad \text{and} \qquad n = 4(6.5) = 26$$

Algebraic Solution

$$
\begin{aligned}
PV &= PMT\left[\frac{1-(1+i)^{-n}}{i}\right] \\
&= \$500\left[\frac{1-(1.015)^{-26}}{0.015}\right] \\
&= \$500\left(\frac{1-0.67902052}{0.015}\right) \\
&= \$500(21.398632) \\
&= \$10{,}699.32
\end{aligned}
$$

Financial Calculator Solution

We do not know whether the payments are cash inflows or outflows. Let us assume they are inflows.

500 (PMT) 0 (FV) 1.5 (i) 26 (n) (COMP) (PV) | −10,699.32 |

The present value of the annuity is \$10,699.32.

Contribution of Each Payment to an Annuity's Present Value

When you use formula (10-2) or a calculator's financial functions to calculate an annuity's present value, the amount each payment contributes to the present value is not apparent. Figure 10.5 helps us see the pattern. Five \$10 payments are represented by columns at one-year intervals along the time axis. Using a discount rate of 10% compounded annually, each payment's contribution to the \$37.91 present value is indicated at the left side of the diagram. Not surprisingly, each successive payment contributes a smaller amount to the present value. But notice that the *difference* between the contributions from two successive payments gets smaller as you look at later payments. For example, the second payment contributes \$0.83 less than the first payment, the third payment contributes \$0.75 less than the second payment, and so on. Eventually, distant payments contribute an insignificant amount to the present value. As an indication, suppose the annuity in Figure 10.5 is extended to 30 years. The total present value is \$94.27, to which the thirtieth payment contributes only \$0.57 (0.6%). If a further 20 payments are added (in Years 31 to 50), they will add only \$4.88 or 5.2% to the present value.

Applications of the Present Value of an Annuity

There are more applications of the present-value calculation than of the future-value calculation. Fundamentally, all present value applications are some form of *valuation*—placing a price tag on the "package" of annuity payments that are about to start. Three categories of applications are discussed in this section. A key issue in each category is how to choose the discount rate for the present-value calculation.

The Market Value of an Annuity Clearly, the right to receive a series of future payments has value today. The *market* value of an annuity is the price at which it could

Figure 10.5 *Contribution of Each Payment to an Annuity's Present Value*

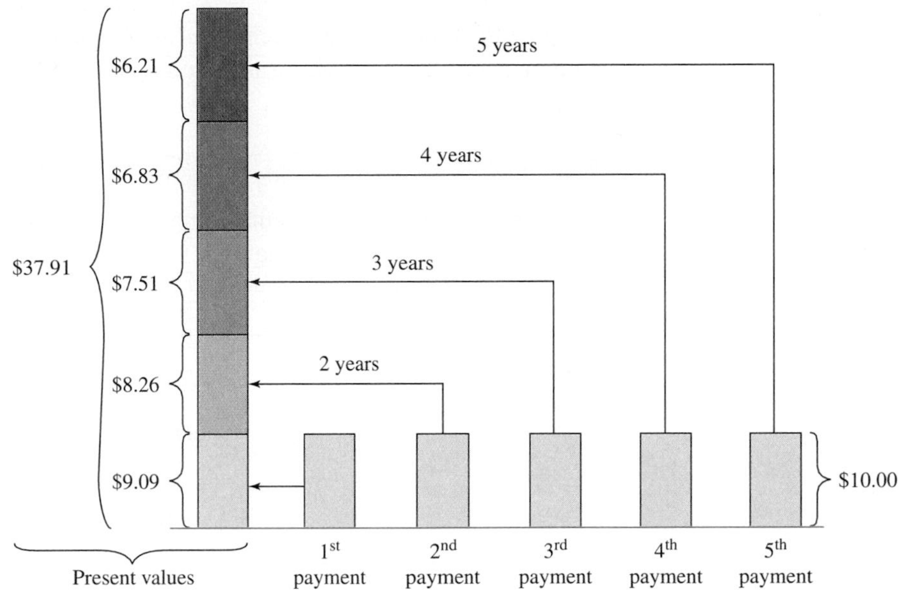

CAUGHT IN THE WEB

Most annuities are now sold to retirees who use money accumulated in their RRSPs to purchase Registered Retirement Income Funds (RRIFs) providing a steady stream of income.

You can find current rates of return paid on RRIFs at a few Web sites. Rates may be quoted for annuity terms of up to 25 years. Two examples are www.londonlife.com/irp/rates/RRIF_r_e.asp and www.canoe.ca/MoneyRates/rrifs10.html

be bought or sold among investors who are fully aware of investment alternatives. We look to the Valuation Principle (Section 7.2) for guidance in calculating the fair market value of any series of cash flows. It instructs us to calculate the present value of the cash flows, discounting them at the prevailing market rate of return (on investments of similar risk and duration). That is,

$$\begin{matrix}\text{Fair market value} \\ \text{of an annuity}\end{matrix} = \begin{matrix}\text{Present value of the annuity payments} \\ \text{(discounted at the } \textit{market rate of return}\text{)}\end{matrix}$$

Current market rates offered by insurance companies to purchasers of annuities are periodically reported in the major financial papers. Alternatively, market rates on annuities of various terms may be obtained from annuity brokers.

The present-value calculation also allows you to estimate the amount you must accumulate by the time you retire in order to purchase, for example, a 25-year annuity paying $3000 per month. (You would have to make an assumption about the market rate of return at time of the annuity purchase.)

The cash flows from some investments include an annuity component. For example, some types of bonds pay a fixed dollar amount of interest every six months until the face value of the bond is repaid at maturity. Some preferred shares pay fixed quarterly dividends until the "par value" of the share is repaid on the redemption date. These two types of investments may be bought or sold in the financial markets. Consequently, valuation at *prevailing market* rates of return is important on a day-by-day basis. The fair market value is the present value of *all* remaining payments. The annuity *component* can be valued separately and added to the present value of the *other* expected payments.

Example 10.3B *Calculating the Purchase Price of an Annuity*

Suppose the funds used to purchase an annuity earn 6% compounded monthly. What amount is needed to purchase an annuity paying $1000 at the end of each month for 20 years?

Solution

The annuity is an ordinary simple annuity with $PMT = \$1000$ and $n = 12(20) = 240$ payments. The amount required to purchase the annuity is the present value of the payments discounted at $i = \frac{6\%}{12} = 0.5\%$ per month.

Algebraic Solution

$$
\begin{aligned}
PV &= PMT\left[\frac{1-(1+i)^{-n}}{i}\right] \\
&= \$1000\left[\frac{1-(1.005)^{-240}}{0.005}\right] \\
&= \$1000\left(\frac{1-0.30209614}{0.005}\right) \\
&= \$139{,}580.77
\end{aligned}
$$

Financial Calculator Solution

1000 (PMT) 0 (FV) 240 (n) 0.5 (i) (COMP) (PV) [−139,580.77]

The purchase price of the annuity is $139,580.77.

Example 10.3C *The Present Value of an Annuity and a Terminal Lump Payment*

A certain investment will pay $50 at the end of every six months for 17 years. At the end of the 17 years, the investment will pay an additional $1000 along with the last regular $50 payment. What is the fair market value of the investment if the prevailing rate of return on similar investments is 8.5% compounded semiannually?

Solution

The fair market value of the investment is the present value of *all* of the payments discounted at the prevailing rate of return. The semiannual payments form an ordinary simple annuity having

$$PMT = \$50 \qquad n = 2(17) = 34 \text{ payments} \qquad i = \frac{8.5\%}{2} = 4.25\%$$

Algebraic Solution

The combined present value of the annuity and the terminal lump payment is

$$PV = \underbrace{PMT\left[\frac{1-(1+i)^{-n}}{i}\right]}_{\text{Formula (10-2)}} + \underbrace{FV(1+i)^{-n}}_{\text{Formula (8-2)}}$$

$$= \$50\left[\frac{1-(1.0425^{-34})}{0.0425}\right] + \$1000(1.0425)^{-34}$$

$$= \$50\left(\frac{1-0.2428923}{0.0425}\right) + \$1000(0.2428923)$$

$$= \$890.715 + \$242.892$$

$$= \$1133.61$$

Financial Calculator Solution

The financial calculator can simultaneously calculate the combined present value of an annuity and a lump payment occurring at the end of the annuity.

50 (PMT) 1000 (FV) 4.25 (*i*) 34 (*n*) (COMP) (PV) | −1133.61 |

The fair market value of the investment is $1133.61.

Example 10.3D *The Present Value of Two Annuities in Series*

How much will it cost to purchase a two-level retirement annuity that will pay $2000 at the end of each month for the first 10 years, and $3000 per month for the next 15 years? Assume that the payments represent a rate of return to the annuitant (the person receiving the payments) of 7.5% compounded monthly.

Solution

The purchase price will be the present value of all of the payments. Since we have month-end payments and monthly compounding, the payments form two ordinary simple annuities in sequence. The given information and a three-step solution strategy are presented in the time diagram.

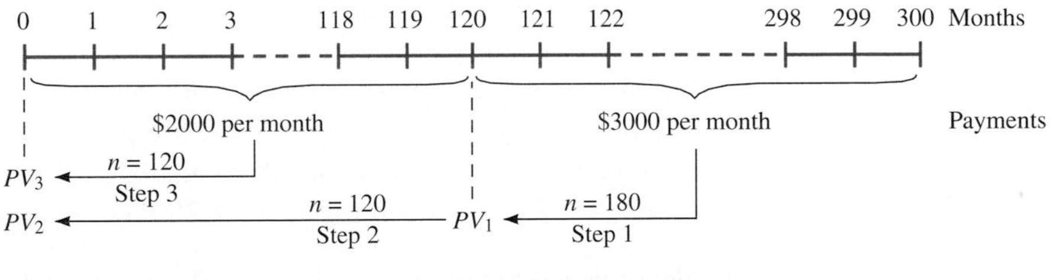

Algebraic Solution

Step 1: Calculate the present value, PV_1, of the $3000 annuity at its beginning.

$$PV_1 = PMT\left[\frac{1-(1+i)^{-n}}{i}\right] = \$3000\left(\frac{1-1.00625^{-180}}{0.00625}\right) = \$323{,}620.28$$

Step 2: Calculate the present value, PV_2, of the Step 1 result at time 0.

$$PV_2 = FV(1+i)^{-n} = \$323{,}620.28(1.00625)^{-120} = \$153{,}224.61$$

Step 3: Calculate the present value, PV_3, of the \$2000 annuity at time 0. The total present value will be $PV_2 + PV_3$.

$$PV_3 = \$2000\left[\frac{1-(1.00625)^{-120}}{0.00625}\right] = \$168{,}489.49$$

The purchase price of the two-level retirement annuity will be

$$PV_2 + PV_3 = \$321{,}714.10$$

Financial Calculator Solution

Step 1: Calculate the present value, PV_1, of the \$3000 annuity at its beginning.

3000 (PMT) 0 (FV) 180 (n) 0.625 (i) (COMP) (PV) | −323,620.28 |

Steps 2 and 3 may be combined. The Step 1 result must be included as a terminal cash *inflow*. The following keystrokes assume that the Step 1 result is still in the display as you begin.

(+/−) (FV) 2000 (PMT) 120 (n) (COMP) (PV) | −321,714.10 |

The purchase price of the two-level retirement annuity will be \$321,714.10.

Example 10.3E *Pricing an Annuity to Provide a Required Rate of Return*

Crazy Ed's Furniture Mart is holding a "nothing-down-and-no-interest-to-pay" promotion on purchases exceeding \$1000. Customers can pay six equal month-end payments with no interest charged. On such instalment sales, the customer signs a conditional sale contract.[3] Crazy Ed's immediately sells the conditional sale contract to Consumers Finance Company. The finance company purchases the contract at a discounted price that builds in a rate of return (on the purchase price) of 15% compounded monthly. What will Consumers Finance pay for a \$1200 contract (consisting of six payments of \$200)?

Solution

The six instalment payments form an ordinary simple annuity. To build the required rate of return into the purchase price, the payments must be discounted at the required rate of return. So we need to calculate the present value of $n = 6$ payments of $PMT = \$200$, discounting at $i = 1.25\%$ per month.

Algebraic Solution

$$PV = PMT\left[\frac{1-(1+i)^{-n}}{i}\right] = \$200[\frac{1-(1+0.0125)^{-6}}{0.0125}] = \$1149.20$$

[3] It is common for furniture retailers to sell such conditional sale contracts to a finance company. The retailer gets immediate cash and avoids having to set up a credit department.

Financial Calculator Solution

200 (PMT) 0 (FV) 6 (n) 1.25 (i) (COMP) (PV) | −1149.20 |

The finance company paid \$1149.20 for the contract.

Loan Balance and Market Value of a Loan Contract In Section 8.3, we established the general principle that

$$\text{Original loan} = \begin{bmatrix}\text{Present value of all of the payments} \\ \text{(discounted at the } \textit{contractual} \\ \textit{rate of interest on the loan}\text{)}\end{bmatrix}$$

Furthermore, the balance owed on a loan at any point is

$$\text{Principal balance} = \begin{bmatrix}\text{Present value of the remaining payments} \\ \text{(discounted at the } \textit{contractual} \\ \textit{rate of interest on the loan}\text{)}\end{bmatrix}$$

Both principles apply to any pattern of loan payments. However, most loans require equal periodic payments. In these cases, we use formula (10-2) for the present value calculation.

Most loan contracts permit the lender to sell the contract to another investor at any time during the term of the loan. The investor/buyer is then entitled to receive subsequent loan payments from the borrower. To determine a price for the loan contract, the buyer and seller first agree upon the rate of return the buyer should earn. (Current interest rates offered by financial institutions on new loans provide a reference point for negotiating the buyer's rate of return.) Then this rate of return is "built in" or "locked in" by using it as the discount rate for calculating the present value of the remaining loan payments.

$$\text{Selling price of a loan contract} = \begin{matrix}\text{Present value of the remaining payments} \\ \text{(discounted at the } \textit{negotiated rate of return}\text{)}\end{matrix}$$

Example 10.3F *Calculating the Original Loan and a Subsequent Balance*

The required monthly payment on a five-year loan bearing interest at 9% compounded monthly is \$249.10.

a. What was the original principal amount of the loan?

b. What is the balance owed just after the seventeenth payment?

Solution

The loan payments form an ordinary simple annuity having $PMT = \$249.10$, $n = 12(5) = 60$, and $i = \frac{9\%}{12} = 0.75\%$ per month. Applying the first two principles discussed in this section, we can write

a. Original principal = Present value of all 60 payments

b. Balance after 17 payments = Present value of the remaining 43 payments

Algebraic Solution

a. Original principal

$$= \$249.10\left(\frac{1 - 1.0075^{-60}}{0.0075}\right)$$

$$= \$249.10\left(\frac{1 - 0.63869970}{0.0075}\right)$$

$$= \$11{,}999.99$$

b. Balance

$$= \$249.10\left(\frac{1 - 1.0075^{-43}}{0.0075}\right)$$

$$= \$249.10\left(\frac{1 - 0.72520810}{0.0075}\right)$$

$$= \$9126.76$$

The original loan was \$12,000 and the balance after 17 payments is \$9126.76.

Financial Calculator Solution

Taking the borrower's point of view for the sign convention,

a: 249.10 (+/−) (PMT) 60 (n) 0.75 (i) 0 (FV) (COMP) (PV) [11,999.99]

b: 43 (n) (COMP) (PV) [9126.76]

The original loan was \$12,000 and the balance after 17 payments is \$9126.76.

Example 10.3G Calculating the Selling Price of a Loan Contract

Suppose the original lender in Example 10.3F wishes to sell the loan just after the seventeenth payment. What is the selling price if the negotiated rate of return to the buyer is to be:

a. 7.5% compounded monthly?

b. 9% compounded monthly (the same as the interest rate on the loan)?

c. 10.5% compounded monthly?

Solution

In each case,

Selling price = Present value of the remaining 43 payments (discounted at the negotiated rate of return)

The periodic rates are

a. $i = \frac{7.5\%}{12} = 0.625\%$ **b.** $i = \frac{9\%}{12} = 0.75\%$ **c.** $i = \frac{10.5\%}{12} = 0.875\%$

Algebraic Solution

a. Selling price $= \$249.10\left(\frac{1 - 1.00625^{-43}}{0.00625}\right) = \$9367.20$

b. Selling price $= \$249.10\left(\frac{1 - 1.0075^{-43}}{0.0075}\right) = \$9126.76$

c. Selling price $= \$249.10\left(\frac{1 - 1.00875^{-43}}{0.00875}\right) = \$8894.86$

Financial Calculator Solution

Taking the buyer's point of view for the sign convention, the purchase price is:

a: 249.10 (PMT) 43 (n) 0.625 (i) 0 (FV) (COMP) (PV) [−9367.20]

b: 0.75 (i) (COMP) (PV) [−9126.76]

c: 0.875 (i) (COMP) (PV) [−8894.86]

The answers are negative because the buyer must pay *out* the purchase price.

Postscript: Note that the answer in part (b) equals the actual loan balance (which we calculated in part (b) of Example 10.3F). The current Example 10.3G illustrates three scenarios summarized below.

Part	Rate of return vs. Interest rate on loan	Selling price vs. Balance on loan
a.	Rate of return < Interest rate on loan	Selling price > Balance on loan
b.	Rate of return = Interest rate on loan	Selling price = Balance on loan
c.	Rate of return > Interest rate on loan	Selling price < Balance on loan

Expressing the same relationships in another way,

- If the price you pay to purchase a loan is *equal* to the balance on the loan, the rate of return on your investment will be the *same* as the interest rate on the loan.
- Consequently, if you pay *more* than the loan balance, your rate of return will be *less* than the interest rate on the loan.
- Conversely, if you pay *less* than the loan balance, your rate of return will be *more* than the interest rate on the loan.

The Economic Value of an Annuity The *economic* value of a payment stream on a particular date (focal date) refers to a *single* amount that is an economic substitute for the payment stream. You will end up in the same financial position if you accept the economic value (on its focal date) instead of the scheduled payment stream.

The economic value of an annuity at the beginning of the annuity is just its present value (using the time value of money as the discount rate). A suitable value for the time value of money is the rate of return currently available on Government of Canada bonds (whose time until maturity is similar to the term of the annuity).

Example 10.3H *Comparing the Economic Values of Two Annuities*

An eligible individual may elect to start collecting the Canada Pension Plan monthly retirement pension at any time between the ages of 60 and 65. The payments are then reduced by 0.5% for each month the pension is collected before age 65. For example, if the pension starts at age 60, the monthly payment will be decreased by (60 months) × (0.5%) = 30%. The reduction is permanent, extending to payments after age 65 as well.

The average life expectancy of a woman aged 60 is another 22 years. If a woman aged 60 lives just the expected 22 years, compare the economic values at age 60 of the following two alternatives:

- Collect a 100% pension from age 65.
- Collect a 70% pension from age 60.

Assume that money is worth 6% compounded monthly.

Solution

The economic value of a stream of pension payments at age 60 will be the present value of the payments discounted at $i = \frac{6\%}{12} = 0.5\%$ per month.

The alternative retirement annuities are illustrated in the following time diagrams. x represents the full (100%) monthly pension payment commencing at age 65. Therefore, $0.70x$ is the monthly payment on a reduced (70%) pension starting at age 60. In the first diagram, PV_1 represents the present value at age 60 of the reduced pension payments.

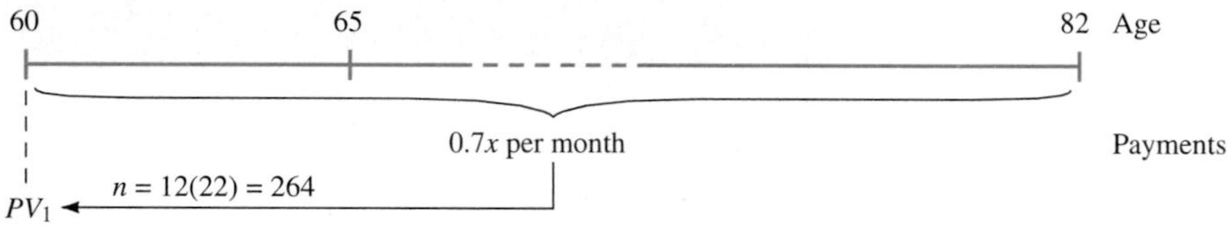

In the next diagram, PV_2 is the present value at age 65 of the full pension payments. PV_3 is the present value at age 60 of PV_2.

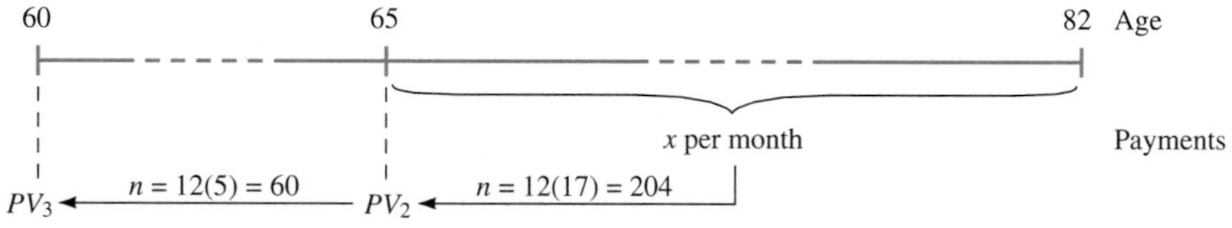

Algebraic Solution

$$PV_1 = PMT\left[\frac{1-(1+i)^{-n}}{i}\right] = 0.7x\left(\frac{1-1.005^{-264}}{0.005}\right) = 102.48x$$

$$PV_2 = x\left[\frac{1-(1.005)^{-204}}{0.005}\right] = 127.70x$$

$$PV_3 = FV(1+i)^{-n} = 127.70x(1.005)^{-60} = 94.67x$$

The economic value at age 60 of the early pension option is $102.48x$. The economic value, also at age 60, of the full pension option is $94.67x$. Based on our assumptions for life expectancy and the time value of money, the early pension option is worth

$$\frac{102.48x - 94.67x}{94.67x} \times 100\% = 8.25\%$$

more than the age 65 option.

Financial Calculator Solution

PV_1: 0.7 (PMT) 0 (FV) 264 (n) 0.5 (i) (COMP) (PV) | −102.48 |

PV_2: 1 (PMT) 204 (n) (COMP) (PV) | −127.70 |

PV_3: (+/−) (FV) 0 (PMT) 60 (n) (COMP) (PV) | −94.67 |

The economic value at age 60 of the early pension option is $102.48x$. The economic value, also at age 60, of the full pension option is $94.67x$. Based on our assumptions for life expectancy and the time value of money, the early pension option is worth

$$\frac{102.48x - 94.67x}{94.67x} \times 100\% = 8.25\%$$

more than the age 65 option.

POINT OF INTEREST

THE "MAGIC" OF COMPOUND INTEREST—IN REVERSE!

No doubt you have seen it on TV—a Publishers Clearing House Prize Patrol van pulls up to a neat little bungalow in suburbia. Then with all cameras rolling, the guy in the expensive suit knocks on the door, waits for the occupant to appear, and then bellows something about "winner of the Publishers Clearing House $1,000,000 SuperPrize." The winner goes through the usual denial–shock–bananas stages, and is finally shown being presented with a billboard-size certificate with $1,000,000 appearing in huge letters.

However, there's a little detail we do not pick up from the TV commercial—the winner does not receive a *cash* prize of $1,000,000. The Official Rules of the Sweepstakes provide that the winner of a $1 million SuperPrize "will receive $50,000 in the first year, $25,000 per year thereafter, plus a final payment of $500,000 in the 20th year." So $1 million is just the nominal sum of $50,000, 18 payments of $25,000, and $500,000.

Questions

Assume that all payments are made at the end of each year and the time value of money is 7% compounded annually.

1. On the date of winning the prize, what is the economic value of the last payment?
2. What is the economic value of the entire prize?
3. Repeat Questions 1 and 2 using 8% compounded annually as the time value of money. The changes from the previous answers provide an indication of how sensitive the economic value calculations are to the rate used for the time value of money.

Concept Questions

1. Annuity A has the same n and i as Annuity B. A's *PMT* is double B's *PMT*. Will A's present value be (pick one): (i) double, (ii) more than double, or (iii) less than double the amount of B's present value? Give the reason for your choice.
2. Suppose the discount rate used to calculate the present value of an annuity is increased (leaving n and *PMT* unchanged). Will the annuity's present value be (pick one): (i) larger or (ii) smaller than before? Give the reason for your choice.
3. Annuity G has the same i and *PMT* as Annuity H. G has twice as many payments as H. Is G's present value (pick one): (i) double, (ii) more than double, or (iii) less than double the amount of H's present value? Give the reason for your choice.
4. Is the economic value of an annuity (at its beginning) higher if the time value of money is larger? Explain.
5. Think of a 20-year annuity paying \$2000 per month. If prevailing market rates decline over the next year, will the price to purchase a 20-year annuity increase or decrease? Explain.

Exercise 10.3

Answers to the odd-numbered problems are at the end of the book.

Determine the present value of each of the ordinary annuities in Problems 1 through 8.

Problem	Periodic payment (\$)	Payment interval	Term	Discount rate (%)	Compounding frequency
1.	500	1 year	13 years	11.5	Annually
2.	100	3 months	$5\frac{1}{2}$ years	10	Quarterly
3.	75	1 month	$2\frac{1}{2}$ years	8	Monthly
4.	2000	6 months	$12\frac{1}{2}$ years	7.5	Semiannually
5.	175	1 month	$8\frac{1}{4}$ years	11	Monthly
6.	700	1 quarter	7 years, 9 months	9	Quarterly
7.	1240	6 months	$9\frac{1}{2}$ years	9.9	Semiannually
8.	350	1 month	11 years, 5 months	8.75	Monthly

9. What is the present value of end-of-quarter payments of \$1000 for four years? Use a discount rate (interest rate) of 6% compounded quarterly.
10. Determine the present value of payments of \$100 at the end of each month for 20 years. Use a discount rate (interest rate) of 6% compounded monthly.
11. This problem demonstrates the dependence of the present value of an annuity on the number of payments. Using 10% compounded annually as

the discount rate, calculate the present value of an ordinary annuity paying \$1000 per year for:

a. 5 years **b.** 10 years **c.** 20 years

d. 30 years **e.** 100 years **f.** 1000 years

Observe that the present value increases with increasing *n*, but at a diminishing rate. In this case, the 970 payments from Year 30 to Year 1000 cause the present value to increase by only about 6%.

12. This problem demonstrates the dependence of the present value of an annuity on the discount rate. For an ordinary annuity consisting of 20 annual payments of \$1000, calculate the present value using an annually compounded discount rate of:

a. 5% **b.** 10% **c.** 11% **d.** 15%

Observe that the present value decreases as you increase the discount rate. However, the present value decreases proportionately less than the increase in the discount rate.

13. Mr. and Mrs. Dafoe are doing some estimates of the amount of funds they will need in their RRSP to purchase an annuity paying \$3000 at the end of each month. For each combination of term and monthly compounded interest rate in the following table, calculate the initial amount required to purchase the annuity.

Term of annuity	Interest rate 8%	9%
20 years	?	?
25 years	?	?

14. If money can earn 9.75% compounded monthly, how much more money is required to fund an ordinary annuity paying \$200 per month for 30 years than to fund the same monthly payment for 20 years?

•15. An annuity contract pays \$2000 semiannually for 15 years. What is the present value of the annuity six months before the first payment, if money can earn 8% compounded semiannually for the first six years, and 10% compounded semiannually for the next nine years?

•16. A Government of Canada bond will pay \$50 at the end of every six months for the next 15 years, and an additional \$1000 lump payment at the end of the 15 years. What is the appropriate price to pay if you require a rate of return of 9% compounded semiannually?

•17. Bosco Class A preferred shares pay quarterly dividends of \$1.00. The shares must be redeemed at \$50 by Bosco $15\frac{1}{4}$ years from now, when the last dividend is paid. What is the fair market value of the shares if the rate of return required by the market on similar preferred shares is:

a. 7% compounded quarterly?

b. 8% compounded quarterly?

c. 9% compounded quarterly?

18. Harold and Patricia Abernathy made a loan to their son, Jason. To repay the loan, Jason will make payments of $2000 at the end of each of the next 10 years. If the interest rate on the loan is 7% compounded annually, what was the amount of the original loan? (Source: CIFP course on Personal Financial Planning.)

19. A 20-year loan requires semiannual payments of $1333.28 including interest at 10.75% compounded semiannually.

    a. What was the original amount of the loan?

    b. What will be the loan's balance $8\frac{1}{2}$ years later (just after the scheduled payment)?

20. The monthly payments on a five-year loan at 7.5% compounded monthly are $200.38.

    a. What was the original amount of the loan?

    b. What is the balance after the thirtieth payment?

21. Kent sold his car to Carolynn for $2000 down and monthly payments of $160.70 for $3\frac{1}{2}$ years, including interest at 12% compounded monthly. What was the selling price of the car?

22. Manuel purchased a boat for $2000 down with the balance to be paid by 36 monthly payments of $224.58 including interest at 10% compounded monthly.

    a. What was the purchase price of the boat?

    b. What is the balance owed just after the ninth payment?

23. A conditional sale contract between Classic Furniture and the purchaser of a dining room set requires month-end payments of $250 for 15 months. Classic Furniture sold the contract to Household Finance Co. at a discount to yield 19.5% compounded monthly. What price did Household pay Classic Furniture?

24. Osgood Appliance Centre is advertising refrigerators for six monthly payments of $199, including a payment on the date of purchase. What cash price should Osgood accept if it would otherwise sell the conditional sale agreement to a finance company to yield 18% compounded monthly?

•25. A mortgage broker offers to sell you a mortgage loan contract that will pay $800 at the end of each month for the next $3\frac{1}{2}$ years, at which time the principal balance of $45,572 is due and payable. What is the highest price you should pay for the contract if you require a return of at least 10.5% compounded monthly?

•26. What is the maximum price you should pay for a contract guaranteeing month-end payments of $500 for the next 12 years if you require a rate of return of at least 8% compounded monthly for the first five years and at least 9% compounded monthly for the next seven years?

27. The Ottawa Senators fired their coach two years into his five-year contract, which paid him $30,000 at the end of each month. If the team owners buy out the remaining term of the coach's contract for its economic value at the

time of firing, what will be the settlement amount? Use 7.5% compounded monthly as the time value of money.

28. The Montreal Canadiens have just announced the signing of Finnish hockey sensation Gunnar Skoroften to a 10-year contract at $1.2 million per year. The media are reporting the deal as being worth $12 million to the young Finn. What current economic value would you place on the contract if Skoroften will be paid $100,000 at the end of each month and money can earn 9% compounded monthly?

29. Colin and Marie have received two purchase offers on their boat. One is for $7900 cash, and the other is for $1000 down plus four payments of $2000 at six-month intervals beginning six months from now. Which offer should they accept if money can earn 10% compounded semiannually?

30. You can purchase a residential building lot for $45,000 cash, or for $10,000 down and quarterly payments of $2500 for four years. The first payment would be due three months after the purchase date. If the money you would use for a cash purchase can earn 8% compounded quarterly during the next four years, which option should you choose? What is the economic advantage in current dollars of the preferred alternative?

31. You have received two offers on the used car you wish to sell. Mr. Lindberg is offering $8500 cash, and Mrs. Martel's offer is five semiannual payments of $1900, including one on the purchase date. Which offer has the greater economic value if money can earn 10% compounded semiannually? What is the economic advantage in current dollars of the preferred alternative?

•32. A lottery offers the winner the choice between a $150,000 cash prize or month-end payments of $1000 for $12\frac{1}{2}$ years, increasing to $1500 per month for the next $12\frac{1}{2}$ years. Which alternative would you choose if money can earn 8.25% compounded monthly over the 25-year period?

•33. For its "One-Year No-Interest Sale," Flemmings Furniture advertises that, on any purchase over $499, the customer's down payment needs to cover only 10% of the ticketed price plus any sales tax not already included in the ticketed price. The balance of the purchase price is then paid in 12 equal monthly payments with no interest charges. Money is worth 11.5% compounded monthly to Flemmings, because it can use surplus cash to pay down the balance on its operating loan on which interest accrues at 11.5% compounded monthly. What cash amount (not including sales tax) should Flemmings be willing to accept (instead of the no-interest plan) on an item ticketed at $1000?

••34. An individual qualifying for Canada Pension Plan benefits may elect to start collecting the CPP monthly retirement benefit at any time between the ages of 60 and 70. If the retirement benefit starts after age 65, the pension payments are increased (from the amount that would otherwise be paid at age 65) by 0.5% for each month after age 65. For example, if the retiree chooses to begin receiving the benefit after turning 68, the CPP payments will be increased by (36 months) $\times$ (0.5%) = 18%.

The average life expectancy of a man aged 65 is another 15 years. If a man aged 65 lives just the expected of 15 years, compare the economic values at age 65 of the two alternatives of collecting a 100% pension from age 65 versus a 118% pension from age 68. Assume that money is worth 7.5% compounded monthly.

••35. The British Columbia Teachers' Pension Plan allows a teacher to begin collecting a retirement pension before age 60, but the pension is reduced by 3% for each year the retiring teacher's age is under 60. For example, a teacher retiring at age 56 would receive 88% of the monthly pension that she would receive at age 60 (with the same number of years of service). The reduction is permanent, extending to payments beyond age 60.

Suppose that a female teacher will live the average life expectancy of 28 additional years for a woman aged 55. Compare the economic values at age 55 of the two alternatives of collecting an 85% pension from age 55 versus collecting a 100% pension from age 60. Assume that money is worth 7.5% compounded monthly.

10.4 Deferred Annuities

A **deferred annuity** may be viewed as an *ordinary* annuity that does not begin until a time interval (named the **period of deferral**) has passed. Figure 10.6 shows a deferred annuity on a time line. In the figure,

$$d = \text{Number of payment intervals in the period of deferral}$$

Note that the period of deferral ends one payment interval *before* the first payment. Viewed from the *end* of the period of deferral, the payments then form an ordinary annuity.

Figure 10.6 *Time Diagram for a Deferred Annuity*

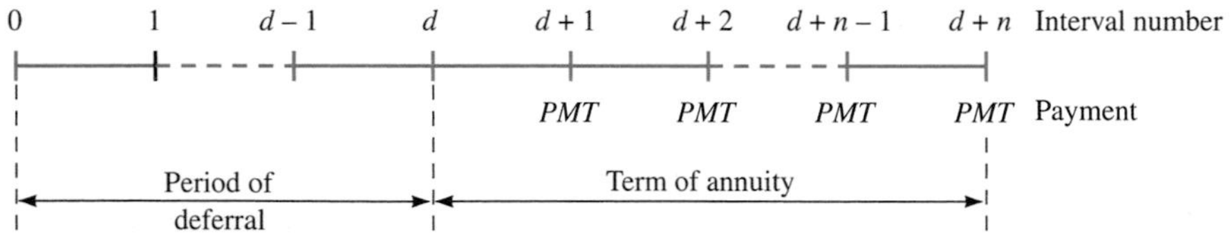

The future value of a deferred annuity is the future value of all of the payments at the end of the last payment interval. Can you see what needs to be done to determine the future value? Looking back from the end of the last payment interval, the payments form an ordinary annuity. So it is a simple matter of doing the same future value calculation you learned in Section 10.2 for ordinary annuities.

The present value of a deferred annuity is the present value of all of the payments at the beginning of the period of deferral. How can it be obtained using ideas you have already learned? The two regions identified in Figure 10.6 suggest a two-step procedure:

1. Calculate the present value, PV_1, of the payments at the end of the period of deferral—this is just the present value of an ordinary annuity.
2. Calculate the present value, PV_2, of the Step 1 amount at the beginning of the period of deferral.

The two steps are indicated pictorially in Figure 10.7.

Figure 10.7 *The Present Value of a Deferred Annuity*

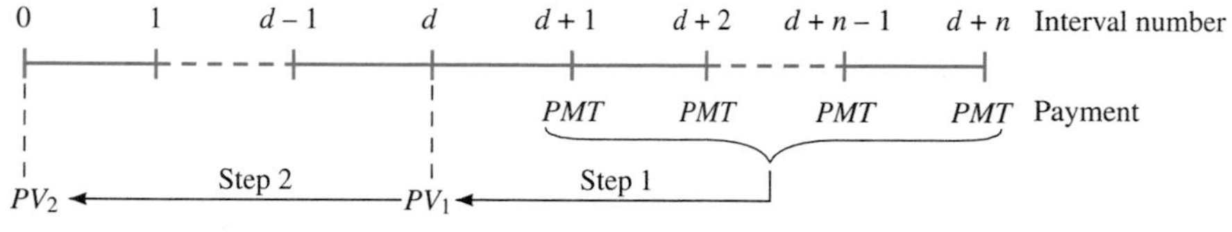

Example 10.4A *Calculating the Present Value of a Deferred Annuity*

Mr. and Mrs. Templeton are setting up a fund to help finance their granddaughter's college education. They want her to be able to withdraw $1000 at the beginning of every three months for three years when she starts college. Her first withdrawal will be $5\frac{1}{2}$ years from now. If the fund can earn 7.2% compounded quarterly, what single amount contributed today will provide for the withdrawals?

Solution

The money the Templetons invest now will have $5\frac{1}{2}$ years to grow before withdrawals start. Thereafter, the ongoing earnings of money still in the fund will help support the periodic withdrawals. The one-time "up front" contribution is the present value of the withdrawals.

The time diagram is presented below. Viewed from today, the withdrawals form a deferred annuity. In order to have an *ordinary* annuity following the period of deferral, the period of deferral must end three months before the first payment. This makes the period of deferral $5\frac{1}{4}$ years.

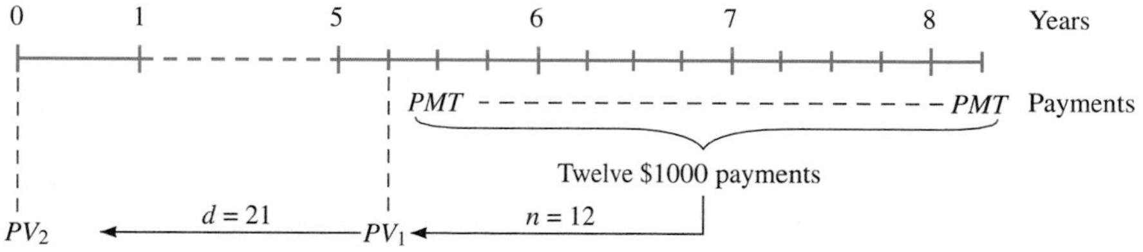

Since payments and compounding both occur quarterly, we have a deferred *simple* annuity with

$$PMT = \$1000 \qquad n = 4(3) = 12 \qquad d = 4(5.25) = 21 \qquad \text{and} \qquad i = \frac{7.2\%}{4} = 1.8\%$$

Algebraic Solution

The present value of the payments $5\frac{1}{4}$ years from now is

$$PV_1 = PMT\left[\frac{1-(1+i)^{-n}}{i}\right] = \$1000\left(\frac{1-1.018^{-12}}{0.018}\right) = \$10{,}706.41$$

The present value of the payments today is

$$PV_2 = FV(1+i)^{-n} = \$10{,}706.41(1.018)^{-21} = \$7361.06$$

The Templetons can provide the desired financial support for their granddaughter by putting \$7361.06 into the fund today.

Financial Calculator Solution

The present value of the payments $5\frac{1}{4}$ years from now is

1000 (PMT) 0 (FV) 12 (n) 1.8 (i) (COMP) (PV) | −10,706.41 |

The present value of the payments today is

(+/−) (FV) 0 (PMT) 21 (n) (COMP) (PV) | −7361.06 |

The Templetons can provide the desired financial support for their granddaughter by putting \$7361.06 into the fund today.

Example 10.4B Calculating the Length of the Deferral Period

Mrs. Sevard purchased a deferred annuity from an insurance company for \$9697. The money used to purchase the annuity will earn 8% compounded quarterly. The annuity will provide sixteen quarterly payments of \$1000. If the first payment is to be received on October 1, 2004, when did Mrs. Sevard purchase the deferred annuity?

Solution

The key idea on which we base the solution is that the purchase price, \$9697, is the present value on the date of purchase of all sixteen annuity payments. The payments form a deferred simple annuity with $PMT = \$1000$, $n = 16$, and $i = 2\%$. The data and solution steps are presented in the diagram below.

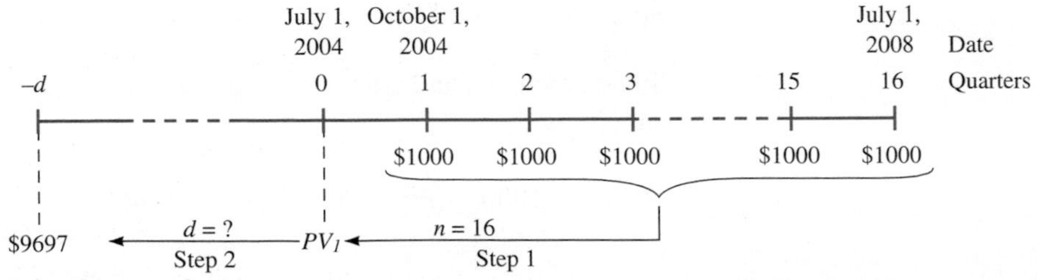

For the payments to be treated as an *ordinary* annuity, the period of deferral must end on July 1, 2004 (one payment interval before the first payment).

Algebraic Solution

The present value of the payments on July 1, 2004 is

$$PV_1 = PMT\left[\frac{1-(1+i)^{-n}}{i}\right] = \$1000\left(\frac{1-1.02^{-16}}{0.02}\right) = \$13{,}577.71$$

This amount is the future value of the \$9697 purchase price at the end of the period of deferral. We must now use formula (9-2) to calculate the number of compounding periods required for \$9697 to grow to \$13,577.71.

$$d = \frac{\ln\left(\frac{FV}{PV}\right)}{\ln(1+i)} = \frac{\ln\left(\frac{\$13{,}577.71}{\$9697}\right)}{\ln 1.02} = \frac{\ln 1.400197}{\ln 1.02} = 17$$

The period of deferral is therefore 17.00 calendar quarters (four years, three months) before July 1, 2004. That places the date of purchase of the deferred annuity at April 1, 2000.

Financial Calculator Solution

Compute the present value of the payments on July 1, 2004.

1000 (PMT) 0 (FV) 16 (*n*) 2 (*i*) (COMP) (PV) [−13,577.71]

This amount is the future value of the \$9697 purchase price at the end of the period of deferral. We must now compute the number of compounding periods required for \$9697 to grow to \$13,577.71.

(+/−) (FV) 0 (PMT) 9697 (+/−) (PV) (COMP) (*n*) [17.00]

The period of deferral is therefore 17.00 calendar quarters (four years, three months) before July 1, 2004. That places the date of purchase of the deferred annuity at April 1, 2000.

Concept Questions

1. What is meant by a deferred annuity?
2. How long is the period of deferral if the first quarterly payment of a deferred annuity will be paid $3\frac{1}{2}$ years from today?
3. Why do we terminate the period of deferral one payment interval before the first payment?
4. For the same *n, PMT,* and *i,* is the present value of a deferred annuity larger or smaller than the present value of an ordinary annuity? Explain.
5. For the same *n, PMT,* and *i,* is the future value of a deferred annuity larger or smaller than the future value of an ordinary annuity? Explain.
6. For the same *n, PMT,* and *i,* would it cost more or less to purchase a deferred annuity than an ordinary annuity? Explain.

Exercise 10.4

Answers to the odd-numbered problems are at the end of the book.

Determine the unknown value for each of the deferred annuities in Problems 1 through 6. In every case, the annuity is understood to be an ordinary annuity after the period of deferral.

Problem	Deferral period	Periodic payment ($)	Interest rate (%)	Compounding and payment frequency	Term (years)	Present value ($)
1.	5 years	2000.00	7	Semiannually	10	?
2.	$3\frac{1}{2}$ years	750.00	8	Quarterly	5	?
3.	$2\frac{3}{4}$ years	500.00	9	Monthly	$3\frac{1}{2}$	?
4.	?	1500.00	7.9	Annually	8	6383.65
5.	?	1076.71	7	Quarterly	$12\frac{1}{2}$	30,000.00
6.	?	400.00	9.75	Monthly	15	33,173.03

7. What amount of money invested now will provide monthly payments of \$200 for five years, if the ordinary annuity is deferred for $3\frac{1}{2}$ years and the money earns 7.5% compounded monthly?

8. Mr. Haddit plans to retire eight years from today. He projects that he will need \$30,000 per year in his retirement, which he guesses will be for 15 years. The first payment will be nine years from today. To fund his retirement, Mr. Haddit will invest a lump amount today and later use it to sustain the 15 withdrawals. If his investment earns 10% compounded annually, how much must he invest today? (Source: ICB course on Wealth Valuation.)

9. Marion's grandfather's will established a trust that will pay her \$1500 every three months for 11 years. The first payment will be made six years from now, when she turns 19. If money is worth 9% compounded quarterly, what is the economic value today of the bequest?

10. Using an inheritance he recently received, Sam wants to purchase a deferred annuity that will pay \$5000 every three months between age 60 (when he plans to retire) and age 65 (when his permanent pension will begin). The first payment is to be three months after he reaches 60, and the last is to be on his sixty-fifth birthday. If Sam's current age is 50 years and six months, and the invested funds will earn 6% compounded quarterly, what amount must he invest in the deferred annuity?

•11. If money can earn 10% compounded annually for the next 20 years, which of the following annuities has the greater economic value today: \$1000 paid at the end of each of the next 10 years, or 10 annual payments of \$2500 with the first payment occurring 11 years from today?

12. A conditional sale contract requires the debtor to make six quarterly payments of \$569, with the first payment due in six months. What amount will a finance company pay to purchase the contract on the date of sale if the finance company requires a rate of return of 20% compounded quarterly?

13. What price will a finance company pay to a merchant for a conditional sale contract that requires 15 monthly payments of \$231 beginning in six months? The finance company requires a rate of return of 18% compounded monthly.

•14. A \$35,000 loan bearing interest at 10% compounded quarterly was repaid, after a period of deferral, by quarterly payments of \$1573.83 over 12 years. What was the time interval between the date of the loan and the first payment?

•15. A finance company paid a merchant \$3975 for a conditional sale contract after discounting it to yield 18% compounded monthly. If the contract is for 20 monthly payments of \$256.96 following a payment-free period, what is the time interval between the date of sale and the first payment?

•16. To the nearest month, how long (before the first withdrawal) must a \$10,000 deposit earning 8.5% compounded semiannually be allowed to grow before it can provide 40 semiannual withdrawals of \$1000?

•17. Mrs. Corriveau has just retired at age 58 with \$160,360 in her RRSP. She plans to live off other savings for a few years and allow her RRSP to continue to grow on a tax-deferred basis until there is an amount sufficient to purchase a 25-year annuity paying \$2000 at the end of each month. If her RRSP and the annuity each earn 7.5% compounded monthly, how much longer must she let her RRSP grow (before she buys the annuity)?

10.5 Ordinary General Annuities

To this point, we have considered only ordinary simple annuities (in which the payment interval *equals* the compounding interval). We will now learn how to handle ordinary general annuities (in which the payment interval *differs* from the compounding interval). Actually, we have already covered all you need to know to calculate the future value and present value of an ordinary general annuity. We need only to "link" two topics whose connection is not obvious.

Let us begin with formula (10-1) for the future value of an ordinary simple annuity.

$$FV = PMT\left[\frac{(1+i)^n - 1}{i}\right] \qquad (10\text{-}1)$$

Keep in mind that this formula may be used *only* in cases where the compounding interval equals (or "matches") the payment interval. But if we can find a way to *transform* a general annuity into a simple annuity, then we can still use formula (10-1).

Sometimes an insight comes more easily if we consider a specific numerical example. Suppose we wish to find the future value of an ordinary annuity comprising 12 semiannual payments of \$100 that earn 8% compounded quarterly. We are given:

$$PMT = \$100 \text{ every six months} \qquad i = \frac{8\%}{4} = 2\% \text{ per quarter} \qquad n = 12$$

Since the payment interval is six months but the compounding interval is three months, the payments form an ordinary *general* annuity. In order to use formula (10-1), we need the periodic rate for six months (the payment interval) that is *equivalent* to the given periodic rate of 2% per quarter. This is precisely the type of calculation for which formula (9-4) was derived in Section 9.4.

$$i_2 = (1 + i_1)^{m_1/m_2} - 1 \qquad (9\text{-}4)$$

For the case at hand,

i_1 = The given periodic rate ($i = 2\%$)
m_1 = Number of compoundings per year (4) at the given interest rate
m_2 = Number of compoundings per year at the *equivalent* interest rate [This will equal the number of annuity payments per year (2).]
i_2 = Periodic interest rate for a payment interval

In this case, the exponent m_1/m_2 in formula (9-4) is

$$\frac{m_1}{m_2} = \frac{\text{Number of compoundings per year (at the given interest rate)}}{\text{Number of payments per year}} = \frac{4}{2} = 2$$

Substituting in formula (9-4), the periodic rate per payment interval (six months) is

$$i_2 = (1 + i_1)^{m_1/m_2} - 1 = 1.02^{4/2} - 1 = 1.02^2 - 1 = 0.0404 = 4.04\%$$

Now substitute this value of i_2 for i in formula (10-1).

$$FV = PMT\left[\frac{(1+i)^n - 1}{i}\right] = \$100\left[\frac{(1.0404)^{12} - 1}{0.0404}\right] = \$1506.03$$

The future value of the general annuity is \$1506.03.

Let us streamline formula (9-4) for use in general annuity problems. As noted in the preceding problem,

$$i_1 = i \quad \text{and} \quad \frac{m_1}{m_2} = \frac{\text{Number of compoundings per year}}{\text{Number of payments per year}}$$

Since $\frac{m_1}{m_2}$ is a standard "package" in general annuities, we can simplify formula (9-4) and the presentation of our solutions if we define a new symbol:

NUMBER OF COMPOUNDINGS PER PAYMENT INTERVAL **(10-3)**

$$c = \frac{\text{Number of compoundings per year}}{\text{Number of payments per year}}$$

Then we can write formula (9-4) as

EQUIVALENT PERIODIC RATE FOR GENERAL ANNUITIES **(9-4*c*)**

$$i_2 = (1 + i)^c - 1$$

TIP *SOME THINGS JUST HAVE TO BE MEMORIZED*

You need to commit the definition of c to memory. The symbol "c" reminds us that "**c**ompoundings per year" comes first (in the numerator).

We have used the future value calculation to introduce the mathematics of ordinary general annuities. The approach we have developed works in all types of general annuity calculations. It is summarized below.

APPROACH FOR SOLVING GENERAL ANNUITY PROBLEMS:
Transform the general annuity problem into a simple annuity problem by:

1. Using $i_2 = (1 + i)^c - 1$ to calculate the equivalent periodic rate that matches the payment interval.
2. Using this equivalent periodic rate as the value for i in the appropriate simple annuity formula, or as the value entered into the (i) memory of the financial calculator.

Example 10.5A *Calculating the Equivalent Periodic Interest Rate*

To five-figure accuracy, calculate the periodic interest rate that matches the payment interval for:

a. Semiannual payments at 5% compounded annually.

b. Monthly payments at 6% compounded quarterly.

Solution

a. $i = \frac{5\%}{1} = 5\%$ per year and $c = \frac{1 \text{ compounding per year}}{2 \text{ payments per year}} = 0.5$

Thus,

$$i_2 = (1 + i)^c - 1 = 1.05^{0.5} - 1 = 0.024695 = 2.4695\% \text{ per half year}$$

TIP *ESTIMATING i_2*

You can easily *estimate* the value of i_2, the periodic rate for a payment interval. It is a good idea to do this to check the "reasonableness" of the value you calculate for i_2. In part (a), the interest rate for six months (the payment interval) will be about half the nominal annual rate of 5%; that is, $i_2 \approx 2.5\%$. (This number is only an approximation because it ignores compounding.) If formula (9-4) does not give you a value close to 2.5%, you have made an error in your calculations. To estimate i_2 in general, simply divide the given nominal rate by the number of payments per year.

b. $i = \frac{6\%}{4} = 1.5\%$ per quarter and $c = \frac{4 \text{ compoundings per year}}{12 \text{ payments per year}} = 0.\bar{3}$

Thus,

$$i_2 = (1 + i)^c - 1 = 1.015^{0.\bar{3}} - 1 = 0.0049752 = 0.49752\% \text{ per month}$$

TIP

IMPROVING THE ACCURACY OF CALCULATED RESULTS

Sometimes the value for c is a *repeating* decimal. This happened in part (b) of the preceding example, where we obtained $c = 0.\overline{3}$. In such cases, use your calculator in a way that optimizes the accuracy of the value you obtain for i_2. For example, immediately after dividing 4 by 12 in the preceding part (b), save the quotient to memory. The calculator then retains at least two more digits than you see in the display. Later, when you need the exponent for the y^x function, recall the value for c from the memory.

Typically, the value you calculate fo i_2 will be used in further calculations. Again, to optimize accuracy, i_2's value should be saved in memory as soon you calculate it using formula (9-4). The value in memory will have two or three more digits than you see in the display. Whenever i_2 is needed in a subsequent calculation, recall it from the memory. This procedure will improve both your efficiency in using the calculator and the accuracy of your results.

Example 10.5B *Calculating the Future Value of an Ordinary General Annuity*

If \$1000 is invested at the end of every year at 8% compounded semiannually, what will be the total value of the periodic investments after 25 years?

Solution

Since the compounding period differs from the payment interval, the regular investments form a general annuity having

$$PMT = \$1000 \qquad n = 25 \qquad \text{and} \qquad i = \frac{8\%}{2} = 4\%$$

The total value of the investments will be their future value. Before we start calculating the future value, we must first determine the periodic interest rate for the one-year payment interval. (It will be *about* 8%.) Since

$$c = \frac{2 \text{ compoundings per year}}{1 \text{ payment per year}} = 2$$

then

$$i_2 = (1 + i)^c - 1 = 1.04^2 - 1 = 0.0816 = 8.16\%$$

Algebraic Solution

Substitute this value of i_2 for i in formula (10-1).

$$FV = PMT\left[\frac{(1 + i)^n - 1}{i}\right] = \$1000\left[\frac{(1.0816)^{25} - 1}{0.0816}\right] = \$1000(74.836806) = \$74,836.81$$

The total value after 25 years will be \$74,836.81.

Financial Calculator Solution

Save the value calculated for i_2 in the (i) memory.

8.16 (i) 1000 (+/-) (PMT) 25 (n) 0 (PV) (COMP) (FV) | 74,836.81 |

The total value after 25 years will be \$74,836.81.

Example 10.5C Calculating the Present Value of a Deferred General Annuity

Maureen has just had her fifty-fifth birthday and plans to retire from teaching at age 60. While reviewing Maureen's personal net worth statement, her financial adviser points out that she has overlooked a significant asset—the current economic value of her future pension. The adviser calculates that the 25 years of service Maureen has already accumulated entitle her to a pension of \$3500 at each month's end starting at age 60. Based on a 22-year life expectancy from age 60 and a time value of money equal to 8% compounded semiannually, estimate the current economic value of Maureen's pension.

Solution

The current economic value of the pension can be estimated by calculating the present value of the expected pension payments discounted at the time value of money. With monthly payments and semiannual compounding, the pension (viewed from her fifty-fifth birthday) constitutes a *deferred* ordinary *general* annuity. The period of deferral is five years. We are given

$$PMT = \$3500 \quad n = 12(22) = 264 \quad d = 12(5) = 60 \quad i = \frac{8\%}{2} = 4\%$$

The diagram below indicates the two main steps in the solution.

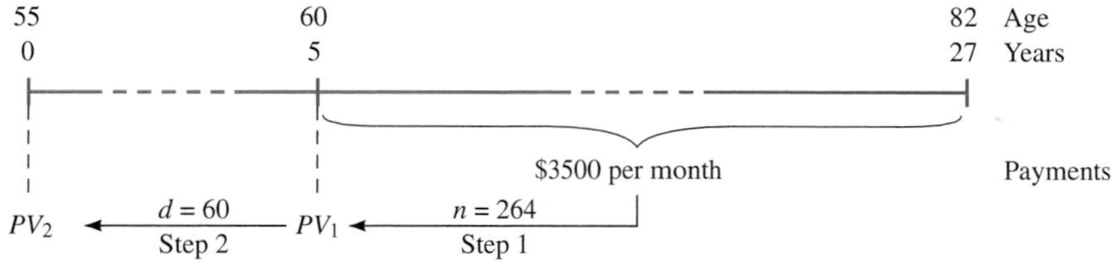

But first we must calculate the periodic rate that matches the one-month payment interval. (It will be about 8%/12 = 0.67%.)

$$c = \frac{2 \text{ compoundings per year}}{12 \text{ payments per year}} = 0.1\overline{6}$$

Using formula (9-4c),

$$i_2 = (1 + i)^c - 1 = 1.04^{0.1\overline{6}} - 1 = 0.0065581969 = 0.65581969\% \text{ per month}$$

Algebraic Solution

Substitute this value of i_2 for i in formula (10-2) to obtain the present value of the pension at age 60.

$$PV_1 = PMT\left[\frac{1-(1+i)^{-n}}{i}\right] = \$3500\left[\frac{1-(1.0065581969)^{-264}}{0.0065581969}\right] = \$438{,}662.92$$

Using formula (8-2) in the form $PV = FV(1+i)^{-n}$, the present value of \$438,662.92 five years earlier is

$$PV_2 = \$438{,}662.92(1+i_2)^{-d} = \$438{,}662.92(1.0065581969)^{-60} = \$296{,}345$$

Financial Calculator Solution

Compute the present value of the pension at age 60.

3500 (PMT) 0 (FV) 264 (n) 0.65581969 (i) (COMP) (PV) | −438,662.92 |

Compute the present value of this lump amount five years earlier.

(+/−) (FV) 0 (PMT) 60 (n) (COMP) (PV) | −296,344.95 |

The current economic value of Maureen's pension is \$296,345. The significance of this number is that, if Maureen did not belong to the pension plan, she would need current savings of \$296,345 in a personal RRSP earning 8% compounded semiannually in order to duplicate the future pension benefits to age 82.

Example 10.5D *Calculating the Fair Market Value of a Preferred Share*

The preferred shares of Dominion Trust Co. will pay a \$0.75 per share dividend at the end of every calendar quarter until they are redeemed (that is, bought back by Dominion Trust) $8\frac{1}{2}$ years from now. On the redemption date, a shareholder will receive the \$40 par value of each share in addition to the last regular dividend. What is the fair market value of a share if preferred shares of similar risk are currently generating a total rate of return of 6.5% compounded semiannually?

Solution

This is a valuation application of present value. The fair market value of a share will be the combined present value of the dividends and the \$40 payment of the par value. The dividend stream constitutes an *ordinary general* annuity having

$$PMT = \$0.75 \qquad n = 4(8.5) = 34 \qquad \text{and} \qquad i = \frac{6.5\%}{2} = 3.25\%$$

Then

$$c = \frac{2 \text{ compoundings per year}}{4 \text{ payments per year}} = 0.5$$

and

$$i_2 = (1+i)^c - 1 = 1.0325^{0.5} - 1 = 0.0161201 = 1.61201\% \text{ per quarter}$$

Algebraic Solution

Fair market value = Present value of dividends + Present value of par value

$$= PMT\left[\frac{1-(1+i)^{-n}}{i}\right] + FV(1+i)^{-n}$$

$$= \$0.75\left(\frac{1-1.0161201^{-34}}{0.0161201}\right) + \$40(1.0161201^{-34})$$

$$= \$19.513 + \$23.224$$
$$= \$42.74$$

The fair market value of a preferred share is \$42.74.

Financial Calculator Solution

The combined present value of the dividends and the \$40 payment may be obtained in a single computation.

0.75 (PMT) 40 (FV) 34 (n) 1.61201 (i) (COMP) (PV) **−42.74**

The fair market value of a preferred share is \$42.74.

Concept Questions

1. What are the distinguishing characteristics of an ordinary general annuity.
2. An annuity has quarterly payments at 6% compounded monthly. What is the value of c? What is the approximate value of i_2? Will the correct value be larger or smaller than the estimate? Explain.
3. An annuity has monthly payments at 6% compounded semiannually. What is the value of c? What is the approximate value of i_2? Will the correct value be larger or smaller than the estimate? Explain.

Exercise 10.5

Answers to the odd-numbered problems are at the end of the book.

To the nearest 0.001%, calculate the periodic interest rate that matches the payment interval for each of the annuities in Problems 1 through 10.

Problem	Payment frequency	Compounding frequency	Nominal interest rate (%)
1.	Annually	Quarterly	10
2.	Quarterly	Monthly	9
3.	Semiannually	Quarterly	8
4.	Annually	Monthly	7.5
5.	Monthly	Quarterly	11
6.	Monthly	Semiannually	9.5
7.	Quarterly	Annually	7.75
8.	Semiannually	Annually	9.25
9.	Monthly	Annually	10.25
10.	Quarterly	Semiannually	8.5

Determine the future value (accurate to the cent) of the ordinary general annuities in Problems 11 through 16.

Problem	Periodic payment ($)	Payment interval	Term (years)	Nominal rate (%)	Compounding frequency
11.	400	3 months	11	11.5	Annually
12.	150	1 month	$6\frac{1}{2}$	10	Quarterly
13.	2750	6 months	$3\frac{1}{2}$	8	Monthly
14.	1500	3 months	$13\frac{1}{2}$	7.5	Semiannually
15.	3500	1 year	17	10.5	Monthly
16.	950	6 months	$8\frac{1}{2}$	9	Quarterly

Determine the present value (accurate to the cent) of the ordinary general annuities in Problems 17 through 22.

Problem	Periodic payment ($)	Payment interval	Term	Discount rate (%)	Compounding frequency
17.	400	3 months	11 years	11.5	Annually
18.	150	1 month	$6\frac{1}{2}$ years	10	Quarterly
19.	2750	6 months	$3\frac{1}{2}$ years	8	Monthly
20.	1500	3 months	$13\frac{1}{2}$ years	7.5	Semiannually
21.	3500	1 year	17 years	10.5	Monthly
22.	950	6 months	$8\frac{1}{2}$ years	9	Quarterly

Determine the unknown value at "?" for each of the deferred annuities in Problems 23 through 28. In every case, the annuity is understood to be an ordinary annuity following the period of deferral.

Problem	Deferral period	Periodic payment ($)	Payment interval (months)	Interest rate (%)	Compounding frequency	Term (years)	Present value ($)
23.	5 years	2000.00	6	7	Quarterly	10	?
24.	$3\frac{1}{2}$ years	750.00	3	8.25	Monthly	5	?
25.	$2\frac{3}{4}$ years	500.00	1	9	Quarterly	$3\frac{1}{2}$	?
•26.	?	1500.00	3	7.9	Annually	8	28,355.14
•27.	?	356.83	1	7	Quarterly	$12\frac{1}{2}$	30,000.00
•28.	?	400.00	6	9.75	Monthly	15	4608.07

29. An ordinary annuity consists of 25 annual payments of $1000. Calculate its future value if the funds earn:

a. 9% compounded annually.

b. 9% compounded quarterly.

c. 9% compounded monthly.

30. Mr. and Mrs. Krenz are contributing to a Registered Education Savings Plan (RESP) they have set up for their children. What amount will they have in the RESP after eight years of contributing $500 at the end of every calendar quarter if the plan earns 9% compounded monthly? How much of the total amount is interest?

31. What is the future value eight years from now of each of the following cash-flow streams if money can earn 9% compounded semiannually?

a. A single payment of $5000 today.

b. An ordinary annuity starting today with eight annual payments of $900.

c. An ordinary annuity starting in three years with 20 quarterly payments of $400.

32. How much larger will the value of an RRSP be at the end of 25 years if the RRSP earns 9% compounded monthly instead of 9% compounded annually? In both cases a contribution of $1000 is made at the end of every three months.

33. What amount will be required to purchase a 20-year annuity paying $2500 at the end of each month, if the annuity provides a return of 8.75% compounded annually?

34. An Agreement for Sale contract on a house requires payments of $4000 at the end of every six months. The contract has seven years to run. The payee wants to sell her interest in the contract. What will an investor pay in order to realize an annually compounded rate of return on the purchase price of:

a. 8%? **b.** 10%? **c.** 12%?

35. Kent sold his car to Carolynn for $2000 down and monthly payments of $160.70 for $3\frac{1}{2}$ years, including interest at 12% compounded quarterly. What was the selling price of the car?

36. With great fanfare, a provincial minister of public works announces a program of highway construction in his province "worth $100 million." Details of the program reveal that $5 million will be spent each calendar quarter for the next five years. If the first $5 million expenditure takes place three months from now, what is the current economic value (to the nearest $1000) of the program if money is worth 8% compounded annually?

37. Ms. Ho is buying a 25% interest in an accounting partnership by end-of-month payments of $537.66, including interest at 8% compounded semiannually, for 12 years.

a. What valuation was placed on the partnership at the beginning of the payments?

b. What total amount of interest will she pay over the 12 years?

•38. How much larger will the value of an RRSP be at the end of 25 years if the contributor makes month-end contributions of $300 instead of year-end contributions of $3600? In both cases the RRSP earns 8.5% compounded semiannually.

•39. An ordinary annuity consists of 40 semiannual payments of $600. What is its future value if the funds earn 9% compounded quarterly for the first

$8\frac{1}{2}$ years, and 8% compounded semiannually for the remainder of the term of the annuity?

•40. A savings plan requires end-of-month contributions of $100 for 25 years. What will be the future value of the plan if it earns 7% compounded quarterly for the first half of the annuity's term, and 8% compounded semiannually for the last half of the term?

•41. An investment plan requires year-end contributions of $1000 for 25 years. What will be the future value of the plan if it earns $7\frac{1}{2}$% compounded monthly for the first 10 years and 8% compounded semiannually thereafter?

•42. Monty expects to contribute $300 to his RRSP at the end of every month for the next five years. For the subsequent 10 years, he plans to contribute $2000 at the end of each calendar quarter. How much will be in his RRSP at the end of the 15 years if the funds earn 8% compounded semiannually?

•43. Gloria has just made her ninth annual $2000 contribution to her RRSP. She now plans to make semiannual contributions of $2000. The first contribution will be made six months from now. How much will she have in her RRSP 15 years from now if the plan has earned and will continue to earn 8% compounded quarterly?

•44. The Toronto Raptors announce the signing of their top draft pick to a "seven-year deal worth $21.6 million." The player will earn $200,000 at the end of each month for the first three years, and $300,000 at the end of each month for the subsequent four years. How do the Raptors get the $21.6 million figure? To the nearest $1000, what is the current economic value of the deal if money can earn 7% compounded annually?

•45. An annuity contract pays $2000 semiannually for 15 years. What is the present value of the annuity six months before the first payment, if money can earn 7.5% compounded monthly for the first five years, and 9% compounded annually for the next 10 years?

•46. An annuity paying $800 at the end of each quarter for the first $4\frac{1}{2}$ years is followed by a second annuity paying $2000 at the end of each half year for the subsequent $4\frac{1}{2}$ years. What is the combined present value of the two annuities at the beginning of the first annuity? Assume the time value of money is 8% compounded quarterly.

•47. An annuity paying $500 at the end of each month for the first $2\frac{1}{2}$ years is followed by a second annuity paying $2000 at the end of each quarter for the subsequent $3\frac{1}{2}$ years. What is their combined present value at the beginning of the first annuity? Assume the time value of money is 7% compounded semiannually.

•48. What amount must be invested today to allow for quarterly payments of $2500 at the end of every quarter for 15 years after a six-year deferral period? Assume that the funds will earn 9% compounded semiannually.

•49. What is the current economic value of an inheritance that will pay $2000 to the beneficiary at the beginning of every three months for 20 years, starting when the beneficiary reaches 20 years of age, $4\frac{1}{2}$ years from now? Assume that money is worth 9% compounded monthly.

•50. To sell a farm that it had acquired in a foreclosure action, the Royal Bank agreed to monthly payments of $2700 for 20 years, with the first payment due 15 months from the date of sale. If the purchaser paid 15% down and the interest rate on the balance is 9% compounded annually, what was the purchase price?

•51. How long (before the first withdrawal) must a $19,665 deposit earning 9.5% compounded semiannually be allowed to grow before it can provide 60 quarterly withdrawals of $1000?

•52. Duncan retired recently and plans to utilize other savings for a few years while his RRSP continues to grow on a tax-deferred basis. The RRSP is currently worth $142,470. How long will it be until the amount in the RRSP is large enough to purchase a 25-year annuity paying $1700 at the end of each month? Assume that the RRSP and the annuity will earn 8.75% compounded semiannually.

••53. What will be the amount in an RRSP after 25 years if contributions of $3000 are made at each year-end for the first seven years and month-end contributions of $500 are made for the next 18 years? Assume that the plan earns 8% compounded quarterly for the first 12 years, and 7% compounded semiannually for the next 13 years.

Review Problems

Answers to the odd-numbered review problems are at the end of the book.

1. You can purchase a residential building lot for $60,000 cash, or for $10,000 down and month-end payments of $1000 for five years. If money is worth 7.5% compounded monthly, which option should you choose?
2. A victim of a car accident won a judgment for wages lost over a two-year period ended nine months before the date of the judgment. In addition, the court awarded interest at 6% compounded monthly on the lost wages from the date they would have otherwise been received to the date of the judgment. If the monthly salary had been $5500, what was the total amount of the award (on the date of the judgment)?
3. Dr. Wilson is buying a 50% interest in a veterinary practice by end-of-month payments of $714.60, including interest at 7% compounded semiannually for 15 years.
   a. What valuation was placed on the partnership at the beginning of the payments?
   b. What total amount of interest will she pay over the 15 years?
4. What minimum amount of money earning 7% compounded semiannually will sustain withdrawals of $1000 at the end of every month for 12 years?
5. A 15-year loan requires monthly payments of $587.33 including interest at 8.4% compounded monthly.
   a. What was the original amount of the loan?
   b. What is the balance on the loan after half of the payments have been made?
6. What amount of money invested now will provide payments of $500 at the end of every month for five years following a four-year period of deferral? The money will earn 7.2% compounded monthly.
7. What price will a finance company pay to a merchant for a conditional sale contract that requires 12 monthly payments of $249, with the first payment due six months from now? The finance company requires a return of 16.5% compounded monthly.
8. ◆ Calculate the future value of an ordinary annuity consisting of monthly payments of $300 for five years, if the rate of interest was 9% compounded monthly for the first two years, and will be 7.5% compounded monthly for the last three years.
9. ◆ How much larger will the value of an RRSP be at the end of 20 years if the contributor makes month-end contributions of $500, instead of year-end contributions of $6000? In both cases the RRSP earns 7.5% compounded semiannually.
10. ◆ Charlene has made contributions of $3000 to her RRSP at the end of every half year for the past seven years. The plan has earned 9% compounded semiannually. She has just moved the funds to another plan paying 7.5% compounded quarterly, and will now contribute $2000 at the end of every three months. What total amount will she have in the plan five years from now?
11. ◆ What percentage more funds will you have in your RRSP 20 years from now if you make fixed contributions of $3000 at the end of every six months for the next 20 years, instead of waiting 10 years and making semiannual contributions that are twice as large for half as many years? Assume that the RRSP earns 8% compounded semiannually.
12. ◆ A mortgage broker offers to sell you a mortgage loan contract that will pay $900 per month for the next $2\frac{3}{4}$ years, at which time the principal balance of $37,886 is due and payable. What should you pay for the contract, if you require a return of 7.2% compounded monthly?
13. ◆ What is the appropriate price to pay for a contract guaranteeing payments of $1500 at the end of each quarter for the next 12 years, if you require a rate of return of 8% compounded quarterly for the first five years, and 9% compounded quarterly for the next seven years?

◆ **14.** Suppose Evan contributes $2000 to his RRSP at the end of every quarter for the next 15 years, and then contributes $1000 at each month's end for the subsequent 10 years. How much will he have in his RRSP at the end of the 25 years? Assume that the RRSP earns 8% compounded semiannually.

◆ **15.** What is the current economic value of an inheritance that will pay $2500 to the beneficiary at the beginning of every three months for 20 years starting when the beneficiary reaches 21 years of age, $5\frac{1}{4}$ years from now? Assume that money can earn 6% compounded monthly.

◆◆ **16.** A $30,000 loan bearing interest at 9% compounded monthly was repaid, after a period of deferral, by monthly payments of $425.10 for 10 years. What was the time interval between the date of the loan and the first payment?

Self-Test Exercise

Answers to the self-test problems are at the end of the book.

1. Calculate the amounts that will be accumulated after 20 years if:

a. $1000 is invested at the end of every six months at 8.5% compounded semiannually.

b. $2000 is invested at the end of every year at 8.5% compounded annually.

2. Louiselle purchased a recreational vehicle for $9000 down, with the balance to be paid by 60 monthly payments of $812.47 including interest at 10.5% compounded monthly.

a. What was the purchase price of the recreational vehicle?

b. If the principal balance may be prepaid at any time, what is the payout amount two years after the purchase date (not including the scheduled payment on that date)?

3. What price will a finance company pay for a conditional sale contract requiring 15 monthly payments of $180.50, if the company requires a rate of return of 21% compounded semiannually? The first payment is due one month from now.

◆ **4.** Dr. Krawchuk made deposits of $2000 to his RRSP at the end of each calendar quarter for six years. He then left general practice for specialist training and did not make further contributions for $2\frac{1}{2}$ years. What amount was in his RRSP at the end of this period, if the plan earned 10% compounded quarterly over the entire $8\frac{1}{2}$ years?

◆ **5.** A Province of Ontario bond has $14\frac{1}{2}$ years remaining until it matures. The bond pays $231.25 interest at the end of every six months. At maturity, the bond also repays its $5000 face value. What is the fair market value of the bond, if similar provincial bonds are currently providing investors with a return of 7.8% compounded semiannually?

◆ **6.** A court-ordered award for family support calls for payments of $800 per month for five years, followed by payments of $1000 per month for 10 more years. If money is worth 10.5% compounded monthly, what is the economic value of the award one month before the first payment?

◆ **7.** Calculate the future value of an annuity consisting of payments of $800 at the end of each calendar quarter for seven years. The rate of interest earned will be 10% compounded quarterly for the first 30 months and 9% compounded semiannually for the remainder of the annuity's term.

◆ **8.** C&D Stereo sold a stereo system on a plan that required no down payment and nothing to pay until January 1 (four months away). Then the first of 12 monthly payments of $226.51 must be made. The payments were calculated to provide a return on the account receivable of 16.5% compounded monthly. What was the selling price of the stereo system?

CASE

The Tobacco Companies Get Burned!

In November of 1998, a historic settlement proposal was announced in Washington, D.C. The proposal included the largest financial recovery in history.

More than 40 states had sued tobacco companies, alleging that the industry had violated antitrust and consumer protection laws. In addition, the states alleged that the companies had conspired to withhold information about adverse health effects of tobacco, and that the companies had manipulated nicotine levels to keep smokers addicted.

To settle the lawsuits, the industry agreed to dozens of new restrictions and public health initiatives aimed at changing the way the industry does business. The main components of the financial portion of the proposed settlement were as follows:

- Five annual payments of $2.4 billion in January of years 1999 to 2003 inclusive.
- Annual payments on April 15 of each year from 1999 to 2025 inclusive as follows:
  - ☐ 1999–2000: $4.5 billion
  - ☐ 2001: $5 billion
  - ☐ 2002–2003: $6.5 billion
  - ☐ 2004–2025: $9 billion

Reports in the media added the dollar amounts and referred to the proposed financial settlement as a "$219 billion settlement."

Question

1. What was the economic value of the settlement on April 15, 1999? Assume that money is worth 6% compounded annually. To simplify the calculation, assume that the five annual payments of $2.4 billion are paid on April 15 of years 1999 to 2003 inclusive.

www.Exercise.com

Current Amounts Needed to Purchase an Annuity Go to the Web site www.canoe.ca/MoneyRates/rrifs10.html and obtain high, low, and "in-between" interest rate quotes from three financial institutions for a 20-year RRIF annuity. Assuming the interest rates are compounded monthly, calculate the amount required in each case to purchase a 20-year annuity paying $3000 at the end of each month.

Summary of Notation and Key Formulas

PMT = Size of each payment in an annuity

n = Number of payments in the annuity

FV = Future value of an ordinary annuity

PV = Present value of an ordinary annuity

i = (Given) periodic interest rate

i_2 = Equivalent periodic interest rate (per payment interval for a general annuity)

$$c = \frac{\text{Number of compoundings per year}}{\text{Number of payments per year}}$$

d = Number of payment intervals in the period of deferral

The financial calculator keys have the following definitions in annuity problems:

(*n*) = Number of annuity payments, *n*

(*i*) = Periodic interest rate (per payment interval). This is the given *i* for a simple annuity or the equivalent i_2 for a general annuity.

When calculating the present value of an annuity,

(FV) = Lump payment at the end of the annuity

(COMP) (PV) computes the *combined* present value of the annuity and the terminal lump payment

When calculating the future value of an annuity,

(PV) = Lump payment at the end of the annuity

(COMP) (FV) computes the *combined* future value of the annuity and the initial lump payment

Formula (10-1) $FV = PMT\left[\frac{(1+i)^n - 1}{i}\right]$ Finding the future value of an ordinary simple annuity

Formula (10-2) $PV = PMT\left[\frac{1-(1+i)^{-n}}{i}\right]$ Finding the present value of an ordinary simple annuity

Formula (10-3) $c = \frac{\text{Number of compoundings per year}}{\text{Number of payments per year}}$ Finding the number of compoundings per payment interval

Formula (9-4c) $i_2 = (1+i)^c - 1$ Finding the periodic interest rate that matches the payment interval in a general annuity

List of Key Terms

Annuity *(p. 392)*
Deferred annuity *(p. 420)*
Future value of an annuity *(p. 393)*
General annuity *(p. 392)*
Ordinary annuity *(p. 392)*
Payment interval *(p. 392)*
Period of deferral *(p. 420)*
Present value of an annuity *(p. 404)*
Simple annuity *(p. 392)*
Term (of an annuity) *(p. 392)*

LEARNING OBJECTIVES

After completing this chapter, you will be able to:

- Calculate the payment size in ordinary and deferred annuities
- Calculate the number of payments in ordinary and deferred annuities
- Calculate the interest rate in ordinary annuities

CHAPTER

11

Ordinary Annuities: Payment Size, Term, and Interest Rate

IN CHAPTER 10, our discussion of ordinary annuities was restricted to applications of the future value and present value calculations. But there are many circumstances in which one of the other variables must be determined. Consider the following questions.

- How do you calculate the monthly payment required to repay a $10,000 loan at 9% compounded monthly in four years?
- At a forecast rate of return, how long will it take to accumulate $500,000 in an RRSP if you contribute $300 per month?
- What rate of return is required for RRSP contributions of $400 per month to grow to $600,000 in 25 years?
- What interest rate are you being charged when you purchase equipment, furniture, insurance, memberships, magazine subscriptions, etc., on an instalment plan instead of paying cash?

Clearly, the ability to answer such questions is important both in business and in your personal financial affairs.

In this chapter, you will learn how to answer these questions if the payments form an *ordinary* annuity. (Chapter 13 will examine cases in which the payments are at the *beginning* of each payment interval.) The introduction to Chapter 10 stated that its contents would be "the foundation we will build upon throughout Chapters 11 to 15." As you will soon discover, you already have the fundamentals in place for the topics in this chapter. You need only to adapt familiar concepts and formulas to new situations.

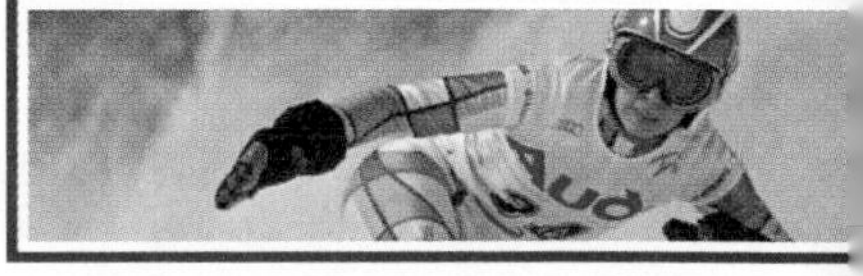

11.1 Calculating the Periodic Payment

Some circumstances in which the periodic payment, *PMT,* must be calculated are:

- Determining the monthly payments on a loan.
- Determining the amount that must be saved on a regular basis to reach a savings goal.
- Determining the periodic payment from an annuity purchased with a lump investment.

In order to calculate *PMT,* the number of payments, *n,* and the periodic interest rate, *i,* must be given (or readily determined from the given information). In addition, you must know *either* the present value, *PV, or* the future value, *FV,* of the annuity.

Algebraic Method The calculation of *PMT* may require up to four steps.

Step 1: If the payments form a simple annuity, go directly to Step 2.

If the payments form a general annuity, use $i_2 = (1 + i)^c - 1$ to calculate the periodic interest rate that matches the payment interval. Use i_2 as the value for i in Step 2.

Step 2: If the annuity's *FV* is known, substitute values of *FV, n,* and *i* into

$$FV = PMT\left[\frac{(1+i)^n - 1}{i}\right] \quad (10\text{-}1)$$

Step 2: If the annuity's *PV* is known, substitute values of *PV, n,* and *i* into

$$PV = PMT\left[\frac{1-(1+i)^{-n}}{i}\right] \quad (10\text{-}2)$$

Step 3: Calculate the quantity within the square brackets.

Step 4: Rearrange the equation to solve for *PMT.*

Financial Calculator Method Remember to obey the cash-flow sign convention for amounts entered in FV and PV.

Step 1: If the payments form a simple annuity, go directly to Step 2.

If the payments form a general annuity, use $i_2 = (1 + i)^c - 1$ to calculate the periodic interest rate that matches the payment interval. Enter the value for i_2 in *i*.

Step 2: If *FV* is known, enter it in FV. In the PV memory, enter any *initial lump* payment whose future value is included in the FV amount. Otherwise, enter "0" in PV.

Step 2: If *PV* is known, enter it in PV. In the FV memory, enter any *final lump* payment whose present value is included in the PV amount. Otherwise, enter "0" in FV.

Step 3: Enter values for *n* (and *i* if not already done in Step 1).

Step 4: COMP PMT

Example 11.1A *Calculating the Periodic Investment Needed to Reach a Savings Target*

Markham Auto Body wishes to accumulate a fund of $300,000 during the next 18 months in order to open at a second location. At the end of each month, a fixed amount will be invested in a money market savings account with an investment dealer. What should the monthly investment be in order to reach the savings objective? The planning assumption is that the account will earn 3.6% compounded monthly.

Solution

The savings target of \$300,000 represents the future value of the fixed monthly investments. Since earnings are compounded *monthly,* the *end-of-month* investments form an *ordinary simple* annuity. We are given:

$$FV = \$300{,}000 \qquad n = 18 \qquad \text{and} \qquad i = \frac{3.6\%}{12} = 0.3\% \text{ per month}$$

Algebraic Solution
Substituting the given values into formula (10-1),

$$FV = PMT\left[\frac{(1+i)^n - 1}{i}\right]$$

Step 2: $$\$300{,}000 = PMT\left[\frac{1.003^{18} - 1}{0.003}\right]$$

Step 3: $$\$300{,}000 = PMT(18.4662733)$$

Step 4: $$PMT = \frac{\$300{,}000}{18.4662733} = \$16{,}245.70$$

Markham Auto Body should make monthly investments of \$16,245.70 in order to accumulate \$300,000 after 18 months.

Financial Calculator Solution

Steps 2 and 3: 300000 (FV) 0 (PV) 18 (n) 0.3 (i)

Step 4: (COMP) (PMT) | −16,245.70 |

Markham Auto Body should make monthly investments of \$16,245.70 in order to accumulate \$300,000 after 18 months.

Example 11.1B *Calculating Loan Payments Which Form an Ordinary General Annuity*

A \$5000 loan requires payments at the end of each quarter for four years. If the interest rate on the loan is 9% compounded monthly, what is the size of each payment?

Solution

The original loan equals the present value of all payments discounted at the rate of interest on the loan. Since interest is compounded *monthly* and payments are made at the *end* of each *quarter,* we have an *ordinary general* annuity with

$$PV = \$5000 \qquad n = 4(4) = 16 \qquad \text{and} \qquad i = \frac{9\%}{12} = 0.75\% \text{ per month}$$

Then,

Step 1: $c = \dfrac{12 \text{ compoundings per year}}{4 \text{ payments per year}} = 3$

and $i_2 = (1 + i)^c - 1 = (1.0075)^3 - 1 = 0.02266917$ per quarter

Algebraic Solution

Substituting the preceding values into formula (10-2),

$$PV = PMT\left[\frac{1 - (1 + i)^{-n}}{i}\right]$$

Step 2: $$\$5000 = PMT\left(\frac{1 - 1.02266917^{-16}}{0.02266917}\right)$$

Step 3: $$\$5000 = PMT(13.29497)$$

Step 4: $$PMT = \frac{\$5000}{13.29497} = \$376.08$$

The size of each quarterly payment is \$376.08.

Financial Calculator Solution

Steps 2 and 3: 5000 (PV) 0 (FV) 16 (n) 2.266917 (i)

Step 4: (COMP) (PMT) [−376.08]

The size of each quarterly payment is \$376.08.

Example 11.1C *Calculating the Size of Loan Payments Required to Reach a Target Balance*

Mr. and Mrs. Morisseau obtained a \$20,000 home improvement loan from their bank at an interest rate of 10.5% compounded monthly. What amount paid monthly will reduce the balance to \$10,000 after five years?

Solution

Again we will use the fundamental principle that

Original principal = Present value of all payments

This principle applies whether or not all payments are equal. (The \$10,000 balance after five years can be viewed as the amount which, along with the last monthly payment, would pay off the loan.)

$$\$20{,}000 = \left(\begin{array}{c}\text{Present value of the}\\ \text{loan payment annuity}\end{array}\right) + \left(\begin{array}{c}\text{Present value of}\\ \text{the \$10,000 balance}\end{array}\right) \qquad (1)$$

Since we have *end-of-month* payments and *monthly* compounding, the payments form an *ordinary simple* annuity. For both the annuity and the terminal payment,

$$n = 12(5) = 60 \qquad \text{and} \qquad i = \frac{10.5\%}{12} = 0.875\%$$

Algebraic Solution

Using formulas (10-2) and (8-2) on the right side of equation (1),

$$PV = PMT\left[\frac{1-(1+i)^{-n}}{i}\right] + FV(1+i)^{-n}$$

$$\$20{,}000 = PMT\left(\frac{1-1.00875^{-60}}{0.00875}\right) + \$10{,}000(1.00875)^{-60}$$

$$\$20{,}000 = PMT(46.52483) + \$5929.08$$

Solving for *PMT*,

$$46.52483PMT = \$20{,}000 - \$5929.08 = \$14{,}070.92$$

$$PMT = \frac{\$14{,}070.92}{46.52483} = \$302.44$$

Monthly payments of \$302.44 will reduce the balance to \$10,000 after five years.

Financial Calculator Solution

We must treat the \$10,000 balance as a terminal cash *outflow.*

20000 (PV) 10000 (+/−) (FV) 0.875 (i) 60 (n) (COMP) (PMT) [−302.44]

Monthly payments of \$302.44 will reduce the balance to \$10,000 after five years.

Example 11.1D *Calculating the Periodic Investment Required to Purchase a Specified Annuity on a Future Date*

Douglas and Margaret Kuramoto together have already accumulated \$125,000 in their RRSPs. They are attempting to estimate the combined annual contributions they must make in order to retire in 15 years, when Doug turns 60. Their goal is to have enough funds in the RRSPs to purchase a 25-year annuity that will pay \$5000 at the end of each month. For their financial projections, they are assuming returns of 8% compounded annually on their RRSPs, and 8.1% compounded monthly on the annuity purchased with their RRSP funds. In order to fulfill the plan, what combined RRSP contribution should they make at the end of each of the next 15 years?

Solution

The given information and the steps in the solution are presented in the following time diagram.

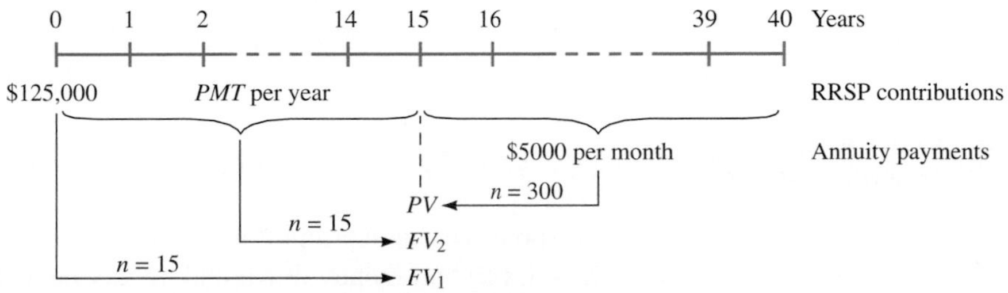

The total amount in the RRSPs 15 years from now will be the future value, FV_1, of the \$125,000 already in the RRSPs *plus* the future value, FV_2, of 15 more annual contributions of size *PMT.* The amount needed to purchase the annuity paying \$5000 per month will be the present value, *PV,* of the 12(25) = 300 payments discounted at $i = \frac{8.1\%}{12} = 0.675\%$. Each series of payments forms an ordinary simple annuity.

In order to have enough money in their RRSPs 15 years from now to purchase the desired annuity, the Kuramotos require

$$FV_1 + FV_2 = PV \qquad (1)$$

Algebraic Solution

The future value of the initial \$125,000 is

$$FV_1 = PV(1 + i)^n = \$125{,}000(1.08)^{15} = \$396{,}521.14$$

The future value of the 15 annual contributions of *PMT* is

$$FV_2 = PMT\left[\frac{(1 + i)^n - 1}{i}\right] = PMT\left(\frac{1.08^{15} - 1}{0.08}\right) = 27.152114\ PMT$$

The amount that will be needed to purchase the annuity is

$$PV = PMT\left[\frac{1 - (1 + i)^{-n}}{i}\right] = \$5000\left(\frac{1 - 1.00675^{-300}}{0.00675}\right) = \$642{,}300.03$$

Substituting these values into equation (1), we obtain

$$\begin{aligned} \$396{,}521.14 + 27.152114\ PMT &= \$642{,}300.03 \\ 27.152114\ PMT &= \$245{,}778.89 \\ PMT &= \$9051.92 \end{aligned}$$

The Kuramotos must make annual RRSP contributions of \$9051.92.

Financial Calculator Solution

First calculate *PV,* the amount that will be needed to purchase the annuity.

5000 (PMT) 0 (FV) 300 (*n*) 0.675 (*i*) (COMP) (PV) | −642,300.03 |

According to equation (1), this amount also represents the combined future value of both the RRSP contributions and the initial \$125,000. Save the displayed *PV* value in (FV) as a cash inflow (when the Kuramotos receive their RRSP funds 15 years from now).

(+/−) (FV) 125000 (+/−) (PV) 15 (*n*) 8 (*i*) (COMP) (PMT) | −9051.92 |

The Kuramotos must make annual RRSP contributions of \$9051.92.

Example 11.1E Calculating the Payment Size in a Deferred Annuity

Budget Appliances has a promotion on a washer-dryer combination selling for \$1750. Buyers will pay "no money down and no payments for six months." The first of 12 equal monthly payments is required six months from the purchase date. What should the monthly payments be if Budget Appliances is to earn 15% compounded monthly on its account receivable during both the deferral period and the repayment period?

Solution

Viewed from the date of the sale, the payments form a deferred simple annuity—a 12-payment ordinary simple annuity following a five-month period of deferral. That is,

$$n = 12 \qquad d = 5 \qquad \text{and} \qquad i = \frac{15\%}{12} = 1.25\%$$

In effect, Budget Appliances makes a $1750 loan to the customer on the date of the sale. The balance owed on the loan will increase over the next five months as interest accrues. Then the 12 monthly payments will pay off this balance. Hence,

$$\begin{pmatrix}\text{Future value of \$1750}\\ \text{at the end of Month 5}\end{pmatrix} = \begin{pmatrix}\text{Present value of the payments}\\ \text{at the end of Month 5}\end{pmatrix}$$

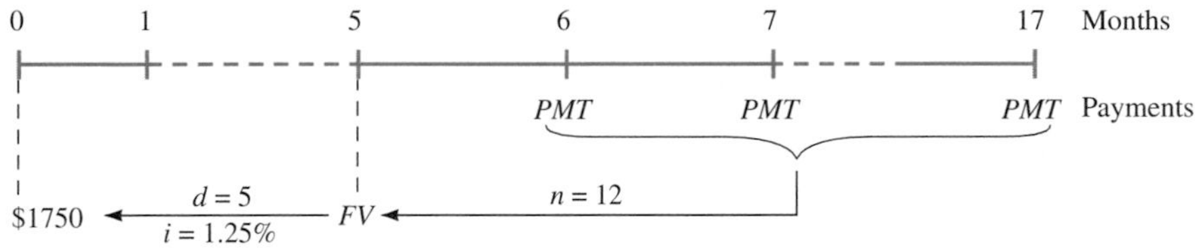

Algebraic Solution

The amount owed after five months will be

$$FV = PV(1 + i)^n = \$1750(1.0125)^5 = \$1862.14$$

This amount is the present value of the 12-payment ordinary simple annuity. Substituting in formula (10-2),

$$\$1862.14 = PMT\left[\frac{1 - (1.0125)^{-12}}{0.0125}\right]$$

$$\$1862.14 = PMT(11.07931)$$

Hence,

$$PMT = \frac{\$1862.14}{11.07931} = \$168.07$$

Monthly payments of $168.07 will provide Budget Appliances with a return of 15% compounded monthly on its account receivable.

Financial Calculator Solution

Calculate the amount owed after five months. We will take Budget Appliances' point of view for the signs of the cash flows.

1750 (+/–) (PV) 0 (PMT) 5 (n) 1.25 (i) (COMP) (FV) [1862.14]

This amount is also the present value of the 12 loan payments which form an ordinary simple annuity. Calculate the monthly payment needed to pay off this balance.

(+/–) (PV) 0 (FV) 12 (n) (COMP) (PMT) [168.07]

Monthly payments of $168.07 will provide Budget Appliances with a return of 15% compounded monthly on its account receivable.

POINT OF INTEREST

Hello! Let's Be Realistic!

The cover story in the September 29, 1997 issue of Maclean's magazine was "Getting Ready for Retirement." One of the key points made in the article was the mismatch between Canadians' financial dreams and the reality of their financial affairs. For example, a poll conducted for Maclean's found that 49% of respondents hoped to retire before age 60. However, only 7% of Canadian households in the 45–54 age group had savings in excess of $250,000 (exclusive of real estate). As pollster Dan Richards bluntly put it: "Clearly, Canadians are living in a state of mass delusion. There is no way on God's green earth that the average person is going to be able to retire in comfort at age 58, given what we know about the savings rate."

In a side box to the feature article, Maclean's presented some estimates of the savings required to retire comfortably at age 65. It is presented verbatim below.

Building a Golden Nest Egg

How much do you need to put aside for retirement? The answer depends partly on when you start. The following figures show how much someone would have to save every year to generate a retirement income (excluding government and company pension benefits) equal to $50,000 in today's dollars, assuming the individual stops work at age 65 and lives to 90. The calculations are based on 3% annual inflation and an 8% return on investments. Experts say that, in general, a person needs 70% of his or her pre-retirement income to maintain a similar standard of living after retirement.

Starting at age:	Savings required at age 65	Annual savings
20	$2,018,387	$5222
35	$1,295,523	$17,154
50	$831,544	$45,938

Source: *Maclean's,* September 29, 1997. Reprinted with permission.

Questions

1. For the starting-at-age-20 case, what income at age 65 will have the same purchasing power as $50,000 today?
2. For the starting-at-age-20 case, show how the amounts for the "Savings required" and "Annual savings" are obtained.
3. The annual savings figures given by Maclean's for age 35 and age 50 are, in fact, incorrect. What are the correct values?

Concept Questions

1. If you pay off a loan over 10 years instead of five years, are the monthly payments only half as large? (Assume the same interest rate in both cases.) Explain your answer.
2. If you wish to accumulate \$100,000 in 10 years instead of 20 years, will your monthly investment have to be twice as large? (Assume the same rate of return in both cases.) Explain your answer.
3. Annuity A and Annuity B have the same values for n and i. $PV(\text{of A}) = 2 \times PV(\text{of B})$. Which of the following is true? Give the reason for your choice.
   (i) $PMT(\text{in A}) = 2 \times PMT(\text{in B})$
   (ii) $PMT(\text{in A}) < 2 \times PMT(\text{in B})$
   (iii) $PMT(\text{in A}) > 2 \times PMT(\text{in B})$
4. Annuity C and Annuity D have the same values for n and i. $FV(\text{of C}) = 2 \times FV(\text{of D})$. Which of the following is true? Give the reason for your choice.
   (i) $PMT(\text{in C}) = 2 \times PMT(\text{in D})$
   (ii) $PMT(\text{in C}) < 2 \times PMT(\text{in D})$
   (iii) $PMT(\text{in C}) > 2 \times PMT(\text{ in D})$
5. Annuity E and Annuity F have the same values for FV and i. $n(\text{for E}) = \frac{1}{2}n(\text{for F})$. Which of the following is true? Give the reason for your choice.
   (i) $PMT(\text{in E}) = 2 \times PMT(\text{in F})$
   (ii) $PMT(\text{in E}) < 2 \times PMT(\text{in F})$
   (iii) $PMT(\text{in E}) > 2 \times PMT(\text{in F})$

Exercise 11.1

Answers to the odd-numbered problems are at the end of the book.

Calculate the periodic payment for each of the ordinary annuities in Problems 1 through 12.

Problem	Present or future value (\$)	Payment interval	Term	Nominal interest rate (%)	Compounding frequency
1.	FV = 76,055	1 year	13 years	10.5	Annually
2.	FV = 35,790	3 months	$5\frac{1}{2}$ years	10	Quarterly
3.	FV = 4357	1 month	$2\frac{1}{2}$ years	7.5	Monthly
4.	FV = 50,000	6 months	$12\frac{1}{2}$ years	8	Semiannually
5.	PV = 20,832	1 month	$8\frac{1}{4}$ years	13.5	Monthly
6.	PV = 35,531	1 quarter	7 years, 9 months	9.9	Quarterly
7.	PV = 20,049	6 months	19 years	9.25	Semiannually
8.	PV = 35,104	1 month	6 years, 7 months	8.4	Monthly
9.	PV = 25,000	3 months	$8\frac{1}{2}$ years	9.5	Semiannually
10.	PV = 50,000	1 month	12 years	8.9	Annually
11.	FV = 100,000	1 year	15 years	9	Quarterly
12.	FV = 30,000	6 months	7 years	8.25	Monthly

Determine the payment size in each of the deferred annuities in Problems 13 through 18. In every case, the annuity is an ordinary annuity following the period of deferral.

Problem	Deferral period	Payment interval (months)	Interest rate (%)	Compounding frequency	Term (years)	Present value ($)
13.	4 years	12	7.75	Annually	10	20,000.00
14.	6 years	6	9.5	Semiannually	$7\frac{1}{2}$	25,000.00
15.	27 months	3	10	Quarterly	20	50,000.00
•16.	4 years	6	7.5	Monthly	10	20,000.00
•17.	6 years	1	9.5	Semiannually	$7\frac{1}{2}$	25,000.00
•18.	27 months	1	10	Quarterly	20	50,000.00

19. In order to accumulate $200,000 after 25 years, calculate the amounts that must be invested at the end of each year at:

a. 8% compounded annually. **b.** 10% compounded annually.

20. Calculate the amounts that must be invested at the end of each year at 9% compounded annually in order to accumulate $200,000 after:

a. 25 years. **b.** 30 years.

21. John has $20,000 available to purchase an annuity. What end-of-month payments can he expect if the funds earn 7.5% compounded monthly and the payments run for:

a. 10 years? **b.** 20 years?

22. What payments can be expected at the end of each quarter from a 10-year annuity purchased for $25,000 if the funds earn:

a. 10% compounded quarterly?

b. 8% compounded quarterly?

23. The interest rate charged on a $20,000 loan is 12% compounded monthly. Calculate the monthly payments and the total interest paid during the life of the loan if the loan is to be paid off over:

a. 5 years. **b.** 10 years. **c.** 15 years.

d. 20 years. **e.** 25 years.

24. The interest rate on a four-year $10,000 loan to purchase a car is 7.2% compounded monthly. What is the amount of the monthly payment? (Source: CIFP course on Personal Financial Planning.)

25. Karen obtained a $20,000 loan at 10.5% compounded monthly. What semi-annual payment will repay the loan in $7\frac{1}{2}$ years?

26. Brenda and Tom want to save $30,000 over the next four years for a down payment on a house. What amount must they regularly save from their month-end pay cheques if their savings can earn 5.5% compounded semi-annually?

27. Henry can buy a farm for $350,000 with terms of $50,000 down and the balance payable over 20 years by quarterly payments including interest at 8% compounded annually. What will be the size of the payments?

28. Seth is supposed to pay $10,000 to Megan today. What payments at the end of each quarter for the next two years would be economically equivalent to the scheduled payment if money can earn 7.5% compounded quarterly?

29. Ardith is scheduled to make a lump payment of $25,000, 11 months from now, to complete a real estate transaction. What end-of-month payments for the next 11 months should the vendor be willing to accept instead of the lump payment if he can invest the funds at 5.4% compounded monthly?

30. In order to purchase another truck, Beatty Transport obtained a $50,000 term loan for five years at 11% compounded semiannually.

a. What are the monthly payments on the loan?

b. What will be the loan's balance at the end of the second year?

31. Mr. Bean wants to borrow $7500 for three years. The interest rate is 9% compounded monthly. (Source: ICB course on Wealth Valuation.)

a. What are the monthly payments?

b. What is the effective rate of interest?

c. What will be the balance owed on the loan at the start of the third year?

•32. The interest rate on a $200,000 loan is 11% compounded quarterly.

a. What payments at the end of every quarter will reduce the balance to $150,000 after $3\frac{1}{2}$ years?

b. If the same payments continue, what will be the balance seven years after the date that the loan was received?

•33. As of Betty's fifty-sixth birthday, she has accumulated $195,000 in her RRSP. What end-of-month payments in a 20-year annuity will these funds purchase at age 65 if she makes no further contributions but continues to earn 8.4% compounded monthly on her RRSP? Assume that the funds in the annuity will earn 7.2% compounded monthly.

•34. On the date of his granddaughter's birth, Mr. Parry deposited $5000 in a trust fund earning 8.25% compounded annually. After the granddaughter's nineteenth birthday, the trust account is to make end-of-month payments to her for four years to assist her with the costs of post-secondary education. If the trust account earns 7.5% compounded monthly during these four years, what will be the size of the monthly payments?

•35. Elizabeth has been able to transfer a $25,000 retiring allowance into an RRSP. She plans to let the RRSP accumulate earnings at the rate of 8.75% compounded annually for 10 years, and then purchase a 15-year annuity making payments at the end of each quarter. What size of payment can she expect if the funds in the annuity earn 9% compounded quarterly?

•36. Ken and Barbara have two children, aged three and six. At the end of every six months for the next $12\frac{1}{2}$ years, they wish to contribute equal amounts to a Registered Education Savings Plan (RESP). Six months after the last RESP contribution, the first of 12 semiannual withdrawals of $5000 will be made. If the RESP earns 8.5% compounded semiannually, what must be the size of their regular RESP contributions?

•37. Four years from now, Tim and Justine plan to take a year's leave of absence from their jobs and travel through Asia, Europe, and Africa. They want to accumulate enough savings during the next four years so they can withdraw $3000 at each month-end for the entire year of leave. What amount must they pay into the fund at the end of every calendar quarter for the next four years to reach their goal? The planning assumptions are that their savings will earn 6% compounded quarterly for the next four years and 4.2% compounded monthly during the fifth year.

•38. Beth and Nelson want to accumulate a combined total of $600,000 in their RRSPs by the time Beth reaches age 60, which will be 30 years from now. They plan to make equal contributions at the end of every six months for the next 25 years, and then to make no further contributions for the subsequent five years of semiretirement. For planning purposes, assume that their RRSPs will earn 7% compounded semiannually for the next 30 years.

a. What should be their combined semiannual RRSP contributions?

b. What combined monthly amount can they expect if they use the $600,000 in their RRSPs 30 years from now to purchase 25-year ordinary annuities? Assume that the funds used to purchase the annuities will earn 7.2% compounded monthly.

•39. Dr. Collins wants the value of her RRSP 30 years from now to have the purchasing power of $500,000 in current dollars.

a. Assuming an inflation rate of 2% per year, what nominal dollar amount should Dr. Collins have in her RRSP after 30 years?

b. Assuming her RRSP will earn 8.5% compounded semiannually, what contributions should she make at the end of every three months to achieve the goal?

•40. Harold, just turned 27, wants to accumulate by age 60 an amount in his RRSP that will have the purchasing power of $300,000 in current dollars. What annual contributions on his twenty-eighth through sixtieth birthdays are required to meet this goal if the RRSP earns 8.5% compounded annually and the rate of inflation is 2.5% per year?

•41. As of Brice's fifty-fourth birthday, he has accumulated $154,000 in his Registered Retirement Savings Plan (RRSP). What size of end-of-month payments in a 20-year annuity will these funds purchase at age 65 if he makes no further contributions? Assume that his RRSP and the investment in the annuity will earn 8.25% compounded monthly.

•42. Leslie received a $40,000 settlement when her employer declared her job redundant. Under special provisions of the Income Tax Act, she was eligible to place $22,000 of the amount in an RRSP. Fifteen years from now, she intends to transfer the money from the RRSP to a Registered Retirement Income Fund (RRIF). Thereafter, Leslie will make equal withdrawals at the end of each quarter for 20 years. If both the RRSP and the RRIF earn 8.5% compounded quarterly, what will be the amount of each withdrawal?

•43. A firm obtained a $3 million low-interest loan from a government agency to build a factory in an economically depressed region. The loan is to be repaid in semiannual payments over 15 years, and the first payment is due three years from today, when the firm's operations are expected to be well established.

a. What will the payments be if the interest rate on the loan is 6% compounded semiannually?

b. What is the nominal amount of interest that will be paid over the lifetime of the loan?

•44. During a one-week promotion, Al's Appliance Warehouse is planning to offer terms of "nothing down and nothing to pay for four months" on major appliances priced above $500. Four months after the date of sale, the first of eight equal monthly payments is due. If the customer is to pay interest at the rate of 12% compounded monthly on the outstanding balance from the date of sale, what will be the monthly payments on an automatic dishwasher priced at $995?

•45. Mr. Donatelli moved from Toronto to Winnipeg to take a job promotion. After selling their Toronto home and buying a home in Winnipeg, the Donatellis have $85,000 in cash on hand. If the funds are used to purchase a deferred annuity from a life insurance company providing a rate of return of 8.25% compounded annually, what payments will they receive at the end of every six months for 20 years after a nine-year deferral period?

•46. Fred asked two life insurance companies to give quotes on a 20-year deferred annuity (with a five-year deferral period) that can be purchased for $100,000. Northwest Mutual quoted payments of $1205 payable at the end of each month. Liberty Standard stated that all their annuity options provide a rate of return equal to 8% compounded annually. Which company offers the better rate of return?

••47. Jack Groman's financial plan is designed to accumulate sufficient funds in his RRSP over the next 28 years to purchase an annuity paying $6000 at the end of each month for 25 years. He will be able to contribute $7000 to his RRSP at the end of each year for the next 10 years. What year-end contribution must he make for the subsequent 18 years to achieve his objective? For these projections, assume that Jack's RRSP will earn 7.5% compounded annually, and that the annuity payments are based on a return of 7.5% compounded monthly.

••48. Cynthia currently has $31,000 in her RRSP. She plans to contribute $5000 at the end of each year for the next 17 years, and then use the accumulated funds to purchase a 20-year annuity making month-end payments.

a. If her RRSP earns 8.75% compounded annually for the next 17 years, and the fund from which the annuity is paid will earn 8.25% compounded monthly, what monthly payments will she receive?

b. If the rate of inflation for the next 17 years is 4% pa, what will be the purchasing power (in today's dollars) of the monthly payments at the start of the annuity?

••49. Mr. Parmar wants to retire in 20 years and purchase a 25-year annuity that will make equal payments at the end of every quarter. The first payment should have the purchasing power of $6000 in today's dollars. If he already has $54,000 in his RRSP, what contributions must he make at the end of every half-year for the next 20 years to achieve his retirement goal? Assume that the rate of inflation for the next 20 years will be 4.5% pa, the RRSP will earn 8% compounded semiannually, and the rate of return on the fund from which the annuity is paid will be 8% compounded quarterly.

11.2 Calculating the Number of Payments

Circumstances in which the number of payments, *n*, must be calculated include:

- Determining the time required for periodic payments to pay off a loan.
- Determining the time required for a periodic savings plan to reach a savings target.
- Determining how long a lump investment can sustain periodic withdrawals.

In order to calculate the number of annuity payments, *PMT* and *i* must be given (or readily determined from the given information). In addition, we must know either the *PV* or the *FV* of the annuity.

Algebraic Method Suppose you substitute known values for *FV, PMT,* and *i* in formula (10-1) for the future value of an annuity, and then proceed to solve for *n*. The procedure is less straightforward than it was for isolating *PMT*—it requires some familiarity with manipulating logarithms. Similar comments apply to formula (10-2) for the present value of an annuity. For these reasons, we present the following versions of formulas (10-1) and (10-2) rearranged to calculate *n*.

$$n = \frac{\ln\left(1 + \frac{i \times FV}{PMT}\right)}{\ln(1+i)} \qquad (10\text{-}1n) \qquad n = -\frac{\ln\left(1 - \frac{i \times PV}{PMT}\right)}{\ln(1+i)} \qquad (10\text{-}2n)$$

Since these are merely new versions of formulas (10-1) and (10-2), we will refer to them as (10-1*n*) and (10-2*n*). (The derivation of formula (10-1*n*) from formula (10-1) is presented in Appendix A.) If the payments form a general annuity, the periodic interest rate that matches the payment interval (that is, i_2) must be substituted for *i*.

Financial Calculator Method The financial calculator method is similar to that for computing *PMT*. Enter the known values for (PMT), (PV), (FV), and (*i*). Then press (COMP) (*n*).

TIP

INTERPRETATION OF "n" WHEN IT IS NOT AN INTEGER

The value obtained for *n* will not necessarily be an integer. To illustrate the interpretation of a non-integer value, suppose $n = 21.3$ in a particular case. This means that there are 22 payments, but the last payment is smaller than the others. Prevailing business practice is to allow a full payment interval for the final reduced payment. Even though the fractional part of *n* in this case is 0.3, it is only an approximation to say that the last payment is 30% of the size of the others. The method for calculating the exact size of the final payment will be presented in Chapter 14.

TIP

OBTAINING THE TERM OF AN ANNUITY FROM "n"

A problem may ask for the *term* of the annuity rather than the number of payments. To obtain the term of the annuity from the number of payments, remember that n (rounded to the next *larger* integer) also represents the number of *payment* intervals. Therefore,

$$\text{Term of annuity} = n\text{ (rounded upward)} \times \text{Payment interval}$$

If the term exceeds 12 months, common practice is to quote the term in years and months (rather than in months, quarters, or half-years).

Example 11.2A *Calculating n Given the Future Value of an Ordinary General Annuity*

One month from now, Maurice will make his first monthly contribution of $250 to an RRSP. In the long run, he expects to earn 8% compounded annually. Rounded to the nearest month, how long will it take for the contributions and accrued interest to reach $100,000?

Solution

Since compounding occurs annually but the contributions are made monthly, the payments form a *general* annuity having

$$FV = \$100{,}000 \qquad PMT = \$250 \qquad \text{and} \qquad i = 8\%$$

To obtain the periodic rate matching the monthly payment interval, first calculate

$$c = \frac{1 \text{ compounding per year}}{12 \text{ payments per year}} = 0.08\overline{3}$$

Then

$$i_2 = (1 + i)^c - 1 = 1.08^{0.08\overline{3}} - 1 = 0.00643403$$

Algebraic Solution

Substitute these values into formula (10-1n).

$$n = \frac{\ln\left(1 + \dfrac{i \times FV}{PMT}\right)}{\ln(1 + i)} = \frac{\ln\left[1 + \dfrac{0.00643403(\$100{,}000)}{\$250}\right]}{\ln(1.00643403)} = \frac{1.27357}{0.0064134} = 198.58$$

The annuity has 199 payments taking 199 months. We need to express the time required in years and months.

$$199 \text{ months} = \frac{199}{12}\text{ yr} = 16.583\text{ yr} = 16\text{ yr} + (0.5833 \times 12\text{ months}) = 16\text{ yr, }7\text{ months}$$

It will take 16 years and seven months for Maurice to accumulate $100,000.

Financial Calculator Solution

250 (+/–) (PMT) 0 (PV) 100000 (FV) 0.643403 (i) (COMP) (n) [198.58]

It will take 16 years and seven months for Maurice to accumulate $100,000. (Refer to the algebraic solution for the conversion of 199 months to 16 years and seven months.)

Example 11.2B *Calculating the Time Required to Pay Off a Loan*

Roy and Lynn are discussing the terms of a $20,000 home improvement loan with their bank's lending officer. The interest rate on the loan will be 12% compounded monthly.

a. How long will it take to repay the loan if the monthly payments are $220?

b. How long will it take to repay the loan if they pay an extra $20 per month?

c. Calculate the approximate total nominal interest savings over the life of the loan as a result of making payments of $240 instead of $220 per month.

Solution

The original loan equals the present value of all the payments. The payments form an ordinary simple annuity with $PV = \$20{,}000$ and $i = 1\%$. In part (a), $PMT = \$220$, while in part (b), $PMT = \$240$.

Algebraic Solution

a. Substitute $PV = \$20{,}000$, $i = 1\%$, and $PMT = \$220$ into formula (10-2n).

$$n = -\frac{\ln\left(1 - \frac{i \times PV}{PMT}\right)}{\ln(1+i)} = -\frac{\ln\left[1 - \frac{0.01(\$20{,}000)}{\$220}\right]}{\ln(1.01)} = -\frac{\ln(0.\overline{09})}{\ln(1.01)} = -\frac{-2.3979}{0.0099503} = 240.99$$

It will take 241 payments, requiring 241 months to pay off the loan. (The last payment will be slightly less than $220.)

$$241 \text{ months} = \frac{241}{12}\text{ yr} = 20.0833 \text{ yr} = 20 \text{ yr} + (0.0833 \times 12) \text{ months} = 20 \text{ yr, } 1 \text{ month}$$

b. Again, we can substitute $PV = \$20{,}000$, $i = 1\%$, and $PMT = \$240$ into formula (10-2n). For those who prefer to work from first principles (and reduce the number of formulas with which they work), we will give one demonstration of calculating n from the basic PV formula (10-2). Substituting the above values into formula (10-2), we obtain

$$PV = PMT\left[\frac{1-(1+i)^{-n}}{i}\right]$$

$$\$20{,}000 = \$240\left(\frac{1-1.01^{-n}}{0.01}\right)$$

Multiplying both sides by $\frac{0.01}{\$240}$ yields

$$\frac{\$20{,}000}{\$240}(0.01) = 1 - 1.01^{-n}$$

Rearranging the equation to isolate 1.01^{-n} on the left-hand side, we have

$$1.01^{-n} = 1 - 0.8\overline{3} = 0.1\overline{6}$$

Taking logarithms of both sides,

$$-n \ln 1.01 = \ln 0.1\overline{6}$$

Hence,

$$n = -\frac{\ln(0.16667)}{\ln(1.01)} = -\frac{-1.79176}{0.0099503} = 180.07$$

It will take 181 months (15 years and one month) to pay off the loan. The last payment will be *approximately* 0.07($240) = $17.

c. With monthly payments of $220, the total of all payments is approximately

$$241(\$220) = \$53{,}020$$

With monthly payments of $240, the total of all payments is approximately

$$180(\$240) = \$43{,}200$$

Ignoring the time value of money, the saving of interest is approximately

$$\$53{,}020 - \$43{,}200 = \$9820$$

Postscript: By increasing their monthly payments by less than 10%, Roy and Lynn will pay off the loan in about 25% less time (essentially 15 years instead of 20 years). Their total interest costs on the $20,000 loan will be reduced by about 30% (from $33,020 to $23,200). This outcome is typical for long-term debt. It is one of the main reasons why personal financial planners encourage us to make even slightly larger payments on long-term debt.

Financial Calculator Solution

a. 20000 (PV) 220 (+/–) (PMT) 1 (i) 0 (FV) (COMP) (n) [240.99]

It will take 241 payments, requiring 241 months to pay off the loan. (The last payment will be slightly less than $220.)

$$241 \text{ months} = \frac{241}{12} \text{ yr} = 20.0833 \text{ yr} = 20 \text{ yr} + (0.0833 \times 12) \text{ months} = 20 \text{ yr, } 1 \text{ month}$$

b. 240 (+/–) (PMT) (COMP) (n) [180.07]

It will take 181 months (15 years and one month) to pay off the loan. The last payment will be *approximately* 0.07($240) = $17.

c. See part (c) and the postscript in the algebraic solution.

Example **11.2C**

Calculating the Time Required to Reach a Savings Goal and the Length of Time a Fund Will Sustain Regular Withdrawals

a. Annual contributions of $5000 will be made at every year-end to an RRSP. To the nearest year, how long will it take for the funds in the RRSP to grow to $500,000 if they earn 7.5% compounded annually?

b. If the \$500,000 will be used to purchase an annuity earning 6% compounded quarterly and paying \$12,000 at the end of each quarter, how long after the purchase date will the annuity payments continue?

Solution

In part (a), the future value of the contributions is to be \$500,000. The contributions form an ordinary simple annuity with $PMT = \$5000$ and $i = 7.5\%$.

In part (b), the accumulated \$500,000 becomes the present value of an ordinary simple annuity having $PMT = \$12{,}000$ and $i = 1.5\%$.

Algebraic Solution

a. Substitute the known values into formula (10-1n)

$$n = \frac{\ln\left(1 + \frac{i \times FV}{PMT}\right)}{\ln(1 + i)} = \frac{\ln\left[1 + \frac{0.075(\$500{,}000)}{\$5000}\right]}{\ln(1.075)} = \frac{2.1401}{0.07232} = 29.59135$$

The interest earned during the thirtieth year[1] will allow the RRSP to reach \$500,000 before the thirtieth contribution is made. Rounded to the nearest year, it will take 30 years for the RRSP to accumulate \$500,000.

b. Substitute the known values into formula (10-2n)

$$n = -\frac{\ln\left(1 - \frac{i \times PV}{PMT}\right)}{\ln(1 + i)} = -\frac{\ln\left[1 - \frac{0.015(\$500{,}000)}{\$12{,}000}\right]}{\ln(1.015)} = -\frac{-0.980829}{0.014889} = 65.88$$

There will be 66 quarterly payments, with the last payment being about 12% smaller than the others. Therefore, the annuity payments will run for

$$\frac{66}{4} = 16.5 \text{ years} = 16 \text{ years and 6 months}$$

Financial Calculator Solution

a. 5000 (+/−) (PMT) 7.5 (i) 500000 (FV) 0 (PV) (COMP) (n) [29.59]

See the discussion in part (a) of the algebraic solution. Rounded to the nearest year, it will take 30 years for the RRSP to accumulate \$500,000.

b. 500000 (+/−) (PV) 12000 (PMT) 1.5 (i) 0 (FV) (COMP) (n) [65.88]

There will be 66 quarterly payments, with the last payment being about 12% smaller than the others. Therefore, the annuity payments will run for

$$\frac{66}{4} = 16.5 \text{ years} = 16 \text{ years and 6 months}$$

---

[1] The math is actually telling us that the RRSP will reach \$500,000 after 29.59135 years if a 30th payment of (essentially) $0.59135 \times \$5000$ is paid into the plan after only 0.59135 of the 30th year. This is not what actually happens—no contribution will be made before the end of the 30th year. To calculate precisely when the RRSP will reach \$500,000 (including accrued interest),

- Calculate the amount in the RRSP after 29 contributions (years).
- Use formula (9-2) to calculate the fraction of a year required for the preceding amount to grow to \$500,000 through the accrual of interest.

Example 11.2D *Calculating the Number of Payments in a Deferred Annuity*

\$10,000 is invested in a fund earning 9.25% compounded semiannually. Five years later, the first semiannual withdrawal of \$1000 will be taken from the fund. After how many withdrawals will the fund be depleted? (The final payment that extinguishes the fund will be smaller than \$1000. Include it in the count.)

Solution

Viewed from the date of the investment, the withdrawals form a deferred simple annuity. The period of deferral is $4\frac{1}{2}$ years long. We have

$$PMT = \$1000 \qquad d = 2(4.5) = 9 \qquad \text{and} \qquad i = \frac{9.25\%}{2} = 4.625\%$$

In effect, the accumulated funds after 4.5 years purchase a "home-made" annuity. As indicated in the following diagram,

$$\begin{pmatrix}\text{Future value of \$10,000} \\ \text{4.5 years from now}\end{pmatrix} = \begin{pmatrix}\text{Present value of the withdrawals} \\ \text{4.5 years from now}\end{pmatrix}$$

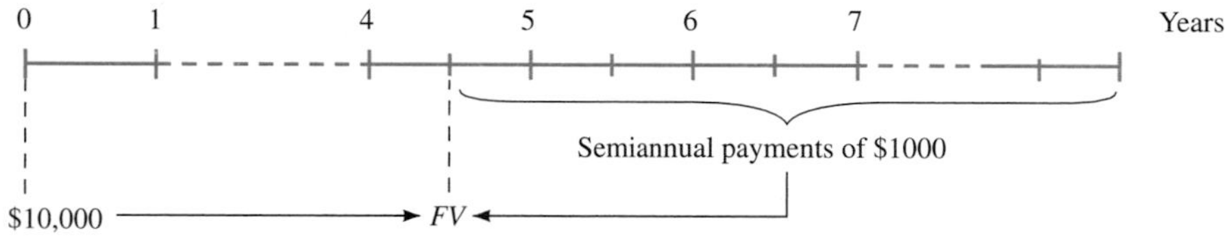

Algebraic Solution

The future value of \$10,000 after $4\frac{1}{2}$ years will be

$$FV = PV(1 + i)^n = \$10{,}000(1.04625)^9 = \$15{,}021.70$$

Now use formula (10-2n) to obtain n.

$$\begin{aligned} n &= -\frac{\ln\left(1 - \dfrac{i \times PV}{PMT}\right)}{\ln(1 + i)} \\ &= -\frac{\ln\left(1 - \dfrac{0.04625 \times \$10{,}000}{\$1000}\right)}{\ln(1.04625)} \\ &= -\frac{\ln(0.305246)}{\ln(1.04625)} \\ &= 26.25 \end{aligned}$$

The fund will be depleted after 27 withdrawals. (The last withdrawal will be about $0.25 \times \$1000 = \$250$.)

Financial Calculator Solution

Calculate the future value of $10,000 after $4\frac{1}{2}$ years.

10000 (+/–) (PV) 0 (PMT) 9 (n) 4.625 (i) (COMP) (FV) | 15,021.71 |

Next calculate the number of withdrawals this amount will sustain.

(+/–) (PV) 1000 (PMT) 0 (FV) (COMP) (n) | 26.25 |

The fund will be depleted after 27 withdrawals. (The last withdrawal will be about $0.25 \times \$1000 = \$250$.)

POINT OF INTEREST

How the Rich Got Rich

Two American professors, Thomas Stanley and William Danko, have studied and written about wealthy Americans for over 25 years. Their recent book, *The Millionaire Next Door: The Surprising Secrets of America's Wealthy* (Pocket Books, 1998), was on the New York Times bestseller list for more than one year. In the book, Stanley and Danko present their findings on who the wealthy are and how they became wealthy. They define "wealthy" as having a *household* net worth (assets minus debts) of at least $1,000,000.

Stanley and Danko determined that, in 1996, 3.5% of American households were millionaires. (With C$1,000,000 equal to about US$700,000, the percentage of Canadian households with a net worth of at least C$1,000,000 is also probably close to 3.5%.)

As the title of their book suggests, typical millionaires do not flaunt the trappings of wealth. Their lifestyles are surprisingly modest. In the words of Stanley and Danko:

> *"Many people who live in expensive homes and drive luxury cars do not have much wealth. Many people who have a great deal of wealth do not live in upscale neighbourhoods. . . . They buy cars that are, on average, only slightly more expensive than the cars less wealthy Americans buy."*

Who are the wealthy? According to Stanley and Danko,

- The average age of American millionaires is 57.
- About 80% are first-generation affluent.
- More than 50% never received a single dollar of inheritance. Only 20% got wealthy through inheritance.
- Two-thirds are self-employed.

How did they become wealthy?

- Most live well below their means. They believe financial independence is more important than displaying high economic status. Most drive domestic cars and own rather than lease their vehicles. They wear inexpensive clothing.

- They plan and budget. Two-thirds of millionaires set short-term and long-term goals. Sixty-two percent know how much their family spends on food, clothing and shelter.
- Most invest at least 15% of household income.
- 95% of millionaires own stocks but most are not active traders. In any year, almost half of them make no trades.

Saving 15% of household income seems a daunting prospect. But many Canadians contribute about 5% off the top of their income to a pension plan. This is usually matched by their employers. In such cases, employees are already saving 10% of their income before they begin a personal savings plan.

Many people often overlook the economic value of accrued pension benefits when they calculate their net worth. An individual retiring at age 60 on an indexed pension of $25,000 per year owns, in effect, an asset worth over $300,000. [You will be able to confirm this in Chapter 12 using formula (12-3). Calculate the present value of a 22-payment annuity starting at $25,000 per year and growing at 2.5% per year with money worth 7% compounded annually.] There are many millionaires who do not realize they are millionaires!

Concept Questions

1. If you double the size of the monthly payment you make on a loan, will you pay it off in (pick one): (i) half the time? (ii) less than half the time? (iii) more than half the time? Give the reason for your choice.
2. If you contribute $250 per month to an RRSP instead of $500 per month, will the time required to reach a particular savings target be (pick one): (i) twice as long? (ii) less than twice as long? (iii) more than twice as long? Give the reason for your choice.
3. The unit for PV and FV is (usually) "$". What is the natural unit for n? (Hint: What is n actually counting?)

Exercise 11.2

Answers to the odd-numbered problems are at the end of the book.

Calculate the term, expressed in years and months, of each of the ordinary annuities in Problems 1 through 12.

Problem	Present or future value ($)	Payment interval	Periodic payment ($)	Nominal interest rate (%)	Compounding frequency
1.	PV = 50,000	6 months	4352.53	9.5	Semiannually
2.	FV = 100,000	1 year	900.46	8.9	Annually
3.	PV = 200,000	3 months	5807.91	9	Quarterly
4.	FV = 30,000	1 month	209.59	8.25	Monthly
5.	PV = 100,000	1 year	10,000.00	8.75	Annually

Problem	Present or future value ($)	Payment interval	Periodic payment ($)	Nominal interest rate (%)	Compounding frequency
6.	$PV = 100{,}000$	1 month	1000.00	9	Monthly
7.	$FV = 100{,}000$	6 months	5000.00	7.5	Semiannually
8.	$FV = 100{,}000$	3 months	3000.00	10	Quarterly
9.	$FV = 74{,}385$	3 months	1200.00	8.75	Annually
10.	$FV = 22{,}500$	6 months	1075.68	9	Monthly
11.	$PV = 5825.85$	1 year	1000.00	7.5	Semiannually
12.	$PV = 20{,}000$	1 month	358.87	10	Quarterly

Determine the term, expressed in years and months, for each of the deferred annuities in Problems 13 through 18. In every case, the annuity is understood to be an ordinary annuity following the period of deferral.

Problem	Deferral period	Periodic payment ($)	Payment interval (months)	Interest rate (%)	Compounding frequency	Term	Present value ($)
13.	7 years	9427.11	12	8.7	Annually	?	40,000.00
14.	$4\frac{1}{2}$ years	2500.00	6	8.5	Semiannually	?	25,498.39
15.	$5\frac{1}{2}$ years	253.89	1	6.75	Monthly	?	15,000.00
•16.	7 years	3764.77	6	8.7	Annually	?	40,000.00
•17.	$4\frac{1}{2}$ years	2500.00	3	8.5	Semiannually	?	37,958.58
•18.	$5\frac{1}{2}$ years	752.43	3	6.75	Monthly	?	15,000.00

19. Rounded to the nearest month, how long will it take end-of-month deposits of $100 to accumulate $10,000 in a savings account that pays interest of 5.25% compounded monthly?

20. How long will $10,000, in a savings account that earns 5.25% compounded monthly, sustain month-end withdrawals of $100?

21. If $300,000 is used to purchase an annuity earning 7.5% compounded monthly and paying $2500 at the end of each month, what will be the term of the annuity?

22. How much longer will it take month-end RRSP contributions of $100 to accumulate $100,000 than month-end contributions of $110? Assume that the RRSP earns 7.5% compounded monthly. Round the time required in each case to the nearest month.

23. How much longer will it take to pay off a $100,000 loan with monthly payments of $1000 than with monthly payments of $1100? The interest rate on the loan is 10.5% compounded monthly.

24. How much longer will it take monthly payments of $1000 to pay off a $100,000 loan if the monthly compounded rate of interest on the loan is 10.5% instead of 9.75%?

25. What duration of annuity paying \$5000 at the end of every quarter can be purchased with \$200,000 if the invested funds earn 8.5% compounded semiannually?

26. Bonnie and Clyde want to take a six-month leave of absence from their jobs to travel extensively in South America. Rounded to the nearest month, how long will it take them to save \$40,000 for the leave if they make month-end contributions of \$700 to their employer's salary deferral plan? The salary deferral plan earns 7.5% compounded semi-annually.

27. Finest Furniture will sell a colour television set priced at \$1395 for \$50 down and payments of \$50 per month, including interest at 13.5% compounded monthly. How long after the date of purchase will the final payment be made?

•28. a. How long will it take monthly payments of \$500 to repay a \$50,000 loan if the interest rate on the loan is 10.25% compounded semiannually?

b. How much will the time to repay the loan be reduced if the payments are \$50 per month larger?

•29. A 65-year-old male can purchase either of the following annuities from a life insurance company for \$50,000. A 25-year term annuity will pay \$386 at the end of each month. A life annuity will pay \$485 at month-end until the death of the annuitant. Beyond what age must the man survive for the life annuity to have the greater economic value? Use 8% compounded monthly as the time value of money.

•30. A 60-year-old woman can purchase either of the following annuities from a life insurance company for \$50,000. A 30-year term annuity will pay \$367 at the end of each month. A life annuity will pay \$405 at month-end until the death of the annuitant. Beyond what age must the woman survive for the life annuity to have the greater economic value? Use 8% compounded monthly as the time value of money.

•31. \$10,000 was invested in a fund earning 7.5% compounded monthly. How many monthly withdrawals of \$300 beginning $3\frac{1}{2}$ years after the date of the initial investment can be taken? Count the final smaller withdrawal.

•32. Nancy borrowed \$8000 from her grandfather to buy a car when she started college. The interest rate being charged is only 4.5% compounded monthly. Nancy is to make the first \$200 monthly payment on the loan three years after the date of the loan. Measured from the date of the first payment, how long will it take her to pay off the loan?

•33. Twelve years ago, Mr. Lawton rolled a \$17,000 retiring allowance into an RRSP that subsequently earned 10% compounded semiannually. Three years ago he transferred the funds to an RRIF. Since then, he has been withdrawing \$1000 at the end of each quarter. If the RRIF earns 8% compounded quarterly, how much longer can the withdrawals continue?

•**34.** Novell Electronics recently bought a patent that will allow it to bring a new product to market in $2\frac{1}{2}$ years. Sales forecasts indicate that the product will increase the quarterly profits by $28,000. If the patent cost $150,000, how long after the date of the patent purchase will it take for the additional profits to repay the original investment along with a return on investment of 15% compounded quarterly? Assume that the additional profits are received at the end of each quarter.

•**35.** Helen and Morley borrowed $20,000 from Helen's father to make a down payment on a house. The interest rate on the loan is 8% compounded annually, but no payments are required for two years. The first monthly payment of $300 is due on the second anniversary of the loan. How long after the date of the original loan will the last payment be made?

•**36.** A property development company obtained a $2.5 million loan to construct a commercial building. The interest rate on the loan is 12% compounded semiannually. The lender granted a period of deferral until rental revenues become established. What quarterly payments, the first occurring 18 months from the date of the loan, are required to pay off the loan over a 20-year period?

•**37.** Bernice is about to retire with $139,000 in her RRSP. She will make no further contributions to the plan, but will allow it to accumulate earnings for another six years. Then she will purchase an annuity providing payments of $5000 at the end of each quarter. Assume that the RRSP will earn 8.5% compounded annually and the funds invested in the annuity will earn 7.5% compounded monthly. How long after the purchase of the annuity will its payments continue?

••**38.** Harold's RRSP is already worth $56,000. Rounded to the nearest month, how long will it take the RRSP to reach $250,000 if additional contributions of $2000 are made at the end of every six months? Assume the RRSP earns 9.75% compounded monthly.

11.3 Calculating the Interest Rate

Circumstances in which you need to calculate the interest rate include:

- Determining the rate of return required for periodic savings to reach a target in a particular length of time.
- Determining the rate of return earned on money used to purchase an annuity.
- Determining the interest rate implied by specified loan payments.
- Determining the interest rate being charged when an instalment payment plan is offered as an alternative to a "cash" payment.
- Determining the interest rate built into the payments on a vehicle or equipment lease.

CAUGHT IN THE WEB

Financial "calculator" worksheets are commonly available at the Web sites of financial institutions and financial services providers. Most are single-purpose calculators designed to do one calculation on a set of input data.

The Capital Builder Calculator in the Toolkit at the Altamira Investment Services Inc. Web site (www.altamira.com/) is more versatile than most Web-based financial calculators. It will allow you to calculate any variable for an ordinary simple annuity if you first enter values for the other four variables. Still, it is less versatile than your own financial calculator because it cannot handle annuities due (Chapter 13) and it does not use the standard cash-flow sign convention.

The interest rate most readily calculated is the periodic interest rate, i. To determine i, you must know the values for PMT, n, and either FV or PV.

Algebraic Method Problems requiring the calculation of i pose some special difficulties for an algebraic approach. Formulas (10-1) for FV and (10-2) for PV cannot be rearranged through algebraic manipulations to isolate i. Consequently, no formulas can be given for i (corresponding to those for n in Section 11.2).

In Appendix B, an approximation technique called "the trial-and-error method" is presented. It is a systematic but time-consuming procedure for improving upon an *estimate* of an equation's solution. With each repetition or *iteration* of the procedure, the approximation gets closer to the correct solution. Solutions for example problems in this section will use only the financial calculator method. The trial-and-error method is illustrated in Appendix B by using it to solve Example 11.3A a second time.

Financial Calculator Method The financial calculator approach for computing i presents no complications. Enter the known values for (PMT), (PV), (FV), and (n). The keystrokes (COMP) (i) will complete the computation.[2]

Calculation of Nominal and Effective Interest Rates If an annuity problem requires the calculation of an interest rate, it will want the *nominal* rate of interest, j, or the *effective* interest rate, f. However, the interest rate you can calculate directly is i, the periodic interest rate (per payment interval). To convert i to j and f, use formulas (8-1) and (9-3), respectively. We present them again for convenient reference.

$$j = mi \quad (8\text{-}1) \qquad \text{and} \qquad f = (1 + i)^m - 1 \quad (9\text{-}3)$$

In both formulas, m is the number of times that the *periodic* rate, i, compounds in a year. Unless you are instructed otherwise, calculate interest rates accurate to the nearest 0.01%.

Example 11.3A *Finding the Rate of Return on Funds Used to Purchase an Annuity*

A life insurance company advertises that \$50,000 will purchase a 20-year annuity paying \$341.13 at the end of each month. What nominal rate of return and effective rate of return does the annuity investment earn?

Solution

The purchase price of an annuity equals the present value of all of its payments. Hence, the rate of return on the \$50,000 purchase price is the discount rate that

[2] The calculator takes longer (up to five seconds) to compute i because the calculator also uses an iterative procedure.

makes the present value of the payments equal to \$50,000. The payments form an ordinary annuity with

$$PV = \$50{,}000 \qquad PMT = \$341.13 \qquad \text{and} \qquad n = 12(20) = 240$$

Solving for i,

50000 (+/–) (PV) 341.13 (PMT) 240 (n) 0 (FV) (COMP) (i) [0.4500]

This is the periodic rate for one payment interval (one month). Therefore, $i = 0.45\%$ per month. Then

$$j = mi = 12(0.4500\%) = 5.40\% \text{ compounded monthly}$$

and the effective interest rate is

$$f = (1 + i)^m - 1 = 1.00450^{12} - 1 = 0.05536 = 5.54\%$$

Example 11.3B Calculating the Rate of Return Required to Reach a Savings Goal in a Specified Time Period

What annually compounded rate of return must Rachel earn in her RRSP in order for month-end contributions of \$500 to accumulate \$600,000 after 25 years?

Solution

The contributions form an ordinary annuity whose future value after 25 years is to be \$600,000. That is,

$$FV = \$600{,}000 \qquad PMT = \$500 \qquad \text{and} \qquad n = 12(25) = 300$$

Solving for i (per payment interval),

600000 (FV) 500 (+/–) (PMT) 300 (n) 0 (PV) (COMP) (i) [0.78386]

That is, $i = 0.78386\%$ per month. The annually compounded rate of return is the same as the effective rate.

$$f = (1 + i)^m - 1 = 1.0078386^{12} - 1 = 0.09823 = 9.82\%$$

Rachel's RRSP must earn 9.82% compounded annually to reach her savings goal.

Example 11.3C Calculating the Implied Interest Rate for an Instalment Payment Option

Rolling Meadows Golf and Country Club allows members to pay the annual membership fee by a single payment of \$2400 at the beginning of the year, or by payments of \$220 at the beginning of each month. What effective rate of interest is paid by members who choose the monthly payment plan?

Solution

The first monthly payment is due on the same date as the full annual fee. In effect, the golf club initially lends \$2400 – \$220 = \$2180 to a member choosing the monthly payment option. The member then repays the "loan" by 11 month-end payments of \$220.

Again we use the fundamental principle that the original "loan" equals the present value of all payments. We need to calculate the discount rate that makes \$2180 the present value of 11 payments of \$220.

2180 (PV) 220 (+/–) (PMT) 11 (n) 0 (FV) (COMP) (i) **1.7824**

With $i = 1.7824\%$ per month, the corresponding effective interest rate is

$$f = (1 + i)^m - 1 = 1.017824^{12} - 1 = 0.236153 = 23.62\%$$

Members on the monthly payment plan are paying an effective rate of 23.62%.

Example 11.3D *Calculating the Interest Rate Equivalent of a Forgone Cash Rebate*

An automobile manufacturer's advertisement announces: "1.8% factory financing over 48 months or \$1000 cash back." If a car buyer finances \$15,000 of a car's purchase price at the low interest rate instead of paying cash and qualifying for the \$1000 rebate, what is the buyer's effective rate of interest?

Solution

An additional front-end cost of the "cheap" 1.8% financing is the forgone \$1000 rebate. To determine the true cost of the 1.8% financing, we will consider the following alternatives.

- Borrow \$15,000 from the manufacturer at 1.8% (compounded monthly) for four years.
- Obtain a four-year loan for \$14,000 elsewhere at the prevailing market interest rate. Pay cash for the car and thereby qualify for the \$1000 rebate.

The alternatives are equivalent if the monthly loan payments are equal. Therefore, we will determine the interest rate in the second case that results in the same monthly payment as for the factory-financed loan. If we can find financing at a *lower* rate, we should borrow \$14,000 from that source and choose the "\$1000 cash back" option.

Step 1: Calculate the monthly payment on a factory-financed \$15,000 four-year loan. The payments form an ordinary annuity having

$$PV = \$15{,}000 \qquad n = 48 \qquad \text{and} \qquad i = \frac{1.8\%}{12} = 0.15\% \text{ per month}$$

15000 (PV) 48 (n) 0.15 (i) 0 (FV) (COMP) (PMT) **−324.12**

Step 2: Determine the interest rate on a four-year \$14,000 loan that would result in the *same* monthly payment.

14000 (PV) (COMP) (i) **0.4391**

With $i = 0.4391\%$ per month,

$$j = mi = 12(0.4391\%) = 5.27\% \text{ compounded monthly}$$

This result means that you will make the same monthly payment (\$324.12) on either of the following loans:

- \$15,000 for four years at 1.8% compounded monthly
- \$14,000 for four years at 5.27% compounded monthly

Therefore, forgoing the cash rebate and financing at 1.8% compounded monthly has the same effect as external financing at 5.27% compounded monthly. (The buyer should arrange external financing if it can be obtained at any rate below 5.27% compounded monthly.)

POINT OF INTEREST

SHOULD YOU CHOOSE "CASH BACK" OR LOW-INTEREST-RATE FINANCING?

To encourage vehicle sales, it is common for automobile manufacturers to offer purchasers of new vehicles a choice between:

- A cash rebate (or discount) on a "cash" purchase, or
- Financing at an interest rate that is significantly lower than may be obtained from financial institutions.

For example, in early 1999 Chrysler advertised:

NEW DODGE CARAVANS

$23,894	**Price includes $1250 Factory Cash or choose . . .**	**0%** financing up to 48 months

The offer means the cash price is $23,894, but if you choose to take advantage of 0% financing, the purchase price is

$$\$23{,}894 + \$1250 = \$25{,}144$$

You should view any forgone rebate or "cash back" as a cost of the "cheap" financing. But how do you decide which alternative to choose?

If you require financing to purchase the vehicle, another option is to borrow the needed funds from a financial institution. This will enable you to take advantage of the $1250 "Factory Cash" offer. The following questions lead you through an analysis of the two financing alternatives.

Questions:

Let us assume you have enough cash savings to cover sales taxes and all other charges. Also assume your bank will lend you $23,894 to be repaid over 48 months.

1. What will the monthly payment be if you use the dealer's 0% financing for 48 months?
2. If, by a remarkable coincidence, the monthly payment on the bank loan is exactly the same amount, what interest rate is the bank charging?
3. What, then, should be your decision criterion for whether to choose the bank loan and take the cash discount, or to choose the 0% financing?
4. Suppose you have investments that you could sell and use the proceeds to purchase the vehicle. What criterion should you use to decide which purchase option to choose?

Concept Questions

1. When you calculate i for an annuity, to what time interval does it apply?
2. Annuity A and Annuity B have the same values for n and PMT. If A's PV is greater than B's PV, which annuity has the larger value of i? Explain briefly.
3. In Example 11.3C, what is wrong with calculating the effective interest rate as follows?

   The total interest charged is

   $$12(\$220) - \$2400 = \$240.00$$

   The interest rate being charged is

   $$\frac{\text{Total interest charged}}{\text{Initial amount of the loan}} \times 100\% = \frac{\$240}{\$2180} \times 100\% = 11.01\%$$

Exercise 11.3

Answers to the odd-numbered problems are at the end of the book.

Calculate all interest rates accurate to the nearest 0.01%.

Calculate the nominal and effective rates of interest for each of the ordinary annuities in Problems 1 through 10. Determine the nominal interest rate whose compounding interval equals the payment interval.

Problem	Present or future value ($)	Payment interval	Periodic payment ($)	Term of annuity
1.	PV = 27,207.34	1 year	4000.00	10 years
2.	PV = 100,000	6 months	6918.51	$12\frac{1}{2}$ years
3.	PV = 50,000	3 months	2377.16	7 years, 9 months
4.	PV = 35,820	1 month	500.00	$8\frac{3}{4}$ years
5.	FV = 500,000	6 months	3030.02	25 years
6.	FV = 291,955	3 months	2500.00	$13\frac{1}{4}$ years
7.	FV = 100,000	1 month	251.33	15 years, 5 months
8.	FV = 138,809	1 month	775.00	$9\frac{1}{4}$ years
9.	FV = 75,000	1 month	318.07	11 years
10.	PV = 48,215	1 year	5000.00	20 years

11. If $100,000 will purchase a 20-year annuity paying $830 at the end of each month, what monthly compounded nominal (annual) rate and effective rate of interest will the funds invested in the annuity earn?
12. If regular month-end deposits of $200 in a savings account amounted to $7727.62 after three years, what monthly compounded nominal (annual) rate and effective rate of interest were paid on the account?
13. After $10\frac{1}{2}$ years of contributions of $2000 at the end of every six months to an RRSP, the accumulated amount stood at $65,727.82. What semiannually compounded nominal rate and effective annual rate of return were earned by the funds in the RRSP?

14. What quarterly compounded nominal rate and effective rate of interest are being charged on a \$5000 loan if quarterly payments of \$302.07 will repay the loan in $5\frac{1}{2}$ years?

15. A \$9000, four-year term loan requires monthly payments of \$234.36. What are the monthly compounded nominal rate and the effective rate of interest on the loan?

16. A finance company paid a furniture retailer \$1050 for a conditional sale contract requiring 12 end-of-month payments of \$100. What effective rate of return will the finance company realize on the purchase?

17. For \$150,000, Continental Life Insurance Co. will sell a 20-year annuity paying \$1200 at the end of each month. What effective rate of return does the annuitant earn?

18. In an insurance settlement for bodily injury, a court awarded Mr. Goodman \$103,600 for two years' loss of wages of \$4000 per month plus interest on the lost wages to the end of the two years. What effective rate of interest has the court allowed on the lost wages?

19. A major daily newspaper charges \$240 for an annual subscription paid in advance, or \$26 per month payable at the end of each month to the carrier. What is the effective interest rate being charged to the monthly payment subscribers?

••20. An advertisement for General Motors trucks offered "2.9% 12-month financing or \$1000 cash back." A truck buyer financed \$17,000 at the low interest rate instead of paying \$16,000 cash (after the \$1000 rebate). What was the effective rate of interest on the loan if the forgone cash rebate was treated as part of the cost of financing? (The 2.9% interest rate was a monthly compounded nominal annual rate.)

••21. A Chrysler advertisement offered "\$1250 cash back or 4.9% factory financing over 48 months" to purchasers of a Dodge Shadow or Plymouth Sundance. A customer financed \$10,000 at the low interest rate instead of paying \$8750 cash (after the \$1250 rebate). What was the effective rate of interest on the loan if the forgone cash rebate was treated as part of the cost of financing? (The 4.9% interest rate was a monthly compounded nominal annual rate.)

*Appendix A: Derivation of the Formula for *n* From the Formula for *FV*

The formula for the future value of an ordinary annuity is

$$FV = PMT\left[\frac{(1+i)^n - 1}{i}\right] \qquad (10\text{-}1)$$

Multiplication of both sides of the equation by $\dfrac{i}{PMT}$ gives

$$\frac{i \times FV}{PMT} = (1+i)^n - 1$$

Rearranging this equation to isolate $(1 + i)^n$ on the left-hand side, we obtain

$$(1 + i)^n = 1 + \frac{i \times FV}{PMT}$$

Now take (natural) logarithms of both sides and use the rule that $\ln(a^k) = k(\ln a)$.

$$n \ln(1 + i) = \ln\left(1 + \frac{i \times FV}{PMT}\right)$$

Therefore,

$$n = \frac{\ln\left(1 + \frac{i \times FV}{PMT}\right)}{\ln(1 + i)} \qquad (10\text{-}1n)$$

*Appendix B: The Trial-and-Error Method for Calculating the Interest Rate per Payment Interval

The trial-and-error method is a procedure for beginning with an *estimate* of the solution to an equation and then improving upon the estimate. The procedure may be repeated as often as needed to obtain the desired degree of accuracy in the answer. Each repetition of the procedure is called an *iteration.*

To describe the procedure in general terms, let us contemplate a situation where *FV, PMT,* and n are known, and we need to calculate the value for i. Since *FV* is known, the appropriate formula to work with is:

$$FV = PMT\left[\frac{(1 + i)^n - 1}{i}\right] \qquad (10\text{-}1)$$

The steps in the procedure are listed in the following table. [The steps are the same if we are given *PV* and start with formula (10-2) instead of (10-1).]

Step	Comment
1. Using the most recent estimate for i, evaluate the right-hand side (RHS).	For the very first estimate, make an educated guess at a reasonable value. For example, try $i = 3\%$ for a three-month payment interval, or $i = 1\%$ for a one-month payment interval.
2. Compare the value obtained in Step 1 to the left-hand side (LHS).	Is the calculated RHS larger or smaller than the LHS?
3. Choose a new value for i that will make the RHS's value closer to the LHS's value.	Use some intuition here. A larger i makes the future value and the RHS larger. (On the other hand, a larger i makes the present value and the RHS of formula (10-2) smaller.)
4. Repeat Steps 1, 2, and 3 until i is obtained to the desired accuracy.	

Example 11.3A, previously solved using the financial calculator method, will now be repeated as Example 11B to illustrate the trial-and-error method.

Example 11B Finding the Rate of Return on Funds Used to Purchase an Annuity

A life insurance company advertises that $50,000 will purchase a 20-year annuity paying $341.13 at the end of each month. What nominal rate of return and effective rate of return does the annuity investment earn? (Calculate these rates accurate to 0.1%.)

Solution

The purchase price of an annuity equals the present value of all of its payments. Hence, the rate of return on the $50,000 purchase price is the discount rate that makes the present value of the payments equal to $50,000. The payments form an ordinary annuity with

$$PV = \$50{,}000 \qquad PMT = \$341.13 \qquad \text{and} \qquad n = 12(20) = 240$$

Substitute these values in formula (10-2).

$$\$50{,}000 = \$341.13\left[\frac{1-(1+i)^{-240}}{i}\right]$$

The general trial-and-error procedure suggested an initial guess of $i = 1\%$ for each month in the payment interval. The payment interval here is just one month. Therefore, choose $i = 1\%$ as the initial guess.

The results of successive iterations should be tabulated.

Iteration number	Estimate of i	$(1+i)^{-240}$	Right-hand side (RHS)
1	0.01	0.0918	$30,981 (Note 1)
2	0.005	0.3021	$47,615 (Note 2)
3	0.004	0.3836	$52,566 (Note 3)
4	0.0045	0.3404	$50,001 (Note 4)

Note 1: We have missed our target value ($50,000) by a "country mile." Present values are larger for lower discount rates. Try $i = 0.5\%$ next.

Note 2: Now we are getting warm. Since we want a larger present value, reduce i some more. Try $i = 0.4\%$.

Note 3: At this point we can see that our target value ($50,000) for the RHS is about midway between $47,615 and $52,566. Therefore, the next estimate for i should be midway between 0.005 and 0.004. Try $i = 0.45\%$.

Note 4: It is pure luck that we happen to hit the target value with our fourth estimate for i. In general, you will need two or three more iterations to obtain a good estimate of the value for i that satisfies the equation. If you hit the target to two-figure accuracy, your interest rate will be accurate to two figures.

The nominal interest rate is

$$j = mi = 12(0.45\%) = 5.4\% \text{ compounded monthly}$$

and the effective interest rate is

$$f = (1+i)^m - 1 = 1.0045^{12} - 1 = 0.0554 = 5.5\%$$

Review Problems

Answers to the odd-numbered problems are at the end of the book.
Interest rates should be calculated accurate to the nearest 0.01%.

1. Calculate the amounts that must be invested at the end of every six months at 7.75% compounded semiannually in order to accumulate $500,000 after:

a. 20 years. **b.** 30 years.

2. What month-end payments discounted at 8.25% compounded monthly will have a present value of $50,000 if the payments run for:

a. 15 years? **b.** 30 years?

3. For $100,000, Royal Life Insurance Co. will sell a 20-year annuity paying $802.76 at the end of each month. What monthly compounded nominal rate and effective rate of return does the annuitant earn on the invested funds?

4. If $400,000 accumulated in an RRSP is used to purchase an annuity earning 7.2% compounded monthly and paying $4500 at the end of each month, what will be the term of the annuity?

5. After contributing $2000 at the end of each quarter for $13\frac{3}{4}$ years, Foster has accumulated $205,064 in his RRSP. What effective annual rate of return was earned by the RRSP over the entire period?

6. What semiannually compounded nominal rate and effective rate of interest are being charged on a $12,000 loan if semiannual payments of $1204.55 will repay the loan in seven years?

7. The interest rate on a $100,000 loan is 9% compounded monthly. How much longer will it take to pay off the loan with monthly payments of $1000 than with monthly payments of $1050?

8. If $100,000 will purchase a 20-year annuity paying $739 at each month's end, what monthly compounded nominal rate and effective rate of interest are earned by the funds?

9. An annuity purchased for $175,000 pays $4000 at the end of every quarter. How long will the payments continue if the funds earn 7% compounded semiannually?

10. A finance company paid a furniture retailer $1934 for a conditional sale contract requiring 12 end-of-month payments of $175. What effective rate of return does the finance company earn on the purchase?

11. Howardson Electric obtained a $90,000 loan at 9.75% compounded monthly. What size of semi-annual payments will repay the loan in 10 years?

◆ **12.** The interest rate on a $100,000 loan is 9.5% compounded quarterly.

a. What quarterly payments will reduce the balance to $75,000 after five years?

b. If the same payments continue, what will be the balance 10 years after the date that the loan was received?

◆ **13.** Mr. Braun wants the value of his RRSP 25 years from now to have the purchasing power of $400,000 in current dollars.

a. Assuming an inflation rate of 4% per year, what nominal dollar amount should Mr. Braun have in his RRSP after 25 years?

b. What contributions should he make at the end of every three months to achieve the goal if his RRSP earns 7.5% compounded semiannually?

◆ **14. a.** How long will it take monthly payments of $600 to repay a $65,000 loan if the interest rate on the loan is 9.5% compounded semiannually?

b. How much will the time to repay the loan be reduced if the payments are $50 per month larger?

◆ **15.** A 70-year-old male can purchase either of the following annuities for the same price from a life insurance company. A 20-year-term annuity will pay \$394 at each month-end. A life annuity will pay \$440 at the end of each month until the death of the annuitant. Beyond what age must the man survive for the life annuity to have the greater economic value? Use 7.2% compounded monthly as the time value of money.

◆ **16.** Noreen's RRSP is currently worth \$125,000. She plans to contribute for 10 more years and then let the plan continue to grow through internal earnings for an additional five years. If the RRSP earns 8% compounded annually, how much must she contribute at the end of every six months during the 10-year period to have \$500,000 in the RRSP 15 years from now?

◆ **17.** \$30,000 is placed in a fund earning 7% compounded quarterly. How many quarterly withdrawals of \$2000 can be made if the first withdrawal occurs three years from today? Count the final withdrawal, which will be less than \$2000.

◆ **18.** A conditional sale contract for a \$1450 transaction required a 10% down payment with the balance to be paid by 12 equal monthly payments. The first payment is due six months after the date of the purchase. The retailer charges an interest rate of 13% compounded semiannually on the unpaid balance. What is the monthly payment?

◆ **19.** After selling their Vancouver home and buying another in Saskatoon, the Martels have \$120,000 cash on hand. If the funds are used to purchase a deferred annuity providing a rate of return of 7.25% compounded annually, what payments will they receive at the end of every six months for a 25-year term starting eight years from now?

◆ **20.** Georgina is about to retire with \$188,000 in her RRSP. She will make no further contributions to the plan, but will allow it to accumulate earnings for another five years. Then she will purchase an annuity providing payments of \$6000 at the end of each quarter. What will be the annuity's term if the RRSP earns 8% compounded annually and the funds invested in the annuity earn 7.5% compounded monthly?

◆ **21.** By the time he turns 60, Justin (just turned age 31) wants the amount in his RRSP to have the purchasing power of \$250,000 in current dollars. What annual contributions on his 32nd through 60th birthdays inclusive are required to meet this goal if the RRSP earns 8% compounded annually and the rate of inflation is 4% per year?

◆◆ **22.** An advertisement for Ford trucks offered "5.9% financing (for 48 months) or \$2000 cash back." A truck buyer financed \$20,000 at the low interest rate instead of paying \$18,000 cash (after the \$2000 rebate). What was the effective rate of interest on the loan if the forgone cash rebate is treated as part of the cost of financing? (The 5.9% interest rate is a monthly compounded nominal annual rate.)

Self-Test Exercise

Answers to the self-test problems are at the end of the book.

1. The interest rate on a \$30,000 loan is 11.25% compounded monthly.

a. What monthly payments are required to pay off the loan in eight years?

b. What monthly payments would be required to reduce the balance to \$10,000 after five years?

2. How much sooner will a \$65,000 loan at 10.5% compounded monthly be paid off if the monthly payments are \$625 instead of \$600? What will be the approximate saving in total (nominal) interest costs over the life of the loan?

3. \$2000 will be contributed to an RRSP at the end of every six months for 20 years. What effective rate of return must the funds in the plan earn if it is to be worth \$250,000 at the end of the 20 years?

4. What payments must be made at the end of each quarter to an RRSP earning 7.5% compounded annually so that its value $8\frac{1}{2}$ years from now will be \$15,000?

◆ **5.** The McGowans are arranging a \$90,000 mortgage loan from their bank. The interest rate on the loan will be 7.9% compounded semiannually.

a. What will the monthly payments be if the loan has a 20-year term?

b. If the McGowans choose to pay \$800 per month, how long will it take to pay off the loan?

◆ **6.** A series of \$500 contributions were made at three-month intervals to a fund earning 7.5% compounded quarterly. The accumulated amount continued to earn 7.5% compounded quarterly for three years after the last contribution, ending the period at \$13,232.56. How many \$500 contributions were made?

◆ **7.** Weston Holdings Ltd. loaned \$3.5 million to a subsidiary to build a plant in Winnipeg. No payments are required for two years, to allow the operations of the plant to become well established. The first monthly payment of \$40,000 is due two years after the date the loan was received. If the interest rate charged on the intercompany loan is 9% compounded monthly, how long (measured from the date of the first payment) will it take the subsidiary to pay off the loan?

◆ **8.** Mr. Sandstrom's will directed that \$20,000 be placed in each of two investment trusts for his grandchildren, Lena and Axel. On each grandchild's eighteenth birthday, he or she is to receive the first of a series of equal quarterly payments running for 15 years. Lena has just turned 13, and Axel's age is eight years, six months. If the funds earn 9.25% compounded semiannually, what size of payment will each grandchild receive?

CASE

Should You Borrow to Make an RRSP Contribution?

Answering this question occupies dozens of newspaper columns and financial commentaries as the March 1 RRSP contribution deadline approaches each year. Many financial institutions and mutual fund companies promote the idea of arranging an "RRSP loan" to obtain money for an RRSP contribution. They sometimes present a scenario giving the impression that borrowing to contribute to an RRSP is so advantageous it is virtually a "no-brainer." The conventional wisdom among financial planners seems to be that it is a good idea with two qualifications—the tax refund from the RRSP contribution should be applied to paying down the loan, and the loan should be paid off within a year. However, as often happens in financial analyses of even moderate complexity, the thinking is usually muddled and flawed.

In this case study, we will identify the key variable(s) for answering the question in the heading. We will discover that the answer (based strictly on financial considerations) turns on a single criterion. Here is the scenario. Suppose your marginal tax rate is 40%. Consequently, if you contribute \$1000 to an RRSP, your taxable income will be reduced by \$1000 and your income tax will be reduced by \$400 (40% of \$1000). To obtain the money for a \$1000 RRSP contribution, you borrow \$1000 at 9% compounded monthly and immediately use the \$400 tax saving to reduce the loan balance to \$600.

Questions

1. What is the monthly loan payment required to pay off the $600 balance in one year?
2. To what amount will the single $1000 contribution grow over the next 20 years if your RRSP earns 9% compounded monthly?

Virtually all analyses of the issue fail to mention a logical alternative to borrowing money for an RRSP contribution. If your budget permits monthly payments on an RRSP loan over the next year, then an alternative to borrowing for an immediate lump RRSP contribution is to use the same budget "room" to start monthly contributions to an RRSP. A subtle but key point will now be developed. In the loan scenario, you immediately applied the tax saving to reduce the loan balance. In effect, you needed to borrow only $600 to make a $1000 RRSP contribution. The $1000 contribution cost you only $600. Similarly, if you make a monthly RRSP contribution of $100, it will really cost you only $60 because of the $40 tax saving. In other words, your after-tax cost is only 60% of your monthly contribution.

Let's turn the last point around and answer this question: How much can you contribute to an RRSP if the after-tax cost to you is to be, say, $50? In this case, the $50 cost represents 60% of your contribution. Therefore, the contribution is $\frac{\$50}{0.6} = \$83.33$.

Questions

3. What monthly RRSP contribution will have the same after-tax cost to you as the monthly loan payment calculated in Question 1?
4. Suppose you make these monthly RRSP contributions. What amount will you have in the RRSP just after the twelfth contribution?
5. To what future value will the Question 4 amount grow over the subsequent 19 years?
6. The future values calculated in Questions 2 and 5 are the amounts in your RRSP 20 years from now under *two alternatives that have the same cost to you.* Comment on the outcome. If the interest rate on an "RRSP loan" is the same as the rate of return earned by your RRSP investments, what is your response to the question in the case's title?
7. Suppose the RRSP earns 12% compounded monthly instead of 9% compounded monthly. Answer Questions 2, 4, and 5 again. Should you borrow for the RRSP contribution in this case?
8. What will be the nature of the outcome if the rate of return earned by the RRSP is *less* than the interest rate on the loan?
9. Summarize your findings as a general decision criterion. (Under what circumstance should you borrow to make an RRSP contribution?)

www.Exercise.com

A "Bug" in a Calculator Web-based calculators do not always give the correct answer. Use the Loan Calculator at www.tdbank.ca/sitemap.html/ to calculate the monthly payment to repay a $10,000 loan at 12% compounded monthly over a five-year term. Also calculate the payment using your financial calculator or formula (10-2). Compare the answers. Try other cases to see if any sort of pattern emerges for the direction and amount of the error. (There is always the possibility that the Loan Calculator may be fixed by the time you try this.)

Summary of Notation and Key Formulas

Formula (10-1*n*) $n = \frac{\ln\left(1 + \frac{i \times FV}{PMT}\right)}{\ln(1 + i)}$ Finding the number of annuity payments given *FV*, *PMT* and *i*

Formula (10-2*n*) $n = -\frac{\ln\left(1 - \frac{i \times PV}{PMT}\right)}{\ln(1 + i)}$ Finding the number of annuity payments given *PV*, *PMT* and *i*

Formula (8-1) $j = mi$ Finding the nominal interest rate corresponding to *i*

Formula (9-3) $f = (1 + i)^m - 1$ Finding the effective interest rate corresponding to *i*

CHAPTER OUTLINE

12.1 Ordinary Perpetuities
*12.2 Constant-Growth Annuities

LEARNING OBJECTIVES

After completing this chapter, you will be able to:

- Calculate the present value of a perpetuity and a deferred perpetuity
- Calculate the present value and future value of an annuity whose payment size grows at a constant rate

C H A P T E R

12

Annuities: Special Situations

TWO SPECIAL CASES OF ANNUITIES are examined in this chapter. The first is *perpetuities*—annuities whose payments continue forever. For example, a college might receive a $200,000 gift or bequest to offer an annual scholarship in perpetuity. The mathematics of perpetuities turns out to be surprisingly simple.

The second special case is constant growth annuities—annuities whose payments increase at a steady rate. We often make a "constant growth assumption" in long-term financial planning. A growing annuity is usually a better approximation of our saving pattern than a constant payment annuity. As wages increase over time (even if only through inflation), most people are able to save more each year. Many pension plans index or link pension payments to the Consumer Price Index. The payments increase over time by the same percentage as the CPI. Again, a growing annuity is a good representation of this payment pattern.

12.1 Ordinary Perpetuities

A **perpetuity** is an annuity whose payments continue forever. An individual might, for example, donate or bequeath a substantial amount of money to a college to establish a scholarship fund. A typical stipulation is that the fund pay out a fixed dollar amount of scholarship awards each year forever. The initial amount used to establish a perpetuity is sometimes called an endowment. The endowment is invested and the perpetuity payments are made from the investment earnings.

Figure 12.1 presents a time diagram for an ordinary perpetuity with payments of size *PMT* at the end of each payment interval.

Figure 12.1 *Time Diagram for the Payments of an Ordinary Perpetuity*

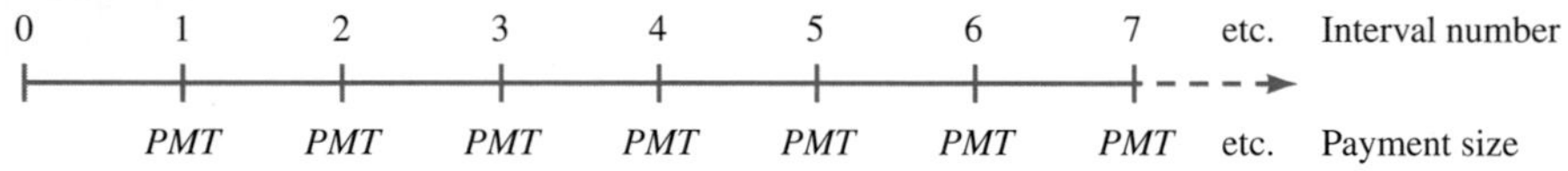

Suppose, for example, that a \$100,000 bequest is made to Seneca College to establish a perpetual bursary fund. If the college invests the funds to earn 6% compounded annually, the maximum amount that can be paid out on each anniversary of the bequest is

$$\$100{,}000 \times 0.06 = \$6000$$

The principal amount will then remain at \$100,000. If a larger amount is paid out, a portion of it will be principal. The fund will eventually be consumed if payments continue at this level. If less than \$6000 is paid out at the end of each year, the retained portion of the annual earnings will compound. The principal balance will then grow over time, enabling the college to increase the annual payout from time to time as costs of post-secondary education rise.

Let us use formula (10-2) to calculate the present value of annual payments of \$6000 in perpetuity, discounting at 6% compounded annually. (Do you have any hunch what the present value will be?) We have $PMT = \$6000$ and $i = 6\% = 0.06$. But what value shall we use for n? To answer this question, recall that payments far in the future make a negligible contribution to present value. So let us just use $n = 1000$. (If you have any doubts about doing this, calculate the present value of the thousandth payment by itself.) We obtain

$$PV = PMT\left[\frac{1-(1+i)^{-n}}{i}\right] = \$6000\left[\frac{1-(1.06)^{-1000}}{0.06}\right] = \$100{,}000$$

We could have anticipated this result from our knowledge that the present value of an annuity represents the amount required to purchase the annuity. For the Seneca College bursary fund, \$100,000 purchased a perpetuity of \$6000 per year. Therefore, the \$100,000 bequest is also the present value, *PV*, of the perpetuity. Let us generalize our earlier calculation.

$$\begin{array}{ccccc} \$100{,}000 & \times & 0.06 & = & \$6000 \\ \uparrow & & \uparrow & & \uparrow \\ PV & & i & & PMT \end{array}$$

Hence,

$$PV \times i = PMT$$

PRESENT VALUE OF AN ORDINARY PERPETUITY

(12-1) $$PV = \frac{PMT}{i}$$

If the payment interval equals the compounding interval, the perpetuity is an ordinary *simple* perpetuity. Otherwise, it is an ordinary *general* annuity. We must then use $i_2 = (1 + i)^c - 1$ to obtain the periodic interest rate that matches the payment interval, and substitute this value for i in formula (12-1).

The future value of a perpetuity is an undefined quantity. Since payments continue forever, the future value is infinite.

Example 12.1A *Calculating the Endowment and Rate of Return Required to Sustain an Ordinary Perpetuity*

A chartered bank is considering the establishment in perpetuity of a Visiting Professor Chair in Public Policy at a university. The ongoing cost will be $7500 at the end of each month.

a. If money can earn 6% compounded monthly in perpetuity, what endowment is required to fund the position?

b. What monthly compounded nominal rate of return must an endowment of $1.25 million earn to fully fund the position?

Solution

a. The payments form an ordinary simple perpetuity having

$$PMT = \$7500 \qquad \text{and} \qquad i = 0.5\% \text{ per month.}$$

The required endowment is

$$PV = \frac{PMT}{i} = \frac{\$7500}{0.005} = \$1,500,000$$

b. With $PV = \$1,250,000$ and $PMT = \$7500$ per month, the required interest rate per payment interval is

$$i = \frac{PMT}{PV} = \frac{\$7500}{\$1,250,000} = 0.006 = 0.6\% \text{ per month}$$

The required nominal rate of return is

$$j = mi = 12(0.6\%) = 7.2\% \text{ compounded monthly}$$

Example 12.1B *Calculating the Price of a Perpetual Preferred Share*

Some preferred shares promise a fixed periodic dividend in perpetuity.

a. What is the fair market value of a perpetual preferred share just after payment of a quarterly $0.50 dividend? The market requires a return of 5% compounded annually on preferred shares of similar risk.

b. What will be an investor's annually compounded rate of return if she is able to purchase these shares at $36.00 each?

Solution

According to the Valuation Principle, the fair market value of a share is the present value of the expected dividend payments (discounted at the rate of return required in the financial market). Since a dividend has just been paid, the first dividend the purchaser will receive will be three months from now. Viewed from the purchase date, the dividend payments form an ordinary perpetuity. Since the payment interval is three months but the compounding interval is one year, the dividend payments form a general perpetuity.

a. Given: $PMT = \$0.50$ and $i = \frac{5\%}{1} = 5\%$

We must first calculate the equivalent periodic rate for the three-month payment interval. (It will be *about* $\frac{5\%}{4} = 1.25\%$ per quarter.)

$$c = \frac{\text{Number of compoundings per year}}{\text{Number of payments per year}} = \frac{1}{4} = 0.25$$

Then

$$i_2 = (1 + i)^c - 1 = 1.05^{0.25} - 1 = 0.0122722 = 1.22722\% \text{ per quarter}$$

and

$$PV = \frac{PMT}{i_2} = \frac{\$0.50}{0.0122722} = \$40.74$$

Thus, the fair market value of a share is \$40.74.

b. If the investor can purchase the shares at a lower price than the fair market value in (a), her rate of return will be greater than 5% compounded annually (because she will receive the same dividends from a smaller investment). The return per payment interval will be

$$i = \frac{PMT}{PV} = \frac{\$0.50}{\$36.00} = 0.01\overline{38} = 1.\overline{38}\% \text{ per quarter}$$

The annually compounded nominal rate of return is the same as the effective rate of return. Using formula (9-3),

$$f = (1 + i)^m - 1 = (1.01\overline{38})^4 - 1 = 0.0567 = 5.67\% \text{ compounded annually}$$

Example 12.1C *Calculating the Initial Endowment for a General Perpetuity*

What amount must be placed in a perpetual fund today if it earns 4.8% compounded semiannually, and monthly payments of \$500 in perpetuity are to start:

a. one month from today?

b. one year from today?

Solution

In both cases, the required initial amount is the present value of the payments. Since payments are made monthly but compounding takes place semiannually, the payments form a *general* perpetuity having

$$PMT = \$500 \text{ per month} \qquad \text{and} \qquad i = \frac{4.8\%}{2} = 2.4\% \text{ per six months}$$

We must calculate the equivalent periodic rate for the one-month payment interval. (It will be *approximately* $\frac{4.8\%}{12} = 0.4\%$ per month.)

$$c = \frac{\text{Number of compoundings per year}}{\text{Number of payments per year}} = \frac{2}{12} = 0.1\overline{6}$$

and

$$i_2 = (1 + i)^c - 1 = (1.024)^{0.1\overline{6}} - 1 = 0.00396057686 = 0.396057686\% \text{ per month}$$

a. The required initial endowment is

$$PV = \frac{PMT}{i_2} = \frac{\$500}{0.00396057686} = \$126{,}244.24$$

The initial amount required to fund the perpetuity is \$126,244.24.

b. The perpetuity is shown on a time line in the following diagram. Viewed from a date 11 months from now, the payments form an ordinary perpetuity. Viewed from today, the payments form a deferred perpetuity with an 11-month period of deferral.

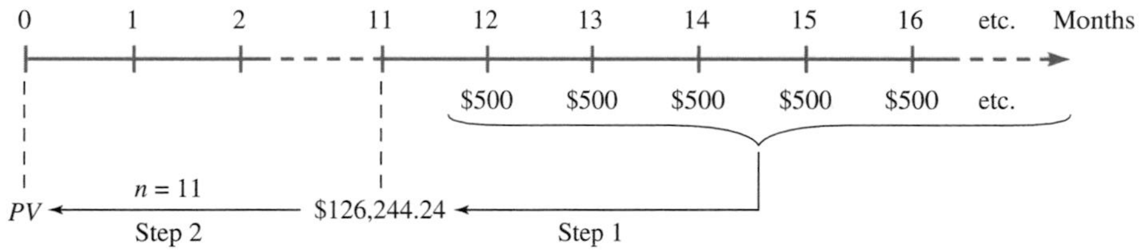

The calculation of today's present value of payments must be done in two steps. First determine the present value, 11 months from today, of the ordinary perpetuity. (This is the same as the \$126,244.24 amount we calculated in part (a).) The amount that must be placed in the fund today is the present value of \$126,244.24, 11 months earlier. Using formula (8-2), this present value is

$$PV = FV(1+i_2)^{-n} = \$126{,}244.24(1.00396057686)^{-11} = \$120{,}872.73$$

The initial amount that must be placed in the perpetual fund is \$120,872.73.

Example 12.1D Calculating the Payment in a Deferred General Perpetuity

Mrs. Paquette is setting up a trust fund with an initial contribution of \$150,000. The funds are to be immediately invested, and the first semiannual payment of a perpetuity is to be made five years from now. The payments are to be used for the care of her son for the rest of his life, and then are to be paid to the Canadian Foundation for Multiple Sclerosis. If the funds in trust earn 5% compounded annually, what is the maximum payment the trust can make in perpetuity?

Solution

The data and solution idea are shown in the time diagram below. Viewed from a focal date $4\frac{1}{2}$ years from now, the payments form an ordinary perpetuity. Since the payment interval (six months) does not equal the compounding interval (one year), the payments form a general annuity.

The future value of the \$150,000 contribution after $4\frac{1}{2}$ years will be the amount (present value) sustaining the perpetuity. That is,

$$\begin{pmatrix} FV \text{ of } \$150{,}000, \\ 4.5 \text{ years from now} \end{pmatrix} = \begin{pmatrix} PV \text{ of the ordinary general} \\ \text{perpetuity } 4.5 \text{ years from now} \end{pmatrix} \qquad ①$$

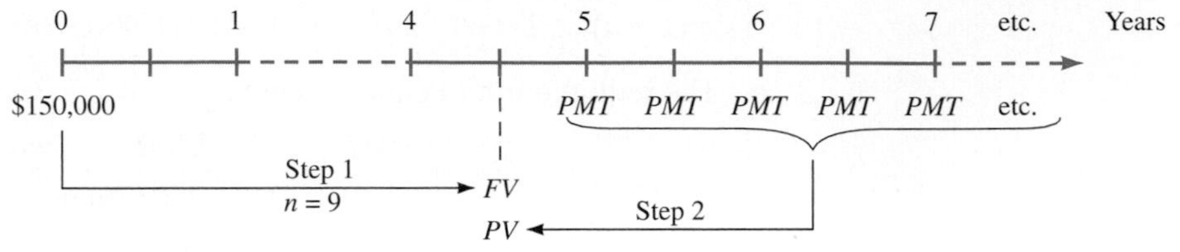

Since

$$i = \frac{5\%}{1} = 5\% \qquad \text{and} \qquad c = \frac{\text{Number of compoundings per year}}{\text{Number of payments per year}} = \frac{1}{2} = 0.5$$

then

$$i_2 = (1 + i)^c - 1 = 1.05^{0.5} - 1 = 0.024695077 = 2.4695077\% \text{ per 6 months}$$

The left side of equation ① is

$$FV = PV(1 + i_2)^n = \$150{,}000(1.024695077)^9 - 1 = \$186{,}828.49$$

The right side is

$$PV = \frac{PMT}{i_2} = \frac{PMT}{0.024695077}$$

Substitute these values into ① giving

$$\$186{,}828.49 = \frac{PMT}{0.024695077}$$

Hence,

$$PMT = 0.024695077 \times \$186{,}828.49 = \$4613.74$$

The trust can make semiannual payments of \$4613.74 in perpetuity.

Concept Questions

1. A perpetuity and an annuity both have the same values for *PMT* and *i*. Which has the larger present value? Give a brief explanation.
2. If market interest rates rise, will it require a larger endowment to sustain a perpetuity with a particular payment size? Give a brief explanation.
3. Will the market value of a perpetual preferred share (paying a fixed periodic dividend) rise if the rate of return required by investors declines? Give a brief explanation.

Exercise 12.1 *Answers to the odd-numbered problems are at the end of the book.*

1. Mrs. O'Reilly gave $125,000 to Medicine Hat College for a perpetual scholarship fund for women in business studies. What amount can be awarded on each anniversary, if the scholarship fund earns 5% compounded annually?
2. What amount is required to fund a perpetuity that pays $2000 at the end of each quarter? The funds can be invested to earn 5% compounded quarterly.
3. A perpetuity is to pay $10,000 at the end of every six months. How much less money is required to fund the perpetuity if the money can be invested to earn 7% compounded semiannually instead of 5% compounded semiannually?
4. Mrs. Fitzgerald wishes to set up a trust paying $500 at each month-end in perpetuity to the foreign missions operated by her church. What initial amount must she place in the trust if it earns 6% compounded monthly on long-term investments?
5. How much more money is required to fund an ordinary perpetuity than a 30-year ordinary annuity if both pay $1000 quarterly and money can earn 6% compounded quarterly?
6. The alumni of the Northern Alberta Institute of Technology (NAIT) donated a total of $37,500 during a special drive to raise money for the institution's scholarship and bursary fund. If the fund earns 5.5% compounded semiannually, what additional annual amount of awards can NAIT grant in perpetuity starting one year from now?
7. An old agreement requires a town to pay $500 per year in perpetuity to the owner of a parcel of land for a water well dug on the property in the 1920s. The well is no longer used, and the town wants to buy out the contract, which has become an administrative nuisance. What amount (including the regular scheduled payment) should the landowner be willing to accept on the date of the next scheduled payment if long-term low-risk investments now earn 5.8% compounded annually?
8. The alumni association of a university is initiating a one-year drive to raise money for a perpetual scholarship endowment fund. The goal is to offer ten scholarships per year, each worth $2000.
   - **a.** How large a fund is required to begin awarding the scholarships one year after the funds are in place if the funds can be invested to earn 5% compounded annually in perpetuity?
   - **b.** Suppose that, during its fund-raising year, the alumni association finds an insurance company that will pay 5.5% compounded annually in perpetuity. How much less money does the association need to raise?
   - **c.** What dollar amount in scholarships can be awarded annually if the alumni association raises only $300,000? Use the interest rate from part (b).
9. A city sells plots in its cemetery for $500 plus an amount calculated to provide for the cost of maintaining the grounds in perpetuity. This cost is figured at $15 per plot due at the end of each quarter. If the city can invest the funds to earn 6.5% compounded annually in perpetuity, what is the price of a plot?

10. A company's preferred shares pay a $2 dividend every six months in perpetuity. What is the fair market value of the shares just after payment of a dividend if the rate of return required by the market on shares of similar risk is

a. 6% compounded semiannually?

b. 7% compounded semiannually?

11. A company's perpetual preferred shares pay a semiannual dividend of $3.00. The next dividend will be paid very soon.

a. At what price would the shares provide an investor with a 6.5% semiannually compounded rate of return?

b. If the shares are trading at $85, what nominal rate of return will they provide to a purchaser?

12. Mr. O'Connor set up a trust account paying $500 per month in perpetuity to the local SPCA. These payments consume all of the interest earned monthly by the trust. Between what amounts does the balance in the trust account fluctuate if it earns 6% compounded monthly?

•**13.** What sum of money, invested today in a perpetual fund earning 5.5% compounded semiannually, will sustain quarterly perpetuity payments of $1000 starting

a. three months from today?

b. one year from today?

•**14.** The common shares of Unicorp. are forecast to pay annual dividends of $2 at the end of each of the next five years, followed by dividends of $3 per year in perpetuity. What is the fair market value of the shares if the market requires a 12% annually compounded rate of return on shares having a similar degree of risk?

•**15.** Mr. Chan has donated $1 million to a college to set up a perpetuity for the purchase of books and journals for a new library to be built and named in his honour. The donation will be invested and earnings will compound for three years, at which time the first of the quarterly perpetuity payments will be made. If the funds earn 6% compounded quarterly, what will be the size of the payments?

•**16.** A wealthy benefactor has donated $1,000,000 to establish a perpetuity that will be used to support the operating costs of a local heritage museum scheduled to open in three years' time. If the funds earn 7.2% compounded monthly, what monthly payments, starting three years from now, can the museum expect?

•**17.** A legal dispute delayed for 18 months the disbursement of a $500,000 bequest designated to provide quarterly payments in perpetuity to a hospice. While under the jurisdiction of the court, the funds earned interest at the rate of 5% compounded semiannually. The hospice has just invested the $500,000 along with its earnings in a perpetual fund earning 5.2% compounded semiannually. What payments will the hospice receive beginning three months from now?

*12.2 Constant-Growth Annuities

In some financial projections, we may wish to incorporate expected growth in a series of regular payments. Some of the growth may be just nominal increases reflecting rising price levels from inflation. In addition, there may be real growth in sales, income, dividends, savings, etc. For example, a business may forecast revenue growth of 5% per year based on annual unit sales growth of about 3% and inflationary unit price increases of 2% per year.

Up to this point, we have considered only annuities having fixed payments. It is a modest mathematical step to learn how to handle **constant-growth annuities**—annuities in which the payments change by the *same percentage* from one payment to the next. Let

g = Rate of growth in payment size between successive payments

For example, if each quarterly payment is 1.5% larger than the preceding payment, then $g = 0.015 = 1.5\%$. In general, if we let PMT represent the amount of the *first* payment, then

$$\begin{aligned}
\text{Second payment} &= PMT + g \times PMT \\
&= PMT(1+g) \\
\text{Third payment} &= (\text{Second payment}) + g \times (\text{Second payment}) \\
&= (\text{Second payment}) \times (1+g) \\
&= PMT(1+g) \times (1+g) \\
&= PMT(1+g)^2
\end{aligned}$$

You can now see the pattern. Each payment is a factor $(1 + g)$ larger than the preceding payment. In other words, the payment's growth rate, g, compounds every payment interval.

The formulas for the future value and the present value of a constant-growth ordinary simple annuity are:

FUTURE VALUE OF A CONSTANT-GROWTH ORDINARY ANNUITY

(12-2) $$FV = PMT\left[\frac{(1+i)^n - (1+g)^n}{i-g}\right]$$

PRESENT VALUE OF A CONSTANT-GROWTH ORDINARY ANNUITY

(12-3) $$PV = PMT\left[\frac{1-(1+g)^n(1+i)^{-n}}{i-g}\right]$$

Note that these formulas have a structure somewhat similar to formulas (10-1) and (10-2). If you substitute $g = 0$ (no growth in the size of payments) into formulas (12-2) and (12-3), you will obtain formulas (10-1) and (10-2). Hence, we can conclude that (10-1) and (10-2) are the "zero-growth case" of the more general formulas (12-2) and (12-3). Formulas (12-2) and (12-3) are not programmed into most financial calculators.

Valuation of Common Shares According to the Valuation Principle, the fair market value of common shares is the present value of all future dividends (discounted at the market's required rate of return). The further we look into the future, the more difficult it becomes to forecast the dividends. Because of this high degree of uncertainty, the rate of return at which investors discount the future dividends is appropriately high.

One approach to stock valuation is to forecast separate dividend growth rates for the short run (three to five years during which forecasts are more reliable) and the long run (where the "crystal ball" becomes cloudy). For example, an analyst might forecast dividends growing at 15% per year for four years and 5% per year thereafter. During the first four years we have a growing annuity; thereafter we have a growing perpetuity. However, at the high discount rates employed in common stock valuation, dividends beyond 30 years contribute little to the present value of the dividend stream.

POINT OF INTEREST

Such a Deal!

In early 1998, the Canada Pension Plan (CPP) was amended to phase in a dramatic increase in the required contribution rates over the next five years. The planned annual increases take the annual contribution rate from 6% of Pensionable Earnings in 1997 to 9.9% in 2003. The contribution rate for 1999 was 7%. (The contribution rate was only 1.8% in 1966 when the CPP system was inaugurated.) Pensionable Earnings are basically annual employment or self-employment income falling between \$3500 and an upper amount that is inflation-indexed. In 1999, this upper limit was \$37,400. Consequently, if your employment income in 1999 was \$40,000, you and your employer each paid half of the maximum CPP contribution for 1999 of:

$$0.07 \times (\$37{,}400 - \$3500) = \$2373$$

Assuming an inflation rate of 1.5% per year for the subsequent four years, the maximum CPP contribution in 2003 will be

$$\text{Contribution rate} \times \text{Pensionable earnings} = 0.099 \times [\$37{,}400(1.015)^4 - \$3500] = \$3583$$

The primary benefit that contributors expect to receive from the CPP is the Retirement Pension. This pension is indexed to the CPI. To be eligible for the maximum CPP pension, you must be age 65 and have made the maximum annual CPP contribution for about 85% of the years since 1965 or age 18, whichever is the shorter period. In 2003, the maximum annual CPP Retirement Pension will be approximately \$9600.

In this Point of Interest, we will estimate the rate of return that CPP contributions must earn to deliver the expected pension. The assumptions are:

- Shona begins to make maximum CPP contributions (\$3583) at age 25 in 2003.
- Thereafter, the rate of inflation (and consequently, the annual increase in the CPP contribution and the Retirement Pension) will be 2%.
- Shona will retire and begin drawing the maximum Retirement Pension at age 65.
- Shona will live to age 90 (well above normal life expectancy).
- CPP contributions and pension payments will be made at the end of each year.

CAUGHT IN THE WEB

Life expectancy tables are based on overall population averages for each age group. Your life expectancy may differ from the overall average for your age group due to factors such as genetics, health, gender, and lifestyle.

At the Northwestern Mutual Life Insurance Company's Web site (www.northwesternmutual.com/games/longevity/), you can respond to questions about factors affecting your life expectancy. Your life expectancy is then calculated and you are given the amount each factor causes your life expectancy to deviate from the population average.

If the pension is funded by Shona's own contributions, then

$$\begin{pmatrix}\text{Future value, at age 65,}\\ \text{of CPP contributions}\end{pmatrix} = \begin{pmatrix}\text{Present value, at age 65,}\\ \text{of pension payments}\end{pmatrix}$$

Since both the contributions and the pension payments grow at the constant rate of inflation, formulas (12-2) and (12-3) must be used for these calculations.

Questions

1. What is the future value, at age 65, of Shona's CPP contributions if the rate of return they earn is:
   a. 3% compounded annually? **b.** 4% compounded annually?
2. What will the (indexed) CPP Retirement Pension be in Shona's first year of retirement? (Assume that the maximum annual CPP Retirement Pension in 2003 is $9600.)
3. What is the present value, at age 65, of Shona's pension payments if the discount rate is:
   a. 3% compounded annually? **b.** 4% compounded annually?
4. What is your *estimate* of the minimum rate of return required for Shona to "self-fund" her CPP Retirement Pension through her CPP contributions?
5. Are you underwhelmed? (No explanation required.)

Example 12.2A *Future Value of Growing RRSP Contributions*

Monica intends to make RRSP contributions on February 28 of each year. She plans to contribute $3000 in the first year and increase the contribution by 3% every year thereafter.

a. Rounded to the nearest dollar, how much will she have in her RRSP at the time of her thirtieth contribution if the plan earns 8% compounded annually?

b. What will be the amount of her last contribution?

Solution

a. The amount in the RRSP will be the future value of the 30 contributions. Viewed from the date of the thirtieth payment, the contributions form a constant-growth ordinary simple annuity having

$$PMT = \$3000 \qquad i = 8\% \qquad n = 30 \qquad \text{and} \qquad g = 3\%$$

Substitute these values into formula (12-2).

$$FV = PMT\left[\frac{(1+i)^n - (1+g)^n}{i - g}\right]$$

$$= \$3000\left(\frac{1.08^{30} - 1.03^{30}}{0.08 - 0.03}\right)$$

$$= \$3000\left(\frac{10.062657 - 2.4272625}{0.05}\right)$$

$$= \$458{,}124$$

Monica will have \$458,124 in her RRSP at the time of her thirtieth contribution.

b. The final payment will be the future value of \$3000 after 29 compoundings at 3%.

$$\text{Final payment} = \$3000(1.03)^{29} = \$7069.70$$

Example 12.2B Amount Required to Purchase an Indexed Annuity

If the money accumulated in an RRSP is used to purchase a fixed payment annuity, the payments will steadily lose purchasing power due to inflation. For this reason, some retirees purchase indexed annuities in which the payments increase at a predetermined rate.

Rounded to the nearest dollar, how much will it cost to purchase a 20-year ordinary annuity making semiannual payments that grow at the rate of 2% compounded semiannually? The first payment is \$10,000 and the funds used to purchase the annuity earn 6% compounded semiannually.

Solution

The cost will be the present value of the payments. The payments form a constant-growth ordinary simple annuity having

$$PMT = \$10{,}000 \quad i = \frac{6\%}{2} = 3\% \text{ per half-year} \quad n = 20 \quad g = \frac{2\%}{2} = 1\% \text{ per half-year}$$

Substitute these values into formula (12-3).

$$PV = PMT\left[\frac{1 - (1+g)^n(1+i)^{-n}}{i - g}\right] = \$10{,}000\left[\frac{1 - (1.01^{20})(1.03^{-20})}{0.03 - 0.01}\right] = \$162{,}205$$

The indexed annuity will cost \$162,205.

Example 12.2C Calculating the Initial Payment in a Constant-Growth Annuity

Derek is 30 years old and intends to accumulate \$1 million in his RRSP by age 60. He expects his income and annual RRSP contributions to keep pace with inflation which he assumes will be 2.5% per year. Rounded to the nearest dollar, what will be his initial contribution one year from now if he assumes the RRSP will earn 8% compounded annually?

Solution

\$1 million is the future value of a constant-growth ordinary simple annuity having

$$FV = \$1{,}000{,}000 \qquad i = 8\% \qquad n = 30 \qquad \text{and} \qquad g = 2.5\%$$

Substitute these values into formula (12-2).

$$FV = PMT\left[\frac{(1+i)^n - (1+g)^n}{i - g}\right]$$

$$\$1{,}000{,}000 = PMT\left(\frac{1.08^{30} - 1.025^{30}}{0.08 - 0.025}\right)$$

$$\$1{,}000{,}000 = PMT\,(144.8198)$$

$$PMT = \frac{\$1{,}000{,}000}{144.820} = \$6905$$

Derek's initial contribution one year from now will be $6905.

Concept Questions

1. In this section, does constant growth mean that each successive payment increases by the same dollar amount? If not, what does it mean?
2. How would you handle cases where successive annuity payments decrease by the same percentage every payment interval?

Exercise 12.2

Answers to the odd-numbered problems are at the end of the book.

1. Suppose year-end contributions to an RRSP start at $3000 and increase by 2.5% per year thereafter. What will be the amount in the RRSP after 25 years if the plan earns 9% compounded annually?
2. Barb Wyre will make year-end contributions for 30 years to an RRSP earning 8% compounded annually.
   a. How much will she have after 30 years if the annual contribution is $2000?
   b. How much more will she have after 30 years if she increases the contributions by 2% every year?
3. Randall wants to accumulate $750,000 in his RRSP by the end of his 30-year working career. What should be his initial year-end contribution if he intends to increase the contribution by 3% every year and the RRSP earns 10% compounded annually?
4. How much will it cost to purchase a 20-year indexed annuity in which the end-of-quarter payments start at $5000 and grow by 0.5% every quarter? Assume that the money used to purchase the annuity earns 6% compounded quarterly.
5. Ken Tuckie is about to buy a 25-year annuity that will deliver end-of-month payments. The first payment will be $1000. How much more will it cost to add an indexation feature providing payment growth at the rate of 2.4% compounded monthly? Assume the money used to purchase the annuity earns 5.4% compounded monthly.
6. Mrs. Sippy (age 65) is about to begin receiving a CPP retirement pension of $9000 per year. This pension is indexed to the Consumer Price Index (CPI). Assume that the annual pension will be paid in a single year-end lump, the CPI will rise 3% per year, and money is worth 6% compounded annually. What is the current economic value of:
   a. 20 years of pension benefits? **b.** 25 years of pension benefits?

•7. Ida Ho is about to retire from a government job with a pension that is indexed to the Consumer Price Index (CPI). She is 60 years old and has a life expectancy of 25 years. Estimate the current economic value of her pension, which will start at $20,000 per year? For the purpose of this estimation, assume that Ida will draw the pension for 25 years, the annual pension will be paid in a single year-end lump, the CPI will rise 2.5% per year, and money is worth 5% compounded annually. How much of the current economic value comes from the indexation feature?

•8. Della Ware has accumulated $300,000 in her RRSP and is about to purchase a 25-year annuity from which she will receive month-end payments. The money used to purchase the annuity will earn 4.8% compounded monthly.

a. What will be the monthly payment without indexing?

b. What will be the initial payment if she chooses an indexation option with growth of 2.4% compounded monthly?

c. How long will it be until the monthly payment from the indexed annuity exceeds the monthly payment from the constant-payment annuity?

•9. Dean has already implemented the first stage of his financial plan. Over a 30-year period, he will continue to increase his annual year-end RRSP contributions by 3% per year. His initial contribution was $2000. At the end of the 30 years, he will transfer the funds to an RRIF and begin end-of-month withdrawals that will increase at the rate of 1.8% compounded monthly for 25 years. Assume that his RRSP will earn 9% compounded annually and his RRIF will earn 6% compounded monthly. What will be the size of his initial RRIF withdrawal?

10. Suppose that a firm's next year-end dividend will be $2.00 per share. An analyst expects that the dividend on the common shares will grow by 3% compounded annually. If the discount rate for this firm is 12% per year, calculate the current market value of the shares. Ignore dividends beyond 40 years. (Source: ICB course on Wealth Valuation.)

•11. The dividends on the common shares of Mosco Inc. are forecast to grow at 10% per year for the next five years. Thereafter, the best guess is that the annual dividend will grow at the same 3% annual rate as the nominal GNP. A $2.00 dividend for the past year was recently paid. Assume that the required rate of return is 14% compounded annually. What is the fair market value of the shares if we ignore all dividends beyond a 30-year time horizon?

Review Problems

Answers to the odd-numbered review problems are at the end of the book.

1. If money can earn 6% compounded annually, what percentage more money is required to fund an ordinary perpetuity paying $1000 at the end of every year, than to fund an ordinary annuity paying $1000 per year for 25 years?
2. A company's preferred shares pay a $1.25 dividend every three months in perpetuity. What is the fair market value of the shares just after payment of a dividend if the rate of return required by the market on shares of similar risk is:

   a. 8% compounded quarterly?

   b. 9% compounded quarterly?
3. ◆ What minimum amount will have to be dedicated today to a fund earning 5.6% compounded quarterly, if the first quarterly payment of $2000 in perpetuity is to occur:

   a. three months from now?

   b. five years from now?
4. ◆ The common shares of Bancorp Ltd. are forecast to pay annual dividends of $3 at the end of each of the next five years, followed by dividends of $2 per year in perpetuity. What is the fair market value of the shares if the market requires a 14% annually compounded rate of return on shares having a similar degree of risk?
5. ◆ How much more money is required to fund an ordinary perpetuity than a 25-year ordinary annuity, if the funds can earn 7% compounded quarterly, and both pay $500 monthly?

Self-Test Exercise

Answers to the self-test problems are at the end of the book.

1. Dr. Pollard donated $50,000 to the Canadian National Institute for the Blind. The money is to be used to make semiannual payments in perpetuity (after a period of deferral) to finance the recording of books on tape for the blind. The first perpetuity payment is to be made five years from the date of the donation. If the funds are invested at 7.5% compounded semiannually, what will be the size of the payments?
2. Mr. Larsen's will directed that $200,000 be invested to establish a perpetuity making payments at the end of each month to his wife for as long as she lives and subsequently to the Canadian Heart Foundation. What will the payments be if the funds can be invested to earn 5.4% compounded monthly?
3. Mrs. McTavish wants to establish an annual $5000 scholarship in memory of her husband. The first scholarship is to be awarded two years from now. If the funds can earn 8.25% compounded annually, what amount must Mrs. McTavish pay now to sustain the scholarship in perpetuity?
4. ◆ What percentage more money is required to fund an ordinary perpetuity than to fund a 30-year ordinary annuity, if the funds can earn 5.8% compounded semiannually? The perpetuity and the annuity each pay $1000 semiannually.

CASE

Should You Choose to Start Receiving the CPP Retirement Pension at Age 60 Instead of Age 65?

Subject to certain restrictions, you may elect to start collecting the Canada Pension Plan (CPP) monthly Retirement Pension at any time after you reach age 60. The payments are then reduced by 0.5% for each month the pension is collected before age 65. For example, if the pension starts at age 60, the monthly payment will be decreased by

$$(60 \text{ months}) \times (0.5\%) = 30\%.$$

The reduction is permanent, extending to payments after age 65 as well.

In Example 10.3H, we compared the economic values of a pension starting at age 60 and a pension starting at age 65. At that point, we ignored an important feature of the CPP Retirement Pension. The payments are indexed to the cost-of-living—every January the payments are increased by the percent change in the CPI index during a recent one-year period.

After studying constant growth annuities, we can do a more rigorous analysis by incorporating an estimate of the rate of inflation in future years. Turn back the clock to consider Neil as he approaches age 60 at the end of 1999. The maximum CPP Retirement Pension in the year 2000 is about \$9200. If he elects to start receiving the pension at age 60, it will be 0.7 × \$9200 = \$6440 per year. In our analysis, we will assume the pension is received as a single payment at each year-end. The payments then form an ordinary annuity. Also assume a 2% annual rise in the Consumer Price Index (CPI) in the years ahead. The CPP pension will then increase by 2% per year.

Questions

1. Assuming that Neil lives another 20 years (the life expectancy of a 60-year-old male), what is the economic value (at the beginning of 2000) of the reduced pension if the time value of money is 6% compounded annually?
2. What will Neil's initial pension be if he waits until age 65 to start receiving it?
3. What is the economic value (at the beginning of 2000) of the full pension if Neil receives it for 15 years from age 65 to age 80? Again use 6% compounded annually for the time value of money.
4. Compare the economic values. Which choice should Neil make?
5. Repeat Questions 1, 3, and 4 using 4.5% compounded annually as the time value of money.

Summary of Notation and Key Formulas

g = Rate of growth in payment size between successive payments

Formula (12-1) $PV = \dfrac{PMT}{i}$ Finding the present value of an ordinary perpetuity

Formula (12-2) $FV = PMT\left[\dfrac{(1+i)^n - (1+g)^n}{i-g}\right]$ Finding the future value of a constant-growth ordinary annuity

Formula (12-3) $PV = PMT\left[\dfrac{1-(1+g)^n(1+i)^{-n}}{i-g}\right]$ Finding the present value of a constant-growth ordinary annuity

List of Key Terms

Constant-growth annuity *(p. 487)* Perpetuity *(p. 480)*

CHAPTER OUTLINE

LEARNING OBJECTIVES

After completing this chapter, you will be able to:

- Calculate the future value and present value of annuities due
- Calculate the payment size, number of payments, and interest rate for annuities due

13

Annuities Due

IF YOU LEASE EQUIPMENT, a vehicle, or a rental property, the typical lease contract requires payments at the beginning of each month. Insurance premiums must be paid at the beginning of each period of coverage. Membership dues are usually paid in advance. These are all examples of annuities *due* in which the payments occur at the *beginning* of each payment interval.

In recent years, the proportion of equipment and vehicles being leased has been increasing. For example, more than half of new vehicles are now leased rather than purchased. Therefore, it is increasingly important that you understand the mathematics of annuities due. As you will soon learn, only a small modification to the mathematics of ordinary annuities is needed to handle annuities due.

13.1 Future Value of an Annuity Due

In an **annuity due**,[1] the payments are made at the *beginning* of each payment interval. Note that we now have two *independent* criteria for classifying annuities. Based on the *timing* of the payment within the payment interval, an annuity is classified as *either* an *ordinary* annuity *or* an annuity *due*. Based on whether or not the payment interval equals the compounding interval, an annuity is *either* a *simple* annuity *or* a *general* annuity. These two independent criteria result in four categories of annuities, which are summarized in Table 13.1.

Table 13.1 *Distinguishing Characteristics of Annuity Categories*

Annuity category	Is the payment at the *end* or at the *beginning* of each payment interval?	Compare the payment interval to the compounding interval.
Ordinary simple annuity	End	Equal
Ordinary general annuity	End	Not equal
Simple annuity due	Beginning	Equal
General annuity due	Beginning	Not equal

Figure 13.1 presents the time diagram for an annuity due consisting of n payments, each of size *PMT*. The serial number for each payment interval is placed above the tick mark at the *end* of the interval.

Figure 13.1 *Time Diagram for an n-Payment Annuity Due*

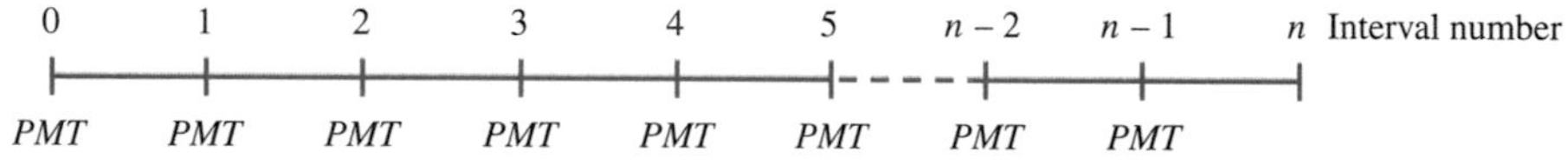

The future value of an annuity due is the sum of the future values of all of the payments (evaluated at the end of the annuity). We will use the symbol *FV*(due) for the future value of an annuity due. The symbols *PMT*, n, and i have the same meaning as for ordinary annuities.

TRAP *WHAT IS MEANT BY THE END OF AN ANNUITY?*

Don't confuse "the end of an annuity" with "the end of the payments" or "the date of the last payment." The end of an annuity means "the end of the annuity's *term*" or "the end of the last payment interval." It occurs one payment interval *after* the last payment in an annuity *due*.

Similarly, the *beginning of an annuity* refers to "the start of the annuity's term" or "the start of the first payment interval." It does coincide with the first payment in an annuity due.

[1] An annuity *due* is sometimes referred to as an annuity *in advance*. An *ordinary* annuity is then called an annuity *in arrears*.

CAUGHT IN THE WEB

Fidelity Investments presents an interactive and very instructive chart as part of its Growth Calculator at www.fidelity.ca/planning/tools/growth/growth.html. Each column in the chart breaks down the future value of a simple annuity due at the end of each year into three components: "invested capital, simple earnings, and compound earnings." *Simple earnings* represent interest earned on invested capital on a simple interest basis. *Compound earnings* represent interest earned on converted interest.

As you change the value for any input variable by moving its "slider," you can watch the impact on each component. (Data may also be entered manually.) When you move the cursor over any column of the chart, the dollar amount is displayed.

Future Value Using the Algebraic Method

The formula for the future value of an annuity *due* may be quickly derived from the formula for the future value of an *ordinary* annuity. Figure 13.2 helps us to see the connection between them. In the figure, n annuity payments of size PMT are shown on each of two time lines.

In the upper part of the figure, the payments are viewed as an annuity due. The focal date for its future value, FV(due), is at the end of the annuity (one payment interval after the last payment). In the lower part of the figure, the payments are viewed as an ordinary annuity. The focal date for its future value, FV, is at the end of the annuity (coincident with the last payment).

Figure 13.2 *The Relationship between FV(due) and FV*

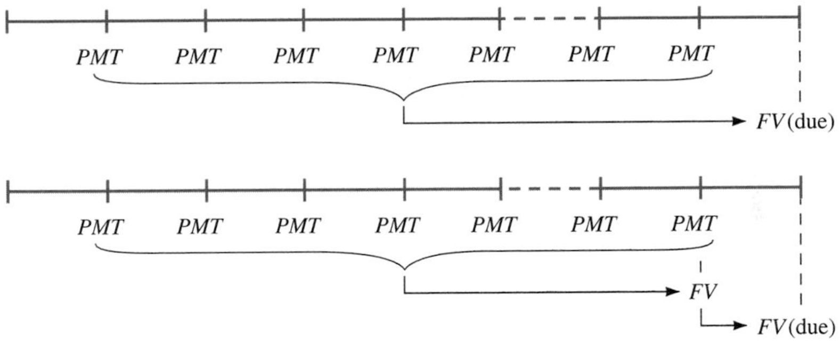

Each of these future values is the single amount (at the respective focal date) that is equivalent to the *same* series of payments. The two future values are thus equivalent to each other, allowing for the time interval between them. Therefore, FV(due) equals the future value of FV, one payment interval later. That is,

$$FV(\text{due}) = FV \times (1 + i)$$

We see that the future value of an annuity due is simply $(1 + i)$ times the future value of an ordinary annuity. Substituting from formula (10-1) for FV, we obtain

FUTURE VALUE OF A SIMPLE ANNUITY DUE

$$\begin{aligned} FV(\text{due}) &= FV \times (1 + i) \\ &= PMT\left[\frac{(1 + i)^n - 1}{i}\right] \times (1 + i) \end{aligned} \quad (13\text{-}1)$$

If the payments form a *general* annuity due, use $i_2 = (1 + i)^c - 1$ to calculate the periodic interest rate that matches the payment interval. Then substitute this value for i in formula (13-1).

Future Value Using the Financial Calculator Functions

Since $FV(\text{due}) = FV \times (1 + i)$, the approach that probably occurs to you is to compute the annuity's future value as though it were an *ordinary* annuity, and then multiply the result by $(1 + i)$. Even this simple step may be avoided if the financial calculator is first "informed" that the annuity is an annuity *due*. Refer to the Appendix for specific instructions on how to set your particular calculator to the annuity due mode. In example problems, "**BGN mode**" indicates that the calculator should be set to the annuity due mode.

Example 13.1A *Calculating the Future Value of a Simple Annuity Due*

To the nearest dollar, how much will Stan accumulate in his RRSP by age 60 if he makes semiannual contributions of \$2000 starting on his twenty-seventh birthday? Assume that the RRSP earns 8% compounded semiannually and that no contribution is made on his sixtieth birthday.

Solution

The accumulated amount will be the future value of the contributions on Stan's sixtieth birthday. Viewed from a focal date at his sixtieth birthday, the RRSP contributions form an annuity *due.* Since the payment interval equals the compounding interval, we have a *simple* annuity due with:

$$PMT = \$2000 \qquad i = \frac{8\%}{2} = 4\% \qquad \text{and} \qquad n = 2(33) = 66 \text{ payments}$$

Algebraic Solution

Substitute the preceding values into formula (13-1).

$$\begin{aligned} FV(\text{due}) &= PMT\left[\frac{(1+i)^n - 1}{i}\right] \times (1+i) \\ &= \$2000\left(\frac{1.04^{66} - 1}{0.04}\right) \times (1.04) \\ &= \$2000\left(\frac{13.310685 - 1}{0.04}\right)(1.04) \\ &= \$640{,}156 \end{aligned}$$

Financial Calculator Solution

Set the calculator to the **BGN mode**.

2000 (+/−) (PMT) 0 (PV) 4 (i) 66 (n) (COMP) (FV) [640,156]

Stan will have \$640,156 in his RRSP at age 60.

Example 13.1B *Calculating the Future Value of a General Annuity Due*

Repeat Example 13.1A with the change that interest is 8% compounded annually instead of 8% compounded semiannually.

Solution

We now have a general annuity since the compounding interval (one year) differs from the payment interval (six months). The value we must use for i in the FV formula is the periodic rate for the six-month payment interval. (It will be about $\frac{8\%}{2} = 4\%$.) Substitute

$$i = \frac{8\%}{1} = 8\% \quad \text{and} \quad c = \frac{\text{Number of compoundings per year}}{\text{Number of payments per year}} = \frac{1}{2} = 0.5$$

into

$$i_2 = (1 + i)^c - 1 = (1.08)^{0.5} - 1 = 0.03923048 = 3.923048\% \text{ per six months}$$

Algebraic Solution

Use the value of i_2 for i in formula (13-1) giving

$$\begin{aligned} FV(\text{due}) &= PMT\left[\frac{(1+i)^n - 1}{i}\right] \times (1+i) \\ &= \$2000\left(\frac{1.03923048^{66} - 1}{0.03923048}\right) \times (1.03923048) \\ &= \$2000\left(\frac{12.676046 - 1}{0.03923048}\right)(1.03923048) \\ &= \$618{,}606 \end{aligned}$$

Financial Calculator Solution

Set the calculator to the **BGN mode.**

2000 (+/–) (PMT) 0 (PV) 3.923048 (i) 66 (n) (COMP) (FV) [618,606]

Stan will have $618,606 in his RRSP at age 60.

Example 13.1C *Calculating the Future Value of an Annuity Due where an Interest Rate Change Occurs During the Term of the Annuity*

Stephanie intends to contribute $2500 to her RRSP at the beginning of every six months starting today. If the RRSP earns 8% compounded semiannually for the first seven years and 7% compounded semiannually thereafter, what amount will she have in the plan after 20 years?

Solution

The amount in the plan will be the future value of the contributions.

Note: We should understand from the wording of this question that we are to determine the amount in the RRSP after *20 years' contributions.* There will be 40 contributions in 20 years. The fortieth contribution will occur $39\frac{1}{2}$ years from now. The 40 contributions form an annuity due when viewed from the focal date at 20 years. (If Stephanie makes a forty-first contribution 20 years from today, that payment will not be included in *FV*(due) calculated at a focal date 20 years from today.)

The future value cannot be calculated in one step because the interest rate changes after seven years. The solution strategy is indicated in the following time diagram. Since the payment interval equals the compounding interval throughout, the payments form a simple annuity in both segments of the 20 years.

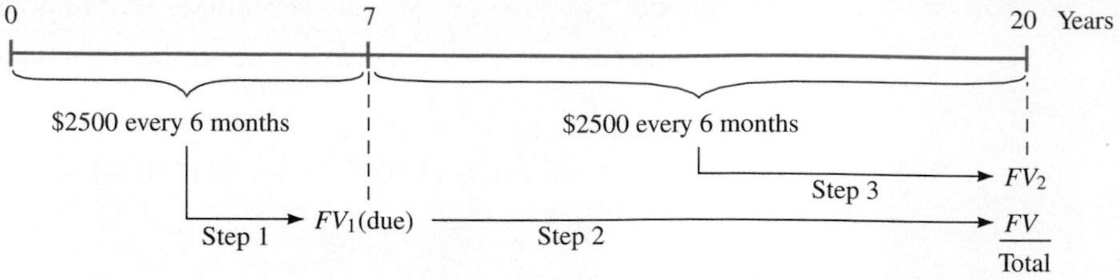

For the first seven years, $i = \frac{8\%}{2} = 4\%$ and $n = 2(7) = 14$

For the next 13 years, $i = \frac{7\%}{2} = 3.5\%$ and $n = 2(13) = 26$

Algebraic Solution

The future value of the first 14 contributions after seven years will be

$$\begin{aligned} FV_1(\text{due}) &= PMT\left[\frac{(1+i)^n - 1}{i}\right] \times (1+i) \\ &= \$2500\left(\frac{1.04^{14} - 1}{0.04}\right) \times (1.04) \\ &= \$2500(18.291911)(1.04) \\ &= \$47{,}558.97 \end{aligned}$$

The future value of $47,558.97 an additional 13 years later will be

$$FV = PV(1+i)^n = \$47{,}558.97(1.035)^{26} = \$116{,}327.27$$

The future value, 20 years from now, of the last 26 payments will be

$$\begin{aligned} FV_2(\text{due}) &= \$2500\left[\frac{(1.035)^{26} - 1}{0.035}\right] \times (1.035) \\ &= \$2500(41.3131017)(1.035) \\ &= \$106{,}897.65 \end{aligned}$$

The total amount in the RRSP after 20 years will be

$$FV + FV_2(\text{due}) = \$116{,}327.27 + \$106{,}897.65 = \$223{,}224.92$$

Financial Calculator Solution

BGN mode

Calculate the future value of the first 14 contributions after seven years.

2500 (+/–) (PMT) 0 (PV) 4 (i) 14 (n) (COMP) (FV) 47,558.97

Steps 2 and 3 in the diagram can be combined. Calculate the combined future value, 20 years from now, of the preceding amount and the next 26 contributions.

(+/–) (PV) 3.5 (i) 26 (n) (COMP) (FV) 223,224.92

Stephanie will have $223,224.92 in her RRSP after 20 years.

POINT OF INTEREST

The Ten-Percent Solution (for Achieving Financial Security)

In 1989 *The Wealthy Barber* by David Chilton was first published by Stoddart Publishing Co. Ltd. Its engaging style and common-sense approach to personal financial planning made it the all-time Canadian best-seller. In the book, the principles of financial planning and money management are revealed through conversations between an unlikely financial hero, barber shop proprietor Roy Miller, and his patrons.

In Chapter 4, titled "The Ten Percent Solution," Tom and Dave arrive for their biweekly haircut accompanied by Dave's sister Cathy. They are all in their late twenties and eager to hear Roy reveal his "golden secret" that "guarantees . . . someday you'll be rich."

To impress the wealth-building potential of compound interest upon Tom, Dave, and Cathy, Roy poses two questions. (The questions and their answers are underlined below for later reference.) With your current knowledge of annuities, you should be able to obtain the answers that amaze Tom, Dave, and Cathy. Roy is speaking as we join the dialogue.

"Wealth beyond your wildest dreams is possible if you learn the golden secret: Invest ten percent of all you make for long-term growth. If you follow that one simple guideline, someday you'll be a very rich man."

"That's it?" asked Tom. "I could get that from a Bank of Nova Scotia commercial!"

"Patience, Tom," replied Roy. "I'll tell you things that turn a seemingly simple sentence into an extremely powerful thought.

"Cathy, if you invested $2400 a year, say $200 a month, for the next 30 years, and averaged a 15% return per year, how much money do you think you'd end up with?" challenged Roy.

"Well, $2400 times 30 is $72,000 . . .

plus growth . . .

I don't know . . .

"I'd say $200,000. Maybe not quite that much," Cathy concluded.

"Wrong. The answer is $1,402,000," Roy declared.

"Get real!" was Tom's initial reaction. When he realized that Roy was serious, he paled. "What about inflation? And where am I going to get 15%? For that matter, where am I going to get $200 per month?" he stammered.

"All good questions, Tom, and we'll get to them in due course. Dave, you try one. If you had started putting $30 a month away, the equivalent of a dollar a day, at age 18 and you continued until age 65, averaging a 15% annual return, how much would you end up with?"

"I hate math, Roy, but I'll give it a shot," replied Dave. "Thirty dollars a month is $360 a year, times 47 years . . . Anybody have a calculator?"

"It's just under $17,000," injected Roy.

"Plus growth, I'll say about $70,000."

"Close," responded Roy. "The answer is $2,679,000."

"Bull," scoffed Tom.

"No, not bull . . . magic. The magic of compound interest—interest on principal and interest, not just simple interest on principal. The eighth wonder of the world. Thirty dollars a month, a dollar a day, will magically turn into over two and a half million. And do you know what's even more impressive? You know someone who has done it," Roy said proudly.

"Thirty-five years ago, I started my savings with $30 a month, which was approximately 10% of my earnings. I have achieved a 15% average annual return, actually a little higher. In addition, as my income rose, my 10% saving component rose accordingly. Thirty dollars a month became $60, then $100, and eventually hundreds of dollars a month. You three are looking at a very wealthy man!"

"Are you trying to tell us that by saving 10% of every pay cheque, you've turned yourself into a millionaire?" an intense Tom demanded.

"Precisely," was the incredible response.

Roy Miller, a millionaire! Dave sat stunned. Roy was clearly deriving great pleasure from the disbelief on their faces.

"Compound interest . . . mind-boggling, isn't it?" he went on. "It's a real tragedy that most people don't understand compound interest and its wondrous powers."

Questions

1. Regarding Roy's first question (to Cathy), how does he arrive at the $1,402,000 figure? Does he use $2400 per year or $200 per month? Is the rate of return 15% compounded annually or 15% compounded monthly? Does he assume that the payments are at the beginning or at the end of each payment interval?
2. Regarding Roy's second question (to Dave), how does he arrive at the $2,679,000 figure? Does he assume that the $30 payments are at the beginning or end of each month?
3. Roy's advice is sound, but the assumption of a long-term rate of return of 15% is unrealistic. During the 1990s, the average Canadian Equity fund had a compound annual return of about 9%. In the same period, the average diversified International Equity fund had a compound annual return of about 11%. Only investors who were wise (or lucky) enough to have most of their investments in U.S. equities during the 1990s would have earned an annual return of close to 15%. What would the answers to Roy's two questions be if we assume a more realistic rate of return of 10.5% compounded monthly?

Concept Questions

1. Give three examples of an annuity due.
2. For the future value of an annuity due, where is the focal date located relative to the final payment?
3. Other things being equal, why is the future value of an annuity due larger than the future value of an ordinary annuity?

Exercise 13.1 *Answers to the odd-numbered problems are at the end of the book.*

In Problems 1 through 14, determine the future value of each annuity due.

Problem	Periodic payment ($)	Payment interval	Term	Nominal rate (%)	Compounding frequency
1.	400	1 year	11 years	11.5	Annually
2.	150	3 months	$6\frac{1}{2}$ years	10	Quarterly
3.	275	1 month	$3\frac{1}{2}$ years	8	Monthly
4.	1500	6 months	$13\frac{1}{2}$ years	7.5	Semiannually
5.	325	1 month	$7\frac{1}{4}$ years	11	Monthly
6.	950	1 quarter	8 years, 9 months	9	Quarterly
7.	329	6 months	8 years, 6 months	8.75	Semiannually
8.	1000	12 months	25 years	7.25	Annually
9.	500	3 months	12 years	11	Annually
10.	200	1 month	$7\frac{1}{2}$ years	10	Quarterly
11.	3000	6 months	$4\frac{1}{2}$ years	8	Monthly
12.	1700	3 months	$11\frac{1}{2}$ years	7.5	Semiannually
13.	2500	1 year	16 years	10.5	Monthly
14.	750	6 months	$6\frac{1}{2}$ years	9	Quarterly

15. Michael Raby has subscribed to a dollar cost averaging program in which he invests $1000 at the beginning of each month. If his rate of return is 6% compounded monthly, what will be the value of his account five years later? (Source: ICB course on Wealth Valuation.)

16. Mary and Steve Farmer plan to invest $2000 at the beginning of each year in an RRSP. What will be the value of the plan after 12 years if it earns 11% compounded annually? (Source: CIFP course on Personal Financial Planning.)

17. If Hans contributes $1500 to his RRSP on February 1, 1990, and every six months thereafter to and including February 1, 2017, what amount will he accumulate in the RRSP by August 1, 2017? Assume that the RRSP will earn 8.5% compounded semiannually. How much of the total will be interest?

18. Many people make their annual RRSP contribution for a taxation year close to the end of the year. Financial advisers encourage clients to contribute as early in the year as possible. How much more will there be in an RRSP at the end of 25 years if annual contributions of $5000 are made at the beginning of each year instead of at the end? Assume that the RRSP will earn:

a. 8% compounded annually. **b.** 8% compounded monthly.

19. What will be the value of an RRSP 25 years from now if $2000 is contributed at the beginning of every six months and the RRSP earns $8\frac{1}{4}$% compounded annually?

•**20.** What will be the amount in an RRSP after 25 years if contributions of \$2000 are made at the beginning of each year for the first 10 years, and contributions of \$4000 are made at the beginning of each year for the subsequent 15 years? Assume that the RRSP will earn 8% compounded quarterly.

•**21.** Fay contributed \$3000 per year to her RRSP on every birthday from age 21 to 30 inclusive. She then ceased employment to raise a family and made no further contributions. Her husband Fred contributed \$3000 per year to his RRSP on every birthday from age 31 to 64 inclusive. Assuming that both plans earn 8% compounded annually over the years, calculate and compare the amounts in their RRSPs at age 65.

13.2 Present Value of an Annuity Due

The present value of an annuity due is the sum of the present values, at the beginning of the annuity, of all payments. Since payments occur at the *beginning* of each payment interval, the beginning of the annuity coincides with the first payment. We will use the symbol PV(due) for the present value of an annuity due.

Present Value Using the Algebraic Method

The formula for PV(due) may be derived from the formula for the present value of an ordinary annuity. The line of reasoning is the same as used in Section 13.1 to derive the formula for FV(due). The outcome is that PV(due) is related to PV in the same way that FV(due) is related to FV. That is,

$$PV(\text{due}) = PV \times (1 + i)$$

Substituting from formula (10-2) for PV, we obtain

PRESENT VALUE OF A SIMPLE ANNUITY DUE

(13-2)

$$\begin{aligned} PV(\text{due}) &= PV \times (1 + i) \\ &= PMT\left[\frac{1-(1+i)^{-n}}{i}\right] \times (1 + i) \end{aligned}$$

If the payments form a *general* annuity due, use $i_2 = (1 + i)^c - 1$ to calculate the periodic interest rate that matches the payment interval. Then substitute this value for i in formula (13-2).

Present Value Using the Financial Calculator Functions

Set the calculator to the annuity due mode ("BGN" or "Begin" showing in the display). Then proceed as you would to compute the present value of an ordinary annuity.

Applications of the Present Value Calculation

As with ordinary annuities, most applications of the present value of an annuity due involve some aspect of valuation. Since the payments on most leases form an annuity due, we are now able to address an additional valuation topic.

The Book Value of a Lease When a business purchases equipment, its accountant records the acquisition of an asset (equipment). If instead, the business leases the equipment, you might think the accountant would just record the monthly lease payments as they are made. However, there is an additional issue.

Most leases for a fixed term are "noncancelable." This means that the lessee is required to continue the lease payments for the full term of the lease, even if the leased equipment is no longer needed. When a business enters into such a lease, Generally Accepted Accounting Principles (GAAP) stipulate that a liability must be created for the "amount" of the obligation. A leasehold asset is also recorded. (The lease represents a long-term asset in the sense that the right to use the equipment will produce a stream of benefits over the term of the lease.)

The question we will address is: "What should be the amount recorded for the lease liability and the (initial) leasehold asset?" Should we simply add up all of the payments for the entire term of the lease? No—that would place the same value on a dollar paid at the end of the lease as a dollar paid at the beginning. Instead, we should record the current economic value of the future lease payments. This raises a follow-up question: "What discount rate should be used in the present value calculation?"

To answer the second question, consider that the usual alternative to leasing equipment is purchasing the equipment using borrowed funds. For this reason, GAAP stipulates that the discount rate should be the interest rate the business would pay to finance the purchase of the equipment.[2]

As time passes, the decreasing number of remaining payments represents a declining lease liability and a diminishing leasehold asset. In accordance with GAAP, the values of the lease liability and the leasehold asset[3] are regularly reduced. At any point during the term of the lease, the present value of the remaining lease payments is known as the **book value of the lease** liability.

$$\begin{array}{c}\text{Book value of a}\\ \text{long-term lease liability}\end{array} = \begin{array}{c}\text{Present value of the remaining payments}\\ \text{(discounted at the interest rate on debt financing)}\end{array}$$

Example 13.2A *Finding the Economic Value of a Simple Annuity Due*

A lottery offers the winner a choice between a $300,000 cash prize, or quarterly payments of $7000 beginning immediately and continuing for 20 years. Which alternative should the winner pick if money is worth:

a. 8% compounded quarterly? **b.** 7% compounded quarterly?

[2] This is consistent with a broader principle in accounting. The reported value of *any* long-term liability is the present value of future contractual payments discounted at the firm's borrowing rate (on the date the liability was incurred).

[3] GAAP allows a leasehold asset to be amortized on a different basis than the write-down of the lease liability. Although they start out equal, later "book" values of the leasehold asset and the lease liability differ. Amortization of a leasehold *asset* is discussed in accounting textbooks.

Solution

The annuity should be chosen if its economic value today exceeds \$300,000. In other words, choose the annuity if its present value, discounted at the time value of money, exceeds \$300,000.

Since the first quarterly payment is paid immediately, the payments constitute an annuity due with

$$PMT = \$7000 \qquad \text{and} \qquad n = 4(20) = 80 \text{ payments}$$

Since the payment interval equals the compounding interval, the payments form a simple annuity. In part *a*, $i = \frac{8\%}{4} = 2\%$ per quarter; in part *b*, $i = \frac{7\%}{4} = 1.75\%$ per quarter.

Algebraic Solution

a. Substituting in formula (13-2), we obtain

$$\begin{aligned} PV(\text{due}) &= PMT\left[\frac{1-(1+i)^{-n}}{i}\right] \times (1+i) \\ &= \$7000\left(\frac{1-1.02^{-80}}{0.02}\right)(1.02) \\ &= \$7000\left(\frac{1-0.20510973}{0.02}\right)(1.02) \\ &= \$283{,}776 \text{ (to the nearest dollar)} \end{aligned}$$

The \$300,000 lump prize should be chosen because it is worth \$16,224 more (in current dollars).

b. $PV(\text{due}) = \$7000\left(\frac{1-1.0175^{-80}}{0.0175}\right)(1.0175) = \$305{,}412$ (to the nearest dollar)

The annuity should be chosen because it is worth \$5412 more (in current dollars).

Financial Calculator Solution

BGN mode

a. 7000 (+/–) (PMT) 0 (FV) 2 (*i*) 80 (*n*) (COMP) (PV) [283,776]

The \$300,000 lump prize should be chosen because it is worth \$16,224 more (in current dollars).

b. 1.75 (*i*) (COMP) (PV) [305,412]

The annuity should be chosen because it is worth \$5412 more (in current dollars).

Example 13.2B The Book Value of a Lease Liability

National Engineering Services (NES) acquired a machine under a capital lease agreement. National pays the lessor \$2400 at the beginning of every three months for five years. If National can obtain five-year financing at 10% compounded quarterly,

a. What long-term lease liability will NES initially report in its financial statements?

b. What liability will be reported two years later?

Solution

The initial liability (book value) is the present value of all of the lease payments. At any later date, the liability reported in the financial statements is the present value of the remaining payments. In both cases, the discount rate should be the interest rate at which the firm could have borrowed at the time of signing the lease. When viewed from the date of the financial statements in either part (a) or part (b), the lease payments form a simple annuity due having $PMT = \$9600$ and $i = 2.5\%$. In part (a), $n = 4(5) = 20$. In part (b), $n = 4(3) = 12$.

Algebraic Solution

a. The initial lease liability is

$$PV\,(\text{due}) = PMT\left[\frac{1-(1+i)^{-n}}{i}\right] \times (1+i)$$

$$= \$2400\left(\frac{1-1.025^{-20}}{0.025}\right)(1.025) = \$38{,}349.34$$

b. After two years, the book value of the lease liability is

$$PV(\text{due}) = \$2400\left(\frac{1-1.025^{-12}}{0.025}\right)(1.025) = \$25{,}234.10$$

Financial Calculator Solution

BGN mode

a. 2400 (+/–) (PMT) 0 (FV) 2.5 (i) 20 (n) (COMP) (PV) [38,349.34]

The initial lease liability is \$38,349.34.

b. 12 (n) (COMP) (PV) [25,234.10]

The lease liability after two years is \$25,234.10.

Example 13.2C *Purchase or Lease a Computer?*

PaperClips Inc. advertises a computer system for \$2995. The same system may be leased for 24 months at \$130 per month (at the beginning of each month). At the end of the lease, the system may be purchased for 10% of the retail price. Should you lease or purchase the computer if you can obtain a two-year loan at 12% compounded annually to purchase the computer?

Solution

We cannot answer the problem by simply comparing the monthly loan payments to the monthly lease payments, for two reasons. Under the lease, you must pay an additional \$299.50 two years from now to own the system. Also, lease payments are made at the beginning of each month while loan payments are made at the end of each month.

We will compare the present values of the two alternatives. Since we are paying out money instead of receiving it, we should choose the alternative with the *lower* present value.

From basic principles, we know that the present value of the loan payments equals the initial loan ($2995). For a fair comparison, we should discount the lease payments (including the terminal payment to acquire ownership) using the same rate.

Since the payment interval (one month) differs from the compounding interval (one year), the lease payments form a *general* annuity due having

$$PMT = \$130 \text{ per month} \qquad n = 24 \qquad \text{and} \qquad i = 12\% \text{ per year}$$

First calculate the periodic interest rate for the one-month payment interval. (It will be about $\frac{12\%}{12} = 1\%$.)

$$c = \frac{\text{Number of compoundings per year}}{\text{Number of payments per year}} = \frac{1}{12} = 0.08\overline{3}$$

$$i_2 = (1 + i)^c - 1 = 1.12^{0.08\overline{3}} - 1 = 0.009488793 = 0.9488793\% \text{ per month}$$

Substitute this value for i in subsequent calculations.

Algebraic Solution

The present value of the monthly lease payments is

$$\begin{aligned} PV(\text{due}) &= PMT\left[\frac{1 - (1 + i)^{-n}}{i}\right] \times (1 + i) \\ &= \$130\left[\frac{1 - 1.009488793^{-24}}{0.009488793}\right](1.009488793) \\ &= \$2804.88 \end{aligned}$$

The present value of the end-of-lease lump payment to purchase the computer is

$$PV = FV(1 + i)^{-n} = 0.1(\$2995)(1.009488793)^{-24} = \$238.76$$

The combined present value is $2804.88 + $238.76 = $3043.64. Since the economic cost (in current dollars) of the lease exceeds the economic cost of purchasing the computer using borrowed funds, the computer system should be purchased.

Financial Calculator Solution

BGN mode

We can obtain the combined present value of the lease payments and the end-of-lease lump payment in a single calculation.

130 (+/−) (PMT) 299.50 (+/−) (FV) 0.9488793 (i) 24 (n) (COMP) (PV) [3043.64]

Since the economic cost (in current dollars) of the lease exceeds the economic cost of purchasing the computer system using borrowed funds, the computer system should be purchased.

Concept Questions

1. For the present value of an annuity due, where is the focal date located relative to the first payment?
2. Other things being equal, why is the present value of an annuity due larger than the present value of an ordinary annuity?
3. If the periodic interest rate for a payment interval is 3%, by what percentage will *PV*(due) exceed *PV?*
4. Other things remaining the same, is the *PV* of an annuity due larger if the given nominal discount rate is compounded monthly instead of annually? Explain briefly.

Exercise 13.2

Answers to the odd-numbered problems are at the end of the book.

In Problems 1 through 14, determine the present value of each annuity due.

Problem	Periodic payment ($)	Payment interval	Term	Nominal rate (%)	Compounding frequency
1.	400	1 year	11 years	11.5	Annually
2.	150	3 months	$6\frac{1}{2}$ years	10	Quarterly
3.	275	1 month	$3\frac{1}{2}$ years	8	Monthly
4.	1500	6 months	$13\frac{1}{2}$ years	7.5	Semiannually
5.	325	1 month	$7\frac{1}{4}$ years	11	Monthly
6.	950	1 quarter	8 years, 9 months	9	Quarterly
7.	329	$\frac{1}{2}$ year	8 years, 6 months	8.75	Semiannually
8.	1000	12 months	25 years	7.25	Annually
9.	500	3 months	12 years	11	Annually
10.	200	1 month	$7\frac{1}{2}$ years	10	Quarterly
11.	3000	6 months	$4\frac{1}{2}$ years	8	Monthly
12.	1700	3 months	$11\frac{1}{2}$ years	7.5	Semiannually
13.	2500	1 year	16 years	10.5	Monthly
14.	750	6 months	$6\frac{1}{2}$ years	9	Quarterly

15. The Associated Press newswire carried the following story on June 6, 1995.

An eight-month-pregnant university student who recently moved back in with her parents to save money is clear on what she intends to do with her Powerball jackpot of nearly $87.6 million: "If I want it, I'll buy it. Today we're all getting new cars for the whole family."

Pam Hiatt, 26, accepted the first $4.38 million cheque from Idaho governor Phil Batt. She will receive the fortune in 20 yearly payments of $4.38 million.

On the date she received the first cheque, what, in fact, was the economic value of the jackpot if the time value of money was:

a. 7% compounded annually? **b.** 9% compounded annually?

16. Under the headline "Local Theatre Project Receives $1 Million!" a newspaper article explained that the Theatre Project had just received the first of ten annual grants of $100,000 from the Hinton Foundation. What is the current economic value of all of the grants if money is worth 7.5% compounded monthly?

17. You have received two offers on the used car you wish to sell. Mr. Lindberg is offering $8500 cash, and Mrs. Martel's offer is five semi-annual payments of $1900, including a payment on the purchase date. Which offer has the greater economic value if money can earn 10% compounded semiannually? What is the economic advantage (in current dollars) of the preferred alternative?

18. Osgood Appliance Centre is advertising refrigerators for six monthly payments of $199, including a payment on the date of purchase. What cash price should Osgood accept if it would otherwise sell the conditional sale agreement to a finance company to yield 18% compounded monthly?

19. The life expectancy of the average 65-year-old Canadian male is about 15 years. Karsten wants to have sufficient funds in his RRIF at age 65 to be able to withdraw $32,500 at the beginning of each year for the expected survival period of 15 years. If his RRIF earns 7% compounded annually, what amount must he have in the RRIF at the time he turns 65? (Source: CIFP course on Wealth Accumulation.)

20. A rental agreement requires the payment of $900 at the beginning of each month.

a. What single payment at the beginning of the rental year should the landlord accept instead of monthly payments if money is worth 9% compounded monthly?

b. Show that the landlord will be equally well off at the end of the year under either payment arrangement if rental payments are invested at 9% compounded monthly.

21. What amount of money earning 9% compounded semiannually will sustain withdrawals of $1200 at the beginning of every month for 15 years?

22. The lease contract for a computer workstation requires quarterly payments of $2100 at the beginning of every three-month period for five years. The lessee would otherwise have to pay an interest rate of 13% compounded quarterly to borrow funds to purchase the workstation.

a. If the lease is treated as a capital lease, what amount will the lessee initially report in its financial statements as the long-term lease liability?

b. What will the liability be at the end of the fourth year?

23. Beaudoin Haulage has signed a five-year lease with GMAC on a new dump truck. Beaudoin intends to capitalize the lease and report it as a long-term liability. Lease payments of $1700 are made at the beginning of each month. To purchase the truck, Beaudoin would have had to borrow funds at 11.25% compounded monthly.

a. What initial liability should Beaudoin report on its balance sheet?

b. How much will the liability be reduced during the first year of the lease?

•24. What is the current economic value of an annuity due consisting of 22 quarterly payments of $700, if money is worth 9% compounded quarterly for the first three years, and 10% compounded quarterly thereafter?

•25. Calculate and rank the economic values of the following cash flow streams:

(i) A single payment of $10,000 eight years from now.

(ii) An annuity due starting today with eight annual payments of $850.

(iii) An annuity due starting in eight years with eight annual payments of $1700.

Do the calculations and ranking for each of two cases:

a. Money can earn 8% compounded annually for the next 16 years.

b. Money can earn 10% compounded annually for the next 16 years.

••26. Two insurance companies gave the following quotations on premiums for essentially the same long-term disability insurance coverage for a 25-year-old. Paul Revere Insurance Co. quoted monthly premiums of $54.83 from ages 26 to 30 inclusive, and $78.17 from ages 31 to 64 inclusive. The monthly premiums from Provident Insurance Co. are "flat" at $69.35 from ages 26 to 64 inclusive. All premiums are paid at the beginning of each month. The insurance broker recommended the Provident coverage because the aggregate lifetime premiums up to the client's sixty-fifth birthday are $32,455.80 versus $35,183.16 for the Paul Revere policy. Is the choice that simple? (*Hint:* Calculate and compare the economic value on the client's twenty-sixth birthday of each policy's stream of premiums assuming a time value of money of 9% compounded monthly.)

••27. The lease on the premises occupied by the accounting firm of Heath and Company will soon expire. The current landlord is offering to renew the lease for seven years at $2100 per month. The developers of a new building, a block away from Heath's present offices, are offering the first year of a seven-year lease rent-free. For the subsequent six years the rent would be $2500 per month. All rents are paid at the beginning of each month. Other things being equal, which lease should Heath accept if money is worth 10.5% compounded monthly?

13.3 Calculating the Periodic Payment, Number of Payments, and Interest Rate

To calculate any one of these three quantities for an annuity due, follow the same procedure you would for an ordinary annuity, but with one change. You must use the annuity due formula that is the counterpart of the ordinary annuity formula. These counterparts are listed in the following table. Formulas (13-1n) and (13-2n) have not been presented before. They are versions of formulas (13-1) and (13-2), respectively, rearranged to isolate n.

Ordinary Annuity Formula		Annuity Due Formula	
$FV = PMT\left[\frac{(1+i)^n - 1}{i}\right]$	(10-1)	$FV(\text{due}) = PMT\left[\frac{(1+i)^n - 1}{i}\right] \times (1+i)$	(13-1)
$PV = PMT\left[\frac{1-(1+i)^{-n}}{i}\right]$	(10-2)	$PV(\text{due}) = PMT\left[\frac{1-(1+i)^{-n}}{i}\right] \times (1+i)$	(13-2)
$n = \frac{\ln\left(1 + \frac{i \times FV}{PMT}\right)}{\ln(1+i)}$	(10-1*n*)	$n = \frac{\ln\left[1 + \frac{i \times FV(\text{due})}{PMT(1+i)}\right]}{\ln(1+i)}$	(13-1*n*)
$n = -\frac{\ln\left(1 - \frac{i \times PV}{PMT}\right)}{\ln(1+i)}$	(10-2*n*)	$n = -\frac{\ln\left[1 - \frac{i \times PV(\text{due})}{PMT(1+i)}\right]}{\ln(1+i)}$	(13-2*n*)

Calculating i algebraically requires the trial-and-error method described in Appendix 11B. We will use only the financial calculator method to solve for i in example problems. When using a calculator's financial functions to calculate *PMT*, n, or i for an annuity due, make certain your calculator is in the annuity due mode.

The Mathematics of Vehicle Leasing The popularity of leasing has grown rapidly in recent years. In 1994, 20% of new vehicles were leased. The percentage increased to over 30% in 1996. Now, more than half of all new vehicles are leased. The main elements of a typical lease contract are as follows:

- The lessee makes fixed beginning-of-month payments for the term of the lease. The most common term is three years.
- The lessee is responsible for all vehicle operating costs (including insurance) during the term of the lease. In this respect, leasing does not differ from owning a vehicle.
- Most leases are "closed-end" or "walk away" leases. At the end of the term, the lessee can simply return the vehicle to the car dealer. Alternatively, at the option of the lessee, the vehicle may be purchased for a *predetermined* amount (called the **residual value** in the lease contract). The residual value represents the dealer's estimate of the market value of the vehicle at the end of the lease.

We will use a particular example to develop our understanding of the economics and mathematics of leasing. Suppose your down payment on a three-year lease is \$2000. The car's purchase price is \$20,000 and its residual value after three years is \$10,000. We will now explain how the lease payment is calculated.

From the car dealer's point of view, the \$18,000 "balance" is paid by 36 beginning-of-month payments plus a final lump payment of \$10,000 after three years. This final payment will either come from you (if you exercise the purchase option) or from the sale of the vehicle at the end of the lease. Consequently, the final lump payment is not known with certainty. The lease payments are calculated on the assumption that the lump payment will be \$10,000.

Except for the uncertainty in the amount of the terminal lump payment, the situation is similar to repaying an \$18,000 loan by 36 beginning-of-month payments plus a final lump payment of \$10,000 after three years. In that case, we know that the present value of all loan payments (discounted at the interest rate on the loan) is \$18,000. Similarly, the present value of all lease payments plus the residual value (discounted at the interest rate charged on the lease) is \$18,000. In general,

$$\begin{pmatrix}\text{Purchase}\\ \text{price}\end{pmatrix} - \begin{pmatrix}\text{Down}\\ \text{payment}\end{pmatrix} = \begin{pmatrix}\text{Present value of}\\ \text{the lease payments}\end{pmatrix} + \begin{pmatrix}\text{Present value of}\\ \text{the residual value}\end{pmatrix}$$

Although it is rarely clearly stated, the interest rate on leases is applied as a monthly compounded rate. Therefore, the monthly lease payments form a simple annuity due.

Sometimes lease advertisements do not give enough information for you to piece together the full financial picture. There are six variables embedded in the preceding mathematical relationship. They are the purchase price, the down payment, the residual value, the number of payments, the amount of the monthly payment, and the interest rate on the lease. If five of the variables are given, you can calculate the sixth. However, the advertisements may omit information about two of the variables. (It is usually two of the following three: the interest rate, the purchase price, and the residual value.) When that happens, you need to contact the dealer to fill in the missing information (which is probably the reason full information wasn't given in the first place).

CAUGHT IN THE WEB

The "Car Lease Calculator" at the Web site www.imoney.com/bm_apps/calculators/html/lease.html allows you to calculate the monthly payment or the residual value or the interest rate if you first enter values for the other five variables.

While such "calculators" are convenient and efficient, you should also be able to do the calculations working from the fundamental relationship developed in this section.

Example 13.3A *Calculating the Size of Lease Payments*

A lease that has $2\frac{1}{2}$ years to run is recorded on a company's books as a liability of \$27,369. If the company's cost of borrowing was 12% compounded monthly when the lease was signed, what is the lease payment at the beginning of each month?

Solution

The "book value" of the lease liability is the present value of the remaining lease payments. The discount rate employed should be the interest rate the company would have paid to borrow funds. The lease payments constitute a simple annuity due with

$$PV(\text{due}) = \$27{,}369 \quad n = 12(2.5) = 30 \quad \text{and} \quad i = \frac{12\%}{12} = 1\% \text{ per month}$$

Algebraic Solution

Substitute the given values into formula (13-2) and solve for *PMT.*

$$PV(\text{due}) = PMT\left[\frac{1-(1+i)^{-n}}{i}\right] \times (1+i)$$

$$\$27{,}369 = PMT\left(\frac{1-1.01^{-30}}{0.01}\right)(1.01)$$

$$= PMT\,(25.80771)(1.01)$$

$$= PMT\,(26.06579)$$

$$PMT = \$1050.00$$

Financial Calculator Solution

BGN mode

27369 (PV) 0 (FV) 30 (n) 1 (i) (COMP) (PMT) [−1050.00]

The monthly lease payment is $1050.00.

Example 13.3B *Calculating the PMT Needed to Attain a Savings Goal*

Mr. Walters has already accumulated $104,000 in his Registered Retirement Savings Plan (RRSP). His goal is to build it to $250,000 with equal contributions at the beginning of each six-month period for the next seven years. If his RRSP earns 8.5% compounded semiannually, what must be the size of further contributions?

Solution

The $250,000 target will be the combined future value of the $104,000 already in the RRSP and the simple annuity due formed by the next 14 payments. That is,

$$\$250{,}000 = \text{Future value of } \$104{,}000 + FV(\text{due}) \quad ①$$

with $n = 14$ and $i = \dfrac{8.5\%}{2} = 4.25\%$ per half year.

Algebraic Solution

The future value of the $104,000 lump amount will be

$$FV = PV(1+i)^n = \$104{,}000(1.0425)^{14} = \$186{,}250.84$$

The future value of the 14 contributions will be

$$FV(\text{due}) = PMT\left[\frac{(1+i)^n - 1}{i}\right](1+i) = PMT\left(\frac{1.0425^{14} - 1}{0.0425}\right)(1.0425) = PMT(19.39966)$$

Substituting these amounts into equation ①, we obtain

$$\$250{,}000 = \$186{,}250.84 + PMT(19.39966)$$

$$PMT = \frac{\$250{,}000 - \$186{,}250.84}{19.39966} = \$3286.10$$

Mr. Walters must make semiannual contributions of $3286.10 to reach the $250,000 target in seven years.

Financial Calculator Solution

The financial calculator can simultaneously accommodate the initial lump amount (entered in (PV)) and the annuity due.

BGN mode

104000 (+/−) (PV) 250000 (FV) 14 (n) 4.25 (i) (COMP) (PMT) [−3286.10]

Mr. Walters must make semiannual contributions of $3286.10 to reach the $250,000 target in seven years.

Example 13.3C *Calculating the Payment on a Car Lease*

An automobile manufacturer is calculating the lease payments to charge on the SLX model whose selling price is \$27,900. During a month-long promotion, the manufacturer will offer an interest rate of only 1.8% compounded monthly on a three-year lease. If the residual value is \$14,500, what will be the lease payments assuming a \$2500 down payment?

Solution

Earlier in this section, we developed the leasing equation:

$$\begin{pmatrix}\text{Purchase}\\ \text{price}\end{pmatrix} - \begin{pmatrix}\text{Down}\\ \text{payment}\end{pmatrix} = \begin{pmatrix}\text{Present value of}\\ \text{the lease payments}\end{pmatrix} + \begin{pmatrix}\text{Present value of}\\ \text{the residual value}\end{pmatrix}$$

For the SLX lease,

$$\$27{,}900 - \$2500 = \begin{pmatrix}\text{Present value of}\\ \text{the lease payments}\end{pmatrix} + \begin{pmatrix}\text{Present value}\\ \text{of } \$14{,}500\end{pmatrix} \qquad ①$$

The lease payments form a simple annuity due with $i = \frac{1.8\%}{12} = 0.15\%$ and $n = 36$.

Algebraic Solution

The present value of the lease payments is

$$PMT\left[\frac{1-(1+i)^{-n}}{i}\right](1+i) = PMT\left[\frac{1-1.0015^{-36}}{0.0015}\right](1.0015) = PMT(35.07224)$$

The present value of the \$14,500 residual value is

$$PV = FV(1+i)^{-n} = \$14{,}500(1.0015)^{-36} = \$13{,}738.32$$

Substitute these values into equation ① and solve for *PMT*.

$$\$25{,}400 = PMT\,(35.07224) + \$13{,}738.32$$

$$PMT = \frac{\$25{,}400 - \$13{,}738.32}{35.07224} = \$332.50$$

The beginning-of-month lease payment is \$332.50.

Financial Calculator Solution

The calculation may be done in one step. We know the present value (\$25,400), the terminal lump payment (\$14,500), *n*, and *i*. Enter these values and compute *PMT*.

BGN mode

25400 (+/−) (PV) 14500 (FV) 0.15 (i) 36 (n) (COMP) (PMT) [332.50]

The beginning-of-month lease payment is \$332.50.

Example 13.3D Calculating n Given the Future Value of a Simple Annuity Due

Rounded to the nearest month, how long will it take to accumulate \$1,000,000 in an RRSP if the first quarterly contribution of \$2000 is made today? Assume the RRSP earns 8% compounded quarterly. (Part way through a compounding period, include *accrued* interest in the value of the RRSP.)

Solution

First, we need to find the number of contributions required for the future value to reach \$1,000,000. Since the compounding interval equals the payment interval, the contributions form a simple annuity having

$$PMT = \$2000 \qquad i = \frac{8\%}{4} = 2\% \qquad \text{and} \qquad FV(\text{due}) = \$1,000,000$$

Algebraic Solution

Substitute these values into formula (13-1*n*).

$$n = \frac{\ln\left[1 + \frac{i \times FV(\text{due})}{PMT(1+i)}\right]}{\ln(1+i)} = \frac{\ln\left[1 + \frac{0.02 \times \$1,000,000}{\$2,000(1.02)}\right]}{\ln(1.02)} = \frac{2.3799}{0.019803} = 120.18$$

Read the discussion and conclusion in the financial calculator solution below.

Financial Calculator Solution

BGN mode

2000 (+/–) (PMT) 0 (PV) 2 (i) 1000000 (FV) (COMP) (n) [120.18]

Interpreting the fractional part of n can be tricky, particularly for annuities due. You cannot simply conclude that the time required is

$$120.18 \times 3 \text{ months} = 360.54 \text{ months}$$

If you calculate the future value of the RRSP after 120 contributions, you obtain \$996,047. The 121st contribution will be made at the beginning of the 121st payment interval, 360 months or 30 years from now. At that moment, the amount in the RRSP jumps to \$998,047, less than \$2000 short of the \$1 million target. The amount in the RRSP will grow by $i = 2\%$ over the next three months. This will add almost \$20,000 (0.02 × \$998,000) to the amount in the RRSP. To accrue just the additional \$2000 interest needed for the RRSP to reach \$1 million will require only about one-tenth ($\frac{\$2000}{\$20,000}$) of the three-month payment interval—about 0.3 month or nine days. Hence, the RRSP (including accrued interest) will reach the \$1 million target only nine or 10 days into the 361st month.

Rounded to the nearest month, it will take 360 months or 30 years for the RRSP to reach \$1,000,000.

Example 13.3E Calculating n Given the Present Value of a General Annuity Due

An investment fund is worth \$210,000 and earns 9% compounded semiannually. If \$2000 is withdrawn at the beginning of each month starting today, when will the fund be depleted?

Solution

The initial amount in the account equals the present value of the future withdrawals. Since the first withdrawal occurs today, and the payment interval differs from the compounding interval, the withdrawals form a *general* annuity *due* having

$$PV(\text{due}) = \$210{,}000 \qquad PMT = \$2000 \qquad \text{and} \qquad i = \frac{9\%}{2} = 4.5\%$$

The value we must use for i in formula (13-2n) and in the (i) memory is the periodic rate for the one-month payment interval. Substitute

$$c = \frac{\text{Number of compoundings per year}}{\text{Number of payments per year}} = \frac{2}{12} = 0.1\overline{6}$$

into

$$i_2 = (1 + i)^c - 1 = (1.045)^{0.1\overline{6}} - 1 = 0.00736312 = 0.736312\% \text{ per month}$$

Algebraic Solution

Substitute the known values into formula (13-2n).

$$n = -\frac{\ln\left[1 - \frac{i \times PV(\text{due})}{PMT(1 + i)}\right]}{\ln(1 + i)} = -\frac{\ln\left[1 - \frac{0.00736312(\$210{,}000)}{\$2000(1.00736312)}\right]}{\ln(1.00736312)} = -\frac{-1.45876}{0.0073361} = 198.85$$

Read the discussion and conclusion in the financial calculator solution below.

Financial Calculator Solution

BGN mode

210000 (PV) 2000 (+/–) (PMT) 0.736312 (i) 0 (FV) (COMP) (n) 198.85

The fund will permit 199 monthly withdrawals. The final withdrawal, smaller than \$2000, will occur at the beginning of the 199th payment interval. But that will be 198 months from now. So the fund will be depleted at the time of the 199th payment, 198 months or 16 years and six months from now.

Example 13.3F *Calculating the Interest Rate for an annuity Due*

Therese intends to contribute \$3000 at the beginning of each six-month period to an RRSP. What rate of return must her RRSP earn in order to reach \$600,000 after 25 years?

Solution

The payments form an annuity due whose future value after 25 years is to be \$600,000. That is,

$$FV(\text{due}) = \$600{,}000 \qquad PMT = \$3000 \qquad \text{and} \qquad n = 2(25) = 50$$

Operating in the **BGN mode**,

3000 (+/-) (PMT) 600000 (FV) 50 (*n*) 0 (PV) (COMP) (*i*) [4.713]

The periodic rate for a payment interval (six months) is 4.713%. The corresponding annual rate that Therese's RRSP must earn is

$$j = mi = 2(4.713\%) = 9.43\% \text{ compounded semiannually}$$

Example 13.3G *Calculating the Interest Rate Built into an Instalment Payment Option*

A \$100,000 life insurance policy requires an annual premium of \$420 or a monthly premium of \$37.00. In either case, the premium is payable at the beginning of the period of coverage. What is the effective rate of interest policyholders pay when they choose the monthly payment plan?

Solution

In effect, the insurance company lends the \$420 annual premium to policyholders choosing the monthly payment option. These policyholders then repay the "loan" by 12 beginning-of-month payments of \$37.00. Hence, \$420 is the present value of the 12 payments which form an annuity due. We have

$$PV(\text{due}) = \$420 \qquad PMT = \$37 \qquad \text{and} \qquad n = 12$$

Operating in the **BGN mode**,

420 (PV) 37 (+/-) (PMT) 0 (FV) 12 (*n*) (COMP) (*i*) [1.0269]

The periodic rate for a payment interval (one month) is 1.0269%. The effective interest rate being charged on the monthly payment plan is

$$f = (1 + i)^m - 1 = 1.010269^{12} - 1 = 0.1304 = 13.04\%$$

Example 13.3H *Calculating the Interest Rate Built into Lease Payments*

In February of 1999, a dealer advertised 1999 Isuzu Rodeo S trucks for sale at \$30,485. A truck could also be leased for three years at \$344 per month, based on a \$3000 down payment. At the end of the lease, the lessee may purchase the vehicle for \$18,901. What monthly compounded interest rate is built into the lease?

Solution

Mathematically, the problem is the same as calculating the interest rate charged on a loan if the balance is reduced from \$27,485 (\$30,485 – \$3000) to \$18,901 by 36 beginning-of-month payments of \$344. That is, \$27,485 is the present value of 36 payments of \$344 and a terminal payment of \$18,901. Thus, we have

$$PV(\text{due}) = \$27{,}485 \qquad PMT = \$344 \qquad n = 36 \qquad \text{and} \qquad FV = \$18{,}901$$

Operating in the **BGN mode**,

27485 (PV) 344 (+/–) (PMT) 18901 (+/–) (FV) 36 (n) (COMP) (i) 0.45724

The periodic rate built into the lease is 0.45724% per month. The annual interest rate is

$$j = mi = 12(0.45724\%) = 5.49\% \text{ compounded monthly}$$

POINT OF INTEREST

Is It Less Costly to Lease or Buy a New Vehicle?

This debate usually "bogs down" on issues such as the maintenance costs of older vehicles (under the purchase alternative) and the psychological appeal of driving newer vehicles. There is one scenario that avoids these issues. If it is your intention to exercise the purchase option at the end of the lease, then purchasing at the outset usually has a lower economic cost. This happens for one or both of the following reasons. Except in special promotions, dealers usually charge a higher interest rate on leases than they charge on loans.[4] In addition, an administration fee is often added to each lease payment.

The main reason for the growth in popularity of leasing is that lease payments are usually significantly smaller than the loan payments to finance the purchase of the same vehicle. Even when the lease transaction involves a *higher* interest rate and *smaller* down payment than a purchase transaction, it usually turns out that the lease payments are smaller than the loan payments. A narrow fixation on monthly payments leads to confused and flawed thinking about the lease vs. purchase alternatives.

Consider the following data obtained from General Motors' Web site (SMARTLEASE page) in early 1999. Browsers were invited to "*Compare SMARTLEASE with traditional financing on a new $20,000 GM vehicle.*"

	SMARTLEASE	Traditional financing
Vehicle selling price	$20,000	$20,000
Down payment	$1000	$1700
Interest rate	7.7%	9.75%
Monthly payment	$345	$462
Number of payments	36	48
Option price (residual value)	$10,000	N/A
Total of payments (including the down payment)	$13,420	$23,876

[4] The reason for this "spread" is that a lessor takes on a higher risk than a lender. The lessor faces the possibility that the market price of the vehicle at the end of the lease will be less than the residual value. Furthermore, the lessor has less security than the lender in the event of default. A lessee's monthly payments basically cover interest and the vehicle's actual depreciation. In contrast, an owner builds equity in the vehicle by making loan payments that are larger than lease payments.

The interest rates in the table are compounded monthly and the monthly payments have been rounded to the nearest dollar.

General Motors drew no conclusion from the data. However, a casual reader might put a flawed interpretation on the data. Each of the following observations seems to indicate an advantage to leasing. With leasing, the down payment is lower, the interest rate is lower, the monthly payment is lower, and the total of all payments (including the down payment) is much lower.

Questions

1. The only questionable assumption in the data is using a higher interest rate for financing (9.75%) than for leasing (7.7%). Except for special promotions, it is unusual for the financing interest rate to exceed the leasing interest rate. For example, when automobile manufacturers advertise *both* financing and leasing options on the same vehicle, the interest rate for financing is usually lower than or equal to the interest rate for leasing. In order to remove the interest rate differential as a factor in the analysis, recalculate the monthly payment and the "total of payments" for "traditional financing" using 7.7% compounded monthly. Use these figures along with the given SMARTLEASE figures to answer Questions 2 and 3.
2. What is wrong with drawing the conclusion that leasing is cheaper because it has the lower monthly payment?
3. What is wrong with drawing the conclusion that leasing is cheaper because its "total of payments" is lower?

Concept Questions

1. An ordinary annuity and an annuity due have the same future value, *n*, and *i*. Which annuity has the larger payment? Give the reason for your answer.
2. An ordinary annuity and an annuity due have the same present value, *n*, and *i*. Which annuity has the smaller payment? Give the reason for your answer.
3. An ordinary annuity and an annuity due have the same present value, *PMT*, and *i*. Which annuity has the greater number of payments? Give the reason for your answer.
4. Other variables being the same, how will the amount of the down payment on a lease affect the size of the lease payments?

5. Other variables being the same, how will the size of the residual value affect the size of the lease payments?

6. The term of the lease on a vehicle is about to expire. Answer parts (a) and (b) strictly on financial considerations.

a. If the market value of the vehicle is less than the residual value, what should the lessee do?

b. If the market value of the vehicle exceeds the residual value, what should the lessee do?

c. In view of your answers to (a) and (b), will the interest rate on a lease contract tend to be higher or lower than the interest rate on a loan to purchase the same vehicle? Explain.

Exercise 13.3

Answers to the odd-numbered problems are at the end of the book.

Calculate the periodic payment for each of the annuities due in Problems 1 through 8.

Problem	Present or future value ($)	Payment interval	Term	Nominal interest rate (%)	Compounding frequency
1.	PV = 25,000	6 months	$8\frac{1}{2}$ years	9.5	Semiannually
2.	PV = 50,000	12 months	12 years	8.9	Annually
3.	FV = 100,000	3 months	15 years, 3 months	9	Quarterly
4.	FV = 30,000	1 month	7 years, 9 months	8.25	Monthly
5.	PV = 30,000	3 months	$10\frac{1}{2}$ years	8.5	Semiannually
6.	PV = 45,000	1 month	11 years	9.9	Annually
7.	FV = 150,000	1 year	16 years	11	Quarterly
8.	FV = 25,000	6 months	$7\frac{1}{2}$ years	8.25	Monthly

Calculate the term, expressed in years and months, of each of the annuities due in Problems 9 through 16.

Problem	Present or future value ($)	Payment interval	Periodic payment ($)	Nominal interest rate (%)	Compounding frequency
9.	FV = 117,896	1 year	3000.00	8.75	Annually
10.	FV = 22,500	1 month	150.75	9	Monthly
11.	PV = 13,405	6 months	1000.00	7.5	Semiannually
12.	PV = 20,000	3 months	858.67	10	Quarterly
13.	FV = 58,898.50	3 months	1200.00	10.25	Annually
14.	FV = 30,000	6 months	636.22	9	Monthly
15.	PV = 6601.13	1 year	1000.00	8.5	Semiannually
16.	PV = 20,000	1 month	236.18	12	Quarterly

Calculate the nominal and effective interest rates accurate to the nearest 0.01% for each of the annuities due in Problems 17 through 22. Determine the nominal rate whose compounding interval equals the payment interval.

Problem	Present or future value ($)	Payment interval	Periodic payment ($)	Term of annuity
17.	$FV = 75{,}000$	6 months	1557.78	11 years, 6 months
18.	$PV = 18{,}143$	1 year	2000.00	18 years
19.	$FV = 37{,}670$	3 months	500.00	$9\frac{1}{2}$ years
20.	$PV = 45{,}000$	1 month	533.42	13 years, 8 months
21.	$FV = 75{,}000$	1 month	357.29	10 years
22.	$PV = 39{,}936$	1 year	5000.00	25 years

The data in Problems 23 to 33 were taken from newspaper advertisements in 1999. Calculate the missing value at "?" in each case.

Make and model	MSRP† ($)	Down payment ($)	Monthly payment ($)	Interest rate on lease‡ (%)	Term of lease (months)	Residual value ($)
23. Saturn SLI	14,903	2000	?	5.1	36	7899
24. Saturn SLI	14,903	?	212.88	5.1	36	7899
25. Toyota 4Runner	?	6270	398	6.8	48	18,017
26. Ford Explorer Sport	30,328	4995	?	2.9	36	17,630
27. Ford Explorer Sport	30,328	?	381	2.9	36	17,630
28. Saturn SCI	17,123	1000	231	?	36	9931
29. Hyundai Sonata	20,090	2545	229	?	48	9304
30. Mazda Millenia S	35,790	5000	399	1.9	48	?
31. Hyundai Elantra	?	1250	199	1.71	48	4995
32. Hyundai Tiburon	18,455	1500	218	5.31	48	?
33. Isuzu Rodeo S	30,485	3000	344	5.5	?	18,901

†Manufacturer's Suggested Retail Price
‡Annual rate with monthly compounding.

34. To accumulate $200,000 after 20 years, what amount must be invested each year if the investment earns 9% compounded annually and the contributions are made:

a. At the beginning of each year? **b.** At the end of each year?

35. What maximum annual withdrawals will a $200,000 fund earning 9% compounded annually sustain for 20 years if the withdrawals are made:

a. At the beginning of each year? **b.** At the end of each year?

36. Heather wants to accumulate $4000 for a trip to Europe one or two years from now. Her investment account pays 6% compounded monthly. What amount must she deposit at the beginning of each month to reach the target in:

a. one year? **b.** two years?

37. Fletcher's Machine Shop wants to start a fund to accumulate half of the expected $1,000,000 cost of expanding the facilities in nine years. What semiannual amount must be paid into the fund earning 7.5% compounded semiannually in order to reach the target if the payments are made:

a. at the beginning of every six months?

b. at the end of every six months?

38. Triex Manufacturing wants to accumulate $500,000 for an expansion planned to begin in five years. If today Triex makes the first of equal quarterly payments into a fund earning 8.25% compounded monthly, what size should these payments be?

39. Erin wants to accumulate $10,000 in four years for his son's college education. He can earn 9% compounded monthly on his investment. What amount must Erin invest at the beginning of each month for the next four years? (Source: CIFP course on Personal Financial Planning.)

40. An insurance company wishes to offer customers a monthly instalment alternative to the annual premium plan. All premiums are payable at the beginning of the period of coverage. The monthly payment plan is to include an interest charge of 15% compounded monthly on the unpaid balance of the annual premium. What will be the monthly premium per $100 of annual premium?

41. Advance Leasing calculates the monthly payments on its three-year leases on the basis of recovering the capital cost of the leased equipment and earning an 18% compounded monthly rate of return on its capital investment. What will be the monthly lease payment on equipment that costs $8500?

42. Shane is about to have his twenty-fifth birthday. He has set a goal of retiring at age 55 with $700,000 in an RRSP. For planning purposes he is assuming that his RRSP will earn 8% compounded annually.

a. What contribution on each birthday from age 25 to 54 inclusive will be required to accumulate the desired amount in his RRSP?

b. If he waits five years before starting his RRSP, what contribution on each birthday from age 30 to 54 inclusive will be required to accumulate the target amount?

43. Wendy will soon turn 33. She wants to accumulate $500,000 in an RRSP by her sixtieth birthday. How much larger will her annual contributions have to be if they are made at the end of each year (from age 33 to age 60) instead of at the beginning of each year? Assume that her RRSP will earn 9% compounded annually.

44. CompuLease leases computers and peripheral equipment to businesses. What lease payments must CompuLease charge at the beginning of each quarter of a five-year lease if it is to recover the $20,000 capital cost of a system and earn 16% compounded quarterly on its investment?

45. Island Water Taxi has decided to lease another boat for five years rather than to finance the purchase of the boat at an interest rate of 13.5% compounded monthly. It is treating the lease as a capital lease and has set up a long-term lease liability of $43,000. What is the lease payment at the beginning of each month?

46. Murray is about to have his twenty-eighth birthday. He wants to accumulate $600,000 in an RRSP by age 60. How much larger will his annual contributions have to be if they are made at the end of each year instead of at the beginning of each year? Assume that his RRSP will earn 8% compounded semiannually.

47. Kim wants to save half of the $16,000 purchase price of a new car by making monthly deposits of $300, beginning today, into a T-bill savings account earning 5.25% compounded monthly. How long will it take him to reach his goal?

48. Central Personnel's accountant set up a long-term lease liability of $11,622.73 to recognize a new contract for the lease of office furniture. She used the firm's 10.5% monthly compounded cost of borrowing as the discount rate. If the lease payments at the beginning of each month are $295, what is the term of the lease?

49. The payments required on a contractual obligation are $500 per month. The contract was purchased for $13,372 just *before* a regular payment date. The purchaser determined this price based on his required rate of return of 9.75% compounded monthly. How many payments will he receive?

50. How much longer will a $100,000 fund earning 9% compounded monthly sustain beginning-of-month withdrawals of $900 than beginning-of-month withdrawals of $1000?

51. How much less time will it take to accumulate savings of $100,000 with beginning-of-month deposits of $220 than with beginning-of-month deposits of $200? The savings earn 6% compounded monthly.

52. If a furniture retailer offers a financing plan on a $1500 purchase requiring four equal quarterly payments of $400 including the first payment on the purchase date, what effective rate of interest is being charged on the unpaid balance?

53. An RRSP is now worth $223,000 after contributions of $2500 at the beginning of every six months for 14 years. What effective rate of return has the plan earned?

54. Pembroke Golf Club's initiation fee is $5500. It offers an instalment payment alternative of $1000 down and $1000 at the end of each year for five years. What effective rate of interest is being charged on the instalment plan?

55. If contributions of $1500 at the beginning of every three months resulted in an RRSP worth $434,960 after 20 years, what quarterly compounded nominal rate and effective rate of return did the RRSP earn?

56. As of the date of Victory Machine Shop's most recent financial statements, three years remained in the term of a capital lease reported as a long-term liability of \$13,824. If the beginning-of-month lease payments are \$450, what monthly compounded nominal (annual) discount rate was used in valuing the lease?

57. If a furniture store offers to sell a refrigerator priced at \$1195 on a conditional sale contract requiring 12 monthly payments of \$110 (including a payment on the date of sale), what effective rate of interest is being charged to the customer?

58. For the past 13 years, Ms. Perrault has contributed \$2000 at the beginning of every six months to a mutual fund. If the mutual fund statement at the end of the 13 years reports that her fund units are worth a total of \$131,483, what has been the semiannually compounded nominal rate and the effective rate of return on her investments over the 13 years?

•59. Advantage Leasing calculates its five-year lease rates so that it recovers the capital cost of the equipment plus an 18% compounded quarterly return on investment over the term of the lease. What will be the required lease payments on a machine that cost \$25,000 if the lease payments are made:

a. At the beginning of every month?

b. At the beginning of each six-month period?

•60. Mr. and Mrs. Friedrich have just opened a Registered Education Savings Plan (RESP) for their daughter. They want the plan to pay \$3000 at the beginning of each half year for four years, starting nine years from now when their daughter will enter college or university. What semiannual contributions, including one today, must they make for the next nine years if the RESP earns 8.25% compounded semiannually?

•61. Ambleside Golf Club's board of directors has set next year's membership fee at \$1900 payable at the beginning of the year. The board has instructed its accountant to calculate beginning-of-quarter and beginning-of-month payment plans that provide a 15% semiannually compounded rate of return on the unpaid balance of the annual fee. What will be the amounts of the quarterly and monthly payments?

•62. RRSP contributions of \$1000 are made at the beginning of every six months. How many more contributions will it take to reach \$150,000 if the RRSP earns 8% compounded semiannually than if it earns 10% compounded semiannually?

•63. Mrs. McPherson wants to use \$10,000 from her late husband's estate to assist her grandson when he enters college in seven years. If the \$10,000 is invested immediately at 8% compounded monthly, how long can the grandson make beginning-of-month withdrawals of \$500 (or less if a final withdrawal) once he starts college?

•64. If you contribute \$500 to an RRSP at the beginning of every three months for 25 years and then use the accumulated funds to purchase an annuity paying \$1500 at the beginning of each month, what will be the term of the annuity? Assume that the RRSP earns 8.5% compounded quarterly, and the funds invested in the annuity earn 7.5% compounded monthly.

•65. Quantum Research Ltd. has arranged debt financing from its parent company to complete the development of a new product. Quantum "draws down" \$10,000 at the beginning of each month. If interest accumulates on the debt at 12% compounded quarterly, how long will it take to reach the credit limit of \$1 million?

•66. Jamshid borrowed \$350 from his mother at the beginning of every month for $2\frac{1}{2}$ years while he attended Seneca College.

a. If the interest rate on the accumulating debt was 6% compounded semi-annually, what amount did he owe his mother at the end of the $2\frac{1}{2}$-year period?

b. If he made the first monthly payment of \$175 on the loan at the end of the first month following the $2\frac{1}{2}$-year period, how long after the date he entered college will he have the loan repaid?

•67. The annual membership dues in the Rolling Meadows Golf and Country Club can be paid by four payments of \$449.40 at the beginning of each calendar quarter, instead of by a single payment of \$1714 at the beginning of the year. What effective rate of interest is the club charging the quarterly instalment payers on the unpaid balance of their annual dues?

•68. The Lifestyle Fitness and Exercise Centre charges annual membership fees of \$300 (in advance) or six "easy" payments of \$60 at the beginning of every two months. What effective interest rate is being charged on the instalment plan?

•69. A magazine offers a one-year subscription rate of \$63.80 and a three-year subscription rate of \$159.80, both payable at the start of the subscription period. Assuming that you intend to continue to subscribe for three years and that the one-year rate does not increase for the next two years, what rate of "return on investment" will be earned by paying for a three-year subscription now instead of three consecutive one-year subscriptions?

•70. Continental Life Insurance Company of Canada offered \$250,000 of term life insurance to a 40-year-old female nonsmoker for an annual premium of \$447.50 (in advance) or for monthly premium payments (in advance) of \$38.82 by preauthorized cheques. What effective rate of interest is charged to those who pay monthly?

•71. The same disability insurance policy offers four alternative premium payment plans: an annual premium of \$666.96, semiannual premiums of \$341.32, quarterly premiums of \$172.62, and monthly premiums of \$58.85. In every case, the premiums are payable in advance. What effective rate of interest is the insurance company charging clients who pay their premiums:

a. Semiannually? **b.** Quarterly? **c.** Monthly?

•72. A \$500,000 life insurance policy for a 26-year-old offers four alternative premium payment plans: an annual premium of \$470.00, semiannual premiums of \$244.40, quarterly premiums of \$123.37, and monthly premiums of \$42.30. In every case, the premiums are payable in advance. What effective rate of interest is the insurance company charging if the premium is paid:

a. Semiannually? **b.** Quarterly? **c.** Monthly?

••**73.** Mr. Ng contributed $500 to an RRSP at the beginning of each calendar quarter for the past 20 years. The plan earned 10% compounded quarterly for the first 10 years and 12% compounded quarterly for the last 10 years. He is converting the RRSP to a Registered Retirement Income Fund (RRIF) and intends to withdraw equal amounts at the beginning of each month for 15 years. If the funds in the RRIF earn 8.25% compounded monthly, what maximum monthly amount can be withdrawn?

•**74.** As a result of the closure of the mine at which he had been employed, Les Orr received a $27,000 severance settlement on his fifty-third birthday. He "rolled" the severance pay into a new RRSP and then, at age 62, used the accumulated funds to purchase an annuity paying $491.31 at the beginning of each month. If the RRSP and the annuity earn 8.5% compounded annually, what is the term of the annuity?

••**75.** Mr. van der Linden has just used the funds in his RRSP to purchase a 25-year annuity earning 8% compounded semiannually and paying $3509 at the beginning of each month. Mr. van der Linden made his last regular semiannual contribution of $2500 to his RRSP six months before purchasing the annuity. How long did he contribute to the RRSP if it earned 8% compounded annually?

*13.4 Integrated Applications

The example problems and exercises in each section of the text have been chosen to illustrate the concepts and techniques introduced in that section. Each problem is an application primarily within the narrow scope of the section. This makes Step 3 of the problem-solving procedure (suggested in Section 2.4) virtually self-evident. (Step 3 is: "Identify the principle, concept, or idea that can be used to construct a word equation.") However, when applications arise in business, the connections to the underlying concept and a solution idea are usually not so apparent.

The purpose of this section is to present some interesting, comprehensive, and challenging problems that may involve any type of annuity as well as lump payments. A problem's solution may call upon any topic in Chapters 8 through 13 (except Section 12.2).

The flowchart in Figure 13.3 presents a procedure for identifying the type of annuity and the relevant formulas.

TIP *IDENTIFY THE TYPE OF ANNUITY AT THE OUTSET*

Immediately after extracting the raw data from an annuity problem, you should write down the type of annuity involved. If you intend to use the financial calculator functions, set the calculator in the proper mode (ordinary or due) at this time. By doing these small steps at the outset, you are less likely to overlook them later when you become preoccupied with more profound aspects of the solution.

Figure 13.3[5] *Annuity Classification Flowchart*

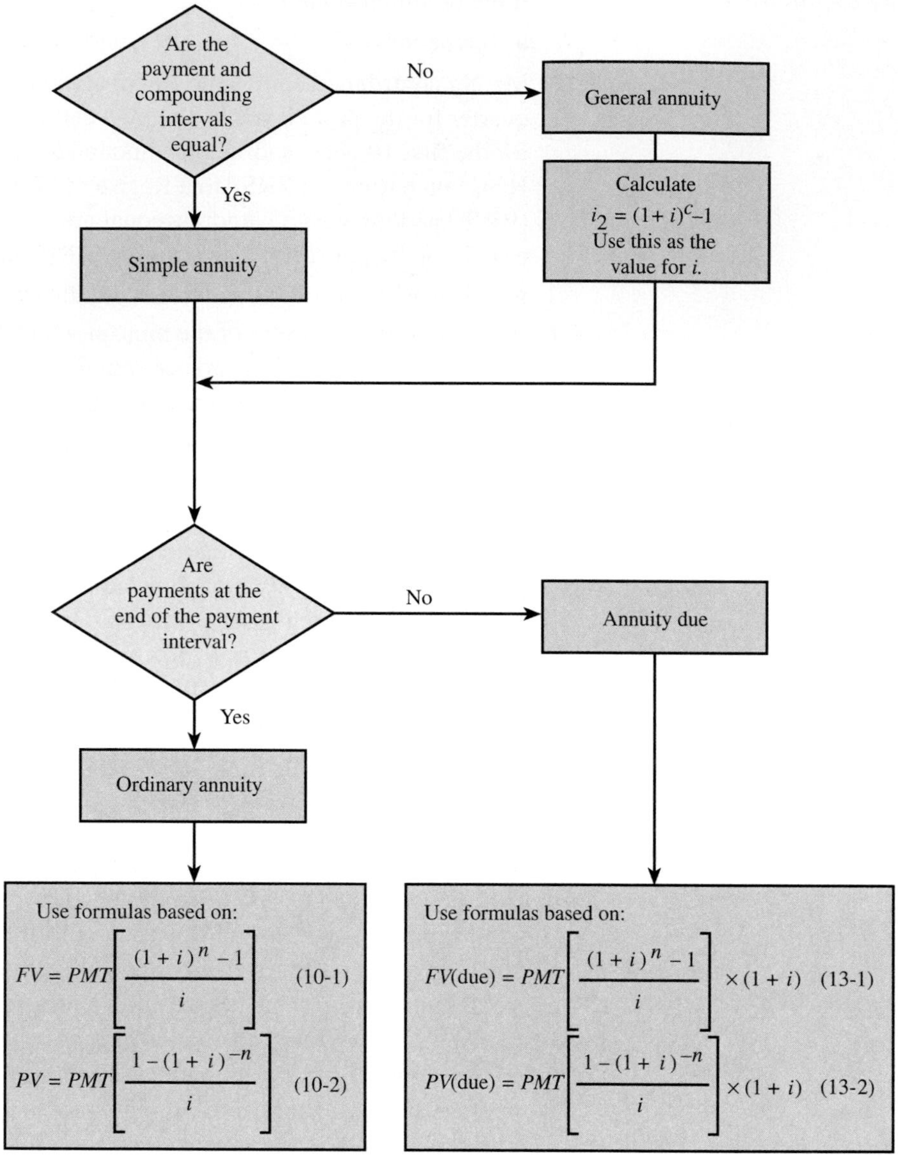

TIP

Clues to the Type of Annuity

Information enabling you to make the ordinary annuity vs. annuity due decision may lie in subtle wording of the problem. Look for a key word or phrase that provides the clue. Some examples of wording that indicates an annuity *due* are:

- "Payments at the beginning of each . . ."
- "Payments . . . in advance"
- "First payment . . . made today"
- "Payments . . . starting now"

[5] This figure was suggested by Bill Inkster of Capilano College.

Example 13.4A *Reducing a Loan's Term by Making More Frequent, Smaller Payments*

Calculate the time required to pay off a \$25,000 loan at 8.25% compounded monthly if the loan is repaid by:

a. Quarterly payments of \$600.

b. Monthly payments of \$200.

c. Semimonthly payments of \$100.

d. In every case, a total of \$600 is paid every three months. Explain why the time required to repay the loan shortens as smaller payments are made more frequently.

Solution

In every case, the present value of the payments is \$25,000. The payments form an ordinary general annuity in parts (a) and (c) where the payment interval differs from the compounding interval. In part (b), they form an ordinary simple annuity having $i = \frac{8.25\%}{12} = 0.6875\%$. The periodic interest rate that matches the payment interval is calculated in the following table.

	PMT	*c*	$i_2 = (1 + i)^c - 1$
a.	\$600	$\frac{12}{4} = 3$	$1.006875^3 - 1 = 0.020767122$
b.	\$200	$\frac{12}{12} = 1$	0.006875
c.	\$100	$\frac{12}{24} = 0.5$	$1.006875^{0.5} - 1 = 0.003431612$

Algebraic Solution

The calculation of *n* for the case of quarterly payments is presented below. Formula (10-2*n*) may be similarly employed for the other two payment frequencies.

$$n = -\frac{\ln\left(1 - \frac{i \times PV}{PMT}\right)}{\ln(1 + i)} = -\frac{\ln\left(1 - \frac{0.020767122 \times \$25{,}000}{\$600}\right)}{\ln(1.020767122)} = 97.53$$

	PMT	*n*	Number of payments	Term of the loan
a.	\$600	97.53	98	98 quarters = 24 years, 6 months
b.	\$200	286.31	287	287 months = 23 years, 11 months
c.	\$100	569.58	570	570 half-months = 23 years, 9 months

The results are summarized below.

It is apparent that the loan's term shortens as a given total annual amount is allocated to smaller, more frequent payments. This happens because the more frequent the payments, the earlier the principal balance is reduced. Subsequent interest charges are then lower. Consider, for example, the cases of monthly and quarterly payments. The first $200 monthly payment will reduce the principal balance. The interest charged in the second month will be less than in the first month because it is calculated on the *reduced* principal. In contrast, the first quarterly payment must include interest on the *full* $25,000 for each of the first three months. Therefore, the *interest* component of the first quarterly $600 payment will be *greater* than the sum of the interest components of the first three $200 monthly payments. Accordingly, the *principal* component of the $600 payment will be *smaller* than the sum of the principal components of the first three $200 monthly payments. This same effect will repeat and compound every quarter. Therefore, monthly payments will reduce the principal balance faster (and pay off the loan sooner) than quarterly payments.

Financial Calculator Solution

a. 25000 (PV) 0 (FV) 600 (+/–) (PMT) 2.0767122 (i) (COMP) (n) 97.53

b. 200 (+/–) (PMT) 0.6875 (i) (COMP) (n) 286.31

c. 100 (+/–) (PMT) 0.3431612 (i) (COMP) (n) 569.58

For the completion of the solution, refer to the table and explanation in the Algebraic Solution.

Example 13.4B A Multiple-Step Problem in Personal Financial Planning

Victor and his financial adviser are checking whether Victor's savings plan will allow him to achieve his retirement goals. Victor wishes to retire in 30 years at age 58. His plan is to use some of the funds in his RRSP at age 58 to purchase a 10-year annuity paying $5000 at the end of each month. Then, at age 68, he intends to use the balance of the funds in his RRSP to purchase a 20-year annuity paying at least $7000 at each month's end.

Victor anticipates that he will be able to contribute $5000 to his RRSP at the beginning of each of the next 15 years and $10,000 at the beginning of each of the subsequent 15 years. Can Victor achieve the desired retirement income if the RRSP earns 8% compounded semiannually and the funds used to purchase the annuities earn 7.5% compounded monthly?

Solution

Victor's savings plan is presented in the following time diagram.

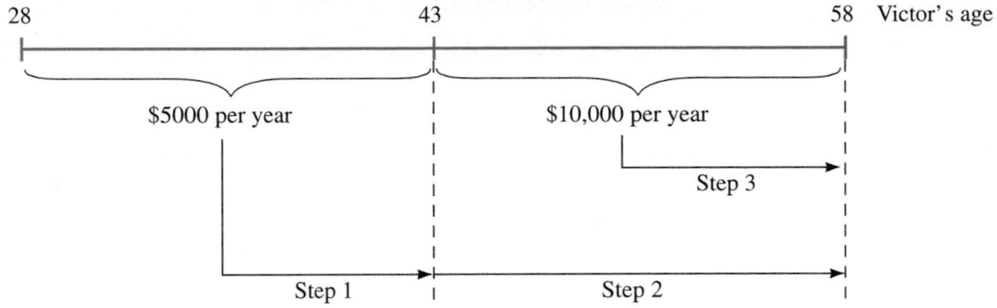

His desired retirement income stream is shown in the following diagram.

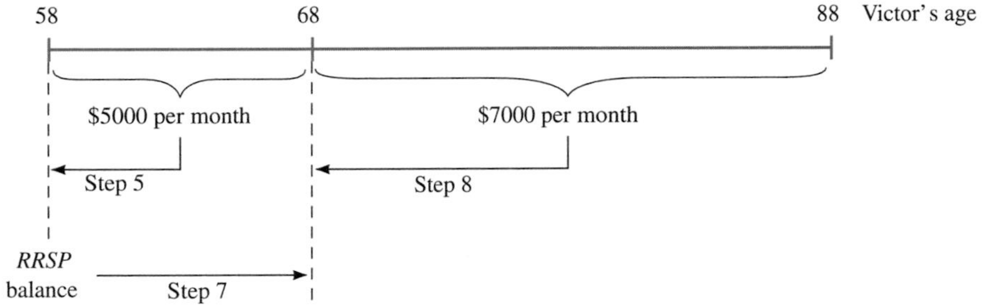

The key test to determine if Victor can achieve his objective for retirement income is whether there will be sufficient funds in his RRSP at age 68 to purchase a 20-year annuity paying $7000 at the end of each month. In general terms, our strategy for the solution is to:

- Calculate the expected amount in the RRSP at age 58. (Steps 1, 2, and 3 in the first diagram. Then as Step 4, add the results of Steps 2 and 3.)
- Deduct the amount required to purchase the 10-year annuity. (Step 5 in the second diagram. Then as Step 6, subtract the Step 5 result from the Step 4 result to obtain the "RRSP balance.")
- Calculate the expected amount in the RRSP at age 68. (Step 7.)
- Calculate the amount required to purchase the 20-year annuity. (Step 8. Then as Step 9, compare the Step 8 amount to the Step 7 amount.)

The two RRSP contribution streams are general annuities due for which

$$i = \frac{8\%}{2} = 4\% \qquad \text{and} \qquad c = \frac{\text{Number of compoundings per year}}{\text{Number of payments per year}} = \frac{2}{1} = 2$$

The periodic interest rate for the one-year payment interval is

$$i_2 = (1 + i)^c - 1 = 1.04^2 - 1 = 0.0816 = 8.16\% \text{ per year}$$

The retirement income annuities are ordinary simple annuities for which

$$i = \frac{7.5\%}{12} = 0.625\% \text{ per month.}$$

Algebraic Solution

Step 1: Calculate the future value at age 43 of the RRSP contributions of \$5000 per year.

$$FV(\text{due}) = PMT\left[\frac{(1+i)^n - 1}{i}\right](1+i) = \$5000\left(\frac{1.0816^{15} - 1}{0.0816}\right)(1.0816) = \$148{,}680.07$$

Step 2: Calculate the future value at age 58 of the Step 1 result.

$$FV = PV(1+i)^n = \$148{,}680.07(1.0816)^{15} = \$482{,}228.57$$

Step 3: Calculate the future value at age 58 of the contributions of \$10,000 per year.

$$FV(\text{due}) = \$10{,}000\left(\frac{1.0816^{15} - 1}{0.0816}\right) \times (1.0816) = \$297{,}360.14$$

Step 4: Calculate the total amount in the RRSP at age 58.

$$\$428{,}228.57 + \$297{,}360.14 = \$779{,}588.71$$

Step 5: Calculate the amount required (present value) to purchase the 10-year annuity paying \$5000 per month.

$$PV = PMT\left[\frac{1-(1+i)^{-n}}{i}\right] = \$5000\left[\frac{1-(1.00625)^{-120}}{0.00625}\right] = \$421{,}223.71$$

Step 6: Calculate the "RRSP balance" at age 58.

$$\$779{,}588.71 - \$421{,}223.71 = \$358{,}365.00$$

Step 7: Calculate the amount (future value) in the RRSP at age 68.

$$FV = \$358{,}365.00(1.0816)^{10} = \$785{,}221.84$$

Step 8: Calculate the amount (present value) required to purchase the 20-year annuity paying \$7000 per month.

$$PV = \$7000\left[\frac{1-(1.00625)^{-240}}{0.00625}\right] = \$868{,}924.92$$

Step 9: Compare the Step 7 and Step 8 results.

When Victor reaches age 68, the RRSP will not have enough funds to purchase the 20-year annuity paying \$7000 per month. The projected shortage is

$$\$868{,}925 - \$785{,}222 = \$83{,}703$$

Financial Calculator Solution

Step 1: Calculate the future value at age 43 of the RRSP contributions of \$5000 per year.

BGN mode

5000 (+/–) (PMT) 8.16 (i) 15 (n) 0 (PV) (COMP) (FV) | 148,680.07 |

Steps 2, 3, and 4: Calculate the total amount in the RRSP at age 58.

BGN mode

(+/−) (PV) 10000 (+/−) (PMT) (COMP) (FV) | 779,588.71 |

Step 5: Calculate the amount required (present value) to purchase the 10-year annuity paying $5000 per month.

5000 (PMT) 0.625 (i) 120 (n) 0 (FV) (COMP) (PV) | −421,223.71 |

Step 6: Calculate the RRSP balance at age 58.

(+) 779588.71 (=) | 358,365.00 |

Step 7: Calculate the amount (future value) in the RRSP at age 68.

(+/−) (PV) 8.16 (i) 10 (n) 0 (PMT) (COMP) (PV) | 785,221.84 |

Step 8: Calculate the amount (present value) required to purchase the 20-year annuity paying $7000 per month.

7000 (PMT) 0.625 (i) 240 (n) 0 (FV) (COMP) (PV) | −868,924.92 |

Step 9: Compare the Step 7 and Step 8 results.
When Victor reaches age 68, the RRSP will not have enough funds to purchase the 20-year annuity paying $7000 per month. The projected shortage is

$$\$868{,}925 - \$785{,}222 = \$83{,}703$$

Exercise 13.4

Answers to the odd-numbered problems are at the end of the book.

•**1.** Monthly payments were originally calculated to repay a $20,000 loan at 12.75% compounded monthly over a 10-year period. After one year, the debtor took advantage of an option in the loan contract to increase the loan payments by 15%. How much sooner will the loan be paid off?

•**2.** On May 23, 1992, a woman won a US$9,346,862 jackpot on a $1 slot machine at Harrah's in Reno, Nevada. The payoff was not made as a single payment, but in 20 equal annual instalments, with the first instalment paid on the date of the win.

a. What was the economic value of this jackpot on May 23, 1992, if money was worth 7% compounded semiannually?

b. When will the stream of payments have an economic value equal to the reported nominal value of US$9,346,862? (Name the month and year.)

•**3.** Sheila already has $67,000 in her RRSP. How much longer must she contribute $4000 at the end of every six months to accumulate a total of $500,000 if the RRSP earns 9% compounded quarterly?

•**4.** What amount is required to purchase an annuity that pays \$5000 at the end of each quarter for the first 10 years and then pays \$2500 at the beginning of each month for the subsequent 10 years? The rate of return on the invested funds is 8.5% compounded quarterly.

•**5.** Natalie's RRSP is currently worth \$133,000. She plans to contribute for another seven years, and then let the plan continue to grow through internal earnings for an additional three years. If the RRSP earns 8.25% compounded annually, how much must she contribute at the end of every six months for the next seven years in order to have \$350,000 in the RRSP 10 years from now?

•**6.** Mr. Palmer wants to retire in 20 years and purchase a 25-year annuity that will make end-of-quarter payments. The payment size is to be the amount which, 20 years from now, has the purchasing power of \$6000 today. If he already has \$54,000 in his RRSP, what semiannual contributions must he make for the next 20 years to achieve his retirement goal? Assume that the annual rate of inflation for the next 20 years will be 4.5%, the RRSP will earn 8% compounded semiannually, and the rate of return on the fund from which the annuity is paid will be 8% compounded quarterly.

•**7.** Interprovincial Distributors Ltd. is planning to open a distribution centre in Calgary in five years. It can purchase a suitable piece of land for the distribution warehouse now for \$450,000. Annual taxes on the vacant land, payable at the end of each year, would be close to \$9000. What price would the property have to exceed five years from now to make it financially advantageous to purchase the property now instead of five years from now? Assume that Interprovincial can otherwise earn 12% compounded semiannually on its capital.

•**8.** Canadian Pacific Class B preferred shares have just paid their quarterly \$1.00 dividend and are trading on the Toronto Stock Exchange (TSE) at \$50. What will the price of the shares have to be three years from now for a current buyer of the shares to earn 10% compounded annually on the investment?

•**9.** If Gayle contributes \$1000 to her RRSP at the end of every quarter for the next 10 years and then contributes \$1000 at each month's end for the subsequent 15 years, how much will she have in her RRSP at the end of the 25 years? Assume that the RRSP earns 8.5% compounded semiannually.

•**10.** It will cost A-1 Courier \$1300 to convert a van from gasoline to natural gas fuel. The remaining useful life of the van is estimated at five years. To financially justify the conversion, what must be the reduction in the monthly cost of fuel to repay the original investment along with a return on investment of 12% compounded monthly? Assume that the fuel will be purchased at the beginning of each month.

••**11.** Conrad has two loans outstanding, which he can repay at any time. He has just made the eleventh monthly payment on an \$8500 loan at 13.5% compounded monthly for a three-year term. The twenty-second monthly payment of \$338.70 was also made today on the second loan, which has a five-year term and an interest rate of 13% compounded semiannually. Conrad is finding the total monthly payments too high, and interest rates on similar loans are now down to 11.25% compounded monthly. He wishes to reduce his monthly cash outflow by obtaining a debt consolidation loan just sufficient to pay off the balances on the two loans. What would his monthly payment be on a five-year term loan at the new rate?

•**12.** Jeanette wishes to retire in 30 years at age 55 with retirement savings that have the purchasing power of $300,000 in today's dollars.

a. If the rate of inflation for the next 30 years is 2% per year, how much must she accumulate in her RRSP?

b. If she contributes $3000 at the end of each year for the next five years, how much must she contribute annually for the subsequent 25 years to reach her goal? Assume that her RRSP will earn 8% compounded annually.

c. The amount in part (a) will be used to purchase a 30-year annuity. What will the month-end payments be if the funds earn 8.25% compounded monthly?

••**13.** The average annual costs to support a child born today are estimated as follows:

Years 1–6	$8400
Years 7–12	5400
Years 13–17	7200
Years 18–19	9600

The costs in the early years include child care expenses or forgone earnings of the care-giving parent.

a. What is the aggregate total cost (ignoring the time value of money) of raising a child to age 19?

b. What is the total economic value, at the date of birth of a child, of these future expenditures, allowing for a time value of money of 6% compounded monthly? Assume that the annual costs are paid in equal end-of-month amounts.

c. What will be the economic value at age 19 of the past expenditures, allowing for a time value of money of 6% compounded monthly?

••**14.** To compensate for the effects of inflation during their retirement years, the Pelyks intend to purchase a combination of annuities that will provide the following pattern of month-end income:

Calendar years, inclusive	Income ($)
2005 to 2009	5000
2010 to 2014	6000
2015 to 2019	7500
2020 to 2030	10,000

How much will they need in their RRSPs when they retire at the beginning of 2005 to purchase the annuities, if the annuity payments are based on a rate of return of 8% compounded semiannually?

••15. For its "Tenth Anniversary Salebration," Pioneer Furniture is offering terms of 10% down, no interest, and no payments for six months. The balance must then be paid in six equal payments, with the first payment due six months after the purchase date. The conditional sale contract calculates the monthly payments to include interest at the rate of 15% compounded monthly after the end of the interest-free period. Immediately after the sale of the furniture, Pioneer sells the contract to Afco Finance at a discount to yield Afco 18% compounded semiannually from the date of the sale. What cash payment will Pioneer receive from Afco on a piece of furniture sold for $2000?

••16. Patrick contributes $1000 at the beginning of every quarter to his RRSP. In addition, he contributes another $2000 to the RRSP each year from his year-end bonus. If the RRSP earns 9.5% compounded semiannually, what will be the value of his RRSP after 23 years?

••17. Reg is developing a financial plan that would enable him to retire 30 years from now at age 60. Upon reaching age 60, he will use some of the funds in his RRSP to purchase an eight-year annuity that pays $5000 at the end of each month. Then, at age 68, he will use the remaining funds to purchase a 20-year annuity paying $6000 at each month's end. What contributions must he make to an RRSP at the beginning of each quarter for 30 years to achieve his retirement goal, if the RRSP and the annuities earn 7.5% compounded monthly?

•18. Cynthia currently has $31,000 in her RRSP. She plans to contribute $5000 at the end of each year for the next 17 years and then use the accumulated funds to purchase a 20-year annuity making end-of-month payments.

a. Assume that her RRSP earns 8.75% compounded annually for the next 17 years, and the fund from which the annuity is paid will earn 8.25% compounded monthly. What monthly payments will she receive?

b. If the average annual rate of inflation for the next 17 years is 4%, what will be the purchasing power in today's dollars of the monthly payments 17 years from now?

••19. A major car manufacturer is developing a promotion offering new car buyers the choice between "below market" four-year financing at 6.9% compounded monthly or a cash rebate. On the purchase of a $20,000 car, what cash rebate would make a car buyer indifferent between the following alternatives?

- Financing through the car dealer at the reduced interest rate.
- Taking the cash rebate and obtaining bank financing at 10.5% compounded monthly for the net "cash" price.

••20. The monthly payments on a $30,000 loan at 10.5% compounded monthly were calculated to repay the loan over a 10-year period. After 32 payments were made, the borrower became unemployed and, with the approval of the lender, missed the next three payments.

a. What amount paid along with the regular payment at the end of the thirty-sixth month will put the loan repayment back on the original schedule?

b. Instead of the "make-up" arrangement in part (a), suppose the regular loan payments (beginning with the payment at the end of the thirty-sixth month) are recalculated to put the loan back on its 10-year repayment "track." What will be the new payments?

••21. Martha's RRSP is currently worth $97,000. She plans to contribute $5000 at the beginning of every six months until she reaches age 58, 12 years from now. Then she intends to use half of the funds in the RRSP to purchase a 20-year annuity making month-end payments. Five years later she will use half of the funds then in her RRSP to purchase another 20-year annuity making month-end payments. Finally, at age 68, she will use all of the remaining funds to purchase a third 20-year annuity also making end-of-month payments. What will be her monthly income at age 65 and at age 70 if her RRSP and the annuities earn 7.5% compounded monthly?

Appendix: Setting Your Calculator in the Annuity Due Mode

This appendix illustrates how to set your calculator for annuity due calculations.

SHARP EL-733A	SHARP EL-735	Texas Instruments BA-35 Solar	Texas Instruments BA II PLUS	Hewlett Packard 10B
BGN "BGN" appears in the display when in this mode.	2nd F BGN/END "BGN" appears in the display when in this mode.	2nd BGN "Begin" appears in the display when in this mode.	2nd BGN 2nd SET 2nd QUIT "BGN" appears in the display when in this mode.	[blank key] BEG/END "BEGIN" appears in the display when in this mode.

Any time you perform these instructions, your calculator will "toggle" or switch between the ordinary annuity mode (no indicator in the display) and the annuity due mode ("BGN" or "Begin" in the display). The calculator will remain in the most recently selected mode, even after being turned off.

Review Problems

Answers to the odd-numbered review problems are at the end of the book.
Interest rates should be calculated accurate to the nearest 0.01%.

1. Brunswick Trucking has signed a five-year lease with Ford Credit Canada Ltd. on a new truck. Lease payments of $1900 are made at the beginning of each month. To purchase the truck, Brunswick Trucking would have had to borrow funds at 10.5% compounded monthly.

   a. What initial liability should Brunswick report on its balance sheet?

   b. How much will the liability be reduced during the first year of the lease?

2. What minimum amount of money earning 7% compounded semiannually will sustain withdrawals of $1000 at the beginning of every month for 12 years?

3. What maximum annual withdrawals will a $300,000 fund earning 7.75% compounded annually sustain for 25 years if the withdrawals are made:

   a. At the beginning of each year? **b.** At the end of each year?

4. Regular investments made at the beginning of each quarter earn 6% compounded quarterly. How many more $1000 investments than $1100 investments will it take to accumulate $100,000?

5. An RRSP is now worth $316,000 after contributions of $3500 at the beginning of every six months for 17 years. What effective rate of return has the plan earned?

6. Suppose that $5000 is contributed at the beginning of each year to an RRSP that earns 8% compounded annually.

   a. How many contributions will it take to accumulate the first $500,000?

   b. How many more contributions will it take for the RRSP to reach $1,000,000?

7. The membership dues at Shoreline Golf and Country Club are $1410 payable at the beginning of the year, or four payments of $368.28 payable at the beginning of each quarter. What effective rate of interest is the club charging members who pay their dues quarterly?

8. Apex Fabricating wants to accumulate $800,000 for an expansion expected to begin in four years. If today Apex makes the first of equal quarterly payments into a fund earning 6.75% compounded monthly, what should the size of these payments be?

9. How many more RRSP contributions of $300 at the beginning of every month are required to reach $200,000 if the funds earn 8% compounded monthly than if they earn 10% compounded monthly?

10. As of the date of Colony Farm's most recent financial statements, $3\frac{1}{2}$ years remained in the term of a capital lease reported as a long-term liability of $26,244. If the beginning-of-month lease payments are $750, what monthly compounded nominal (annual) discount rate was used in valuing the lease?

11. If a furniture store offers to sell a washer-dryer combination priced at $1395 on a conditional sale contract requiring 12 monthly payments of $125 (including a payment on the date of sale), what effective rate of interest is being charged?

12. Sovereign Life Insurance Company of Canada offers $250,000 of term life insurance to a 45-year-old male for an annual premium of $716 (in advance) or for monthly premium payments (in advance) of $62.50 by preauthorized cheques. What effective rate of interest is charged to those who pay monthly?

13. Fred is about to have his twenty-seventh birthday. He has set a goal of retiring at age 58 with \$1,000,000 in his RRSP. For planning purposes, he is assuming that his RRSP will earn 8% compounded annually.

a. What contributions on each birthday from age 27 to 57 inclusive will be required to accumulate the desired amount in his RRSP?

b. If he waits five years before starting his RRSP, what contributions on each birthday from age 32 to 57 inclusive will be required to reach the target?

◆ **14.** What is the initial economic value of an annuity due if it consists of 19 semiannual payments of \$1500? Money is worth 9% compounded semiannually for the first five years, and 10% compounded semiannually thereafter.

◆ **15.** What will be the amount in an RRSP after 30 years if contributions of \$4000 are made at the beginning of each year for the first 10 years, and contributions of \$6000 are made at the beginning of each year for the subsequent 20 years? Assume that the RRSP will earn 8.25% compounded annually.

◆ **16.** A rental agreement requires the payment of \$1000 at the beginning of each month.

a. What single payment at the beginning of the rental year should the landlord accept instead of monthly payments if money is worth 8% compounded monthly?

b. Show that the landlord will be equally well off at the end of the year under either payment arrangement if rental payments are invested at 8% compounded monthly.

◆ **17.** Mick contributed \$5000 at the beginning of each year for 25 years to his RRSP. Assume that the RRSP earned 8% compounded annually. What percentage of the RRSP's value after 25 years comes from contributions made in the first five years?

◆ **18.** What amount is required to purchase an annuity that pays \$4000 at the end of each quarter for the first five years and then pays \$2500 at the beginning of each month for the subsequent 15 years? Assume that the annuity payments are based on a rate of return of 7.5% compounded quarterly.

◆ **19.** Suppose that \$5000 is contributed at the beginning of each year for 25 years to an RRSP that earns 10% compounded annually. By what percentage would annual contributions have to be increased in order to have the same future value after 25 years if the plan earns only 8% compounded annually?

◆ **20.** Suppose you contribute \$2000 to an RRSP at the beginning of every six months for 25 years, and then use the accumulated funds to purchase an annuity paying \$2500 at the beginning of each month. How long after the start of the annuity will the last payment be made? Assume that the RRSP earns 8% compounded semiannually and the funds invested in the annuity earn 7.5% compounded monthly.

◆ **21.** Capital Leasing calculates its five-year lease rates so that it recovers the capital cost of the equipment plus a rate of return on investment of 16% compounded semiannually over the term of the lease. What will be the required lease payments on a machine that cost \$35,000 if the lease payments are made:

a. At the beginning of every month?

b. At the beginning of each six-month period?

Self-Test Exercise

Answers to the self-test problems are at the end of the book.

1. Calculate the amount that will be accumulated after 20 years if:

   a. $1000 is invested at the beginning of every six months at 8.5% compounded semiannually.

   b. $2000 is invested at the beginning of every year at 8.5% compounded annually.

2. A life insurance company quoted an annual premium of $387.50 (payable at the beginning of the year) for a $250,000 term insurance policy on a 35-year-old male nonsmoker. Alternatively, the insured can pay $33.71 at the beginning of each month by preauthorized cheques. Which payment plan would an applicant choose solely on the basis of money being worth 10% compounded monthly?

3. A seven-year capital lease of an executive jet requires semiannual payments of $200,000 at the beginning of each six-month period. The company can borrow funds for five to 10 years at 10.75% compounded semiannually.

   a. What long-term lease liability will the firm set up at the start of the term of the lease?

   b. What liability will remain halfway through the term of the lease?

◆ 4. Calculate the future value of an annuity consisting of payments of $800 at the beginning of each calendar quarter for seven years. Assume that the rate of interest earned will be 10% compounded quarterly for the first 30 months and 9% compounded semiannually for the remainder of the annuity's term.

5. Excel Leasing calculates the payments on long-term equipment leases so that it earns a rate of return of 15% compounded quarterly on its investment in the equipment. What beginning-of-month payments will Excel charge on a four-year lease of a photocopier costing $7650? (Assume no residual value at the end of the lease.)

◆ 6. Ms. Bowers wants to be able to purchase a 20-year annuity at age 62 that will pay her $3500 at the beginning of each month. If she starts quarterly contributions to an RRSP on her thirty-fifth birthday and continues them up to but not including her sixty-second birthday, what should be the size of each contribution? Assume that her RRSP will earn 8% compounded quarterly and that the money used to purchase the annuity fund will earn 7.5% compounded monthly.

◆ 7. Mr. and Mrs. Zolob contributed $50 on the first of each month to an RESP they set up for their grandson Jeff. By the time he entered Mohawk College, 14 years and five months of contributions had accumulated. The grandparents' contributions stopped, and Jeff started beginning-of-month withdrawals of $500. How long will these payments last if the RESP has earned and will continue to earn 8.25% compounded monthly?

◆ 8. New Look Fitness Centre offers a one-year membership for $250 in advance, or a three-month membership for $80 in advance. What effective rate of interest is an individual paying if she buys four consecutive three-month memberships instead of a one-year membership?

◆ 9. A life insurance company is calculating the monthly premium that it will offer clients as an alternative to paying the full annual premium. With both alternatives, premiums are payable at the beginning of the period of coverage. If the monthly payment by preauthorized cheque is calculated to yield the insurance company 16% compounded semiannually on the unpaid balance of the annual premium, what should be the monthly premium per $100 of annual premium?

CASE

THE TRADE-OFF BETWEEN THE DOWN PAYMENT AND THE LEASE PAYMENT

In early 1999, the Ford Motor Company of Canada advertised both lease and purchase options for the 1999 Explorer Sport utility vehicle. A 2.9% interest rate (compounded monthly) was offered on both 36-month leases and 48-month loans-to-purchase. The purchase price was $30,328 and the residual value used for the lease payments was $17,630.

Three monthly lease payments were quoted for three different down payments.

Down payment	Lease payment
$4995	$266 per month
?	$298 per month
$995	? per month

QUESTIONS

1. What values did Ford quote where a "?" is found in the preceding table?
2. On rare occasions, you might see mention of a "one-payment lease plan." The idea is that a single lump payment is made at the beginning of the lease. If Ford had offered such a plan on the 1999 Explorer Sport, what would have been the lump payment?
3. What is the monthly loan payment if the Explorer Sport is purchased with a $4995 down payment?
4. Assuming the Explorer's market value after three years equals the residual value, what equity will the buyer (in Question 3) have in the vehicle at the end of the third year? (The owner's equity is the amount by which the Explorer's market value exceeds the loan's balance?)

www.Exercise.com

COMPONENTS OF THE FUTURE VALUE OF AN ANNUITY DUE Go to Fidelity Investments' Growth Calculator referred to in the "Caught in the Web" box in Section 13.1 (www.fidelity.ca/planning/tools/growth/growth.html). A sample of the chart you will find at the Web site is shown below. (You may need to click on the Reset button to make the chart appear.)

Each column in the chart shows the components of the future value of a simple annuity due at the year-end. Fidelity refers to the three components as invested capital, simple earnings, and compound earnings. *Simple earnings* represent interest earned on invested capital on a simple interest basis. *Compound earnings* represent interest earned on converted interest.

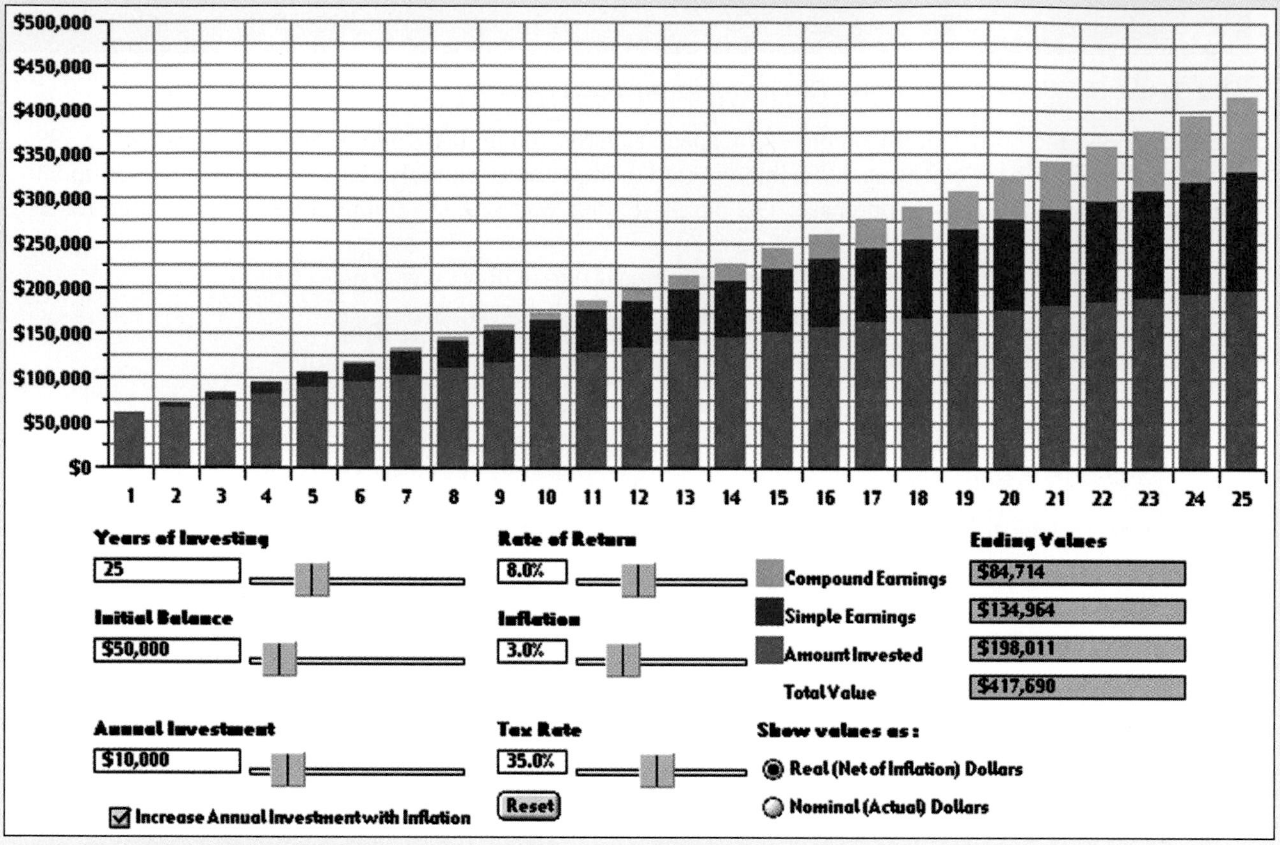

Source: Reproduced with permission of *Fidelity Investments Canada Limited.*

The calculator will adjust for inflation in two respects. If you intend to increase your annual contributions to keep pace with the rate of inflation, check the "Increase Annual Investment With Inflation" box. (This is the type of scenario covered in Section 12.2). For *fixed* annual investments, delete the check mark from this box. The second optional inflation adjustment is to display the future value (and its components) in constant purchasing power dollars. This feature is activated by selecting the "Real (Net of Inflation) Dollars" option.

The calculator will also display results on a before-income-tax basis (by setting "Tax Rate" at 0%) or on an after-tax basis. The number you enter in "Tax Rate" is the percentage of each year's investment earnings that will be paid in income tax. For example, if you enter 40% in "Tax Rate" and 10% in "Rate of Return," the after-tax rate of growth will be only 10% – 0.4(10%) = 6%.

Answer the following questions for a "Rate of Return" of 10% compounded annually and a fixed annual investment of $1000. The calculator assumes the payments are at the beginning of each year. Unless otherwise indicated, enter "0" for the "Tax Rate" to simulate growth within an RRSP.

1. How long does it take for the "Compound Earnings" component to exceed the "Simple Earnings" component?
2. After 10 years, what is each component's percentage of the future value?
3. After 25 years, what is each component's percentage of the future value?

4. If the annual rate of inflation is 2%, what is the future value after 25 years in constant purchasing power (real) dollars?
5. If the investments are held outside an RRSP and the annual earnings are taxed at 30%, how much less will you have (in nominal dollars) after 25 years than in Question 3?

Summary of Notation and Key Formulas

$FV(\text{due})$ = Future value of an n-payment annuity due
$PV(\text{due})$ = Present value of an n-payment annuity due

Formula (13-1) $$FV(\text{due}) = PMT\left[\frac{(1+i)^n - 1}{i}\right] \times (1+i)$$ Finding the future value of an annuity due

Formula (13-2) $$PV(\text{due}) = PMT\left[\frac{1-(1+i)^{-n}}{i}\right] \times (1+i)$$ Finding the present value of an annuity due

Formula (13-1*n*) $$n = \frac{\ln\left[1 + \frac{i \times FV(\text{due})}{PMT(1+i)}\right]}{\ln(1+i)}$$ Finding the number of payments given $FV(\text{due})$

Formula (13-2*n*) $$n = -\frac{\ln\left[1 - \frac{i \times PV(\text{due})}{PMT(1+i)}\right]}{\ln(1+i)}$$ Finding the number of payments given $PV(\text{due})$

List of Key Terms

Annuity due *(p. 498)*

Book value (of a lease liability) *(p. 507)*

Residual value *(p. 514)*

CHAPTER OUTLINE

LEARNING OBJECTIVES

After completing this chapter, you will be able to:

- Calculate the principal balance after any payment using both the Prospective Method and the Retrospective Method
- Calculate the final loan payment when it differs from the others
- Calculate the principal and interest components of any payment
- Construct a loan's amortization schedule
- Calculate mortgage payments for the initial loan and its renewals
- Calculate mortgage loan balances and amortization periods to reflect prepayments of principal
- Calculate the effective cost of borrowing when a brokerage fee is charged on a mortgage loan
- Calculate the market value of mortgage loans
- Calculate the equivalent cash value of a real estate transaction involving a vendor take-back mortgage

CHAPTER

14

Amortization of Loans

THE TERM "LOAN AMORTIZATION" is used in two ways. One meaning is the process of repaying the original principal by equal periodic payments. (The final payment may differ from the others.) Loan amortization also refers to the accounting treatment of loan payments. Although all payments are the same size, each one consists of a different combination of principal and interest. There are several applications in which we need to separate the principal and interest components of one or more payments. In Sections 1 and 2, you will learn the concepts needed to do these calculations.

The largest single amount most of us will ever borrow is a mortgage loan for the purchase of a home. At the end of 1998, total residential mortgage debt represented 72% of all household debt (over $550 billion) in Canada. Mortgage financing is also very common in the commercial sector. In fact, a higher proportion of commercial properties and residential rental properties have mortgage loans against them than do owner-occupied dwellings. How well you manage mortgage debt is a key factor in growing your personal and your business's net worth.

14.1 Loan Balances and Details of Individual Payments

A loan for a specific major purchase such as a vehicle, machinery, or real estate, is usually set up as a term loan. In a **term loan**, the payments are calculated to repay the loan over a predetermined length of time called the **amortization period**. This period is typically three to five years for a vehicle or a machine, and 20 or 25 years for residential and commercial real estate.

Calculating the Loan Balance

In previous chapters we have been using the fundamental concepts:

$$\text{Original loan} = \begin{bmatrix} \text{Present value of all of the payments} \\ \text{(discounted at the } \textit{contractual} \\ \textit{rate of interest on the loan}\text{)} \end{bmatrix}$$

and

$$\text{Principal balance} = \begin{bmatrix} \text{Present value of the remaining payments} \\ \text{(discounted at the } \textit{contractual} \\ \textit{rate of interest on the loan}\text{)} \end{bmatrix}$$

It turns out that the way we have been using this method for calculating a loan's balance usually results in a small inaccuracy. In the following example, we will illustrate why the inaccuracy arises. Then we will develop two ways of avoiding it—we can either change the way we apply this concept or we can use an entirely different method. Both approaches will be presented.

Example 14.1A *Consequences of Rounding the Calculated Payment*

A $20,000 mortgage loan at 9% compounded monthly requires monthly payments during its 20-year amortization period.

a. Calculate the monthly payment rounded to the nearest cent.

b. Using the rounded monthly payment from part (a), calculate the present value of all payments.

c. Why does the answer in (b) differ from $20,000?

Solution

The payments form an ordinary simple annuity having

$$PV = \$20{,}000 \qquad i = \frac{9\%}{12} = 0.75\% \text{ per month} \qquad \text{and} \qquad n = 12(20) = 240$$

Solve for *PMT* using the principle that

$$\text{Original loan} = \text{Present value of all payments}$$

Algebraic Solution

a. Substitute the given values into

$$PV = PMT\left[\frac{1-(1+i)^{-n}}{i}\right]$$

giving

$$\$20{,}000 = PMT\left[\frac{1-(1.0075)^{-240}}{0.0075}\right]$$

Solving for *PMT,* we obtain *PMT* = \$179.9452, which we round to \$179.95.

b. Now calculate the *PV* of 240 payments of \$179.95.

$$PV = \$179.95\left[\frac{1-(1.0075)^{-240}}{0.0075}\right] = \$20{,}000.53$$

c. The present value of the payments is \$0.53 larger than the original loan! This difference is due to rounding the monthly payment to the nearest cent. (In everyday commerce we do not usually deal in fractions of a cent.) We rounded the calculated payment *up* from \$179.9452 to \$179.95. This means that each payment is actually

$$\$179.95 - \$179.9452 = \$0.0048$$

more than mathematically necessary to repay (or amortize) the loan. The calculation in part (b) tells us that 240 payments of \$179.95 would, in fact, amortize a loan of \$20,000.53. (The 240 overpayments of \$0.0048 repay the extra \$0.53. You can verify this by calculating the present value of 240 payments of \$0.0048.)

Financial Calculator Solution

a. 20000 (PV) 0.75 (*i*) 240 (*n*) 0 (FV) (COMP) (PMT) [−179.9452]

b. 179.95 (+/−) (PMT) (COMP) (PV) [20,000.53]

The present value of 240 payments of \$179.95 is \$20,000.53.

c. See part (c) in the Algebraic Solution.

Postscript: In practice, a lender would adjust for the 239 overpayments by reducing the size of the final payment. (We will return to the calculation of the final payment later in this section.)

If the calculated payment is rounded *down* to the nearest cent, each actual payment represents a small underpayment. The present value of all payments will be *less* than the original loan. Consequently, the final payment must be larger[1] than the regular payment to compensate for the preceding underpayments.

---

[1] Borrowers are much more likely to inquire (and complain) if the final payment is increased than if it is decreased. Since the reason for the adjustment is a rather subtle point (which most borrowers would not understand even if bank personnel could explain it), some lenders strictly round the regular payment upward so that the final payment will always be smaller than the others. In this book, we will follow the standard rules for rounding and always round to the *nearest* cent.

Calculating the Loan Balance When the Final Payment Differs from the Others As a result of rounding the calculated payment to the nearest cent, the final payment almost always differs from the others. Consequently, a loan's balance calculated from the present value of the remaining payments will not be strictly correct if all payments are assumed to be equal. To obtain the precise value of the balance, you must employ a two-step approach.

1. Using the *rounded* value of *PMT,* calculate the revised non-integer value for *n,* the total number of payments required to pay off the loan. The fractional part of *n* corresponds to the final smaller payment.
2. The balance just after any payment is the present value of the remaining payments (with the fractional part of *n* being retained to represent the final payment).

The following example illustrates this approach.

Example 14.1B Precise Calculation of a Loan's Balance

For the mortgage loan ($20,000 at 9% compounded monthly with monthly payments for 20 years) in Example 14.1A,

a. Calculate the balance after five years assuming the final payment will be the same as the rounded regular payment ($179.95).

b. Calculate the exact balance after five years assuming the final payment will be adjusted for the effect of rounding the regular payment.

Solution

We have

$$PMT = \$179.95 \qquad \text{and} \qquad i = \frac{9\%}{12} = 0.75\% \text{ per month}$$

After 5 years, 240 − 12(5) = 180 monthly payments remain to pay off or amortize the loan.

Algebraic Solution

a. Balance (after five years) = *PV* of 180 payments of $179.95

$$= \$179.95\left[\frac{1 - (1.0075)^{-180}}{0.0075}\right]$$

$$= \$17{,}741.88$$

b. Step 1: Calculate the exact *n* for monthly payments of $179.95 to repay a $20,000 loan. Using formula (10-2n), we obtain

$$n = -\frac{\ln\left(1 - \dfrac{i \times PV}{PMT}\right)}{\ln(1 + i)} = -\frac{\ln\left(1 - \dfrac{0.0075 \times \$20{,}000}{\$179.95}\right)}{\ln(1.0075)} = 239.9820863$$

Step 2: After five years, 239.9820863 − 60 = 179.9820863 payments remain. Hence,

$$\text{Balance (after five years)} = PV \text{ of } 179.9820863 \text{ payments of } \$179.95$$

$$= \$179{,}95\left[\frac{1-(1.0075)^{-179.9820863}}{0.0075}\right]$$

$$= \$17{,}741.05$$

The strictly correct balance after five years is $17,741.05.

Financial Calculator Solution

a. Balance (after five years) = *PV* of 180 payments of $179.95

179.95 (+/–) (PMT) 180 (*n*) 0.75 (*i*) 0 (FV) (COMP) (PV) [17,741.88]

The balance after five years is $17,741.88 (assuming all payments are the same).

b. Step 1: Calculate the exact *n* for monthly payments of $179.95 to repay a $20,000 loan.

20000 (PV) (COMP) (*n*) [239.9820863]

Step 2: After five years, 239.9820863 − 60 = 179.9820863 payments remain. Hence,

Balance (after five years) = *PV* of 179.9820863 payments of $179.95

Rather than keying in the new value for (*n*), subtract 60 from the old (*n*) still in the display.

(–) 60 (=) (*n*) (COMP) (PV) [17,741.05]

The correct balance after five years is $17,741.05.

Postscript: So there you have the bad news—to avoid an error of only several cents, you must do a two-step calculation involving ugly values of *n*. The good news is that there is another method that avoids non-integer values of *n*. (In other words, there is another way to "come to your proper cents.") There is an additional bonus for users of financial calculators—the alternative method entails a single calculation requiring less time than it takes to overcome the shock of seeing a number like $n = 239.9820863$.

Retrospective Method for Loan Balances This name for the alternative method will make sense after you understand the concept underlying it.

Recall that the equation

$$\text{Original loan} = \left[\begin{array}{c}\text{Present value of all of the payments} \\ \text{(discounted at the } \textit{contractual} \\ \textit{rate of interest on the loan}\text{)}\end{array}\right]$$

is really a statement that the original loan is economically equivalent to all of the loan payments (if money can earn a rate of return equal to the interest rate on the loan).

The balance at any point is the single amount that will replace all remaining payments. The equation

$$\text{Balance} = \left[\begin{array}{c}\text{Present value of the remaining payments}\\ \text{(discounted at the } \textit{contractual}\\ \textit{rate of interest on the loan}\text{)}\end{array}\right]$$

is really a statement that the balance is economically equivalent to all remaining payments. In Figure 14.1, the loan balance at the time of payment number x replaces the subsequent $n - x$ payments.

It follows from the two preceding statements that the original loan is economically equivalent to the first x payments plus the balance. With a focal date at the time of the original loan, the statement of this equivalence is

$$\left(\begin{array}{c}\text{Original}\\ \text{loan}\end{array}\right) = \left(\begin{array}{c}\text{Present value of}\\ \text{the first } x \text{ payments}\end{array}\right) + \left(\begin{array}{c}\text{Present value of the balance}\\ \text{just after the } x\text{th payment}\end{array}\right)$$

Suppose we locate the focal date at the date of the xth payment as indicated in Figure 14.2.

The statement of economic equivalence becomes

$$\left(\begin{array}{c}\text{Future value of}\\ \text{the original loan}\end{array}\right) = \left(\begin{array}{c}\text{Future value of the}\\ \text{payments already made}\end{array}\right) + \text{Balance}$$

Rearranging this equation to isolate the "Balance," we obtain

$$\text{Balance} = \left(\begin{array}{c}\text{Future value of}\\ \text{the original loan}\end{array}\right) - \left(\begin{array}{c}\text{Future value of the}\\ \text{payments already made}\end{array}\right)$$

This result provides an alternative method for calculating a loan's balance immediately after any payment. Note that it is based on the payments we see when *looking back* from the focal date. A dictionary definition of "retrospective" is "look-

Figure 14.1 *A Loan Is Equivalent to a Series of Payments and the Principal Balance After the Payments*

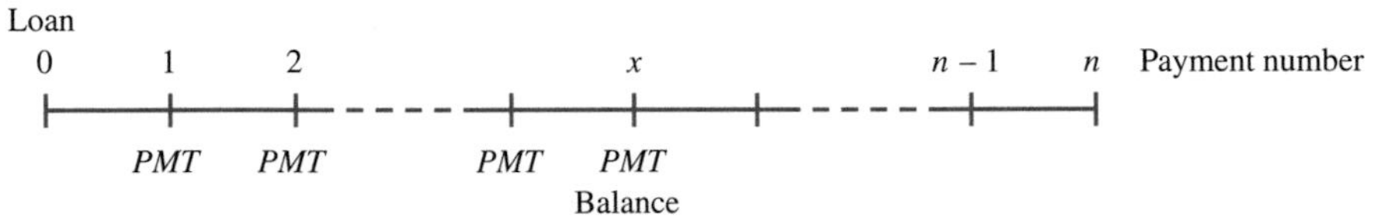

Figure 14.2 *Placing the Focal Date at the Balance Date*

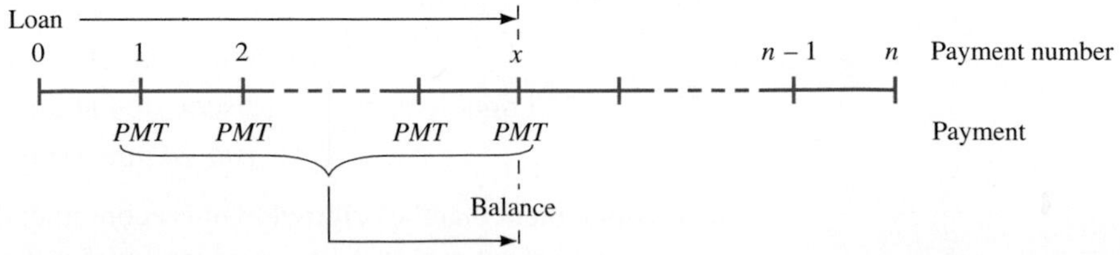

ing back on or dealing with the past." Now you see the reason for the name **Retrospective Method**. It is based on payments already made.

In contrast, our former method (Balance = Present value of remaining payments) is based on payments still to come. We will now refer to it as the **Prospective Method** because "prospective" means "concerned with or applying to the future."

Let us illustrate the Retrospective Method by using it to again answer part (b) of Example 14.1B. This will allow you to compare the Retrospective Method to the Prospective Method.

Example 14.1C *Loan Balance Using the Retrospective Method*

Part (b) of Example 14.1B was: Calculate the exact balance after five years of the loan in Example 14.1A. (The loan in Example 14.1A was for $20,000 at 9% compounded monthly with monthly payments of $179.95 for 20 years, except for a smaller final payment.)

Solution

We have

$$PMT = \$179.95 \qquad \text{and} \qquad i = \frac{9\%}{12} = 0.75\% \text{ per month}$$

After five years, 12(5) = 60 payments have been made. According to the Retrospective Method,

$$\text{Balance} = \begin{pmatrix} \text{Future value of} \\ \$20{,}000 \text{ after five years} \end{pmatrix} - \begin{pmatrix} \text{Future value of the 60} \\ \text{payments already made} \end{pmatrix}$$

Algebraic Solution

$$\begin{aligned} \text{Balance} &= PV(1+i)^n - PMT\left[\frac{(1+i)^n - 1}{i}\right] \\ &= \$20{,}000(1.0075)^{60} - \$179.95\left[\frac{(1.0075)^{60} - 1}{0.0075}\right] \\ &= \$31{,}313.62 - \$13{,}572.57 \\ &= \$17{,}741.05 \end{aligned}$$

Financial Calculator Solution

The financial calculator will do both future value calculations simultaneously. The subtraction is an automatic by-product of the sign convention.

20000 (PV) 179.95 (+/-) (PMT) 60 (n) 0.75 (i) (COMP) (FV) [−17,741.05]

The balance after five years is $17,741.05.

Postscript: A comparison of this solution to the solution in part (b) of Example 14.1B leads to the following observations.

- If strict accuracy is required in an algebraic solution, the Retrospective Method for calculating the loan balance involves shorter and simpler calculations with fewer opportunities to make a mistake.
- If strict accuracy is required in a financial calculator solution, the Retrospective Method is clearly faster and easier to use than the Prospective Method. In fact, the *correct* balance using the Retrospective Method is as readily calculated as the *approximate* balance using the Prospective Method!

Calculating the Final Payment

The final payment must cover the principal balance remaining after the second-to-last payment *plus* the interest on that balance for one payment interval. Therefore, if the payments form a simple annuity,

$$\begin{pmatrix}\text{Final}\\ \text{payment}\end{pmatrix} = \begin{pmatrix}\text{Balance after the}\\ \text{second-to-last payment}\end{pmatrix} + i \times \begin{pmatrix}\text{Balance after the}\\ \text{second-to-last payment}\end{pmatrix}$$

Since

$$\begin{pmatrix}\text{Balance after the}\\ \text{second-to-last payment}\end{pmatrix}$$ is a common factor on the right side, then

$$\text{Final payment} = (1 + i) \times \begin{pmatrix}\text{Balance after the}\\ \text{second-to-last payment}\end{pmatrix}$$

If the loan payments form a general annuity, replace i by i_2, the equivalent periodic rate that matches the payment interval. [Recall that $i_2 = (1 + i)^c - 1$.]

Example 14.1D *Calculating the Size of the Final Payment*

Calculate the final payment for the mortgage loan we have been using in Examples 14.1A, 14.1B, and 14.1C. It was a $20,000 loan at 9% compounded monthly with a 20-year amortization. We previously calculated the monthly payment to be $179.95.

Solution

The final payment is the balance after Payment 239 plus one month's interest on that balance. Using the general result we derived in the preceding discussion,

$$\text{Final payment} = 1.0075 \times \text{Balance after 239 payments}$$

According to the Retrospective Method,

$$\begin{pmatrix}\text{Balance after}\\ \text{239 payments}\end{pmatrix} = \begin{pmatrix}\text{Future value of}\\ \$20{,}000 \text{ after 239 months}\end{pmatrix} - \begin{pmatrix}\text{Future value of the 239}\\ \text{payments already made}\end{pmatrix}$$

Algebraic Solution

$$\begin{aligned}\text{Balance} &= PV(1+i)^n - PMT\left[\frac{(1+i)^n - 1}{i}\right]\\ &= \$20{,}000(1.0075)^{239} - \$179.95\left[\frac{(1.0075)^{239} - 1}{0.0075}\right]\\ &= \$119{,}288.367 - \$119{,}112.945\\ &= \$175.42\end{aligned}$$

$$\begin{aligned}\text{Final payment} &= 1.0075 \times \text{Balance after 239 payments}\\ &= 1.0075 \times \$175.42\\ &= \$176.74\end{aligned}$$

Financial Calculator Solution

First calculate the balance after 239 payments.

20000 (PV) 179.95 (+/−) (PMT) 239 (*n*) 0.75 (*i*) (COMP) (FV) −175.42

$$\begin{aligned}\text{Final payment} &= 1.0075 \times \text{Balance after 239 payments}\\ &= 1.0075 \times \$175.42\\ &= \$176.74\end{aligned}$$

Example 14.1E *Calculating a Loan Balance and the Final Payment*

Meditech Laboratories borrowed $28,000 at 10% compounded quarterly to purchase new testing equipment. Payments of $1500 are made every three months.

a. Calculate the balance after the tenth payment.

b. Calculate the final payment.

Solution

The loan in this example has been set up so the regular payment is a "nice round" easily remembered number. In all likelihood, the final payment will differ substantially from $1500. The loan payments form an ordinary simple annuity having

$$PV = \$28{,}000,\ PMT = \$1500 \text{ (except for the last payment), and } i = \frac{10\%}{4} = 2.5\%$$

Note that to answer part (a) using the Retrospective Method, we do not need to know the total number of payments.

$$\begin{pmatrix}\text{Balance after}\\ \text{10 payments}\end{pmatrix} = \begin{pmatrix}\text{Future value of}\\ \text{\$28,000 after 10 quarters}\end{pmatrix} - \begin{pmatrix}\text{Future value of the 10}\\ \text{payments already made}\end{pmatrix}$$

To answer part (b), we need to know the balance after the second-to-last payment. Before we can calculate this balance, we must determine the total number of payments.

Algebraic Solution

a. $$\begin{pmatrix}\text{Balance after}\\ \text{10 payments}\end{pmatrix} = PV(1+i)^n - PMT\left[\frac{(1+i)^n - 1}{i}\right]$$

$$= \$28{,}000(1.025)^{10} - \$1500\left[\frac{(1.025)^{10} - 1}{0.025}\right]$$

$$= \$35{,}842.367 - \$16{,}805.073$$

$$= \$19{,}037.29$$

b. First calculate the total number of payments to repay the loan.

$$n = -\frac{\ln\left(1 - \frac{i \times PV}{PMT}\right)}{\ln(1+i)} = -\frac{\ln\left(1 - \frac{0.025 \times \$28{,}000}{\$1500}\right)}{\ln(1.025)} = -\frac{\ln(0.5\overline{3})}{\ln(1.025)} = 25.457357$$

The second-to-last payment will be the twenty-fifth payment. Again using the Retrospective Method,

$$\begin{pmatrix}\text{Balance after}\\ \text{25 payments}\end{pmatrix} = \$28{,}000(1.025)^{25} - \$1500\left[\frac{(1.025)^{25} - 1}{0.025}\right]$$

$$= \$51{,}910.435 - \$51{,}236.646$$

$$= \$673.79$$

$$\text{Final payment} = 1.025 \times \text{Balance after 25 payments}$$

$$= 1.025 \times \$673.79$$

$$= \$690.63$$

Financial Calculator Solution

a. 28000 (PV) 1500 (+/–) (PMT) 10 (*n*) 2.5 (*i*) (COMP) (FV) | –19,037.29 |

b. First calculate the total number of payments to settle the loan.

0 (FV) (COMP) (*n*) | 25.457357 |

The second-to-last payment will be the twenty-fifth payment. Again using the Retrospective Method to obtain the balance after 25 payments,

25 (*n*) (COMP) (FV) | –673.79 |

$$\text{Final payment} = 1.025 \times \text{Balance after 25 payments}$$

$$= 1.025 \times \$673.79$$

$$= \$690.63$$

TRAP *An Incorrect Interpretation of the Fractional Part of "n"*

It is tempting but incorrect to calculate the size of the last payment simply by multiplying *PMT* by the fractional part of *n*. This calculation will give only an approximate value for the size of the last payment. In the preceding example, the actual final payment was $690.63, whereas

$$(\text{Fractional part of } n) \times PMT = 0.457357 \times \$1500 = \$686.03$$

This amount is neither the final payment nor the principal component of the final payment.

Example 14.1F *Calculating the Amount of the New Loan Payment When a New Interest Rate Takes Effect*

Foothills Fabricating obtained a \$75,000 loan from the Business Development Bank of Canada to purchase machinery. The monthly payments are based on an interest rate of 10.2% compounded monthly and a 10-year amortization period. However, the interest rate is fixed for only a five-year term. The payments will then be recalculated so that, at the new market-based interest rate, the balance will be paid off over the remaining five years. What will the payments (except for the final payment) be for the last five years if the interest rate becomes 9% compounded monthly?

Solution

The answer will come from the last of three steps in the solution.

Step 1: Calculate the monthly payments during the first five years. For this calculation we know that $PV = \$75{,}000$ and $i = \frac{10.2\%}{12} = 0.85\%$ per month. Even though this interest rate applies to the first five years only, we calculate the monthly payments as though the rate applies to the entire 10-year amortization period. Hence, $n = 12(10) = 120$ payments.

Step 2: Calculate the loan's balance after five years (60 payments). Using the Retrospective Method,

$$\begin{pmatrix}\text{Balance after}\\ \text{five years}\end{pmatrix} = \begin{pmatrix}\text{Future value of}\\ \text{\$75,000 after five years}\end{pmatrix} - \begin{pmatrix}\text{Future value of the}\\ \text{first 60 payments}\end{pmatrix}$$

Step 3: Calculate the new monthly payment that will amortize this balance over five years at an interest rate of 9% compounded monthly. The Step 2 result becomes the present value of the remaining 60 payments with $i = \frac{9\%}{12} = 0.75\%$ per month.

Algebraic Solution

Step 1: Substitute the known values into formula (10-2) and solve for *PMT*.

$$PV = PMT\left[\frac{1-(1+i)^{-n}}{i}\right]$$

$$\$75{,}000 = PMT\left[\frac{1-(1.0085)^{-120}}{0.0085}\right]$$

Then

$$PMT = \frac{\$75{,}000}{75.040862} = \$999.4555$$

Step 2: Round the payment to \$999.46. Then calculate the balance after five years.

$$\begin{aligned}\begin{pmatrix}\text{Balance after}\\ \text{five years}\end{pmatrix} &= \$75{,}000(1.0085)^{60} - \$999.46\left(\frac{1.0085^{60}-1}{0.0085}\right)\\ &= \$124{,}627.940 - \$77{,}805.711\\ &= \$46{,}822.23\end{aligned}$$

Step 3: Solve for *PMT* in

$$\$46{,}822.23 = PMT\left[\frac{1-(1.0075)^{-60}}{0.0075}\right]$$

$$PMT = \frac{\$46{,}822.23}{48.173374} = \$971.9525 = \$971.95$$

The payments for the last five years will be \$971.95 per month.

Financial Calculator Solution

Step 1: \$75,000 (PV) 120 (n) 0 (FV) 0.85 (i) (COMP) (PMT) [−999.455]

Step 2: Round the payment to \$999.46. Then calculate the balance after five years.

999.46 (+/−) (PMT) 60 (n) (COMP) (FV) [−46,822.23]

Step 3: (+/−) (PV) 0 (FV) 0.75 (i) 60 (n) (COMP) (PMT) [−971.95]

The payments for the last five years will be \$971.95 per month.

Calculating the Interest and Principal Components of a Payment

Proper accounting procedures require a business to identify the principal and interest components of a loan payment. Only the interest portion of a loan payment is an accounting expense for the borrower and an accounting revenue for the lender. Individual investors must also determine the interest portion of any loan payments received in order to report interest income on their tax returns.

For demand loans in Section 7.4, we used the daily-interest method to determine the interest portion of monthly payments. We calculated interest for the *exact number of days* in each payment interval. For term loans, the interest portion of a payment is based on the *same interest rate per payment interval,* regardless of small variations in the actual interval length. For example, a term loan requiring monthly payments uses the same interest rate per month, regardless of whether the month has 28, 30, or 31 days.

The interest portion of a payment is the interest for one payment interval on the loan's balance (after the preceding payment). For example, the interest portion of the thirty-third monthly payment is one month's interest on the balance after the thirty-second payment. If the loan payments form a simple annuity,

$$\text{Interest component} = i \times (\text{Balance after the previous payment})$$

If the loan payments form a general annuity, replace i by i_2, the equivalent periodic rate that matches the payment interval.

The principal portion of a payment reduces the loan's balance. For example, the principal portion of the thirty-third monthly payment reduces the balance from the value it had after the thirty-second payment to the new lower balance after the thirty-third payment. In general, the principal component of a payment is just the difference between the previous balance and the new balance after the payment.

$$\text{Principal component} = \begin{pmatrix}\text{Balance after the}\\ \text{previous payment}\end{pmatrix} - \begin{pmatrix}\text{Balance after}\\ \text{the payment}\end{pmatrix}$$

TIP *A SHORTCUT*

Don't forget that

$$PMT = \text{Principal component} + \text{Interest component}$$

Once *either* the principal component *or* the interest component of any payment has been calculated, simply subtract it from the payment to obtain the other component.

Interest and Principal Components of an Investment-Annuity Payment We can use the concepts developed for loan payments to separate investment-annuity payments into interest and principal components. The justification for doing so becomes apparent when you realize that, by granting a loan requiring equal periodic payments, a lender is in effect purchasing an annuity from the borrower. The price the lender "pays" for the annuity (or the amount "invested" in the annuity) is the principal amount of the loan. Conversely, when we buy an annuity, we are in a sense lending the funds to the annuity issuer, who subsequently repays the "loan" with interest. The rate of return on our annuity investment may be viewed as the rate of interest we charge on the "loan."

Example 14.1G *Calculating the Interest and Principal Components of a Payment and of a Group of Consecutive Payments*

A \$9500 personal loan at 10.5% compounded monthly is to be repaid over a four-year term by equal monthly payments.

a. Calculate the interest and principal components of the twenty-ninth payment.

b. How much interest will be paid in the second year of the loan?

Solution

The loan payments form an ordinary simple annuity with

$$PV = \$9500 \qquad n = 12(4) = 48 \qquad \text{and} \qquad i = \frac{10.5\%}{12} = 0.875\%$$

In part (a), the size of the loan payments must be obtained before any balances can be calculated. A "brute force" approach to part (b) would be to calculate the interest component of each of the 12 payments in Year 2, and then add them. A much less laborious procedure uses the two following ideas.

$$\text{Total } \textit{interest} \text{ paid in Year 2} = 12(PMT) - \text{Total } \textit{principal} \text{ paid in Year 2}$$

where

$$\text{Total } \textit{principal} \text{ paid in Year 2} = \text{Balance after Year 1} - \text{Balance after Year 2}$$

$$= \begin{pmatrix}\text{Balance after}\\ \text{12 payments}\end{pmatrix} - \begin{pmatrix}\text{Balance after}\\ \text{24 payments}\end{pmatrix}$$

Substituting the second equation for the "Total *principal* paid in Year 2" into the first equation, we obtain

$$\text{Total interest paid in Year 2} = 12(PMT) - \left[\begin{pmatrix}\text{Balance after}\\ \text{12 payments}\end{pmatrix} - \begin{pmatrix}\text{Balance after}\\ \text{24 payments}\end{pmatrix}\right]$$

Algebraic Solution

a. Calculate the size of the payments by solving for *PMT* in

$$\$9500 = PMT\left[\frac{1-(1.00875)^{-48}}{0.00875}\right] = PMT(39.05734)$$

$$PMT = \frac{\$9500}{39.05734} = \$243.23$$

We next want

$$\begin{pmatrix}\text{Interest component}\\ \text{of the twenty-ninth payment}\end{pmatrix} = i \times \begin{pmatrix}\text{Balance after}\\ \text{28 payments}\end{pmatrix}$$

Using the Retrospective Method to calculate the balance after 28 payments,

$$\begin{aligned}\begin{pmatrix}\text{Balance after}\\ \text{28 payments}\end{pmatrix} &= \begin{pmatrix}\text{Future value of}\\ \text{\$9500 after 28 months}\end{pmatrix} - \begin{pmatrix}\text{Future value of the 28}\\ \text{payments already made}\end{pmatrix}\\ &= PV(1+i)^n - PMT\left[\frac{(1+i)^n - 1}{i}\right]\\ &= \$9500(1.00875)^{28} - 243.23\left[\frac{(1.00875)^{28} - 1}{0.00875}\right]\\ &= \$12{,}124.47 - \$7670.41\\ &= \$4445.06\end{aligned}$$

Hence,

$$\begin{pmatrix}\text{Interest component}\\ \text{of the twenty-ninth payment}\end{pmatrix} = 0.00875 \times \$4445.06 = \$38.89$$

and

$$\begin{aligned}\text{Principal component} &= PMT - \text{Interest component}\\ &= \$243.23 - \$38.89\\ &= \$204.34\end{aligned}$$

b. $$\begin{pmatrix}\text{Total interest}\\ \text{paid in Year 2}\end{pmatrix} = 12(PMT) - \left[\begin{pmatrix}\text{Balance after 12}\\ \text{payments}\end{pmatrix} - \begin{pmatrix}\text{Balance after}\\ \text{24 payments}\end{pmatrix}\right]$$

where

$$\begin{aligned}\begin{pmatrix}\text{Balance after}\\ \text{12 payments}\end{pmatrix} &= \begin{pmatrix}\text{Future value of}\\ \text{\$9500 after 12 months}\end{pmatrix} - \begin{pmatrix}\text{Future value of the 12}\\ \text{payments already made}\end{pmatrix}\\ &= \$9500(1.00875)^{12} - \$243.23\left[\frac{(1.00875)^{12} - 1}{0.00875}\right]\\ &= \$7483.53\end{aligned}$$

and

$$\begin{pmatrix}\text{Balance after}\\ \text{24 payments}\end{pmatrix} = \begin{pmatrix}\text{Future value of}\\ \text{\$9500 after 24 months}\end{pmatrix} - \begin{pmatrix}\text{Future value of the 24}\\ \text{payments already made}\end{pmatrix}$$
$$= \$9500(1.00875)^{24} - \$243.23\left[\frac{(1.00875)^{24} - 1}{0.00875}\right]$$
$$= \$5244.84$$

Therefore,

Total interest paid in Year 2 = 12($243.23) − ($7483.53 − $5244.84) = $680.07

Financial Calculator Solution

a. First calculate the *PMT.*

9500 (PV) 0 (FV) 0.875 (i) 48 (n) (COMP) (PMT) −243.232

We next want

$$\begin{pmatrix}\text{Interest component}\\ \text{of the twenty-ninth payment}\end{pmatrix} = i \times \begin{pmatrix}\text{Balance after}\\ \text{28 payments}\end{pmatrix}$$

Using the Retrospective Method to calculate the Balance after 28 payments,

243.23 (+/−) (PMT) 28 (n) (COMP) (FV) −4445.06

Hence,

$$\begin{pmatrix}\text{Interest component}\\ \text{of the twenty-ninth payment}\end{pmatrix} = 0.00875 \times \$4445.06 = \$38.89$$

and

$$\begin{aligned}\text{Principal component} &= PMT - \text{Interest component}\\ &= \$243.23 - \$38.89\\ &= \$204.34\end{aligned}$$

b. $$\begin{pmatrix}\text{Total interest}\\ \text{paid in Year 2}\end{pmatrix} = 12(PMT) - \left[\begin{pmatrix}\text{Balance after}\\ \text{12 payments}\end{pmatrix} - \begin{pmatrix}\text{Balance after}\\ \text{24 payments}\end{pmatrix}\right]$$

Calculate the balance after 12 months.

12 (n) (COMP) (FV) −7483.53

Calculate the balance after 24 months.

24 (n) (COMP) (FV) −5244.84

Therefore,

Total interest paid in Year 2 = 12($243.23) − ($7483.53 − $5244.84) = $680.07

Example **14.1H** *Interest and Principal Components of Loan Payments Which Form a General Annuity*

Monthly payments of $300 are made on a $10,000 loan at 9% compounded semi-annually.

a. What is the interest component of the tenth payment?

b. What is the principal component of the twentieth payment?

Solution

The loan payments form a general annuity having

$PV = \$10{,}000$, $PMT = \$300$ (except for the final payment), $i = \frac{9\%}{2} = 4.5\%$, and

$$c = \frac{\text{Number of compoundings per year}}{\text{Number of payments per year}} = \frac{2}{12} = 0.1\overline{6}$$

We must use the periodic rate that matches the one-month payment interval.

$$i_2 = (1 + i)^c - 1 = 1.045^{0.1\overline{6}} - 1 = 0.00736312301 = 0.736312301\% \text{ per month}$$

In this problem we are given the regular payment amount but not the amortization period or number of payments. To use the Prospective Method, we would have to first determine n. But we can use the Retrospective Method without knowing the total number of payments.

Algebraic Solution

a. $$\begin{pmatrix}\text{Interest component}\\ \text{of the tenth payment}\end{pmatrix} = i \times \begin{pmatrix}\text{Balance after}\\ \text{nine payments}\end{pmatrix}$$

Using the Retrospective Method to calculate the balance after nine payments,

$$\begin{pmatrix}\text{Balance after}\\ \text{nine payments}\end{pmatrix} = \begin{pmatrix}\text{Future value of}\\ \text{\$10,000 after nine months}\end{pmatrix} - \begin{pmatrix}\text{Future value of the nine}\\ \text{payments already made}\end{pmatrix}$$

$$= \$10{,}000(1.007363123)^9 - \$300\left[\frac{(1.007363123)^9 - 1}{0.007363123}\right]$$

$$= \$7901.63$$

Hence,

$$\begin{pmatrix}\text{Interest component}\\ \text{of the tenth payment}\end{pmatrix} = 0.007363123 \times \$7901.63 = \$58.18$$

b. $$\begin{pmatrix}\text{Principal component}\\ \text{of the twentieth payment}\end{pmatrix} = \begin{pmatrix}\text{Balance after}\\ \text{19 payments}\end{pmatrix} - \begin{pmatrix}\text{Balance after}\\ \text{20 payments}\end{pmatrix}$$

where

$$\begin{pmatrix}\text{Balance after}\\ \text{19 payments}\end{pmatrix} = \begin{pmatrix}\text{Future value of}\\ \text{\$10,000 after 19 months}\end{pmatrix} - \begin{pmatrix}\text{Future value of the 19}\\ \text{payments already made}\end{pmatrix}$$

$$= \$10{,}000(1.007363123)^{19} - \$300\left[\frac{1.007363123)^{19} - 1}{0.007363123}\right]$$

$$= \$5401.72$$

and

$$\begin{pmatrix}\text{Balance after}\\ \text{20 payments}\end{pmatrix} = \begin{pmatrix}\text{Future value of}\\ \text{\$10,000 after 20 months}\end{pmatrix} - \begin{pmatrix}\text{Future value of the 20}\\ \text{payments already made}\end{pmatrix}$$

$$= \$10{,}000(1.007363123)^{20} - \$300\left[\frac{(1.007363123)^{20} - 1}{0.007363123}\right]$$

$$= \$5141.50$$

Therefore,

$$\begin{pmatrix}\text{Principal component}\\ \text{of the twentieth payment}\end{pmatrix} = \$5401.72 - \$5141.50 = \$260.22$$

Financial Calculator Solution

a. $$\begin{pmatrix}\text{Interest component}\\ \text{of the tenth payment}\end{pmatrix} = i \times \begin{pmatrix}\text{Balance after}\\ \text{nine payments}\end{pmatrix}$$

Using the Retrospective Method to calculate the balance after nine payments,

10000 (PV) 300 (+/–) (PMT) 9 (n) 0.7363123 (i) (COMP) (FV) [−7901.63]

Hence,

$$\begin{pmatrix}\text{Interest component}\\ \text{of the tenth payment}\end{pmatrix} = 0.007363123 \times \$7901.63 = \$58.18$$

b. $$\begin{pmatrix}\text{Principal component}\\ \text{of the twentieth payment}\end{pmatrix} = \begin{pmatrix}\text{Balance after}\\ \text{19 payments}\end{pmatrix} - \begin{pmatrix}\text{Balance after}\\ \text{20 payments}\end{pmatrix}$$

Using the Retrospective Method to calculate the balance after 19 payments,

19 (n) (COMP) (FV) [−5401.72]

Using the Retrospective Method to calculate the balance after 20 payments,

20 (n) (COMP) (FV) [−5141.50]

Therefore,

$$\begin{pmatrix}\text{Principal component}\\ \text{of the twentieth payment}\end{pmatrix} = \$5401.72 - \$5141.50 = \$260.22$$

Example 14.11 *Calculating the Interest and Principal Components of Annuity Payments*

Joanna purchased a 20-year annuity with $100,000 accumulated in her RRSP. The payments are received at the end of every three months. They include a rate of return of 7.5% compounded semiannually on the $100,000 investment in the annuity.

a. Calculate the interest and principal components of the fifteenth payment.

b. How much of the payments received in the second year represents the recovery of principal from her initial investment of $100,000?

Solution

The payments form an ordinary *general* annuity having

$$PV = \$100{,}000 \qquad n = 4(20) = 80 \qquad i = \frac{7.5\%}{2} = 3.75\% \qquad \text{and} \qquad c = \frac{2}{4} = 0.5$$

The periodic rate matching the three-month payment interval is

$$i_2 = (1 + i)^c - 1 = 1.0375^{0.5} - 1 = 0.018577438 = 1.8577438\% \text{ per quarter}$$

The size of the quarterly payments must first be determined from the requirement that

$$\$100{,}000 = \text{Present value of all 80 payments}$$

Algebraic Solution

$$\$100{,}000 = PMT\left[\frac{1-(1.018577438)^{-80}}{0.018577438}\right]$$

$$= PMT(41.483766)$$

$$PMT = \$2410.58$$

a. $$\begin{pmatrix}\text{Interest component}\\ \text{of the fifteenth payment}\end{pmatrix} = i \times \begin{pmatrix}\text{Balance after}\\ \text{14 payments}\end{pmatrix}$$

Using the Retrospective Method to calculate the balance after 14 payments,

$$\begin{pmatrix}\text{Balance after}\\ \text{14 payments}\end{pmatrix} = \begin{pmatrix}\text{Future value of}\\ \text{\$100,000 after 14 quarters}\end{pmatrix} - \begin{pmatrix}\text{Future value of the 14}\\ \text{payments already made}\end{pmatrix}$$

$$= \$100{,}000(1.018577438)^{14} - \$2410.58\left[\frac{(1.018577438)^{14}-1}{0.018577438}\right]$$

$$= \$91{,}252.56$$

Hence,

$$\begin{pmatrix}\text{Interest component}\\ \text{of the fifteenth payment}\end{pmatrix} = 0.018577438 \times \$91{,}252.56 = \$1695.24$$

$$\text{Principal component} = PMT - \text{Interest component}$$

$$= \$2410.58 - \$1695.24$$

$$= \$715.34$$

b. Payments 5 to 8 inclusive are received in the second year.

$$\begin{pmatrix}\text{Total principal in}\\ \text{Payments 5 to 8}\end{pmatrix} = \begin{pmatrix}\text{Balance after}\\ \text{four payments}\end{pmatrix} - \begin{pmatrix}\text{Balance after}\\ \text{eight payments}\end{pmatrix}$$

where

$$\begin{pmatrix}\text{Balance after}\\ \text{four payments}\end{pmatrix} = \begin{pmatrix}\text{Future value of \$100,000}\\ \text{after four quarters}\end{pmatrix} - \begin{pmatrix}\text{Future value of the four}\\ \text{payments already made}\end{pmatrix}$$

$$= \$100{,}000(1.018577438)^{4} - \$2410.58\left[\frac{(1.018577438)^{4}-1}{0.018577438}\right]$$

$$= \$97{,}726.27$$

Similarly, the balance after eight payments is \$95,278.81.

Therefore,

$$\text{Principal received in Year 2} = \$97{,}726.27 - \$95{,}278.81 = \$2447.46$$

Financial Calculator Solution

First calculate the amount of the quarterly payment.

100000 (+/–) (PV) 0 (FV) 1.8577438 (i) 80 (n) (COMP) (PMT) [2410.58]

a. $$\begin{pmatrix}\text{Interest component}\\ \text{of the fifteenth payment}\end{pmatrix} = i \times \begin{pmatrix}\text{Balance after}\\ \text{14 payments}\end{pmatrix}$$

Using the Retrospective Method to calculate the balance after 14 payments,

2410.58 (PMT) 14 (n) (COMP) (FV) [91,252.56]

Hence,

$$\begin{pmatrix}\text{Interest component}\\ \text{of the fifteenth payment}\end{pmatrix} = 0.018577438 \times \$91{,}252.56 = \$1695.24$$

$$\begin{aligned}\text{Principal component} &= PMT - \text{Interest component}\\ &= \$2410.58 - \$1695.24\\ &= \$715.34\end{aligned}$$

b. Payments 5 to 8 inclusive are received in the second year.

$$\begin{pmatrix}\text{Total principal in}\\ \text{Payments 5 to 8}\end{pmatrix} = \begin{pmatrix}\text{Balance after}\\ \text{four payments}\end{pmatrix} - \begin{pmatrix}\text{Balance after}\\ \text{eight payments}\end{pmatrix}$$

Calculate the balance after four payments.

4 (n) (COMP) (FV) [97,726.27]

Calculate the balance after eight payments.

8 (n) (COMP) (FV) [95,278.81]

Therefore,

$$\text{Principal received in Year 2} = \$97{,}726.27 - \$95{,}278.81 = \$2447.46$$

Concept Questions

1. A \$100,000 loan and a \$50,000 loan both have the same interest rate and the same amortization period (10 years).
   - **a.** Will the monthly payment on the \$100,000 loan be double the monthly payment on the \$50,000 loan? Explain briefly.
   - **b.** Will the balance after five years on the \$100,000 loan be double the balance on the \$50,000 loan? Explain briefly.
2. Will a loan's balance midway through its amortization period be (pick one):

   (i) more than (ii) less than or (iii) equal to

   half of the original principal? Explain.
3. If the loan payments and interest rate remain unchanged, will it take longer to reduce the balance from \$20,000 to \$10,000 than to reduce the balance from \$10,000 to \$0? Explain briefly.
4. The calculated monthly payment on a loan amortized over five years is rounded up by 0.2 cents to get to the nearest cent.
   - **a.** Will the adjusted final payment be more than or less than the regular payment?
   - **b.** Will the difference between the regular and the final payment be (pick one):

     (i) more than (ii) less than or (iii) equal to

     0.2 cents $\times$ 59 = 11.8 cents? Explain.
5. The calculated monthly payment on a loan amortized over 10 years is rounded down by 0.3 cents to get to the nearest cent.

a. Will the adjusted final payment be more than or less than the regular payment?

b. Will the difference between the regular and the final payment be (pick one):

(i) more than (ii) less than or (iii) equal to
0.3 cents × 119 = 35.7 cents? Explain.

6. A loan has a 10-year amortization period. If the interest rate is fixed, will the principal repaid in the third year be (pick one):

(i) more than (ii) less than or (iii) equal to
the principal repaid in the seventh year? Explain.

7. A loan has a five-year amortization period. If the interest rate is fixed, will the interest paid in the fourth year be (pick one):

(i) more than (ii) less than or (iii) equal to
the interest paid in the second year? Explain.

8. Loan A is for $20,000 while Loan B is for $10,000. Both have the same interest rate and amortization period. Will the total interest paid on Loan A be (pick one):

(i) more than (ii) less than or (iii) equal to
twice the total interest paid on Loan B? Explain.

Exercise 14.1

Answers to the odd-numbered problems are at the end of the book.

Each of the loans in Problems 1 through 6 requires equal payments at the end of each payment interval. The compounding period equals the payment interval. Calculate the principal portion of the payment having the serial number listed in the second-to-last column, and the interest portion of the payment having the serial number listed in the last column.

Problem	Original principal ($)	Amortization period (years)	Payment interval (months)	Nominal rate (%)	Principal portion of Payment	Interest portion of Payment
1.	12,000	3	3	10.5	5	9
2.	40,000	8	1	11	75	43
3.	14,000	6	6	12.5	8	10
4.	25,000	5	3	11	15	6
5.	45,000	15	1	9.75	117	149
6.	30,000	10	1	12	99	41

Each of the loans in Problems 7 through 14 requires equal payments at the end of each payment interval. The loan payments in these problems form ordinary general annuities. Calculate the principal portion of the payment having the serial number listed in the second-to-last column, and the interest portion of the payment having the serial number is listed in the last column.

Problem	Original principal ($)	Amortization period (years)	Payment interval	Nominal rate (%)	Compounding period (months)	Principal portion of Payment	Interest portion of Payment
7.	7000	10	1 year	10	6	7	4
8.	9000	8	1 year	11	1	4	7
9.	10,000	7	6 months	9.5	12	6	10
10.	25,000	5	1 month	10.25	12	38	4
11.	70,000	12	3 months	10.75	6	11	30
12.	4000	2	1 month	13	3	21	13
13.	45,000	15	1 month	10.5	6	117	149
14.	30,000	10	6 months	12	3	19	9

All payments in Problems 15 through 22 are made at the end of the payment interval. Calculate the principal portion of the payment having the serial number listed in the second-to-last column, and the interest portion of the payment having the serial number listed in the last column. *Also determine the amount of the final payment for each loan.*

Problem	Original principal ($)	Payment ($)	Payment interval (months)	Nominal rate (%)	Compounding period (months)	Principal portion of Payment	Interest portion of Payment
15.	12,000	1000	3	10.5	3	9	5
16.	40,000	600	1	11	1	43	77
17.	14,000	1200	6	12.5	6	7	12
18.	25,000	500	1	10.25	12	11	41
19.	70,000	2500	3	10.75	6	30	11
20.	4000	150	1	13	3	14	22
21.	45,000	500	1	10.5	6	149	117
22.	30,000	2500	6	12	3	9	19

Each of the loans in Problems 23 through 30 requires equal payments at the end of each payment interval. Calculate the total principal paid in the year listed in the second-to-last column and the total interest paid in the year listed in the last column.

Problem	Original principal ($)	Amortization period (years)	Payment interval (months)	Nominal rate (%)	Compounding period (months)	Principal paid in Year	Interest paid in Year
•23.	14,000	6	6	12.5	6	2	5
•24.	25,000	5	3	11	3	4	2
•25.	45,000	15	1	9.75	1	11	6
•26.	30,000	10	1	12	1	3	8
•27.	25,000	5	1	10.25	12	2	4
•28.	70,000	12	3	10.75	6	9	4
•29.	4000	7	1	13	3	6	3
•30.	45,000	15	1	10.5	6	5	10

31. A $37,000 loan at 10.8% compounded semiannually is to be repaid by equal semiannual payments over 10 years.

a. What amount of principal will be repaid by the sixth payment?

b. What will be the interest portion of the sixteenth payment?

c. How much will the principal be reduced by Payments 6 to 15 inclusive?

d. How much interest will be paid in the third year?

e. What will be the final payment?

32. A 10-year annuity providing a rate of return of 8% compounded quarterly was purchased for $25,000. The annuity makes payments at the end of each quarter.

a. How much of the twenty-fifth payment will be interest?

b. What will be the principal portion of the thirteenth payment?

c. How much interest will be paid by Payments 11 to 20 inclusive?

d. How much will the principal be reduced in the second year?

e. What will be the final payment?

•33. Guy borrowed $6000 at 12.75% compounded monthly and agreed to repay the loan in equal quarterly payments over four years.

a. How much of the fifth payment will be interest?

b. What will be the principal repaid by the eleventh payment?

c. How much interest will be paid by Payments 5 to 12 inclusive?

d. How much will the principal be reduced in the second year?

e. What will be the final payment?

•34. A 25-year annuity was purchased with $225,000 that had accumulated in a Registered Retirement Savings Plan (RRSP). The annuity provides a semi-annually compounded rate of return of 9.5% and makes equal month-end payments.

a. What amount of principal will be included in Payment 206?

b. What will be the interest portion of Payment 187?

c. How much will the principal be reduced by Payments 50 to 100 inclusive?

d. How much interest will be paid in the fourteenth year?

e. What will be the final payment?

Problems 35 to 38 are variations of Problems 31 to 34, respectively. The size of the regular payment is given instead of the duration of the loan or investment annuity.

35. A $37,000 loan at 10.8% compounded semiannually is to be repaid by semiannual payments of $3000 (except for a smaller final payment).

a. What amount of principal will be repaid by the sixteenth payment?

b. What will be the interest portion of the sixth payment?

c. How much will the principal be reduced by Payments 8 to 14 inclusive?

d. How much interest will be paid in the fifth year?

e. What will be the final payment?

36. An annuity providing a rate of return of 8% compounded quarterly was purchased for $27,000. The annuity pays $1000 at the end of each quarter (except for a smaller final payment).

a. How much of the sixteenth payment will be interest?

b. What will be the principal portion of the thirty-third payment?

c. How much interest will be paid by Payments 20 to 25 inclusive?

d. How much principal will be repaid in the sixth year?

e. What will be the final payment?

•37. Guy borrowed $6000 at 12.75% compounded monthly and agreed to make quarterly payments of $500 (except for a smaller final payment).

a. How much of the eleventh payment will be interest?

b. What will be the principal repaid by the sixth payment?

c. How much interest will be paid by Payments 3 to 9 inclusive?

d. How much will the principal be reduced in the third year?

e. What will be the final payment?

•38. An annuity paying $2000 at the end of each month (except for a smaller final payment) was purchased with $225,000 that had accumulated in an RRSP. The annuity provides a semiannually compounded rate of return of 9.5%.

a. What amount of principal will be included in Payment 137?

b. What will be the interest portion of Payment 204?

c. How much will the principal be reduced by Payments 145 to 156 inclusive?

d. How much interest will be paid in the twentieth year?

e. What will be the final payment?

•39. Ms. Esperanto obtained a $40,000 home equity loan at 12% compounded monthly.

a. What will she pay monthly if the amortization period is 15 years?

b. How much of the payment made at the end of the fifth year will go towards principal and how much will go towards interest?

c. What will be the remaining balance on the loan after five years?

d. How much interest did she pay during the fifth year?
(Taken from ICB course on Wealth Valuation.)

•40. Elkford Logging's bank will fix the interest rate on a $60,000 loan at 10.5% compounded monthly for the first four-year term of an eight-year amortization period. Monthly payments are required on the loan.

a. If the prevailing interest rate on four-year loans at the beginning of the second term is 9% compounded monthly, what will be the monthly payments for the last four years?

b. What will be the interest portion of the twenty-third payment?

c. Calculate the principal portion of the fifty-third payment.

••41. Christina has just borrowed $12,000 at 11% compounded semiannually. Since she expects to receive a $10,000 inheritance in two years when she turns 25, she has arranged with her credit union to make monthly payments that will reduce the principal balance to exactly $10,000 in two years.

a. What monthly payments will she make?

b. What will be the interest portion of the ninth payment?

c. Determine the principal portion of the sixteenth payment.

••42. Elkford Logging's bank will fix the interest rate on a $60,000 loan at 10.5% compounded monthly for the first four years. After four years, the interest rate will be fixed at the prevailing three-year rate. Monthly payments of $1000 (except for a smaller final payment) are required on the loan.

a. If the interest rate after four years is 9% compounded monthly, when will the loan be paid off?

b. What will be the amount of the final payment?

c. What is the interest portion of the thirty-second payment?

d. Calculate the principal portion of the fifty-eighth payment.

14.2 Loan Amortization Schedule

A **loan amortization schedule** is a table that:

- Breaks down each payment into its interest and principal components, and
- Gives the principal balance outstanding after each payment.

Typical headings for the columns of an amortization schedule are presented in Table 14.1.

Each payment occupies a row in the schedule. The values entered in the last three columns are calculated as follows:

1. Calculate the "Interest portion" of the payment using

$$\text{Interest portion} = i \times \text{Balance after the previous payment}$$

2. Calculate the "Principal portion" of the payment from

$$\text{Principal portion} = PMT - \text{Interest portion}$$

3. Calculate the new "Principal balance" from

$$\text{Principal balance} = \text{Previous balance} - \text{Principal portion}$$

Table 14.1 *Column Headings for an Amortization Schedule*

Payment number	Payment	Interest portion	Principal portion	Principal balance
0	—	—	—	Loan
1				
etc.	etc.			

Recall that a consequence of rounding the calculated payment to the nearest cent is that the last payment may be several cents more or less than the other payments. The second and third of the preceding steps must be altered for the final payment because its precise amount is not initially known. For the *final payment,*

2. The principal portion of the payment is simply the previous principal balance (making the new balance zero).
3. Calculate the final payment using

$$\text{Final payment} = \text{Interest portion} + \text{Principal portion}$$

Partial Amortization Schedule A particular circumstance may require only a portion of a loan's amortization schedule. Suppose, for example, details are needed for only the monthly payments made in the fourth year of a five-year loan. The partial schedule must, therefore, present details of Payments 37 to 48 inclusive. The key number needed to "get started" is the principal balance after the thirty-sixth payment. After this amount is obtained (by either the Prospective Method or, preferably, the Retrospective Method), the three-step routine for each successive payment can begin.

Example 14.2A *Constructing A Full Amortization Schedule*

Marpole Carpet Cleaning borrowed $7000 from Richmond Credit Union at 12.5% compounded quarterly. The loan is to be repaid by equal quarterly payments over a two-year term. Construct an amortization schedule for the loan. Calculate the total interest paid.

Solution

The loan payments form an ordinary simple annuity having

$$PV = \$7000 \qquad n = 8 \qquad \text{and} \qquad i = \frac{12.5\%}{4} = 3.125\%$$

The payment amount must be calculated before beginning the amortization schedule.

Algebraic Solution

Solve for PMT in

$$\$7000 = PMT\left[\frac{1-(1.03125)^{-8}}{0.03125}\right]$$

$$PMT = \frac{\$7000}{6.98282389} = \$1002.46$$

The amortization schedule follows the financial calculator solution.

Financial Calculator Solution

7000 (PV) 3.125 (i) 8 (n) 0 (FV) (COMP) (PMT) [−1002.46]

Payment number	Payment	Interest portion	Principal portion	Principal balance
0	—	—	—	\$7000.00
1	\$1002.46	\$218.75 ①	\$783.71 ②	6216.29 ③
2	1002.46	194.26	808.20	5408.09
3	1002.46	169.00	833.46	4574.63
4	1002.46	142.96	859.50	3715.13
5	1002.46	116.10	886.36	2828.77
6	1002.46	88.40	914.06	1914.71
7	1002.46	59.83	942.63	972.08
8	1002.46	30.38	972.08	0.00
Total	\$8019.68	\$1019.68	\$7000.00	

① Interest portion $= i \times$ Previous balance
$= 0.03125(\$7000)$
$= \$218.75$

② Principal portion = PMT − Interest portion
$= \$1002.46 - \$218.75$
$= \$783.71$

③ Balance after payment = Previous balance − Principal portion
$= \$7000 - \$783.71$
$= \$6216.29$

The total interest paid may be determined either by adding the "Interest portion" column or from the difference between the total of the payments and the original principal. That is,

$$\text{Interest paid} = 8(\$1002.46) - \$7000 = \$1019.68$$

Example 14.2B *Constructing a Full Amortization Schedule Where the Payments Form a General Annuity*

Healey Fishing obtained a \$40,000 loan for a major refit of a troller. The loan contract requires seven equal annual payments including interest at 11.5% compounded semiannually. Construct the full amortization schedule for the loan. Calculate the total interest paid over the life of the loan.

Solution

The loan payments form an ordinary *general* annuity in which

$$PV = \$40{,}000 \qquad n = 7 \qquad i = \frac{11.5\%}{2} = 5.75\% \qquad \text{and} \qquad c = \frac{2}{1} = 2$$

The periodic interest rate that matches the one-year payment interval is

$$i_2 = (1+i)^c - 1 = 1.0575^2 - 1 = 0.11830625 = 11.830625\% \text{ per year}$$

The payment size is the value of the payment in

$$\$40{,}000 = \text{Present value of seven payments}$$

Algebraic Solution

Solve for *PMT* in

$$\$40{,}000 = PMT\left[\frac{1-(1.11830625)^{-7}}{0.11830625}\right]$$

$$PMT = \frac{\$40{,}000}{4.5883725} = \$8717.69$$

The amortization schedule follows the financial calculator solution.

Financial Calculator Solution

40000 (PV) 11.830625 (i) 7 (n) 0 (FV) (COMP) (PMT) | −8717.69 |

Payment number	Payment	Interest portion	Principal portion	Principal balance
0	—	—	—	$40,000.00
1	$8717.69	$4732.25	$3985.44	36,014.56
2	8717.69	4260.75	4456.94	31,557.62
3	8717.69	3733.46 ①	4984.23 ②	26,573.39 ③
4	8717.69	3143.80	5573.89	20,999.50
5	8717.69	2484.37	6233.32	14,766.18
6	8717.69	1746.93	6970.76	7795.42
7	8717.67 ④	922.25	7795.42	0.00
	Total	$21,023.81	$40,000.00	

① Interest portion = 0.11830625($31,557.62) = $3733.46

② Principal portion = $8717.69 − $3733.46 = $4984.23

③ Balance after payment = $31,557.62 − $4984.23 = $26,573.39

④ Last payment = $7795.42 + $922.25 = $8717.67

$$\begin{aligned}\text{Total interest paid} &= (\text{Total of payments}) - \$40{,}000\\ &= 6(\$8717.69) + \$8717.67 - \$40{,}000\\ &= \$21{,}023.81\end{aligned}$$

Example 14.2C *A Partial Loan Amortization Schedule*

Kimberleigh obtained a loan from her bank for $11,000 at 10.5% compounded monthly to purchase a new car. The monthly payments were set at $250. Construct a partial amortization schedule showing details of the first two payments, Payments 27 and 28, and the last two payments. Calculate the total interest charges.

Solution

The loan payments constitute an ordinary simple annuity in which

$$PV = \$11{,}000 \qquad i = \frac{10.5\%}{12} = 0.875\% \qquad \text{and} \qquad PMT = \$250$$

except for the final payment. Obtain n by solving

$$\$11{,}000 = \text{Present value of } n \text{ payments of } \$250$$

Algebraic Solution

$$n = -\frac{\ln\left(1 - \dfrac{i \times PV}{PMT}\right)}{\ln(1+i)} = -\frac{\ln\left(1 - \dfrac{0.00875 \times \$11{,}000}{\$250}\right)}{\ln(1.00875)} = 55.800772$$

The amortization schedule follows the financial calculator solution.

Financial Calculator Solution

11000 (PV) 0.875 (i) 0 (FV) 250 (+/–) (PMT) (COMP) (n) [55.800772]

Payment number	Payment	Interest portion	Principal portion	Principal balance
0	—	—	—	$11,000.00
1	$250	$96.25 ①	$153.75 ②	10,846.25 ③
2	250	94.90	155.10	10,691.15
·	·	·	·	·
·	·	·	·	·
26				6533.07 ④
27	250	57.16	192.84	6340.23
28	250	55.48	194.52	6145.71
·	·	·	·	·
·	·	·	·	·
54				444.74 ⑤
55	250	3.89	246.11	198.63
56	200.37 ⑥	1.74	198.63	0.00
Total	$13,950.37	$2950.37 ⑦	$11,000.00	

① Interest portion $= i \times$ Previous balance
$= 0.00875(\$11{,}000)$
$= \$96.25$

② Principal portion $= PMT -$ Interest portion
$= \$250 - \$96.25$
$= \$153.75$

③ New balance = Former balance − Principal portion
$= \$11{,}000 - \$153.75$
$= \$10{,}846.25$

④ Balance = Present value of the remaining 29.800772 payments
$= \$6533.07$

⑤ Balance = Present value of the remaining 1.800772 payments
$= \$444.74$

⑥ Final payment = Balance after 55 payments $\times (1 + i)$
$= \$198.63(1.00875)$
$= \$200.37$

⑦ Total interest = Total of payments − Initial loan
$= 55(\$250) + \$200.37 - \$11{,}000$
$= \$2950.37$

POINT OF INTEREST

Starting Life with Debt

Personal debt is soaring as more and more young people get bogged down in loans and credit card debt. "We have a societal crisis," says Laurie Campbell, program manager of the Credit Counselling Service of Toronto. "Debt has become crippling. Savings and assets are being depleted as people try to service their debts."

The Toronto-Dominion Bank reports that total household debt (including mortgages, car loans, and credit card debt) climbed to 100% of personal disposable income in 1998, compared to 77.6% in 1990. "We are seeing people here in our office with higher and higher debt loads," says Ms. Campbell. "It's very hard to help them."

As of the third quarter of 1998, Canadians owed close to $98 billion on personal loans and credit cards. That's a national average of $4467 per person (over the age of 19) before we start to add residential mortgage debt.

The figures show that young people are carrying a bigger burden than ever before. Students are courted by the credit card industry, and have easy access to credit and student loans. Ms. Campbell says 20% of her office's clients now are recent graduates; two decades ago, the figure was only 1%. Even formal bankruptcy will not discharge debts (such as student loans) owed to the government.

Most of those in trouble, however, are working people who keep charging to plastic. Unlike the old days, "50% of the population do not pay off their cards monthly. These credit card interest rates can be as high as 28.8%," says Ms. Campbell. "If you are paying only the minimum payment, it can take close to 20 years to pay off a $5000 balance."

There were 54.2 million credit cards in circulation in Canada in 1998, or 2.31 cards for every Canadian over the age of 18. Of those, 35.3 million were Visa or MasterCard (up from 31.9 million in 1997). Outstanding balances on major credit cards in October 1998 totalled more than $17 billion. The average credit card sale rose from $82.50 in 1997 to $90 in 1998.

As a last-ditch effort to buy time and figure out how to earn more income, many people use credit cards to make payments on other debts. Ms. Campbell recommends having only one "evil dog" credit card or swearing off cards altogether.

Exercise 14.2

Answers to the odd-numbered problems are at the end of the book.
Formatted spreadsheet templates (Excel 97) are available for these problems on the diskette accompanying this text.

SPATS

1. Monica bought a $1250 stereo system for 20% down, with the balance to be paid with interest at 15% compounded monthly in six equal monthly payments. Construct the full amortization schedule for the debt. Calculate the total interest paid.

2. Dr. Alvano borrowed $8000 at 10% compounded quarterly to purchase a new X-ray machine for his clinic. The agreement requires quarterly payments during a two-year amortization period. Prepare the full amortization schedule for the loan. Calculate the total interest charges.

•3. Golden Dragon Restaurant obtained a $9000 loan at 12.75% compounded annually to replace some kitchen equipment. Prepare a complete amortization schedule if the loan is to be repaid by semiannual payments over a three-year term.

•4. Valley Produce received $50,000 in vendor financing at 11.5% compounded semiannually for the purchase of harvesting machinery. The contract requires equal annual payments for seven years to repay the debt. Construct the amortization schedule for the debt. How much interest will be paid over the seven-year term?

•5. Suppose that the loan in Problem 2 permits an additional prepayment of principal on any scheduled payment date. Prepare another amortization schedule that reflects a prepayment of $1500 with the third scheduled payment.

•6. Suppose that the loan in Problem 4 permits an additional prepayment of principal on any scheduled payment date. Prepare another amortization schedule that reflects a prepayment of $10,000 with the second scheduled payment. How much interest is saved as a result of the prepayment?

•7. Cloverdale Nurseries obtained a $60,000 loan at 10.5% compounded monthly to build an additional greenhouse. Monthly payments were calculated to amortize the loan over six years. Construct a partial amortization schedule showing details of the first two payments, Payments 43 and 44, and the last two payments.

•8. Jean and Walter Pereira financed the addition of a swimming pool using a $24,000 home improvement loan from their bank. Monthly payments were based on an interest rate of 11% compounded semiannually and a five-year amortization. Construct a partial amortization schedule showing details of the first two payments, Payments 30 and 31, and the last two payments. What total interest will they pay over the life of the loan?

The following problems are variations of the preceding eight problems. The size of the regular loan payment is given instead of the duration of the loan.

9. Monica bought a $1250 stereo system for 20% down and payments of $200 per month (except for a smaller final payment) including interest at 15% compounded monthly. Construct the full amortization schedule for the debt. Calculate the total interest paid.

10. Dr. Alvano borrowed $7500 at 10% compounded quarterly to purchase a new X-ray machine for his clinic. The agreement requires quarterly payments of $1000 (except for a smaller final payment). Prepare the full amortization schedule for the loan. Calculate the total interest charges.

•11. Golden Dragon Restaurant obtained a $9000 loan at 12.75% compounded annually to replace some kitchen equipment. Prepare a complete amortization schedule if payments of $2000 (except for a smaller final payment) are to be made semiannually.

•**12.** Valley Produce received $50,000 in vendor financing at 11.5% compounded semiannually for the purchase of harvesting machinery. The contract requires annual payments of $12,000 (except for a smaller final payment). Construct the complete amortization schedule for the debt. How much interest will be paid over the entire life of the loan?

•**13.** Suppose that the loan in Problem 10 permits an additional prepayment of principal on any scheduled payment date. Prepare another amortization schedule that reflects a prepayment of $1000 with the third scheduled payment.

•**14.** Suppose that the loan in Problem 12 permits an additional prepayment of principal on any scheduled payment date. Prepare another amortization schedule that reflects a prepayment of $10,000 with the second scheduled payment. How much interest is saved as a result of the prepayment?

•**15.** Cloverdale Nurseries obtained a $60,000 loan at 10.5% compounded monthly to build an additional greenhouse. Construct a partial amortization schedule for payments of $1000 per month (except for a smaller final payment) showing details of the first two payments, Payments 56 and 57, and the last two payments.

•**16.** Jean and Walter Pereira financed the addition of a swimming pool using a $24,000 home improvement loan from their bank. Monthly payments of $500 (except for a smaller final payment) include interest at 11% compounded semiannually. Construct a partial amortization schedule showing details of the first two payments, Payments 28 and 29, and the last two payments. What total interest will the Pereiras pay over the life of the loan?

14.3 Mortgage Loans: Fundamentals

Basic Concepts and Definitions

A mortgage loan is a loan secured by some *physical* property. Often the borrowed money is used to purchase the property. If the property securing the loan is not real estate, the mortgage is called a *chattel* mortgage. This section will deal only with mortgage loans secured by real property.

The **face value** of the mortgage is the original principal amount that the borrower promises to repay. In legal language, the borrower is called the **mortgagor** and the lender is called the **mortgagee**. The mortgage contract sets out the terms and conditions of the loan. It also specifies the lender's remedies should the borrower default on repaying of the loan. The key remedy is the ultimate power to foreclose on the property and force its sale to recover the amounts owed. At the time a mortgage loan is granted, the lender registers the mortgage on the title of the property at the provincial government's land titles office. Anyone can search the title to determine potential claims against the property.

Even though a homeowner may already have a mortgage loan, the remaining equity in the home can sometimes be used as security for another mortgage loan. The second lender's claim will rank behind the existing claim of the first lender. In the event the borrower defaults on the first mortgage loan, the first lender's claim must be satisfied before any claim of the second lender. Because of this ranking of the claims, the existing mortgage is referred to as the *first mortgage* and the additional mortgage as the *second mortgage.* Also, the interest rate on a second mortgage is significantly higher than the rate on a first mortgage. Loans advertised by financial institutions as "home equity loans" or "home improvement loans" will often be secured by a second mortgage.

The most common amortization periods for mortgage loans are 20 and 25 years. Usually a lender will commit to a fixed interest rate for only a shorter period or term. The **term** of a mortgage loan is the length of time from the date on which the loan is advanced to the date on which the remaining principal balance is due and payable. Most institutional lenders offer terms of six months to seven years. At the expiry of the loan's term, the lender will normally renew the loan for another term, but at the prevailing market rate of interest on the date of renewal. The payments are adjusted so that the borrower continues with the original amortization period but at the new interest rate.

Calculating the Payment and Balance

The federal Interest Act requires that the mortgage contract "contains a statement showing . . . the rate of interest chargeable, calculated yearly or half-yearly, not in advance." In our terminology, the interest rate must be disclosed as the equivalent semiannually compounded nominal rate or the equivalent annually compounded rate.[2] The semiannually compounded rate has become the industry standard for disclosure in the mortgage contract. Mortgage interest rates advertised by most financial institutions are also semiannually compounded rates (even though the compounding frequency is not usually stated). The majority of mortgages require monthly payments. With interest compounded semiannually, the monthly payments form an ordinary *general* annuity having

$$c = \frac{\text{Number of compoundings per year}}{\text{Number of payments per year}} = \frac{2}{12} = \frac{1}{6} = 0.1\overline{6}$$

The mortgage interest rates quoted by a minority of credit unions and a majority of independent mortgage brokers are monthly compounded rates. Monthly payments then form an ordinary *simple* annuity.

Most people receive their wages semimonthly, biweekly, or weekly. Budgeting and cash flow planning are simplified if a constant loan payment is made in each pay period. In addition, there will be significant interest savings over the life of a mortgage if the total amount paid in a year is by more frequent, smaller payments than

---

[2] The Interest Act makes the lender liable for a very severe penalty for failing to disclose the rate of interest as required by the Act. In that event, the Interest Act states that "no interest whatever shall be chargeable, payable, or recoverable, on any part of the principal money advanced." The borrower would be entitled to a refund of any interest already paid and consequently would have the loan on an interest-free basis.

by less frequent, larger payments. Mortgage lenders are becoming increasingly flexible in structuring mortgages for more frequent payments.

Usually the borrower chooses a standard amortization period of 15, 20, or 25 years. The payments for the initial term are then calculated *as though* the interest rate is fixed for the *entire* amortization period. Occasionally, the borrower has a preference for a particular payment size. As long as the resulting amortization period is no more than 25 years, most mortgage lenders will agree to such a proposal.

The principal balance on the mortgage loan after any payment may be calculated using either the Prospective Method or (preferably) the Retrospective Method. The balance at the end of a mortgage's term becomes, in effect, the beginning loan amount for the next term. The lender calculates a new payment size based on current interest rates and (normally) a continuation of the original amortization period. Part (b) of Example 14.3A demonstrates this procedure.

The principal and interest components of any mortgage payment may be calculated as described in Section 14.1 for other term loans. Particularly when the amortization period is 20 or 25 years, the payments in the first few years are primarily interest. Consider a mortgage loan at 8.5% compounded semiannually with a 25-year amortization period. Figure 14.3 shows how the interest and principal components of the fixed monthly payments change over the lifetime of the loan.

At any point in the 25-year amortization, the interest portion of a payment is the vertical distance *below* the curve. The principal portion of the payment is the remainder of the 100%, that is, the vertical distance *above* the curve. For example, the payment at the end of Year 14 is about 60% interest and 40% principal. During the first five years, more than 80% of every payment is interest. Consequently, the principal balance declines very slowly during the early years (as you will see in Figure 14.4).

Figure 14.4 illustrates how the balance owed on a $100,000 mortgage loan at 8.5% compounded semiannually declines during its 25-year amortization period. As expected from the preceding discussion, the balance decreases slowly in the early

CAUGHT IN THE WEB

Canada Trust has a Mortgage Calculator at www.canadatrust.com/credit/tool/mtgcalc. It will calculate the "Payment" or the "Principal" or the "Amortization period" if you enter values for the relevant variables. You can select a weekly, biweekly, semimonthly, or monthly payment frequency. If you enter the number of remaining payments for the amortization period (in months) and calculate the "Principal," the calculator gives you the mortgage balance using the Prospective Method. The answer will have the usual small error that results when you assume the final payment is equal to the others.

Figure 14.3 *The Composition of Mortgage Payments During a 25-Year Amortization*

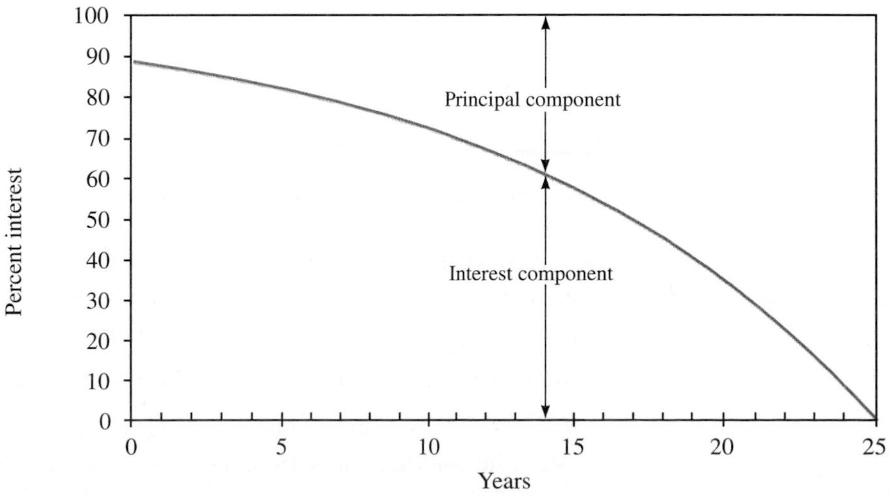

Figure 14.4 *A Mortgage's Declining Balance During a 25-Year Amortization*

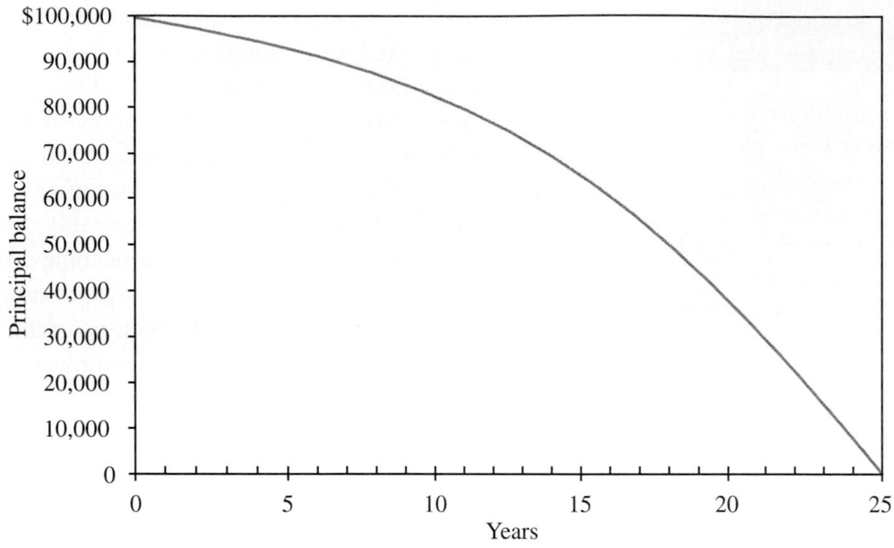

years. It takes about one-quarter of the amortization period to pay off the first \$10,000 (10% of the original loan). Almost *three-quarters* of the amortization period are required to reduce the balance to *one-half* of the original principal. The rate at which the principal is reduced accelerates in later years as an ever-increasing portion of each payment is applied to the principal.

Example 14.3A *Calculating the Payments on a Mortgage Loan at its Beginning and at Renewal*

A \$50,000 mortgage loan is written with a 20-year amortization period, a three-year term, and an interest rate of 9.5% compounded semiannually. Payments are made monthly. Calculate:

a. The balance at the end of the three-year term.

b. The size of the payments upon renewal for a five-year term at 10.5% compounded semiannually (with the loan maintaining its original 20-year amortization).

Solution

The mortgage payments constitute an ordinary general annuity having

$$PV = \$50{,}000 \quad n = 12(20) = 240 \quad i = \frac{9.5\%}{2} = 4.75\% \quad \text{and} \quad c = \frac{2}{12} = 0.1\overline{6}$$

The periodic interest rate that matches the one-month payment interval is

$$i_2 = (1+i)^c - 1 = 1.0475^{0.1\overline{6}} - 1 = 0.00776438317 = 0.776438317\% \text{ per month}$$

Before the balance can be obtained in part (a), the monthly payment must be determined. The amortization period rather than the term of the mortgage is relevant for the payment calculation. That is, calculate the monthly payment that will repay the loan in 20 years if the interest rate remains at 9.5% compounded semiannually.

Part (b) is handled in the same way as a new mortgage whose original principal equals the balance from part (a), but with a 17-year amortization period and an interest rate of 10.5% compounded semiannually. In part (b),

$$i_2 = (1 + i)^c - 1 = 1.0525^{0.1\bar{6}} - 1 = 0.00856451515 = 0.856451515\% \text{ per month}$$

Algebraic Solution

a. Solving

$$\$50{,}000 = PMT\left[\frac{1 - 1.007764383^{-240}}{0.007764383}\right]$$

gives $PMT = \$460.12$. Using the Retrospective Method, the balance after three years (36 payments) will be

$$\begin{pmatrix}\text{Balance after}\\ \text{36 payments}\end{pmatrix} = \begin{pmatrix}\text{Future value of}\\ \text{\$50,000 after 36 months}\end{pmatrix} - \begin{pmatrix}\text{Future value of the 36}\\ \text{payments already made}\end{pmatrix}$$

$$= \$50{,}000(1.007764383)^{36} - \$460.12\left[\frac{1.007764383^{36} - 1}{0.007764383}\right]$$

$$= \$47{,}026.83$$

The balance after the initial three-year term will be \$47,026.83.

b. The monthly payment upon renewal is the value of PMT such that the present value of 17 years' payments ($n = 12 \times 17 = 204$) discounted at the new periodic interest rate ($i_2 = 0.856451515\%$) equals the balance obtained in part (a). That is,

$$\$47{,}026.83 = PMT\left[\frac{1 - 1.00856451515^{-204}}{0.00856451515}\right]$$

Solving gives $PMT = \$488.53$. Upon renewal of the mortgage at 10.5% compounded semiannually, the payments will rise to \$488.53 per month.

Financial Calculator Solution

a. Calculate the payments at 9.5% compounded semiannually.

50000 (PV) 0 (FV) 0.776438317 (i) 240 (n) (COMP) (PMT) [−460.115]

Calculate the balance after three years (36 payments).

460.12 (+/−) (PMT) 36 (n) (COMP) (FV) [−47,026.83]

b. The monthly payment upon renewal is the value of PMT such that the present value of 17 years' payments ($n = 12 \times 17 = 204$) discounted at the new periodic interest rate ($i_2 = 0.856451515\%$) equals the balance obtained in part (a).

(+/−) (PV) 0.856451515 (i) 0 (FV) 204 (n) (COMP) (PMT) [−488.533]

The monthly payment upon renewal will be \$488.53.

Example 14.3B Calculations Where the Mortgage Payment is Rounded to the Next Higher $10

The monthly payments for the first five-year term of a $20,000 mortgage loan were based on a 10-year amortization and an interest rate of 9.9% compounded semiannually. The payments were rounded up to the next higher $10.

a. Calculate the size of the monthly payments.

b. What is the principal balance at the end of the five-year term?

c. If the interest rate at renewal is 9% compounded semiannually for a second five-year term, calculate the new monthly payments also rounded to the next higher $10.

d. Calculate the size of the final payment.

Solution

The calculations in parts (a), (b), and (c) run parallel to those in parts (a) and (b) of Example 14.3A. Therefore, only the financial calculator approach will be presented for this solution.

Financial Calculator Solution

a. The payments form an ordinary general annuity with

$$PV = \$20{,}000 \quad n = 12(10) = 120 \quad i = \frac{9.9\%}{2} = 4.95\% \quad \text{and} \quad c = \frac{2}{12} = 0.1\overline{6}$$

Then

$$i_2 = (1 + i)^c - 1 = 1.0495^{0.1\overline{6}} - 1 = 0.0080848171 = 0.80848171\% \text{ per month}$$

20000 (PV) 120 (n) 0.80848171 (i) 0 (FV) (COMP) (PMT) [−261.01]

The monthly payment rounded to the next higher $10 is $270.

b. Calculate the balance after five years ($n = 60$) using the Retrospective Method.

60 (n) 270 (+/−) (PMT) (COMP) (FV) [−11,679.06]

The principal balance at the end of the five-year term is $11,679.06.

c. At the new nominal rate of 9% compounded semiannually,

$$i_2 = (1 + i)^c - 1 = 1.045^{0.1\overline{6}} - 1 = 0.007363123 = 0.7363123\% \text{ per month}$$

11679.06 (PV) 0.7363123 (i) 60 (n) 0 (FV) (COMP) (PMT) [−241.51]

The monthly payment on renewal will be $250 (rounded to the next higher $10).

d. Since the payment size was rounded up, fewer than 60 payments will be required to extinguish the debt, and the last payment will be less than $250.

Calculating the number of payments needed to pay off the loan,

250 (+/−) (PMT) (COMP) (n) [57.4634]

Therefore, only 58 payments will be required. The final payment will be the balance after 57 payments plus one month's interest. That is,

$$\text{Last payment} = \text{Balance after 57 payments} \times (1 + i)$$

Calculate the balance after 57 payments.

57 (n) (COMP) (FV) [−115.23]

Hence,

$$\text{Last payment} = \$115.23 \times (1.007363123) = \$116.08$$

Qualifying for a Mortgage Loan

Mortgage lenders must determine whether a mortgage loan is adequately secured by the property, and whether the borrower has the financial capacity to make the mortgage payments. To do this, they calculate and set upper limits on three ratios:[3]

1. *Loan-to-Value Ratio* $= \dfrac{\text{Principal amount of the loan}}{\text{Lending value of the property}} \times 100\% \leq 75\%$

   The 75% maximum for this ratio means the borrower's minimum down payment is 25% of the "lending value." (The lending value is the lesser of the purchase price and the market value as determined by a certified appraiser.)

2. *Gross Debt Service Ratio* (GDS ratio):

$$\text{GDS ratio} = \frac{\begin{pmatrix}\text{Total monthly payments for}\\ \text{mortgage, property taxes, and heat}\end{pmatrix}}{\text{Gross monthly income}} \times 100\% \leq 32\%$$

   The upper limit on this ratio means that the major costs of home ownership should not require more than 32% of the borrower's gross income.

3. *Total Debt Service Ratio* (TDS ratio):

$$\text{TDS ratio} = \frac{\begin{pmatrix}\text{Total monthly payments for mortgage,}\\ \text{property taxes, heat, and other debt}\end{pmatrix}}{\text{Gross monthly income}} \times 100\% \leq 40\%$$

   The upper limit on this ratio means that payments related to home ownership *and all other debt* should not require more than 40% of the borrower's gross income.

A borrower must qualify on *all* three ratios. The upper limits for the GDS and TDS ratios vary somewhat from one lender to another. Depending on the lender, the maximum GDS ratio can range[4] from 30% to 33% and the maximum TDS ratio from 37% to 42%.

[3] The indicated upper limits are typical for what are called "conventional first mortgages."

[4] If a prospective homeowner is eligible for Canada Mortgage and Housing Corporation's First-Home Loan Insurance, the upper limits are 95% for the loan-to-value ratio, 35% for the GDS ratio, and 42% for the TDS ratio. To qualify under this program, at least one of the buyers must not have owned a home as a principal residence during the preceding five years. The home must also become the buyer's principal residence.

Example 14.3C Determining the Maximum Mortgage Loan for which a Borrower Qualifies

The Schusters have saved \$35,000 for the down payment on a home. Their gross monthly income is \$3200. They want to know the maximum conventional mortgage loan for which they can qualify in order to determine the highest price they can pay for a home. They have 18 payments of \$300 per month remaining on their car loan. Their bank has upper limits of 32% for the GDS ratio and 40% for the TDS ratio.

a. Allowing for property taxes of \$150 per month and heating costs of \$100 per month, what maximum monthly mortgage payment do the GDS and TDS ratios permit?

b. What is the maximum mortgage loan for which the Schusters can qualify? (Use a 25-year amortization and an interest rate of 8% compounded semiannually for a five-year term. Round the answer to the nearest \$100.)

c. Based on a \$35,000 down payment and the maximum loan from part (b), what is the highest price they can pay for a home? Round the answer to the nearest \$100.

Solution

a. The GDS ratio allows

$$\frac{\left(\begin{array}{c}\text{Maximum mortgage payment}\\ +\text{ property taxes }+\text{ heating costs}\end{array}\right)}{\text{Gross income}} = 0.32$$

That is,

$$\frac{\text{Maximum mortgage payment} + \$150 + \$100}{\$3200} = 0.32$$

Hence,

$$\begin{aligned}\text{Maximum mortgage payment} + \$150 + \$100 &= 0.32(\$3200)\\ \text{Maximum mortgage payment} &= 0.32(\$3200) - \$250 = \$774\end{aligned}$$

The TDS ratio allows

$$\frac{\left(\begin{array}{c}\text{Maximum payments on all debt}\\ +\text{ property taxes }+\text{ heating costs}\end{array}\right)}{\text{Gross income}} = 0.40$$

Hence,

$$\begin{aligned}\text{Maximum mortgage payment} + \$150 + \$100 + \$300 &= 0.40(\$3200)\\ \text{Maximum mortgage payment} &= 0.40(\$3200) - \$550 = \$730\end{aligned}$$

For the Schusters' situation, the TDS ratio is the more restrictive ratio. It limits the maximum mortgage payment to \$730 per month.

b. The TDS ratio restricts the Schusters to a maximum mortgage payment of \$730 per month. For a loan at 8% compounded semiannually with a 25-year amortization,

$n = 12(25) = 300 \quad i = 4\% \quad c = 0.1\overline{6} \quad \text{and} \quad i_2 = 1.04^{0.1\overline{6}} - 1 = 0.006558197$

The maximum loan permitted by the TDS ratio is

$$\begin{aligned} PV &= \text{Present value of 300 payments of \$730} \\ &= \$730\left[\frac{1 - 1.006558197^{-300}}{0.006558197}\right] \\ &= \$95{,}600 \text{ rounded to the nearest \$100} \end{aligned}$$

c. The maximum loan-to-value ratio for a conventional first mortgage loan is 75%. Therefore, if the Schusters borrow the maximum amount ($95,600) permitted by the TDS ratio,

$$\frac{\$95{,}600}{\text{Minimum house value}} = 0.75$$

Hence,

$$\text{Minimum house value} = \frac{\$95{,}600}{0.75} = \$127{,}500$$

At this price, the minimum down payment required is

$$\$127{,}500 - \$95{,}600 = \$31{,}900$$

Since the Schusters have $35,000 for a down payment, they satisfy the loan-to-value criterion with $3100 to spare. Therefore, the maximum price[5] they can pay for a home is

$$\$127{,}500 + \$3100 = \$130{,}600$$

POINT OF INTEREST

AN ANALYSIS OF THE INTEREST "SAVINGS" FROM CHOOSING A SHORTER AMORTIZATION PERIOD

Many financial planners and commentators make a great ballyhoo about the large amount of interest that can be saved by choosing a shorter mortgage amortization period. Their typical analysis goes as follows. (We will use monthly compounding rather than semiannual compounding to simplify the math.)

Suppose you obtain a $100,000 mortgage loan at 7.2% compounded monthly. The following table compares 20- and 25-year amortizations.

---

[5] Mortgage lenders usually base the loan-to-value ratio on the *lesser* of the purchase price or the value placed on the property by an independent appraiser. In this example, the appraised value would have to be $127,500 or more for the Schusters to qualify for a $95,600 mortgage loan.

The Schusters also need to keep in mind that they will have significant legal, appraisal, survey, and registration costs in connection with the purchase transaction. If they have not otherwise provided for these costs, the $3100 "surplus" down payment might better be viewed as a reserve to cover these transaction costs.

Amortization period	Monthly payment	Total of all payments	Total interest
25 years	$719.59	$215,877	$115,877
20 years	$787.35	$188,964	$ 88,964
Difference:	($ 67.76)	$ 26,913	$ 26,913

By choosing a 20-year amortization, you will have "interest savings" of $26,913. The "savings" result from eliminating payments of $719.59 per month during Years 21 to 25 by spending an extra $67.76 per month during Years 1 to 20. That is,

$$\text{Interest savings} = (5 \times 12 \times \$719.59) - (20 \times 12 \times \$67.76) = \$26{,}913$$

It seems quite astounding—increasing the monthly mortgage payment by less than 10% reduces the total interest costs by over 23%! The usual conclusion is that reduction of your mortgage's amortization period should be one of your highest financial priorities because of the amazing "interest savings." In the present example, you will be "$26,913 ahead" by choosing the 20-year amortization.

Do you see any flaws in this conventional analysis? Is it complete? Does it violate any basic concept you have learned? (Clearly, the analysis must be problematic—otherwise, we would not be making an issue of it. But before reading on, cover the remainder of the discussion and take five minutes to see if you can gain the satisfaction of identifying the error made by so many "experts.")

The main flaw in the analysis is that the most basic concept in finance—the time value of money—has been ignored. Whenever you add nominal dollar amounts that are paid on different dates, you are ignoring the time value of money. The longer the time frame over which the payments are spread, the more serious will be the resulting error. In the present case, a dollar in Year 25 is treated as having the same value as a dollar in Year 1. In fact, individual dollars saved in Years 21 to 25 have, on average, significantly less economic value than extra dollars spent in Years 1 to 20.

Let us do a rigorous analysis to determine the amount of the economic advantage of the shorter amortization period.

Questions

1. With a 25-year amortization, suppose you invest the $67.76 difference between the monthly payments. If you earn the same rate of return as the interest rate you pay on the mortgage, how much will you accumulate after 20 years?
2. What will be the balance owed after 20 years on the 25-year mortgage? Compare this balance to the Question 1 result. Which mortgage alternative puts you in a better financial position 20 years from now? Does either alternative put you in a better position at any date? Where did all of the "interest savings" go?
3. How will the outcome differ if the rate of return on your investments is higher than the interest rate you pay on your mortgage?
4. Write a "decision rule" that your friends (who have not had the good fortune of taking this course) can use to decide whether to select a longer or a shorter mortgage amortization period.

Postscript: We do not want to leave the impression that we disagree with advice that paying off your mortgage as fast as possible should be a high financial priority. We merely make the point that the usual rationale is flawed and overstated. Legitimate reasons for the advice are:

- When you use extra money to reduce the principal on your mortgage, you are *certain* of earning an *after-tax* rate of return equal to the interest rate on the mortgage. After you adjust returns from alternative investments for their *risk* and *tax exposure,* the mortgage "investment" is very attractive in comparison.
- Human nature is such that we are more readily motivated to accelerate mortgage repayment than to undertake some other investment plan.
- Reduction of household debt improves our ability to absorb financial shocks such as loss of income due to sickness or job loss.

Post-postscript: In the next section, you will learn about other possibilities for accelerating the repayment of a mortgage loan. Some books present calculations of the resulting "interest savings." We play down this fundamentally flawed perspective for the reasons discussed in this Point of Interest.

Common Prepayment Privileges and Penalties

Any payments other than the regular contractual payments on a mortgage loan are called **prepayments**. Unless they include a penalty, prepayments are applied entirely to the reduction of principal since the regular payments already cover interest charges. Mortgages that place no restrictions or penalties on extra payments by the borrower are called **fully open mortgages**. At the other extreme are **closed mortgages** which do not allow any prepayment without a penalty. A borrower must pay a higher interest rate on an open mortgage than on a closed mortgage having the same term—0.3% to 0.5% higher for a six-month-term open mortgage and 0.6% to 1% higher for a one-year-term open mortgage.

Between the two extremes just described are **partially open mortgages** which grant limited penalty-free prepayment privileges. The more common prepayments allowed on partially open mortgage loans are one or more of the following.

- **Lump or Balloon Payments** Each year the borrower can prepay without penalty up to 10% of the original amount of the mortgage loan. (A few lenders permit lump payments each year of up to 15% of the original loan.)
- **Increasing the Regular Payment** Once each year, the borrower can permanently increase the size of the regular payments by up to 10%. (A few lenders allow an annual increase of as much as 15%.)
- **"Double-Up"** On any payment date, the borrower can pay twice the regular monthly payment. Taken to the extreme, the borrower could double *every* payment.

If the mortgage contract allows more than one of these options, the borrower can take advantage of two or more simultaneously. However, the privileges are usually *not* cumulative. For example, if you do not use a 10% lump prepayment privilege in the first year, you cannot carry it forward enabling you to prepay up to 20% in the second year.

Details of these prepayment privileges vary among lending institutions. For example, lump payments may be permitted only once each year or several times (subject to the 10% or 15% annual limit). "Each year" might mean a calendar year or it might refer to a year between mortgage anniversary dates. Prepayment privileges may be allowed only after an initial "closed period." Examples of typical closed periods are: the first year of a two-year term mortgage, the first two years of a three-year term mortgage, and the first three years of a four- or five-year term mortgage.

Another increasingly common feature of mortgages is a "skip-a-payment" provision. This allows the borrower to miss one monthly payment each year. Whereas a prepayment will shorten the time required to ultimately pay off a mortgage, skipping a payment will lengthen the time.

It is not unusual for homeowners to sell their house part way through the term of a closed or partially open mortgage. If a mortgage has a *portability* clause, the balance owed may be transferred to the next property purchased by the borrower. A small proportion of mortgages are *assumable.* An assumable mortgage loan may be transferred to (or "assumed by") the purchaser of the property securing the mortgage *if* the purchaser satisfies the lender's GDS and TDS ratios. The most typical scenario, however, is for the vendor to "pay out" the balance owed on the mortgage. Such a pay-out is usually treated as a prepayment. The mortgage contract provides for a financial penalty on any prepayment not specifically permitted by the contract. The most common prepayment penalty is the *greater* of:

- Three months' interest on the amount prepaid, or
- The lender's reduction in interest revenue from the prepaid amount (over the remainder of the mortgage's term[6]).

CAUGHT IN THE WEB

CM Canada Mortgage Corporation has a very informative Mortgage Graphing Calculator at the Web site www.canadamortgage.com/tools/amortization.cgi. After you enter the relevant values, the calculator plots a bar chart showing the interest and principal portions of each year's payments. When you move the mouse cursor over a particular bar, the actual dollar amounts of the components are displayed in a ribbon above the bar chart.

The calculator also allows you to enter an extra annual year-end balloon payment and/or an increase to the regular payment. The amortization chart then shows the effect of the extra payments on the amortization period and on the total interest paid over the life of the loan.

Example 14.3D *The Consequences of a 10% Lump Prepayment*

The interest rate for the first five-year term of an $80,000 mortgage loan is 10.5% compounded semiannually. The mortgage requires monthly payments over a 25-year amortization period. The mortgage contract gives the borrower the right to prepay up to 10% of the original mortgage loan, once each year, without interest

---

[6] The following is an extract from a mortgage contract describing this penalty.

"The amount, if any, by which interest at the rate on this mortgage exceeds interest at the current reinvestment interest rate, calculated on the amount prepaid by you, for the remaining term of the mortgage. The 'current reinvestment interest rate' at the time of prepayment means the rate at which we would lend to you on the security of a similar mortgage of your property for a term commencing on the date of prepayment and expiring on the balance due date of the mortgage."

penalty. Suppose that, at the end of the second year of the mortgage, the borrower makes a prepayment of $8000.

a. How much will the amortization period be shortened?

b. What will be the principal balance at the end of the five-year term?

Solution

a. The $8000 prepayment at the time of the twenty-fourth regular monthly payment will be applied entirely to reducing the principal. To answer part (a), we must take the following steps:

Step 1. Calculate the payments based on a 25-year amortization.

Step 2. Calculate the balance after 24 payments.

Step 3. Reduce this balance by $8000.

Step 4. Calculate the number of monthly payments needed to pay off this new balance.

Step 5. Calculate the reduction in the original 25-year amortization period.

Only the financial calculator solution will be presented.

Step 1: Solve for *PMT* so that

$$\$80{,}000 = \text{Present value of 300 payments}$$

where the periodic rate matching the one-month payment interval is

$$i_2 = (1 + i)^c - 1 = 1.0525^{0.1\bar{6}} - 1 = 0.00856451514 = 0.856451514\%$$

80000 (PV) 0.856451514 (i) 0 (FV) 300 (n) (COMP) (PMT) [−742.664]

The size of the monthly payment is $742.66.

Step 2: Calculate the balance after 24 payments.

742.66 (+/−) (PMT) 24 (n) (COMP) (FV) [−78,475.18]

Step 3: The balance after the $8000 prepayment is $70,475.18.

Step 4: Calculate the number of payments of $742.66 required to have a present value of $70,475.18.

70475.18 (PV) 0 (FV) (COMP) (n) [196.44]

After the $8000 prepayment, 197 more payments will pay off the loan.

Step 5: Without the prepayment, 300 − 24 = 276 payments remain after the twenty-fourth payment. Therefore, the $8000 prepayment reduces the amortization period by

$$276 - 197 = 79 \text{ months} = 6 \text{ years, } 7 \text{ months.}$$

b. Beginning with the balance of $70,475.18 after the $8000 prepayment, calculate the new balance after another 36 payments are made.

36 (n) (COMP) (FV) [−64,639.83]

The balance at the end of the five-year term will be $64,639.83

Example 14.3E *The Consequences of a 10% Increase in the Payment Size*

Two and one-half years ago the Simpsons borrowed \$90,000 secured by a mortgage against the home they purchased at the time. The monthly payments, based on an interest rate of 11% compounded semiannually for a five-year term, would amortize the debt over 25 years. The mortgage has a prepayment clause that allows the Simpsons to increase the monthly payments up to 10% once in each year after a two-year closed period. Any increase is to be a permanent increase. If the Simpsons increase future payments by 10% starting with the thirty-first payment:

a. How much will the amortization period be shortened?

b. What will be the principal balance at the end of the first five-year term?

Solution

a. The following steps are required to answer the question.

Step 1: Calculate the original size of the payments.

Step 2: Calculate the balance after $2\frac{1}{2}$ years (30 payments).

Step 3: Calculate the size of the payments after a 10% increase.

Step 4: Calculate the number of the new, larger payments needed to amortize the balance from Step 2.

Step 5: Calculate the reduction from the original 25-year amortization period.

Only the financial calculator solution will be presented.

Step 1: The interest rate per payment interval is

$$i_2 = (1 + i)^c - 1 = 1.055^{0.1\overline{6}} - 1 = 0.0089633939 = 0.89633939\%$$

90000 (PV) 0 (FV) 0.89633939 (i) 300 (n) (COMP) (PMT) [−866.276]

The Simpsons have been making monthly payments of \$866.28.

Step 2: 866.28 (+/−) (PMT) 30 (n) (COMP) (FV) [−87,959.81]

Step 3: The increased monthly payment will be

$$1.1(\$866.28) = \$952.91$$

Step 4: Now solve for the number of payments of \$952.91 required to pay off the \$87,959.81 balance.

87959.81 (PV) 0 (FV) 952.91 (+/−) (PMT) (COMP) (n) [196.86]

Only 197 of the larger payments are needed to pay off the loan.

Step 5: The total time to amortize the loan will be 30 + 197 = 227 months instead of the original 300 months. Therefore, the amortization period will be shortened by 300 − 227 = 73 months, or six years, one month. (Note that the 10% increase in the size of the payments after $2\frac{1}{2}$ years will reduce the time required to pay off the loan by about 25%!)

b. By the end of the five-year term, another 30 payments of $952.91 will have been made.

30 (n) (COMP) (FV) [−82,326.64]

The balance at the end of the initial five-year term will be $82,326.64.

Exercise 14.3

Answers to the odd-numbered problems are at the end of the book.

1. A $100,000 mortgage loan at 8.2% compounded semiannually requires monthly payments bared on a 25-year amortization. Assuming that the interest rate does not change for the entire 25 years,

Complete the following table.

Interval	Balance at the end of the interval	Principal reduction during the interval	Interest paid during the interval
0 to 5 years			
5 to 10 years			
10 to 15 years			
15 to 20 years			
20 to 25 years			

2. The interest rate on a $100,000 mortgage loan is 9% compounded semiannually.

a. Calculate the monthly payment for each of 15-, 20-, and 25-year amortizations.

b. By what percentage must the monthly payment be increased for a 20-year amortization instead of a 25-year amortization?

c. By what percentage must the monthly payment be increased for a 15-year amortization instead of a 25-year amortization?

d. For each of the three amortization periods in part (a), calculate the total interest paid over the entire amortization period (assuming that the interest rate and payments do not change).

3. A $100,000 mortgage loan has a 25-year amortization.

a. Calculate the monthly payment at interest rates of 8%, 9%, and 10% compounded semiannually.

b. By what percentage does the monthly payment on the 10% mortgage exceed the monthly payment on the 9% mortgage?

c. Calculate the total interest paid over the entire 25-year amortization period at each of the three interest rates. (Assume the final payment equals the others.)

4. The Graftons can afford a maximum mortgage payment of $1000 per month. The current interest rate is 8.25% compounded semiannually. What is the maximum mortgage loan they can afford if the amortization period is:

a. 15 years? **b.** 20 years? **c.** 25 years?

5. The Tarkanians can afford a maximum mortgage payment of $1000 per month. What is the maximum mortgage loan they can afford if the amortization period is 25 years and the interest rate is:

a. 8% compounded semiannually? **b.** 9% compounded semiannually?

6. Calculate the monthly payment on a $100,000 mortgage loan:

a. At 8.5% compounded semiannually with a 20-year amortization.

b. At 9.5% compounded semiannually with a 25-year amortization. (Other things being the same, mortgage payments are larger for higher interest rates and smaller for longer amortization periods. Note in part (b) that the 1% higher interest rate more than offsets the effect of the five-year increase in the amortization period.)

•7. The Switzers are nearing the end of the first five-year term of a $100,000 mortgage loan with a 25-year amortization. The interest rate has been 8.5% compounded semiannually for the initial term. How much will their monthly payments increase if the interest rate upon renewal is 9.5% compounded semiannually?

•8. The Melnyks are nearing the end of the first three-year term of a $100,000 mortgage loan with a 20-year amortization. The interest rate has been 9% compounded semiannually for the initial term. How much will their monthly payments decrease if the interest rate upon renewal is 8% compounded semiannually?

•9. The interest rate for the first three years of an $80,000 mortgage loan is 10.5% compounded semiannually. Monthly payments are calculated using a 25-year amortization.

a. What will be the principal balance at the end of the three-year term?

b. What will the monthly payments be if the loan is renewed at 9.5% compounded semiannually (and the original amortization period is continued)?

•10. Five years ago, Ms. Halliday received a mortgage loan from the Bank of Nova Scotia for $60,000 at 11.25% compounded semiannually for a five-year term. Monthly payments were based on a 25-year amortization. The bank is agreeable to renewing the loan for another five-year term at 10% compounded semiannually. Calculate the principal reduction that will occur in the second five-year term if:

a. The payments are recalculated based on the new interest rate and a continuation of the original 25-year amortization.

b. Ms. Halliday continues to make the same payments as she made for the first five years (resulting in a reduction of the amortization period).

•11. A $40,000 mortgage loan charges interest at 9.75% compounded *monthly* for a four-year term. Monthly payments were calculated for a 15-year amortization and then rounded up to the next higher $10.

a. What will be the principal balance at the end of the first term?

b. What will the monthly payments be on renewal for a three-year term if it is calculated for an interest rate of 9% compounded monthly and an 11-year amortization period, but again rounded to the next higher $10?

•**12.** Polly is shopping for a mortgage loan to purchase a house for $110,000. She has accumulated enough money to make a 25% down payment and she prefers monthly instalments. She makes it clear that she cannot afford mortgage payments much more than $800 per month. However, Polly would like to pay back her mortgage loan as soon as possible. The current interest rate on mortgages with a five-year term is 10.50% compounded semiannually.

a. What is the size of the mortgage loan Polly needs?

b. How long will it take Polly to pay back the mortgage if her mortgage payment is exactly $800 and the interest rate stays constant over the duration of the mortgage?

c. Polly indicates that she might be able to pay a little more than $800. How much would Polly's monthly payment be to amortize the loan over exactly 20 years? (Taken from ICB course on Wealth Valuation.)

•**13.** The interest rate for the first five years of a $27,000 mortgage loan was 11.25% compounded semiannually. The monthly payments computed for a 10-year amortization were rounded to the next higher $10.

a. Calculate the principal balance at the end of the first term.

b. Upon renewal at 10.5% compounded semiannually, monthly payments were calculated for a five-year amortization and again rounded up to the next $10. What will be the amount of the last payment?

•**14.** The Delgados have a gross monthly income of $6000. Monthly payments on personal loans total $500. Their bank limits the gross debt service ratio at 33% and the total debt service ratio at 42%.

a. Rounded to the nearest $100, what is the maximum 25-year mortgage loan for which they can qualify on the basis of their income? Assume monthly heating costs of $120 and property taxes of $200 per month. Current mortgage rates are 8.6% compounded semiannually.

b. Rounded to the nearest $100, what minimum down payment must they have to qualify for the maximum conventional mortgage on a new home?

•**15.** The Archibalds are eligible for Canada Mortgage and Housing Corporation's First Home Loan Insurance. Consequently, their limits are 95% for the loan-to-value ratio, 35% for the GDS ratio, and 42% for the TDS ratio.

a. Rounded to the nearest $100, what is the maximum 25-year mortgage loan for which they can qualify if their gross monthly income is $5000 and their payments on personal debt amount to $600 per month? Assume monthly heating costs of $100 and property taxes of $175 per month. Current mortgage rates are 8.25% compounded semiannually.

b. If they make the minimum down payment, what is the maximum price (rounded to the nearest $100) they can pay for a home? (Assume the purchase price equals the appraised value.)

•**16.** A mortgage loan requires monthly payments of $683.52 for the initial five-year term of a 25-year amortization. If the loan was for $75,000, calculate the semiannually compounded nominal rate of interest on the loan.

•**17.** The interest rate on a $100,000 mortgage loan is 8.75% compounded semi-annually.

a. What are the monthly payments for a 25-year amortization?

b. Suppose that the borrower instead makes weekly payments equal to one-fourth of the monthly payment calculated in part (a). When will the loan be paid off if the interest rate does not change? Assume there are exactly 52 weeks in a year.

•**18.** A $100,000 mortgage at 8.2% compounded semiannually with a 25-year amortization requires monthly payments. The mortgage allows the mortgagor to prepay up to 10% of the original principal once each year. How much will the amortization period be shortened if, on the first anniversary of the mortgage, the mortgagor makes (in addition to the regular payment) a prepayment of:

a. $5000? **b.** $10,000?

•**19.** A $100,000 mortgage at 8.2% compounded semiannually with a 20-year amortization requires monthly payments. The mortgage allows the mortgagor to prepay up to 10% of the original principal once each year. How much will the amortization period be shortened if, on the first anniversary of the mortgage, the mortgagor makes (in addition to the regular payment) a prepayment of:

a. $5000? **b.** $10,000?

•**20.** A $100,000 mortgage at 8% compounded semiannually with a 25-year amortization requires monthly payments. The mortgage entitles the mortgagor to increase the regular payment by up to 10% once each year. How much will the amortization period be shortened if, after the twelfth payment, the payments are increased by:

a. 5%? **b.** 10%?

•**21.** A $100,000 mortgage at 8% compounded semiannually with a 20-year amortization requires monthly payments. The mortgage allows the mortgagor to increase the regular payment by up to 10% once each year. How much will the amortization period be shortened if, after the twelfth payment, the payments are increased by:

a. 5%? **b.** 10%?

•**22.** A $100,000 mortgage at 8.5% compounded semiannually with a 25-year amortization requires monthly payments. The mortgage allows the mortgagor to "double up" on a payment once each year. How much will the amortization period be shortened if the mortgagor doubles the tenth payment?

•**23.** A $100,000 mortgage at 8.8% compounded semiannually with a 20-year amortization requires monthly payments. The mortgage allows the mortgagor to "double up" on a payment once each year. How much will the amortization period be shortened if the mortgagor doubles the eighth payment?

•**24.** A $100,000 mortgage at 8.75% compounded semiannually with a 20-year amortization requires monthly payments. The mortgage allows the mortgagor to miss a payment once each year. How much will the amortization period be lengthened if the mortgagor misses the ninth payment? (The interest that accrues during the ninth month is converted to principal at the end of the ninth month.)

•25. A $100,000 mortgage at 8.25% compounded semiannually with a 25-year amortization requires monthly payments. The mortgage allows the mortgagor to miss a payment once each year. How much will the amortization period be lengthened if the mortgagor misses the twelfth payment? (The interest that accrues during the twelfth month is converted to principal at the end of the twelfth month.)

•26. A $100,000 mortgage at 9.1% compounded semiannually with a 20-year amortization requires monthly payments. How much will the amortization period be shortened if a $10,000 lump payment is made along with the twelfth payment and payments are increased by 10% starting in the third year?

•27. A $100,000 mortgage at 8.8% compounded semiannually with a 25-year amortization requires monthly payments. How much will the amortization period be shortened if payments are increased by 10% starting in the second year, and a $10,000 lump payment is made along with the twenty-fourth payment?

•28. Monthly payments on a $70,000 mortgage are based on an interest rate of 11.5% compounded semiannually and a 20-year amortization. If a $5000 prepayment is made along with the thirty-second payment,

a. How much will the amortization period be shortened?

b. What will be the principal balance after four years?

•29. The interest rate for the first five years of a $120,000 mortgage is 9.9% compounded semiannually. Monthly payments are based on a 25-year amortization. If a $5000 prepayment is made at the end of the second year,

a. How much will the amortization period be shortened?

b. What will be the principal balance at the end of the five-year term?

•30. A $100,000 mortgage loan at 9% compounded *monthly* has a 25-year amortization.

a. What prepayment at the end of the first year will reduce the time required to pay off the loan by one year?

b. Instead of the prepayment in part (a), what prepayment at the end of the tenth year will reduce the time required to pay off the loan by one year?

•31. After three years of the first five-year term at 10.25% compounded semiannually, Dean and Cindy decide to take advantage of the privilege of increasing the payments on their $100,000 mortgage loan by 10%. The monthly payments were originally calculated for a 20-year amortization.

a. How much will the amortization period be shortened?

b. What will be the principal balance at the end of the five-year term?

•32. The MacLellans originally chose to make payments of $800 per month on a $69,000 mortgage written at 10.5% compounded semiannually for the first five years. After three years they exercised their right under the mortgage contract to increase the payments by 10%.

a. If the interest rate does not change, when will they extinguish the mortgage debt?

b. What will be the principal balance at the end of the five-year term?

••33. The monthly payments on the Wolskis' $83,000 mortgage were originally based on a 25-year amortization and an interest rate of 9.9% compounded semiannually for a five-year term. After two years, they elected to increase their monthly payments by $50, and at the end of the fourth year they made a $5000 prepayment.

a. How much have they shortened the amortization period?

b. What was the principal balance at the end of the five-year term?

••34. A recent innovation is the "cash-back mortgage" wherein the lender gives the borrower an up-front bonus cash payment. For example, if you borrow $100,000 on a 3% cash-back mortgage loan, the lender will give you $3000 in addition to the $100,000 loan. You pay back only the $100,000 principal over the amortization period. The $3000 can be immediately applied as a prepayment to reduce the principal balance (to $97,000) or it can be used for any other purpose. You must keep your mortgage with the lender for at least five years.

The cash-back mortgage seems like a good deal but there is more you need to know about advertised mortgage interest rates. The rates you see posted in your local financial institution are just a starting point for negotiations. You can get $\frac{1}{4}$% knocked off just by asking for it. With some firm negotiating, you can probably get a $\frac{1}{2}$% reduction. If the institution really wants your business, you can get a $\frac{3}{4}$% reduction. However, if you take advantage of some other promotion such as a cash-back offer, you will not get any rate discount. So the cash-back offer is not as good as it initially appears.

Which of the following loans should be chosen by the borrower?

- A standard $100,000 mortgage loan at 6.5% compounded semiannually?
- A 3% cash-back mortgage loan for $100,000 at 7.25% compounded semiannually?

In both cases, the interest rate is for a five-year term and the payments are based on a 25-year amortization. For the cash-back mortgage, assume that the $3000 cash bonus is immediately applied to reduce the balance to $97,000. (Since the monthly payments are based on the $100,000 face value, the prepayment will shorten the time required to pay off the loan.) Use 7.2% compounded monthly as the time value of money.

*14.4 Mortgage Loans: Additional Topics

A mortgage loan sometimes involves costs in addition to interest charges. In this section you will learn how to incorporate these additional costs into an overall effective cost of borrowing. This is the best figure to use when comparison shopping for a mortgage loan.

A mortgage loan represents an investment of funds by the lender. Most mortgage contracts can be sold by the lender to another investor at any time during the term of the mortgage. This section also explains how you determine the fair market value of a mortgage contract. This topic is also relevant to real estate transactions in which the vendor provides mortgage financing at a below-market interest rate.

The Effective Cost of Borrowing

Some mortgage lenders, particularly individual investors, use the services of a mortgage broker. The broker finds a party in need of mortgage financing, determines the party's financial condition and creditworthiness, and conducts the negotiations. All or a substantial portion of the broker's remuneration for these services is taken out of the principal amount of any loan that is advanced. Consequently, the borrower receives *less* than the face value or **gross amount** of the mortgage loan, but must repay the full gross amount over the amortization period. The amount retained to compensate the broker is variously called the brokerage fee, bonus, placement fee, commission, finder's fee, or discount.[7]

A brokerage fee or bonus represents a cost of borrowing in addition to the interest charges. Particularly from the borrower's point of view, it is desirable to combine the interest charges and brokerage fee in some measure of the overall "true" cost of borrowing.[8] The costs must be combined in a way that takes into account the time value of money. Borrowers can then use this measure to compare alternatives available from various mortgage lenders.

Most provinces in Canada have passed legislation requiring disclosure of the impact of brokerage fees on the cost of borrowing. The most common requirement is for the disclosure of an effective annual interest rate that impounds the brokerage fee. We can gain an insight into how to calculate this effective interest rate by taking the following view. The borrower initially receives net or "useful" loan proceeds of only

Net amount of the loan = (Gross amount of the loan) − (Brokerage fee)

The effective interest rate we want is the interest rate on a loan in which the *same* payments reduce a

Beginning balance = *Net amount* of the mortgage loan

to an

Ending balance = End-of-term balance of the mortgage loan

[7] A mortgage loan in which an amount, by whatever name, is retained by the broker or lender, is called a *bonused mortgage.* Who do you think chose this name—mortgage brokers or borrowers?

[8] Mortgage lenders routinely require an official land survey, an official appraisal of the property's market value, and a title search of the property. Most mortgages make provision for the lender to directly pay the survey and appraisal costs, legal fees, and other disbursements, and to deduct them from the loan proceeds. These are not considered a cost of borrowing in the same sense as interest and brokerage fees. A prudent purchaser of real estate will incur most of these expenses even if a mortgage loan is not required. Therefore, these other charges are not deducted from the face value of the loan for the purpose of calculating the "true" cost of borrowing.

That is,

EFFECTIVE COST OF BORROWING
The effective or "true" cost of borrowing for a mortgage loan is the annually compounded discount rate that makes
Net amount of the loan = (*PV* of payments) + (*PV* of end-of-term balance)

This definition of the effective cost of borrowing implies a two-step procedure for obtaining it.

1. Solve for i, the interest rate per payment interval, that satisfies the preceding equation.
2. Calculate the effective annual interest rate using $f = (1 + i)^m - 1$ where m is the number of compoundings in a year (which in this context equals the number of payments in a year.)

Example 14.4A Calculating the "True" or Effective Cost of Borrowing

A mortgage broker arranged a \$50,000 gross mortgage loan at 10.75% compounded semiannually. The loan has a five-year term with monthly payments based on a 20-year amortization. A brokerage fee of \$3767.45 was deducted from the gross amount. What is the borrower's effective annual cost of borrowing (over the five-year term)?

Solution

The borrower receives only

$$\$50{,}000 - \$3767.45 = \$46{,}232.55$$

but must make payments that amortize \$50,000 over 20 years. The brokerage fee of \$3767.45 is viewed, for the purpose of this calculation, as a "front-end" interest charge. The steps in the solution are:

Step 1: Calculate i_2 corresponding to 10.75% compounded semiannually.

Step 2: Calculate the payment size.

Step 3: Calculate the balance at the end of the term.

Step 4: Calculate the value for i that makes the net amount actually received (\$46,232.55) equal to the combined present value of the 60 payments and the balance owed (from Step 3) at the end of the five-year term.

Step 5: Convert the periodic rate from Step 4 to the effective annual rate.

Only the financial calculator solution will be presented.

Step 1: $i_2 = (1 + 0.05375)^{0.1\overline{6}} - 1 = 0.876405309\%$ per month

Step 2:

50000 (PV) 0 (FV) 0.876405309 (i) 240 (n) (COMP) (PMT) [−499.756]

Step 3: 499.76 (+/−) (PMT) 60 (n) (COMP) (FV) [−45,167.50]

Step 4: 46232.55 (PV) (COMP) (i) [1.05324]

Step 5: The corresponding effective annual rate is

$$f = (1 + i)^m - 1 = 1.0105324^{12} - 1 = 0.13397 = 13.40\%$$

The impact of the brokerage fee is to make the effective annual rate for the overall cost of borrowing 13.40% (compared to

$$f = 1.05375^2 - 1 = 0.11039 = 11.04\%$$

for the quoted interest rate of 10.75% compounded semiannually).

Example 14.4B *Determining Which Mortgage Loan Has the Lower "True" Cost of Borrowing*

William intends to raise $50,000 for his business by obtaining a mortgage loan secured by his home. He is considering two alternatives. A mortgage broker will approve a $52,000 face value loan at 10.5% compounded semiannually but will retain a $2000 commission. A credit union will grant a $50,000 loan at 11.5% compounded semiannually with no other fees. Both loans would have a five-year term and require monthly payments based upon a 15-year amortization. Which loan is a better deal for William?

Solution

Clearly, William should not simply choose the loan with the lower interest rate because that would ignore the $2000 commission. Less clearly, William should not necessarily select the loan with the lower payments because when the loans are renewed after five years, their balances will not be equal. The best decision criterion is to choose the loan with the lower effective rate of interest (including any brokerage fee).

For the credit union loan, the cost of borrowing is just the interest rate. The effective annual interest rate is

$$f = (1 + i)^m - 1 = 1.0575^2 - 1 = 0.118306 = 11.83\%$$

For the loan from the broker, the commission or brokerage fee is also a cost of borrowing. The $2000 front-end commission cost must be combined with the actual interest costs and expressed as an effective rate of interest for the five-year term. To determine this rate, we will:

Step 1: Calculate i_2 corresponding to 10.5% compounded semiannually.

Step 2: Calculate the payments on the brokered loan.

Step 3: Calculate the balance on the brokered loan at the end of the five-year term.

Step 4: Calculate the periodic rate that makes the combined present value of the payments in Step 2 and the balance in Step 3 equal to $52,000 − $2000 = $50,000.

Step 5: Convert the periodic rate from Step 4 to an effective annual rate.

Only the financial calculator solution will be presented.

Step 1: $i_2 = (1 + 0.0525)^{0.1\overline{6}} - 1 = 0.0085645151 = 0.85645151\%$ per month

Step 2:

52000 (PV) 0 (FV) 0.85645151 (i) 180 (n) (COMP) (PMT) **−567.653**

Step 3: 567.65 (+/−) (PMT) 60 (n) (COMP) (FV) **−42,460.06**

Step 4: 50000 (PV) (COMP) (i) **0.947521**

Step 5: The corresponding effective annual rate is

$$f = (1 + i)^m - 1 = 1.00947521^{12} - 1 = 0.11982 = 11.98\%$$

The credit union loan has a slightly (0.15%) lower effective annual cost of borrowing, making it the better choice.

POINT OF INTEREST

BEWARE! FINANCIAL QUICKSAND!

"Psst! Hey buddy—need a loan? OK, here's duh deal. Duh boss lends yuh $25 grand. Yuh make monthly payments for 25 years. Oh ya, a couple udder t'ings. A year from now yuh owe us almost $30 grand. Seven years from now, yuh still owe us more than 25 big ones. Wha' da yuh say?"

You can get a deal like this from your local loan shark. Or, if you prefer more refined English, you can probably find a registered mortgage broker offering similar loans in your city. The data in the following table were obtained from a mail flyer distributed by a store-front lender[9] in a mid-size Canadian city. Some cells are left blank for you to calculate the missing amounts later.

The monthly payment in every case is based on an interest rate of 5.5% compounded monthly, a 25-year amortization, and the *gross amount* of the loan. The rate of 5.5% compounded monthly was, if anything, lower than mortgage rates offered at the time by mainstream lenders. However, the term of the loan was only one year, after which the borrower would face market rates.

Gross amount of loan	Net amount of loan	Monthly payment
$30,400	$25,000	$186.68
	50,000	357.40
	75,000	525.04
113,000	100,000	
139,500	125,000	

Actually, only the net amount of the loan (which was called the "cash advance") and the monthly payment were shown on the front of the flyer. To find the gross amount, you had to look on the back panel (just where the tiny print

[9] The author's fondness for the current shape of his knee-caps precludes naming names!

all but disappeared against the background of the lender's logo) and squint really hard. The amount retained for brokerage and other charges in each case is shocking.

Questions:

1. Do the calculations to determine the missing amounts in the table.
2. What will be the balance on each loan at the end of the one-year term?
3. In each case, what is the borrower's effective annual cost of borrowing (for the one-year term)?
4. Even though the borrower will likely pay a higher interest rate upon renewal in one year, assume for the moment that the interest rate and monthly payment will not change. In each case, how long from the date of the original loan will it take the borrower to reduce the balance owed to the original *net* amount of the loan? (Now you understand the choice of title for this Point of Interest!)

Valuation of Mortgages

A mortgage loan represents an investment by the lender in the form of a loan to the borrower. The mortgage contract specifies the stream of future payments to which the lender is entitled. If they are received as scheduled, the lender's rate of return will be the rate of interest charged on the loan.

The original lender can sell his legal interest in the mortgage contract to another investor without the consent of the borrower. This might be done, for example, if the lender needs to raise a substantial amount of cash before the expiry of the current term of the mortgage. The central question for both the original lender and the new investor is: What price should be paid for the right to receive the remaining payments?

Suppose there are two years remaining in the five-year term of a mortgage loan. Also suppose that interest rates in general have *risen* over the past three years. If the new investor pays an amount equal to the current principal balance, her rate of return on investment will equal the contractual interest rate on the mortgage loan. Since the prevailing interest rate is now higher than that contractual rate, she will prefer the alternative of making a new loan at the prevailing market rate. Consequently, the owner of the existing mortgage must expect to receive a price lower than the outstanding balance on the mortgage. The price must be low enough that the remaining scheduled payments provide a rate of return to the purchaser equal to the *prevailing* rate on new two-year-term mortgages. Then investors will be indifferent between the alternatives of buying the existing mortgage or making a new loan.

We again turn to the Valuation Principle (presented in Section 7.2) for guidance. The fair market value of an investment is the present value of the expected payments discounted at the *prevailing market* rate of return. Adapting the Valuation Principle to the specific case of mortgage valuation,

$$\begin{pmatrix}\text{Fair market value}\\\text{of a mortgage}\end{pmatrix}=\begin{pmatrix}\text{Present value of the}\\\text{payments remaining}\\\text{in the current term}\end{pmatrix}+\begin{pmatrix}\text{Present value of the}\\\text{principal balance}\\\text{at the end of the term}\end{pmatrix}$$

TIP *The Different Roles of the Contractual Interest Rate and the Market Interest Rate*

The *contractual* rate of interest on the mortgage loan is used to calculate the size of the payments and the loan's balance at any point. The *prevailing market* rate is used as the discount rate for calculating the mortgage's fair market value at any later date.

Example 14.4C *Calculating the Fair Market Value of a Mortgage Loan Partway Through Its Term*

A \$65,000 mortgage loan was made three years ago at 11% compounded semiannually. The monthly payments for the first five-year term were based on a 20-year amortization. What price can the lender expect to receive by selling the mortgage if the current rate on new mortgage loans for a two-year term is:

a. 12% compounded semiannually?

b. 11% compounded semiannually?

c. 10% compounded semiannually?

Solution

The fair market value of the mortgage is the present value of the 24 payments remaining in the five-year term *plus* the present value of the principal balance due at the end of the term. The discount rate used should be the prevailing rate of return required on similar investments in the capital markets. From the point of view of an investor, the existing mortgage has two years to go until the end of its term. It must offer a rate of return that is competitive with the rate on new two-year term mortgage loans.

There are three steps in the solution.

Step 1: Calculate the size of the monthly payment.

Step 2: Calculate the principal balance after five years.

Step 3: Calculate the combined present value of the remaining 24 payments and the balance from Step 2. The discount rate should be the current market rate on new two-year term mortgages.

Step 1: The interest rate per payment interval for the existing mortgage is

$$i_2 = 1.055^{0.1\overline{6}} - 1 = 0.0089633939 = 0.89633939\% \text{ per month}$$

65000 (PV) 0 (FV) 0.89633939 (i) 240 (n) (COMP) (PMT) | −660.166 |

Step 2: 660.17 (+/−) (PMT) 60 (n) (COMP) (FV) | −58,873.28 |

Step 3: Calculate i_2 for each of the three current market rates.

a. $i_2 = 1.06^{0.1\overline{6}} - 1 = 0.0097587942 = 0.97587942\%$ per month

b. $i_2 = 1.055^{0.1\overline{6}} - 1 = 0.0089633939 = 0.89633939\%$ per month

c. $i_2 = 1.05^{0.1\overline{6}} - 1 = 0.0081648461 = 0.81648461\%$ per month

Using each of these discount rates, calculate the combined present value of the remaining 24 payments and the balance from Step 2.

a. 0.97587942 (i) 24 (n) (COMP) (PV) | −60,697.75 |

b. 0.89633939 (i) (COMP) (PV) | −61,722.33 |

c. 0.81648461 (i) (COMP) (PV) | −62,770.61 |

The price that the lender can expect to receive for the mortgage is:

a. $60,697.75 **b.** $61,722.33 **c.** $62,770.61

Notes: The outstanding balance on the mortgage at the time of sale (after 36 payments) is $61,722.33. The market prices calculated above provide specific examples of the three following general results.

1. When the prevailing market return *equals* the contractual rate on the mortgage, the fair market value is the *actual* principal balance currently owed on the mortgage (part **b**).
2. When the prevailing market return is *greater* than the contractual rate, investors pay *less* than the principal balance in order to obtain the higher rate of return (part **a**).
3. When the prevailing market return is *less* than the contractual rate, investors will pay *more* than the principal balance owed and still earn the competitive rate of return (part **c**).

Vendor Take-Back Mortgage The prospective purchaser of a property may propose to buy the property with a cash down payment and with the balance of the purchase price set up as a loan payable by the purchaser to the vendor. The loan would normally be secured by a mortgage on the property. A mortgage arising in this way is called a **vendor take-back mortgage**.

On a vendor take-back mortgage, it is common for the borrower to try to negotiate an interest rate that is below the current market rate. A below-market rate confers a financial benefit to the buyer at the expense of the vendor. (If the vendor were instead to receive the full purchase price in cash, he could invest the money by granting another mortgage loan at the higher current market rate.) The value of the financial benefit to the purchaser of the property is the difference between the *face* value and the *fair market* value of the vendor take-back mortgage.

Example 14.4D *Calculating the Equivalent Cash Price on a Property Sale That Includes a Vendor Take-Back Mortgage*

A house is listed for $125,000. A potential purchaser makes a "full price" offer of $125,000 subject to the vendor taking back a $75,000 mortgage at 8% compounded semiannually. Monthly payments would be based on a 25-year amortization. The prevailing market rate for mortgages with terms of five years and longer is 10% compounded semiannually. To the nearest dollar, calculate the equivalent cash value of the offer if the term of the vendor take-back mortgage is:

a. 25 years. **b.** Five years.

Solution

The equivalent cash value of the offer is the cash price that would put the vendor in the same economic position as the actual offer. Since the vendor could sell the proposed mortgage for its fair market value, the equivalent cash value of the offer is the down payment of $50,000 plus the fair market value of the vendor take-back mortgage. The steps for obtaining the mortgage's fair market value are:

Step 1: Calculate the payments on the vendor take-back mortgage loan.

Step 2: Calculate the balance owed at the end of the mortgage's term.

Step 3: Calculate the combined present value of the mortgage payments during the term and the balance payable at the end of the term. Use the prevailing market rate as the discount rate.

Step 1: The interest rate per payment interval on the take-back mortgage is

$$i_2 = 1.04^{0.1\overline{6}} - 1 = 0.0065581969 = 0.65581969\% \text{ per month}$$

75000 (PV) 0 (FV) 0.65581969 (i) 300 (n) (COMP) (PMT) | −572.410 |

a. Step 2: If the term equals the full amortization period, the balance at the end of the term will be $0.

Step 3: The market interest rate per payment interval is

$$i_2 = 1.05^{0.1\overline{6}} - 1 = 0.0081648461 = 0.81648461\% \text{ per month}$$

Discount all 300 payments at the prevailing market rate.

572.41 (+/−) (PMT) 0.81648461 (i) (COMP) (PV) | 63,993.09 |

The equivalent cash value of the offer is $50,000 + $63,993 = $113,993.

b. Step 2:

75000 (PV) 0.65581969 (i) 60 (n) (COMP) (FV) | −69,101.83 |

Step 3: Discount 60 payments and the balance at the prevailing market rate.

0.81648461 (i) (COMP) (PV) | 69,489.78 |

The equivalent cash value of the offer is $50,000 + $69,490 = $119,490.

Exercise 14.4

Answers to the odd-numbered problems are at the end of the book.

Problems 1 through 6 concern the effective cost of borrowing when a mortgage loan involves brokerage fees.

•**1.** The Gills have arranged a second mortgage loan with a face value of $21,500 at an interest rate of 13.5% compounded monthly. The face value is to be fully amortized by equal monthly payments over a five-year period. The Gills received only $20,000 of the face value, the difference being a bonus retained by the lender. What is the actual cost of borrowing, including the bonus, expressed as an effective annual rate?

•**2.** A mortgage loan having a face value of $63,000 is arranged by a mortgage broker. From this face value, the broker deducted her fee of $3000. The mortgage is written at a contract rate of 8% compounded semiannually for a five-year term. Monthly payments are calculated on a 25-year amortization. What is the annual cost of borrowing including the brokerage fee, expressed as an effective annual rate?

•**3.** A borrower has arranged a $105,000 face value, bonused mortgage loan with a broker at an interest rate of 10.8% compounded semiannually. Monthly payments are based on a 15-year amortization. A $5000 placement fee will be retained by the broker. What is the effective annual cost of the funds actually advanced to the borrower if the contractual interest rate is for:

a. A five-year term?

b. A 10-year term?

c. The entire 15-year amortization period?

•**4.** A local mortgage broker has arranged a mortgage loan with a face value of $77,500, which included a finder's fee of $2500. The loan is to be amortized by monthly payments over 20 years at 12% compounded semiannually. What is the actual cost of borrowing, expressed as an effective annual rate, if the contractual interest rate is for:

a. A three-year term?

b. A seven-year term?

c. The entire 20-year amortization period?

•**5.** A borrower has the choice between two mortgage loans. Both are to be amortized by monthly payments over 10 years. A mortgage broker will charge a fee of $2200 for an $82,200 face value loan at 10.25% compounded semiannually. A trust company will grant an $80,000 loan (with no other fees) at 10.75% compounded semiannually. Determine which loan has the lower effective annual cost of borrowing if the contractual interest rates are for:

a. A five-year term.

b. The entire 10-year amortization period.

•**6.** Calculate the effective annual cost of borrowing for each of the following three financing alternatives. All interest rates are for a seven-year term and all mortgages use a 20-year amortization to calculate the monthly payments. Bank B will lend $90,000 at 10.75% compounded semiannually. Credit union C will lend $90,000 at 10.5% compounded monthly. Mortgage broker M will lend $93,000 at 10.25% compounded semiannually but will retain $3000 as a brokerage fee.

Problems 7 through 16 require the calculation of the fair market value of mortgage loans.

•**7.** The vendor of a residential property accepted a $40,000 take-back mortgage to facilitate the sale. The agreement calls for quarterly payments to amortize the loan over 10 years at an interest rate of 7% compounded semiannually. What was the cash value (or fair market value) of the mortgage at the time of the sale if the market interest rate on 10-year term mortgages was:

a. 10.5% compounded semiannually?

b. 9% compounded semiannually?

•**8.** The vendor of a property agrees to take back a $55,000 mortgage at a rate of 7.5% compounded semiannually with monthly payments of $500 for a two-year term. Calculate the market value of the mortgage if financial institutions are charging 9.5% compounded semiannually on two-year term mortgages.

•**9.** A mortgagee wishes to sell his interest in a closed mortgage contract that was written 21 months ago. The original loan was for $60,000 at 12% compounded semiannually for a five-year term. Monthly payments are being made on a 20-year amortization schedule. What price can the mortgagee reasonably expect to receive if the current semiannually compounded interest rate on three- and four-year term mortgages is:

a. 11%? **b.** 12%? **c.** 13%?

•**10.** An investor is considering the purchase of an existing closed mortgage that was written 20 months ago to secure a $45,000 loan at 10% compounded semiannually paying $500 per month for a four-year term. What price should the investor pay for the mortgage if she requires a semiannually compounded rate of return on investment of:

a. 11%? **b.** 10%? **c.** 9%?

•**11.** A property is listed for $175,000. A potential purchaser makes an offer of $170,000, consisting of $75,000 cash and a $95,000 mortgage back to the vendor bearing interest at 8% compounded semiannually with monthly payments for a 10-year term and a 10-year amortization. Calculate the equivalent cash value of the offer if 10-year mortgage rates in the market are at 10.25% compounded semiannually.

•**12.** What is the equivalent cash value of the offer in Problem 11 if the vendor financing arrangement is for the same 10-year amortization but with:

a. A five-year term? **b.** A one-year term?

•**13.** The owner of a property listed at $145,000 is considering two offers. Offer C is for $140,000 cash. Offer M is for $50,000 cash and a mortgage back to the vendor for $100,000 at a rate of 8% compounded semiannually and payments of $750 per month for the five-year term. If current five-year rates are 10.25% compounded semiannually, what is the cash equivalent value of M's offer?

•**14.** You are interested in purchasing a house listed for \$180,000. The owner seems quite determined to stay at the asking price, but you think that the true market value is \$165,000. It may be that the owner would accept an offer whose nominal value is the psychologically important \$180,000 figure but whose cash value is close to your \$165,000 figure. What would be the cash value of the following offer if long-term mortgage rates were 10.5% compounded semiannually? The offer is for the "full" price of \$180,000, consisting of \$60,000 down and the balance by a \$120,000 mortgage in favour of the vendor. Monthly payments for a 20-year term are to be based on a 20-year amortization and an interest rate of 8.5% compounded semiannually.

•**15.** The Phams are two years into the first five-year term of a 25-year \$80,000 mortgage loan at 10.5% compounded semiannually. Interest rates on three-year term mortgage loans are now 9% compounded semiannually. A job transfer necessitates the sale of the Phams' home. To prepay the closed mortgage, the mortgage contract requires that the Phams pay a penalty equal to the greater of:

a. Three months' interest on the balance.

b. The difference between the fair market value of the mortgage and the balance.

What would be the amount of the penalty if they paid out the balance after two years of monthly payments?

•**16.** A \$75,000 mortgage loan at 9% compounded semiannually has a five-year term and a 25-year amortization. Prepayment of the loan at any time within the first five years leads to a penalty equal to the greater of:

a. Three months' interest on the balance.

b. The difference between the fair market value of the mortgage and the balance.

What would be the amount of the penalty if the balance were paid out just after the nineteenth monthly payment and the prevailing rate on three- and four-year-term mortgages were 8% compounded semiannually?

Review Problems

Answers to the odd-numbered review problems are at the end of the book.

1. Jessica bought a $1150 television set for 25% down and the balance to be paid with interest at 11.25% compounded monthly in six equal monthly payments. Construct the full amortization schedule for the debt. Calculate the total interest paid.

◆ 2. Givens, Hong, and Partners obtained a $7000 term loan at 10.75% compounded annually for new boardroom furniture. Prepare a complete amortization schedule in which the loan is repaid by equal semiannual payments over three years.

3. A $28,000 loan at 10.5% compounded quarterly is to be repaid by equal quarterly payments over a seven-year term.
   a. What amount of principal will be repaid by the sixth payment?
   b. What will be the interest portion of the twenty-second payment?
   c. How much will the principal be reduced by Payments 10 to 15 inclusive?
   d. How much interest will be paid in the second year?

◆ 4. A 20-year annuity was purchased with $180,000 that had accumulated in an RRSP. The annuity provides a semiannually compounded rate of return of 7.5% and makes equal month-end payments.
   a. What amount of principal will be included in Payment 134?
   b. What will be the interest portion of Payment 210?
   c. How much will the principal be reduced by Payments 75 to 100 inclusive?
   d. How much interest will be paid in the sixth year?

5. Metro Construction received $60,000 in vendor financing at 10.5% compounded semiannually for the purchase of a loader. The contract requires semiannual payments of $10,000 until the debt is paid off. Construct the complete amortization schedule for the debt. How much total interest will be paid over the life of the loan?

6. Suppose that the loan in Problem 5 permits an additional prepayment of principal on any scheduled payment date. Prepare another amortization schedule that reflects a prepayment of $5000 with the third scheduled payment. How much interest is saved as a result of the prepayment?

7. An annuity providing a rate of return of 7.5% compounded monthly was purchased for $45,000. The annuity pays $500 at the end of each month.
   a. How much of the thirty-seventh payment will be interest?
   b. What will be the principal portion of the ninety-second payment?
   c. How much interest will be paid by Payments 85 to 96 inclusive?
   d. How much principal will be repaid in the fifth year?
   e. What will be the final payment?

◆ 8. Niagara Haulage obtained an $80,000 loan at 9.75% compounded monthly to build a storage shed. Construct a partial amortization schedule for payments of $1200 per month showing details of the first two payments, Payments 41 and 42, and the last two payments.

◆ 9. The interest rate for the first five years of a $90,000 mortgage loan is 9.25% compounded semiannually. Monthly payments are calculated using a 20-year amortization.
   a. What will be the principal balance at the end of the five-year term?
   b. What will be the new payments if the loan is renewed at 10.5% compounded semiannually (and the original amortization period is continued)?

◆ **10.** A mortgage calls for monthly payments of $802.23 for 25 years. If the loan was for $95,000, calculate the semiannually compounded nominal rate of interest on the loan.

◆ **11.** A $25,000 home improvement (mortgage) loan charges interest at 9.75% compounded monthly for a three-year term. Monthly payments are based on a 10-year amortization and rounded up to the next $10. What will be the principal balance at the end of the first term?

◆ **12.** The interest rate for the first five years of a $95,000 mortgage is 9.5% compounded semiannually. Monthly payments are based on a 25-year amortization. If a $3000 prepayment is made at the end of the third year:

a. How much will the amortization period be shortened?

b. What will be the principal balance at the end of the five-year term?

◆ **13.** After two years of the first five-year term at 10.25% compounded semiannually, Dan and Laurel decide to take advantage of the privilege of increasing the payments on their $110,000 mortgage loan by 10%. The monthly payments were originally calculated for a 25-year amortization.

a. How much will the amortization period be shortened?

b. What will be the principal balance at the end of the five-year term?

◆ **14.** A mortgage broker has arranged a mortgage loan with a face value of $46,500, which includes a finder's fee of $1500. The loan is to be amortized by monthly payments over a 15-year period at 10.25% compounded semiannually. What is the actual cost of borrowing, expressed as an effective annual rate, if the contractual interest rate is for:

a. A three-year term? **b.** A five-year term?

◆ **15.** Ms. Finch wishes to sell a closed mortgage contract just after receiving the twenty-ninth payment. The original loan was for $60,000 at 11% compounded semiannually for a five-year term. Monthly payments are being made on a 25-year amortization schedule. What price can she reasonably expect to receive if the current semiannually compounded interest rate on two- and three-year term mortgages is:

a. 10%? **b.** 12%?

◆ **16.** The owner of a property listed at $195,000 is considering two offers. Mr. and Mrs. Sharpe are offering $191,000 cash. The Conlins' "full-price" offer consists of $65,000 cash and a mortgage back to the vendor for $130,000 at a rate of 7.5% compounded semiannually with payments of $1000 per month for a five-year term. If current five-year rates are 8.5% compounded semiannually, what is the equivalent cash value of the Conlins' offer? Which offer should be accepted?

Self-Test Exercise

Answers to the self-test problems are at the end of the book.

1. A $16,000 loan is to be amortized by monthly payments over a five-year period. The interest rate on the loan is 10.8% compounded monthly.

a. What is the interest portion of the twenty-ninth payment?

b. Determine the principal portion of the forty-sixth payment.

c. How much will the principal be reduced in the second year?

d. How much interest will be paid in the third year?

◆ **2.** The interest rate on a $6400 loan is 10% compounded semiannually. If the loan is to be repaid by monthly payments over a four-year term, prepare a partial amortization schedule showing details of the first two payments, Payments 34 and 35, and the last two payments.

◆◆ **3.** A $255,000 amount from an RRSP is used to purchase an annuity paying $7500 at the end of each quarter. The annuity provides an annually compounded rate of return of 10%.

a. What will be the amount of the final payment?

b. What will be the interest portion of the twenty-seventh payment?

c. What will be the principal portion of the fifty-third payment?

d. How much will the principal balance be reduced by Payments 14 to 20 inclusive?

e. How much interest will be paid by the payments received in the sixth year?

◆ **4.** A mortgage contract for $45,000 written 10 years ago is just at the end of its second five-year term. The interest rates were 13% compounded semiannually for the first term and 11.75% compounded semiannually for the second term. If monthly payments throughout have been based on a 25-year amortization, calculate the principal balance at the end of the second term.

◆ **5.** The interest rate for the first three years of an $87,000 mortgage is 9.5% compounded semiannually. Monthly payments are based on a 20-year amortization. If a $4000 prepayment is made at the end of the sixteenth month:

a. How much will the amortization period be shortened?

b. What will be the principal balance at the end of the three-year term?

◆ **6.** Calculate the annual cost of borrowing, expressed as an effective interest rate, if a mortgage broker retains $3300 from a $110,000 face value mortgage loan written at 11% compounded semiannually for a five-year term. The required monthly payments would amortize the face value in 25 years.

◆ **7.** There are two offers on a property listed at $185,000. Mr. Smith is offering $183,000 cash. Ms. Jones's offer consists of $100,000 cash and a mortgage back to the vendor for $90,000 at a rate of 7.5% compounded semiannually and payments of $700 per month for a three-year term. If current three-year rates are 9.5% compounded semiannually, what is the equivalent cash value of Ms. Jones's offer?

www.Exercise.com

Go to the CM Canada Mortgage Web site (www.canadamortgage.com/tools/amortization.cgi) referred to in Section 14.3. Enter the data for the base case of a $100,000 mortgage loan at 7.2% compounded semiannually with monthly payments, a five-year term, and a 25-year amortization.

a. What is the total interest paid over the life of the loan? What is the balance at the end of the five-year term?

b. What is the first year in which the principal portion of the 12 payments exceeds the interest portion?

c. How much will the amortization period be shortened if each loan payment is increased by $50? What is the reduction in the total interest paid?

d. How much will the amortization period be shortened (from the base case) if a $500 balloon payment is made at the end of each year? What is the reduction in the total interest paid?

e. Returning to the base case, what will the monthly payment be upon renewal at 8% compounded semiannually if the original 25-year amortization is continued?

Summary of Notation and Key Formulas

In all but the last of the following equations, the relevant interest rate or discount rate is the loan's contractual rate of interest (per payment interval).

$$\text{Original loan} = \left[\begin{array}{c}\text{Present value of all of the payments} \\ \text{(discounted at the } \textit{contractual} \\ \textit{rate of interest on the loan}\text{)}\end{array}\right]$$

We frequently use this concept to calculate the payment size or amortization period given the original loan.

$$\text{Principal balance} = \left[\begin{array}{c}\text{Present value of the remaining payments} \\ \text{(discounted at the } \textit{contractual} \\ \textit{rate of interest on the loan}\text{)}\end{array}\right]$$

Prospective Method for calculating a loan's balance.

$$\text{Balance} = \left(\begin{array}{c}\text{Future value of} \\ \text{the original loan}\end{array}\right) - \left(\begin{array}{c}\text{Future value of the} \\ \text{payments already made}\end{array}\right)$$

Retrospective Method for calculating a loan's balance.

$$\text{Final payment} = (1 + i) \times \left(\begin{array}{c}\text{Balance after the} \\ \text{second-to-last payment}\end{array}\right)$$

The final loan payment usually differs from the others.

$$\text{Interest component} = i \times (\text{Balance after the previous payment})$$

$$\text{Principal component} = \left(\begin{array}{c}\text{Balance after the} \\ \text{previous payment}\end{array}\right) - \left(\begin{array}{c}\text{Balance after the} \\ \text{current payment}\end{array}\right)$$

The interest and principal components of a loan payment may be calculated from nearby balances.

$$\left(\begin{array}{c}\text{Fair market value} \\ \text{of a mortgage}\end{array}\right) = \left(\begin{array}{c}\text{Present value of the} \\ \text{payments remaining} \\ \text{in the current term}\end{array}\right) + \left(\begin{array}{c}\text{Present value of the} \\ \text{principal balance} \\ \text{at the end of the term}\end{array}\right)$$

Use the prevailing mortgage interest rate as the discount rate.

List of Key Terms

CHAPTER OUTLINE

LEARNING OBJECTIVES

After completing this chapter, you will be able to:

- Calculate the market price of a bond on any date
- Calculate the yield to maturity of a bond on an interest payment date
- Calculate the payment for a sinking fund
- Prepare a sinking fund schedule

CHAPTER

15

Bonds and Sinking Funds

THE PRIMARY MEANS BY WHICH our three levels of government and publicly traded corporations finance their long-term debt is by issuing the type of bonds described in this chapter. At the end of 1998, over $325 billion of the Government of Canada's debt was financed by these "marketable" bonds (compared to about $96 billion by Treasury Bills and $29 billion by Canada Savings Bonds). The aggregate total of provincial bonds exceeds that of Government of Canada bonds! Corporate bonds totalling almost $140 billion represented about two-thirds of all corporate long-term debt at the end of 1998.

Even though you may never directly invest in them, these bonds affect your financial future in two significant ways. Interest and any reduction of principal on federal and provincial debt are paid primarily from tax revenues. A significant portion (in the 20% to 25% range) of your federal and provincial taxes is required to pay interest on federal and provincial debts. On the other hand, when you contribute to a pension plan or invest in a balanced mutual fund or a bond mutual fund, you will indirectly receive interest payments from these bonds.

The purchaser of a bond is not "locked in" for the entire lifetime of the bond. There is an active, efficient "bond market" for the sale and purchase of bonds after their initial issue. In this chapter, you will learn how to calculate the bond prices that are reported in the financial news.

15.1 Basic Concepts and Definitions

A bond is a certificate representing the borrower's debt obligation to the bond holder. The borrower is usually called the bond issuer. We will adopt the widespread practice of using the term *bond* loosely to refer to both true bonds and debentures. The technical distinction between a bond and a debenture is that a **bond** is secured by specific assets of the borrower, whereas a **debenture** is backed only by the general credit of the borrower. Therefore, Government of Canada "bonds" are, in fact, debentures since no particular assets secure them. The distinction is not important for the mathematics of bonds.

Unlike term loans where each payment includes a principal portion that reduces the debt, bonds require the borrower to make periodic payments of interest only. Then, on the **maturity date** of the bond, the full principal amount is repaid along with the final interest payment. Bonds are issued with maturities ranging from two to 30 years.

The bond certificate sets out the main features of the loan contract. The following items are part of the information you need to calculate a bond's market price.

- The **issue date** is the date on which the loan was made and on which interest starts to accrue.
- The **face value** (or *denomination*) is the principal amount that the issuer is required to pay the bond holder on the maturity date. The face value is usually the principal amount borrowed when the bond was issued. The most common face values are $1000, $5000, and $25,000, although larger denominations are often issued to institutional investors.
- The **coupon rate**[1] is the contractual rate of interest paid on the face value of the bond. It is a *semiannually* compounded rate and is normally fixed for the life of the bond. The vast majority of bonds pay interest at six-month intervals measured from the issue date.[2] Therefore, such interest payments form an ordinary *simple* annuity.

You should be clear on the distinction between *savings* bonds (such as Canada Savings Bonds described in Section 8.5) and *marketable* bonds discussed in this chapter. You can cash in a *savings* bond before its scheduled maturity date and receive the full face value plus accrued interest. *Marketable* bonds such as Government of Canada bonds do not have this open-redemption privilege. If you

---

[1] This term originated many years ago when it was customary for the bond certificate to have interest coupons attached to its margin. At each interest payment date, the bond holder would clip off the matured coupon and present it at a bank to receive payment in cash. Most bonds are now registered in the owner's name, and interest payments are made by cheques sent through the mail.

[2] If a bond's maturity date is the last day of a month, both semiannual coupons are paid on the *last* days of the appropriate months. For example, a bond maturing on September 30 pays its March coupon on March 31 (rather than on March 30). A bond maturing on October 31 pays an April coupon on April 30.

If a bond's maturity date is August 29 or 30, it pays a February coupon on February 28 (or February 29 in a leap year).

want to liquidate a marketable bond before it matures, you must sell it through an investment dealer who participates in the "bond market."[3] Let us now address the question of what determines the market value of a bond.

15.2 Bond Price on an Interest Payment Date

Most bonds pay interest semiannually, offer no early redemption privileges, and are redeemed for their face value at maturity. In this section we are concerned with pricing bonds having these typical features. But before we begin the mathematics of bond pricing, you should understand *why* bond prices change in the bond market.

Dependence of Bond Price on Prevailing Interest Rates

On the date a bond is issued, its coupon rate must be a competitive rate of return. The bond issuer cannot expect a prudent investor to buy a new 7% coupon bond (for the full face value) if the investor can earn an 8% rate of return from other investments of similar risk.

Subsequent to the issue date, prevailing interest rates in the financial markets change (and the coupon rate offered on *subsequent new* bond issues must change accordingly). However, the coupon rate on a previously issued bond is *fixed* for the life of the bond. If its coupon rate *exceeds* the current competitive rate of return, investors will be willing to pay *more* than face value to acquire the bond. If the bond's coupon rate is *less* than the current competitive rate of return, investors will not buy it unless its price is a suitable amount *below* face value.

To make our discussion more specific, consider the four hypothetical Government of Canada bonds listed in Table 15.1. The issue dates and initial terms have been chosen so that, as of today's date, every bond has five years remaining until maturity. Consequently, the four $1000 face-value bonds represent identical investments except for differing coupon rates. The coupon rate on the *newly issued* Bond A is 10% compounded semiannually. Therefore, we can conclude that the prevailing competitive rate of return for five-year maturity bonds is also 10% compounded semiannually.

Table 15.1 *Relative Prices of $1000 Face Value Bonds*

Bond	Issue date	Initial term (years)	Coupon rate (%)	Bond price
A	Today	5	10	$1000
B	5 years ago	10	12	More than $1000
C	10 years ago	15	10	$1000
D	15 years ago	20	8	Less than $1000

[3] For the most part, bonds are not bought and sold at a particular physical location corresponding to the stock exchanges for common shares. The "bond market" consists of investment dealers who are linked by telecommunications networks, and who act as intermediaries between bond buyers and sellers.

We will now develop the reasoning for the relative bond prices indicated in the last column. Bonds C and A both carry a 10% coupon and have five years remaining until maturity. Therefore, Bond C is identical to Bond A from this point onward. Its market value will always be the same as the market value of Bond A. Today that value is $1000. When a bond trades at its face value, it is said to trade "at par." Any bond will trade at par if its coupon rate equals the prevailing rate of return required in the bond market.

Bond B carries a coupon rate that is 2% above the current competitive rate. It will pay $120 interest per year ($60 every six months), whereas Bond A will pay only $100 per year. If you could buy Bond B for $1000, you would earn a 12% rate of return on your investment. Since the prevailing rate of return is only 10%, investors will prefer Bond B and bid its price above $1000. As the purchase price rises, the rate of return on the purchase price declines (because the future interest payments to the bond holder remain fixed, regardless of prevailing rates and regardless of the amount paid for the bond).

TRAP *Don't Overlook the Capital Gain or Capital Loss Component of Total Return*

You might be inclined to conclude that Bond B's price will rise to $1200 for the following reason. The $120 annual interest from Bond B represents a 10% rate of return on an investment of $1200. This will provide an investor with the prevailing competitive rate of return. Is there any error or omission in this line of reasoning?

Yes. If you pay $1200 for Bond B, you will suffer a $200 capital loss over the next five years because you will receive only the $1000 face value at maturity. One year's "share" of the capital loss is $\frac{\$200}{5} = \$40$. This is 3.3% of the $1200 investment. Hence, the average annual rate of *total* return on a $1200 purchase price will be only about 10% − 3.3% = 6.7%. When you pay *more* than face value for a bond, you must factor in the effect of the overall *capital loss.* In the present example, the market value of the bond will be above $1000 but well below $1200 in order to deliver a rate of *total* return of 10% compounded semiannually.

The market value of Bond B is the price at which the interest payments, combined with the *capital loss,* provide a rate of *total* return equal to 10% compounded semiannually.

Bond D pays only $80 interest per year ($40 every six months). Investors will not buy Bond D until its price falls to an appropriate level below $1000. If you buy a bond for *less* than its face value, you will realize a capital *gain* when the face value is received at maturity. The market value of Bond D is the price at which the interest payments, combined with the capital gain, provide a rate of *total* return equal to 10% compounded semiannually.

Summary The market value of Bond B is more than its face value because its coupon rate exceeds the required rate of return in the bond market. In other words, if the market rate *falls below* the coupon rate, the bond's price *rises above* its face value. The market value of Bond D is less than its face value because its coupon rate is less than the required rate of return in the bond market. In other words, if the market rate *rises above* the coupon rate, the bond's price *falls below* its face value. This inverse relation between market rate of return and market value is easily remembered using the "teeter-totter model" shown in Figure 15.1.

Figure 15.1 *Effects of Interest Rate Changes on Bond Prices*

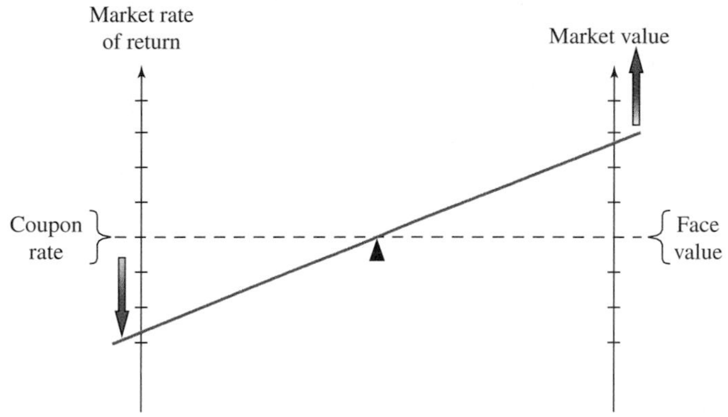

In the particular case shown in the diagram, the market rate of return has fallen below the bond's coupon rate. "Pushing" the market rate of return "end" of the teeter-totter down below the coupon rate "raises" the market value "end" above the bond's face value. (This is the Bond B case.) The more the market rate falls below the coupon rate, the higher the bond price will rise above the face value. If prevailing rates in the bond market start to rise (from the level depicted in the diagram), all bond prices will start to decline. But a particular bond's price will not fall below face value until the market's required rate of return rises above that bond's coupon rate.

Later in this section we will add another feature to the model that will make it particularly helpful.

Calculating a Bond's Price on an Interest Payment Date

The pricing or valuation of bonds is yet another application where we use the Valuation Principle to determine an investment's fair market value. To apply the Valuation Principle to bonds, we need to:

1. Determine the amount and timing of future payments.
2. Determine the rate of return currently required in the bond market.
3. Calculate the present value of the future payments using this rate of return as the discount rate.

If we let

$$2b = \text{Coupon rate (compounded semiannually) and}$$
$$FV = \text{Face value of the bond}$$

then the interest rate for the six-month interest payment interval is b and the semiannual interest payment is:

$$b \times (\text{Face value}) = b \times FV$$

In this section we consider the special case where a bond is being sold on an interest payment date (with the interest payment going to the seller). Figure 15.2

CAUGHT IN THE WEB

The current rate of return required in the bond market on Government of Canada bonds may be found at www.bank-banque-canada.ca/english/bonds.htm. The rate is given for four different maturities on each of the preceding five business days. An inspection of the table will give you a sense of the size of the day-to-day changes in the market's required rate of return.

Figure 15.2 *Expected Payments from a Bond*

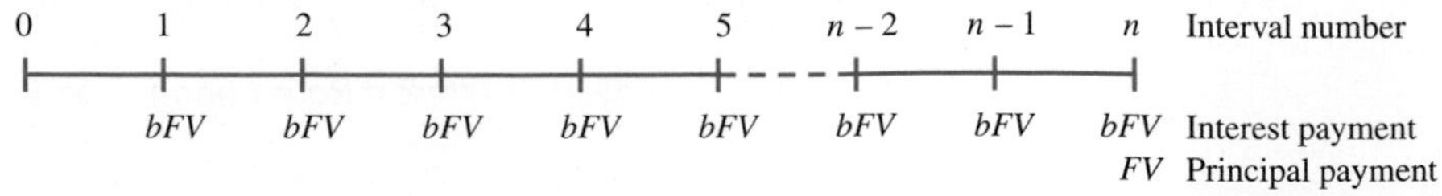

illustrates the future payments that a prospective purchaser/investor can expect to receive. There are n interest payments remaining until the bond matures. Each interest payment is $b(FV)$. At the time of the final interest payment, the face value FV will also be received. According to the Valuation Principle, the fair market value of the bond is the present value of these future payments discounted at the *prevailing rate of return* in the bond market. That is,

$$\begin{pmatrix}\text{Fair market}\\\text{value of a bond}\end{pmatrix} = \begin{pmatrix}\text{Present value of the}\\\text{interest payments}\end{pmatrix} + \begin{pmatrix}\text{Present value of}\\\text{the face value}\end{pmatrix}$$

Since the interest payments form an ordinary annuity, we will use formula (10-2) to obtain the present value of the interest payments. The present value of the face value can be calculated using $PV = FV(1 + i)^{-n}$. Hence, the combined present value is

BOND PRICE (ON AN INTEREST PAYMENT DATE)

$$\textbf{(15-1)} \qquad \text{Bond price} = b(FV)\left[\frac{1-(1+i)^{-n}}{i}\right] + FV(1+i)^{-n}$$

TIP *THE DIFFERENT ROLES OF THE COUPON RATE AND THE BOND MARKET RATE OF RETURN*

The bond's coupon rate is used only to determine the size of the periodic interest payments. The prevailing rate of return in the bond market is used to discount the future payments when calculating the bond's price.

POINT OF INTEREST

SHORT-TERM INVESTING IN LONG-TERM BONDS

The dollar value of transactions in the Canadian bond market averaged about \$100 billion per month in 1998. It's an astounding number that, standing alone, is hard to put into perspective. The following information is helpful in gaining a sense of the activity in and the importance of the bond market.

Stocks and the stock market receive vastly more coverage in the media than bonds and the bond market. But the dollar value of transactions in the bond market in 1998 was essentially twice the aggregate dollar value of share transactions on all four Canadian stock exchanges!

About 90% of bond market trading is in Government of Canada issues. The value of 1998 transactions in Government of Canada bonds was about \$1100 billion. But the aggregate dollar value of all outstanding Government of Canada bonds was only (only?) about \$325 billion. How can the value of transactions in a year exceed the amount potentially available for sale? By selling the same bonds more than once in the year. In effect, the entire \$325 billion of outstanding Government of Canada bonds were sold more than three times during the year! This makes the average holding period less than four months. Now you understand why institutional bond traders are always draped in telephones (and why bond "trading" is a more common term than bond "investing").

Example 15.2A *Calculating the Price of a Bond on an Interest Payment Date*

Calculate the market value of Bonds B, C, and D in Table 15.1.

Solution

Since the new issue of five-year bonds carries a 10% coupon rate, the current competitive rate of return on five-year bonds is 10% compounded semiannually. Therefore, we will use $i = 5\%$ to discount the payments from all three bonds.

For Bond B, $FV = \$1000$, $n = 10$, $b = 6\%$, $b(FV) = \$60$.
For Bond C, $FV = \$1000$, $n = 10$, $b = 5\%$, $b(FV) = \$50$.
For Bond D, $FV = \$1000$, $n = 10$, $b = 4\%$, $b(FV) = \$40$.

Algebraic Solution

$$\begin{aligned}
\text{Price of Bond B} &= b(FV)\left[\frac{1-(1+i)^{-n}}{i}\right] + FV(1+i)^{-n} \\
&= \$60\left(\frac{1-1.05^{-10}}{0.05}\right) + \$1000(1.05^{-10}) \\
&= \$463.304 + \$613.913 \\
&= \$1077.22 \\
\text{Price of Bond C} &= \$50\left(\frac{1-1.05^{-10}}{0.05}\right) + \$1000(1.05^{-10}) \\
&= \$386.087 + \$613.913 \\
&= \$1000.00 \\
\text{Price of Bond D} &= \$40\left(\frac{1-1.05^{-10}}{0.05}\right) + \$1000(1.05^{-10}) \\
&= \$308.869 + \$613.913 \\
&= \$922.78
\end{aligned}$$

Financial Calculator Solution

The combined present value of the interest payments and the face value can be obtained in a single step. For Bond B,

60 (PMT) 1000 (FV) 5 (*i*) 10 (*n*) (COMP) (PV) [−1077.22]

For Bond C,

50 (PMT) (COMP) (PV) [−1000.00]

For Bond D,

40 (PMT) (COMP) (PV) $\boxed{-922.78}$

The prices of Bonds B, C, and D are \$1077.22, \$1000, and \$922.78, respectively. These prices confirm the relative prices deduced in the last column of Table 15.1.

Postscript: Note how the purchaser of Bond B will earn the market rate of return (10% compounded semiannually) that the Valuation Principle impounds in the market price. The \$120 annual interest by itself represents an income yield of

$$\frac{\$120}{\$1077.22} \times 100\% = 11.1\%$$

However, over the entire five years there will be a capital *loss* of \$1077.22 − \$1000 = \$77.22. The capital loss per year is

$$\frac{\$77.22}{5} = \$15.44 \text{ representing a capital loss yield of } \frac{\$15.44}{\$1077.22} \times 100\% = 1.4\%$$

The rate of *total* return per year is *approximately* 11.1% − 1.4% = 9.7%. (The reason this is an approximation is that the timing of payments and compounding have been ignored.)

Example 15.2B *Calculating a Bond's Price Change Resulting from a Change in the Prevailing Interest Rate*

A \$5000 face value bond has a coupon rate of 6.6% and a maturity date of March 1, 2018. Interest is paid semiannually. On September 1, 2000, the prevailing interest rate on long-term bonds abruptly rose from 6% to 6.2% compounded semiannually. What were the bond's prices before and after the interest rate change?

Solution

Given: $FV = \$5000,\ b = \dfrac{6.6\%}{2} = 3.3\%$

September 1, 2000 was an interest payment date, after which $15\frac{1}{2}$ years remain until maturity of the bond ($n = 31$). The semiannual interest paid on the bond is

$$b(FV) = 0.033(\$5000) = \$165$$

On September 1, 2000, the prevailing periodic market rate rose from

$$i = \frac{6\%}{2} = 3\% \qquad \text{to} \qquad i = \frac{6.2\%}{2} = 3.1\%$$

Algebraic Solution

$$\begin{aligned}\text{Bond price before rate increase} &= \$165\left(\frac{1 - 1.03^{-31}}{0.03}\right) + \$5000(1.03^{-31})\\ &= 3300.071 + \$1999.936\\ &= \$5300.01\end{aligned}$$

$$\text{Bond price after rate increase} = \$165\left(\frac{1 - 1.031^{-31}}{0.031}\right) + \$5000(1.031^{-31})$$
$$= \$3256.708 + \$1940.669$$
$$= \$5197.38$$

The bond's price dropped from \$5300.01 to \$5197.38 as a result of the interest rate increase. [Although the bond's price remained above the face value (since $b > i$), the bond price decreased by \$128.51.]

Financial Calculator Solution

Calculate the bond price before the market rate increase.

165 (PMT) 5000 (FV) 3 (i) 31 (n) (COMP) (PV) [−5300.01]

Calculate the bond price after the market rate increase.

3.1 (i) (COMP) (PV) [−5197.38]

The bond's price dropped from \$5300.01 to \$5197.38 as a result of the interest rate increase. [Although the bond's price remained above the face value (since $b > i$), the bond price decreased by \$128.51.]

Example 15.2C Calculating the Capital Gain from an Investment in Bonds

David Healey purchased 10 bonds, each with a face value of \$1000 and paying an 8% coupon rate. On the purchase date, the bonds still had $9\frac{1}{2}$ years remaining until maturity, and the market rate of return for bonds of this maturity was 10% compounded semiannually. Two and one-half years later, when the interest rate had declined to 8.5% compounded semiannually, he sold the bonds. What was the capital gain (or loss) on the bond investment?

Solution

Capital gain = 10(Selling price per bond − Purchase price per bond)
For calculating the purchase price of each bond,

$$FV = \$1000,\ b = \frac{8\%}{2} = 4\%,\ b(FV) = \$40,\ n = 2(9.5) = 19, \text{ and } i = \frac{10\%}{2} = 5\%$$

For calculating the selling price of each bond,

$$FV = \$1000,\ b = 4\%,\ b(FV) = \$40,\ n = 2(7) = 14, \text{ and } i = \frac{8.5\%}{2} = 4.25\%$$

Algebraic Solution

$$\text{Purchase price} = \$40\left(\frac{1-1.05^{-19}}{0.05}\right) + \$1000(1.05^{-19})$$
$$= \$483.413 + \$395.734$$
$$= \$879.15$$

$$\text{Selling price} = \$40\left(\frac{1-1.0425^{-14}}{0.0425}\right) + \$1000(1.0425^{-14})$$
$$= \$415.636 + \$558.387$$
$$= \$974.02$$

$$\text{Capital gain} = 10(\$974.02 - \$879.15)$$
$$= \$948.70$$

Financial Calculator Solution

Compute the purchase price of each bond.

40 (PMT) 1000 (FV) 5 (i) 19 (n) (COMP) (PV) | −879.15 |

Compute the selling price of each bond.

4.25 (i) 14 (n) (COMP) (PV) | −974.02 |

$$\text{Capital gain} = 10(\$974.02 - \$879.15) = \$948.70$$

Bond Premium and Bond Discount Figure 15.3 shows graphs of bond price versus the prevailing market rate of return for two 10% coupon, $1000 face value bonds. One bond has five years remaining until maturity, and the other has 10 years until maturity.

Figure 15.3 *Bond Price versus Market Rate of Return for Two Maturities of 10% Coupon Bonds*

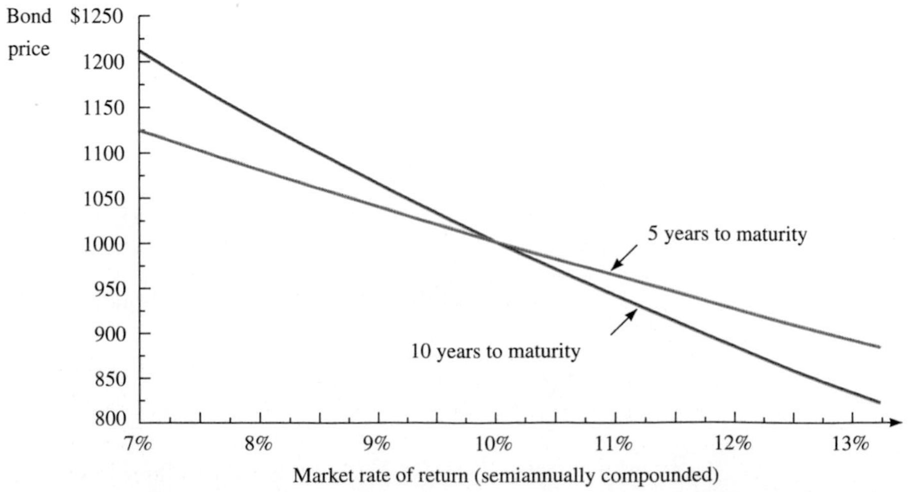

For the reasons discussed earlier, the market values of both bonds are below their \$1000 face value when the market rate of return exceeds the 10% coupon rate. In this circumstance, we say that both bonds trade at a discount. The amount of the discount is

$$\textbf{Bond discount} = \text{Face value} - \text{Bond price} \qquad \text{when } i > b$$

The discount is larger for the bond with the longer maturity.

Similarly, the market values of both bonds are above their face value when the market rate of return is less than the 10% coupon rate. In this circumstance, we say that both bonds trade at a premium. The amount of the premium is

$$\textbf{Bond premium} = \text{Bond price} - \text{Face value} \qquad \text{when } i < b$$

The premium is larger for the bond with the longer maturity.

The dependence of the discount or premium on the time remaining until maturity can be included on our teeter-totter model as shown in Figure 15.4. Think of bonds with longer maturities as "sitting" further out from the pivot point on the right arm of the teeter-totter. For a given interest rate movement of the left arm, bonds further away from the pivot point will move through a larger vertical distance. That is, longer-term bonds will undergo a greater change in market value than shorter-term bonds.

Figure 15.4 *Dependence of Bond Premium on Time to Maturity*

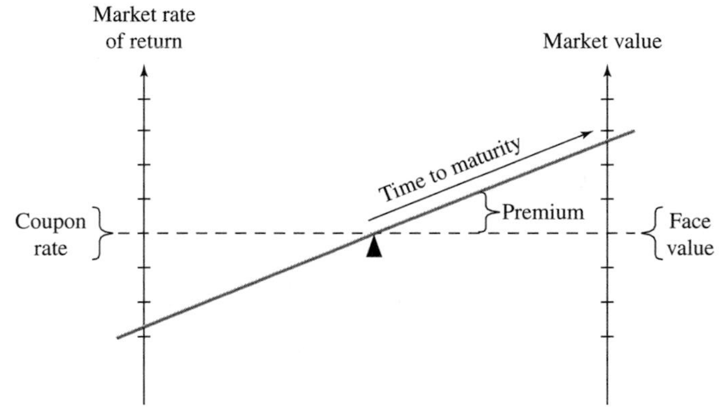

Concept Questions

1. Name four variables that affect a bond's price. Which ones, if any, have an inverse effect on the bond's price? That is, for which variables does a lower value of the variable result in a higher bond price?
2. Under what circumstance can you realize a capital gain on a bond investment?
3. Assuming that the bond issuer does not default on any payments, is it possible to lose money on a bond investment? Discuss briefly.
4. On a recent interest payment date, a bond's price exceeded its face value. If the prevailing market rate of return does not change thereafter, will the bond's premium be different on later interest payment dates? Explain.

5. If you are firmly convinced that prevailing interest rates will decline, what adjustment should you make to the average maturity of bonds in your bond portfolio?

Exercise 15.2

Answers to the odd-numbered problems are at the end of the book.

Note: Unless otherwise indicated, assume that:

- The face value of a bond is $1000.
- Bond interest is paid semiannually.
- The bond was originally issued at its face value.
- Bonds are redeemed at their face value at maturity.
- Market rates of return are compounded semiannually.

Calculate the purchase price of each of the $1000 face value bonds in Problems 1 through 8.

Problem	Issue date	Maturity date	Purchase date	Coupon rate (%)	Market rate (%)
1.	June 1, 1993	June 1, 2013	June 1, 1996	8.2	7.5
2.	March 15, 1992	March 15, 2017	Sept 15, 1999	9.0	6.0
3.	Jan 1, 1997	Jan 1, 2012	July 1, 1997	7.3	6.3
4.	Sept 20, 1996	Sept 20, 2006	Sept 20, 1997	7.4	6.1
5.	Aug 1, 1998	Aug 1, 2028	Aug 1, 2000	5.9	6.2
6.	July 1, 1999	July 1, 2019	Jan 1, 2001	5.6	6.5
7.	June 1, 1994	June 1, 2019	June 1, 1998	9.6	9.0
8.	Nov 1, 1998	Nov 1, 2028	May 1, 2000	5.1	6.1

9. A $1000, 9.5% coupon bond has $13\frac{1}{2}$ years remaining until maturity. Calculate the bond premium if the required return in the bond market is 8.2% compounded semiannually.

10. A $1000, 11.25% coupon bond has $8\frac{1}{2}$ years remaining until maturity. Calculate the bond premium if the required return in the bond market is 8.5% compounded semiannually.

11. A $1000, 9% coupon bond has 16 years remaining until maturity. Calculate the bond discount if the required return in the bond market is 10.2% compounded semiannually.

12. A $1000, 8.25% coupon bond has $21\frac{1}{2}$ years remaining until maturity. Calculate the bond discount if the required return in the bond market is 9.7% compounded semiannually.

13. What would you expect to pay for a $1000 face value bond with 15 years remaining to maturity and a coupon rate of 11% compounded semiannually? The yield to maturity on similar bonds is 8.75% compounded semiannually. (Source: ICB course on Wealth Valuation.)

14. You have two $1000 face value bonds that are identical in every respect except maturity. Bond A matures in two years and Bond B matures in

10 years. They currently trade at par and pay 6% compounded semiannually. Suppose the required rate of return for these bonds suddenly drops to 5.5% compounded semiannually. What are their new prices? Is there a general rule which this problem demonstrates? (Source: ICB course on Wealth Valuation.)

15. Eight years ago, Mary bought a $20,000, 15-year bond with a coupon rate of 10% compounded semiannually. The prevailing rate of return on bonds of this quality is now 6.5% compounded semiannually. How much will Mary receive for her bond if she sells it? (Source: CIFP course on Wealth Accumulation.)

16. Jared wants to buy a four-year, $30,000 bond having a coupon rate of 11% compounded semiannually. At the moment, comparable investments are realizing a return of 7% compounded semiannually. What price can Jared expect to pay for the bond? (Source: CIFP course on Strategic Investment Planning.)

17. Bonds A, B, C, and D all have a face value of $1000 and carry a 10% coupon. The time remaining until maturity is five, 10, 15, and 25 years for A, B, C, and D, respectively. Calculate their market prices if the rate of return required by the market on these bonds is 8% compounded semiannually. Summarize the observed pattern or trend in a brief statement.

18. Bonds E, F, G, and H all have a face value of $1000 and carry a 10% coupon. The time remaining until maturity is five, 10, 15, and 25 years for E, F, G, and H, respectively. Calculate their market prices if the rate of return required by the market on these bonds is 12% compounded semiannually. Summarize the observed pattern or trend in a brief statement.

19. Bonds J, K, and L all have a face value of $1000 and all have 20 years remaining until maturity. Their respective coupon rates are 10%, 11%, and 12% compounded semiannually. Calculate their market prices if the rate of return required by the market on these bonds is 9% compounded semiannually. Summarize the observed pattern or trend in a brief statement.

20. Bonds M, N, and Q all have a face value of $1000 and all have 20 years remaining until maturity. Their respective coupon rates are 8%, 7%, and 6% compounded semiannually. Calculate their market prices if the rate of return required by the market on these bonds is 9% compounded semiannually. Summarize the observed pattern or trend in a brief statement.

21. Bonds E and F both have a face value of $1000 and 12 years remaining until maturity. Their coupon rates are 8% and 12%, respectively. Calculate the price of both bonds if the required rate of return is 10% compounded semiannually.

•22. A $1000, 10% coupon bond has 15 years remaining until maturity. The rate of return required by the market on these bonds has recently been 10% (compounded semiannually). Calculate the price change if the required return abruptly:

a. Rises to 11%.

b. Rises to 12%.

c. Falls to 9%.

d. Falls to 8%.

e. Is the price change caused by a 2% interest rate increase twice the price change caused by a 1% interest rate increase?

f. Is the price change caused by a 1% interest rate increase equal in magnitude to the price change caused by a 1% interest rate decrease?

•23. This problem investigates the sensitivity of the prices of bonds with different maturities to interest rate changes. Bonds G, H, and J all have a face value of \$1000 and carry a 10% coupon. The time remaining until maturity is five, 10, and 25 years for G, H, and J, respectively. Calculate the price change of each bond if the prevailing market rate increases from 10% to 11% compounded semiannually. Briefly describe the observed trend.

•24. This problem investigates the sensitivity of the prices of bonds having differing coupon rates to interest rate changes. Bonds K and L both have a face value of \$1000 and 15 years remaining until maturity. Their coupon rates are 8% and 12%, respectively. If the prevailing market rate decreases from 10% to 9% compounded semiannually, calculate the price change of each bond:

a. In dollars.

b. As a percentage of the initial price.

c. Are high-coupon or low-coupon bonds more sensitive to a given interest rate change? Justify your response using the results from part (b).

•25. Three years after the issue of a \$10,000, 8.75% coupon, 25-year bond, the rate of return required in the bond market on long-term bonds is 8.1% compounded semiannually.

a. At what price would the bond sell?

b. What capital gain or loss (expressed as a percentage of the original investment) would the owner realize by selling the bond at that price?

•26. Four and one-half years ago Gavin purchased 20 \$1000 bonds in a new Province of Ontario issue with a 20-year maturity and an 8.5% coupon. If the prevailing market rate is now 9.6% compounded semiannually:

a. What would be the proceeds from the sale of Gavin's bonds?

b. What would be the capital gain or loss (expressed as a percentage of the original investment)?

•27. Three years ago Quebec Hydro sold an issue of 20-year, 10.5% coupon bonds. Calculate an investor's percent capital gain for the entire three-year holding period if the current semiannually compounded return required in the bond market is:

a. 9%. **b.** 10.5%. **c.** 12%.

•28. Two and one-half years ago the Province of Saskatchewan sold an issue of 25-year, 11% coupon bonds. Calculate an investor's percent capital gain for the entire $2\frac{1}{2}$-year holding period if the current rate of return required in the bond market is:

a. 12%. **b.** 11%. **c.** 10%.

••**29.** During periods of declining interest rates, long-term bonds can provide investors with impressive capital gains. The best example in recent times occurred in the early 1980s. In September 1981 the bond market was pricing long-term bonds to provide a rate of return of over 18.5% compounded semiannually. Suppose you had purchased 10% coupon bonds in September 1981 with 20 years remaining until maturity, priced to yield 18.5%. Four and one-half years later (in March 1986) the bonds could have been sold at a prevailing market rate of 9.7% compounded semiannually. What would have been your semiannually compounded rate of total return on the bonds during the $4\frac{1}{2}$-year period?

••**30.** The downside of the long-term bond investment story occurs during periods of rising long-term interest rates, when bond prices fall. During the two years preceding September 1981, long-term bond yields rose from 11% to 18.5%. Suppose you had purchased 10% coupon bonds with 22 years remaining until maturity in September 1979 and sold them in September 1981. What would have been your semiannually compounded rate of total return on the bonds during the two-year period?

15.3 Yield to Maturity on an Interest Payment Date

If you purchase a bond at the price given by formula (15-1) and keep the bond *until it matures,* your rate of return will be the market rate of return used as the discount rate in formula (15-1). In the language of bonds, this rate of return is called the **yield to maturity**[4] (YTM). It is standard practice to quote the YTM as a semiannually compounded nominal rate. The yield to maturity is "locked in" by the price you pay for the bond—the higher the purchase price, the lower the bond's YTM.

If you purchase a bond at the price given by formula (15-1) and subsequently *sell it before it matures,* we cannot say what your rate of return will be. The actual rate of return depends on the selling price which, in turn, depends on the market rate of return on the date of sale. The prevailing market rate of return on a future date is not known in advance.

In Section 15.2, we learned how to answer the following question. Given the prevailing market rate of return (that is, given the yield to maturity required by the bond market), what is the market value of a bond? The other question a bond investor commonly faces is: What yield to maturity will a bond provide if it is purchased at its offered price?

To answer the second question, the mathematical task is to solve formula (15-1) for i given the bond price. The (semiannually compounded) yield to maturity is then

[4] The yield to maturity is sometimes called simply the "yield" or the "bond yield." For example, quotations of bond yields to maturity in the financial pages use just "yield" or "bond yield" to mean yield to maturity. However, "yield" is also used to refer to a bond's "current yield" (defined as the annual coupon interest as a percentage of the bond's market price). Therefore, use of the simple term "yield" to mean "yield to maturity" should be discouraged because of this ambiguity.

$2i$. The algebraic approach requires the trial-and-error method (Appendix 11B). In this method, you substitute estimates of i into the formula until you find an estimate that comes close to satisfying the formula. Since the financial calculator method for calculating the yield to maturity is more accurate and much more efficient, the algebraic method will be demonstrated in only one of the following examples.

Example 15.3A Calculating the Yield to Maturity of a Bond

A $1000 face value Province of Manitoba bond, bearing interest at 9.75% payable semiannually, has 11 years remaining until maturity. What is the bond's yield to maturity (YTM) at its current market price of $1021?

Solution

This bond's yield to maturity is the discount rate that makes the combined present value of all remaining interest payments and the face value equal to the bond's market value. We are given:

$$FV = \$1000, \quad b = \frac{9.75\%}{2} = 4.875\%, \quad b(FV) = \$48.75, \quad n = 22,$$

and bond price = $1021

Substitute these values into

$$\text{Bond price} = b(FV)\left[\frac{1-(1+i)^{-n}}{i}\right] + FV(1+i)^{-n}$$

The YTM is the value of $2i$, where i is the solution to

$$\$1021 = \underbrace{\$48.75\left[\frac{1-(1+i)^{-22}}{i}\right]}_{\text{Term ①}} + \underbrace{\$1000(1+i)^{-22}}_{\text{Term ②}}$$

Algebraic Solution

In the trial-and-error method, we try various values for i on the right-hand side (RHS) until we get values for the RHS within 0.5% above and 0.5% below $1021. For an initial estimate, we can deduce that i will be less than $b = 4.875\%$ since the bond price is more than its face value. Let us try $i = 4.75\%$ for the initial estimate. The results of substituting this and a second estimate for i are presented in the following table. We show the two estimates "bracketing" the correct value of the RHS and the unknown correct value of i.

Trial number	Estimated i	Term ①	Term ②	RHS
1	0.0475	656.58	360.26	1016.84
	i			1021.00
2	0.047	659.62	364.06	1023.68

By inspecting the table, you can see that the correct value for i will be closer to 0.0470 than to 0.0475. Therefore, $i = 0.0472 = 4.72\%$ is a logical choice for the best estimate. The bond's YTM is $2i = 9.44\%$ compounded semiannually.

Financial Calculator Solution

48.75 (PMT) 22 (n) 1000 (FV) 1021 (+/–) (PV) (COMP) (i) [4.7195]

The bond's YTM is $2i = 2(4.7195\%) = 9.44\%$ compounded semiannually.

Example 15.3B *Calculating the Yield to Maturity of a High-Risk or "Deep-Discount" Bond*

A corporation's financial condition may deteriorate to the point where there is some doubt about its ability to make future interest payments on its bonds or to redeem the bonds at maturity. Investors are then unwilling to buy the bonds at a price based on market rates of return on bonds of healthy corporations. The price of bonds of the financially distressed corporation will fall to a level determined more by the perceived risk rather than by the prevailing market rates of return. It is still useful to calculate the YTM on such "deep-discount" bonds. The YTM represents the rate of return the bond purchaser will realize if (1) the corporation does manage to meet all of the scheduled payments on time, and (2) the bond is held until the maturity date.

Calculate the YTM on the \$1000, 12% coupon bonds of Beaucamp Corp., which are trading at \$500. The bonds have $7\frac{1}{2}$ years remaining until maturity.

Solution

Given: $FV = \$1000$, $b = \dfrac{12\%}{2} = 6.0\%$, $b(FV) = \$60$, $n = 15$, and bond price $= \$500$

The YTM is the value of $2i$, where i is the solution to

$$\$500 = \$60\left[\frac{1-(1+i)^{-15}}{i}\right] + \$1000(1+i)^{-15}$$

Financial Calculator Solution

60 (PMT) 15 (n) 1000 (FV) 500 (+/–) (PV) (COMP) (i) [14.237]

The bond's YTM is $2i = 2(14.237\%) = 28.47\%$ compounded semiannually.

Exercise 15.3

Answers to the odd-numbered problems are at the end of the book.

Note: Unless otherwise indicated, assume that:

- The face value of a bond is \$1000.
- Bond interest is paid semiannually.
- The bond was originally issued at its face value.
- Bonds are redeemed at their face value at maturity.
- Market rates of return and yields to maturity are compounded semiannually.

1. A bond with a face value of $1000 and 15 years remaining until maturity pays a coupon rate of 10%. Calculate its yield to maturity if it is priced at $900.
2. A bond with a face value of $1000 and 15 years remaining until maturity pays a coupon rate of 10%. Calculate its yield to maturity if it is priced at $1100.
3. Bonds A and C both have a face value of $1000 and pay a coupon rate of 9%. They have five and 20 years, respectively, remaining until maturity. Calculate the yield to maturity of each bond if it is purchased for $950.
4. Bonds D and E both have a face value of $1000 and pay a coupon rate of 9%. They have five and 20 years, respectively, remaining until maturity. Calculate the yield to maturity of each bond if it is purchased for $1050.

•5. A $1000 Government of Canada bond carrying a 10% coupon is currently priced to yield 10% compounded semiannually until maturity. If the bond price abruptly rises $20, what is the change in the yield to maturity if the bond has:

   a. Three years remaining to maturity?

   b. 15 years remaining to maturity?

•6. A $1000 Nova Corporation bond carrying an 11% coupon is currently priced to yield 10% compounded semiannually until maturity. If the bond price abruptly falls $25, what is the change in the yield to maturity if the bond has:

   a. Two years remaining to maturity?

   b. 12 years remaining to maturity?

•7. In the spring of 1992 it became apparent that Olympia & York (O&Y) would have serious difficulty in servicing its debt. Because of this risk, investors were heavily discounting O&Y's bond issues. On April 30, 1992 an Olympia & York bond issue, paying an 11.25% coupon rate and maturing on October 31, 1998, traded at $761.50 (per $1000 of face value). (This was at a time when Government of Canada bonds with a similar coupon and maturity date were trading at a premium of about 10% above par.) If O&Y had managed to make the contractual payments on these bonds, what yield to maturity would investors who purchased those bonds on April 30, 1992 have realized? (P.S.: They didn't!)

15.4 Bond Price on Any Date

In Section 15.2, we learned how to calculate a bond's price on an interest payment date. This limits us to valuing a particular bond on just the two days in a year when the interest payments are made. But bonds trade in the financial markets *every* business day. We need to develop the further steps required to calculate a bond's price on any date.

Calculating a Bond's Price on Any Date

Regardless of the date of sale, a bond's market value will be the present value of the future payments discounted at the market's required rate of return. For a date of sale lying between interest payment dates, it appears that each payment must be discounted over a non-integral number of compounding intervals. We can, however, use our understanding of equivalent values to develop a simpler procedure. The present value of all payments on the date of sale may be obtained by the two steps indicated in Figure 15.5.

Step 1: Calculate the present value of the remaining payments on the *preceding* interest payment date. For the discount rate, use the market rate of return as of the date of sale.

Step 2: The bond price is the future value, on the date of sale, of the Step 1 result. Use $FV = PV(1 + i)^n$ with

$$i = \frac{\text{Market's required rate of return}}{2}$$

and

$$n = \frac{\text{Number of days since the preceding interest payment}}{\text{Total number of days in the full payment interval}}$$

Figure 15.5 *Calculating a Bond's Price on Any Date*

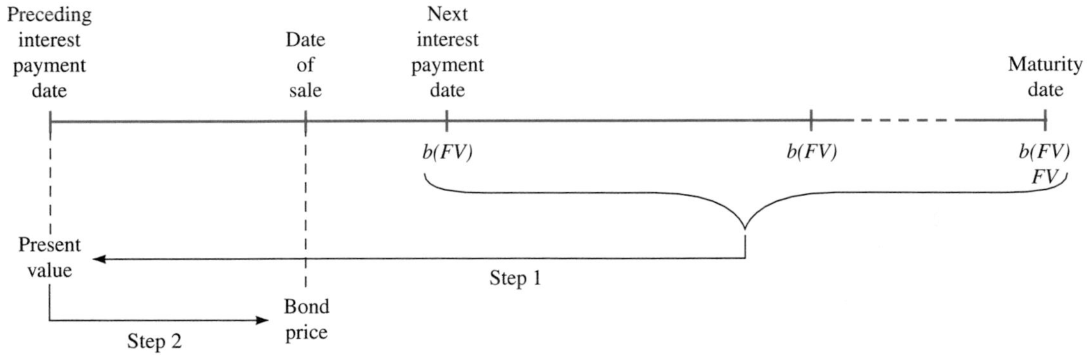

Example 15.4A *Pricing a Bond between Interest Payment Dates*

A $1000, 20-year, 6% coupon bond was issued on August 15, 1998. It was sold on November 3, 2000, to yield the purchaser 6.5% compounded semiannually until maturity. At what price did the bond sell?

Solution

Given: $FV = \$1000$, $b = 5.5\%$, $b(FV) = \$55$, $i = 4.4\%$,
and $n = 36$ coupon payments remaining.

Step 1: Calculate the present value of the remaining payments at the most recent interest payment date (August 15, 2000) using formula (15-1).

Step 2: Calculate the future value on the date of sale (November 3, 2000) of the amount from Step 1. The interval from August 15 to November 3, 2000 (a leap year) is 308 − 228 = 80 days. The total length of the interest payment interval from August 15, 2000, to February 15, 2001, is

$$46 + (366 - 228) = 184 \text{ days}$$

On the date of sale, the fraction of the payment interval that had elapsed was

$$n = \frac{80}{184} = 0.4347826$$

Algebraic Solution

Step 1: Present value (August 15) $= \$30\left(\frac{1 - 1.0325^{-36}}{0.0325}\right) + \$1000(1.0325^{-36})$

$= \$631.203 + \$316.197$

$= \$947.40$

Step 2: Price (November 3) $= \$947.40(1.0325^{0.4347826}) = \$960.67$

The bond sold for $960.67 on November 3, 2000.

Financial Calculator Solution

Step 1: 30 (PMT) 1000 (FV) 36 (n) 3.25 (i) (COMP) (PV) [−947.40]

Step 2: 0 (PMT) 0.4347826 (n) (COMP) (FV) [960.67]

The bond sold for $960.67 on November 3, 2000. (It sold at a discount because the coupon rate was less than the market's required rate of return.)

Example 15.4B Pricing a Bond between Interest Payment Dates

On January 15, 1992, Westcoast Energy Inc. issued 20-year bonds having a 7.6% coupon rate. At what price did $1000 face value bonds trade on April 10, 2000, if the required return was 6.2% compounded semiannually?

Solution

Given: $FV = \$1000$, $b = 3.8\%$, $b(FV) = \$38$, $i = 3.1\%$, and $n = 24$ coupon payments remaining.

Step 1: Calculate the present value of the remaining payments at the most recent interest payment date (January 15, 2000).

Step 2: Calculate the future value on the date of sale (April 10, 2000) of the amount from Step 1. The interval from January 15 to April 10, 2000 (a leap year) is 101 − 15 = 86 days long. The total length of the interest payment interval from January 15, 2000 to July 15, 2000 was 197 − 15 = 182 days.

On the date of sale, the fraction of the payment interval that had elapsed was

$$n = \frac{86}{182} = 0.4725275$$

Algebraic Solution

Step 1: Present value (January 15) $= \$38\left(\frac{1 - 1.031^{-24}}{0.031}\right) + \$1000(1.031^{-24})$

$= \$636.673 + \$480.609$

$= \$1117.28$

Step 2: Price (April 10) $= \$1117.28(1.031^{0.4725275}) = \$1133.52$

The bonds traded at \$1133.52 on April 10, 2000.

Financial Calculator Solution

Step 1: 38 (PMT) 1000 (FV) 24 (n) 3.1 (i) (COMP) (PV) [−1117.28]

Step 2: 0 (PMT) 0.4725275 (n) (COMP) (FV) [1133.52]

The bonds traded at \$1133.52 on April 10, 2000. (They traded at a premium because the coupon rate was greater than the market's required rate of return.)

Quotation of Bond Prices

Even if prevailing interest rates do not change, the price of a bond will change as time passes, for two reasons. First, the accrual of interest causes a bond's price to steadily rise after an interest payment. Then the price will abruptly fall by the amount $b \times FV$ on the day interest is paid. The result of this cycle repeating every six months is a "saw-tooth" pattern for the graph of bond price versus time. Figure 15.6 illustrates the pattern for the case of a bond selling at a premium. Figure 15.7 presents the corresponding graph for a bond selling at a discount. The graphs show how the market value of a \$1000 face value bond changes over the last six interest payment intervals before the maturity date (assuming that prevailing market rates of return do not change). Note that much of the bond price axis between \$0 and \$1000 has been omitted to show the details of bond price changes on a larger scale. Keep in mind that $b \times FV$ will be in the \$30 to \$60 range for coupon rates in the 6% to 12% range.

Figure 15.6 *Price Change Over Time for a Bond Trading at a Premium*

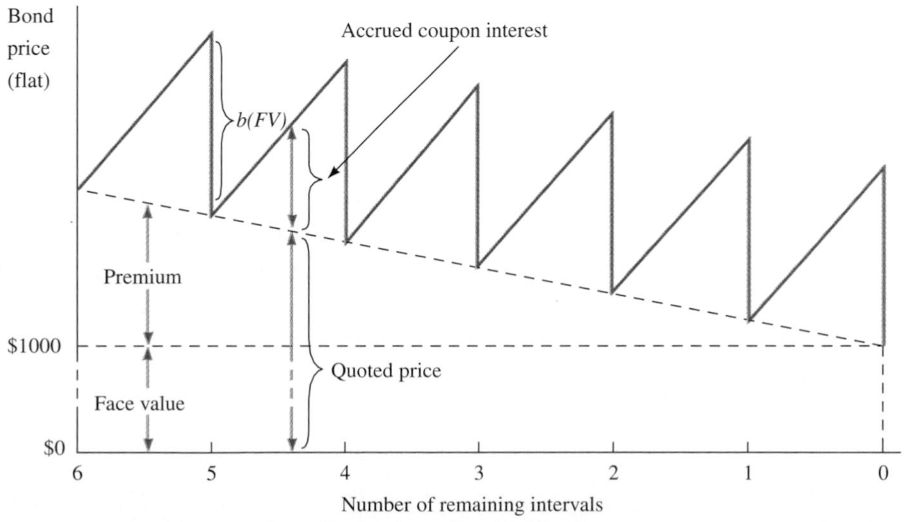

The second reason the bond's price will change is that the premium or discount will diminish over time. The premium on any date in Figure 15.6 is the distance between the downward-sloping dashed line and the horizontal line at $1000. The discount on any date in Figure 15.7 is the distance between the horizontal line at $1000 and the upward-sloping dashed line. The premium or discount decreases as time passes because the difference between the market rate of return and a bond's coupon rate becomes less important as the number of remaining payments decreases. It is the same reason that causes a long-term bond to sell at a larger premium or discount than a short-term bond (other variables being the same for both bonds). By the time a bond reaches its maturity date, any bond premium or discount has shrunk to zero.

Figure 15.7 *Price Change Over Time for a Bond Trading at a Discount*

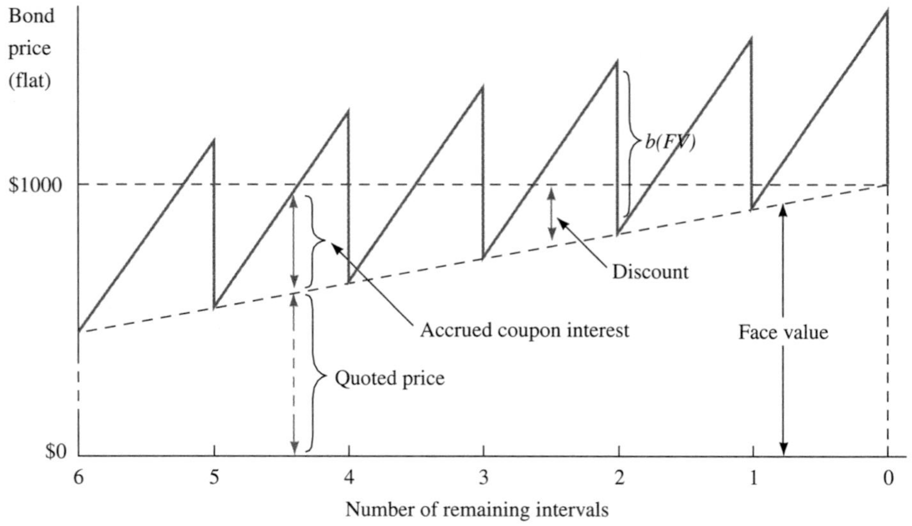

Flat Price vs. Quoted Price In bond terminology, the bond price we have been calculating (and plotting in Figures 15.6 and 15.7) is called the **flat price**. It is the *actual* amount paid by the purchaser and received by the seller (ignoring brokerage charges). The flat price includes coupon interest that has accrued since the preceding interest payment date.

Before an investor can make meaningful comparisons among bond prices, the prices must be adjusted for their differing amounts of accrued coupon interest. As an extreme example, the flat prices of two otherwise identical bonds will differ by almost $b \times FV$ if one bond paid coupon interest yesterday and the other bond will pay interest tomorrow. The accrued interest should be deducted from the flat prices of both bonds to obtain prices that may be fairly compared. For this reason, bond prices are quoted in the financial media and in the bond market with the accrued coupon interest already deducted from the flat price. That is,

$$\textbf{Quoted price} = \text{Flat price} - \text{Accrued coupon interest}$$

In Figures 15.6 and 15.7, the flat price on one particular date is broken down into its "accrued coupon interest" and "quoted price" components. The quoted price includes the premium or discount but does not include accrued coupon interest. When they purchase bonds, investors are aware that accrued coupon interest will be *added* to the quoted price, giving the flat price they will pay.

Table 15.2 lists some bond quotations at the close of the bond market on May 28, 1999. Since there can be several face value denominations in any bond issue, bond prices are quoted as a *percentage* of face value. The dollar price of any denomination may then be readily calculated. For example, the price of a \$5000 face value bond quoted at 102.25(%) is

$$\$5000 \times 1.0225 = \$5112.50$$

Even though the bond yield (meaning yield to maturity) can be calculated from the other information in the table, it is nevertheless quoted because many bond investors are unable to perform the calculation.

Table 15.2 *Bond Price Quotations (May 28, 1999)*

Issuer	Coupon rate (%)	Maturity Date	Quoted price (%)	Bond yield (%)
Government of Canada	11.50	March 1, 2009	144.97	5.48
Government of Canada	10.50	March 15, 2021	161.04	5.61
Province of Nova Scotia	9.60	January 30, 2022	142.33	6.12
Province of New Brunswick	7.75	June 19, 2006	111.63	5.72
Ontario Hydro	8.90	August 18, 2022	136.21	5.99
Bell Canada	10.35	December 15, 2009	132.79	6.09
Canadian Tire	6.25	April 13, 2028	94.71	6.66
Trans Canada Pipeline	6.50	December 9, 2030	95.82	6.82

Calculating the Accrued Coupon Interest We have mentioned that the buyer of a bond pays accrued coupon interest in addition to the quoted price. The prevailing practice is to calculate accrued coupon interest on a *simple-interest* basis. Therefore,

$$\text{Accrued coupon interest} = P \times r \times t = FV \times b \times t$$

where t is the fraction of the payment interval (containing the date of sale) that has elapsed since the preceding interest payment. That is,

$$t = \frac{\text{Number of days since the preceding interest payment}}{\text{Total number of days in the full payment interval}}$$

Example 15.4C Calculating the Accrued Coupon Interest and Quoted Price, Given the Flat Price

In Example 15.4B, we calculated the (flat) price on April 10, 2000, of a $1000 face value, 7.6% coupon Westcoast Energy Inc. bond maturing January 15, 2012. The calculated price for a yield to maturity of 6.2% compounded semiannually was $1117.28.

a. How much of that price was interest that had accrued (in favour of the previous owner) since the preceding interest payment date?

b. What price did the financial media and securities brokers quote for these bonds on April 10, 2000?

Solution

a. The number of days from the preceding interest payment on January 15, 2000 to the April 10, 2000 date of sale was

$$101 - 15 = 86$$

The number of days in the full payment interval (from January 15 to July 15) was

$$197 - 15 = 182$$

The coupon interest that accrued over these 86 days was

$$I = Prt = (FV)bt = \$1000 \times 0.038 \times \frac{86}{182} = \$17.96$$

Hence, $17.96 of the $1117.28 flat price was accrued interest.

b. Brokers and financial media report the quoted price. (Bond investors understand that they must pay the accrued interest of $17.96 in addition to the quoted price.)

$$\begin{aligned}\text{Quoted price} &= \text{Flat price} - \text{Accrued interest}\\ &= \$1117.28 - \$17.96\\ &= \$1099.32\end{aligned}$$

Example 15.4D Calculating the Accrued Coupon Interest and Quoted Price Given the Yield to Maturity

For the Canadian Tire Corp. bond listed in Table 15.2, show how the quoted price may be calculated from the other information provided in the table. What additional accrued interest did the purchaser of a $10,000 face value bond on May 28, 1999 have to pay?

Solution

From the table, we see that the Canadian Tire bond maturing April 13, 2028 pays a coupon rate of 6.25%. The bond market was valuing these bonds on May 28, 1999 to yield 6.66% (compounded semiannually) until maturity. We will base our calculations on a $1000 face value bond. Thus,

$$FV = \$1000 \quad b = \frac{6.25\%}{2} = 3.125\% \quad b(FV) = \$31.25 \quad i = \frac{6.66\%}{2} = 3.33\%$$

and $n = 2(29) = 58$ payments remaining

We must calculate the flat price before we can determine the quoted price. The steps in the solution are:

Step 1: Calculate the present value of the remaining payments on the preceding interest payment date (April 13, 1999).

Step 2: Calculate the flat price on May 28, 1999 by calculating the future value of the Step 1 result with interest at 6.66% compounded semiannually.

Step 3: Calculate the accrued coupon interest.

Step 4: Deduct the accrued coupon interest from the flat price to get the quoted price.

In both the algebraic solution and the financial calculator solution, we need the fraction of the payment interval that has elapsed up to May 28, 1999. That fraction is

$$\frac{148 - 103}{286 - 103} = \frac{45}{183} = 0.2459016$$

Algebraic Solution

Step 1:

$$\begin{aligned}\text{Present value (April 13)} &= \$31.25\left(\frac{1 - 1.0333^{-58}}{0.0333}\right) + \$1000(1.0333^{-58}) \\ &= \$149.578 + \$480.609 \\ &= \$947.65\end{aligned}$$

Step 2: Flat price (May 28) $= \$947.65(1.0333^{0.2459016}) = \$955.31$

Step 3: Accrued coupon interest $= Prt = (FV)bt = \$1000 \times 0.03125 \times \frac{45}{183}$

$$= \$7.68$$

Step 4:

$$\begin{aligned}\text{Quoted price} &= \text{Flat price} - \text{Accrued interest} \\ &= \$955.31 - \$7.68 \\ &= \$947.63\end{aligned}$$

This price is 94.76% of the $1000 face value. The quoted price in Table 15.2 is 94.71% of face value. (The reason for the difference is that the yield we used in our calculations was quoted in the financial pages to only three-figure accuracy. Therefore our answer can have a rounding error showing up in the third figure. The yield that gives a quoted price of 94.71 is actually 6.664%. Rounded to three figures, this becomes the 6.66% figure quoted in Table 15.2.)

The purchaser of a $10,000 face value bond must pay ten times the accrued interest calculated above for a $1000 face value bond. That is, the purchaser paid an extra 10($7.68) = $78.60 for accrued coupon interest.

Exercise 15.4

Answers to the odd-numbered problems are at the end of the book.

Note: Unless otherwise indicated, assume that:

- The face value of a bond is $1000.
- Bond interest is paid semiannually.
- The bond was originally issued at its face value.
- Bonds will be redeemed for their face value at maturity.
- Market rates of return and yields to maturity are compounded semiannually.

Calculate the purchase price of each of the $1000 face value bonds in Problems 1 through 8.

Problem	Issue date	Maturity date	Purchase date	Coupon rate (%)	Market rate (%)
1.	June 1, 1991	June 1, 2011	June 15, 2000	10	9.75
2.	March 15, 1990	March 15, 2015	Oct 5, 1996	12.5	7.4
3.	Jan 1, 1995	Jan 1, 2010	April 15, 1995	8.9	9.9
4.	Sept 20, 1994	Sept 20, 2014	June 1, 1997	9.0	6.8
5.	Aug 1, 1994	Aug 1, 2014	Dec 15, 1998	9.5	5.4
6.	July 1, 1997	July 1, 2017	April 9,1998	9.7	5.9
7.	Dec 1, 1998	Dec 1, 2018	Mar 25, 2000	5.2	5.7
8.	April 1, 1998	April 1, 2023	June 20, 1999	5.1	5.8

Problems 9 through 16 require the calculation of bond prices between interest payment dates.

•**9.** A $1000, 11% coupon bond issued by Bell Canada matures on October 15, 2011. What was its price on June 11, 1992 if its yield to maturity was 9.9% compounded semiannually?

•**10.** A $1000, 8.5% coupon, 25-year Government of Canada bond was issued on June 1, 1986. At what price did it sell on April 27, 1990 if the market's required return was 11.2% compounded semiannually?

•**11.** A $1000, 9.25% coupon bond issued by Ontario Hydro on January 6, 1979 matures on January 6, 2004. What was its market price on August 8, 1981 when the required yield to maturity was 17% compounded semiannually?

•**12.** A $1000, 15.5% coupon, 25-year Government of Canada bond was issued on March 15, 1982. At what price did it trade on June 4, 1986, when the market's required return was 9.2% compounded semiannually?

•**13.** A $1000, 9% coupon, 20-year Province of Ontario bond was issued on March 15, 1992. Calculate its price on March 15, April 15, May 15, June 15, July 15, August 15, and September 15, 1993, if the yield to maturity on every date was 10% compounded semiannually.

•**14.** A $1000, 11% coupon, 15-year Province of Quebec bond was issued on November 20, 1991. Calculate its price on May 20, June 20, July 20, August 20, September 20, October 20, and November 20, 1993, if the yield to maturity on every date was 9.6% compounded semiannually.

••**15.** A $5000, 9% coupon, 20-year bond issued on August 1, 1986, was purchased on April 25, 1990, to yield 11.5% to maturity, and then sold on

December 27, 1991, to yield 8.8% to maturity. What was the investor's capital gain or loss:

a. In dollars?

b. As a percentage of her original investment?

••16. A $10,000, 14% coupon, 25-year bond issued on June 15, 1984, was purchased on March 20, 1987, to yield 9% to maturity, and then sold on April 20, 1990, to yield 11.5% to maturity. What was the investor's capital gain or loss:

a. In dollars?

b. As a percentage of his original investment?

Problems 17 through 22 require the calculation of quoted bond prices and accrued interest.

•17. A $1000 face value, 11% coupon bond pays interest on May 15 and November 15. If its flat price on August 1 was $1065.50, at what price (expressed as a percentage of face value) would the issue have been reported in the financial pages?

•18. A $5000 bond was sold for $4860 on September 17. If the bond pays $200 interest on June 1 and December 1 of each year until maturity, what price (expressed as a percentage of face value) would have been quoted for bonds of this issue on September 17?

•19. If a broker quotes a price of 108.50 for a bond on October 23, what amount will a client pay per $1000 face value? The 10.5% coupon rate is payable on March 1 and September 1 of each year. The relevant February has 28 days.

•20. Calculate the quoted price on April 15, 1995 of the bond described in Problem 3.

•21. Calculate the quoted price on June 1, 1997, of the bond described in Problem 4.

•22. Using the given bond yields, verify the May 28, 1999 quoted prices in Table 15.2 for the following bonds:

a. Government of Canada 11.5% coupon, maturing March 1, 2009.

b. Government of Canada 10.5% coupon, maturing March 15, 2021.

c. Province of Nova Scotia 9.6% coupon, maturing January 30, 2022.

d. Province of New Brunswick 7.75% coupon, maturing June 19, 2006.

e. Ontario Hydro 8.9% coupon, maturing August 18, 2022.

f. Bell Canada 10.35% coupon, maturing December 15, 2009.

g. Trans Canada Pipeline 6.5% coupon, maturing December 9, 2030.

*15.5 Sinking Funds

A **sinking fund** is an interest-earning account into which periodic deposits are made for the purpose of accumulating a required amount of money by a particular date. The accumulated funds are typically used to acquire an asset requiring a substantial capital expenditure, or to retire the principal amount of a debt.

Sinking Fund for a Capital Expenditure

A sinking fund can be established by a business to accumulate funds for a future project, replacement of equipment, expansion of production facilities, or an acquisition.

The simplest sinking fund arrangement requires *equal periodic* contributions. The payment size is calculated so that, at the expected rate of return, the *future value* of the payments on the target date equals the amount needed. We will deal only with cases where the interval between contributions equals the compounding interval. The payments then form a *simple* annuity. If the sinking fund payments are made at the *end* of each payment interval, you calculate their size by solving for *PMT* in:

(10-1) $$FV = PMT\left[\frac{(1+i)^n - 1}{i}\right]$$

If the sinking fund payments are made at the *beginning* of each payment interval, solve for *PMT* in:

(13-1) $$FV(\text{due}) = PMT\left[\frac{(1+i)^n - 1}{i}\right] \times (1+i)$$

A table presenting details of the increase in the sinking fund each period is called a **sinking fund schedule.** The balance or accumulated amount in the sinking fund at the *end* of any interval is the future value of payments already made. The following relationships are used in constructing a sinking fund schedule.

$$\left(\begin{matrix}\text{Balance at the end of}\\ \text{any payment interval}\end{matrix}\right) = \left(\begin{matrix}\text{Future value of the}\\ \text{payments already made}\end{matrix}\right)$$

$$\left(\begin{matrix}\text{Interest earned in}\\ \text{any payment interval}\end{matrix}\right) = i \times \left(\begin{matrix}\text{Amount in the sinking fund}\\ \text{at the beginning of the interval}\end{matrix}\right)$$

TRAP *Interest Earned When Payments Form an Annuity Due*

Be careful when using the preceding idea to calculate the interest earned during a payment interval of an annuity due. The interest-earning amount at the beginning of an interval is the previous interval's ending balance *plus* the new contribution at the beginning of the current interval.

$$\left(\begin{matrix}\text{Increase in the sinking fund's balance}\\ \text{during any payment interval}\end{matrix}\right) = PMT + \left(\begin{matrix}\text{Interest earned}\\ \text{during the interval}\end{matrix}\right)$$

This increase can be added to the balance from the end of the preceding interval to obtain the new balance at the end of the current interval. The format for a sinking fund schedule is presented in the following examples.

Example 15.5A *Preparation of a Complete Sinking Fund Schedule in Which the Payments Form an Ordinary Annuity*

Borland Engineering plans to undertake a \$900,000 expansion six years from now. By that time, Borland wants to accumulate half of the cost of the expansion by making payments into a sinking fund at the end of each of the next six years. It is anticipated that the money in the sinking fund will earn 7% compounded annually.

a. What should be the size of the annual payments?

b. How much of the money in the sinking fund at the end of the six years will be interest earnings?

c. Prepare a sinking fund schedule. Verify the answer to part (b) by summing the "interest earned" column.

Solution

a. The future value of the six sinking fund payments, invested at 7% compounded annually, must be \$450,000.

Algebraic Solution

Solve for *PMT* in

$$\$450{,}000 = PMT\left[\frac{(1.07)^6 - 1}{0.07}\right]$$

$$= PMT(7.1532907)$$

$$PMT = \frac{\$450{,}000}{7.1532907} = \$62{,}908.11$$

The annual sinking fund payment should be \$62,908.11.

Financial Calculator Solution

450000 (FV) 0 (PV) 6 (n) 7 (i) (COMP) (PMT) [−62,908.11]

The annual sinking fund payment should be \$62,908.11.

b. The total of the payments to the sinking fund will be

$$6 \times \$62{,}908.11 = \$377{,}448.66$$

The remainder of the \$450,000 will be interest earned. That is,

$$\text{Interest earned} = \$450{,}000 - \$377{,}448.66 = \$72{,}551.34$$

c.

Payment interval number	Payment (at end)	Interest earned	Increase in the fund	Balance in fund (end of interval)
0	—	—	—	0
1	\$62,908.11	0	\$ 62,908.11	\$ 62,908.11
2	\$62,908.11	\$4403.57 ①	67,311.68 ②	130,210.79 ③
3	\$62,908.11	9115.39	72,023.50	202,243.29
4	\$62,908.11	14,157.03	77,065.14	279,308.43
5	\$62,908.11	19,551.59	82,459.70	361,768.13
6	\$62,908.11	25,323.77	88,231.88	450,000.01
	\$377,448.66	\$72,551.35 ④	\$450,000.01 ⑤	

① Interest earned = 0.07(Amount at the beginning of the interval)
= 0.07(\$62,908.11)
= \$4403.57

② Increase in the fund = Interest earned + Payment
= \$4403.57 + \$62,908.11
= \$67,311.68

③ Balance = Previous balance + Increase in the fund
= \$62,908.11 + \$67,311.68
= \$130,210.79

④ Column total = \$72,551.35
= Total interest earned (confirming the answer in part *b*)

⑤ The total of the increases to the fund should equal the final total in the sinking fund.

Example 15.5B ***Preparation of a Complete Sinking Fund Schedule in Which the Payments Form an Annuity Due***

Repeat Example 15.5A, with the change that the sinking fund payments are made at the beginning of each year.

Solution

a. The future value of the six sinking fund payments, invested at 7% compounded annually, must be $450,000.

Algebraic Solution

Solve for *PMT* in

$$\$450{,}000 = PMT\left[\frac{(1.07)^6 - 1}{0.07}\right](1.07)$$
$$= PMT(7.6540211)$$
$$PMT = \frac{\$450{,}000}{7.6540211} = \$58{,}792.63$$

Financial Calculator Solution

BGN mode

450000 (FV) 0 (PV) 6 (*n*) 7 (*i*) (COMP) (PMT) [−58,792.63]

The annual sinking fund payment should be $58,792.63.

b. Interest earned = $450,000 − Total of payments
= $450,000 − (6 × $58,792.63)
= $97,244.22

c.

Payment interval number	Payment (at start)	Interest earned	Increase in the fund	Balance in fund (end of interval)
0	—	—	—	0
1	$ 58,792.63	$ 4115.48	$62,908.11	$ 62,908.11
2	$ 58,792.63	8519.05①	67,311.68②	130,219.79③
3	$ 58,792.63	13,230.87	72,023.50	202,243.29
4	$ 58,792.63	18,272.51	77,065.14	279,308.43
5	$ 58,792.63	23,667.07	82,459.70	361,768.13
6	$ 58,792.63	29,439.25	88,231.88	450,000.01
	$352,755.78	$97,244.23	$450,000.01	

① Interest earned = 0.07(Amount at the beginning of the interval)
= 0.07(Balance at end of previous interval + *PMT*)
= 0.07($62,908.11 + $58,792.63)
= $8519.05

② Increase in the fund = Interest earned + Payment
= $8519.05 + $58,792.63
= $67,311.68

③ Balance = Previous balance + Increase in the fund
= $62,908.11 + $67,311.68
= $130,219.79

Example 15.5C Preparation of a Partial Sinking Fund Schedule

The board of directors of Borland Engineering decide that the firm's cash flows can be managed better if the sinking fund payments are made quarterly instead of annually (as in Example 15.5A). The goal is still to accumulate \$450,000 after six years, but now with end-of-quarter payments. The sinking fund would earn 6.8% compounded quarterly. Construct a partial sinking fund schedule showing details of Payments 1, 2, 15, 16, 23, and 24.

Solution

The first step is to calculate the size of the payments so that their future value will be \$450,000. The payments form an ordinary simple annuity with $n = 24$ and $i = \frac{6.8\%}{4} = 1.7\%$.

Algebraic Solution

Solve for *PMT* in

$$\$450{,}000 = PMT\left[\frac{(1.017)^{24} - 1}{0.017}\right]$$

$$= PMT(29.332891)$$

$$PMT = \frac{\$450{,}000}{29.332891} = \$15{,}341.14$$

Financial Calculator Solution

450000 (FV) 0 (PV) 24 (n) 1.7 (i) (COMP) (PMT) [−15,341.14]

Payment interval number	Payment (at end)	Interest earned	Increase in the fund	Balance in fund (end of interval)
0	—	—	—	0
1	\$15,341.14	0	\$15,341.14	\$ 15,341.14
2	\$15,341.14	\$260.80 ①	15,601.94 ②	30,943.08 ③
.	.	.	.	.
14				240,200.61 ④
15	\$15,341.14	4083.41	19,424.55	259,625.16
16	\$15,341.14	4413.63	19,754.77	279,379.93
.	.	.	.	.
22				405,164.24⑤
23	\$15,341.14	6887.79	22,228.93	427,393.17
24	\$15,341.14	7265.68	22,606.82	449,999.99
	\$368,187.36	\$81,812.63	\$449,999.99	

① $0.017 \times \$15{,}341.14 = \$260.80$

② $\$260.80 + \$15{,}341.14 = \$15{,}601.94$

③ $\$15{,}601.94 + \$15{,}341.14 = \$30{,}943.08$

④ Future value after 14 payments $= \$15{,}341.14\left[\frac{(1.017)^{14} - 1}{0.017}\right] = \$240{,}200.61$

⑤ Future value after 22 payments $= \$15{,}341.14\left[\frac{(1.017)^{22} - 1}{0.017}\right] = \$405{,}164.24$

Sinking Fund for Debt Retirement

Recall from the discussion of bonds earlier in this chapter that no principal is repaid to the bond owner before the maturity of the bond. In some circumstances, bond investors may have concerns about the ability of the borrower to repay the full principal amount at a maturity date several years in the future. To ease this concern, many corporate, regional government, and municipal government bonds carry a sinking fund provision.[5] The purpose of the sinking fund is to provide for the repayment of all or a substantial portion of the principal amount of the bond issue.

A trust company is usually appointed as the trustee to administer the sinking fund. The bond issuer does not have access to the money in the sinking fund; the funds are accumulated for the express purpose of repaying the principal amount of the debt. There are two ways of setting up a sinking fund for a bond issue:

- The borrower makes periodic payments to the trustee. The trustee invests the funds in low-risk securities (such as federal government bonds and Treasury bills). On the maturity date of the bond issue, the accumulated funds are used to repay all or a substantial portion of the principal amount of the debt.
- The trustee uses the periodic payments received from the bond issuer to retire a portion of the bond issue each year. To do this in any particular year, the trustee chooses the cheaper of the following two alternatives:

  (i) A specified percentage of the issue may be called and redeemed at a predetermined redemption price per bond.

  (ii) If, however, the bonds can be purchased in the bond market for less than the redemption price, the trustee will buy enough bonds for the year's prescribed debt retirement.

The second sinking fund arrangement is more common. However, the first involves the more interesting mathematics, which we will discuss in the remainder of this section.

The simplest contribution arrangement requires *equal* regular payments to the sinking fund after the initial issue[6] of the bonds. The payment size is calculated so that

$$\begin{pmatrix}\text{Future value of the}\\ \text{sinking fund payments}\end{pmatrix} = \begin{pmatrix}\text{Principal amount of}\\ \text{the debt to be retired}\end{pmatrix}$$

---

[5] Sinking funds are primarily associated with debentures rather than with true bonds because debentures are not secured by specific fixed assets of the borrower. A debt issue that has a sinking fund provision usually includes the words *sinking fund* in its full title.

[6] In cases where the sinking fund is structured to retire only a portion of the debt, there may be an initial five- or 10-year "contribution holiday" during which the issuer makes no sinking fund payments.

A conservative compound rate of return is assumed for the sinking fund. We will consider only cases where contributions are made at the end of every six months and compounding occurs semiannually. In these cases, the sinking fund contributions form an ordinary simple annuity.

The sinking fund schedule for a debt retirement usually includes an additional column for the **book value of the debt** defined as:

$$\begin{pmatrix}\text{Book value}\\\text{of the debt}\end{pmatrix} = \begin{pmatrix}\text{Principal amount}\\\text{of the debt}\end{pmatrix} - \begin{pmatrix}\text{Balance in the}\\\text{sinking fund}\end{pmatrix}$$

The book value of a debt can be interpreted as the balance that would still be owed on the debt if the money in the sinking fund were immediately applied to reduce the debt.

Keep in mind that, under a sinking fund arrangement, the borrower is making *two* series of payments, each one constituting an annuity. One is the sinking fund payments to the fund's trustee. The other is the semiannual interest payments to the lenders or bondholders. The combined total of a year's interest payments and a year's sinking fund payments is called the **annual cost of the debt.** It represents the total annual cash outflow arising from the debt obligation.

TIP *THE DIFFERENT ROLES OF THE COUPON RATE AND THE SINKING FUND RATE OF RETURN*

Distinguish the roles of the two interest rates that are involved in sinking fund debt. The contractual rate of interest on the debt determines the regular interest *expense* paid by the borrower to the lender. The rate of return earned by the sinking fund determines the *revenue* earned by the sinking fund. Although the lender does not directly receive the earnings of the sinking fund, the lender still benefits from the interest earnings: they will eventually be used to repay the principal amount of the debt.

Example 15.5D *Calculating the Sinking Fund Payment Size, Annual Cost of Debt, and Book Value of Debt*

Abacus Corp. raised \$20 million from an issue of sinking fund bonds. The bonds have a 12-year term and a 9% coupon rate. The bond indenture requires Abacus to make equal semiannual contributions to a sinking fund to provide for the retirement of the full principal amount of the bond issue at its maturity.

a. If the sinking fund earns 6.5% compounded semiannually, what is the size of the semiannual sinking fund payments?

b. What is the annual cost of the debt?

c. What is the book value of the debt after six years?

Solution

a. The future value of the sinking fund payments invested at 6.5% compounded semiannually for 12 years is to be \$20 million. Therefore, the semiannual payment will be the value of *PMT* that satisfies

$$\$20{,}000{,}000 = PMT\left[\frac{(1.0325)^{24} - 1}{0.0325}\right]$$
$$= PMT(35.525359)$$
$$PMT = \frac{\$20{,}000{,}000}{35.525359}$$
$$= \$562{,}978.13$$

b. The annual cost of the debt is the total of the bond interest and sinking fund payments made in a year. The semiannual interest paid on the debt is

$$\frac{0.09}{2} \times \$20{,}000{,}000 = \$900{,}000$$

Hence,

Annual cost of the debt = 2(\$562,978.13 + \$900,000) = \$2,925,956.26

c. The book value of the debt after six years will be the principal amount of the debt (\$20,000,000) less the amount in the sinking fund. Hence,

$$\text{Book value} = \$20{,}000{,}000 - \$562{,}978.13\left[\frac{(1.0325)^{12} - 1}{0.0325}\right]$$
$$= \$20{,}000{,}000 - \$8{,}104{,}230.90$$
$$= \$11{,}895{,}769.10$$

Example 15.5E Constructing a Partial Sinking Fund Schedule

In order to construct a secondary sewage treatment system, the town of Port Barlow has received approval to borrow \$12 million through the provincial government's Municipal Finance Authority (MFA). The MFA is the central borrowing agency for financing the capital requirements of member municipalities and regional governments. It enters the capital markets to borrow the funds needed by its members. It also manages the collection of money from its members for both the payment of interest and the accumulation of sinking funds to retire the principal portion of each debt issue.

Bond coupon interest at the rate of 10% compounded semiannually is payable every six months. In addition, Port Barlow must make payments at the end of every six months into a sinking fund that will accumulate the full principal amount of the debt after 15 years. The sinking fund earns 8% compounded semiannually. Round sinking fund payments and interest earnings to the nearest dollar.

a. Calculate the combined interest and sinking fund payment that Port Barlow must send to the MFA every six months.

b. What will be the balance in the sinking fund halfway through the term of the debt?

c. How much will the balance in the sinking fund increase during the tenth year?

d. How much interest will the sinking fund earn in the first half of the seventh year?

e. Construct a partial sinking fund schedule showing details of the first three and the last three payments.

Solution

a. The future value of the sinking fund payments after 15 years at 8% compounded semiannually must be \$12,000,000. Solve for *PMT* in

$$\$12{,}000{,}000 = PMT\left[\frac{(1.04)^{30} - 1}{0.04}\right]$$

$$PMT = \$213{,}961$$

The semiannual interest payments are

$$\$12{,}000{,}000(0.05) = \$600{,}000$$

The total semiannual payment is \$213,961 + \$600,000 = \$813,961.

b. The amount in the sinking fund at any point will be the future value of the payments already contributed. After $7\frac{1}{2}$ years (15 payments), the sinking fund balance will be

$$FV = \$213{,}961\left[\frac{(1.04)^{15} - 1}{0.04}\right] = \$4{,}284{,}267$$

c. The increase in the balance during the tenth year will be

$$= \text{Balance after 10 years} - \text{Balance after nine years}$$

$$= \$213{,}961\left[\frac{(1.04)^{20} - 1}{0.04}\right] - \$213{,}961\left[\frac{(1.04)^{18} - 1}{0.04}\right]$$

$$= \$6{,}371{,}347.4 - \$5{,}487{,}118.2$$

$$= \$884{,}229$$

d. The interest earned in the first half of Year 7

$$= 0.04(\text{Amount in the fund at the end of Year 6})$$

$$= 0.04 \times \$213{,}961\left[\frac{(1.04)^{12} - 1}{0.04}\right]$$

$$= 0.04(\$3{,}214{,}936.3)$$

$$= \$128{,}597$$

e. Partial sinking fund schedule:

Payment interval number	Payment	Interest earned	Increase in the fund	Balance in fund (end of interval)	Book value of the debt
0	—	—	—	0	$12,000,000
1	$213,961	0	$213,961	$213,961	11,786,039
2	213,961	$ 8558 ①	222,519 ②	436,480 ③	11,563,520 ④
3	213,961	17,459	231,420	667,900	11,332,100
.	.	.	.	.	
.	.	.	.	.	
.	.	.	.		
27				10,074,186 ⑤	1,925,814
28	213,961	402,967	616,928	10,691,114	1,308,886
29	213,961	427,645	641,606	11,332,720	667,280
30	213,961	453,309	667,270	11,999,990	10
	$6,418,830	$5,581,160	$11,999,990		

① Interest earned = 0.04(Amount at the beginning of the interval)
= 0.04($213,961)
= $8558

② Increase in fund = Interest earned + Payment
= $8558 + $213,961
= $222,519

③ Balance = Previous balance + Increase in the fund
= $213,961 + $222,519
= $436,480

④ Book value = Debt principal − Sinking fund balance
= $12,000,000 − $436,480
= $11,563,520

⑤ Balance in the sinking fund = Future value of the first 27 payments

$$= \$213,961\left[\frac{(1.04)^{27} - 1}{0.04}\right]$$

= $10,074,186

Exercise 15.5 *Answers to the odd-numbered problems are at the end of the book.*

For each of the sinking funds in Problems 1 through 8, calculate (rounded to the nearest dollar):

a. The size of the periodic sinking fund payment.

b. The balance in the sinking fund at the time indicated in the last column. (Round the sinking fund payment to the nearest dollar before calculating the balance.)

Problem	End-of-term amount of sinking fund ($ millions)	Term (years)	Sinking fund rate of return (%)	Payment and compounding interval	Payment at beginning or end of interval?	Balance at the end of Interval
1.	12	10	7	6 months	End	12
2.	7	5	6	3 months	End	6

Problem	End-of-term amount of sinking fund ($ millions)	Term (years)	Sinking fund rate of return (%)	Payment and compounding interval	Payment at beginning or end of interval?	Balance at the end of Interval
3.	15	15	6.5	1 year	End	11
4.	8	10	7.5	1 month	End	65
5.	6	5	5.25	1 month	Beginning	27
6.	10	10	6.5	3 months	Beginning	28
7.	18	15	6.75	6 months	Beginning	19
8.	5	10	5.75	1 year	Beginning	8

Each of the bond issues in Problems 9 through 16 has a sinking fund requirement for retiring the entire principal amount of the issue on its maturity date. In each case calculate (to the nearest dollar):

a. The size of the sinking fund payment at the end of every six months.

b. The annual cost of the debt.

c. The book value of the debt at the end of the indicated interval. (Round the sinking fund payment to the nearest dollar before calculating the book value.)

The coupon rates and rates of return on the sinking fund investments are compounded semiannually.

Problem	Principal amount of bond issue ($ millions)	Term (years)	Sinking fund rate of return (%)	Coupon rate (%)	Book value at the end of Interval
•9.	10	10	7	10	12
•10.	8	5	6	8.5	6
•11.	15	15	6.5	9	21
•12.	12	10	7.5	10.5	15
•13.	7	5	5.75	8	7
•14.	9	10	6.5	9.25	18
•15.	11	15	7.5	10.25	19
•16.	10	10	7	9.75	11

For Problems 17 through 20, construct the complete sinking fund schedule. Calculate the total interest earned by adding up the "interest earned" column and by calculating the difference between the final balance in the fund and the total of the contributed payments. Round the sinking fund payments and periodic interest earnings to the nearest dollar.

Problem	End-of-term amount of sinking fund ($)	Term (years)	Sinking fund rate of return (%)	Payment and compounding interval	Payment at beginning or end of interval?
•17.	800,000	3	7	6 months	End
•18.	675,000	6	6	1 year	End
•19.	1,000,000	5	6.75	1 year	Beginning
•20.	550,000	4	5.75	6 months	Beginning

•**21.** For the sinking fund described in Problem 2, prepare a partial sinking fund schedule showing details of Payments 1, 2, 11, 12, 19, and 20. Round the sinking fund payments and periodic interest earnings to the nearest dollar.

•**22.** For the sinking fund described in Problem 5, prepare a partial sinking fund schedule showing details of Payments 1, 2, 39, 40, 59, and 60. Round the sinking fund payments and periodic interest earnings to the nearest dollar.

•**23.** For the bond sinking fund described in Problem 9, prepare a partial sinking fund schedule (including the book value of the debt) showing details of the first three and the last three payments. Round the sinking fund payments and periodic interest earnings to the nearest dollar.

•**24.** For the bond sinking fund described in Problem 10, prepare a partial sinking fund schedule (including the book value of the debt) showing details of the first three and the last three payments. Round the sinking fund payments and periodic interest earnings to the nearest dollar.

•**25.** To provide for the automation of a production process in five years, Dominion Chemicals is starting a sinking fund to accumulate $600,000 by the end of the five years. Round the sinking fund payments and the periodic interest earnings to the nearest dollar.

a. If the sinking fund earns 7.5% compounded monthly, what monthly payments starting today should be made to the fund?

b. How much interest will be earned in the fourth year?

c. In what month will the fund pass the halfway point?

d. How much interest will be earned in the thirty-fifth month?

•**26.** Repeat Problem 25, with the change that the sinking fund payments are to be made at the end of every month.

••**27.** Thermo-Tech Systems recently sold a $20 million bond issue with a 20-year maturity and a coupon rate of 11% compounded semiannually. The bond indenture contract requires Thermo-Tech to make equal payments at the end of every six months into a sinking fund administered by National Trust. The sinking fund should accumulate the full $20 million required to redeem the bonds at their maturity. Round the sinking fund payments and periodic interest earnings to the nearest dollar.

a. What must the size of the sinking fund payments be if the fund earns 8.5% compounded semiannually?

b. How much interest will the fund earn in the sixth year?

c. How much will the fund increase in the twenty-seventh payment interval?

d. Construct a partial sinking fund schedule showing details of the first two and the last two payments, and the total of the interest earned.

••**28.** The town of Mount Hope is financing a $4.5 million upgrade to its water system through the province's Municipal Finance Authority. The MFA obtained financing via a bond issue with interest at 9.5% per annum payable semiannually. Also, at the end of every six months, the town is to make equal payments into a sinking fund administered by the MFA so that the necessary funds are available to repay the $4.5 million debt when it matures in 17 years.

The sinking fund earns 7.5% compounded semiannually. Round the sinking fund payments and periodic interest earnings to the nearest dollar.

a. Calculate the size of the sinking fund payments.

b. How much will the fund increase in the eighteenth payment interval?

c. How much interest will the fund earn in the tenth year?

d. Construct a partial sinking fund schedule showing details of the ninth, tenth, and last two payments, and the total of the interest earned.

••29. A sinking fund is to be set up to provide for the repayment of 80% of the principal amount of a $1 million debt in 10 years. Equal payments are to be made at the beginning of each quarter. The sinking fund will earn 7% compounded quarterly. Round the sinking fund payments and periodic interest earnings to the nearest dollar.

a. Calculate the size of the sinking fund payments.

b. Construct a partial sinking fund schedule showing details of the first two and the last two payments, and the total of the interest earned.

••30. Repeat Problem 29, with the change that the sinking fund payments are to be made at the end of every quarter.

*Appendix: Amortization of Bond Premiums and Discounts

The origin and calculation of bond premiums and discounts were discussed in Section 15.2. We will now look at the premiums and discounts from an accountant's perspective. The point of view and the schedules developed here provide the basis for the accounting treatment of bond premiums, discounts, and interest payments.

Amortization of a Bond's Premium

Bonds are priced at a premium when the coupon rate *exceeds* the yield to maturity required in the bond market. Suppose that a bond paying a 10% coupon rate is purchased three years before maturity to yield 8% compounded semiannually. The purchase price that provides this yield to maturity is $1052.42.

The accounting view is that a period's *earned interest* is the amount that gives the required rate of return on the bond investment. The interest payment after the first six months that would, by itself, provide the required rate of return (8% compounded semiannually) on the amount invested is

$$\frac{0.08}{2} \times \$1052.42 = \$42.10$$

The earned interest during the first six months from an accounting point of view is $42.10. The actual first coupon payment of $50 pays $50 − $42.10 = $7.90 more than is necessary to provide the required rate of return for the first six months.[7] The

[7] Individual bond investors view the "excess" interest each period as a partial offset for the $52.42 capital *loss* that they will incur when the bond is redeemed for its $1000 face value at maturity. On his income tax returns, an individual investor reports the full coupon payments year by year as interest income. In the year the bond matures, he is allowed to claim the full $52.42 capital loss.

$7.90 is regarded as a refund of a portion of the original premium, leaving a net investment (called the bond's *book value*) of

$$\$1052.42 - \$7.90 = \$1044.52$$

This book value becomes the beginning investment for the next six months. You then apply the same line of reasoning to this amount in the second interval, and so on.

TIP *Calculation of Earned Interest*

Earned interest is always calculated on the *book value* of the bond *after the previous coupon payment.* For the interest rate, use the *yield to maturity* that was "locked in" on the bond's date of purchase.

The effect of this treatment is to periodically *reduce* the book value of the bond (and the book value of the premium). After the final interest payment, the bond's book value will be reduced to the $1000 face value which is received along with the last interest payment. The process of reducing the premium in this way is called *amortization of the bond premium.* The details of the treatment of each coupon payment and the reduction of the bond premium are often tabulated in a bond premium amortization schedule. In the following example, we will develop a full amortization schedule for the bond used in the preceding discussion.

Example 15AA *Construction of a Bond Premium Amortization Schedule*

Prepare a complete bond premium amortization schedule for the 10% coupon bond in the preceding discussion. It was purchased for $1052.42 on a date three years before maturity to yield 8% to maturity. How much of the $300 received in coupon payments over the three years would accountants treat as interest income?

Solution

Coupon number	Coupon payment	Interest on book value	Premium amortized	Book value of bond	Unamortized premium
0	—	—	—	$1052.42	$52.42
1	$ 50	$42.10 ①	$7.90 ②	1044.52 ③	44.52 ④
2	50	41.78	8.22	1036.30	36.30
3	50	41.45	8.55	1027.75	27.75
4	50	41.11	8.89	1018.86	18.86
5	50	40.75	9.25	1009.61	9.61
6	50	40.39	9.61	1000.00	0.00
	$300	$247.58	$52.42		

① Interest on book value = 0.5 × Yield rate × Book value after previous coupon payment
= 0.04 × $1052.42 = $42.10
② Premium amortized = Coupon payment − Interest on book value = $50 − $42.10 = $7.90
③ New book value = Previous book value − Premium amortized = $1052.42 − $7.90 = $1044.52
④ Unamortized premium = Current book value − Face value = $1044.52 − $1000 = $44.52

Of the $300 received in coupon interest payments, accountants would treat $247.58 as interest income during the three years. The remaining $52.42 would be treated as a refund of the bond's premium.

AMORTIZATION OF A BOND'S DISCOUNT

Bonds are priced at a discount when the coupon rate is *less* than the yield to maturity required in the bond market. Suppose that a bond paying a 10% coupon rate is purchased three years before maturity to yield 12% compounded semiannually. The purchase price that provides this yield to maturity is \$950.83.

The accounting view is that a period's *earned interest* is the amount that gives the required rate of return on the bond investment. The interest payment after the first six months that would, by itself, provide the required rate of return (12% compounded semiannually) on the amount invested is

$$\frac{0.12}{2} \times \$950.83 = \$57.05$$

The earned interest during the first six months from an accounting point of view is \$57.05. The actual first coupon payment of \$50 is \$7.05 *less* than the amount needed to provide the required rate of return for the first six months.[8] The \$7.05 deficiency is converted to principal, giving an increased investment or *book value* of

$$\$950.83 + \$7.05 = \$957.88$$

This book value becomes the beginning investment for the next six months. You then apply the same line of reasoning to this amount in the second interval, and so on.

The effect of this amortization procedure is to periodically *increase* the book value of the bond and to simultaneously *reduce* the book value of the discount. After the final interest payment, the bond's book value will reach the \$1000 face value which is received along with the last interest payment. The process of reducing the discount in this way is called *amortization of the bond discount.* The details of the treatment of each coupon payment and the reduction of the bond discount are often tabulated in a bond discount amortization schedule. In the following example, we will develop a full amortization schedule for the bond used in the preceding discussion.

Example 15AB *Construction of a Bond Discount Amortization Schedule*

Prepare the complete bond discount amortization schedule for the 10% coupon bond in the preceding discussion. It was purchased for \$950.83 on a date three years before maturity to yield 12% to maturity. Even though \$300 is received in coupon payments over the three years, what total interest income would accountants recognize for the three years?

[8] Individual bond investors recognize that the interest "deficiency" each period will ultimately be offset by the \$49.17 capital *gain* they will realize when the bond is redeemed for its \$1000 face value at maturity.

Solution

Coupon number	Coupon payment	Interest on book value	Discount amortized	Book value of bond	Unamortized discount
0	—	—	—	$950.83	$49.17
1	$ 50	$ 57.05	$ 7.05	957.88	42.12
2	50	57.47 ①	7.47 ②	965.35 ③	34.65 ④
3	50	57.92	7.92	973.27	26.73
4	50	58.40	8.40	981.67	18.33
5	50	58.90	8.90	990.57	9.43
6	50	59.43	9.43	1000.00	0.00
Total:	$300	$349.17	$49.17		

① Interest on book value = 0.5 × Yield rate × Book value after previous coupon payment
= 0.06 × $957.88 = $57.47

② Discount amortized = Interest on book value − Coupon payment
= $57.47 − $50 = $7.47

③ New book value = Previous book value + Discount amortized
= $957.88 + $7.47 = $965.35

④ Unamortized discount = Face value − Current book value
= $1000 − $965.35 = $34.65

The effect of this amortization procedure is that accountants treat both the $300 from the coupon payments and the original discount as interest revenue during the three years. There is no capital gain or loss in the third year because the face value payment equals the book value of the bond on the redemption date. (In contrast, individual investors will report, for tax purposes, $100 of interest income each year plus a $49.17 capital gain in the year the bond matures.)

TIP *A Shortcut*

You can *directly* obtain the *book value* of a bond after any interest payment without working through an amortization schedule. The book value equals the present value of the *remaining* interest and face value payments from the bond, discounted at the bond's yield to maturity. Use this approach to obtain an intermediate book value in the construction of a *partial* amortization schedule for a bond premium or discount.

Exercise 15A

Answers to the odd-numbered problems are at the end of the book.

Note: Unless otherwise indicated, assume that:

- Bond interest is paid semiannually.
- Bonds will be redeemed at their face value at maturity.
- Market rates of return and yields to maturity are compounded semiannually.

Calculate the purchase price and construct a bond premium amortization schedule for each of the bonds described in Problems 1 through 4. Determine the total interest that will be recorded for accounting purposes from the purchase date until maturity.

••1. A \$1000 face value, 9% coupon, five-year bond is purchased three years before maturity to yield 8% compounded semiannually until maturity.

••2. A \$5000 face value bond with an 11% coupon is purchased $3\frac{1}{2}$ years before maturity to yield 9.5% to maturity.

••3. The yield to maturity on a \$1000 face value, 10% coupon, 20-year bond purchased with 12 years remaining until maturity is 8.8%. Show details of the first three and the last three coupon interest payments in a partial amortization schedule.

••4. A \$10,000 face value, 13% coupon bond is purchased $16\frac{1}{2}$ years before maturity at a price that will yield 10% until maturity. Show details of the first three and the last three coupon payments in a partial amortization schedule.

Calculate the purchase price and construct a bond discount amortization schedule for each of the bonds described in Problems 5 through 8. Determine the total interest that will be recorded for accounting purposes from the purchase date until maturity.

••5. A \$1000 face value, 8% coupon bond is purchased three years before maturity to yield 9.5% compounded semiannually until maturity.

••6. A \$5000 face value, 9% coupon, 10-year bond is purchased $2\frac{1}{2}$ years before the maturity date at a price that will yield 11% until maturity.

••7. The yield to maturity on a \$1000 face value, 8.5% coupon bond purchased with 11 years remaining until maturity is 10.4%. Show details of the first three and the last three coupon interest payments in a partial amortization schedule.

••8. A \$10,000 face value, 8.6% coupon, 25-year bond is purchased $14\frac{1}{2}$ years before maturity at a price that will yield 10% until maturity. Show details of the first three and the last three coupon payments in a partial amortization schedule.

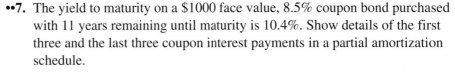

Review Problems

Answers to the odd-numbered review problems are at the end of the book.

1. A $1000, 7.5% coupon bond has $19\frac{1}{2}$ years remaining until maturity. Calculate the bond discount if the required return in the bond market is 8.6% compounded semiannually.

2. Four years after the issue of a $10,000, 9.5% coupon, 20-year bond, the rate of return required in the bond market on long-term bonds was 7.8% compounded semiannually.

a. At what price did the bond then sell?

b. What capital gain or loss (expressed in dollars) would the original owner have realized by selling the bond at that price?

3. Four and one-half years ago, Glenda purchased fifteen $1000 bonds in a Province of New Brunswick issue carrying an 8.5% coupon and priced to yield 9.8% (compounded semiannually). The bonds then had 18 years remaining until maturity. The bond market now requires a yield to maturity on the bonds of 8.0% compounded semiannually. If Glenda sells the bonds today, what will be the dollar amount of her capital gain or loss?

◆ **4.** A $1000, 9.5% coupon Government of Canada bond has 10 years remaining until its maturity. It is currently priced at 108.25 (percent of face value).

a. What is the bond's yield to maturity?

b. If the bond price abruptly rises $25, what is the change in its yield to maturity?

◆ **5.** A $1000, 12.25% coupon, 20-year Government of Canada bond was issued on June 15, 1985. At what price did it trade on December 10, 1989, when the market's required return was 10.2% compounded semiannually?

◆ **6.** If a broker quotes a price of 111.25 for a bond on September 10, what amount will a client pay per $1000 face value? The 11.25% coupon rate is payable on May 15 and November 15 of each year.

SPATS ◆ **7.** Laurentian Airways is preparing for the replacement of one of its passenger jets in three years by making payments to a sinking fund at the beginning of every six months for the next three years. The fund can earn 6% compounded semiannually, and the capital required in three years is $750,000. Prepare a complete sinking fund schedule. Round the sinking fund payments and periodic interest earnings to the nearest dollar.

SPATS ◆ **8.** The municipality of Duncan has financed a sewage treatment plant by issuing $18 million worth of sinking fund debentures. The debentures have a 15-year term and pay a coupon rate of 9% compounded semiannually. Rounding the sinking fund payments, interest payments, and periodic interest earnings to the nearest dollar,

a. What equal payments at the end of every six months will be necessary to accumulate $18 million after 15 years if the sinking fund can earn 6.25% compounded semiannually?

b. What is the annual cost of the debt to Duncan taxpayers?

c. Construct a partial sinking fund schedule (including the book value of the debt) showing details of the first three and the last three payments.

Self-Test Exercise

Answers to the self-test problems are at the end of the book.

1. A $1000 face value, 9.8% coupon, Province of Alberta bond with 18 years to run until maturity is currently priced to yield investors 9.5% compounded semiannually until maturity. How much lower would the bond's price have to be to make the yield to maturity 10% compounded semiannually?

2. Two and one-half years ago, Nova Scotia Power sold an issue of 25-year, 12.5% coupon bonds. If the current semiannually compounded return required in the bond market is 10%, calculate the percent capital gain or loss on the bonds over the entire $2\frac{1}{2}$-year holding period.
3. Calculate the yield to maturity on a bond purchased for \$1034.50 if it carries an 11.5% coupon and has $8\frac{1}{2}$ years remaining until maturity.
4. ◆ A New Brunswick Electric bond issue carrying a 13.25% coupon matures on November 1, 2004. At what price did \$1000 face value bonds trade on June 10, 1992, if the yield to maturity required by the bond market on that date was 9.3% compounded semiannually?
5. Calculate the quoted price on June 10, 1992, of the bond in Problem 4.
6. ◆ The Cowichan Regional District borrowed \$500,000 through the Provincial Finance Authority to purchase fire-fighting equipment. At the end of every six months, the regional district must make a sinking fund payment of a size calculated to accumulate \$500,000 after seven years to repay the principal amount of the debt. The sinking fund earns 7% compounded semiannually. Construct a partial sinking fund schedule showing details of the first two and the last two payments. Round the sinking fund payments and periodic interest earnings to the nearest dollar.

Summary of Notation and Key Formulas

In the context of bond pricing,

FV = Face value of the bond
b = Coupon rate per interest payment interval (normally six months)
i = The bond market's required rate of return per payment interval
n = Number of interest payments remaining until the maturity date

Formula (15-1) Bond price $= b(FV)\left[\frac{1-(1+i)^{-n}}{i}\right] + FV(1+i)^{-n}$ Finding the price of a bond on a coupon interest payment date

The following relationships were developed for sinking funds.

$$\begin{pmatrix}\text{Balance at the end of}\\ \text{any payment interval}\end{pmatrix} = \begin{pmatrix}\text{Future value of the}\\ \text{payments already made}\end{pmatrix}$$

$$\begin{pmatrix}\text{Interest earned in}\\ \text{any payment interval}\end{pmatrix} = i \times \begin{pmatrix}\text{Amount in the sinking fund}\\ \text{at the beginning of the interval}\end{pmatrix}$$

$$\begin{pmatrix}\text{Increase in the sinking fund's balance}\\ \text{during any payment interval}\end{pmatrix} = PMT + \begin{pmatrix}\text{Interest earned}\\ \text{during the interval}\end{pmatrix}$$

$$\begin{pmatrix}\text{Book value}\\ \text{of the debt}\end{pmatrix} = \begin{pmatrix}\text{Principal amount}\\ \text{of the debt}\end{pmatrix} - \begin{pmatrix}\text{Balance in the}\\ \text{sinking fund}\end{pmatrix}$$

List of Key Terms

Annual cost of a debt *(p. 645)*
Bond *(p. 614)*
Bond discount *(p. 623)*
Bond premium *(p. 623)*
Book value of a debt *(p. 645)*
Coupon rate *(p. 614)*
Debenture *(p. 614)*
Face value *(p. 614)*
Flat price *(p. 634)*
Issue date *(p. 614)*
Maturity date *(p. 614)*
Quoted price *(p. 635)*
Sinking fund *(p. 639)*
Sinking fund schedule *(p. 640)*
Yield to maturity *(p. 627)*

CHAPTER OUTLINE

LEARNING OBJECTIVES

After completing this chapter, you will be able to:

- Calculate the net present value (*NPV*) of a capital investment and use the *NPV* to decide whether the investment should be made
- Under conditions of capital rationing, choose the best combination of investments from a group of acceptable capital investment opportunities
- Select the best investment from two or more mutually exclusive investments
- Calculate the internal rate of return (*IRR*) of a capital investment and use the *IRR* to decide whether the investment should be made
- Calculate the payback period of a capital investment

CHAPTER *16

Business Investment Decisions

WHAT ANALYSIS SHOULD A BUSINESS undertake for investment decisions such as expanding production, adding another product line, or replacing the existing plant or equipment?

In this chapter we will study techniques used by managers to make sound financial decisions on capital investments. We will study three criteria widely employed to guide business investment decisions. Two of them rest on a solid economic foundation. The third is flawed in some respects but, nevertheless, is frequently used in business—it is important that you understand its limitations.

Given the long-term nature of capital investments, any rigorous analysis must recognize the time value of money. Most of the concepts and mathematics you need to evaluate business investments have already been presented in previous chapters. What remains is to learn the terminology and procedures for applying this knowledge to analyze potential business investments.

16.1 Comparing Business to Personal Investment Decisions

The fundamental principles that guide both personal and business investment decisions are the same. The Valuation Principle is as relevant to business investments as it is to personal investments. Use of the Valuation Principle to determine the fair market value of an investment requires three steps:

1. Identify or estimate the cash flows expected from the investment. If there are cash outflows as well as cash inflows in any particular period, estimate the period's

$$\text{Net cash flow} = \text{Cash inflows} - \text{Cash outflows}$$

2. Determine the rate of return appropriate for the type of investment.
3. Calculate the sum of the present values of the net cash flows estimated in Step 1, discounted at the rate of return determined in Step 2.

If cash flows are actually received as forecast in Step 1, an investor will realize the Step 2 rate of return on the amount of money calculated in Step 3. But a *higher* purchase price or *lower* (than forecast) cash flows will result in a rate of return that is *smaller* than the discount rate used in Step 2. On the other hand, a *lower* price or *higher* cash flows will result in a rate of return *greater* than the discount rate.

The *nature* of investments made by an *operating* business differs markedly from the nature of most personal investments. Personal investments fall primarily in a limited number of categories such as Treasury bills, GICs, bonds, and stocks. With the exception of common stocks, there is a considerable degree of similarity among investments within each category. In addition, an individual investor can usually depend on competitive bidding in the financial markets to set fair prices for widely traded securities. In these cases, the investor may not explicitly use the Valuation Principle in selecting investments.

For investments in plant and equipment by a business, the way in which the asset will be used and the resulting pattern of cash flows tend to make each investment situation unique. Also, there are likely to be ongoing cash outflows as well as cash inflows associated with a business investment. These factors argue for a more comprehensive and rigorous approach in business to handle the great variety of investment possibilities.

Individual investors and business managers take different perspectives in determining the discount rate used with the Valuation Principle. An individual investor looks to the financial markets for benchmark rates of return on each category of investment. A business manager takes the view that a capital investment must be financed by some combination of debt and equity financing. Therefore, a business investment project must provide a rate of return *at least equal to* the return required by the providers of the capital. The weighted average rate of return required by a firm's sources of debt and equity financing is called the firm's **cost of capital**. *This cost of capital is the discount rate that should be used when applying the Valuation Principle* to a proposed capital investment project. The sum of the present values of the project's future cash flows discounted at the firm's cost of capital represents the value of the project to the business. The business should not pay more than this value. The same project may be worth more or less to another business primarily because the project's future cash flows are likely to differ when operated by another business. It could also be the case that different firms would use differing discount rates because of differing costs of capital.

There are three possible outcomes of a comparison between the present value of future cash flows and the initial capital investment required.

1. **Present value of the future cash flows = Initial investment**
   The cash flows will provide a rate of return (on the initial investment) exactly *equal* to the discount rate—the firm's cost of capital. The investment's net cash flows will be just enough to repay the invested capital along with the minimum required rate of return. This is, therefore, the *minimum condition* for acceptance of a capital investment project.
2. **Present value of the future cash flows < Initial investment**
   The project's net cash flows will not be enough to provide the sources of financing with their *full* minimum required rate of return (on top of the return of their capital investment). Note that we are not necessarily saying that the project or the suppliers of capital lose money—we are saying only that the project will not provide the *full* rate of return embodied in the discount rate. In this case, the investment opportunity should be *rejected.*
3. **Present value of the future cash flows > Initial investment**
   The investment will earn a rate of return greater than the discount rate—more than the minimum needed to give the suppliers of capital their minimum required return (as well as their capital investment back). The project should be accepted.

The preceding discussion can be summarized in the following decision criterion:

INVESTMENT DECISION CRITERION

Undertake a business investment opportunity if the present value of the future net cash flows (discounted at the firm's cost of capital) is greater than or equal to the initial investment.

The Economic Value That an Investment Adds to a Firm We have seen that the sources of investment capital receive their required rate of return (the cost of capital) when

$$\text{Present value of (net) cash flows} = \text{Initial investment}$$

In this circumstance, the economic value (present value) of the future cash flows is the same as the amount initially spent to buy the investment. Therefore, undertaking this investment does not change the firm's value. It follows that, in Case 3 of the preceding list, the difference

$$(\text{Present value of cash flows}) - (\text{Initial investment})$$

represents the *value immediately added* to the firm when it makes the initial investment. That is,

$$\begin{matrix}\text{Value added}\\ \text{to the firm}\end{matrix} = \begin{pmatrix}\text{Present value of the}\\ \text{future net cash flows}\end{pmatrix} - \begin{pmatrix}\text{Initial}\\ \text{investment}\end{pmatrix}$$

The providers of debt financing have no claim on this added value. It belongs entirely to the firm's owners (the providers of equity capital).

The following example considers an investment opportunity with features typical of business investment opportunities. Periodic cash flows are unequal and include a cash outflow subsequent to the initial investment. The investment, if undertaken, must be financed with borrowed funds.

Note: Since forecasts of future cash flows are imprecise, all calculations in this chapter will be rounded to the nearest dollar. Even this suggests a degree of precision that does not really exist in this sort of analysis. It does, however, permit you to verify the mathematical accuracy of your calculations.

Example 16.1A *Evaluating a Business Investment Opportunity*

A low-risk, four-year investment promises to pay \$3000, \$6000, and \$5000 at the end of the first, second, and fourth years, respectively. A cash injection of \$1000 is required at the end of the third year. The investment may be purchased for \$10,000, which would have to be borrowed at an interest rate of 10%. Use the Valuation Principle to determine whether the investment should be undertaken.

Solution

The purchase price at which a 10% rate of return would be realized on the amount invested is the present value of the cash flows discounted at 10%.

$$\begin{aligned}\text{Price for a 10\% rate of return} &= \frac{\$3000}{1.10} + \frac{\$6000}{1.10^2} + \frac{(-\$1000)}{1.10^3} + \frac{\$5000}{1.10^4} \\ &= \$2727 + \$4959 - \$751 + \$3415 \\ &= \$10{,}350\end{aligned}$$

The \$10,000 offering price should be accepted. By paying a price that is *below* \$10,350, the purchaser will realize a rate of return on investment *greater* than the 10% cost of capital to finance the investment.

Interpretation: The \$10,350 figure for the present value of the investment's cash flows represents the amount today that is *equivalent* to the cash-flow stream from the investment. By paying \$10,000 today for a payment stream that is worth \$10,350 today, the firm's value is immediately increased by \$350 (in current dollars).

Example 16.1B *Evaluating a Business Investment Opportunity*

Repeat the problem in Example 16.1A, with the change that the interest rate on the loan to finance the investment is 12% instead of 10%.

Solution

The purchase price at which a 12% rate of return would be realized on the amount invested is the present value of the cash flows discounted at 12%.

$$\begin{aligned}\text{Price for a 12\% rate of return} &= \frac{\$3000}{1.12} + \frac{\$6000}{1.12^2} + \frac{(-\$1000)}{1.12^3} + \frac{\$5000}{1.12^4}\\ &= \$2679 + \$4783 - \$712 + \$3178\\ &= \$9928\end{aligned}$$

The \$10,000 offering price should be rejected. Paying a price that is *above* \$9928 would result in a rate of return on investment that is *less* than the 12% cost of capital to finance the investment.

Cost Minimization Suppose the replacement of a piece of machinery is essential to the operation of an entire production line. Either Machine A or Machine B will do the job equally well. In other words, the future benefits will be the same whether we obtain Machine A or Machine B. In such a case, the scope of the financial analysis can be narrowed to finding the lowest-cost alternative. This involves a comparison of the *current* economic values of the future cash *outflows* for each alternative. The best choice is the one having the *lower* present value of cash outflows.[1]

Example 16.1C *Evaluating Lease versus Purchase Alternatives*

Laven and Co., Certified General Accountants, are considering whether to buy or lease a photocopy machine. A five-year lease requires payments of \$550 at the beginning of every three months. The same machine can be purchased for \$9000 and would have a trade-in value of \$1500 after five years. If the accounting firm can borrow funds at 11% compounded quarterly, should it buy or lease a photocopy machine?

Solution

The preferred alternative is the one having the lower present value of expenditures (net of any amounts recovered from resale, salvage, or trade-in).

As discussed in Section 13.2, leasing is usually regarded as an alternative to borrowing the funds to purchase the asset. Therefore, the appropriate discount rate to use in the present-value calculation is the firm's cost of borrowing. The lease payments form a simple annuity due with

$$PMT = \$550 \qquad n = 4(5) = 20 \qquad \text{and} \qquad i = \frac{11\%}{4} = 2.75\%$$

If the photocopy machine is purchased, there is an initial expenditure of \$9000 and a \$1500 recovery from trading it in five years later.

---

[1] If the alternatives do not have equal lifetimes, the analysis must go beyond a simple comparison of the present values of cash outflows for the respective lifetimes. The additional analysis needed will be presented in Section 16.3.

Algebraic Solution

$$PV(\text{lease}) = PMT\left[\frac{1-(1+i)^{-n}}{i}\right] \times (1+i)$$
$$= \$550\left(\frac{1-1.0275^{-20}}{0.0275}\right)(1.0275)$$
$$= \$8605$$

$$PV(\text{purchase}) = \$9000 - FV(1+i)^{-n}$$
$$= \$9000 - \$1500(1.0275^{-20})$$
$$= \$9000 - \$872$$
$$= \$8128$$

Hence, purchasing the photocopying machine is the lower cost alternative. The current economic value of the difference in net costs over the five-year lifetime is $477.

Financial Calculator Solution

Compute the present value of the lease payments.

BGN mode

550 (+/−) (PMT) 0 (FV) 2.75 (i) 20 (n) (COMP) (PV) [8605]

Compute the present value of the trade-in value.

0 (PMT) 1500 (FV) (COMP) (PV) [−872]

The present value of the purchase expenditures is

$$\$9000 - \$872 = \$8128$$

compared to the $8605 present value of the lease payments. In current dollars, the purchase alternative costs $477 less than the lease alternative. Therefore, the accounting firm should purchase the photocopy machine.

Exercise 16.1

Answers to the odd-numbered problems are at the end of the book.

Unless otherwise indicated in the following exercises, assume that the initial capital investment occurs at the beginning of the first year and subsequent cash flows occur at the end of each year.

•**1.** Vencap Enterprises is evaluating an investment opportunity that can be purchased for $30,000. Further product development will require contributions of $30,000 in Year 1 and $10,000 in Year 2. Then returns of $20,000, $60,000, and $40,000 are expected in the three following years.

a. Use the Valuation Principle to determine whether Vencap should make the investment if its cost of capital is 15%.

b. By what amount will the current economic value of Vencap be increased or decreased if it proceeds with purchasing the investment for $30,000?

•**2.** Repeat Problem 1 with the change that Vencap's cost of capital is 18%.

•**3.** What price should Vencap offer for the investment opportunity described in Problem 1 if it requires a 20% return on investment?

•**4.** The timber rights to a tract of forest can be purchased for $90,000. The harvesting agreement would allow 25% of the timber to be cut in each of the first, second, fourth, and fifth years. The purchaser of the timber rights would be required to replant, at its expense, the logged areas in Years 3 and 6. Arrowsmith Lumber calculates that its profit in each of the four cutting years would be $50,000 and that the cost of replanting the harvested areas in each of Years 3 and 6 would be $20,000.

a. Should Arrowsmith Lumber buy the timber rights if its cost of capital is 14%?

b. By what amount would the economic value of Arrowsmith Lumber be increased or decreased if it proceeded with purchasing the timber rights for $90,000?

•**5.** Repeat Problem 4 with the change that Arrowsmith Lumber's cost of capital is 18%.

•**6.** At what price would Arrowsmith Lumber be willing to purchase the timber rights described in Problem 4 if it requires a return on investment of 20%?

•**7.** A machine can be leased for four years at $1000 per month payable at the beginning of each month. Alternatively, it can be purchased for $43,000 and sold for $5000 after four years. Should the machine be purchased or leased if the firm's cost of borrowing is:

a. 12% compounded monthly? **b.** 9% compounded monthly?

•**8.** A real estate salesperson can lease an automobile for five years at $500 per month payable at the beginning of each month, or purchase it for $28,000. She can obtain a loan at 9.75% compounded monthly to purchase the car. Should she lease or buy the car if:

a. The trade-in value after five years is $5000?

b. The trade-in value after five years is $8000?

•**9.** A college can purchase a telephone system for $30,000 or lease a system for five years for a front-end charge of $3000 and regular payments of $1500 at the beginning of every quarter (including the first quarter). The system can be purchased at the end of the lease period for $3000.

a. Should the college lease or buy the system if it can borrow funds at 10% compounded quarterly?

b. What is the current economic value of the savings with the lower-cost option?

•**10.** Rocky Mountain Bus Tours needs an additional bus for three years. It can lease a bus for $2100 payable at the beginning of each month, or it can buy a similar bus for $110,000, using financing at the rate of 12% compounded monthly. The bus's resale value after three years is expected to be $60,000.

a. On strictly financial considerations, should the company lease or buy the bus?

b. What is the financial advantage in current dollars of the preferred choice?

••11. Ralph Harder has been transferred to Regina for five years. He has found an attractive house that he can buy for \$120,000 or rent for \$900 per month, payable at the beginning of each month. He estimates that the resale value of the house in five years will be \$145,000 net of the selling commission. If he buys the house, the average (month-end) costs for repairs, maintenance, and property taxes will be \$250. Should Mr. Harder rent or buy the house if mortgage rates are:

a. 10.5% compounded monthly? **b.** 9% compounded monthly?

16.2 The Net Present Value of an Investment

In this section, we will express the investment criterion and the concepts from Section 16.1 in language customarily used for business investment analysis. Recall that

$$\begin{matrix}\text{Value added}\\ \text{to the firm}\end{matrix} = \begin{pmatrix}\text{Present value of the}\\ \text{future net cash flows}\end{pmatrix} - \begin{pmatrix}\text{Initial}\\ \text{investment}\end{pmatrix}$$

Since an operating period's "net cash flow" means

$$\text{Cash inflows}^2 - \text{Cash outflows}$$

we can expand the first quantity (in brackets on the right side) giving

$$\begin{matrix}\text{Value added}\\ \text{to the firm}\end{matrix} = \begin{pmatrix}\text{Present value of}\\ \text{future cash inflows}\end{pmatrix} - \begin{pmatrix}\text{Present value of}\\ \text{future cash outflows}\end{pmatrix} - \begin{pmatrix}\text{Initial}\\ \text{investment}\end{pmatrix}$$

If we include the "initial investment" among the cash *outflows,* the second and third terms may be combined to give

$$\begin{matrix}\text{Value added}\\ \text{to the firm}\end{matrix} = \begin{pmatrix}\text{Present value of}\\ \text{cash inflows}\end{pmatrix} - \begin{pmatrix}\text{Present value of}\\ \text{cash outflows}\end{pmatrix}$$

The right side can be viewed as the *net* amount by which the *present value* of cash inflows exceeds the *present value* of cash outflows. For this reason, the "value added to the firm" is customarily called the **net present value** (*NPV*) of an investment. That is,

$$NPV = \begin{pmatrix}\text{Present value of}\\ \text{cash inflows}\end{pmatrix} - \begin{pmatrix}\text{Present value of}\\ \text{cash outflows}\end{pmatrix}$$

The Investment Decision Criterion developed in Section 16.1 may be expressed in terms of the *NPV*.

***NPV* INVESTMENT DECISION CRITERION:**

Accept the investment if $NPV \geq 0$.
Reject the investment if $NPV < 0$.

---

[2] A rigorous analysis of capital investments requires the calculation of cash flows *before* interest charges but *after* income tax (including the tax savings from any capital cost allowance on a depreciable asset). You will learn these refinements if you take a course in managerial finance. In this chapter, we will use *profit* or *operating profit* to mean the net before-interest after-tax cash flow from the investment during an accounting period.

The firm's cost of capital (for financing the investment) is used for the discount rate in the *NPV* calculation. To simplify the calculation of present values, the assumption is usually made that the cash inflows and outflows within each year occur at the *end* of the year.[3] The initial capital investment outlay is assumed to take place at the *beginning* of the first year.

> ***Significance of an Investment's NPV***
> The *NPV* of an investment is the amount (in current dollars) by which the economic value of the cash inflows exceeds the economic value of the cash outflows. Therefore, the *NPV* represents the value added to the firm on the date the investment is made.

This added value belongs to the owners of the business and increases the market value of the owners' equity. A negative *NPV* does not necessarily mean that the investment will cause the firm to suffer an accounting loss. It does mean, however, that the project's cash flows are not sufficient to provide the sources of financing with their full minimum required rate of return. As a result, a negative *NPV* project would, if undertaken, reduce the market value of the firm's equity (by the amount of the *NPV*).

Example 16.2A *Using the NPV Criterion to Evaluate a Capital Investment*

A firm is contemplating the purchase of a $10,000 machine that would reduce labour costs by $4000 in each of Years 1 and 2, and by $3000 in each of Years 3 and 4. The machine's salvage value at the end of Year 4 is $1000. Should the machine be purchased if the firm's cost of capital is 15% compounded annually?

Solution

Profits would rise by $4000 in Years 1 and 2 and by $3000 in Years 3 and 4 as a result of purchasing the machine. These profit increases plus the salvage value in Year 4 are the net cash flows that the investment will generate.

Years	0	1	2	3	4
Cash flow ($000s)	(10)	4	4	3	3 1

$$NPV = \$4000(1.15^{-1}) + \$4000(1.15^{-2}) + \$3000(1.15^{-3}) + \$4000(1.15^{-4}) - \$10{,}000$$
$$= \$3478 + \$3025 + \$1973 + \$2287 - \$10{,}000$$
$$= \$763$$

Since the $NPV > 0$, the machine should be purchased. The savings will add $783 to the value of the firm.

[3] The errors introduced by ignoring the time value of money *within* each year are usually smaller than the uncertainties in forecasts of the amounts and timing of the cash flows.

Example 16.2B Using the NPV Criterion When Cash Flows Form Annuities

Digitel Electronics' engineering and marketing departments have prepared forecasts for the development costs and operating profits of the next generation of their digital electrical meters. Development costs for each of the next three years will be \$50,000. Manufacturing equipment costing \$100,000 will be purchased near the end of Year 3. Annual profits for the normal five-year product life (Years 4 to 8 inclusive) are projected to be \$80,000. The salvage value of the manufacturing equipment at the end of Year 8 is \$20,000. Should Digitel proceed with the product development if its annually compounded cost of capital is:

a. 14%? **b.** 15.5%? **c.** 17%?

Solution

The cash flows are presented on a time line below. Our convention is to assume cash flows occur at the year's end unless otherwise indicated. Cash outflows (negative) are placed in parentheses. Digitel should proceed with the product development if the net present value of the cash flows, discounted at the cost of capital, is greater than or equal to zero.

Years	0	1	2	3	4	5	6	7	8
Cash flow (\$000s)		(50)	(50)	(50) (100)	80	80	80	80	80 20

$$NPV = \text{Present value of cash inflows} - \text{Present value of cash outflows}$$

To reduce the number of calculations, do not break up annuities. In this problem, there is an ordinary simple annuity with three \$50,000 payments and a deferred (three years) ordinary simple annuity with five \$80,000 payments.

$$NPV = -\$50{,}000\left[\frac{1-(1+i)^{-3}}{i}\right] - \frac{\$100{,}000}{(1+i)^3}$$

$$+\$80{,}000\left[\frac{1-(1+i)^{-3}}{i}\right] \times \frac{1}{(1+i)^3} + \frac{\$20{,}000}{(1+i)^8}$$

a. For $i = 14\%$,

$$NPV = -\$116{,}082 - \$67{,}497 + \$185{,}379 + \$7011 = \$8811$$

Since $NPV > 0$, Digitel should proceed with the project. The interpretation of the *NPV* is that the current economic value of the funds remaining after repaying the sources of financing is \$8811. This is also the increase in the firm's current market value as a result of investing in the product development project.

b. For $i = 15.5\%$,

$$NPV = -\$113{,}221 - \$64{,}901 + \$172{,}007 + \$6315 = \$200$$

Given the sizes of the cash flows in the forecast, this is basically a zero-*NPV* investment. This does not imply that there is no profit. Rather, it means that the estimated profits will be just sufficient to repay the project's financing along with a 15.5% rate of return on the funds while they are invested in the project. This is acceptable, but represents the threshold for acceptability.

c. For $i = 17\%$, we obtain $NPV = -\$7414$. In this case, the project will fall short (by \$7414 in terms of current dollars) of repaying the financing along with the required 17% rate of return on investment. Digitel should not proceed in this case.

Exercise 16.2

Answers to the odd-numbered problems are at the end of the book.

Use the *NPV* investment criterion to answer the following problems. Unless otherwise indicated, assume that the initial capital investment occurs at the beginning of the first year and that subsequent cash flows occur at the end of the year. Show calculations that justify your decision.

•**1.** St. Lawrence Bus Lines is offered a contract for busing schoolchildren that will produce an annual profit of \$36,000 for seven years. To fulfill the contract, St. Lawrence would have to buy three buses at a total cost of \$165,000. At the end of the contract, the resale value of the buses is estimated to be \$40,000. Should St. Lawrence Bus Lines sign the contract if its cost of capital is:

a. 12%? **b.** 15%? **c.** 18%?

•**2.** An automotive parts plant is scheduled to be closed in 10 years. Nevertheless, its engineering department thinks that some investments in computer-controlled equipment can be justified by savings in labour and energy costs within that time frame. The engineering department is proposing a four-phase program that would require the expenditure of \$100,000 at the beginning of each of the next four years. Each successive phase would produce additional annual savings of \$30,000, \$27,000, \$22,000, and \$22,000. The savings from any phase are in addition to annual savings already realized from previous phases. There will be no significant residual value. The firm's cost of capital is 14%. As the plant's financial analyst, what phases, if any, of the proposal would you accept?

•**3.** The pro forma projections for growing a 20-hectare ginseng crop require the expenditure of \$150,000 in the summer that the crop is planted, and an additional \$50,000 in each of the next two summers to cultivate and fertilize the growing crop. After payment of the costs of harvesting the crop, the profit should be \$200,000 in the third summer after planting, and \$300,000 in the fourth summer. Allowing for a cost of capital of 15% compounded annually, what is the economic value of the project at the time of planting? (*Hint:* The project's economic value is its *NPV*.)

•**4.** A proposed strip mine would require the investment of \$1 million at the beginning of the first year and a further investment of \$1.5 million at the end of the first year. Mining operations are expected to yield annual profits of \$500,000 beginning in Year 2. The ore body will sustain 10 years of mining operations. At the beginning of the twelfth year, the mining company would have to spend \$500,000 on environmental restoration.

Would the project provide the mining company with a rate of return exceeding its 18% cost of capital? (*Hint:* The project will provide a rate of return exceeding the cost of capital if it has a positive *NPV*.)

•5. The development of a new product will require the expenditure of $150,000 at the beginning of each of the next three years. When the product reaches the market in Year 4, it is expected to increase the firm's annual profit by $90,000 for seven years. Then the product will be replaced by a new model, and $100,000 of the original expenditures should be recoverable. If the firm's cost of capital is 14%, should it proceed with the project?

•6. The introduction of a new product will require an initial investment of $45,000. The annual profit expected from the new product is forecast to be $9000 for Years 1 to 3, $6000 for Years 4 to 6, and $4000 for Years 7 to 12. Should the firm proceed with the investment if its required compound annual return is 15%?

••7. Jasper Ski Corp. is studying the feasibility of installing a new chair lift to expand the capacity of its downhill-skiing operation. Site preparation would require the expenditure of $400,000 at the beginning of the first year. Construction would take place early in the second year at a cost of $1.8 million. The lift would have a useful life of 12 years and a residual value of $400,000. The increased capacity should generate increased annual profits of $300,000 at the end of Years 2 to 5 inclusive and $500,000 in Years 6 to 13 inclusive. Should Jasper proceed with the project if it requires a return on investment of 16%?

••8. A capital project would require an immediate investment of $150,000 and a further investment of $40,000 on a date four years from now. On the operating side, the project is expected to lose $30,000 in the first year and $10,000 in the second, to break even in the third year, and to turn annual profits of $60,000 in Years 4 to 7 and $30,000 in Years 8 to 10. The estimated residual value at the end of the tenth year is $50,000. Is the project acceptable if a return on investment of 17% is required?

••9. To manufacture a new product, a company must immediately invest $275,000 in new equipment. At the end of Years 3 and 5, there will have to be a major overhaul of the equipment at a cost of $40,000 on each occasion. The new product is expected to increase annual operating profits by $75,000 in each of the first four years, and by $55,000 in each of the next three years. The equipment will then be salvaged to recover about $30,000. Should the product be manufactured if the company's cost of capital is 14% compounded annually?

••10. A new machine that will lead to savings in labour costs of $16,000 per year can be purchased for $52,000. However, it will cost $1500 per year for the first four years and $2500 per year for the next four years to service and maintain it. In addition, its annual electrical power consumption will cost $1000. After a service life of eight years, the salvage value of the machine is expected to be $5000. Should the machine be acquired if the company requires a minimum return on investment of 15%?

16.3 Comparing Investment Projects

Normally, a firm should accept every investment project that has a positive net present value. Any positive-*NPV* project produces a net economic benefit to the firm after the sources of financing have received their required returns. The *NPV* gives the magnitude of the economic benefit on the date of the initial capital expenditure.

There are two circumstances in which a business will not necessarily proceed with all of the positive-*NPV* investments available to it. In these situations, choosing one of the projects may exclude the selection of other positive-*NPV* projects. Some refinements to our selection criterion are needed to rank or select from projects that, in some sense, are competing alternatives.

Capital Rationing

Capital rationing is the circumstance in which there is a limit on the total amount of capital funds that a firm may invest during a period. In this situation, the firm should *choose the group of projects that have the highest combined NPV* subject to the limitation on the total capital budget. By this choice, the increase in the firm's value is maximized.

Example 16.3A *Selecting Capital Projects Subject to a Capital Rationing Constraint*

The strategic planning group at Hardy Toy Co. has identified the following positive-*NPV* projects, ranked in order of their *NPV*. All projects are independent—selection of any project neither requires nor precludes the selection of any other project.

Capital investment project	Initial capital investment	Project *NPV*
Expand production facilities	$270,000	$195,000
Open western distribution centre	250,000	155,000
Introduce Toy A	90,000	130,000
Buy out regional wood-toy maker	155,000	120,000
Introduce Game B	60,000	80,000
Purchase plastic moulding machine	54,000	70,000
Introduce Toy C	110,000	65,000
Introduce plastic recycling process	56,000	63,000
Replace old packaging machine	62,000	40,000
Introduce new doll	60,000	31,000

The board of directors has imposed a $600,000 capital expenditure limit for the next year. What projects should the company undertake within the capital budget restriction?

Solution

The company will want to choose the group of projects with the largest combined *NPV*, subject to the requirement that the total initial capital investment must not exceed $600,000. To obtain the "biggest bang per invested buck," it is helpful to calculate each project's *NPV* per dollar of initial investment. In the following table, the projects are ranked on the basis of this ratio (presented in the third column).

Project number	Capital investment project	*NPV* per invested dollar	Initial capital investment	Cumulative capital investment
1	Introduce Toy A	$1.44	$ 90,000	$ 90,000
2	Introduce Game B	1.33	60,000	150,000
3	Purchase plastic moulding machine	1.30	54,000	204,000
4	Introduce plastic recycling process	1.13	56,000	260,000
5	Buy out regional wood-toy maker	0.77	155,000	
6	Expand production facilities	0.72	270,000	
7	Replace old packaging machine	0.65	62,000	
8	Open western distribution centre	0.62	250,000	
9	Introduce Toy C	0.59	110,000	
10	Introduce new doll	0.52	60,000	

Until the capital budget constraint becomes a consideration, the projects with the highest *NPV* per invested dollar are automatically selected. The first four projects require a total investment of $260,000, leaving $340,000 available for others. If Project 5 is chosen next, Project 6 cannot be undertaken, because it would take the total investment beyond the $600,000 limit. But Projects 7 and 9 can still be included, along with 5, while remaining within the $600,000 limit. Therefore, one group of projects that must be considered is Projects 1, 2, 3, 4, 5, 7, and 9, for which

Required total capital investment = $587,000
Total net present value = $225,000

If we do not include Project 5, we can proceed with Project 6 and still have enough funds remaining in the $600,000 global budget to undertake Project 7 as well. This second combination (Projects 1, 2, 3, 4, 6, and 7) has

Required total capital investment = $592,000
Total net present value = $235,000

The second group should be selected since it adds $10,000 more economic value to Hardy Toy Co.

Mutually Exclusive Projects

Alternative capital investments, any one of which will substantially satisfy the same need or purpose, are called **mutually exclusive projects**. For example, three different machines that fabricate the same product are mutually exclusive projects if any one of them will satisfy the firm's requirements. Only one will be selected, even if each one has a positive *NPV*.

If the mutually exclusive projects all have the *same* lifetime, a direct comparison may be made among the *NPV*s of the projects. The one with the largest positive *NPV* should be chosen because it provides the greatest economic benefit to the firm.

It projects have *unequal* lifetimes, it is *not* a simple matter of selecting the project with the largest lifetime *NPV*. A fair comparison requires a common time frame that might involve replacement cycles for one or more of the projects. However, we cannot arbitrarily pick the duration of the common time period because net cash flows are generally spread unevenly over each project's lifetime. Either of two methods—the *replacement chain method* or the *equivalent annual cash-flow method*—may be used to deal with unequal investment lifetimes and uneven cash flows.

Replacement Chain Method The replacement chain approach repeats the replacement cycle of one or more of the mutually exclusive alternatives until *all* terminate on the *same* date. Then the *NPV*s of all cash flows within this common time horizon are calculated for each project. The one with the highest positive *NPV* should be selected.

Example 16.3B *Replacement Chain Method with Mutually Exclusive Projects*

A machine shop is trying to decide which of two types of metal lathe to purchase. The more versatile Japanese lathe costs \$32,000, and will generate an annual profit of \$16,000 for three years. Its trade-in value after three years will be about \$10,000. The more durable German lathe costs \$42,000, and will increase profits by \$12,000 per year for six years. Its trade-in value at that point is estimated at \$15,000. Based on an *NPV* calculation at a 10% cost of capital, which lathe should be purchased?

Solution

We will first determine the lifetime *NPV* of a capital investment in each lathe.

Time diagram for the Japanese lathe

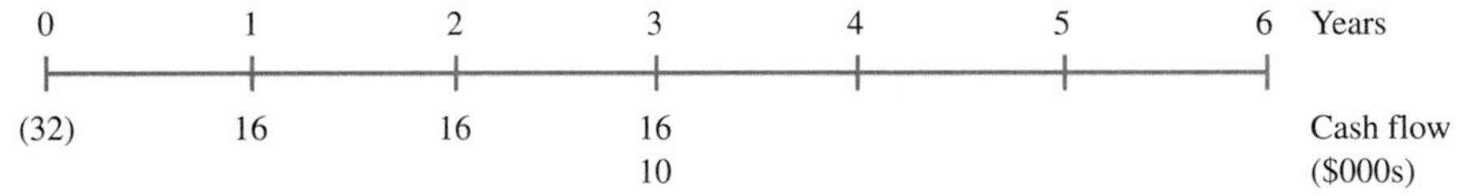

Time diagram for the German lathe

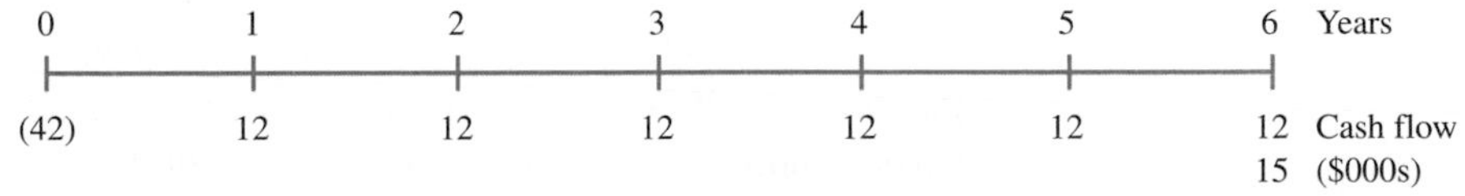

The *NPV* for the acquisition of the Japanese lathe is

$$\begin{aligned} NPV_J &= PMT\left[\frac{1-(1+i)^{-n}}{i}\right] + FV(1+i)^{-n} - \$32{,}000 \\ &= \$16{,}000\left[\frac{1-(1.10)^{-3}}{0.10}\right] + \$10{,}000(1.10)^{-3} - \$32{,}000 \\ &= \$39{,}790 + \$7513 - \$32{,}000 \\ &= \$15{,}303 \end{aligned}$$

The *NPV* for the purchase of the German lathe is

$$NPV_G = \$12{,}000\left[\frac{1-(1.10)^{-6}}{0.10}\right] + \$15{,}000(1.10)^{-6} - \$42{,}000$$
$$= \$18{,}730$$

A comparison of the *NPV*s at this point would not necessarily lead to a valid conclusion (to purchase the higher-*NPV* German lathe). For a fair comparison, an adjustment must be made for the unequal service lives of the two lathes.

Since the machine shop is prepared to commit to the German lathe for six years, it is logical to infer that it is also prepared to have a Japanese lathe for six years. By including one replacement cycle of the Japanese lathe in the analysis, we obtain a common time frame of six years for both alternatives.

To reconsider the Japanese option, it is not necessary to begin again with each year's cash flows. Remember the significance of the present value of a number of cash flows—it is the single amount that is equivalent, at the focal date, to all of the cash flows. Therefore, an investment's *NPV* is equivalent to all of the cash flows included in its calculation. The actual cash flows for six years with the Japanese lathe may be replaced by inflows of \$15,303 at the beginning of each three-year service life. The following equivalent time diagram may be used for six years of operation with the Japanese lathe.

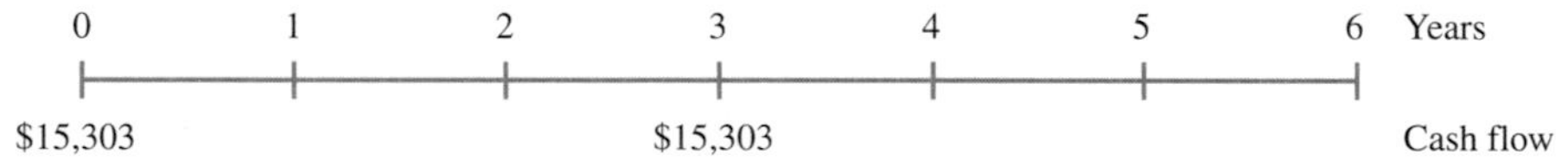

The *NPV* for six years with the Japanese lathe is

$$NPV_J = \$15{,}303 + \$15{,}303(1.10)^{-3} = \$26{,}800$$

With the alternative investments transformed to a common time horizon, the Japanese lathe gives the higher *NPV*. Therefore, it should be selected.

The replacement chain method works well when the service life of one alternative is an integer multiple of the service life of a second alternative (as in Example 16.3B). But what if the service lives of two competing alternatives were five years and seven years? We would have to consider five cycles of the seven-year lifetime and seven cycles of the five-year lifetime to have a common time frame containing a whole number of replacement cycles of both alternatives. If there are more than two alternatives, the replacement chain approach becomes more unwieldy. In these cases the equivalent annual cash-flow method is simpler.

Equivalent Annual Cash-Flow Method In this approach, we calculate the *constant annual* cash flow during each project's lifetime that has the same *NPV* as the *actual* cash flows. Since the equivalent annual flows also apply to any number of replacement cycles, we can directly compare the equivalent annual cash flows of competing projects. *The project with the largest positive equivalent annual cash flow should be selected.*

Example 16.3C *Equivalent Annual Cash-Flow Method with Mutually Exclusive Projects*

Repeat the problem in Example 16.3B using the equivalent annual cash-flow method.

Solution

Recall that the *NPV* for one three-year investment cycle in the Japanese lathe was

$$NPV_J = \$15{,}303$$

and that the *NPV* for one six-year investment cycle in the German lathe was

$$NPV_G = \$18{,}730$$

For the Japanese lathe, the equivalent annual cash flow is the value of PMT_J satisfying

$$\$15{,}303 = PMT_J\left[\frac{1-(1.10)^{-3}}{0.10}\right]$$

The solution is $PMT_J = \$6154$.

For the German lathe, the equivalent annual cash flow is the solution to

$$\$18{,}730 = PMT_G\left[\frac{1-(1.10)^{-6}}{0.10}\right]$$

The solution is $PMT_G = \$4301$.

Since the Japanese lathe has the larger equivalent annual cash flow, it should be selected.

Note: The ratio of the two equivalent annual cash flows in this solution is

$$\frac{PMT_J}{PMT_G} = \frac{\$6154}{\$4301} = 1.431$$

The ratio of the *NPV*s of investments in the two lathes calculated in Example 16.3B for a common six-year time horizon is:

$$\frac{NPV_J \text{ for 6 years}}{NPV_G \text{ for 6 years}} = \frac{\$26{,}800}{\$18{,}730} = 1.431$$

The equality of the two ratios demonstrates the equivalence of the two methods.

TIP UNEQUAL LIVES MATTER ONLY FOR MUTUALLY EXCLUSIVE PROJECTS

Remember that unequal lives do not have to be taken into account when *independent* projects are being selected under conditions of capital rationing. Unequal lives are a consideration only for *mutually exclusive* projects.

Cost Minimization When mutually exclusive alternatives generate the same benefits or cash inflows, it is sufficient to focus on the cash outflows. We should select the lowest-cost alternative, recognizing the time value of money. When the time horizons of the competing alternatives are the same, the present values of the lifetime cash outflows may be directly compared. However, when the time horizons differ, calculate the *equivalent annual cash outflow* for each alternative. Select the one with the *smallest* equivalent annual cash outflow.

Exercise 16.3

Answers to the odd-numbered problems are at the end of the book.

Problems 1, 2, and 3 require the selection of independent capital investments subject to a capital budget limitation.

•**1.** A firm has identified the following four investment opportunities and calculated their net present values. If the firm's capital budget for this period is limited to $300,000, which projects should be selected?

Project	Initial investment	*NPV*
A	$100,000	$ 25,000
B	60,000	40,000
C	130,000	60,000
D	200,000	110,000

•**2.** The investment committee of a company has identified the following seven projects with positive *NPV*s. If the board of directors has approved a $3 million capital budget for the current period, which projects should be selected?

Project	Initial investment	*NPV*
1	$1,000,000	$600,000
2	1,800,000	324,000
3	750,000	285,000
4	600,000	270,000
5	450,000	113,000
6	150,000	21,000
7	250,000	20,000

•**3.** Mohawk Enterprises is considering the following investment opportunities.

Project	Initial investment	Profit for year			
		Year 1	Year 2	Year 3	Year 4
A	$30,000	$12,000	$9000	$ 8000	$20,000
B	36,000	6000	23,000	10,000	14,000
C	18,000	10,000	0	0	20,000
D	22,000	0	18,000	2500	11,000
E	28,000	26,000	0	0	17,000
F	20,000	6000	7000	10,000	11,000

If Mohawk's cost of capital is 15% per annum and its capital budget is limited to $90,000, which projects should it choose?

Problems 4 through 11 require the selection of the best investment from two or more mutually exclusive alternatives.

•4. A small regional airline has narrowed down the possible choices for its next passenger plane purchase to two alternatives. The Eagle model costs \$250,000, and would have an estimated resale value of \$50,000 after seven years. The Albatross model has a \$325,000 price, and would have an estimated resale value of \$150,000 after seven years. The annual operating profit from the Eagle would be \$75,000. Because of its greater fuel efficiency and slightly larger seating capacity, the Albatross's annual profit would be \$95,000. Which plane should the airline purchase if its cost of capital is 15%? In current dollars, what is the economic advantage of selecting the preferred alternative over the other?

•5. Carl Williams does custom wheat combining in southern Alberta. He will purchase either a new Massey or a new Deere combine to replace his old machine. The Massey combine costs \$95,000, and the Deere combine costs \$78,000. Their trade-in values after six years would be about \$25,000 and \$20,000, respectively. Because the Massey cuts an 18-foot swath versus the Deere's 15-foot swath, Carl estimates that his annual profit with the Massey will be 10% higher than the \$35,000 he could make with the Deere. The Massey equipment dealer will provide 100% financing at 11% per annum, and the Deere dealer will approve 100% financing at 10% per annum. Which combine should Carl purchase? How much more, in current dollars, is the better alternative worth?

••6. A business is evaluating two mutually exclusive projects. Project A requires an immediate investment of \$6000, plus another \$8000 in three years. It would produce a profit of \$6000 in the second year, \$18,000 in the fourth year, and \$12,000 in the seventh year. Project B requires an immediate investment of \$5000, another \$8000 in two years, and a further \$5000 in four years. It would produce an annual profit of \$5200 for seven years. Neither project would have any residual value after seven years. Which project should be selected if the required rate of return is 16%? What is the economic advantage, in current dollars, of the preferred project over the other?

••7. A company must choose between two investments. Investment C requires an immediate outlay of \$50,000 and then, in two years, another investment of \$30,000. Investment D requires annual investments of \$25,000 at the beginning of each of the first four years. C would return annual profits of \$16,000 for 10 years beginning with the first year. D's profits would not start until Year 4 but would be \$35,000 in Years 4 to 10 inclusive. The residual values after 10 years are estimated to be \$30,000 for C and \$20,000 for D. Which investment should the company choose if its cost of capital is 15%? How much more is the preferred project worth today?

•8. Machine A costs \$40,000 and is forecast to generate an annual profit of \$15,000 for four years. Machine B, priced at \$60,000, will produce the same annual profits for eight years. The trade-in value of A after four years is expected to be \$10,000, and the resale value of B after eight years is also estimated to be $10,000. If either machine satisfies the firm's requirements, which one should be selected? Use a required return of 14%.

•**9.** A sawmill requires a new saw for cutting small-dimension logs. Model H, with a three-year service life, costs $100,000 and will generate an annual profit of $55,000. Model J, with a four-year service life, costs $140,000 and will return an annual profit of $58,000. Neither saw will have significant salvage value. If the mill's cost of capital is 16%, which model should be purchased?

••**10.** A landscaping business will buy one of three rototillers. The initial cost, expected service life, and trade-in value (at the end of the service life) of each model are presented in the following table. The annual profit from rototilling services is $700.

Model	Cost	Service life (years)	Trade-in value
A	$1000	2	$200
AA	1400	3	450
AAA	2100	6	700

Which model should be purchased if the required return on investment is 20%?

••**11.** An independent trucker is trying to decide whether to buy a 15-ton or a 25-ton truck. A 15-ton vehicle would cost $75,000; it would have a service life of seven years, and a trade-in value of about $15,000 at seven years of age. A 25-ton truck would cost $100,000, and would have a service life of six years and a trade-in value of about $20,000 at six years of age. The estimated annual profit (after provision for a normal salary for the driver–owner) would be $24,000 for the smaller truck and $32,000 for the larger truck. Which truck should be purchased if the cost of financing a truck is 12.5% compounded annually? What is the average annual economic benefit of making the right decision?

Problems 12 through 15 require the selection of the lowest-cost alternative.

•**12.** *Consumer Digest* recently reported that car batteries X, Y, and Z have average service lives of three, four, and six years, respectively. Grace found that the best retail prices for these batteries in her town are $60, $75, and $105. If money is worth 10% compounded annually, which battery has the lowest equivalent annual cost?

•**13.** The provincial government's Ministry of Forest Resources requires a spotter plane for its fire service. The price of a Hawk is $120,000, and its annual operating costs will be $30,000. Given the heavy use it will receive, it will be sold for about $30,000 after five years and replaced. A more durable but less efficient Falcon, priced at $100,000, will cost $40,000 per year to operate, will last seven years, and will have a resale value of $40,000. If the provincial government pays an interest rate of 9% compounded annually on its mid-term debt, which plane has the lower equivalent annual cost?

••**14.** Neil always trades his car in when it reaches five years of age because of the large amount of driving he does in his job. He is investigating whether there would be a financial advantage in buying a two-year-old car every three years instead of buying a new car every five years. His research indicates that, for the make of car he prefers, he could buy a two-year-old car for \$12,000, whereas a new car of the same model sells for \$20,000. In either case, the resale value of the five-year-old car would be \$4000. Repairs and maintenance average \$300 per year for the first two years of the car's life and \$1000 per year for the next three. Which alternative has the lower equivalent annual cost if money is worth 11% compounded annually?

••**15.** A construction company has identified two machines that will accomplish the same job. The Caterpillar model costs \$80,000, and has a service life of eight years if it receives a \$15,000 overhaul every two years. The International model costs \$105,000, and should last 12 years with a \$10,000 overhaul every three years. In either case, the overhaul scheduled for the year of disposition would not be performed, and the machine would be sold for about \$10,000. If the company's cost of capital is 15%, which machine should be purchased?

16.4 Internal Rate of Return

Business managers often prefer to discuss and compare investment opportunities in terms of an annual rate of return on investment. The net present value calculation does not provide the rate of return on the invested funds.

Recall that the net cash flows from an investment project having an *NPV* of zero will be just sufficient to repay the project's financing, including a rate of return *equal* to the discount rate. Therefore, the rate of return on investment for a zero-*NPV* project equals the discount rate (cost of capital) used in the *NPV* calculation. This special case suggests a technique for determining the rate of return on investment from any project. If we can find a discount rate that makes the *NPV* of the project's net cash flows equal to zero, then that discount rate is the project's rate of return on investment. In the context of business capital investments, this rate of return is often called the **internal rate of return** (*IRR*).

INTERNAL RATE OF RETURN (IRR):
An investment's *IRR* is the discount rate that makes the net present value of the investment equal to zero.

When the periodic cash flows from a capital investment form an annuity, you may use a financial calculator to compute *i*. Otherwise, you must employ the trial-and-error approach (Appendix 11B) to solve for the *IRR*.[4] The basic procedure is:

1. Make a reasonable estimate of the investment's *IRR*. (Start with an estimate larger than the cost of capital if the project has a positive *NPV*.)

[4] Advanced models of financial calculators have pre-programmed functions that permit the calculation of the *NPV* and *IRR* for a non-uniform series of cash flows.

2. Calculate the investment's *NPV* using the estimated *IRR* as the discount rate.
3. Make a better estimate of the *IRR*. (If the *NPV* in Step 2 was positive, choose a larger value for the estimated *IRR*. If the *NPV* was negative, choose a smaller value for the *IRR*.) Repeat Steps 2 and 3 until positive and negative *NPV*s are obtained for two *IRR* estimates differing by less than 1%.
4. Interpolate between these two *IRR* estimates to calculate the *IRR* at which the investment's *NPV* is zero. This interpolation step should give you the *IRR* accurate to within ±0.1%.

A positive-*NPV* investment has an *IRR* greater than the cost of capital, whereas a negative-*NPV* investment has an *IRR* less than the cost of capital. The *NPV* Investment Decision Criterion developed in Section 16.2 may be restated in terms of the investment's *IRR*.

***IRR* INVESTMENT DECISION CRITERION:**

Accept the investment if $IRR \geq$ Cost of capital.
Reject the investment if $IRR <$ Cost of capital.

As net cash flows are received from a project, the invested funds are gradually recovered. The *IRR* continues to be earned only on the *unrecovered* portion of the original investment. The recovered funds subsequently earn the rate of return for the next project in which they are reinvested.[5]

Example 16.4A *Calculation of an Investment's IRR by Trial and Error*

A project requires an immediate investment of $20,000, and an additional investment of $10,000 in one year. It will generate an annual profit of $8000 in Years 2 to 8, and have a residual value of $5000 at the end of the eighth year. Calculate the project's internal rate of return. Should the project be undertaken if the firm's cost of capital is 14%?

Solution

The cash flows are presented in the time diagram below.

0	1	2	3	4	5	6	7	8	Years
(20)	(10)	8	8	8	8	8	8	8	Cash flow
								5	($000s)

5 An alternative definition of the *IRR* is "the discount rate that makes the present value of the future cash flows equal to the initial capital outlay." From this version of the definition, it is clearer that the *IRR* is a new name for a familiar concept. The returns on investment that we calculated for various investment instruments in previous chapters are the internal rates of return for those investments. For example, the yield to maturity on a bond (Section 15.3) could also be called the bond's *IRR*. It is merely prevailing business practice that dictates which term is used for the same quantity in different contexts.

The project's net present value at the discount rate i is

$$NPV = -\$20{,}000 - \underbrace{\frac{\$10{,}000}{1+i}}_{\text{Term ①}} + \underbrace{\$8000\left[\frac{1-(1+i)^{-7}}{i}\right] \times \left(\frac{1}{1+i}\right)}_{\text{Term ②}} + \underbrace{\frac{\$5000}{(1+i)^8}}_{\text{Term ③}}$$

The project's internal rate of return is the value for i that makes the NPV zero. Now begin a trial-and-error process to find two values for i that will make the sum of the terms in the NPV expression a few hundred dollars above zero and a few hundred dollars below zero. Then interpolation can be used to improve upon these two estimates of the IRR. A natural choice for the first trial is $i = 14\%$ (the cost of capital).

Trial number	Estimated i	Term ①	Term ②	Term ③	NPV
1	0.14	−$8772	$30,093	$1753	$3074
2	0.15	−8695	28,941	1635	1881
3	0.16	−8621	27,852	1575	756
4	0.165	−8584	27,329	1474	219
	IRR				0
5	0.168	−8562	27,022	1444	−96

Interpolating,

$$\frac{IRR - 0.165}{0.168 - 0.165} \doteq \frac{0 - \$219}{-\$96 - \$219} = \frac{\$219}{\$315} = 0.695$$

$$IRR - 0.165 \doteq 0.003(0.695)$$

$$IRR \doteq 0.165 + 0.0021$$

$$\doteq 0.167$$

$$\doteq 16.7\%$$

The project's IRR is 16.7%. Since the IRR is greater than the cost of capital, the project should be accepted. (This conclusion is consistent with the outcome of the first trial, where the project had a positive NPV when the cost of capital was used as the discount rate.)

Exercise 16.4

Answers to the odd-numbered problems are at the end of the book.

Determine the IRR in the following problems to the nearest 0.1%.

1. A 10-year licence to distribute a product should increase the distributor's profit by $10,000 per year. If the licence can be acquired for $50,000, what is the investment's IRR?
2. Burger Master bought the food concession for a baseball stadium for five years at a price of $1.2 million. If the operating profit is $400,000 per year, what IRR will Burger Master realize on its investment?

•3. Calculate the IRR of each of the four stages of the cost reduction proposal in Problem 2 of Exercise 16.2. Based on the IRR investment criterion, which stages should be approved at a 14% cost of capital?

•**4.** A project requires an initial investment of \$60,000. It will generate an annual profit of \$12,000 for eight years and have a terminal value of \$10,000. Calculate the project's *IRR*. Should it be accepted if the cost of capital is 15%?

•**5.** An investment of \$100,000 will yield annual profits of \$20,000 for 10 years. The proceeds on disposition at the end of the 10 years are estimated at \$25,000. On the basis of its *IRR* and a 16% cost of capital, should the investment be made?

•**6.** Determine the *IRR* on the school bus contract in Problem 1 of Exercise 16.2. At which of the three costs of capital would the contract be financially acceptable?

••**7.** A \$100,000 capital investment will produce annual profits of \$25,000 for the first five years and \$15,000 for the next five years. It will have no residual value. What is its *IRR*? Should it be undertaken if the cost of capital is 15%?

••**8.** A natural resource development and extraction project would require an investment of \$1 million now and \$1 million at the end of each of the next four years. Then it would generate annual profits of \$2 million in each of the following five years. There would be no residual value. What would be the *IRR* of the project? Would it be acceptable to a company requiring a 16% return on investment?

••**9.** The introduction of a new product would require an initial investment of \$120,000. The forecast profits in successive years of the anticipated four-year product life are \$25,000, \$60,000, \$50,000, and \$35,000. Determine the *IRR* of the investment. Should the product be introduced if the firm's cost of capital is 15%?

••**10.** A venture requiring an immediate investment of \$500,000 and an additional investment of \$200,000 in three years' time will generate annual profits of \$150,000 for seven years starting next year. There will be no significant terminal value. Calculate the *IRR* of the investment. Should the investment be undertaken at a 13% cost of capital?

••**11.** Determine the *IRR* on the strip-mine proposal in Problem 4 of Exercise 16.2. Should the mine be developed, given the mining company's 18% cost of capital?

16.5 Comparing *NPV* and *IRR* Approaches

For independent projects, the *NPV* and *IRR* investment decision criteria lead to the same "accept" or "reject" conclusion.[6] If the *NPV* criterion is satisfied, the *IRR* criterion will also be met.

---

[6] An exception sometimes occurs if there is more than one sign reversal among the periodic net cash flows. In such cases there can be more than one discount rate that makes the project's *NPV* equal to zero, and the *IRR* investment criterion will not necessarily apply. These cases will not be encountered in this text; they are considered in texts on managerial finance.

The *NPV* approach has the advantage that it also quantifies the magnitude of the economic benefit to the firm of undertaking a capital investment. The primary objective of the managers of a firm is to maximize the value of the firm. The *NPV* analysis relates directly to this objective since it gives the amount that each potential investment will add to the firm's value. Nevertheless, studies of actual business practice reveal that more managers prefer to base business investment decisions on the *IRR* than on the *NPV*. This seems to reflect a traditional bias toward measures of profitability stated as percentage rates of return. Managers are also inclined to think in terms of the spread between the cost of capital and the (internal) rate of return on an investment.

A flawed investment decision can result if the *IRR* is used to rank projects that are mutually exclusive, or to rank projects that are competing for a limited capital budget. In these cases, it can happen that the project with the larger *IRR* has the smaller *NPV*. The ranking should be based strictly on the projects' *NPV*s. Then you can be sure you are selecting the project that adds the most value to the firm.

In summary, the *NPV* approach to evaluating and ranking capital investment opportunities *always* works. It also gives the amount by which the investment will increase the value of the firm. There are some situations, particularly the ranking of mutually exclusive investments, in which the *IRR* method can lead to a suboptimal decision.[7]

Example 16.5A Ranking Projects with Uneven Cash Flows

The initial investment and subsequent profits for two mutually exclusive, three-year projects are forecast as follows:

	Project S	Project T
Initial investment	$100,000	$100,000
Year 1 profit	100,000	25,000
Year 2 profit	20,000	25,000
Year 3 profit	20,000	110,000

a. Rank the projects on the basis of their *IRR*s.

b. Rank the projects on the basis of their *NPV*s if the firm's cost of capital is 15%.

c. Rank the projects on the basis of their *NPV*s if the firm's cost of capital is 12%?

d. Which project should be selected if the cost of capital is 12%?

---

[7] The fundamental reason for this limitation can be traced to a subtle point. Any valuation of cash flows based on a present-value calculation implicitly assumes that cash flows from the investment may be reinvested at the discount rate used in the present-value calculation. An *NPV* ranking of projects therefore assumes the same reinvestment rate (the cost of capital) for all projects. An *IRR* ranking of projects assumes a different reinvestment rate for each project—namely, each project's own internal rate of return. It is not a fair comparison to rank projects on the basis of a criterion that does not use the same reinvestment rate for all projects being compared. Therefore, an *IRR* ranking of projects may differ from an *NPV* ranking, and the latter should take precedence.

Solution

a. The *IRR* of Project S is the value of *i* in

$$0 = -\$100{,}000 + \underbrace{\frac{\$100{,}000}{1+i}}_{\text{Term ①}} + \underbrace{\frac{\$20{,}000}{(1+i)^2}}_{\text{Term ②}} + \underbrace{\frac{\$20{,}000}{(1+i)^3}}_{\text{Term ③}}$$

Estimate *i* by the trial-and-error method.

Trial number	Estimated i	Term ①	Term ②	Term ③	RHS
1	0.15	$86,957	$15,123	$13,150	$15,230
2	0.20	83,333	13,889	11,574	8796
3	0.25	80,000	12,800	10,240	3040
4	0.28	78,125	12,207	9537	−131
	IRR				0
5	0.278	78,247	12,245	9582	74

Interpolating,

$$\frac{IRR - 0.278}{0.28 - 0.278} \doteq \frac{0 - \$74}{-\$131 - \$74} = \frac{\$74}{\$205} = 0.361$$

$$\begin{aligned} IRR - 0.278 &\doteq 0.002(0.361) \\ IRR &\doteq 0.278 + 0.0007 \\ &\doteq 0.2787 \\ &\doteq 27.87\% \text{ for Project S} \end{aligned}$$

The *IRR* for Project T may be similarly shown to be 20.91%. Therefore, Project S has the greater *IRR* and, on that basis, would rank ahead of Project T.

b. At a cost of capital of 15%, the *NPV* of Project S is

$$\begin{aligned} NPV_S &= \frac{\$100{,}000}{1.15} + \frac{\$20{,}000}{1.15^2} + \frac{\$20{,}000}{1.15^3} - \$100{,}000 \\ &= \$86{,}957 + \$15{,}123 + \$13{,}150 - \$100{,}000 \\ &= \$15{,}230 \end{aligned}$$

The *NPV* of Project T may be calculated in a similar manner to give

$$NPV_T = \$12{,}970$$

Therefore, Project S has the greater *NPV* and ranks ahead of Project T. This is the same as the *IRR* ranking in part (a).

c. At a cost of capital of 12%, the *NPV*s of the two projects can be calculated again using the same method as in part (b). The values are

$$NPV_S = \$19{,}465 \qquad NPV_T = \$20{,}547$$

In this case, T has the larger *NPV* and ranks ahead of S. We note from parts (b) and (c) that the *NPV* ranking can depend on the cost of capital.

d. A project's *IRR* is not affected by the cost of capital. On the basis of the *IRR*, Project S would always be selected over Project T.

At a 12% cost of capital, the *IRR* and *NPV* rankings do not agree. We should let the *NPV* ranking take precedence and select the project that adds the greater value to the firm. Therefore, Project T should be chosen.

Example 16.5B *Ranking Projects with Uniform Cash Flows*

A company is considering two mutually exclusive projects. The initial investment required and the expected profits are presented in the following table. Neither project will have any residual value.

	Project A	Project B
Initial investment	$50,000	$100,000
Year 1 profit	28,000	50,000
Year 2 profit	28,000	50,000
Year 3 profit	28,000	50,000

a. Rank the projects on the basis of their *IRR*s.

b. Which project should be chosen if the company's cost of capital is 17%?

c. Which project should be chosen if the cost of capital is 14%?

Solution

a. Each project's annual profits form a simple annuity. The *IRR* of Project A is the value of i in

$$0 = \$28{,}000\left[\frac{1-(1+i)^{-3}}{i}\right] - \$50{,}000$$

Similarly, the *IRR* of Project B is the solution to

$$0 = \$50{,}000\left[\frac{1-(1+i)^{-3}}{i}\right] - \$100{,}000$$

An algebraic solution to these equations requires a trial-and-error approach.

Financial Calculator Solution

When the periodic cash flows form an annuity, we can use the calculator's basic financial functions to solve for i.

a. Determine the *IRR* of Project A.

50000 (+/–) (PV) 28000 (PMT) 0 (FV) 3 (n) (COMP) (i) 31.21%

Determine the *IRR* of Project B.

100000 (+/–) (PV) 50000 (PMT) (COMP) (i) 23.38%

On the basis of their *IRR*s, Project A should be selected over Project B.

b. At a cost of capital of 17%,

$$NPV_A = \$28{,}000\left[\frac{1 - (1.17)^{-3}}{0.17}\right] - \$50{,}000 = \$11{,}868$$

$$NPV_B = \$50{,}000\left[\frac{1 - (1.17)^{-3}}{0.17}\right] - \$100{,}000 = \$10{,}479$$

Since $NPV_A > NPV_B$, Project A should be selected.

c. At a cost of capital of 14%,

$$NPV_A = \$28{,}000\left[\frac{1 - (1.14)^{-3}}{0.14}\right] - \$50{,}000 = \$15{,}006$$

$$NPV_B = \$50{,}000\left[\frac{1 - (1.14)^{-3}}{0.14}\right] - \$100{,}000 = \$16{,}082$$

Since $NPV_B > NPV_A$, Project B should be selected (even though $IRR_A > IRR_B$).

Exercise 16.5

Answers to the odd-numbered problems are at the end of the book.
Calculate internal rates of return to the nearest 0.1%.

•**1.** Two mutually exclusive investments are available to a firm. Project C, requiring a capital investment of $150,000, will generate an annual profit of $43,000 for six years. Project D is expected to yield an annual profit of $30,000 for six years on an initial investment of $100,000.

a. Calculate the internal rate of return on each project. Based upon their *IRR*s, which project should be selected?

b. Which project should be selected if the firm's cost of capital is 15%?

c. Which project should be selected if the firm's cost of capital is 12%?

•**2.** Academic Publishing is trying to decide which of two books to publish. The larger book will cost $100,000 to publish and print. Sales are expected to produce an annual profit of $32,000 for five years. The smaller book will cost $60,000 to publish and print, and should generate an annual profit of $20,000 for five years.

a. Calculate the internal rate of return on each book. On the basis of their *IRR*s, which book should be published?

b. Which book should be published if the firm's cost of capital is 17%?

c. Which book should be published if the firm's cost of capital is 14%?

••**3.** Due to a restricted capital budget, a company can undertake only one of the following three-year projects. Both require an initial investment of $650,000 and will have no significant terminal value. Project XXX is anticipated to have annual profits of $400,000, $300,000, and $200,000 in successive years, whereas Project YYY's only profit, $1.05 million, comes at the end of Year 3.

a. Calculate the *IRR* of each project. On the basis of their *IRR*s, which project should be selected?

b. Which project should be selected if the firm's cost of capital is 14%?

c. Which project should be selected if the firm's cost of capital is 11%?

••**4.** Two mutually exclusive projects each require an initial investment of $50,000 and should have a residual value of $10,000 after three years. The following table presents their forecast annual profits.

Year	Project 1	Project 2
1	$10,000	$50,000
2	15,000	10,000
3	50,000	5000

a. Calculate the *IRR* of each project. On the basis of their *IRR*s, which project should be selected?

b. Which project should be selected if the firm's cost of capital is 14%?

c. Which project should be selected if the firm's cost of capital is 12%?

••**5.** A company is examining two mutually exclusive projects. Project X requires an immediate investment of $100,000 and produces no profit until Year 3. Then the annual profit is $60,000 for Years 3 to 5 inclusive. Project Y requires an investment of $50,000 now and another $50,000 in one year. It is expected to generate an annual profit of $40,000 in Years 2 to 5.

a. Calculate the *IRR* of each project. On the basis of their *IRR*s, which project is preferred?

b. Which project should be selected if the firm's cost of capital is 15%?

c. Which project should be selected if the firm's cost of capital is 12%?

••**6.** A company is evaluating two mutually exclusive projects. Both require an initial investment of $240,000 and have no appreciable disposal value. Their expected profits over their five-year lifetimes are as follows:

Year	Project Alpha	Project Beta
1	$140,000	$ 20,000
2	80,000	40,000
3	60,000	60,000
4	20,000	100,000
5	20,000	180,000

The company's cost of capital is 12%. Calculate the *NPV* and *IRR* for each project. Which project should be chosen? Why?

16.6 The Payback Period

Many smaller firms still use the payback period as a measure of the attractiveness of a capital investment. The **payback period** is the number of years it takes to recover an initial investment from the investment's future operating profits. For example, if an initial capital investment of $450,000 generates an annual profit of

\$100,000 for 10 years, it has a $4\frac{1}{2}$-year payback. A firm that uses this approach establishes a maximum payback period for an acceptable investment. Investment opportunities that have a payback period shorter than or equal to the maximum should be accepted.

The payback approach to investment selection has three serious shortcomings. The first is that the payback calculation ignores the time value of money—there is no discounting of the future cash flows. In the example above, \$1 in Year 5 is treated as having the same value as \$1 of the initial investment. A second flaw is that the payback calculation ignores the profits and residual value that would be received beyond the maximum payback period. The third weakness is that the maximum acceptable payback period is set by the firm in a rather arbitrary manner without rigorous economic justification. The payback method is included in our coverage of investment decision criteria not because it has any great merit, but only because it is still widely used.

Example 16.6 *Calculation of the Payback Period; Comparison of Decisions Based on Payback versus NPV*

A firm is considering three independent projects. They all require the same initial investment of \$90,000 and have no residual value after eight years. All three generate the same aggregate total of profits (\$160,000), but the profits are distributed differently over the eight-year period, as presented in the following table.

		Annual profit	
Year	**Project A**	**Project B**	**Project C**
1	\$25,000	\$20,000	\$ 0
2	25,000	20,000	0
3	25,000	20,000	45,000
4	25,000	20,000	45,000
5	15,000	20,000	15,000
6	15,000	20,000	15,000
7	15,000	20,000	20,000
8	15,000	20,000	20,000

a. Which projects should be accepted if the firm has a four-year payback requirement?

b. Which projects would be accepted on the *NPV* criterion if the firm's cost of capital is 14%?

Solution

a. To be accepted on the payback criterion, a project must have cumulative profits after four years that equal or exceed the original capital investment (\$90,000). The following table presents the cumulative profits from the three projects at the end of each year.

Year	Project A	Cumulative profits Project B	Project C
1	\$ 25,000	\$ 20,000	\$ 0
2	50,000	40,000	0
3	75,000	60,000	45,000
4	100,000	80,000	90,000
5	115,000	100,000	105,000
6	130,000	120,000	120,000
7	145,000	140,000	140,000
8	160,000	160,000	160,000

Assuming that the profits accumulate uniformly within each year, the payback periods are:

$$\text{Project A:} \quad 3 + \frac{\$15{,}000}{\$25{,}000} = 3.6 \text{ years}$$

$$\text{Project B:} \quad 4 + \frac{\$10{,}000}{\$20{,}000} = 4.5 \text{ years}$$

$$\text{Project C:} \quad 4.0 \text{ years}$$

Projects A and C will be accepted because they recover the original investment within the four-year payback period. Project B will be rejected on the same criterion.

b. The net present value of Project A is

$$NPV_A = \$25{,}000\left[\frac{1-(1.14)^{-4}}{0.14}\right] + \$15{,}000\left[\frac{1-(1.14)^{-4}}{0.14}\right](1.14)^{-4} - \$90{,}000$$
$$= \$72{,}843 + \$25{,}877 - \$90{,}000$$
$$= \$8720$$

The net present value of Project B is

$$NPV_B = \$20{,}000\left[\frac{1-(1.14)^{-8}}{0.14}\right] - \$90{,}000 = \$2777$$

The net present value of Project C is

$$NPV_C = \frac{\$45{,}000}{1.14^3} + \frac{\$45{,}000}{1.14^4} + \frac{\$15{,}000}{1.14^5} + \frac{\$15{,}000}{1.14^6} + \frac{\$20{,}000}{1.14^7} + \frac{\$20{,}000}{1.14^8} - \$90{,}000$$
$$= \$30{,}374 + \$26{,}644 + \$7790 + \$6834 + \$7993 + \$7011 - \$90{,}000$$
$$= -\$3354$$

Since Projects A and B both have a positive *NPV*, they should be accepted. Project C, with a negative *NPV*, should be rejected.

Note: Since there is no fundamental economic rationale behind the payback period, we should not expect a high degree of consistency between investment decisions based on a payback period and decisions based on the *NPV* criterion. In this example Project B was accepted based on its *NPV* but was rejected because its payback period exceeded four years. Conversely, Project C failed to satisfy the *NPV* criterion but met the payback requirement. A general statement that can be made is that the shorter a project's payback period, the more likely it is to have a positive *NPV*.

POINT OF INTEREST

The Actual Use of Investment Criteria by Businesses

Discounted-cash-flow techniques—primarily the net present value (*NPV*) and internal rate of return (*IRR*) methods—started to be used by large corporations in the early 1950s. An early study concluded that, in 1955, only 9% of large American firms used some form of discounted-cash-flow analysis in making capital investment decisions.[8] A 1965 survey of 105 Canadian companies revealed that 30% of them employed a discounted-cash-flow method as their primary investment selection criterion. Most of the others used the payback method or some other rule of thumb.[9]

The shift to increased usage of *NPV* and *IRR* techniques continued as more and more accounting and business school graduates were educated in discounted-cash-flow techniques. A 1976 survey of 99 Canadian corporations indicated that a small majority of large corporations were employing a discounted-cash-flow method as the primary standard for selecting capital investments.[10]

In 1985 Blazouske, Carlin, and Kim surveyed the chief financial officers of all the corporations listed in the *Financial Post* 500 industrials to determine the techniques used by large companies for choosing capital investments.[11] The corporations were asked, among other things, to indicate the primary and secondary methods they used in 1980 and in 1985 for evaluating investment projects. The responses received from 208 of the 500 Canadian companies are summarized in the following table.

	Primary method		Secondary method	
Technique	**1980**	**1985**	**1980**	**1985**
IRR	38%	40%	7%	13%
NPV	22	25	10	11
Payback	25	19	41	44
Other method	12	13	11	12
No method used	3	3	31	20

The data indicate that the trend of the previous three decades to more widespread use of discounted-cash-flow methods continued between 1980 and 1985. The percentage of firms employing *IRR* or *NPV* as the primary selection criterion increased from 60% in 1980 to 65% in 1985. The proportion using payback or another method as the primary basis dropped from 37% in 1980 to 32% in 1985.

It is noteworthy that, in 1985, 80% of the firms used more than one project evaluation technique and 63% used payback as either their primary or their secondary

---

[8] Alexander A. Robichek and James G. MacDonald, *Financial Management in Transition, Long-Range Planning Service,* Report no. 268 (Menlo Park, Calif.: Stanford Research Institute, 1966).

[9] J. T. Nicholson and J. D. Ffolliot, "Investment Evaluation Criteria of Canadian Companies," *Business Quarterly* (Summer 1996).

[10] Helen Baumgartner and V. Bruce Irvine, "A Survey of Capital Budgeting Techniques Used in Canadian Companies," *Cost and Management* (January–February 1977), pp. 51–55.

[11] J. D. Blazouske, I. Carlin, and S. H. Kim, "Current Capital Budgeting Practices in Canada," *CMA Magazine* (March 1988), pp. 51–54.

approach. These statistics raise two related questions: Why are multiple techniques used, since an investment's *NPV* seems to directly give what the firm needs to know? Why is the obviously flawed payback method still so widely used?

The answers lie partly in the uncertainty involved in forecasting the revenues and expenses associated with an investment. Particularly for new ventures, marketing and sales personnel tend to make overly optimistic sales projections. Therefore, investment decision-makers commonly employ additional approaches to obtain confirmation of the results of the primary method. For example, a project with a small positive *NPV* is more likely to be undertaken if it has a three-year payback period than if it has a five-year payback. If two mutually exclusive investments have similar *NPV*s, the one with the shorter payback period will normally be preferred because the invested capital will be recovered more quickly. The faster-payback project is usually viewed as less risky because revenue and expenditure forecasts tend to be more reliable for earlier years than for later years.

Studies indicate that small firms use discounted-cash-flow techniques less extensively than large firms. L. R. Runyon conducted a study in the early 1980s of 214 firms whose owners' equity was in the \$0.5 million to \$1 million range.[12] He found that only 14% of them used a discounted-cash-flow approach. Almost 70% of these small companies relied on the payback method or some other seriously flawed technique. Another 9% did not use any formal capital investment analysis at all!

Several factors contribute to the relatively low usage of discounted-cash-flow techniques by small firms for the analysis of investment projects. Three important ones are:

- Small firms are less likely to have individuals with the necessary financial skills to carry out an *NPV* or *IRR* analysis.
- For benefits beyond those already provided by a simple approach such as the payback method, the cost of a rigorous discounted-cash-flow analysis may not be justifiable for small capital investments.
- Since small projects and small firms typically face greater uncertainty in their cash flows, a greater emphasis on short-term cash flows and the payback period is often justified.

Differences exist across countries in the relative importance placed on the various capital investment criteria. For example, the payback method is more widely used in Japan than in Canada and the United States. A 1988 survey[13] of Japanese companies revealed that 47% still used a payback period as the primary investment criterion. Only 30% used either the *NPV* or the *IRR* criterion as the primary basis for investment decisions. Nevertheless, the trend in Japan is toward increased usage of discounted-cash-flow methods.

Where the payback method is used, comparative studies report that Japanese companies use a longer payback period as the cut-off point than do American

---

[12] L. R. Runyon, "Capital Expenditure Decision Making in Small Firms," *Journal of Business Research* (September 1983), pp. 389–97.

[13] N. B. Gultekin and T. Taga, "Financial Management in Japanese Corporations," Working Paper, University of Pennsylvania, 1989.

companies. For example, a 1988 study[14] of firms in advanced manufacturing technologies found that 50% of Japanese companies used a maximum payback period of at least four years. Eighty-eight percent of U.S. companies used a shorter cutoff for payback.

Exercise 16.6 *Answers to the odd-numbered problems are at the end of the book.*

1. The expected profits from a \$52,000 investment are \$8000 in Year 1, \$12,000 in each of Years 2 to 5, and \$6000 in each of Years 6 and 7.

a. What is the investment's payback period?

b. If the firm's required payback period is four years, will it make the investment?

2. A firm is considering the purchase of a \$30,000 machine that would save labour costs of \$5000 per year in the first three years and \$6000 per year for the next four years. Will the firm purchase the machine if the payback requirement is:

a. Five years? **b.** Six years?

•3. Projects X and Y both require an initial investment of \$100,000. Project X will generate an annual operating profit of \$25,000 per year for six years. Project Y produces no profit in the first year, but will yield an annual profit of \$25,000 for the seven subsequent years. Rank the projects based on their payback periods and on their *NPV*s (at a 10% cost of capital).

•4. A capital investment requiring a single initial cash outflow is forecast to have an operating profit of \$50,000 per year for five years. There is no salvage value at the end of the five years. If the investment has an *IRR* of 17%, calculate its payback period.

••5. Investment proposals A and B require initial investments of \$45,000 and \$35,000, respectively. Both have an economic life of four years with no residual value. Their expected profits are as follows:

Year	Proposal A	Proposal B
1	\$16,250	\$12,500
2	17,500	12,500
3	17,500	15,000
4	17,500	15,000

If the firm's cost of capital is 14%, rank the proposals based on their:

a. *NPV*s. **b.** *IRR*s. **c.** Payback periods.

[14] NAA Tokyo Affiliate, "Management Accounting in the Advanced Manufacturing Surrounding: Comparative Study on Survey in Japan and U.S.A.," 1988.

Review Problems

Answers to the odd-numbered review problems are at the end of the book.

◆ **1.** A manufacturer's sales rep can lease an automobile for five years at $385 per month payable at the beginning of each month, or purchase it for $22,500. He can obtain a loan at 9% compounded monthly to purchase the car. Should he lease or buy the car if:

a. The trade-in value after five years is $5000?

b. The trade-in value after five years is $7000?

◆◆ **2.** Jurgen Wiebe has been transferred to Winnipeg for five years. He has found an attractive house that he can buy for $150,000 or rent for $1150 per month, payable at the beginning of each month. He estimates that the resale value of the house in five years will be $175,000 net of the selling commission. If he buys the house, the average (end-of-month) costs for repairs, maintenance, and property taxes will be $300. Should Mr. Wiebe rent or buy the house if the interest rate on five-year mortgage loans is 8.25% compounded monthly?

◆ **3.** A proposed open-pit mine would require the investment of $2 million at the beginning of the first year and a further investment of $1 million at the end of the first year. Mining operations are expected to yield annual profits of $750,000, beginning in Year 2. The ore body will sustain eight years of ore extraction. At the beginning of the tenth year, the mining company must spend $1 million on cleanup and environmental restoration. Will the project provide the mining company with a rate of return exceeding its 16% cost of capital?

◆ **4.** The development of a new product will require the expenditure of $125,000 at the beginning of each of the next two years. When the product reaches the market in Year 3, it is expected to increase the firm's annual profit by $50,000 for eight years. (Assume that the profit is received at the end of each year.) Then $75,000 of the original expenditures should be recoverable. If the firm's cost of capital is 14%, should it proceed with the project?

◆◆ **5.** A new machine that will lead to savings in labour costs of $20,000 per year can be purchased for $60,000. However, it will cost $2000 per year for the first four years, and $3000 per year for the next four years to service and maintain the machine. In addition, its annual fuel consumption will cost $1500. After a service life of eight years, the salvage value of the machine is expected to be $10,000. Should the machine be acquired if the company requires a minimum annual rate of return on investment of 15%?

◆ **6.** The investment committee of a company has identified the following seven projects with positive *NPV*s. If the board of directors has approved a $4.5 million capital budget for the current period, which projects should be selected?

Project	Initial investment	*NPV*
1	$1,125,000	$428,000
2	2,700,000	486,000
3	675,000	170,000
4	375,000	30,000
5	1,500,000	900,000
6	225,000	32,000
7	900,000	405,000

◆ **7.** Machine X costs $50,000 and is forecast to generate an annual profit of $16,000 for five years. Machine Y, priced at $72,000, will produce the same annual profits for 10 years. The trade-in value of X after five years is expected to be $10,000, and the resale value of Y after 10 years is also thought to be $10,000. If either machine satisfies the firm's requirements, which one should be selected? Use a required return of 14%.

◆ **8.** A U-Print store requires a new photocopier. A Sonapanic copier with a four-year service life costs $35,000 and will generate an annual profit of $14,000. A higher-speed Xorex copier with a five-year service life costs $43,500 and will return an annual profit of $17,000. Neither copier will have significant salvage value. If U-Print's cost of capital is 16%, which model should be purchased?

◆ **9.** The provincial government's Ministry of Fisheries requires a new patrol boat. The price of a Songster is $45,000, and its annual operating costs will be $5000. It will be sold for about $10,000 after five years, and replaced. A more durable and more efficient Boston Wailer, priced at $55,000, would cost $4000 per year to operate, last seven years, and have a resale value of $20,000. If the provincial government pays an interest rate of 8% compounded annually on its midterm debt, which boat has the lower equivalent annual cost?

10. A seven-year licence to distribute a product should increase the distributor's profit by $18,000 per year. If the licence can be acquired for $70,000, what is the investment's *IRR*?

◆ **11.** An investment of $300,000 will yield annual profits of $55,000 for eight years. The proceeds on disposition of the investment at the end of the eight years are estimated at $125,000. On the basis of its *IRR* and a 15% cost of capital, should the investment be made?

◆◆ **12.** A $500,000 capital investment will produce annual profits of $100,000 for the first four years and $150,000 for the next four years. It will have no residual value. What is its *IRR*? Should it be undertaken if the cost of capital is 15%?

◆◆ **13.** A company is examining two mutually exclusive projects. Project P requires an immediate investment of $225,000 and produces no profit until the fourth year. Then the expected annual profit is $120,000 for Years 4 to 7 inclusive. Project Q requires an investment of $225,000 now and is expected to generate an annual profit of $55,000 in Years 1 to 7. Neither project has any residual value after seven years.

a. Calculate the *IRR* of each project. On the basis of their *IRR*s, which project is preferred?

b. Which project should be selected if the firm's cost of capital is 16%?

c. Which project should be selected if the firm's cost of capital is 13%?

14. The expected profits from an $80,000 investment are $15,000 in Year 1 and $20,000 in each of Years 2 to 7.

a. What is the investment's payback period?

b. If the firm's required payback period is four years, will it make the investment?

c. If the firm's cost of capital is 14%, will it make the investment?

Self-Test Exercise

Answers to the self-test problems are at the end of the book.

◆ **1.** Rainbow Aviation needs an additional plane for five years. It could buy the plane for $180,000, using funds borrowed at 11.25% compounded monthly and then sell the plane for an estimated $70,000 after five years. Alternatively, it could lease the plane for $2800, payable at the beginning of each month. Which alternative should Rainbow Aviation choose? What is the economic value of the financial advantage on the initial date of the preferred alternative?

◆ **2.** Huron Charters can purchase a sailboat for $50,000 down and a $30,000 payment due in one year. The boat would generate additional annual operating profits of $12,000 for the first five years and $15,000 for the next five years. New sails costing $8000 would be required after five years. After 10 years the boat would be replaced; its resale value would be about $30,000. Should Huron purchase the sailboat if its cost of capital is 15% compounded annually?

◆ **3.** A company's board of directors has imposed an $800,000 limit on capital spending for the current year. Management has identified the following five projects as all providing a return on investment greater than the cost of capital. Which projects should be chosen?

Project	Initial investment	*NPV*
A	$200,000	$ 63,000
B	400,000	100,000
C	350,000	90,000
D	250,000	75,000
E	100,000	20,000

◆ **4.** A company is considering two mutually exclusive investment projects. Each requires an initial investment of $25,000. Project A will generate an annual profit of $6000 for eight years and have a residual value of $5000. Project B's profits are more irregular: $15,000 in the first year, $19,000 in the fifth year, and $24,000 (including the residual value) in the eighth year. Which project should be chosen if the required return on investment is 18% compounded annually?

◆◆ **5.** A firm can manufacture the same product with either of two machines. Machine C requires an initial investment of $55,000 and would earn a profit of $30,000 per year for three years. It would then be replaced, because repairs would be required too frequently after three years. Its trade-in value would be $10,000. Machine D costs $100,000 and would have a service life of five years. The annual profit would be $5000 higher than Machine C's profit because of its lower repair and maintenance costs. Its recoverable value after five years would be about $20,000. Which machine should be purchased if the firm's cost of capital is 16%? What is the average annual economic advantage of the preferred choice?

◆ **6.** A potato farmer needs to buy a new harvester. Two types have performed satisfactorily in field trials. The SpudFinder costs $70,000 and should last for five years. The simpler TaterTaker costs only $40,000 but requires an extra operator at $10,000 per season. This machine has a service life of seven years. The disposal value of either machine is insignificant. If the farmer requires a 13% return on investment, which harvester should she buy?

◆ **7.** A capital investment requiring one initial cash outflow is forecast to have the operating profits listed below. The investment has an *NPV* of $20,850, based on a required rate of return of 12%. Calculate the payback period of the investment.

Year	Operating profit
1	$74,000
2	84,000
3	96,000
4	70,000

◆◆ **8.** The introduction of a new product will require a $400,000 investment in demonstration models, promotion, and staff training. The new product will increase annual profits by $100,000 for the first four years and $50,000 for the next four years. There will be no significant recoverable amounts at the end of the eight years. The firm's cost of capital is 13%. Calculate the expected *IRR* on the proposed investment in the new product. Should the new product be introduced? Why?

◆ **9.** The initial investment and expected profits from two mutually exclusive capital investments being considered by a firm are as follows:

	Investment A	Investment B
Initial investment	$70,000	$65,000
Year 1 profit	30,000	50,000
Year 2 profit	80,000	50,000

a. Calculate the internal rate of return for each investment. Which one would be selected based on an *IRR* ranking?

b. Which investment should be chosen if the firm's cost of capital is 14%?

c. Which investment should be chosen if the firm's cost of capital is 17%?

Summary of Notation and Key Formulas

NPV = Net present value (of an investment)
IRR = Internal rate of return (on an investment)

$$NPV = \begin{pmatrix}\text{Present value}\\\text{of cash inflows}\end{pmatrix} - \begin{pmatrix}\text{Present value}\\\text{of cash outflows}\end{pmatrix}$$

NPV INVESTMENT DECISION CRITERION:

Accept the investment if $NPV \geq 0$.
Reject the investment if $NPV < 0$.

IRR INVESTMENT DECISION CRITERION:

Accept the investment if $IRR \geq$ Cost of capital.
Reject the investment if $IRR <$ Cost of capital.

List of Key Terms

Capital rationing *(p. 671)*
Cost of capital *(p. 660)*
Internal rate of return *(p. 679)*
Mutually exclusive projects *(p. 672)*
Net present value *(p. 666)*
Payback period *(p. 687)*

Answers to Odd-Numbered Problems

Chapter 1 Review and Applications of Basic Mathe

Exercise 1.1

1. 4
3. 24
5. 20
7. 49
9. 0.5
11. 6
13. 255
15. 9

Exercise 1.2

1. 0.875 = 87.5%
3. 2.35 = 235%
5. −1.4 = −140%
7. 0.025 = 2.5%
9. 2.02 = 202%
11. 0.75 = 75%
13. $0.8\overline{3} = 83.\overline{3}\%$
15. $7.\overline{7} = 777.\overline{7}\%$
17. $1.\overline{1} = 111.\overline{1}\%$
19. $-0.0\overline{259} = -2.\overline{592}\%$
21. 11.38
23. 0.5545
25. 1.002
27. 40.10
29. 0.16667 = 16.667%
31. 0.016667 = 1.6667%
33. 0.68493 = 68.493%
35. 0.0091667 = 0.91667%
37. $94.68
39. $410.99
41. $3384.52
43. $720.04
45. $14,435.88
47. $6648.46
49. $7159.48
51. $1830.07

Exercise 1.3

1. $6.13
3. 13.0%
5. $75.00
7. $174.98
9. 200%
11. $90.00
13. $19.47
15. 62.1%
17. $105.26
19. 1.00%
21. $0.05
23. $150.00
25. $593.78
27. $125.00
29. $2000.00
31. 1.50% of sales
17.7% of salary
33. 80
35. $154,000
37. $84,000
39. $75,000
41. 2.60%

Exercise 1.4

1. a. $24.231 per hour
b. $23.774 per hour
3. a. $20.4233 per hour
b. $1858.52
5. $796.50
7. $328.75
9. a. $465.96
b. $4090.91 per week
11. a. $3988.00
b. 7.2668%
13. 3.50%
15. $110,833.33

1.5

1.53
3. 3.50
5. 8.9783%
7. 7.53
9. 43.74 days
11. **a.** \$10.674
 b. \$10.664
 c. \$2548.70
13. 52.2%
15. 25.50
17. 6,250,000

Exercise 1.6

1.

Quarter	GST remittance (Refund)
1	\$10,875.55
2	(23,821.35)
3	28,605.36
4	11,537.26

3. **a.** \$23,433
 b. \$25,185
 c. \$25,190.48
5. **a.** \$3558.18
 b. \$6345.42
7. \$3827.88
9. \$4317.15
11. **a.** 7.4837
 b. 7.1273

Review Problems

1. **a.** 23
 b. −40
 c. \$205.39
 d. \$2275.40
 e. \$343.08
 f. \$619.94
 g. \$457.60
 h. \$1549.56
3. \$125.00
5. $8.\overline{3}\%$
7. **a.** \$29.026 per hour
 b. \$2372.85
9. 4.50%
11. 26.1

Self-Test Exercise

1. **a.** 164
 b. 29
 c. \$1295.88
 d. \$208.62
 e. \$3735.16
2. \$59.70
3. \$84,000
4. \$3894.61
5. \$2667
6. 2.10%
7. \$81,308.33

Chapter 2 Review and Applications of Algebra

Exercise 2.1

1. 0
3. $6x^2y$
5. $7x^2 + 7xy - 4y^2$
7. $8x + 3y$
9. $25x - 16$
11. $-0.7x + 3.45$
13. $18.8x - 8.5$
15. $3.0509P$
17. $2.9307k$
19. $12a^2b - 20a^2 + 24ab$
21. $-10x^3y + 5x^2y^2 + 15xy^3$
23. $20r^2 - 7rt - 6t^2$
25. $2a^2 + 34a + 99$
27. $6x$
29. $x - y$
31. $\dfrac{x^2 - 2x + 3}{4}$
33. $2ab - 3a^2$
35. 23.75
37. −44.8
39. \$315.11
41. \$346.22
43. \$2430.38
45. \$1378.42
47. \$1794.22
49. \$1071.77

Exercise 2.2

1. a^5
3. b^4
5. $(1 + i)^{13}$
7. x^{28}
9. t^2
11. x^2
13. $4(1 + i)^2$
15. $\frac{t^3}{2r}$
17. $\frac{81a^{12}b^8}{(a - b)^4}$
19. $-\frac{y}{2x^4}$
21. 16.0000
23. 18.5203
25. 1,000,000
27. 1.07006
29. 1.00990
31. −4.00000
33. −0.197531
35. 20.1569
37. 15.9637
39. 1.00908

Exercise 2.3

1. 2
3. 43
5. 200
7. 0.5
9. 9
11. 30
13. $286.66
15. $699.47
17. $391.01

Exercise 2.4

1. 2065
3. $2.61
5. $13.00
7. 2 24-exposure rolls
   22 36-exposure rolls
9. Joan will invest $10,800
   Sue will invest $12,960
   Stella will invest $9000
11. 42 units of product *Y*
13. $73,451.62 per child
    $24,483.87 per grandchild
15. $12,040
17. 18 minutes for cutting
    11 minutes for assembly
    6 minutes for painting

Exercise 2.5

1. 5.26%
3. 285.71%
5. 18.18%
7. $118.26
9. 105.2 cm
11. $25.00
13. 11.11%
15. $80.00
17. $42.86
19. 0.62% less
21. $131.25
23. $125.00
25. $658.80
27. $99.96
29. 200.00%
31. $10,075
33. $230.00
35. $375.00
37. $129.00
39. **a.** −15.28%
    b. 2.65%
    c. −13.03%
41. 565
43. −20.00% in 1998
    −25.00% in 1999
45. $665,000
47. 7.14% reduction
49. $1.43
51. $80,000

Exercise 2.6

Problem	Income yield	Capital gain yield	Rate of total return
1.	10.00%	10.00%	20.00%
3.	11.11%	−4.44%	6.67%
5.	10.31%	−16.53%	−6.22%
7.	8.00%	−100.00%	−92.00%

9. Income = \$100.00
Capital gain yield = 10.00%
Rate of total return = 15.00%
11. Income yield = 6.70%
Capital gain yield = −1.70%
Final value = \$3666.50
13. Income yield = 10.00%
Initial value = \$3000.00
Income = \$300.00
15. Income = \$128.00
Capital gain yield = −8.00%
Final value = \$1472.00
17. Income yield = 1.62%
Capital gain yield = 8.11%
Rate of total return = 9.73%
19. Income yield = 6.65%
Capital gain yield = −2.99%
Rate of total return = 3.66%
21. a. 9.50%
b. 3.40%
c. \$1290.00
d. 12.90%
23. 24.07%
25. a. 28.28%
b. 20.94%
27. \$1.50
29. \$1073.34
31. \$1533.33

Exercise 2.7

1. \$16.385 per hour
3. 51.58%
5. 56.25%
7. −33.33%
9. 100%
11. 7.44%
13. 207.13%
15. a. \$192 million
b. \$288 million
17. a. 159.37%
b. 148.83%
The constant 10% increases produce a 10.54% higher cumulative increase.
19. a. 15,075
b. 1194
21. 8.07% decrease
23. a. \$12.82
b. \$3.00
25. 23.36% increase
42.54% underperformance
27. 54.24% increase
11.66% underperformance

Review Problems

1. a. $0.7y + 2.2\overline{6}$
b. $2.996843P$
3. a. \$252.59
b. \$1468.56
5. a. 589.020
b. 0.00826484
7. a. \$34.58
b. \$500.00
c. \$117.65
d. \$199.50
e. \$562.00
f. \$350.00
g. \$210.00
9. a. 238.24%
b. \$7.48
11. a. 8.00%
b. −2.00%
c. \$900.00
d. 6.00%
13. a. \$25.26
b. \$5.13
15. \$4400 in ABC Ltd.
\$3400 in XYZ Inc.

Self-Test Exercise

1. a. $-60y^2 + 45y - 51$
b. $2.925b - 21$
c. $3.05587x$
d. $\dfrac{4m - 3nm}{2n}$
2. \$4505.14
3. a. $-\dfrac{9}{x}$
b. $-\dfrac{8b^3}{a^9}$
4. a. 1.19641
b. 0.00816485
c. 41.1527
d. 9.11858

5. **a.** $280.97
b. $436.96
6. **a.** 79.27%
b. −79.27%
7. 18.40%
8. 36.75%
9. **a.** −57.54%
b. $7.51
10. $46,350 to Hugh
$52,080 to Ken

Chapter 3 Ratios and Proportions

Exercise 3.1

1. 3 : 16
3. 3 : 1 : 2
5. 2 : 3
7. 3 : 5 : 7
9. 8 : 13 : 5
11. 1 : 6
13. 7 : 10
15. 3 : 4
17. 15 : 8
19. 2 : 6 : 3
21. $2.5\overline{3}$: 1
23. 1 : 4.58
25. 1 : 2.61
27. 3.35 : 1 : 1.78
29. 1 : 1.54 : 2.29
31. 1 : 2.47 : 1.37
33. 5 : 7 : 8
35. 3.36 : 1 : 2.18
37. 8 : 7 : 5

Exercise 3.2

1. 42
3. 232.9
5. 28.70
7. 0.0155
9. $\frac{1}{3}$
11. $n = 90; m = 75$
13. $g = 5; f = 375$
15. $r = 11.21; s = 19.01$
17. $2658.86
19. 11.06 hours
21. $18,888.75
23. $459 million in U.S. stocks
$323 million in Japanese stocks
$187 million in British stocks
25. 4.5 litres of fruit juice
1.8 litres of ginger ale
27. Wholesale cost = $2.955 million
Overhead expenses = $1.553 million
29. $1.23 million budget reduction
11 staff reduction
31. $4.345 million
33. **a.** $14,889
b. $19,852

Exercise 3.3

See the answers to Exercise 2.5.

Exercise 3.4

1. $75.85
3. $406.85
5. **a.** $1592.00
b. $1722.49
7. **a.** $168,750 to A
$450,000 to B
$281,250 to C
b. $7,237,500 to A
$19,300,000 to B
$12,062,500 to C
9. **a.** $389,838 to Industrial Products
$265,799 to Fine Paper
$183,363 to Containers & Packaging
b. $480,724 to Industrial Products
$189,342 to Fine Paper
$168,934 to Containers & Packaging
11. **a.** $542,500
b. W will own 443 shares
Y will own 517 shares
Z will own 590 shares
c. $50,050 from W
$58,450 from Y
$66,500 from Z

Exercise 3.5

1. C$2787.71
3. ¥1,168,410

5. C$2692.48
7. C$9381.96
9. £39,089.21
11. DM60,249.26
13. **a.** C$0.2529
b. £0.42285
c. A$0.01296
d. C$0.96834
15. C$71.01
17. C$838.42
19. C$0.28 per pound cheaper in Canada
21. C$ has appreciated by 4.55%
23. US$0.6738 per C$1.00
C$1.4841 per US$1.00
25. US$0.6643 per C$1.00
27. C$0.8429 per DM1.00
29. An increase of C$53.81
31. An increase of C$9.58 per ounce
33. Direct conversion gives £1593.09
Indirect conversion gives £1593.18
(which, to four-figure accuracy, are equal)
35. US$0.68 per pound more in the U.S.

Exercise 3.6

1. 151.3
3. $9001
5. 9.374
7. $3646
9. 122.2
11. $1024.46
13. **a.** $1157.02
b. $1209.03
c. 5.20%
15. 65.75% more
17. **a.** $161.16
b. 8.90% for 1978
9.60% for 1979
11.95% for 1980
11.42% for 1981
8.25% for 1982

Review Problems

1. **a.** 6 : 20 : 15
b. 3 : 2 : 4
c. 3 : 6 : 2
d. 5 : 4 : 3
3. Mark : Ben : Tanya = 5 : 3 : 7
5. 194 nurses; 97 aides
7. $111,111
9. $3774.06 to A
$11,382.08 to B
$4642.69 to C
$8776.18 to D
11. $25,546 to Huey
$28,859 to Dewey
$30,375 to Louie
13. Y0.055298 per X1.00
X18.084 per Y1.00
15. **a.** (i) 2.3% (ii) 3.0%
b. $112.97

Self-Test Exercise

1. **a.** 18.06
b. $a = 332.8$; $b = 205.4$
2. 11 : 14 : 6
3. 95,025 units
4. $3.39 billion for health care
$2.30 billion for social services
5. $1.52
6. Ms. L received $4000
Mr. M received $2666.67
Mr. P received $1333.33
7. $148,798 to Wife
$106,284 to Son
$75,918 to Stepson
8. 1,759,300 lira
9. $23.51 per hour
10. Decrease of C$1304
11. Alberta coal is C$3.25 cheaper per metric ton

Chapter 4 Mathematics of Merchandising

Exercise 4.1

1. $83.00, $166.00
3. $21.33, $16\frac{2}{3}$%
5. $1750.00, $1137.50
7. $27.40, 45.0%
9. $3256.00, $407.00
11. 41.67%, $57.75
13. 37.56%, $149.00

15. $83.70
17. $185.95
19. 22.0%
21. 26.55%
23. $169,900
25. **a.** $5087.50
b. $495.00
27. 46.9 points
29. **a.** $1025.9 million
b. 7382 people
31. **a.** $7579.22
b. $646.88
c. $398.91
33. 6.00%
35. **a.** $100.00
b. $35.00

Exercise 4.2

1. $2317.70
3. $799.18
5. $1337.70, $1000.00
7. $1722.97, $1700.00
9. $1557.66
11. $374.90
13. $2127.36
15. $975.61

Exercise 4.3

1. **a.** $20.00
b. $12.00
c. $8.00
d. 66.67%
e. 40.00%
3. **a.** $23.85
b. $23.85
c. $0
d. 42.86%
e. 30.00%
5. **a.** $23.10
b. $26.95
c. −$3.85
d. 42.86%
e. 30.00%
7. $OE = \$32.10$
$SP = \$199.95$
Rate of markup = 31.11%
Gross profit margin = 23.73%
9. $OP = \$127.00$
$C = \$1555.00$
Rate of markup = 27.97%
Gross profit margin = 21.86%
11. $M = \$15.00$
$SP = \$39.47$
$C = \$24.47$
Rate of markup = 61.29%
13. $SP = \$11.00$
$M = \$4.40$
$OP = \$1.25$
Rate of markup = 66.67%
15. **a.** $SP = \$363.60$
b. Rate of markup = 32.89%
c. Gross profit margin = 24.75%
d. $330.60
17. **a.** $37.90
b. 31.03%
19. 150%
21. **a.** $30.47
b. 45.95%
23. **a.** $21.00
b. 69.10%
c. $1091.07
25. $17.60

Exercise 4.4

1. $SP = \$277.50$
Gross profit margin = 33.33%
Rate of markdown = 21.62%
$RSP = \$217.50$
3. $C = \$24.99$
Rate of markup = 100.0%
$D = \$24.99$
$RSP = \$24.99$
5. $SP = \$29.62$
Rate of markup = 53.87%
$D = \$7.41$
$RSP = \$22.21$
7. $C = \$225.71$
Gross profit margin = 42.86%
$D = \$158.00$
$RSP = \$237.00$
9. **a.** 59.95%
b. 37.48%
c. 37.48%
11. $114.40

13. a. 25.72%
    b. 13.84%

Exercise 4.5

1. SP = \$178.00
   RSP = \$133.50
   ROP = −\$17.80
3. D = \$17.88
   Overhead expenses = 20.00% of C
   Rate of markup = 60.00%
5. SP = \$167.70
   C = \$83.85
   ROP = −\$13.98
7. a. \$285.12
   b. 32.00% of C
9. a. 15%
   b. \$19.76 loss per unit
11. 23.61%
13. a. 25.00%
    b. −\$6.12
    c. 25.00%
15. a. \$950.00
    b. \$1187.50
17. a. \$2975.00
    b. \$39.67 loss

Review Problems

1. \$352.08
3. 27.5%
5. a. \$825.80
   b. \$33,852
7. \$5.00
9. a. 10,657
   b. 341 in 1980–84
   536 in 1985–89
   460 in 1990–94
11. \$859.46
13. 122.2%
15. \$287.00
17. a. \$59.63
    b. 26.83%

Self-Test Exercise

1. Source B is \$1.80 cheaper
2. \$1160.95
3. \$169,300
4. a. \$780.48
   b. \$720.00
   c. 34.69%
   d. \$34.38
5. a. \$6.94
   b. \$2.50
6. \$3089.25
7. 1.75%
8. a. \$67.30
   b. \$61.24
9. a. \$20.65
   b. 76.50%
   c. \$18.59
10. a. 153.3%
    b. 6.52%
11. a. 25.00%
    b. \$25.20 loss per pair
    c. 25.00%

Chapter 5 Applications of Linear Equations

Exercise 5.1

1. $(x,y) = (4,2)$
3. $(a,b) = (3,5)$
5. $(x,y) = (7,14)$
7. $(c,d) = (500,1000)$
9. $(v,w) = \left(\frac{3}{2}, -\frac{1}{3}\right)$
11. $(x,y) = (17.0, 6.24)$
13. $(e,f) = (250,125)$
15. 238 student members
    345 regular members
17. \$1.21 per litre, \$1.98 per dozen
19. Maurice: \$39,000, Marcel: \$44,000
21. \$1.50
23. 23 six-packs, 87 single cans
25. 9 production workers, 9 assembly workers

Exercise 5.2

1. a. \$8.00
b. 150 units per week
c. (i) Loss of \$240 per week
(ii) Profit of \$800 per week
d. 200 units per week

3. a. \$27
b. 2000 borgels per month
c. \$13,500 per month
d. \$10,800 loss per month
e. 84.4% of capacity
f. Decreases by 71 borgels per month

5. a. 8000 units; \$240,000
b. \$100,000; \$27,500
c. \$210,000; \$30.00

7. a. 28 participants
b. \$200 profit
c. 20 participants

9. a. 311 tickets at \$23
205 tickets at \$28
b. \$780 at \$23 per ticket
\$1260 at \$28 per ticket

11. a. \$40.97
b. \$40.58

13. a. 12.72 tonnes per hectare
b. 1.03 tonnes per hectare
c. (i) \$130 per hectare
(ii) \$155 per hectare

Exercise 5.3

1.

x:	−3	0	6
y:	−6	0	12

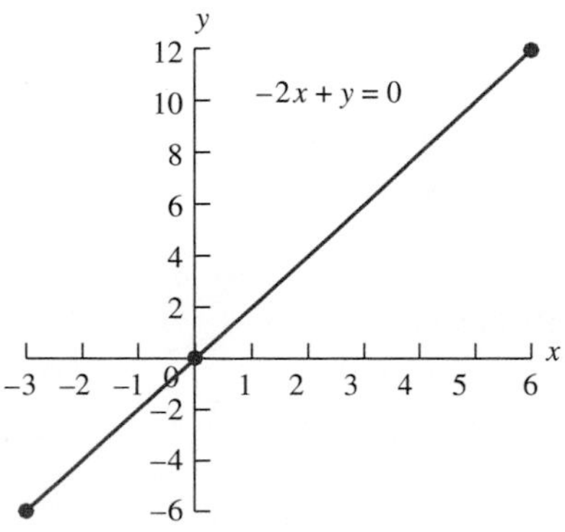

3.

x:	−3	0	6
y:	10	4	−8

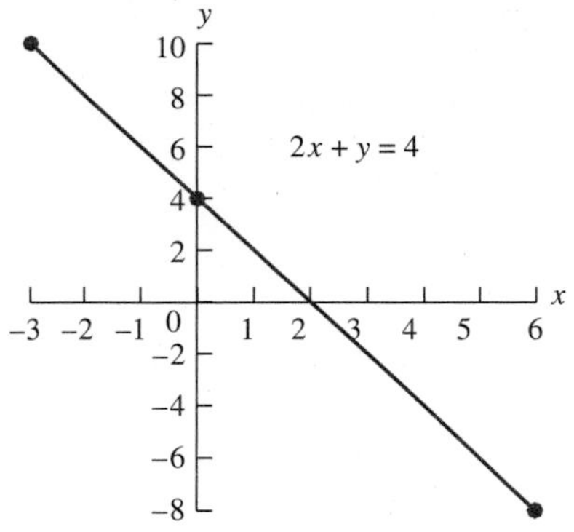

5.

x:	−8	0	12
y:	−3	3	12

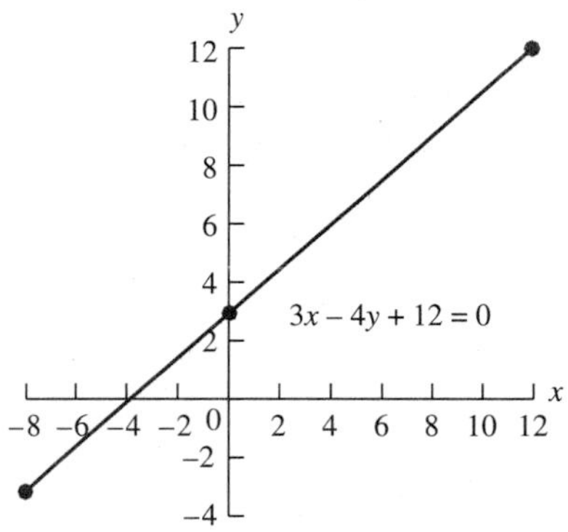

7.

x:	0	3000	6000
y:	5000	18500	32000

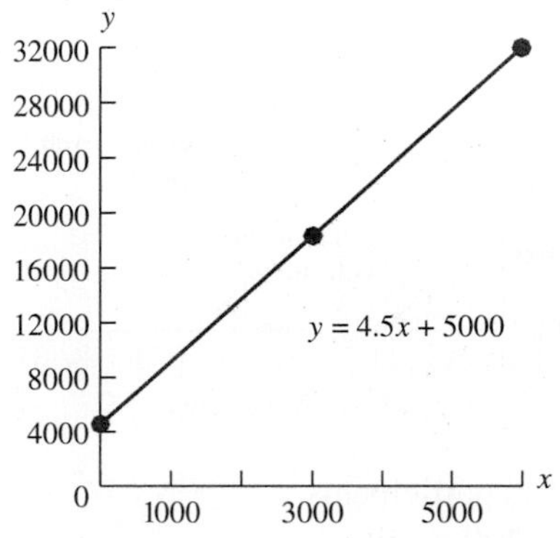

Graphical solution to Problem 1, Exercise 5.2

$TR = \$20X$
$TC = \$1200 + \$12X$

X:	0	250
TR:	\$ 0	\$5000
TC:	\$1200	\$4200

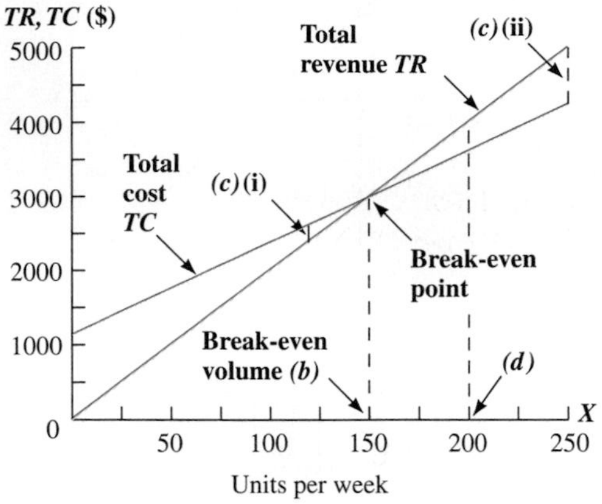

b. 150 units per week
c. (i) Loss of \$240 per week
(ii) Profit of \$800 per week
d. 200 units per week

Graphical solution to Problem 7, Exercise 5.2

$TR = \$135X$
$TC = \$700 + \$110X$

X:	15	36
TR:	\$2025	\$4860
TC:	\$2350	\$4660

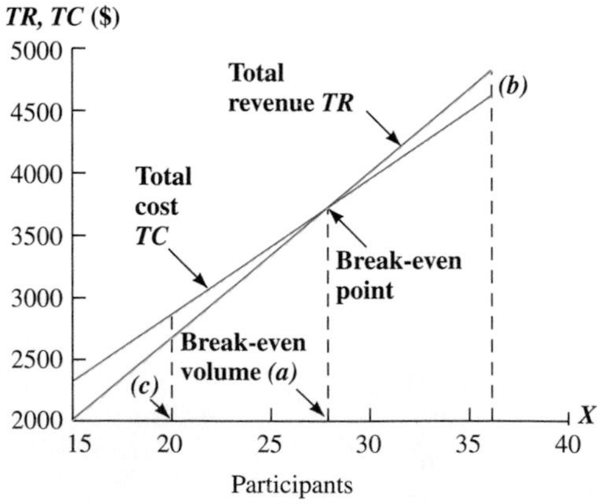

a. 28 participants
b. \$200 profit
c. 20 participants

Review Problems

1. a. $(a,b) = (5,-2)$
b. $(x,y) = (11.4,-6.32)$
3. \$3.55 per kg for ling cod
\$4.10 per kg for red snapper
5. a. $SP = \$12.00$
$NI = \$80,000$
b. $NI = \$100,000$
$VC = \$20.00$
c. Unit sales = 20,000
$FC = \$108,000$
7. a. \$6000
b. \$60 million per year
c. \$12 million
9. a. \$4.0 million
b. \$3,770,778
c. \$4,666,667
d. 50%
e. *NI* will increase to \$533,334

Self-Test Exercise

1. $(x,y) = (7,-2)$
2. 456
3. \$7.80 in the "reds"
\$10.92 in the "blues"
4. a. 2500, 2500
b. (i) \$3000, \$2000
(ii) \$1800 loss, \$1200 loss
c. The 30% commission rate will result in a higher profit if attendance surpasses the break-even point. However, if attendance falls short of break-even, the 30% commission will produce the larger loss.
5. a. 36.2%
b. (i) \$1480 per month
(ii) \$2390 loss per month
c. Reduce the price to \$47

Chapter 6 Simple Interest

Exercise 6.1

1. $83.13
3. 8 months
5. $567.23
7. 7 months
9. $114.58
11. $6500.00
13. 8.10%
15. 13 months
17. $195.00, $198.80

Exercise 6.2

1. $118.63
3. $4149.86
5. $1171.28
7. 8.5%
9. March 9, 1997
11. January 29, 1997
13. $22.09
15. 5.50%
17. 41 days
19. March 18
21. $196.03
23. $3112.28

Exercise 6.3

1. $3182.31
3. $780.00
5. $14,100.00
7. 10.70%
9. 18.50%
11. 182 days
13. 8 months
15. $5169.38
17. $19,324.57
19. 16.00%
21. 7.82%
23. January 8
25. $5604.26
27. $23,542.33

Exercise 6.4

1. $535.99
3. $5460.62
5. 7.25%
7. 90 days
9. 251 days
11. **a.** The later payment
b. 10.86%
13. **a.** The later payment
b. 1.03% per month
15. $974.58
17. $457.49
19. $1146.65
21. $2902.06 today
$2933.99 in two months
$2966.63 in four months
$3000.00 in six months
$3033.75 in eight months
$3067.50 in 10 months
$3101.25 in 12 months
23. Jody's scholarship
25. 7.69%

Exercise 6.5

1. $816.79
3. $1958.60
5. $4442.98
7. $2028.97
9. **a.** $3722.94
b. $3904.76
c. The equivalent value of a given payment stream will be higher at a later date because of the time value of money.
11. $2364.29, $2350.80
The $900 and $1400 payments have a $13.49 greater economic value (in today's dollars).
13. $1856.32

Exercise 6.6

1. $1083.45
3. $876.21

5. $505.54
7. $859.48
9. $1321.52
11. $2719.68
13. $1419.61
15. $2165.97

Review Problems

1. 4.75%
3. $70.96
5. $43,426.53
7. $1028.14
9. $8459.14
11. $2173.14

Self-Test Exercise

1. 11.90%
2. September 8
3. $9736.45
4. $59,430.77
5. **a.** The early-booking price saves $25.51
   b. 11.30%
6. $3762.76
7. **a.** $9571.35
   b. $9663.06

Chapter 7 Applications of Simple Interest

Exercise 7.1

1. **a.** $15,258.90
   b. $15,437.62
3. $166.44
5. $15.48
7. $5.65 more
9. $9.22
11. $52.28

Exercise 7.2

1. **a.** $967.47
   b. $974.54
   c. The closer the purchase date to the payments, the smaller the discount will be for a given time value of money.
3. **a.** $1944.27
   b. $1935.26
   c. The payments from B are received one month later. This makes their value today less than the value of the payments from A.
5. $10,974.71
7. $7854.11

Exercise 7.3

1. $24,651
3. $989,745
5. $99,347 for the 30-day maturity
   $98,702 for the 60-day maturity
   $98,066 for the 90-day maturity
7. $96,079
9. 4.978%
11. 70 days
13. **a.** $97,706
    b. (i) $98,787
    (ii) $98,854
    (iii) $98,920
    c. (i) 4.751%
    (ii) 5.045%
    (iii) 5.335%

Exercise 7.4

1.

Date	Number of days	Interest rate	Interest	Accrued interest	Payment (Advance)	Principal portion	Balance
5-Feb						($15,000)	$15,000
29-Feb	24	8.50%	$83.84	~~$83.84~~	$83.84		15,000
15-Mar	15	8.50%	52.40	52.40		10,000	5,000
31-Mar	16	8.50%	18.63	~~71.03~~	71.03		5,000
30-Apr	30	8.50%	34.93	~~34.93~~	34.93		5,000
1-May	1	8.50%	1.16	1.16		(7,000)	12,000
31-May	30	8.50%	83.84	~~85.00~~	85.00		12,000

The interest charged to Dr. Robillard's account was $83.84 on February 29, $71.03 on March 31, $34.93 on April 30, and $85.00 on May 31.

3.

Date	Number of days	Interest rate	Interest	Accrued interest	Payment (Advance)	Principal portion	Balance
3-Jul						($25,000)	$25,000
20-Jul	17	10.00%	$116.44	~~$116.44~~	$116.44		25,000
29-Jul	9	10.00%	61.64	61.64		(30,000)	55,000
5-Aug	7	10.00%	105.48	167.12			55,000
20-Aug	15	9.75%	220.38	~~387.50~~	387.50		55,000

The amounts of interest charged on July 20 and August 20 were $116.44 and $387.50, respectively.

5.

Date	Number of days	Interest rate	Interest	Accrued interest	Payment (Advance)	Principal portion	Balance
7-Oct						($30,000)	$30,000
15-Oct	8	11.75%	$ 77.26	~~$77.26~~	$77.26		30,000
15-Nov	31	11.75%	299.38	~~299.38~~	299.38		30,000
24-Nov	9	11.75%	86.92	86.92		(15,000)	45,000
15-Dec	21	11.75%	304.21	~~391.13~~	391.13		45,000
17-Dec	2	11.75%	28.97	28.97			45,000
23-Dec	6	11.50%	85.07	114.04		(20,000)	65,000
15-Jan	23	11.50%	471.03	~~585.07~~	585.07		65,000

7.

Date	Number of days	Interest rate	Interest	Accrued interest	Payment (Advance)	Principal portion	Balance
31-Mar						($30,000)	$30,000
18-Apr	18	10.75%	$159.04	~~$159.04~~	$159.04		30,000
28-Apr	10	10.75%	88.36	88.36		(10,000)	40,000
14-May	16	10.75%	188.49	276.85			40,000
18-May	4	11.00%	48.22	~~325.07~~	325.07		40,000
1-Jun	14	11.00%	168.77	168.77		(15,000)	55,000
18-Jun	17	11.00%	281.78	~~450.55~~	450.55	5,000	50,000
3-Jul	15	11.00%	226.03	226.03		10,000	40,000
18-Jul	15	11.00%	180.82	~~406.85~~	406.85		40,000

9.

Date	Number of days	Interest rate	Interest	Accrued interest	Payment (Advance)	Principal portion	Balance
15-Aug							$3,589.80
31-Aug	16	8.75%	$13.77	$13.77	$300.00	$300.00	3,289.80
15-Sep	15	8.75%	11.83	~~25.60~~	100.00	74.40	3,215.40
30-Sep	15	8.75%	11.56	11.56	300.00	300.00	2,915.40
11-Oct	11	8.75%	7.69	19.25			2,915.40
15-Oct	4	8.50%	2.72	~~21.97~~	100.00	78.03	2,837.37
31-Oct	16	8.50%	10.57	10.57	300.00	300.00	2,537.37
15-Nov	15	8.50%	8.86	~~19.43~~	100.00	80.57	2,456.80

11.

Date	Number of days	Interest rate	Interest	Accrued interest	Payment (Advance)	Principal portion	Balance
1-Apr							$6,000.00
1-May	30	11.25%	$ 55.48	~~$55.48~~	$1,000.00	$944.52	5,055.48
1-Jun	31	11.25%	48.30	~~48.30~~	1,000.00	951.70	4,103.78
7-Jun	6	11.25%	7.59	7.59			4,103.78
1-Jul	24	11.00%	29.68	~~37.27~~	1,000.00	962.73	3,141.05
1-Aug	31	11.00%	29.35	~~29.35~~	1,000.00	970.65	2,170.40
27-Aug	26	11.00%	17.01	17.01			2,170.40
1-Sep	5	11.25%	3.34	~~20.35~~	1,000.00	979.65	1,190.75
1-Oct	30	11.25%	11.01	~~11.01~~	1,000.00	988.99	201.76
1-Nov	31	11.25%	1.93	~~1.93~~	203.69	201.76	0.00
	Total of the interest charges =		$203.69				

13.

Date	Number of days	Interest rate	Interest	Accrued interest	Payment (Advance)	Principal portion	Balance
23-Feb							$2,500.00
15-Apr	51	9.00%	$31.44	~~$31.44~~	$500.00	$468.56	2,031.44
15-May	30	9.00%	15.03	~~15.03~~	500.00	484.97	1,546.47
15-Jun	31	9.00%	11.82	~~11.82~~	500.00	488.18	1,058.29
15-Jul	30	9.50%	8.26	~~8.26~~	500.00	491.74	566.55
31-Jul	16	9.50%	2.36	2.36			566.55
15-Aug	15	9.75%	2.27	~~4.63~~	500.00	495.37	71.18
15-Sep	31	9.75%	0.59	~~0.59~~	71.77	71.18	0.00

Exercise 7.5

1. Grace period interest = $430.21

Date	Number of days	Interest rate	Interest	Accrued interest	Payment (Advance)	Principal portion	Balance
1-Dec	—	—	—	—	—	—	$9830.21
31-Dec	30	9.00%	$72.72	~~$72.72~~	$135.00	$62.28	9767.93
17-Jan	17	9.00%	40.95	40.95		0.00	9767.93
31-Jan	14	9.25%	34.66	~~75.61~~	135.00	59.39	9708.54
28-Feb	28	9.25%	68.89	~~68.89~~	135.00	66.11	9642.43

3. Grace period interest = $389.50

Date	Number of days	Interest rate	Interest	Accrued interest	Payment (Advance)	Principal portion	Balance
1-Jan	—	—	—	—	—	—	$7189.50
31-Jan	30	11.25%	$66.48	~~$66.48~~	$200.00	$133.52	7055.98
28-Feb	28	11.25%	60.89	~~60.89~~	200.00	139.11	6916.87
2-Mar	2	11.25%	4.26	4.26			6916.87
25-Mar	23	10.75%	46.85	51.11	500.00	500.00	6416.87
31-Mar	6	10.75%	11.34	~~62.45~~	200.00	137.55	6279.32

5. Grace period interest = $254.19

Date	Number of days	Interest rate	Interest	Accrued interest	Payment (Advance)	Principal portion	Balance
1-Dec	—	—	—	—	—	—	$5454.19
31-Dec	30	9.75%	$43.71	~~$43.71~~	$110.00	$66.29	5387.90
31-Jan	31	9.75%	44.62	~~44.62~~	110.00	65.38	5322.52
14-Feb	14	9.50%	19.39	19.39	300.00	300.00	5022.52
28-Feb	14	9.50%	18.30	~~37.69~~	110.00	72.31	4950.21

Exercise 7A

1. September 19
3. 100 days
5. October 25
7. March 3
9. $1032.53
11. $2600.00
13. 9.0%
15. 45 days
17. $988.09
19. $2760.61
21. 7.5%
23. **a.** March 3, 1998
b. March 1, 1998
25. $1036.23
27. $3257.12
29. $763.17
31. $3000.91

Review Problems

1. $12,128.95
3. $49,169.71
5. 6.385%
7. $98.63
9. $6.73

11.

Date	Number of days	Interest rate	Interest	Accrued interest	Payment (Advance)	Principal portion	Balance
8-Mar						($40,000)	$40,000
24-Mar	16	10.25%	$179.73	~~$179.73~~	$179.73		40,000
2-Apr	9	10.25%	101.10	101.10		(15,000)	55,000
24-Apr	22	10.25%	339.79	~~440.89~~	440.89		55,000
13-May	19	10.25%	293.46	293.46			55,000
24-May	11	10.50%	174.04	~~467.50~~	467.50		55,000
5-Jun	12	10.50%	189.86	189.86		25,000	30,000
24-Jun	19	10.50%	163.97	~~353.83~~	353.83		30,000

The first four interest debits were, in order, $179.73, $440.89, $467.50, and $353.93.

Self-Test Exercise

1. $3780.22
2. a. $24,665.59
   b. 5.815% pa
   c. 4.762% pa
3. $14.90
4.

Date	Number of days	Interest rate	Interest	Accrued interest	Payment (Advance)	Principal portion	Balance
3-Jun	—	—	—	—	—	($50,000)	$ 50,000
26-Jun	23	12.00%	$ 378.08	~~$378.08~~	$378.08		50,000
30-Jun	4	12.00%	65.75	65.75		(40,000)	90,000
5-Jul	5	12.00%	147.95	213.70			90,000
17-Jul	12	12.25%	362.47	576.17		(25,000)	115,000
26-Jul	9	12.25%	347.36	~~923.53~~	923.53		115,000
31-Jul	5	12.50%	196.92	196.92		30,000	85,000
18-Aug	18	12.50%	523.97	720.89		35,000	50,000
26-Aug	8	12.50%	136.99	~~857.88~~	857.88		50,000
			$2,159.49				

5.

Date	Number of days	Interest rate	Interest	Accrued interest	Payment (Advance)	Principal portion	Balance
23-May							$15,000.00
15-Jun	23	9.50%	$ 89.79	~~$89.79~~	$700.00	$610.21	14,389.79
15-Jul	30	9.50%	112.36	~~112.36~~	700.00	587.64	13,802.15
26-Jul	11	9.50%	39.52	39.52			13,802.15
15-Aug	20	9.25%	69.96	~~109.48~~	700.00	590.52	13,211.63
14-Sep	30	9.25%	100.44	100.44			13,211.63
15-Sep	1	9.75%	3.53	~~103.97~~	700.00	596.03	12,615.60
15-Oct	30	9.75%	101.10	~~101.10~~	700.00	598.90	12,016.70

Chapter 8 Compound Interest: Future Value and Present Value

Exercise 8.1

1. 2.7% per quarter
3. 0.875% per month
5. 11.0% compounded monthly
7. Quarterly compounding
9. Monthly compounding

Exercise 8.2

1. $9899.66
3. $15,428.20
5. **a.** $8623.08
b. $9032.64
c. $9254.05
d. $9408.41
7. **a.** $108.30
b. $108.35
c. $108.37
d. $108.30
Choose 8.2% compounded semiannually
9. Maturity value = $3448.13
Interest charged = $448.13
11. $2750.75; 25.39%
13. $3018.67; 53.86%
15.

Interest rate	20 years	25 years	30 years
8%	$4660.96	$6848.48	$10,062.66
10%	$6727.50	$10,834.71	$17,449.40

17. $6865.65
19. $3707.78
21. $3011.67
23. $11,544.93
25. Donna will receive $8340.04
Tim will receive $10,045.40
Gary will receive $12,099.47
27. **a.** $108,366.67
b. $113,743.60
c. $103,219.59
29. $8206.23
31. $2936.09
33. $6473.04

Exercise 8.3

1. $3890.66
3. $7500.00
5. $5548.69
7. $2563.19
9. $2976.38
11. The Araki offer is worth $160.12 more.
13. Do not pay $964. (Worth only $887.30.)
15. $977.59
17. $1528.67
19. $4005.37
21. $2807.83
23. $4965.96
25. $3065.37 in 3.5-year certificate
$3551.16 in 4.5-year certificate
$3881.03 in 5.5-year certificate
27. $2804.32
29. $14,977.31
31. $4694.63
33. $2345.50
35. $2945.55
37. $1200.00

Exercise 8.5

1. $675.00
3. $52,831.32
5. 7.5% compounded semiannually
7. Earn $88.01 more at 5% compounded annually than at 4.75% compounded monthly
9. $678.93 from the BC bonds
$753.06 from the Canada Savings Bonds
11. **a.** $6320.89
b. $6522.37
13. $404.34
15. $2871.26; $186.34
17. $10,209.09; $502.10
19. $1930.03 on the RateRiser GIC
$1931.22 on the fixed-rate GIC
21. RateRiser GIC: $627.63
Fixed-rate GIC: $645.83

23. a. $148.59
b. $180.61
c. $219.11
25. $21.16 per hour
27. a. $47,105.39
b. $54,528.86
c. $72,762.49
29. $34,425,064
31. $244.81
33. $6920.20
35. 28 bonds can be purchased
37. $10,489.74
39. $3599.26

Exercise 8.6

1. $3902.32
3. $1925.11
5. $382.66; $765.32
7. $1539.02
9. $2167.15
11. $1492.77
13. a. Alternative (2) is worth $956.61 more
b. Alternative (1) is worth $852.03 more
15. $3711.68; $7423.35
17. $3124.38; $9373.14
19. $2541.74

Review Problems

1. $67.73
3. a. $14,750.38
b. $906.75
5. Principal = $2012.56
Interest = $285.22
7. $38,288.36
9. $3372.42
11. $7972.59
13. 7.75% compounded annually
15. Current price = $229.44
Increase in value = $25.20
17. $4327.07
19. 16.32%
21. $2500.00
23. $3917.24

Self-Test Exercise

1. a. $14,354.74 for the RateRiser GIC
$14,356.29 for the fixed-rate GIC
b. $854.66 from the RateRiser GIC
$866.72 from the fixed-rate GIC
2. a. $9509.42
b. $2411.71
c. 294.3%
3. $1282.09
4. $979.19
5. $12,322.58
6. $9267.27
7. Offer 1 is worth $37,180.13
Offer 2 is worth $38,164.23
Offer 2 should be accepted
8. $61.80 more will be earned from the Escalator GIC.
9. 59.05%
10. $1975.49
11. $2311.51

Chapter 9 Compound Interest: Further Topics and Applications

Exercise 9.1

1. 8.13% compounded annually
3. 9.00% compounded quarterly
5. 8.50% compounded monthly
7. 4.37% compounded annually
9. 5.25% compounded annually
11. 8.02% compounded annually
13. 35.34% compounded annually
15. −5.77% compounded annually
17. 5.93%
19. 6.98%
21. 14.00% compounded quarterly
23. a. TSE 300: 6.76% compounded annually
S&P 500: 14.46% compounded annually
b. $23,667.42
25. 6.95% compounded annually
27. 10.94% compounded annually
29. 8.08% compounded annually

31. 36.37% compounded annually (3 yr.)
23.71% compounded annually (5 yr.)
21.74% compounded annually (10 yr.)

Exercise 9.2

1. 23 years
3. 6 years and 6 months
5. 2 years and 11 months
7. 3.5 years
9. 14.5 years
11. **a.** 8 years and 7 months
b. 6 years and 9 months
13. **a.** 18 years
b. $15\frac{3}{4}$ years
15. **a.** 14 years and 6 months
b. 7 years and 4 months
17. 23 months
19. 2 years, 11 months, and 24 days
21. 11 years and 129 days
23. 1 year, 9 months, and 57 days

Exercise 9.3

1. 10.78%
3. 11.02%
5. 7.71%
7. 10.24% compounded semiannually
9. 10.03% compounded monthly
11. 7.30% compounded quarterly
13. 12.68%
15. 12.01%
17. 10.00% compounded semiannually
19. 9.57% compounded monthly
21. 23.87%
23. 26.82%
25. 9.10%
27. 10.72%
29. Accept the credit union loan
31. Choose the broker loan (0.02% lower rate)
33. 5.75% compounded annually
5.67% compounded semiannually
5.60% compounded monthly
35. 19.68% compounded monthly

Exercise 9.4

1. 9.76% compounded semiannually
3. 9.57% compounded monthly
5. 9.88% compounded quarterly
7. 10.38% compounded annually
9. 9.92% compounded monthly
11. 10.21% compounded semiannually
13. 9.20% compounded annually
15. 7.95% compounded monthly
17. 7.43% compounded quarterly
19. 8.59% compounded semiannually
21. **a.** 9.20% compounded annually
b. 9.31% compounded annually
c. 9.38% compounded annually
23. 7.39% compounded monthly
25. 12.30% compounded semiannually
27. 7.95% compounded monthly
8.09% compounded semiannually

Exercise 9B

1. Simple rate = 6.00%
Effective rate = 6.15%
3. Simple rate = 9.75%
Effective rate = 10.20%
5. 14.10%
7. 4.67%
9. Simple rate = −9.33%
Effective rate = −9.01%
11. Current yield = 5.06%
Effective yield = 5.19%
13. 6.36%
15. **a.** 972.7%
b. 227.5%

Review Problems

1. 28.47% compounded annually
3. 14.43% compounded annually
5. 4.89%
7. August 1 of the following year
9. 1.75 years
11. 2 years and 118 days
13. 10.73% compounded semiannually
15. 19.56%
17. 7.02%
19. Choose the bank mortgage

Self-Test Exercise

1. 7.40% compounded annually
2. 2.37%

3. a. 11.11%
b. 5 years and 6 months
4. 3.12% compounded annually
5. 13.55%
6. 10 years and 4 months
7. 13 years and 9 months
8. 13 years and 131 days
9. 5.30% compounded semiannually
10. Choose 7.5% compounded monthly
11. 10.52%

Chapter 10 Ordinary Annuities: Future Value and Present Value

Exercise 10.2

1. $13,551.86
3. $2481.66
5. $28,023.46
7. $346,122.02
9. $4557.88
11. $163,066.90
13. $4186.20
15. a. $6105.10
b. $15,937.42
c. $31,772.48
d. $57,275.00
e. $98,347.06
f. $164,494.02
17. a. (i) $9254.65
(ii) $9679.33
(iii) $9826.56
b. (i) $10,717.94
(ii) $10,406.66
(iii) $10,226.04
19. $30,014.43
21. $188,830.07
23. $40,177
25. $176,937

Exercise 10.3

1. $3291.74
3. $2033.16
5. $11,355.21
7. $15,047.05
9. $14,131.26
11. a. $3790.79
b. $6144.57
c. $8513.56
d. $9426.91
e. $9999.27
f. $10,000.00

13.

	8%	9%
20 years	$358,662.88	$333,434.86
25 years	$388,693.57	$357,484.87

15. $33,372.71
17. a. $54.66
b. $50.00
c. $45.87
19. a. $21,750.01
b. $17,365.12
21. $7489.21
23. $3304.30
25. $59,623.78
27. $964,437
29. The multiple-payment offer is worth $191.90 more.
31. Mrs. Martel's offer is worth $137.31 more.
33. $946.36
35. The pension-at-age 55 option has a 31.9% higher economic value.

Exercise 10.4

1. $20,150.88
3. $14,032.77
5. 2 years and 6 months
7. $7682.97
9. $24,949.52
11. The $1000 annuity has the greater economic value.
13. $2861.16
15. 8 months
17. 7 years

Exercise 10.5

1. 10.381%
3. 4.040%
5. 0.908%

7. 1.884%
9. 0.816%
11. $33,515.32
13. $21,764.70
15. $156,049.64
17. $10,120.92
19. $16,464.70
21. $26,388.76
23. $20,035.79
25. $14,074.16
27. 2 years and 6 months
29. **a.** $84,700.90
 b. $88,673.74
 c. $89,635.35
31. **a.** $10,111.85
 b. $9998.73
 c. $9939.94
33. $289,817.81
35. $7499.94
37. **a.** $200,000
 b. $27,423.04
39. $58,720.25
41. $73,953.35
43. $195,703.18
45. $34,429.70
47. $34,513.13
49. $50,239.76
51. 5 years and 6 months
53. $313,490.72

Review Problems

1. Choose the five-year-payment option.
3. **a.** $160,000
 b. $48,628.00
5. **a.** $59,999.80
 b. $39,119.37
7. $2556.57
9. $9118.21
11. 59.56%
13. $45,329.87
15. $85,804.68

Self-Test Exercise

1. **a.** $100,822.83
 b. $96,754.03
2. **a.** $46,800.03
 b. $24,997.20
3. $2376.15
4. $82,819.01
5. $5623.01
6. $81,160.11
7. $30,795.12
8. $2390.05

Chapter 11 Ordinary Annuities: Payment Size, Term, and Interest Rate

Exercise 11.1

1. $3000.00
3. $132.50
5. $349.99
7. $1130.00
9. $1075.51
11. $3324.24
13. $3972.46
15. $1812.48
17. $675.54
19. **a.** $2735.76
 b. $2033.61
21. **a.** $237.40
 b. $161.12
23. **a.** $444.89; $6693.40
 b. $286.94; $14,432.80
 c. $240.03; $23,205.40
 d. $220.22; $32,852.80
 e. $210.64; $43,192.00
25. $1974.83
27. $7419.89
29. $2222.05
31. **a.** $238.50
 b. 9.38%
 c. $2727.23
33. $3261.26
35. $1766.18
37. $1962.61
39. $4075.72

41. $3241.66
43. a. $177,435.91
b. $2,323,077.30
45. $8821.74
47. $12,554.29
49. $3834.66

Exercise 11.2

1. 8 years and 6 months
3. 16 years and 9 months
5. 25 years
7. 8 years
9. 10 years
11. 8 years
13. 13 years
15. 9 years and 9 months
17. 7 years and 6 months
19. 6 years and 11 months
21. 18 years and 7 months
23. 4 years and 8 months
25. 22 years and 3 months
27. 2 years and 9 months
29. Beyond age 79 years and 7 months
31. 51
33. 18 years and 9 months
35. 10 years and 11 months
37. 26 years

Exercise 11.3

1. 7.70% compounded annually; 7.70%
3. 10.50% compounded quarterly; 10.92%
5. 8.50% compounded semiannually; 8.68%
7. 9.00% compounded monthly; 9.38%
9. 9.80% compounded monthly; 10.25%
11. 7.90% compounded monthly; 8.19%
13. 8.50% compounded semiannually; 8.68%
15. 11.40% compounded monthly; 12.01%
17. 7.67%
19. 65.48%
21. 12.53%

Review Problems

1. a. $5418.78
b. $2204.89
3. 7.45% compounded monthly; 7.71%
5. 8.775%
7. 18 months longer
9. 20 years and 9 months
11. $7206.60
13. a. $1,066,335
b. $3737.03
15. 86 years
17. 23
19. $9055.67
21. $7499.21

Self-Test Exercise

1. a. $475.31
b. $531.10
2. 5 years and 3 months; $30,760
3. 10.54%
4. $322.29
5. a. $740.13
b. 16 years and 11 months
6. 18
7. 16 years and 10 months
8. Lena: $946.39
Axel: $1421.64

Chapter 12 Annuities: Special Situations

Exercise 12.1

1. $6250.00
3. $114,285.71
5. $11,168.22
7. $9120.69
9. $1445.28
11. a. $95.31
b. 7.32% compounded semiannually
13. a. $73,223.88
b. $70,303.99
15. $17,669.23
17. $6954.87

Exercise 12.2

1. $312,421.69
3. $3494.84

5. $46,155.28
7. $362,020.14; $80,141.25
9. $1949.10
11. $23.42

Review Problems

1. 30.38%
3. a. $142,857.14
   b. $109,693.48
5. $15,209.95

Self-Test Exercise

1. $2611.53
2. $900.00
3. $55,987.12
4. 21.94%

Chapter 13 Annuities Due

Exercise 13.1

1. $8964.56
3. $13,366.94
5. $43,362.43
7. $8404.79
9. $48,508.71
11. $33,130.87
13. $108,964.03
15. $70,118.88
17. $326,252.08; $243,752.08
19. $321,965.55
21. Fay will have $128,616.00 more.

Exercise 13.2

1. $2707.11
3. $10,111.90
5. $19,603.86
7. $4058.70
9. $13,865.77
11. $23,142.25
13. $20,457.00
15. a. $49.65 million
    b. $43.58 million
17. Mrs. Martel's offer is worth $137.31 more
19. $316,727.71
21. $120,339.78
23. a. $78,470.45
    b. $12,389.23
25. a. Highest value: $1700 annuity
       Lowest value: $850 annuity
    b. Highest value: $850 annuity
       Lowest value: $1700 annuity
27. Accept the lease on the new location (saving of $4678)

Exercise 13.3

1. $2077.58
3. $762.57
5. $1060.28
7. $3298.84
9. 17 years
11. 9 years
13. 8 years
15. 9 years
17. 11.50% compounded semiannually
    11.83%
19. 13.00% compounded quarterly
    13.65%
21. 10.28% compounded monthly
    10.78%
23. $182.99
25. $36,786.56
27. $1012.46
29. 5.12% compounded monthly
31. $15,154.43
33. 36-month lease
35. a. $20,100.27
    b. $21,909.30
37. a. $19,227.29
    b. $19,948.31
39. $172.56
41. $302.75
43. $401.90
45. $978.42
47. 25 months from today (26th deposit)

49. 30 payments
51. 13 months
53. 14.89%
55. 11.00% compounded quarterly
11.46%
57. 24.79%
59. a. $622.06
b. $3599.09
61. $501.07 quarterly
$169.04 monthly
63. 3 years and 3 months
65. 5 years and 9 months (after the first draw)
67. 13.74%
69. 21.26% compounded annually
71. a. 9.86%
b. 9.78%
c. 13.45%
73. $1459.87
75. 27 years

Exercise 13.4

1. 1 year and 11 months
3. 15 years
5. $2412.64
7. $863,467
9. $572,376.63
11. $367.67
13. a. $138,000
b. $82,857.57
c. $258,342
15. $1643.51
17. $1692.37
19. $1330.69
21. $3031.42 at age 65
$4885.46 at age 70

Review Problems

1. a. $89,170.65
b. $14,312.37
3. a. $25,527.54
b. $27,505.93
5. 10.36%
7. 12.55%
9. 29
11. 17.43%
13. a. $7506.74
b. $11,580.67
15. $615,447.79
17. 37.4%
19. 37.0%
21. $4829.66

Self-Test Exercise

1. a. $105,107.80
b. $104,978.12
2. The monthly payment plan is slightly better.
3. a. $2,037,008
b. $1,203,077
4. $31,516.97
5. $209.61
6. $1144.74
7. 3 years and 2 months
8. 103.54%
9. $8.93

Chapter 14 Amortization of Loans

Exercise 14.1

	Principal portion	Interest portion	Last payment
1.	$958.05	$116.05	
3.	1250.18	281.51	
5.	284.00	108.76	
7.	779.37	569.91	
9.	656.25	200.41	
11.	959.81	1017.07	
13.	284.62	117.32	
15.	$842.78	$240.19	$604.28
17.	467.58	566.86	664.87
19.	1374.54	1644.11	2130.46
21.	404.87	191.82	373.51

	Total principal	Total interest
23.	$1904.23	$646.03
25.	3681.81	3454.84
27.	4492.22	883.95
29.	714.50	382.87

31. a. $1395.08
b. $709.99
c. $17,878.32
d. $3422.31
e. $3070.45

33. a. $153.74
b. $401.63
c. $910.28
d. $1393.78
e. $485.78

35. a. $2205.35
b. $1696.62
c. $11,933.60
d. $2865.32
e. $2563.45

37. a. $78.86
b. $359.40
c. $979.13
d. $1659.12
e. $208.50

39. a. $480.07
b. Principal = $144.02
Interest = $336.05
c. $33,460.71
d. $4123.64

41. a. $182.62
b. $102.01
c. $85.81

Exercise 14.2

1.

Payment number	Payment	Interest portion	Principal portion	Principal balance
0				$1000.00
1	$174.03	$12.50	$161.53	838.47
2	174.03	10.48	163.55	674.92
3	174.03	8.44	165.59	509.33
4	174.03	6.37	167.66	341.67
5	174.03	4.27	169.76	171.91
6	174.06	2.15	171.91	0.00
		$44.21		

3.

Payment number	Payment	Interest portion	Principal portion	Principal balance
0				$9000.00
1	$1840.85	$556.54	$1284.31	7715.69
2	1840.85	477.12	1363.73	6351.96
3	1840.85	392.79	1448.06	4903.90
4	1840.85	303.25	1537.60	3366.30
5	1840.85	208.17	1632.68	1733.62
6	1840.82	107.20	1733.62	0.00

5.

Payment number	Payment	Interest portion	Principal portion	Principal balance
0				$8000.00
1	$1115.74	$200.00	$ 915.74	7084.26
2	1115.74	177.11	938.63	6145.63
3	2615.74	153.64	2462.10	3683.53
4	1115.74	92.09	1023.65	2659.88
5	1115.74	66.50	1049.24	1610.64
6	1115.74	40.27	1075.47	535.17
7	548.55	13.38	535.17	0.00
		$742.99		

7.

Payment number	Payment	Interest portion	Principal portion	Principal balance
0				$60,000.00
1	$1126.74	$525.00	$601.74	59,398.26
2	1126.74	519.73	607.01	58,791.25
.	.	.	.	.
.	.	.	.	.
42				29,616.38
43	1126.74	259.14	867.60	28,748.78
44	1126.74	251.55	875.19	27,873.59
.	.	.	.	.
.	.	.	.	.
70				2224.07
71	1126.74	19.46	1107.28	1116.79
72	1126.56	9.77	1116.79	0.00

9.

Payment number	Payment	Interest portion	Principal portion	Principal balance
0				$1000.00
1	$200.00	$12.50	$187.50	812.50
2	200.00	10.16	189.84	622.66
3	200.00	7.78	192.22	430.44
4	200.00	5.38	194.62	235.82
5	200.00	2.95	197.05	38.77
6	39.25	0.48	38.77	0.00
		$39.25		

11.

Payment number	Payment	Interest portion	Principal portion	Principal balance
0				$9000.00
1	$2000.00	$556.54	$1443.46	7556.54
2	2000.00	467.28	1532.72	6023.82
3	2000.00	372.50	1627.50	4396.32
4	2000.00	271.86	1728.14	2668.18
5	2000.00	164.99	1835.01	833.17
6	884.69	51.52	833.17	0.00

13.

Payment number	Payment	Interest portion	Principal portion	Principal balance
0				$7500.00
1	$1000.00	$187.50	$812.50	6687.50
2	1000.00	167.19	832.81	5854.69
3	2000.00	146.37	1853.63	4001.06
4	1000.00	100.03	899.97	3101.09
5	1000.00	77.53	922.47	2178.62
6	1000.00	54.47	945.53	1233.09
7	1000.00	30.83	969.17	263.92
8	270.52	6.60	263.92	0.00
		$770.52		

15.

Payment number	Payment	Interest portion	Principal portion	Principal balance
0				$60,000.00
1	$1000.00	$525.00	$475.00	59,525.00
2	1000.00	520.84	479.16	59,045.84
.	.	.	.	.
.	.	.	.	.
.	.	.	.	.
55				26,629.91
56	1000.00	233.01	766.99	25,862.92
57	1000.00	226.30	773.70	25,089.22
.	.	.	.	.
.	.	.	.	.
.	.	.	.	.
84				1435.19
85	1000.00	12.56	987.44	447.75
86	451.67	3.92	447.75	0.00

Exercise 14.3

1.

Interval	Balance at end	Principal reduction	Interest paid
0 to 5 years	$92,340.18	$7659.82	$38,901.38
5 to 10 years	80,892.29	11,447.89	35,113.31
10 to 15 years	63,782.96	17,109.33	29,451.87
15 to 20 years	38,212.41	25,570.56	20,990.64
20 to 25 years	0.00	38,212.41	8345.00

3. a. $763.21 at a rate of 8%
$827.98 at a rate of 9%
$894.49 at a rate of 10%
b. 8.03%
c. $128,963 at 8%
$148,394 at 9%
$168,347 at 10%

5. a. $131,025
b. $120,776

7. $57.14

9. a. $77,587.44
b. $692.26

11. a. $33,866.00
b. $410.00

13. a. $16,456.38
b. $90.45

15. a. $157,200
b. $165,500

17. a. $811.61
b. 19 years and 28 weeks

19. a. 2 years and 1 month
b. 3 years and 10 months

21. a. 1 year and 11 months
b. 3 years and 5 months

23. 5 months

25. 8 months

27. 9 years and 2 months

29. a. 3 years and 1 month
b. $106,008.91

31. a. 3 years and 4 months
b. $87,282.67

33. a. 6 years and 8 months
b. $70,357.69

Exercise 14.4

1. 18.135%

3. a. 12.607%
b. 12.144%
c. 12.068%

5. a. The trust company's loan has an effective rate that is 0.38% lower.
b. The trust company's loan has an effective rate that is 0.19% lower.

7. a. $34,488.28
b. $36,699.09

9. a. $60,024.46
b. $58,538.34
c. $57,100.64

11. $161,588.89

13. $141,749.57

15. $2922.73

17. $566.16

19. 14 years and 5 months

21. a. $107,580; 43.61%
b. $159,348; 53.39%
c. $220,694; 61.33%

23. 40.59%

25. 27 years and 4 months

Review Problems

1.

Payment number	Payment	Interest portion	Principal portion	Principal balance
0				$862.50
1	$148.50	$8.09	$140.41	722.09
2	148.50	6.77	141.73	580.36
3	148.50	5.44	143.06	437.30
4	148.50	4.10	144.40	292.90
5	148.50	2.75	145.75	147.15
6	148.53	1.38	147.15	0.00
		$28.53		

3. **a.** $785.01
   b. $236.32
   c. $5579.53
   d. $2516.16

5.

Payment number	Payment	Interest portion	Principal portion	Principal balance
0				$60,000.00
1	$10,000.00	$ 3150.00	$6850.00	53,150.00
2	10,000.00	2790.38	7209.62	45,940.38
3	10,000.00	2411.87	7588.13	38,352.25
4	10,000.00	2013.49	7986.51	30,365.74
5	10,000.00	1594.20	8405.80	21,959.94
6	10,000.00	1152.90	8847.10	13,112.84
7	10,000.00	688.42	9311.58	3801.26
8	4,000.83	199.57	3801.26	0.00
		$14,000.83		

7. **a.** $226.25
   b. $385.64
   c. $1414.28
   d. $3664.33
   e. $341.08
9. **a.** $79,914.89
   b. $872.38
11. $19,719.03
13. **a.** 5 years and 11 months
    b. $99,423.78
15. **a.** $61,374.33
    b. $58,818.22

Self-Test Exercise

1. **a.** $86.32
   b. $302.74
   c. $2840.92
   d. $992.09
2.

Payment number	Payment	Interest portion	Principal portion	Principal balance
0				$6400.00
1	$161.70	$52.26	$109.44	6290.56
2	161.70	51.36	110.34	6180.22
.	.	.	.	.
.	.	.	.	.
.	.	.	.	.
33				2274.13
34	161.70	18.57	143.13	2131.00
35	161.70	17.40	144.30	1986.70
.	.	.	.	.
.	.	.	.	.
.	.	.	.	.
46				319.47
47	161.70	2.61	159.09	160.38
48	161.69	1.31	160.38	0.00

3. **a.** $7023.10
   b. $4989.79
   c. $4664.05
   d. $13,861.82
   e. $20,976.85
4. $39,453.90
5. **a.** 2 years and 1 month
   b. $77,157.87
6. 12.20%
7. $185,596
8. $144,452
9. 41.54%

Chapter 15 Bonds and Sinking Funds

Exercise 15.2

1. $1066.64
3. $1094.16
5. $960.37
7. $1056.17
9. $104.96
11. $93.70
13. $1185.98
15. $23,887.09

17. Bond A: $1081.11
Bond B: $1135.90
Bond C: $1172.92
Bond D: $1214.82
The longer a bond's maturity, the greater the premium for a given difference: "Coupon rate − Market rate."

19. Bond J: $1092.01
Bond K: $1184.02
Bond L: $1276.02
The greater the difference, "Coupon rate − Market rate," the greater the price premium.

21. Bond E: $862.01
Bond F: $1137.99

23. Bond G: −$37.69
Bond H: −$59.75
Bond J: −$84.66
The longer a bond's maturity, the more sensitive the bond's price is to market interest rate changes.

25. **a.** $10,662.58
b. 6.62%

27. **a.** 12.94%
b. 0%
c. −10.78%

29. 28.49% compounded semiannually

Exercise 15.3

1. 11.41% compounded semiannually

3. Bond A: 10.30% csa
Bond C: 9.57% csa

5. **a.** 0.78% decrease
b. 0.26% decrease

7. 17.54% compounded semiannually

Exercise 15.4

1. $1020.35

3. $948.67

5. $1464.11

7. $959.22

9. $1110.82

11. $563.91

13. March 15: $915.66
April 15: $923.22
May 15: $930.59
June 15: $938.27
July 15: $945.77
August 15: $953.57
September 15: $916.44

15. **a.** $1070.62
b. 25.55%

17. 104.22%

19. $1100.08

21. $1221.62

Exercise 15.5

	Payment	Balance
1.	$424,333	$6,196,094
3.	$620,292	$9,534,856
5.	$ 87,284	$2,506,640
7.	$344,297	$9,268,208

	Payment	Annual cost of debt	Book value
9.	$353,611	$1,707,222	$4,836,586
11.	$302,726	$1,955,452	$6,081,667
13.	$614,137	$1,788,274	$2,311,969
15.	$204,464	$1,536,428	$5,478,509

17.

Payment interval number	Payment (at end)	Interest earned	Increase in the fund	Balance in fund (end of interval)
0	—	—	—	$ 0
1	$122,135	$ 0	$122,135	122,135
2	122,135	4275	126,410	248,545
3	122,135	8699	130,834	379,379
4	122,135	13,278	135,413	514,792
5	122,135	18,018	140,153	654,945
6	122,135	22,923	145,058	800,003
		$67,193	$800,003	

19.

Payment interval number	Payment (at start)	Interest earned	Increase in the fund	Balance in fund (end of interval)
0	—	—	—	$ 0
1	$163,710	$ 11,050	$ 174,760	174,760
2	163,710	22,847	186,557	361,317
3	163,710	35,439	199,149	560,466
4	163,710	48,882	212,592	773,058
5	163,710	63,232	226,942	1,000,000
		$181,450	$1,000,000	

21.

Payment interval number	Payment (at end)	Interest earned	Increase in the fund	Balance in fund (end of interval)
0	—	—	—	$ 0
1	$302,720	$ 0	$302,720	302,720
2	302,720	4541	307,261	609,981
3	302,720	9150	311,870	921,851
⋮	⋮	⋮	⋮	⋮
10				3,239,928
11	302,720	48,599	351,319	3,591,247
12	302,720	53,869	356,589	3,947,836
⋮	⋮	⋮	⋮	⋮
17				5,812,634
18	302,720	87,190	389,910	6,202,544
19	302,720	93,038	395,758	6,598,302
20	302,720	98,975	401,695	6,999,997

23.

Payment interval number	Payment	Interest earned	Increase in the fund	Balance in fund (end of interval)	Book value of the debt
0	—	—	—	$ 0	$10,000,00
1	$353,611	$ 0	$353,611	353,611	9,646,389
2	353,611	12,376	365,987	719,598	9,280,402
3	353,611	25,186	378,797	1,098,395	8,901,605
⋮	⋮	⋮	⋮	⋮	⋮
17				8,028,743	1,971,257
18	353,611	281,006	634,617	8,663,360	1,336,640
19	353,611	303,218	656,829	9,320,189	679,811
20	353,611	326,207	679,818	10,000,007	(7)

25. a. $8221
b. $29,938
c. The 33rd month
d. $2003

27. a. $198,368
b. $217,583
c. $585,395
d.

Payment interval number	Payment	Interest earned	Increase in the fund	Balance in fund (end of interval)	Book value of the debt
0	—	—	—	$ 0	$20,000,000
1	$ 198,368	$ 0	$ 198,368	198,368	19,801,632
2	198,368	8431	206,799	405,167	19,594,833
3	198,368	17,220	215,588	620,755	19,379,245
.	.	.	.	.	.
.	.	.	.	.	.
.	.	.	.	.	.
37				17,104,453	2,895,547
38	198,368	726,939	925,307	18,029,760	1,970,240
39	198,368	766,265	964,633	18,994,393	1,005,607
40	198,368	807,262	1,005,630	20,000,023	(23)
		$12,065,303			

29. a. $13,737
b.

Payment interval number	Payment	Interest earned	Increase in the fund	Balance in fund (end of interval)	Book value of the debt
0	—	—	—	$ 0	$800,000
1	$ 13,737	$ 240	$13,977	13,977	786,023
2	13,737	485	14,222	28,199	771,801
3	13,737	734	14,471	42,670	757,330
.	.	.	.	.	.
.	.	.	.	.	.
.	.	.	.	.	.
37				718,907	81,093
38	13,737	12,821	26,558	745,465	54,535
39	13,737	13,286	27,023	772,488	27,512
40	13,737	13,759	27,496	799,984	16
		$250,504			

Exercise 15A

1. Price: $1026.21; total interest: $243.79.

Coupon number	Coupon payment	Interest on book value	Premium amortized	Book value of bond	Unamortized premium
0	—	—	—	$1026.21	$26.21
1	$ 45.00	$ 41.05	$ 3.95	1022.26	22.26
2	45.00	40.89	4.11	1018.15	18.15
3	45.00	40.73	4.27	1013.87	13.87
4	45.00	40.55	4.45	1009.43	9.43
5	45.00	40.38	4.62	1004.81	4.81
6	45.00	40.19	4.81	1000.00	0.00
	$270.00	**$243.79**	$26.21		

3. Price: $1087.85; total interest: $1112.15.

Coupon number	Coupon payment	Interest on book value	Premium amortized	Book value of bond	Unamortized premium
0	—	—	—	$1087.85	$87.85
1	$ 50.00	$ 47.87	$ 2.13	1085.71	85.71
2	50.00	47.77	2.23	1083.48	83.48
3	50.00	47.67	2.33	1081.16	81.16
.	.	.	.	.	.
.	.	.	.	.	.
.	.	.	.	.	.
21				1016.52	16.52
22	50.00	44.73	5.27	1011.25	11.25
23	50.00	44.50	5.50	1005.75	5.75
24	50.00	44.25	5.75	1000.00	0.00
	$1200.00	**$1112.15**	$87.85		

5. Price: $961.63; total interest: $278.37.

Coupon number	Coupon payment	Interest on book value	Discount amortized	Book value of bond	Unamortized discount
0	—	—	—	$ 961.63	$38.37
1	$ 40.00	$ 45.68	$ 5.68	967.30	32.70
2	40.00	45.95	5.95	973.25	26.75
3	40.00	46.23	6.23	979.48	20.52
4	40.00	46.53	6.53	986.00	14.00
5	40.00	46.84	6.84	992.84	7.16
6	40.00	47.16	7.16	1000.00	0.00
	$240.00	**$278.37**	$38.37		

7. Price: $877.20; total interest: $1057.80.

Coupon number	Coupon payment	Interest on book value	Discount amortized	Book value of bond	Unamortized discount
0	—	—		$877.20	$122.80
1	$42.50	$45.61	$3.11	880.31	119.69
2	42.50	45.78	3.28	883.59	116.41
3	42.50	45.95	3.45	887.04	112.96
.	.	.	.	.	.
.	.	.	.	.	.
.	.	.	.	.	.
19				974.23	25.77
20	42.50	50.66	8.16	982.39	17.61
21	42.50	51.08	8.58	990.97	9.03
22	42.50	51.53	9.03	1000.00	0.00
	$935.00	$1057.80	$122.80		

Review Problems

1. $103.14

3. $2246.55

5. $1217.57

7.

Payment interval number	Payment (at start)	Interest earned	Increase in the fund	Balance in fund (end of interval)
0	—	—	—	$ 0
1	$112,571	$ 3377	$115,948	115,948
2	112,571	6856	119,427	235,375
3	112,571	10,438	123,009	358,384
4	112,571	14,129	126,700	485,084
5	112,571	17,930	130,501	615,585
6	112,571	21,845	134,416	750,001
		$74,575	$750,001	

Self-Test Exercise

1. $42.19
2. 22.22%
3. 10.87% compounded semiannually
4. $1301.18
5. $1286.78
6.

Payment interval number	Payment	Interest earned	Increase in the fund	Balance in fund (end of interval)	Book value of the debt
0	—	—	—	$ 0	$500,000
1	$28,285	$ 0	$28,285	28,285	471,715
2	28,285	990	29,275	57,560	442,440
3	28,285	2015	30,300	87,860	412,140
.	.	.	.	.	.
.	.	.	.	.	.
.	.	.	.	.	.
11				371,721	128,279
12	28,285	13,010	41,295	413,016	86,984
13	28,285	14,456	42,741	455,757	44,243
14	28,285	15,951	44,236	499,993	7

Chapter 16 Business Investment Decisions

Exercise 16.1

1. **a.** Vencap should make the investment since the present value ($33,694) exceeds the required investment.
   b. $3694
3. $24,640
5. $16,346
7. **a.** Leasing saves $1545 in current dollars.
   b. Purchasing saves $979 in current dollars.
9. **a.** Lease.
   b. $1201
11. **a.** $3421 advantage to renting.
   b. $4249 advantage to buying.

Exercise 16.2

1. **a.** Yes ($NPV = \$17,389$).
   b. No ($NPV = -\$187$).
   c. No ($NPV = -\$15,228$).
3. $71,744
5. No ($NPV = -\$109,521$).
7. No ($NPV = -\$135,946$).
9. No ($NPV = -\$16,653$).

Exercise 16.3

1. Select B and D.
3. Select F, E, and A (having a combined *NPV* of $11,639).

5. The Deere's *NPV* is $4482 larger.
7. Project D is worth $3575 more today.
9. Model H has a $2507 higher equivalent annual cash flow.
11. The 25-ton truck has a $997 higher equivalent annual cash flow.
13. The Falcon has a $317 lower equivalent annual cost.
15. The International has a $1422 lower equivalent annual cost.

Exercise 16.4

1. 15.1%
3. Approve phase 1 (*IRR* = 27.3%).
   Approve phase 2 (*IRR* = 22.7%).
   Approve phase 3 (*IRR* = 14.6%).
   Reject phase 4 (*IRR* = 12.1%).
5. Yes (since *IRR* = 16.6% > 16.0%).
7. Yes since the *IRR* of 17.6% exceeds the cost of capital.
9. Yes. The *IRR* of 15% equals the cost of capital.
11. The *IRR* of 12.4% is less than the cost of capital. The mine should not be developed.

Exercise 16.5

1. **a.** Select D since its *IRR* (19.91%) is larger than C's *IRR* (18.10%).
   b. Select D—it has the larger *NPV*.
   c. Select C—it has the larger *NPV*.
3. **a.** Select XXX since its *IRR* (20.82%) is larger than YYY's *IRR* (17.33%).
   b. Select XXX—it has the larger *NPV*.
   c. Select YYY—it has the larger *NPV*.
5. **a.** Select Y since its *IRR* (17.46%) is larger than X's *IRR* (16.04%).
   b. Select Y—it has the larger *NPV*.
   c. Select X—it has the larger *NPV*.

Exercise 16.6

1. **a.** 4.67 years.
   b. No.
3.

Project	*NPV*	Payback
X	$ 8882	4 years
Y	$10,646	5 years

Prefer X on payback; prefer Y on *NPV*.

5.

Project	*NPV*	*IRR*	Payback
A	$4893	19.14%	2.64 years
B	$4589	20.02%	2.67 years

Project rankings:

Project	*NPV*	*IRR*	Payback
A	1	2	1
B	2	1	2

Review Problems

1. **a.** Leasing produces a $621 savings.
   b. Buying produces a $657 savings.
3. No (*NPV* = −$316,666 at a 16% cost of capital).
5. Yes (*NPV* = $15,677).
7. Machine X has a $235 higher equivalent annual cash flow.
9. The Boston Wailer has a $2243 lower equivalent annual cost.
11. No. *IRR* = 13.91%, below the cost of capital.
13. **a.** Project P: *IRR* = 15.03%.
   Project Q: *IRR* = 15.56%.
   Q is preferred on the basis of the *IRR*.
   b. Reject both P and Q. Both have a negative *NPV* and an *IRR* < 16%.
   c. Select P. P's *NPV* ($22,375) is larger than Q's *NPV* ($18,244).

Self-Test Exercise

1. $10,766 advantage to leasing.
2. No. The investment's *NPV* = −$7424.
3. Select A, D, and C.
4. Project B has a $1606 higher *NPV*.
5. C has an annual economic advantage of $996.
6. The TaterTaker produces an equivalent annual cost savings of $858.
7. 2.7 years.
8. *IRR* = 12.02%. Do not introduce the product since the *IRR* is less than the cost of capital.
9. **a.** A: *IRR* = 30.46%
   B: *IRR* = 34.23%
   B is preferred on the basis of the *IRR*.
   b. A has a $540 larger *NPV*.
   c. B has a $179 larger *NPV*.

Glossary

Algebraic expression A statement of the mathematical operations to be carried out on a combination of numbers and variables.

Amortization of a loan The repayment of a loan by periodic payments that, with the possible exception of the last payment, are equal in size.

Amortization of a bond's discount The process of increasing a bond's book value over the time remaining until maturity, by periodically reducing the bond's discount.

Amortization of a bond's premium The process of reducing a bond's book value over the time remaining until maturity, by periodically reducing the bond's premium.

Amortization period The total length of time to repay a loan with equal regular payments.

Annual cost of a debt The combined total of the annual interest payments on the debt and the annual payments into a sinking fund for retirement of the principal amount of the debt.

Annualized rate of return The annual rate of return that results if a short-term rate of return continues for an entire year.

Annuity A series of equal payments at regular intervals.

Annuity due An annuity in which the periodic payments occur at the beginning of each payment interval.

Balloon payment Any payment of principal in addition to the regular periodic payments.

Base (1) The quantity that is multiplied by itself in a power. (2) The initial amount to which a percent change is applied.

Binomial An algebraic expression containing two terms.

Bond A debt instrument secured by specific assets. The bond issuer (borrower) promises to periodically pay accrued interest, and to repay the full principal amount of the debt on the maturity date. The term "bond" is sometimes used in a generic sense to refer to both true bonds and debentures.

Bond discount The amount by which a bond's face value exceeds its quoted price.

Bond premium The amount by which a bond's quoted price exceeds its face value.

Book value of a debt The amount by which the principal balance owed on the debt exceeds the funds accumulated in a sinking fund for retiring the debt.

Book value of a lease liability The present value of the remaining lease payments (discounted at the interest rate on debt financing).

Break-even analysis A procedure for determining the level of sales at which a firm's net income is zero.

Break-even chart A graph presenting both total costs and total revenue as a function of sales volume so that the break-even point may be determined.

Break-even point The sales volume at which net income is zero; the intersection of the total cost and total revenue lines on a break-even chart.

Capital gain The amount by which an investment's value increases during the holding period.

Capital gain yield The capital gain as a percentage of the initial investment.

Capital loss The amount by which an investment's value decreases during the holding period.

Capital rationing The circumstance where there is a limit on the total amount of capital funds that a firm may invest during a period.

Cash discount A discount allowed for a payment within the discount period.

Cash flow Refers to a cash disbursement (cash outflow) or cash receipt (cash inflow).

Cash-flow sign convention Rules for using an algebraic sign to indicate the direction of cash movement. Cash *inflows* (receipts) are positive, and cash *outflows* (disbursements) are negative.

Closed mortgage A mortgage that does not permit any penalty-free prepayments.

Commercial paper Promissory notes issued by large corporations to borrow funds for a short term.

Common logarithm (of a number) The exponent to which the base "10" must be raised in order to equal the number.

Complex fraction A fraction containing one or more other fractions in its numerator or denominator.

Compound interest method The procedure for calculating interest wherein interest is *periodically* calculated and *added* to principal.

Compounding Applying each successive percent change to the cumulative amount after the preceding percent change.

Compounding frequency The number of compoundings that take place per year.

Compounding period The time interval between two successive conversions of interest to principal.

Constant growth annuity An annuity in which the payments change by the *same percentage* from one payment to the next.

Consumer credit Loans acquired by individuals for personal consumption expenditures and personal financing needs.

Contribution margin The amount by which the unit selling price exceeds the unit variable cost.

Contribution rate The contribution margin expressed as a percentage of the unit selling price.

Cost function The total costs expressed in terms of the number of units sold.

Cost of capital The weighted average of the rates of return required by a firm's various sources of financing.

Cost–volume–profit analysis A procedure for estimating a firm's *operating profit* (or net income before taxes) at any sales *volume* given the firm's *cost* structure.

Coupon rate The nominal annual rate of interest paid on the face value of a bond.

Credit period The time period granted to a customer for paying an invoice.

Debenture A debt instrument having most of the characteristics of a bond except that no *specific* assets secure the debt.

Deferred annuity An annuity where the start of the periodic payments is delayed by more than one payment interval.

Demand loan A loan where the lender is entitled to demand full repayment at any time without notice.

Denominator The number under the division line in a fraction. The denominator is also known as the *divisor.*

Discount period The time period within which a payment on an invoice qualifies for a prompt payment discount (called a cash discount).

Discount rate The interest rate used in calculating the present value of future cash flows.

Discounting a payment The process of calculating a payment's present value.

Economically equivalent payments Alternative payments that will result in the same future value at a later date.

Effective interest rate The equivalent annually compounded rate of interest.

End-of-month (EOM) dating Terms of payment where the credit and discount periods start at the end of the month in the date of the invoice.

Equation A statement of the equality of two algebraic expressions.

Equivalent fractions Fractions that have the same value.

Equivalent interest rates Different nominal interest rates that produce the same maturity value of a given principal after one year.

Equivalent payments Alternative payments that will result in the same future value at a later date.

Equivalent ratio A ratio obtained from another ratio by multiplying each term by the same number, or by dividing each term by the same number.

Equivalent value A single payment on a different date that has the same economic value as the scheduled payment or stream of payments.

Exchange rate (between two currencies) The amount of one currency required to purchase one unit of the other currency.

Exponent The number of times that the base is multiplied by itself in a power.

Face value (1) The amount paid at maturity of a Treasury Bill or commercial paper. (2) The principal amount that the issuer will pay to the owner of a marketable bond on its scheduled maturity date. (3) The initial principal amount of a mortgage. (4) The principal amount specified on a promissory note.

Factors The components of a term in an algebraic expression that are separated by multiplication or division signs; the components of a product.

Fair market value A price established by competitive bidding among many buyers and sellers.

Fixed cost A cost that does not change with the volume of sales.

Flat price The actual or full amount paid by a bond purchaser and received by the seller. It is the quoted price plus the accrued coupon interest.

Focal date The date selected for the calculation of equivalent values.

Fully open mortgage A mortgage loan that places no restrictions on extra payments by the borrower.

Future value A payment's equivalent value at a *subsequent* date, allowing for the time value of money.

Future value of an annuity The single amount, at the end of the annuity, that is economically equivalent to the annuity.

General annuity An annuity in which the payment interval does not equal the compounding interval.

General annuity due An annuity in which the payment interval does *not* equal the compounding interval, and payments occur at the *beginning* of each payment interval.

General perpetuity A perpetuity in which the compounding interval differs from the payment interval.

Gross amount (of a loan) The total principal amount that must be repaid over the amortization period.

Gross profit The difference between the selling price and the unit cost of an item of merchandise. (Also called *markup*.)

Gross profit margin The gross profit expressed as a percentage of the selling price.

Guaranteed Investment Certificate (GIC) A fixed-term non-redeemable deposit investment that earns a predetermined rate of interest.

Holding period The time period over which investment income or capital gain is being calculated.

Improper fraction A fraction whose numerator is larger than or equal to the denominator.

Income Revenue earned from an investment without selling any portion of the investment.

Income yield An investment's income expressed as a percentage of the amount invested at the beginning of the period.

Interest The fee or rent that lenders charge to borrowers for the temporary use of the borrowed money.

Interest period See compounding period.

Internal rate of return The discount rate that makes the net present value of an investment's cash flows equal to zero.

Issue date (1) The date on which (i) a loan secured by a bond or Treasury bill was originally made and (ii) interest starts to be earned. (2) The date on which a promissory note was written or "made" and the date from which interest, if any, accrues.

Legal due date The date, three days after expiry of a promissory note's term, beyond which the note is in default if not paid in full.

Like terms Terms having the same literal coefficient.

Linear equation An equation in which the variable is raised only to the first power.

List price The price quoted by a supplier of a product before any trade discounts.

Literal coefficient The non-numerical factor in a term.

Loan amortization schedule A table presenting details of the interest and principal components of each payment, and the balance after each payment.

Loan repayment schedule A table presenting details of interest charges, payments, and outstanding balances on a loan.

Lowest terms (of a ratio) The equivalent ratio having the smallest possible integers for its terms.

Maker The party (debtor) promising to pay the promissory note at its maturity.

Markdown The amount that the price of an item is reduced.

Markup The difference between the selling price and the unit cost of an item of merchandise. (Also called *gross profit.*)

Maturity date (1) The date on which the principal and accrued interest on an investment will be received. (2) The date on which the principal balance and accrued interest on a debt must be paid.

Maturity value The total of principal plus the interest due on the maturity date of a loan or investment.

Mill rate The amount of property tax per $1000 of taxable value.

Mixed number A number consisting of a whole number plus a fraction.

Monomial An algebraic expression containing only one term.

Mortgagee The party lending money on the security of a mortgage.

Mortgagor The party borrowing money and giving a mortgage as security on the loan.

Mutually exclusive projects Alternative capital investments, any one of which will substantially satisfy the same need or purpose.

Net amount (of a loan) The initial loan proceeds that the borrower actually receives.

Net present value The present value of cash inflows minus the present value of cash outflows.

Net price The price paid after the deduction of trade discounts.

Nominal interest rate The stated *annual* interest rate on which the compound-interest calculation is based.

Non-linear equation An equation in which the variable appears with an exponent other than "1", or appears as part of a mathematical function.

Numerator The number above the division line in a fraction. The numerator is also known as the *dividend.*

Numerical coefficient The numerical factor in a term.

Open mortgage See *fully open mortgage* and *partially open mortgage.*

Ordinary dating Terms of payment where the credit and discount periods start on the date of the invoice.

Ordinary annuity An annuity in which the payments are made at the *end* of each payment interval.

Ordinary general annuity An annuity in which the payment interval does *not* equal the compounding interval, and payments are made at the *end* of each payment interval.

Ordinary simple annuity An annuity in which the payment interval *equals* the compounding interval, and payments are made at the *end* of each payment interval.

Partial payment Any payment that is smaller than the initial amount required to fully settle an invoice.

Partially open mortgage A mortgage that grants limited penalty-free prepayment privileges.

Payback period The number of years it will take to recover an initial investment outlay from the investment's future operating profits.

Payee The party to whom a payment is to be made.

Payment interval The length of time between successive payments in an annuity.

Payment stream A series of two or more payments required by a single transaction or contract.

Period of deferral The time interval until the beginning of the first payment *interval* in a deferred annuity.

Periodic interest rate The rate of interest for one compounding period.

Perpetuity An annuity whose payments continue forever.

Perpetuity due An annuity in which the payments are made at the beginning of each payment interval and continue forever.

Polynomial An algebraic expression containing more than one term.

Power A mathematical operation indicating the multiplication of a quantity (the *base*) by itself a certain number (the *exponent*) of times.

Prepayments Any loan payments in addition to the regular contractual payments.

Present value A payment's equivalent value at a *prior* date, allowing for the time value of money.

Present value of an annuity The single amount, at the beginning of the annuity, that is economically equivalent to the annuity.

Prime rate of interest A chartered bank's lowest lending rate.

Principal The original amount borrowed or invested.

Proceeds The selling price of a promissory note. It is the present value, on the date of sale, of the note's maturity value.

Promissory note A written promise by one party to pay a certain sum of money to another party on a specific date, or on demand.

Proper fraction A fraction whose numerator is less than the denominator.

Proportion A statement of the equality of two ratios.

Proration A procedure in which an amount is subdivided and allocated on a proportionate basis.

Quoted price The full purchase price (flat price) of a bond less any accrued coupon interest.

Rate of interest The percentage of the principal that will be charged for a particular period of time, normally one year.

Rate of markdown The markdown expressed as a percentage of the regular price.

Rate of markup The markup expressed as a percentage of the cost of the merchandise.

Rate of total return The investment's combined income and capital gain expressed as a percentage of the beginning investment.

Ratio A comparison, by division, of the relative size of two or more quantities.

Receipt-of-goods (ROG) dating Terms of payment where the credit and discount periods start on the date that the goods are received.

Residual value The amount for which the lessee can purchase a leased vehicle at the end of the lease's term.

Revenue function The total revenue expressed in terms of the number of units sold.

Revolving loan A loan arrangement in which advances and repayments of principal are at the borrower's discretion (subject to a minimum monthly payment and a credit limit).

Root (of an equation) A particular numerical value for the variable that makes the two sides of the equation equal.

Rule of 72 A rule of thumb for a quick estimation of the number of years it will take an investment to double at a known compound annual rate of return.

Savings account A deposit account that offers essentially unrestricted withdrawal privileges.

Simple annuity An annuity in which the payment interval equals the compounding interval.

Simple annuity due An annuity in which the payment interval *equals* the compounding interval, and payments occur at the *beginning* of each payment interval.

Simple interest Interest calculated only on the original principal and paid only at the maturity date.

Sinking fund An interest-earning account into which periodic payments are made for the purpose of accumulating a desired amount of money by a certain date.

Sinking fund schedule A table presenting details of each period's increase in the sinking fund.

Substitution Assigning a numerical value to each of the algebraic variables in an expression.

Tax rate The fraction of a price or taxable amount that is payable as tax.

Term The time period for which a loan or investment is made.

Term Deposit A deposit investment that earns a predetermined rate of interest for a stated term. A reduced interest rate applies if the term deposit is redeemed before maturity.

Term of an annuity The total time from the beginning of the first payment interval to the end of the last payment interval.

Terms The components of an algebraic expression that are separated by addition or subtraction signs.

Terms of a ratio The numbers being compared in the ratio.

Terms of payment The specifications on an invoice of the length of the credit period, any cash discount offered and the corresponding discount period, and the date on which the credit and discount periods start.

Time diagram A time axis showing the dollar amounts and the dates of payments.

Time value of money The property that a given *nominal* amount of money has different economic values on different dates.

Total return The sum of the income and capital gain from an investment during a holding period.

Trade discount A discount granted by the supplier to a purchaser of goods for resale.

Treasury bills Promissory notes issued (at a discount to face value) by the federal government and most provincial governments to borrow money for short terms.

Trinomial An algebraic expression containing three terms.

Variable costs Costs that grow in direct proportion to the volume of output or sales.

Vendor take-back mortgage A mortgage loan granted by the vendor to the purchaser for part of the purchase price of real property.

Yield-to-maturity The market rate of return on the day the bond was purchased. The discount rate that makes the present value of the bond's remaining cash flows equal to its purchase price. The rate of return a bond purchaser will earn if the bond is kept until it matures.

Index

Applications of Algebra

$$V_f = V_i(1 + c_1)(1 + c_2)(1 + c_3)\cdots(1 + c_n)$$

Mathematics of Merchandising

$$N = L(1 - d)$$

$$N = L(1 - d_1)(1 - d_2)(1 - d_3)$$

Cost–Volume–Profit Analysis

$$NI = (CM)X - FC$$

$$TR = (SP)X$$

$$TC = (VC)X + FC$$

$$NI = (SP - VC)X - FC$$

Mathematics of Finance

$$I = Prt$$

$$S = P(1 + rt)$$

$$i = \frac{j}{m}$$

$$n = m \times (\text{Number of years in the term})$$

$$FV = PV(1 + i)^n$$

$$FV = PV(1 + i_1)(1 + i_2)(1 + i_3)\cdots(1 + i_n)$$

$$i = \sqrt[n]{\frac{FV}{PV}} - 1 = \left(\frac{FV}{PV}\right)^{1/n} - 1$$

$$n = \frac{\ln(FV / PV)}{\ln(1 + i)}$$

$$f = (1 + i)^m - 1$$

$$i_2 = (1 + i_1)^{m_1/m_2} - 1$$

$$FV = PMT\left[\frac{(1 + i)^n - 1}{i}\right]$$

$$PV = PMT\left[\frac{1 - (1 + i)^{-n}}{i}\right]$$

$$c = \frac{\text{Number of compoundings per year}}{\text{Number of payments per year}}$$

$$i_2 = (1 + i)^c - 1$$

$$n = \frac{\ln\left(1 + \frac{i \times FV}{PMT}\right)}{\ln(1 + i)}; \quad n = -\frac{\ln\left(1 - \frac{i \times PV}{PMT}\right)}{\ln(1 + i)}$$

$$FV(\text{due}) = PMT\left[\frac{(1 + i)^n - 1}{i}\right] \times (1 + i)$$

$$PV(\text{due}) = PMT\left[\frac{1 - (1 + i)^{-n}}{i}\right] \times (1 + i)$$

$$PV = \frac{PMT}{i}$$

$$\text{Bond price} = b(FV)\left[\frac{1 - (1 + i)^{-n}}{i}\right] + FV(1 + i)^{-n}$$

Summary of Notation

Applications of Algebra

V_i = Initial (or beginning or original or old) value
V_f = Final (or ending or new) value
c = Percent change
c_t = Percent change in period t

Mathematics of Merchandising

L = List price
d = Rate of trade discount
N = Net price
SP = Unit selling price
C = Unit cost
M = Markup
OE = Overhead or operating expenses per unit
OP = Operating profit per unit
D = Markdown
RSP = Reduced selling price
ROP = Reduced operating profit per unit

Cost–Volume–Profit Analysis

SP = Selling price or revenue per unit
VC = Variable costs per unit
FC = (Total) Fixed costs
CM = Contribution margin per unit
CR = Contribution rate
X = Total number of units sold in the period
NI = Net income (or operating profit) for the period
TR = Total revenue (from the sale of X units)
TC = Total costs (for X units)

Summary of Notation (continued)

Mathematics of Finance

V_i = Value of the investment at the beginning of the period
V_f = Value of the investment at the end of the period
P = Principal amount of a loan or investment
= Present value (with simple interest)
r = Annual rate of simple interest
t = Time period (term), in years, of the loan or investment
I = Amount of simple interest paid or received
S = Maturity value of a loan or investment
= Future value (with simple interest)
j = Nominal annual interest rate
m = Number of compoundings per year
i = Periodic interest rate
n = Number of compounding periods (for a lump amount)
= Number of payments in an annuity
PV = Present value
FV = Future value
f = Effective (annual) rate of interest or rate of return
PMT = Amount of each payment in an annuity
c = Number of compoundings per payment interval
i_2 = Equivalent periodic interest rate (per payment interval for a general annuity)
d = Number of payment intervals in the period of deferral
$FV(\text{due})$ = Future value of an annuity due
$PV(\text{due})$ = Present value of an annuity due
FV = Face value of a bond
b = Bond coupon rate per interest payment interval
NPV = Net present value
IRR = Internal rate of return